SCOTLAND: A CONCISE CULTURAL HISTORY

SCOTLAND
A CONCISE CULTURAL HISTORY

Edited by
Paul H. Scott

MAINSTREAM
PUBLISHING
EDINBURGH AND LONDON

First published in Great Britain in 1993 by
MAINSTREAM PUBLISHING COMPANY (EDINBURGH) LTD
7 Albany Street
Edinburgh EH1 3UG

ISBN 1 85158 581 8

A catalogue record for this book is available from the British Library

The publisher gratefully acknowledges the financial assistance of
The Scottish A rts Council
in the production of this book

Typeset in 11/12pt Monophoto Fournier by Servis Filmsetting Ltd, Manchester
Printed in Great Britain by Butler & Tanner Ltd, Frome

I knew a very wise man so much of Sir Christopher's sentiment, that he believed if a man were permitted to make all the ballads, he need not care who should make the laws of a nation.

ANDREW FLETCHER OF SALTOUN

The same age, which produces great philosophers, and politicians, renowned generals and poets, usually abounds with skilful weavers and ship-carpenters. We cannot reasonably expect, that a piece of woollen cloth will be brought to perfection in a nation, which is ignorant of astronomy, or where ethics are neglected.

DAVID HUME

All nations can point to their geniuses in many realms of human endeavour; but, for a country of its size, Scotland's contribution is almost disturbing in its scale.

DOUGLAS DUNN

The peculiar history of the Scots has meant that, man for man, they have probably done more to create the modern world than any other nation. They owe it an explanation.

CHRISTOPHER HARVIE

Contents

Introduction

PAUL H. SCOTT

A writer in the magazine *Cencrastus* recently expressed in two short sentences two of the remarkable things about Scottish culture: 'To the outside world Scotland no doubt appears to be a small and remote place. Thus, it must come as a surprise that such a country should have contributed so much to human thought and endeavour.'[1] These are the two surprising things: that Scotland should have contributed so much; but that this should be so little known, even to the Scottish people themselves.

Many observers have remarked on the importance of the Scottish contribution to civilisation. David Hume said that the Scots were the people 'most distinguished for literature in Europe',[2] and he used the word 'literature' in a very wide sense to include philosophy, history and virtually every other kind of writing. As a Scot, he might be held to be a prejudiced witness on this point; but there is no shortage of observers from other countries who have said much the same.

Three English examples: Horace Walpole said of the Scots: 'the most accomplished nation in Europe; the nation to which, if any country is endowed with a superior partition of sense, I should be inclined to give the preference.'[3] Sydney Smith, who spent about six years in Edinburgh at the end of the eighteenth century: 'They are perhaps in some points of view the most remarkable nation in the world, and no country can afford an example of so much order, morality, economy, and knowledge among the lower classes of society.'[4] H.T. Buckle, the Victorian sage who intended to write a History of Civilisation, but did not proceed much beyond eighteenth-century Scotland: 'That so poor and thinly-peopled a country as Scotland, should, in so short a period, have produced so many remarkable men, is extremely curious.'[5]

And three Americans: Harold Thompson said that to discover comparable achievements by so small a nation we should have to go back to the age of Pericles.[6] In Harold Orel's opinion, 'No nation its size has contributed as much to world culture.'[7]

The economist, J.K. Galbraith, said that the only serious rival to the Scots were the Jews.[8]

These opinions may be a little exaggerated; there are other small countries, such as the city-state of Florence at the time of the Renaissance, which should be taken into account. Still, whatever reservation one might wish to make, it is undeniable that Scotland, in a phrase often quoted by the Saltire Society, has been for many centuries a great creative force in European civilisation. There are many examples in the essays that follow. Alexander Broadie discusses the important contribution which Scots have made to western philosophy for at least eight centuries. Derick Thomson, R.J. Lyall and Roderick Watson deal with the great range of our literature in Latin, Gaelic, Scots and English. John Lenihan has no hesitation in saying that Scottish scientists led the world in the mid-eighteenth and mid-nineteenth centuries. John Purser, Charles McKean and Duncan Macmillan show that in music, architecture and painting, Scotland, in Macmillan's words, 'gave as well as received in the exchange that made Europe vital'. This is a very diverse culture with great strengths in many fields from engineering to folk song or from philosophy to dance. It has a long history, but its great achievements are not all in the past. As Sara Stevenson explains, Scotland in the last century made an outstanding contribution to the new medium of photography. Just as James Watt played an essential part in the age of steam, so did Clerk Maxwell in the present electronic age. We are now in the midst of one of the great periods of our literature, painting and music.

Scottish studies are an expanding subject in universities from America to Japan and there are scholars everywhere at work on some aspect of our cultural history. Even so, this is largely the province of a few specialists who have stumbled with surprise upon a treasure of which the world at large is unconscious. It is possible to go through even a Scottish education at all levels from nursery school to a post-graduate degree and emerge in almost complete ignorance of Scotland's outstanding contribution to civilisation.

The reasons for this curious and unfortunate state of affairs derive in a number of ways from our loss of independence through the Union of the Crowns in 1603 and of the Parliaments in 1707. When James VI flitted to London in 1603, the arts lost the royal patronage on which they then depended all over Europe. The centre of power, fashion and taste moved with him, and the politically and socially ambitious began to feel the need to ape the habits and the language of the ruling circles in London. Even more serious was the loss of international identity. Then (and, as we have recently been reminded in the Maastricht debate, to some extent still) foreign affairs were a matter of the royal prerogative. Scotland was no longer a distinct player on the European and world stage, but, to all appearances, an appendage of England. To the rest of the world, the whole of the now united kingdoms were known simply as England. The process was carried still further by the 'incorporating' parliamentary union of 1707 which reduced Scotland to political impotence.

Scotland had become an invisible country internationally, and the culture of invisible countries is also invisible. Inside Scotland itself the loss of independence was traumatic and it began a decline into a complex of inferiority and powerlessness from which we still suffer. London as the apex of power and prestige became, in James Boswell's words, 'the strong centre of attraction for all of us'.[9] His own life is a sad example of the destructiveness of that attraction. Especially to the snobbish and the ambitious, everything English seemed admirable and desirable and everything Scottish provincial and second-rate. To those who succumbed to this attitude, anything that was not English was called 'parochial'. Even a man of the greatness of David Hume, who deplored 'the Barbarians who inhabit the banks of the Thames',[10] struggled to write English and to suppress his natural and expressive Scots. For lesser mortals this was a recipe for inarticulacy. The literati of the Scottish Enlightenment were so confused by the shame of belonging to a defeated country that they largely expunged references to Scotland in their writing, and even when they had their own country in their mind they disguised it by an allusion to north America or classical Greece or Rome.

As J.G. Lockhart pointed out, Walter Scott did much to restore Scottish self-respect and save us from the worst excesses of this feeling of shame;[11] but its effects are with us still. The art historian, Tom Normand, recently described the effect of this attitude on Scottish painters: 'To be a Scottish artist was to be condemned to parochialism and sentimentalism. This is not to say that these were the inherent characteristics of Scottish art, rather this was the perception of Scottishness fostered by the experience of government from London and the domination of the metropolitan vision. Moreover, this perception was, to some extent, internalised by Scottish artists with the result that the search for an authentic national discourse in art became something of an embarrassment.'[12] In other words, there are strong pressures to shame Scots of all kinds, and not only painters, out of their Scottishness. In this century external pressures have greatly increased because of London's domination of radio and television. These pressures are not only external, but are exerted also by Scots whose minds have been colonised and who have accepted the dominant vision.

This attitude, often called the 'Scottish cringe', has affected many of our educationalists. To them it has seemed quite acceptable that our schools and universities should teach English history and literature in preference to our own. In the days of the Empire, this used to be the normal practice in all of its territories. Now Scotland is almost the last refuge of this particular manifestation of imperialism. It is the reason, of course, why Scots are so ignorant of their own cultural history.

English models, inventions or ideas may often be useful to Scotland, just as they are from many other countries, or in turn the Scottish example to them. To benefit from cultural exchange it is not necessary to be under the same government, and it is much better that each of us should be free to accept the influences that happen to meet our needs. Imposed conformity from one external source is more likely to stifle than inspire. In many matters English tastes and ideas are so different from our own that their imposition can be damaging. Robert Louis Stevenson, for instance, said of Robert Burns that he owed to the English authors that he most read and admired 'nothing but a warning'.[13] DeLancey Ferguson, the biographer of Burns and the editor of his letters, made much the same point about him: 'Had he received a formal eduction, it would have been in the anglifying mould that was standard in late eighteenth-century Scotland. So trained, the poet might have become another Thomson, but he would have been taught to despise the folk tradition which has made him immortal.'[14]

For all these reasons, the drafters of A Claim of Right for Scotland of 1988 were undoubtedly right to conclude that 'the Union has always been, and remains, a threat to the survival of a distinctive culture in Scotland.'[15] Those, like Ian Lang, who argue that on the contrary Scottish culture virtually began with the Union,[16] either reveal ignorance or a wilful disregard of the facts to suit their political argument. The essays by Michael Lynch, Donald Smith, John Purser and many of the others, amply demonstrate the richness of Scottish culture from very early times and its strong lines of continuity.

It has been suggested that the disparagement of our culture (of which Lang's statement is an example) is part of a deliberate policy to bolster control from London. The American sociologist, Michael Hechter, developed this theory in his book, *Internal Colonialism*, first published in 1975. He argued that 'a defining characteristic of imperial expansion is that the centre must disparage the indigenous culture of peripheral groups' and that this is achieved 'through the voluntary assimilation of peripheral élites'.[17] More recently, Craig Beveridge and Ronald Turnbull have applied to Scotland the very similar conclusions of Frantz Fanon that the central process of colonisation was 'a sustained belittling of the colonised culture, which is depicted by the colonisers as impoverished, backward, inferior, primitive'.[18]

It is certainly true that the attitude of the Establishment of the London-Oxbridge triangle and of those of the 'peripheral élite' or Scottish cringe, who swallow it in Scotland, bears an uncanny resemblance to the descriptions of Hechter and Fanon. That does not necessarily mean that it is a consequence of formal policy. I doubt whether Westminster and Whitehall are capable of sustaining anything so subtle and consistent. It is much more likely to be the automatic result of the concentration of political power in London, with the wealth and social prestige that go with it. No doubt it is assisted by what the distinguished historian, Linda Colley, has called the 'enormous conceit'[19] of these ruling circles and by their unquestioning assumption that their standards and tribal customs are a model of excellence which the rest of the world must envy.

Fortunately, this denigration of Scottish culture has failed; if it had not, this book would not have been written. The fact that a distinctive Scottish culture has not merely survived, but is in many ways in robust health, is a proof of its inherent strength. The Union left intact the Church, the law, the burghs, the schools and universities. For more than a hundred years these institutions were of much greater influence in the life of Scotland than a distant parliament which took very little interest in its affairs. In more recent times all of them have been subjected to the pressures of anglicisation; but they, and Scottish culture with them, are still sustained by our habits of strenuous thought, egalitarianism, width of interest and internationalism. In all the arts this Scottishness is now more vigorous and self-confident than at any time since Westminster began to interfere in Scottish affairs after Waterloo.[20]

If Andrew Fletcher's wise man was right and the ballads are more important than the laws, then the recovery of political independence is likely soon to follow. Andrew Marr ends his chapter on politics on a pessimistic note. This is comprehensible because it was written at a depressing time in Scottish affairs when a paradoxical election had been followed by a failure of the political parties to maintain the determination of the impressive demonstration of 12 December 1992. I do not think that Scotland can be at ease with itself, and realise its potential, until its cultural identity is sustained by political identity as well.

It is astonishing, but perhaps symptomatic of the effects of denigration, that hardly any attempt has been made before to study Scottish culture as a whole. Certainly, there are references in works of general history, but they are necessarily incidental. Literature has had several histories since the last century and recently those of Kurt Wittig, Maurice Lyndsay, Roderick Watson and the four volumes edited by Cairns Craig.

Understanding of Scottish painting and music has now been greatly enlarged by the pioneering work of Duncan Macmillan and John Purser. There have, of course, been many other useful books on other particular aspects. The first work to take a serious look at most branches of Scottish culture was an excellent book, edited by David Daiches, *A Companion to Scottish Culture*, published in 1981 and now appearing in a new edition. That was arranged as a work of reference. The present volume is the first on the subject which is intended to be read straight through.

We have been fortunate to have as our contributors leading experts in their fields, including several whom I have just mentioned. I hope that this book will serve various purposes: to help to repair the omissions of which Scottish education is often guilty; to give those who are familiar with one art form an acquaintance with the rest; to serve as an introduction to Scotland to people coming here to work, including academics and students, and perhaps even administrators in the arts. I hope that it might lead to a new appreciation of Scottish culture as a subject of intrinsic value and as an indispensable part of a Scottish education, and to a wider understanding of the Scottish past. In all these ways, I hope that it may contribute to the present revival of national self-confidence on which the future of Scotland depends.

Notes

1. Bill Hare, 'Past and Present: a Historical View of Scottish Art in the 1980s' in *Cencrastus* No.44, New Year 1993, p.21.
2. David Hume, *Letters*, ed. J.Y.T. Greig, 2 vols. (Oxford, 1932), Vol.1, p.255.
3. Horace Walpole, Yale Edition of his *Correspondence*, ed. W.S. Lewis; Vol.15 (London and Yale, 1952), p.41, fn.1.
4. Sydney Smith, *Letters*, ed. N.C. Smith, 2 vols. (Oxford, 1953), Vol.1, pp.21–22.
5. H.T. Buckle, 'On Scotland and the Scotch Intellect', in Vol.2 of H.J. Hanham, *The History of Civilisation* (Chicago, 1970), p.359, fn 236.
6. H.W. Thompson, *Henry Mackenzie: a Scottish Man of Feeling*, (London, 1931), p.1.
7. Harold Orel, *The Scottish World: History and Culture of Scotland*, (London, 1981), p.12.
8. J.K. Galbraith in a BBC television programme in 1977.
9. James Boswell, *Boswell: Laird of Auchinleck* (New York, 1977); p.66. Reprinted in George Bruce and Paul H. Scott (eds.), *A Scottish Postbag* (Edinburgh, 1986), p.72.
10. David Hume, *Letters* (as note 2 above), Vol.1, p.436. Reprinted in *A Scottish Postbag* (as note 9 above), p.43.
11. This point is discussed in Paul H. Scott, *Walter Scott and Scotland* (Edinburgh, 1981), pp.92–96.
12. Tom Normand, 'Scottish Modernism and Scottish Identity' in Wendy Kaplan (ed.), *Scotland Creates* (Glasgow, 1990), pp.170–71.
13. R.L. Stevenson, 'Some Aspects of Robert Burns' in *Familiar Studies of Men and Books* (Everyman's Library Edition, n.d.), p.172.
14. DeLancey Ferguson in his Introduction to *Selected Letters of Robert Burns* (Oxford, 1953), p.x.

15. *A Claim of Right for Scotland* (Report of the Constitutional Steering Committee, July 1988), p.2. Reprinted in a book of the same title, edited by Owen Dudley Edwards (Edinburgh, 1989), p.14.
16. Ian Lang in the Usher Hall debate on 18 January 1992 said: 'Scotland's greatest days have been since the Union. Our greatest economic growth, our cultural flowering, our art and our heritage come from the last 300 years.'
17. Michael Hechter, *Internal Colonialism* (London, 1975), pp.64 and 81.
18. Craig Beveridge and Ronald Turnbull, *The Eclipse of Scottish Culture*, (Edinburgh, 1989), p.5.
19. Linda Colley, *Britons: Forging the Nation, 1707–1837* (Newhaven and London, 1992), p.43.
20. See Sir Walter Scott's *The Letters of Malachi Malagrowther*, especially Letter 1. The most recent edition is one which I edited in 1981 (Edinburgh) and the most relevant passage is on pp.8–15.

Books for Further Reading

David Allan, *Virtue, Learning and the Scottish Enlightenment* (Edinburgh, 1982).

Craig Beveridge and Ronald Turnbull, *The Eclipse of Scottish Culture* (Edinburgh, 1989).

R.H. Campbell and Andrew Skinner (eds.), *The Origin and Nature of the Scottish Enlightenment* (Edinburgh, 1989).

Annand C. Chitnis, *The Scottish Enlightenment* (London, 1976).

David Daiches (ed.), *A Companion to Scottish Culture* (London, 1981).

George Elder Davie, *The Democratic Intellect* (Edinburgh, 1961).

Michael Hechter, *Internal Colonialism* (London, 1975).

William McIlvanney, *Surviving the Shipwreck* (Edinburgh, 1991).

Magnus Magnusson and Robin Denniston (eds.), *Anatomy of Scotland* (Edinburgh, 1992).

Paul H. Scott, *Cultural Independence* (Scottish Centre for Economic and Social Research, 1989).

Paul H. Scott, *In Bed with an Elephant* (Saltire Society, 1985); Reprinted in *Towards Independence: Essays on Scotland* (Edinburgh, 1991).

Sir Walter Scott, *The Letters of Malachi Malagrowther* (1826), edited by Paul H. Scott (Edinburgh, 1981).

Derick S. Thomson (ed.), *The Companion to Gaelic Culture* (Oxford, 1983).

Scottish Culture in its Historical Perspective

MICHAEL LYNCH

The major events or themes in Scottish history – such as the coming to power of Kenneth mac Alpin in 843, the Wars of Independence which afflicted Scotland for almost a hundred years from 1296 onwards, the Reformation of 1559–60, the Union of 1707 and the Enlightenment of the mid-eighteenth century – are easy to list, even if historians' lists would vary a little. The impact of such landmarks on Scotland's cultural history is less easy to evaluate. Each of those listed above, it is possible to argue and it was argued at or near the time, was a turning point, at which the concern of contemporaries was less the past than the present. A series of anonymous chroniclers were intent, after 843, at making Kenneth mac Alpin the symbol of a new kind of kingship as well as the founder of a new dynasty; John Knox, in his *History of the Reformation*, devoted only 300 words to the centuries of Scottish history before the arrival of its first Protestants, the Lollards of Kyle; within a couple of pages he had reached the tragic account of Scotland's first Protestant martyr, Patrick Hamilton, burned at St Andrews in 1528; a long line of later Presbyterian historians would pass over the Middle Ages in a quest for their own roots in the primitive Christianity of the Columban Church. In a similar vein, William Robertson, in his *History of Scotland*, first published in London in 1759, which celebrated the present age of politeness as an escape from a troubled and barbarous past, cast off the centuries of Scotland's history before 1500 as unworthy of consideration. The present 'enlightened' generation was the 'historical age' of David Hume; the 'historical nation', in the words of two distinguished modern historians of the Enlightenment, moved 'almost overnight' in the 1750s from a position of cultural isolation to being the 'centre of the thinking world'.[1] In 1929 Robert Boothby, then a promising young Conservative politician, in turn dismissed Scottish history before the Union of Parliaments:

> Prior to 1707 the Scottish people were a pack of miserable savages, living in incredible poverty and squalor, and playing no part in the development of civilisation. Since 1707, they have been partners in the greatest undertaking the world has ever seen.[2]

1. *David I and Malcolm IV, Kings of Scotland. From a charter of 1159 to Kelso Abbey.*
(Deposited in the National Library of Scotland by the Duke of Roxburghe and reproduced
by his permission)

This was a view which surfaced again during the general election of 1992, which in
Scotland provoked a historical debate about the effects of the Union which might have
taken place in the polite salons of mid-eighteenth-century Edinburgh. When Sir
Nicholas Fairbairn, Conservative MP, opined: 'Look at the food – oatcakes, haggis,
broth – it's all peasant fare. This was a peasant country before the Union',[3] it was clear
that the wheel had again come full circle: North British rhetoric was *redivivus*.

One of the oddities of the position taken by Conservative politicians such as these
is that it owes more to a Whig interpretation of history than a Tory one; the past is seen
as a struggle between progressives and reactionaries with the progressives eventually
winning. Although the crudities of the Whig position have generally rendered it out of
favour with most modern historians, it nonetheless persists – in various forms – in
assessments of Scotland's cultural history.[4] Knox, Robertson and the Unionist view of
Scottish history are all examples of it, highlighting a decisive turning-point which
suddenly brought Scotland into a new godly, 'modern' or more civilised age. Various
schools of Scottish history – Presbyterian, Enlightenment and Unionist – have a vested
interest in the construction of a major watershed somewhere in Scotland's past.

During the past generation, there has been a distinct tendency amongst historians
to stress the overarching continuities – in social and economic history especially –
which give some coherence to the complex story of Scotland's past. In every century
until the nineteenth, it has been asserted, the forces of continuity outweighed those
making for change.[5] In recent years, the same features have notably marked studies of
the major components of Scotland's culture – in art, historiography, music and
philosophy, and, to a lesser extent, in architecture and literature. David Allan, for
example, has traced a 'compelling moral vision', based on a philosophical core of

'Presbyterian humanism', which ran as a consistent thread linking the historical writings of John Knox and George Buchanan not only with half-forgotten seventeenth-century philosopher historians such as the mathematician Thomas Crauford and the lawyer and linguist Sir Robert Spottiswoode but also with the giants of the Enlightenment, including David Hume, Adam Ferguson and William Robertson.[6] Alexander Broadie, focusing on the intellectual ferment of the opening decades of the sixteenth century, has similarly linked the circle of John Mair in the 1520s and 1530s with the philosophers who formed the school of Francis Hutcheson in the generation after 1720.[7]

The Reformation was in a number of significant ways, and not least in culture and learning, less of a watershed than is often assumed. John Durkan has shown how developments in both the universities and grammar schools in the pre-Reformation period prepared the ground for the primacy given by the Protestant reformers of 1560 to establishing a godly, educated society.[8] John Purser has shown that music did not entirely disappear after 1560 and that some of the notable early successes of the new Protestant religion in evangelising society depended on the blunt instruments of new, simple words being set to existing popular tunes.[9] Duncan Macmillan has demonstrated that the power that painting had as public propaganda was too valuable a weapon to be abandoned after the Reformation, by the Crown and even, to an extent, by the reformed Church.[10] The Protestant reformers, confronted by an instinctively conservative society, faced the most formidable obstacles in the spheres where they argued for a new society; the first generation of Protestant preachers, hampered by the insistence on the purging of 'idolatrous' paintings, statues and images and faced by congregations where typically less than a quarter of adult males could read,[11] had less evangelical tools with which to fight the good fight than the parish priests and chaplains of the pre-Reformation Church.

The Reformation, as a result, for a time succeeded most readily in the areas where it could draw on the cultural treasury of late medieval Scotland. Pre-Reformation song schools were not disbanded but refounded as vernacular schools, practising godly psalms, sung to a small batch of common tunes. The inculcation of the simple truths of the Gospel took generations to achieve in a semi-literate society, and the most potent weapon in the Kirk's armoury was the psalter rather than the catechism or bible. As late as the mid-seventeenth century, many congregations relied on a precentor to sing tune, pitch and words, to be repeated line by line; the psalms of David, which had been central to the worship of the Scottish Church since at least the twelfth century, continued, with a new purpose and vigour after the Reformation.[12]

Four other initial sets of points are worth making. Throughout Scottish history, it will be seen, the culture of the present has been informed by a highly developed, self-conscious sense of the past. Even the Reformation, after the first flush of iconoclastic enthusiasm was over, was not an exception to this rule. In 1633, when an elaborate, formal entry was prepared to mark the first visit of Charles I to his capital, one of the centrepieces was a huge, timber Parnassus, built in the middle of the High Street, near where the Tron Kirk now stands. On it, amidst a double-topped mountain 'stopit full with books' were displayed representations of the 'ancient worthies of Scotland for learning'. The contents of this three-dimensional cultural history of Scotland were significant: they featured Duns Scotus, Scotland's most celebrated academic philosopher; Robert Henryson, schoolmaster and the greatest poet of the age of James IV; William Elphinstone, bishop of Aberdeen, a rector of Glasgow University and founder of Scotland's third university, at Aberdeen, doyen of the late medieval class of churchmen who were simultaneously distinguished scholars and skilled administrators of the Crown; Hector Boece, chronicler, who had returned from Paris to become the first rector of Aberdeen's new university; John Mair, logician and historian, a teacher at Glasgow and Paris before he became principal of the new College of St Leonard's at St Andrews; Gavin Douglas, bishop of Dunkeld, royal tutor and translator of Virgil's *Aeneid*; Sir David Lyndsay, royal herald, tutor to James V, poet and playwright; and George Buchanan, another principal of St Leonard's, one of the most celebrated humanists in sixteenth-century Europe, and author of the most widely published history of Scotland to date. The Parnassus of 1633 is clear evidence of the status then given to learning: the 'worthies' included five academics and a schoolmaster; it celebrated three of Scotland's recent and most influential historians; it mirrored some of the best-selling printed works of the early seventeenth century, which included Lyndsay's collected works and Henryson's *Testament of Cresseid*; and it reinforced the

*2. Guthrie Bell Shrine – twelfth century and later, West Highland. Restored by John II, Lord of the Isles, at the end of the fifteenth century. It is made of iron, copper alloy, silver and gilt. (*National Museums of Scotland*)*

justification which Elphinstone had himself given for his new university, founded '*pro patria*'.[13]

The conclusions to be drawn from this temporary national monument, constructed for the benefit of Scotland's first fully absentee king, are clear enough. The works of the Renaissance, fostered in the Courts of James IV and V, had reached, through the new medium of the printing press and a wave of patriotic publishing which marked the three-quarters of a century after 1570, a new and much wider audience. The importance attached to learning and the need for a national system of schooling formed a bridge across the troubled waters of the Reformation century. The continuum of Scotland's culture and learning were perceived to be part of the very fabric of its historical identity. This was a view which remained unchallenged until the polite historians of the Enlightenment.

The second point worth establishing at the outset is that although Scottish culture has habitually celebrated Scotland's own past, it has seldom been 'little Scotlander'. There are temptations to claim the existence of an authentic strain of Scottish culture: it is most often present in discussions of the folk tradition[14] and in a 'nationalist' interpretation, which dwells on what is sometimes called the 'paradox of Scottish culture', seeing a hard-fought conflict since the eighteenth century (or perhaps since 1603) between a vernacular culture and the forces of anglicisation.[15] Each of these schools of thought runs the risk of oversimplifying the historical complexity of Scotland's cultural traditions. Immigrants and migrants have thronged every century of Scotland's recorded history. In the twelfth and thirteenth centuries, as in the eighth, Scotland was, as a result, a racially hybrid society, with a culture to match. An English chronicler recounted with bemusement the make-up of the extraordinary army consisting of Anglo-Norman, French and Fleming settlers as well as Galwegians, Cumbrians and Scots which fought at the Battle of the Standard in 1138 for David I, himself the son of a native Celtic king and a Saxon queen and the product of an upbringing amidst the Anglo-Norman culture of the English Court.

The passage of trade, ideas, patronage as well as peoples ensured that Scotland was a thoroughly cosmopolitan society. Medieval and early modern Scotland was tied to Continental Europe by various umbilical cords, and none was more significant than that provided by the Church. Every monastery, it has been said, was a 'little part of France';[16] the houses of the orders of Tironensian, Cistercian and Cluniac monks were tied closely to their mother houses in Tiron, Cîteaux and Cluny. By the fourteenth century, when the religious houses were almost entirely staffed by native Scots, the nature of the conduit of European influences had changed, but it had not diminished. Until the Wars of Independence, it had been common for Scots to attend the Universities of Oxford and Cambridge as well as the great law schools of Bologna and Padua.[17] By the mid-fifteenth century, most of the promising graduates from the new colleges at St Andrews and Glasgow were going to the new universities at Cologne and Louvain to continue their studies. Such graduates filled not only the ecclesiastical hierarchy but also formed the core of the royal administration during the reigns of James II, III and IV; their highly developed sense of scholarship was both self-consciously patriotic and northern European.[18] The flow of Scots scholars to Continental universities did not slacken after the Reformation, only their destinations changed; by the 1580s Huguenot academies such as Montauban and Saumur and Heidelberg, in the newly Calvinist Palatinate, had replaced Cologne and Paris as favourite destinations. By 1625 Leyden, in the Calvinist Netherlands, had begun to establish itself as the centre attended by Scots intent on a career involving theology or law; by the second half of the seventeenth century Scots pursuing a career in medicine, like Robert Sibbald, had also begun to go there.[19]

In the eighteenth century, much of polite society may have conceived of themselves as North British rather than 'Scotch', but an alternative culture thrived elsewhere, outside the salons of Edinburgh and Glasgow, even if it still usually evades historical headlines. Yet the high Enlightenment of the 1750s was not concerned only with the pursuit of civic virtue, for that (it can be argued) had been a feature of the Scottish intellect since the sixteenth century. It also calculatedly involved a rejection of the Scottish past in favour of the contemplation of a British present.[20] It was a brave experiment, but a profoundly impractical one. A nation needs its historical myths, and in England the new patrician patriotism which would sustain Britain during the Seven Years' War (1756–63), a virtual world war extending from the Elbe to North America, was bolstered by the manufacture of new icons of the past; this was the period when *Rule Britannia!* was written and John Bull was invented (both, ironically, by Scots). In the Enlightenment century, when Edinburgh's 'hotbed of genius' was trying to bury Scotland's past, England was happily reinventing its own; in the 1760s John Bull was found a lineage going back to Saxon times.[21] More British than Great Britain itself but wedded to a culture without historical roots, North British society was quickly caught in an exquisite dilemma of its own making.

The high Enlightenment of David Hume, William Robertson and Adam Smith provoked two counter-currents, each in search of Scottish identity. One was the age of Sir Walter Scott and the new historical clubs, most notably the Bannatyne Club and the Maitland Club. It was a multi-layered phenomenon which ranged from the excesses of a new ersatz, tartan version of Scottishness, triggered by the visit to Edinburgh of George IV in 1822,[22] to Scott's own historical novels for the mass market (furth of Scotland as well as within it) and the production, often by amateur scholars, of more than a thousand works of genuine research, which remain to this day the standard primary texts of pre-1707 Scottish history. The other was an evangelical counter-Enlightenment, led by Presbyterian divines such as Thomas McCrie, who looked to the heroes of Scotland's Protestant past such as John Knox and Andrew Melville to provide a guide to the complexities of the present. The breakdown of a Presbyterian consensus, culminating in the Disruption of 1843, brought a series of denominations, each claiming it represented the authentic strain in Scotland's Protestant tradition. The Free Church may now be little more than an insignificant sect, its influence confined to parts of the Highlands and Western Isles, but it has left an indelible mark on the Scottish psyche: the Wodrow Society, which printed the histories of Knox and Calderwood and much else in the hothouse years of the 1840s, has done more than perhaps any other institution to preserve a vision of Scotland as a Protestant nation. These rival attempts to create a new Caledonia and a new Presbyterian Jerusalem were the first stage of a much longer quest to reconstruct Scottish identity, which has continued into the twentieth century.

It is significant that the first phase of the Industrial Revolution, which saw huge expansion in the textiles industry, mass migration and immigration and the virtual collapse of the old system of poor relief, was also highly concentrated in its effects. Rapid change was confined to certain kinds of towns and a limited number of industries. By the 1840s, Scotland stood on the brink of a new industrial society, but the second, crucial phase of industrialisation, involving the complex of heavy industry, a new skilled workforce and an economy significantly geared to meet the demands of the Empire, had yet to come.

The first Industrial Revolution, which began with the rise of cotton in the 1770s and ended with the crisis faced by the textiles industry in the late 1830s, was played out to the confused search for a new version of Scottish identity. The second Industrial Revolution, which began in the 1850s and dominated the shape of Scottish society until the First World War, was the age of equipoise, when most Scots came to think of themselves as being *both* Scots *and* British, and drew on competing strains of culture as a result.[23] If the novels of the 'Kailyard' and a London-based 'middlebrow' literary culture catered for the interests of Scotland's Victorian middle classes in book form, there was also a sharp increase, during the course of the nineteenth century, of a popular press, seen in journals like the Dundee-based *People's Journal*, which printed, not news as such, but a pot-pourri of Scottish national, local and literary history, folk-tale, and popular fiction, mostly in a vigorous vernacular Scots; in 1864 it had a circulation of 58,000 copies and by the 1890s it claimed a readership of almost 220,000.[24] In effect, the chapbook had found a much wider reading public, amongst the lower middle and respectable working classes, in the novel form of the mass circulation weekly journal.

One of the most telling effects of the strikingly rapid processes of urbanisation and industrialisation which took place in nineteenth-century Scotland was to etch more clearly a distinct sense of class identity. It was not, however, a simple matter of the consolidation of separate sets of middle and working-class values. A series of factors served to underline the habits of the different layers of both the middle classes and the working classes to find new means to secure and distinguish their own identity. Skilled working men found new institutions, such as the craft union, the friendly society, the temperance society, the Orange or Freemason's lodge, different varieties of Presbyterian dissent or surrogate churches like the Salvation Army or the Band of Hope, as well as new leisure pursuits and reading habits to distinguish themselves from the semi-skilled and unskilled working classes.[25]

The consolidation of a distinct, skilled working class belonged to the second Industrial Revolution, when the complex of heavy industry – steel, engineering and marine engineering – established itself. It is striking that it was the same period, the second half of the nineteenth century, which saw a fourfold expansion in newspapers: in 1845 there were already twenty-five burghs with their own newspapers; following the repeal of Stamp Duty in 1855, the number of titles doubled by 1860 and it doubled again by 1900.[26] Their readership lay primarily amongst skilled artisans and the lower middle classes, who were first given the vote in the Second Reform Act of 1868. It is as well to remember, however, the different composition of the electorate in Scotland from that in England and Wales: even after the Third Reform Act of 1884, which in theory granted adult male suffrage, various residential qualifications peculiar to Scotland still operated; the result was that only three out of every five adult males had the vote in practice, whereas south of the Border the figure was two out of every three. The modest demand amongst the Scottish bourgeoisie for creative fiction in book form, as William Donaldson points out, produced either a more anglocentric dependent culture or an ersatz one, in the form of the Kailyard, which also attracted a wider, non-Scots readership.[27] The distinctive shape of the Scottish electorate and the primacy of place enjoyed by the skilled artisan in politics, religion and the workplace, in turn, underpinned the distinctive values of the Victorian popular press in Scotland: douce, sober, thrifty, and intensely conscious of its Presbyterian inheritance and its Scottish identity.

In addition, it is as well to remember that through the centuries many Scots have often seen themselves as Borderers, Galwegians, Shetlanders or teuchters first and Scots second. It is a natural reaction in a society where for centuries 'my country' meant 'my locality'. Instinctively, a society confronted by change clings to its local roots. The arrival of modern transport, an increase in migration and the emergence of a more integrated economy in the nineteenth century at first, as a result, served to heighten rather than diminish this sense of place: the local community found new means to preserve its own identity. But for the one in five Scots (and by 1900 it was one in three) who lived in one of the big four cities – Glasgow, Edinburgh, Dundee or Aberdeen – the great city provided a new kind of identity of the age of rapid urbanisation. 'I belong tae Glesca', ran the words of the song but also, it claimed, 'Glesca belongs tae me'. But which Glasgow was this, for it had many faces? For the evangelists, Glasgow was the Presbyterian 'gospel city', the spiritual home of temperance and of friendly societies; for the late Victorian city reformers, it was the ideal city of the social gospel, a vast working model of Christian enterprise in which notions of space and order, vital to the middle-class view of the world, were given physical form and where the trams, the vital props of a dispersed workforce, ran on time. For its manufacturers and merchants, it was the imperial city, claimed to be 'second city of the Empire'. And for the unskilled and semi-skilled working classes, it was no accident that the big city football teams, which gave either a local or a sectarian identity (or both), were amongst the first to be founded, in the late 1860s and 1870s.[28]

The expansion of the popular press in the nineteenth century took the form of an explosion of *local* newspapers and journals, geared to local preoccupations and culture as well as to a more general Scottish heritage. David Pae's novel of 1863, *Lucy the Factory Girl: or, the Secrets of the Tontine Close* (originally subtitled 'the Dark Places of Glasgow'), was serialised by the *Dundee Advertiser* group, which was based in an industrial city that had, in its jute and textile mills, an unusually large female workforce, disproportionately skewed by first- and second-generation Irish immigrants. William Alexander's *Sketches of Rural Life in Aberdeenshire*, serialised by the *Aberdeen Free Press* in 1853, was, in sharp contrast, a distinctively regional novel of the north-east. This critique of the conflict between rural life and the ruthless economic forces of urban society came out of the same mould as Lewis Grassic Gibbon's *Sunset Song* and *Grey Granite*, which were written more than half a century later. It drew on the experience of an area where the bulk of the urban population explosion in Aberdeen did not come from Irish immigrants or migrant workers from the Highlands, but from its own rural hinterland.[29]

If the locality, the workplace and new middle-class suburbs all served to offer competing versions of identity in the Victorian period, the sense of being both Scots and British offered alternative images which could, paradoxically, project rather than undermine a sense of nationhood. To leave for the moment the complex matter of how Scots thought themselves to be Scottish in the nineteenth century, their sense of Britishness now lay in an imperial mission rather than a North Britain *réchauffé*. This was what underpinned the new-born confidence in a Greater Britain; the Empire provided desk and army jobs for younger sons at least until the 1850s and markets for much of Scotland's industry throughout the nineteenth century. It poses for the student of Scottish culture, however, a conundrum which is difficult to unpick. In the century which transformed Scottish society like no other before it, when so many factors – such as the break-up of the Established Church, mass migration and immigration, intensely rapid urbanisation, and the intensification of class divisions – seemed to make for the disintegration of Scottish society, why was it that this society remained so remarkably stable? An important part of the answer lies in how Scots thought of themselves. Here there seems to be no simple or single image. Essentially, there seems to have been three variable components: a sense of place, sometimes old and sometimes quite new, coalesced with a renewed image of Scottish identity and a novel sense of Britishness.[30] Each of these components fed off a different pattern of culture – local, Scots and imperial.

An expansive English culture existed too, of course, and much attention has been focused on it by those historians who see the Victorian period as one of steady anglicisation of Scottish culture and institutions.[31] It is a phenomenon which threatens to achieve the status of yet another watershed in Scotland's history; but the precise dating of the death of the 'last Scotch age' varies. Some have traced it, *ad hominem*, to the departure of Thomas Carlyle for the literary and intellectual circles of London in the 1830s. Others prefer to point to the late 1840s, which saw the first railway link with England completed and the journey time from Edinburgh to London reduced from forty-three hours to twelve, as bringing a new Union into being, suddenly and unexpectedly more complete than ever before.[32] It was probably no accident that the 1850s saw the first concerted 'nationalist' protest movement, in the shape of the National Association for the Vindication of Scottish Rights, formed in 1853. The real question to be answered is whether anglicisation was rampant in Victorian Scotland or was it held in check? The argument advanced here is that later nineteenth-century Scotland was a melting-pot of different, overlapping identities. In this rich brew of so many ingredients, anglicisation as yet posed only a minor threat. If there is a specific turning-point to be identified, when the constituents of the balance of image, identity and culture shifted significantly, a more plausible case can be made for the First World War and for the serious crisis of Scottish identity which followed in its wake.

THE MAKING OF A SCOTTISH IDENTITY

'Who were the Scots?' is no less a metaphysical question to answer than 'Who are the Scots?'. The chroniclers have left suspiciously clear guidelines. In 843 Kenneth mac Alpin seized the kingdom of the Picts. He is described in a late twelfth-century king list as 'first king of Scots', and there he and his successors were given a regnal order excluding previous kings which was still followed in the sixteenth century, as it is to this day. Yet in reality Kenneth was not the first to hold the kingdoms of the Picts and Scots simultaneously, and he was known to contemporaries as 'king of Picts' rather than king of Scots. Despite appearances and the best efforts of later chroniclers, Kenneth's reign did not mark the introduction of hereditary succession, from father to son. It was a reign which, like many other seemingly key events in Scottish history, gained in importance from the perspective of hindsight.

Dark-Age Scotland has left enigmatic glimpses of a highly sophisticated culture. The haunting, mysterious images found on the standing stones of the Picts, which are to be found sprinkled over the whole of the mainland of present-day Scotland from the Cromarty Forth to the Firth of Forth, have left a sense of a Pictish 'world we have lost', still at best only half understood. The most striking proof that this was a highly developed culture is perhaps the St Andrews tomb shrine, a stone-built sarcophagus nearly six feet in length with elaborately carved panels and corner posts depicting David holding open the jaws of a lion, which was found by workmen digging in the precincts of St Andrews Cathedral in 1833. It was probably the product of the long reign of the Pictish king Constantine (789–820), which saw a flowering of officially sponsored ecclesiastical art. It is the first of countless examples in Scotland's history which indicate that it had a cosmopolitan culture, reflecting and adapting current fashions in Western Europe; the popularity of the cult of the Roman Christian Emperor Constantine reached its highpoint in the reign of Charlemagne, crowned Holy Roman Emperor in 800.[33]

The most powerful image of that other Dark-Age Scotland, the kingdom of Dalriada, located in present-day Argyll, and its alter ego, the Church of Columba, is probably the *Book of Kells*. This magnificent illuminated manuscript, which was begun probably on Iona in the late eighth century but was taken for safety to the new

3. A page from the Book of Kells. *This illuminated manuscript was probably begun in Iona, c.800. Because of its links with Pictish art and the Lindisfarne manuscripts, it is also possible that it was written in eastern Scotland in the eighth century.* (Trinity College, Dublin)

monastery at Kells when Iona was abandoned in the face of Viking threat in 807, is one of a number of surviving artefacts of the Columban Church whose sphere of influence stretched, from its epicentre in Iona, westwards across the Irish Sea as far as Derry and eastwards as far as Holy Island. It demonstrates not only the importance of Iona as one of the great centres of Celtic art but also how cosmopolitan the Christian culture of Iona was: the *Book of Kells* drew on many influences, and not least Byzantine and Coptic cults of the Virgin and Child.[34]

There are, by contrast, few if any striking cultural artefacts which can be traced either to Kenneth's own reign or the mac Alpin dynasty. What Kenneth did was to draw together and harmonise the competing symbols of his composite kingdom. St Andrews, spiritual home of the Pictish kingdom since it had been assigned a biblical saint in the eighth century, remained as an important royal centre; but a counterbalance was created at Dunkeld, to which in 848 the relics of Columba, emblem of authority within the Columban Church, were brought. There were also contemporary references to Kenneth's 'kingdom of Scone' and it is possible that another symbolic gesture belongs to his reign: the bringing to Scone, another old royal centre, of a long-established inauguration stone would have been a characteristic gesture of a usurper king on the make. Whether it was the historic Stone of Destiny or not, it would have made complete the marriage of king to the land and people he ruled. What Kenneth had done was to exploit all the resources of the hybrid kingdom over which he ruled. Its kingship, church and culture were all composite.

The manufacturers of the new imagery of kingship were churchmen. The first duties of holy men, in the time of Columba, had been as the magicians and clerks of kings. By the eighth century, the learned orders had become a mandarin class, promoting the authority and duties of high kings, worthy of Christian record, like kings of Judah and Israel. By then the firm foundations of a distinctive, national church had already been laid: cults of national saints – Columba, Andrew and Ninian – had been established; a close link between Church and king had been formed and the duties of Christian kings set down.

The next recasting of the image of a national Church came in the twelfth and thirteenth centuries, again with a new royal dynasty, the heirs of Malcolm III (1058–93). It was in this period, accelerating from the reign of David I (1124–53) onwards, that the structure of the Scottish Church was transformed. By 1250, well over fifty monasteries and abbeys had been founded, the work of almost a dozen of the new religious orders of Western Europe, and a network of over a thousand parishes had been established.[35] By the 1270s, the shape of the dioceses of the medieval Church had almost reached their final form. Yet, as before, change was cast in the clothes of the old order. It was no accident that the reign of William the Lion (1165–1214) saw a revival of the legends of the origins of kings of Scots and a further elaboration of the cult of St Andrew. It is to the 1160s that can be traced the beginnings of the building of a new cathedral at St Andrews; at 320 feet in length and 168 feet across its transepts, it was far larger than any other church in the realm. Firm foundations had already been laid for what was in effect a national shrine which in 1318 would be reconsecrated in a service of national thanksgiving 'for the notable victory granted to the Scottish people by blessed Andrew protector of the realm' four years earlier at Bannockburn.[36] The intertwined identity of king, Church and people was nearing its mature form.

Three important points are suggested by the immense investment, in money, manpower and national effort, represented by the building programme of the medieval

4. Melrose Abbey. Originally founded by David I in 1136. Wrecked repeatedly in English invasions, particularly in 1322 and 1385. The present remains are of a later rebuilding of the late fourteenth or mid-fifteenth centuries. It was plundered and largely destroyed in the English invasions under the Earl of Hertford in 1544 and 1545.

Church. It is difficult to consider a country which could finance cathedrals such as Glasgow, St Andrews or Elgin and abbeys such as Dunfermline, Kelso or Dryburgh, as being poor or backward. Throughout the medieval period, the clergy were the most important of the many conduits of influence linking Scotland with Europe. But the Wars of Independence made the clergy, who were already the chief patrons of Scotland's culture, also the defenders of national identity. Culture and national identity, as a result, became even more closely intertwined than before. That sense of nationality, which found mature expression in the Declaration of Arbroath (1320), was expanded in a series of officially inspired chronicles of Scottish history, written in the century after the Wars of Independence.[37] All were the work of clerics, ranging from *The Brus* of John Barbour, a canon of Aberdeen, to the massive *Scotichronicon* of Walter Bower, Augustinian abbot of Inchcolm, and they remained the mainspring of Scots' views of themselves until well into the seventeenth century. Yet, beside the growing national consciousness, other churchmen also continued to foster a sense of the Celtic past and the hybrid society which the Scots had once been and, to an extent, still were. In rural parish kirks, Andrew, the national saint, had to compete with local or early saints like Kentigern, Ninian or Machar. The lives of native saints, which had been written or rewritten during the spectacular change of the twelfth century, were revisited in the fifteenth, culminating in the *Aberdeen Breviary*, assembled by William Elphinstone, bishop of Aberdeen, and published in 1510. The *Breviary*, one of Scotland's earliest surviving printed books, had within it more than seventy native saints, each a miniature history in itself. Yet its liturgy also had most of the major new devotions current in Europe, such as St Mary *ad Nives*.[38] The distinctive blend of localist, nationalist and Continental influences which had long marked Scotland's culture had been recast yet again.

A LONG RENAISSANCE?

The fifteenth century should not be thought of as the 'end of an auld sang' but as the first act in a series of cultural patterns which would, for the most part, lead to the Enlightenment of the eighteenth century. In this century, Scotland's first three universities were founded: at St Andrews in 1412; another college (St Salvator's) erected at St Andrews in 1450 to teach theology and philosophy; a College of Arts founded at Glasgow in 1451, and the setting up at Aberdeen in 1495 of the College of St Mary in the Nativity (or King's College). Further colleges shortly followed at St Andrews: St Leonard's, erected in 1513 as a 'college of poor clerks' based on the austere model of the College of Montaigu in Paris, was fuelled by Augustinian piety; St Mary's, first mooted in 1525, given formal foundation in 1538 and reorganised in 1544, would become the centre of the movement for internal reform of the Church in the late 1540s and 1550s. All these foundations were the acts of bishops, who placed them at the centre of their dioceses, and were clerically endowed. Even if the number of graduates was still modest, amounting to perhaps a hundred a year by the 1540s, all this amounted to a national programme for higher learning – Elphinstone referred to his university as being built for the 'glory of the fatherland'.

The most talented and ambitious of these graduates who wished to pursue their studies further, usually by specialisation in those passports to ecclesiastical preferment – canon and civil law – continued to go abroad, to the great universities of Western Europe, as Scots, such as Duns Scotus (d.1308) who had gone to Oxford and Paris, had done for centuries. Yet not the least of the achievements of the new university foundations was that they partly reversed the academic brain drain: Hector Boece, lured home by Elphinstone from the College of Montaigu to become the first Principal of Aberdeen University, was a close friend of the great Erasmus and a devotee of the new learning; and John Mair (or Major), who had gained a European-wide reputation while at Paris, returned to become Provost of St Salvator's College in 1534. This was the generation of scholars which brought the 'humanist revolution' to Scotland: it was based on the study of classical languages, Greek and Hebrew as well as Latin, and a new understanding of Aristotle.[39] Far less is known of the other two sectors of the medieval education system – the grammar schools and the variety of 'little', song and vernacular schools. Duns Scotus had gone to a grammar school at Haddington and it seems likely that the upsurge in university education reflected an increase in the number of grammar schools, which were based mostly in towns. Many were associated with cathedrals or with collegiate churches. Some religious houses, too, had monastic schools which opened their doors, like the Cistercian abbey at Kinloss, to a wider intake of boys. Some friaries had their own 'lector' in theology or arts, and the Dominican house at Ayr had a tutor in grammar in 1420.[40] By the time of the Education Act passed by Parliament in 1496, which encouraged the attainment by the sons of barons and freeholders of 'perfyte latyn', it seems likely that the growing demands of the state for administrators and lawyers may have been threatening to outstrip supply. The course of the sixteenth century would see the increasingly heavy hand of state intervention in both the grammar schools and the universities, but the curriculum remained much the same as in 1530. The nature of the training of the intellect changed before the Reformation rather than after it.

There were many other kinds of schools in medieval Scotland, although they were not necessarily parish schools. The most easy to trace are the song schools attached to both cathedral and collegiate churches, reflecting the reviving interest in the fifteenth century in church music. There were also reading or 'English' schools, situated in rural areas as well as in towns and intended to give only a rudimentary education, probably mostly to boys. There were probably also some small schools designed for girls, sometimes run by women or by nuns, often described as sewing schools. It is likely that many lairds ran private schools for their children and perhaps also those of their kin and tenants. The effect of the Protestant Reformation was felt most keenly in this area of schooling. The generations after 1560, however, saw the consolidation rather than the establishment of an elementary national system of education.

The fifteenth century, which is too easily cast off as the period of a church in the first throes of terminal decline, was in fact an age of great spiritual awakening. This quickening of spiritual life had many facets, too many to be fully described here. It included many religious cults which originated in the Low Countries; the three most important were the new devotions to the Virgin Mary (reflected in the exquisite *Arbuthnot Book of Hours*, composed for the parish church of Arbuthnot by its own vicar, James Sibbald, about 1480), the cult of the Holy Blood, brought direct from Scotland's old staple port of Bruges (and seen in the Fetternear Banner, the elaborate tapestry made for the Holy Blood Fraternity of the Edinburgh merchant guild about 1520), and the cult of the Passion.[41] It is no coincidence that the three opening pieces in the most important surviving manuscript collection of pre-Reformation Scottish devotional verse, Arundel MS 285, are all penitential works on the Passion: the *Tabill of Confessioun* of the court poet and chaplain, William Dunbar; the *Contemplacioun of Synnaris* of the Observant Franciscan William of Touris; and the *Passioun of Crist* of Walter Kennedy, a graduate of Glasgow. The *Contemplacioun* was written specifically for James IV (1488–1513), probably as part of his annual retreat at Eastertide when, girded with an iron belt, he sought expiation for his involvement in the death of his father in the revolt of 1488.[42]

These devotional poems, however, were part of a wider spiritual movement, which also had a popular face. The preparation through the long season of Lent for what was probably for most ordinary men and women an annual celebration of communion at Easter depended on populist representations of the Passion: the Passion plays adopted in a number of burghs in the later fifteenth century, paintings depicting the Crucifixion and Last Judgment on church walls (such as the large painted oak panels dating from c.1453 which remarkably survive from the kirk of Foulis Easter in Angus), or the private ritual of the rosary, were all versions of the same obsession with salvation.[43] Protestantism would reject Marian devotions as a 'richt way to the kingdom of heavin', but it would keep, suitably retouched, a number of other manifestations of late medieval piety. The cult of the Passion, sometimes mistaken as a Protestant devotion half a century before its time, was one such. Much devotional literature and some church music, as a result, survived the Reformation.

Who were the patrons of the quickening of culture in the fifteenth century? The most important patrons, in both religious and secular culture, remained the Crown. The Courts of Stewart kings from James I onwards were employment agencies for all manner of poets, bards, chroniclers, minstrels and entertainers. The royal Court was a forum where multiple strains of both European and native culture might meet, and never more so than in the reign of James IV (1488–1513), who himself probably spoke six languages, including Danish and Gaelic. The construction of a *palatium* or great hall and the lavish endowment of a Chapel Royal at Stirling Castle in his reign is rightly

5. *James IV at prayer, 1503. From the* Book of Hours of James IV and Margaret Tudor. *Attributed to Simon Bening. (*Österreiches Staatsbibliothek, Vienna*)*

taken as the climax of Scotland's medieval monarchy.[44] It was the venue for the brilliant Renaissance Court inhabited by musicians such as Robert Carver, an Augustinian canon of Scone, and by poets such as the Observant, William of Touris, and that better-known churchman, William Dunbar. It combined such fashionable figures as an alchemist (the celebrated John Damian, the butt of vicious satire of that poorer paid Crown pensioner, Dunbar) and the king's Gaelic harpist (an office which can be traced back to the eighth century). As kings had done for centuries, James IV made his court the meeting place of new European fashions and native traditions.

The foreign queens of James II, III, IV and V each added her own distinctive contribution. It was probably the Burgundian princess, Mary of Gueldres, wife of James II (1437–60), who was instrumental in bringing the Observant Franciscans, a new breakaway branch of the mendicant Franciscan friars, to Scotland in the 1450s; by 1500 they had no fewer than nine friaries, based in royal centres such as Edinburgh, Perth, St Andrews and Stirling. The Observants became the favourite religious order of the royal house of Stewart in the century before the Reformation.[45] They mirrored the influence of Burgundy and Flanders on the first phase of the Scottish Renaissance, which was also reflected in the Trinity College altarpiece, the work of the Flemish painter, Hugo van der Goes, in the 1470s.[46] (See Plate 22.) By the reign of James V (1513–42), if not before, the French connection had established itself as the most important single influence operating on the Court. Physical proof lies still in the palace at Stirling, with its series of formal apartments built in the late 1530s, or at Linlithgow Palace, vastly extended to look – according to James's second French bride, Mary of Guise-Lorraine – like a château on the Loire. Yet the same court also acted as patron to native poets like Gavin Douglas, playwrights like the king's Lyon Herald, Sir David Lyndsay, and historians, such as Bellenden, translator of Boece's *History*. The full extent of the cultural influence of the Courts of James IV and V was enormous, yet it still awaits full quantification.

The fifteenth century witnessed the rise of a new nobility, who basked in the reflected glory of the royal Court. Yet nobles were themselves also developing a reputation as patrons of both the arts and the Church. The *Buke of the Howlat* was a long poem written for an entertainment organised by one of the Douglas earls in the 1450s. The Black Douglases were accused of having an almost royal Court, with its own ceremonial offices such as carver and cup-bearer and the walls of castles like Threave hung with elaborate tapestries. Such nobles epitomised the spread of the cult of chivalry and a more leisured style of living. The courtyard castle, which was steadily taking over from the cruder fortified tower house, and the great hall or aula, where nobles might hold court, were further symbols of a Renaissance which already extended to the greater nobility. The collegiate church, devoted to the saying of votive masses for the souls of the dead, was another.

More than fifty collegiate churches were founded between 1400 and 1550.[47] Two of these foundations – Restalrig and Holy Trinity, Edinburgh – were the work of the Crown. A few – St Giles' in Edinburgh and Holy Trinity in St Andrews being the outstanding examples – were burgh parish churches awarded collegiate status as the result of substantial rebuilding, lengthy petitioning and considerable investment by townspeople, and more would follow in the sixteenth century, including St Mary's in Haddington and the Holy Rude at Stirling. Most collegiate kirks, however, were the tangible results of the patronage of nobles or barons; such were Kilmaurs, founded in 1403 by the local Cunningham family before it acquired an earldom, or Crichton,

6. The ceiling of Roslin Chapel. The choir of a collegiate church established by William Sinclair, Earl of Orkney, in 1450, and remarkable for the richness of its stone carving. (RCAHMS)

founded in 1449 by Lord Crichton, chancellor of James II. The most celebrated of these churches is Roslin, marked out by its elaborate architecture and sometimes fantastic internal decoration, including its carving of the dance of death and the 'Prentice Pillar'. Its construction in 1446 was followed by a century of investment which was cut short only by the Reformation. The collegiate church has a double importance in Scotland's cultural history: it was the vehicle of a new, much wider kind of religious patronage, involving the laity from the Crown down to the newly incorporated urban craft guilds who had been given their own altars in the expanded great burgh churches; and it was the venue for a wider range of artistic patronage, involving architecture, decoration, music and music schools, and various kinds of devotional literature, including missals, psalters and books of hours. Nobles, lairds and the larger burghs had already joined the royal Court and the ecclesiastical establishment as patrons of the arts.

The sixteenth century brought a Reformation, but it came late to Scotland and this is immensely significant. The Reformation needs to be set alongside but disentangled from the two other phenomena with which it was intimately connected: the humanist revolution and the arrival of the printing press. Without these twin props, the effects of the Reformation are easily exaggerated or dated too early. There was only a modest return of Scots Protestant exiles from abroad to provide clerical leadership and impetus.

Access to a vernacular Bible had little impact on ordinary Scots much before the 1640s, which was when it first began to figure in significant numbers in booksellers' inventories. For at least three generations after 1560, the Protestant dynamic depended, as it had before 1560, on the conviction of the few, concentrated in the new but modest cadre of ministers and the 'middling sort' of lairds, professional men and merchants, rather than the conversion of the many. The *First Book of Discipline*, blueprint of the Protestant reformers, had more to say about education than any other single subject, but in fact changed little; the real problem was re-endowment and expansion of the schools and universities, not the hewing of virgin ground.

The Reformation is better understood as one part of a three-headed revolution, much of which had already been set in train more than a generation before 1560. When combined with the rise of humanism and access to the new print culture, the impact of Protestantism was startling. It benefited immeasurably from the spread of the new learning in academic circles and from the growth of a new reading public amongst the 'middling sort'. The new humanism continued Scotland's intimate links with the universities of Western Europe. The printing press had by 1600 already become the instrument of a mass culture, which would in the course of the seventeenth century create a new intelligentsia, largely made up of the professions and lairds.[48] For them, printed sermons like those of the Edinburgh minister, Robert Bruce, were best-sellers in the 1590s, and by the 1620s a contemplative piety, seen in the vogue for spiritual autobiographies and manuals of practical divinity, had grounded itself in the psyche of Scottish Calvinism.[49] But the other best-sellers of Jacobean Scotland were histories and works of vernacular literature from the late medieval period. Barbour's *The Brus* and Blind Harry's *Wallace* vied for popularity with George Buchanan's *History*, first published in 1582. Similarly, the works of the poets of the Renaissance Courts of James IV and V, such as Henryson's *Testament of Cresseid* and Gavin Douglas's *Palace of Honour*, were more popular in the revival from the 1570s onwards of the literary masterpieces of Middle Scots than they had been when first written. It was the first example in Scottish history of a patriotic publishing campaign; it would be repeated at regular intervals, most notably in the works of the printer, Thomas Ruddiman, between 1707 and 1715.[50]

The rationale of the wave of historical works produced after the Reformation owed a good deal both to the philosophical tradition established by John Mair and to the vogue for collecting historical documents, which had been seen, for example, in the register of Cambuskenneth Abbey assembled in 1535 by its abbot, Alexander Mylne, scholar, canon lawyer and first President of the newly created Court of Session. The national tradition of historical scholarship became a moral duty and an empirical science in the process.[51] The philosophical tradition, which would culminate in Stair's *Institutions of the Law of Scotland* (1681), also underlay the growing systematisation of the law, where the first milestone was the printed collection of *Acts of Parliament* (1566), the work of a little-known legal circle at the court of Mary, Queen of Scots; by the 1590s collections of legal precedents or practicks had become common. The study of history and law, both of which traced their provenance to the fifteenth century, became the core of Presbyterian humanism which would culminate in the self-styled 'new' philosophical history of Hume and Robertson.

The vital difference which distinguished the seventeenth century from the centuries which preceded it was the loss of the role as cultural patrons of both the Church and the royal Court. The scope of ecclesiastical patronage narrowed after the

7. Head of a King. One of several medallions from the ceiling of the
King's Presence Chamber, Stirling Castle. Carved oak, c.1540.
(National Museums of Scotland)

Reformation, but Presbyterian ministers quickly continued and strengthened the long tradition of the clergy as the guardians of the national memory and university teachers bound to a patriotic programme of learning. The effects of the removal of the Court to London in 1603 are often exaggerated. Poets and chroniclers had already learned to survive in a cold climate; half of the sixteenth century had been taken up with royal minorities. The *Bannatyne Manuscript*, a huge collection of Middle Scots verse assembled in the mid-1560s by an Edinburgh lawyer, George Bannatyne, is ample testimony to the widening circle of literary patronage and interest taking place well before 1603.

For some, the century of the Covenants, conventicling, state repression and the witch hunt produces a dismal story and little literary culture of interest,[52] but if the same standards were applied to the eighteenth century, recent historians would produce a picture of an age of deep anxiety, riven by rebellion, popular riot and a church at odds both with itself and a growing body of Presbyterian dissent. There was, it is true, less creative writing of quality, in Scots or English, in the seventeenth century than in the sixteenth. The focus of culture, however, had shifted to a wider Renaissance of letters, involving architecture, heraldry and music. What Charles McKean has termed the 'Scottish architectural renaissance', manifested in a galaxy of baronial tower houses in both town and country, was only just beginning in 1603.[53] In this century, Latin, still the language of scholarly communication, was the favoured medium of the intellect rather than Scots. The new cultural patrons were the landed classes and the professions.

Their contribution did not replicate the previous roles played by Church and Crown, but established new patterns of cultural interests which would be of great significance for the future. The great libraries were no longer those of religious houses or bishops but of individual lairds and lawyers or the collections of the new professions. This was the age of the collector and the virtuoso. One model of his age was Lauder of Fountainhall, who had amassed 536 books by the time he was admitted as an advocate in 1668 at the age of twenty-two; they straddled the classics, modern histories of European countries as well as of Scotland, and both French and English literature. The most impressive collection of all was that in the Advocates' Library, founded in 1689, which had a catalogue of 158 pages; sixty-nine of them were devoted to non-legal works.[54]

The pursuit of the intellect gathered in pace after 1660, but its rationale was to rediscover Scotland's links with its past, interrupted by a generation of civil war. If there was a break marked by the Restoration of 1660, it came in the universities, where there was a calculated purge of dissident clergy. Newton's theories of light and colour and Harvey's discoveries about the blood were being taught at Edinburgh University from the 1670s onwards. There was a broad-based advance among the Scottish universities in the study of mathematics, law and some of the physical sciences between the 1670s and the 1720s. The schemes for a new medical school at Edinburgh, eventually realised in 1726, built on at least three successive attempts made in the previous century. Enlightened ideas did not burst upon a bare stage in the 1730s; they had been gathering momentun in the universities since at least the 1670s.[55]

The main dynamic in the Restoration period, however, was provided by the professions. Between 1679 and 1688 an astonishing number of institutions and offices were founded; they included the Royal College of Physicians (1681), the Order of the Thistle (1687), the Advocates' Library (1689) and the offices of Royal Physician, Geographer-royal and Historiographer-royal, all introduced between 1680 and 1682.[56] Even if there was no dramatic declaration of the birth of a new age, such as the publicists of the Enlightenment would make in the 1750s, the achievement of the Restoration age was a very real one: it drew together the threads which linked the long Renaissance stretching back to the late fifteenth century with the Enlightenment of the eighteenth. The most lasting effects of the Enlightenment – and not least the growth of the medical profession – were those which depended most heavily on a long tradition.

A MODERN SCOTTISH RENAISSANCE?

In many ways, and not least in its conjunction of the national and the international in its concerns, the self-styled 'Scottish Renaissance' of the 1920s stood firmly within the Scottish cultural tradition. Yet the phrase had begun to be used, for example by Patrick Geddes in his periodical, significantly titled *The Evergreen*, in the 1890s, when it had a rather different point.[57] Geddes was summarising a period lasting from the 1850s until the First World War which, it has been argued, saw the re-creation of Scotland as a nation.[58] In politics, the office of Secretary of State for Scotland had been revived in 1886, Home Rule was firmly on the agenda of Scottish politics, new solutions were being pressed on the Liberal Party by the ginger group, the Young Scots, and the creation of the Scottish Trade Union Congress in 1897 promised to lend a national focus to the labour movement which had hitherto been doggedly localist in its organisation. New institutions were also founded in civil society which gave a renewed focus for Scottish identity and culture; the Scottish National Portrait Gallery had been founded in 1882 and opened in 1889, and a new generation of historical and literary societies – notably the Scottish History Society (1887) and the Scottish Text Society (1884) – had risen to replace the historical clubs of the age of Scott, which had mostly foundered by the 1860s.

This renewed national consciousness also depended on the thriving nature of local identity and culture as well as on 'national' institutions based in Edinburgh (or, like the Scottish Office, in London) or with responsibility for the whole of Scotland. In the 1890s, local periodicals and newspapers were still in a phase of expansion. The second half of the century had been the age of the friendly and savings society, the temperance society and the craft union, all of which (and much more) gave new status to the skilled working man. This new working-class culture, which had a religious as well as a secular face, was inevitably localist in its loyalties, even if part of it involved organisations, ranging from the Rechabites and Good Templars to the Orange Order and the Band of Hope, which had a British or transatlantic network. The 'parish state', in which education and poor relief had been locally run by the Established Church, did not entirely disappear after the Disruption of 1843; with schools, it had survived in the different form of local boards on which the influence of the Presbyterian churches predominated; in poor relief, the shift from kirk sessions to parochial boards kept control in much the same local hands as before. There was certainly intrusion in Scottish affairs by London, but it is significant that accusations of anglicisation were loudest in education, which was already undergoing a process of profound soul-searching. Intrusion into Scots law, however, was probably more substantial, if more subtle; new areas, such as public health and working conditions, which had previously not been covered, in Scots law or any other, required legislation, which inevitably had an anglocentric tone. Yet it is difficult to see any wholesale shift of power from locality to the collectivist British state before the First World War.[59]

The third and final element in the making of a 'nation within a nation', was the British or imperial dimension. As early as the 1850s, much Scottish investment was already concentrated in parts of the Empire. Scots usually preferred to form their own organisations in the new self-help culture of Victorian Britain rather than join British ones; they ranged from trade unions to the Boys' Brigade. The same was true of the evangelical mission to the far-flung parts of the Empire; much of the effort of Scots was concentrated in Scottish organisations (like the Society for Promoting Female Education in India) or local ones (such as the Edinburgh British and Foreign School Society).[60] This – and much more – was the foundation for the familiar claim made amidst the social and economic crises which afflicted Scotland between the two world wars that the Scots were an 'imperial race', who had contributed as much as the English to the making of the Empire.

The 1890s, in sum, were the high summer of a confident, renewed sense of national consciousness, at its strongest amongst the middle and skilled working classes. The 1920s would see a profound crisis of confidence, which would provoke a reaction which was more recognisably 'nationalist', in the modern sense of the word, although much of the reaction was still confined to sections within the established parties. Where does this leave the undoubted phenomenon of a Scottish Renaissance in the 1920s or the suggestion that it tried to address a rather different crisis of confidence, the roots of which were first detected by T.F. Henderson at the end of his highly influential *Scottish*

Vernacular Literature, published in 1898?[61] Even within the world of the creative arts, it is difficult to accept that Henderson's diagnosis of Scottish literature was typical elsewhere. In painting as in politics, rebellion by younger artists against the establishment, in the form of the Royal Scottish Academy, was part of the complex but stimulating vortex of ideas which informed the work of the 'Glasgow Boys' and the Scottish colourists.[62] Too much has often been concluded from the alleged state of creative writing in the nineteenth century, as in the seventeenth; literary critics are more prone even than historians to reach for the word 'crisis'. Too many general crises of Scottish culture have been hung on too narrow an agenda in too many periods of Scottish history.

The 'Scottish Literary Renaissance' of the 1920s was more narrowly based than its nineteenth-century counterpart. Many of its writings were published in new, but short-lived journals. It also depended, however, on many of the local newspapers and small journals which had sustained the nineteenth-century age of equipoise. For some, their last act was to publish the work of the new writers of the 1920s.[63] The infrastructure which underpinned the distinctively local face of Scottish culture was disappearing. It would be replaced by a new kind of 'national' press, in which a handful of daily newspapers predominated; most were stridently Scottish in tone, not least those, like the *Scottish Daily Express*, which were Scottish editions of London-based dailies. Authoritative comment and full political coverage was confined to the *Scotsman* and *Glasgow Herald*, although each, skewed by its base in Edinburgh or Glasgow, remained, in a real sense, less than national newspapers. Regional newspapers remained and some, like Aberdeen's *Press and Journal*, flourished, but the characteristically varied voice of the locality, which had so clearly marked the Victorian age, had gone – probably for good.[64]

This literary Renaissance found it difficult to escape the crisis of Scottish society which gave birth to it. By the 1920s, which not only saw mass unemployment but was the first decade in its history that Scotland suffered a net loss of population, there was a distinct sense of a cultural vacuum and the need to recover a world which had been lost. The Renaissance of the 1920s was the product of a society where many sets of nerves were badly frayed. Both the middle classes and the Church of Scotland were apprehensive of the new working-class consciousness which had emerged during the First World War; the self-confident world of the skilled working man had begun to slip even before the war and the slump which followed it. There were regular predictions in right-wing circles during the 1920s of the end of the Scottish race, not least by John Buchan, who elegantly combined the personae of Scottish, English and imperial patriot. A sustained campaign was waged throughout the 1920s and beyond by an influential element within the Church of Scotland to stop immigration of Catholic Irish, an 'inferior' and 'alien race'. The 1920s witnessed a confused jumble of nationalist solutions of different kinds, which gripped the old, established parties as well as those who sought solutions in a new, explicitly nationalist politics.[65]

There was little consensus amongst the prophets of the Scottish Renaissance as to where the authentic Scottish tradition was to be found. Promotion of the cultural treasury of pre-Reformation Scotland ran up against the anti-Catholicism which still permeated many influential circles in the 1920s. Ideas of a Gaelic revival had briefly flowered in the 1880s, the decade of the Crofters' Wars, the Napier Commission and the Crofters Party, but they had been built, if briefly, on an alliance with Irish land agitation and political protest; that prospect, despite Hugh MacDiarmid's backing, seemed more remote after Ireland gained Home Rule in 1922. Few doubted the centrality of the Reformation in Scotland's history, but many writers felt a sharp distaste for the Calvinism which had underpinned much of the self-help philosophy of the Victorian age and was now so much on the defensive against the new forces of secularism. The Enlightenment, although still acknowledged as a high point in Scotland's cultural past, was disliked by many for its abandonment of Scottish tradition and the barrier which it had erected between Scots and their past.[66]

The dilemmas which confronted Scots in a search for their cultural roots were not easily resolved. It is perhaps only in this present generation that a more inclusive vision of Scottish culture has begun to be formulated. The rediscovery of the quality of music and both lyric and religious poetry of the pre-Reformation period has done much to explain why Scottish poets in the eighteenth century, like Allan Ramsay, looked to the 'good old bards' to regenerate both naturalism and a primitive classicism. Scotland's broad-based humanist Renaissance, grounded on philosophy, historiography and a Latin culture, has established another link between pre- and post-Reformation Scotland; the fact that it survived and flourished throughout the seventeenth century in a 'long Renaissance' more easily explains the widely acknowledged roots of the Enlightenment in the culture of the Restoration period. The most difficult pill to swallow for readers in the Scotland of the 1990s when, as David McCrone has claimed, 'we are all nationalists now',[67] may be to come to accept the nineteenth century as a period when Scotland had regained a national self-consciousness. The fact that it was very different from the national identity of both pre-1707 Scotland and the North Britain which followed it is less of a barrier than its lack of similarity to what we, in the late twentieth century, usually understand as modern nationalism. But history should not be a supermarket which allows us to pick and choose amongst the different phases of our national past.

SOME CONCLUSIONS

The Scottish historical experience is not easy to sum up in short space. Within the geographical entity which by the eleventh century had come to be known as Scotland, locality, different *nationes* and an inchoate but potent sense of nationhood competed. By the fourteenth century, however, there was no doubt that this hybrid society was held together by an overweening loyalty, both to a 'king of Scots' and a compelling sense of nationality. No group was more assertive of Scottish nationality than the clergy of the medieval Church, yet theirs was a cosmopolitan nationalism, deeply influenced by their regular contacts with Europe and by a humanist consensus. The clergy of the new post-Reformation Church fell heirs to both the interwoven identity of Church and nation and the role of guardians of the archives of the national memory. There is, as a result, a direct line to be traced between Barbour, Fordun and Bower, the late medieval architects of a new, more sharply focused Scottish historical identity, and post-Reformation historians such as Buchanan, Calderwood and Spottiswoode, who drew on much the same assumptions about Scottish culture and the moral utility of drawing to the attention of Scotland's rulers 'faithful advisers from history'.

Continuities such as these abound in Scotland's history. Yet the more closely Scotland's cultural heritage is studied, the more varied the influences at work on it appear and the more diverse it seems to become. For centuries a sizeable part of the

Scottish experience stemmed from the absorption of successive waves of immigrants and the importation of foreign artists, architects or craftsmen on the one hand, and the habits of generation after generation of native Scots to study, trade, tour or fight abroad on the other, bringing back with them the tastes, habits and enthusiasms of different parts of Continental Europe. It would be misleading to suggest that the result is a kind of Scottish *doppelgänger*, where native culture has sat uneasily beside a more sophisticated imported foreign culture. There is no need to invent a new 'paradox of Scottish culture' or to provoke a renewed 'Scottish cringe'. It has been the argument of this chapter that this 'paradox' has been exaggerated. It was characteristic only of the North British milieu in the eighteenth century and, sadly, of part of the twentieth century, when the balance between native and anglocentric culture has been lost. What is much more typical of Scotland's long historical experience is a dialogue rather than a cultural conquest; native continuity and tradition have been continually exposed to cross-examination by foreign or cosmopolitan connections, and new patterns have resulted. Three final conclusions may be worth making.

Scottish art, architecture, literature and music have all drawn on a series of foreign influences, yet what is striking are the ways in which each set of influences has usually been absorbed and refined into a distinctively Scottish style. The royal palaces of James IV and V were mostly built by French architects and stonemasons, but by the end of the sixteenth century the spirit of the Renaissance was manifested in what Charles McKean has termed the '*châteaux* of the Scottish Renaissance' – town houses like the Argyll Lodging in Stirling or Acheson House and Moray House in the Canongate or country houses like those at Fyvie, Drum and Inverugie, which were by then mostly the products of indigenous skills and materials. All are testimony to the continuing influence of European fashion and to the ability of Scottish architecture to put its own stamp on a distinctively Renaissance style.[68] In the history of art and decoration, the story is much the same. To give just one example: the exquisite mace of St Salvator's College, commissioned in 1461 by James Kennedy, bishop of St Andrews, was made in France by Jean Mayelle, a leading Parisian goldsmith who may well have been an expatriate Scot. The splendid Galloway mazer, made in 1569 by James Gray, a local Canongate goldsmith, for an Edinburgh merchant, although it shows both English and German influences, is nevertheless 'altogether Renaissance in feeling' and evident of a discrete Scottish style.[69] (See Plate 30.) Some of the best-selling books in James VI's Scotland were either Continental romances or native works cast in the same chivalric tradition like the fifteenth-century *Graysteil* (which could also be set to music).[70] The cult of honour was one of the most basic traits of the European Renaissance; its translation into Scots and Scottish terms produced some of the masterpieces in Scottish literature, including Barbour's epic poem, *The Brus*, and Gavin Douglas's *The Palace of Honour*. In the same vein, Robert Carver, usually taken to represent the climax of the Scottish Renaissance in music was, as an Augustinian canon, part of an international intellectual network which had its most immediate contacts with sister houses in England, the Low Countries and northern Germany. His music reflects all of these influences, but it is not surprising that the foremost was that of the Flemish masters for the religious cults of Flanders were the most significant of the myriad of Continental influences at work on the psyche of the Scottish Church. Yet, within Carver's church music are a number of features which were uniquely Scottish.[71]

Amidst all these foreign influences, it is necessary to remember, as Alexander Broadie has emphasised, that the intellectual traffic was not one way.[72] Scottish academics and artisans for centuries found employment in Europe. Between 1411 and

1560, the University of Paris had no fewer than seventeen Scottish rectors. It was the reversal of this brain drain in the century before the Reformation that provided the humanist core of the Scottish Renaissance. The story of Scotland's Reformation was rather different. Its late arrival and the decades of uncertainty and intermittent persecution which preceded it forced tens of intellectuals and schoolmen and schoolmasters into exile. They are part of the hidden story of the Scottish Reformation. Only a handful of them – such as Alexander Alane (or Alesius) or John MacAlpine (Machabeus) – are well known, but most of the others, like them, fled to northern Germany or Scandinavia, where they made a minor but distinguished contribution to the spread of the Reformation in their adopted homelands. The flight of the intellectuals may help explain the inchoate nature of early Scottish Protestantism, for most never returned to Scotland. With one or two notable and obvious exceptions, its leadership came from laymen rather than clerics.

The number of Scots employed in the universities of the Netherlands, Germany and France increased in the century after the Reformation, and here is a clear case where Scotland gave as much as it received. Sir Thomas Urquhart of Cromarty in his *The Jewel*, written in 1652, celebrated the long procession of scholars working abroad as one of the characteristics of the Scottish nation.[73] This pattern, which confirms that Scotland lay in the cultural mainstream of northern Europe while Latin remained the main vehicle of instruction in its universities, persisted into the early eighteenth century. It is for that reason that a fair case, in terms of its culture, can be made that the second language of Scotland was Latin until about the 1720s, when John Clerk of Penicuik chose it as the medium for a history of Scotland from the Romans to the present time.[74] The main change between the seventeenth and eighteenth centuries was not the emergence either of the virtuoso or a newly enlightened society; it was the replacement of Latin by English as a lingua franca. For the émigré Scot, who for centuries had indulged in a literature of homesickness, a new kind of dilemma was posed. The wandering scholar, Florence Wilson (or Volusenus), found it easier to dream of his native Moray landscape in his Latin poem, *De Animi Tranquilitate*, published at Lyons in 1543, than did James Boswell, cast adrift in London polite society, where he had his Scotticisms to worry about. For Boswell, as for many in the salons of the new North British society of the 1750s, the Scots and English were divided rather than united by their common language. It was not until the Enlightenment was nearly over that their dilemma began to be resolved.

The late eighteenth and the nineteenth centuries brought a new breed of Scots émigrés: administrators, engineers, scientists and medical doctors. By the 1760s, there were already shrill complaints from English politicians and journalists such as John Wilkes that ambitious Scots careerists were depriving true-born Englishmen of jobs and perks. When a new Empire opened up in India after 1784, the Scots and Irish were the two largest contingents to benefit from the expanded network of state patronage. A hugely disproportionate number of Scots merchants, administrators and army officers already thronged Madras and Bengal; they became a flood after 1784. When the French wars brought about a huge expansion of the army and navy after 1793 it was the Scots and Irish who benefited, comprising between them almost a half of the officer corps.[75] A simple explanation for the size of the Scots' contribution to the imperial mission is difficult to find; it may be, as one (non-Scottish) historian has recently speculated, that the Scots had centuries of practice of working or fighting for a foreign culture behind them.[76]

In some fields, however, it was clearly the distinctive nature of Scottish education as well as the numbers produced by it which made the difference. In the field of medicine, Scots had typically gone to Leyden to study in the second half of the seventeenth century. By 1750, the Edinburgh medical school, basing its methods of teaching on those of Leyden, had established a reputation second to none, in Britain or Europe. In the century after 1750, Scotland's universities educated some 10,000 doctors, whereas Oxford and Cambridge produced 500. They and others like them were the tangible products of the age of Enlightenment. The Edinburgh medical school, when it had been set up, had been urged to expose its students to the sciences in general and to stress the social role of science and the scientist. Its impact, as a result, extended beyond the medical profession into a wider scientific world in which botany, natural history and mineralogy particularly figured. This was the broad basis for the continuing links between Edinburgh medicine and America, both before and after the War of Independence.[77]

There is an important clue here to the nature of the Scottish intellect and its ability to thrive in foreign cultures. The methodology and philosophy of medical teaching at Edinburgh quickly conformed to that in the university as a whole. It was a product of the 1720s, the 'age of Improvement', in which lawyers, academics and gentry met, debated and conversed on topics ranging from agricultural improvement to the moral study of mankind. Colin McLaurin, professor of mathematics at Edinburgh University and one of the key figures in the first generation of the literati, opened up his lectures on Newtonian astronomy and methodology to polite society. It was he who had encouraged the new professors of medicine to study science as a whole and to include the antiquities of Scotland.[78]

But were the traits of the virtuoso and the study of the science of man new products of the Enlightenment? Newton's physics had been taught in Scottish universities since the 1670s, before anywhere else. The laws of nature, whether or not they were attributed to God's Providence, had underpinned the writing of history by Scots since the sixteenth century. It had been a characteristic of the Scottish humanist mind to combine an interest in many disciplines, with philosophy and history given central place. Sir Richard Maitland of Lethington, privy councillor and senator of the College of Justice in the reigns of Queen Mary and James VI, was a historian of the nobility (in both Latin and Scots), legal historian, anthologist of Scots verse and a distinguished poet in his own right. He was the prototype for the model of the aristocratic virtuoso which reached new levels of sophistication in the half century before 1720 in figures such as Sir Robert Sibbald (1641–1722) and John Clerk of Penicuik (1676–1755). Sibbald, who had gone to study medicine at Leyden in 1660 and became Geographer-royal as well as the first professor of medicine at Edinburgh University, had interests which ranged from natural history and botany (he was instrumental in founding in 1667 what later became the Royal Botanic Garden in Edinburgh) to archaeology, cartography and local history. In him, as with a series of charismatic thinkers in Scotland's history, a patriotic programme of learning combined the science of man with a desire to preserve the cultural treasures of the past.[79]

The figure of John Clerk of Penicuik illustrates, in almost exaggerated form, the eclectic habits of the Scottish intellect. Another product of Leyden, where he studied law, his interests ranged across agricultural improvement, astronomy, chemistry, geology and medicine, but they also included archaeology, antiquarianism, the classics and Scots poetry; he was a poet (mostly in high-flown Augustan English), a historian (in Latin) and a distinguished musical composer (familiar with the musical lingua franca of Paris and Italy).[80] The history of the Enlightenment often tends to be studied through the development of the clubs of polite society; it produces too easily a sense of cohesive movement towards the ideals of civic virtue and a pigeon-holing of yesterday's men and tomorrow's *philosophes*. Clerk, as a result, can become a Jekyll and Hyde figure: as an apologist for vernacular Scots and as a historian who chose to write a six-volume chronicle of the Scottish nation in Latin he can be said to belong to the dying Scoto-Latin humanist culture of the Ruddiman circle; as an improver, industrialist and musician, he can be said to have earned his membership of the emerging 'hotbed of genius'.

Clerk's multifaceted career, from the different perspective taken by this chapter, provides an accurate snapshot of the competing strains of culture at work in early eighteenth-century Scotland. Most of the swirling ideas of the Enlightenment had deep roots in Scotland's past. The difference, in post-Union society, was the Union itself and the need felt by many of its apologists to redefine the patriotic programme which had characterised Scottish learning since the fifteenth century. That was why, in the century after 1720, many of the different patterns of Scottish culture seemed to be in competition with each other. Hume and Robertson rejected whole sections of Scotland's culture and turned their back on Scotland's past. Clerk tried to absorb and balance the paradoxes within his country's culture and looked to its past to provide a solution to the present. The paradoxes within Clerk's mind and career – a patriotic Scotsman who was also a North Briton, a defender of Scottish culture who sent his eldest son to Eton – reflected the paradoxes in which Scotland found itself in the confusing century which followed the Union of 1707.[81] Yet Clerk was also in some ways the prototype for the century after that, when the Victorian age attempted, amidst new confusions of its own, to subsume a Scottish patriotism within a sense of a British imperialism.

Notes

1. N.T. Phillipson and R. Mitchison (eds.), *Scotland in the Age of Improvement: Essays in Scottish History in the Eighteenth Century* (Edinburgh, 1970), p.1.

2. *The Nation*, 9 March 1929.

3. Reported in the *Observer*, 5 April 1992.

4. A. Hook (ed.), *The History of Scottish Literature*, Vol.2, *1660–1800* (Aberdeen, 1987), pp.1–2.

5. M. Lynch, *Scotland: a New History* (2nd edn., London, 1992), pp.xv–xviii.

6. D. Allan, *Virtue, Learning and the Scottish Enlightenment: Ideas of Scholarship in Early Modern History* (Edinburgh, 1993).

7. A. Broadie, *The Tradition of Scottish Philosophy: a New Perspective on the Enlightenment* (Edinburgh, 1990).

8. J. Durkan, 'Education: the laying of fresh foundations', in J. MacQueen (ed.), *Humanism in Renaissance Scotland* (Edinburgh, 1990), pp.123–60.

9. J. Purser, *Scotland's Music* (Edinburgh, 1992).

10. D. Macmillan, *Scottish Art, 1460–1990* (Edinburgh, 1990), p.40.

11. R.A. Houston, *Scottish Literacy and the Scottish Identity* (Cambridge, 1985).

12. Purser, *Scotland's Music*, p.145.

13. M. Lynch, 'Renaissance and Reformation', in R. Mitchison (ed.), *Why Scottish History Matters* (Edinburgh, 1991), pp.26–36. Details of the 1633 entry are to be found in L.E. Kastner (ed.), *The Poetical Works of William Drummond of Hawthornden*, 2 vols (Scot. Text Soc., 1913).

14. See, for example, E.J. Cowan (ed.), *The People's Past* (Edinburgh, 1980), p.31, where the distinction between a written and unwritten history, which has 'endless appeal', is made.

15. See D. Craig, *Scottish Literature and the Scottish People* (London, 1961); and D. Daiches, *The Paradox of Scottish Culture: the Eighteenth-Century Experience* (London 1964).

16. S. Cruden, *Scottish Medieval Churches* (Edinburgh, 1986), p.63.

17. D.E.R. Watt 'Scottish university men of the 13th and 14th centuries', in T.C. Smout (ed.), *Scotland and Europe, 1200–1850* (Edinburgh, 1986), pp.1–18.

18. R.J. Lyall, 'Scottish students and masters at the Universities of Cologne and Louvain in the 15th century', *Innes Review*, xxxvi (1985), pp.55–73; L.J. Macfarlane, *William Elphinstone and the Kingdom of Scotland, 1431–1514* (Aberdeen, 1985), chs. 1, 3, 5, 7.

19. J. Durkan, 'The French connection in the 16th and early 17th centuries', in Smout (ed.), *Scotland and Europe*, pp.19–44.

20. L. Colley, *Britons: Forging the Nation, 1707–1837* (New Haven and London, 1992), p.168.

21. G. Newman, *The Rise of English Nationalism, 1740–1830* (London, 1987), p.48, pp.116–18; Lynch, *Scotland*, p.324, p.344.

22. J. Prebble, *The King's Jaunt: George IV in Scotland, 1822* (London, 1988).

23. R.J. Morris, 'Scotland, 1830–1914: the making of a nation within a nation', in W.H. Fraser and R.J. Morris (eds.), *People and Society in Scotland*, vol.2, *1830–1914* (Edinburgh, 1990), pp.1–7.

24. W. Donaldson, *Popular Literature in Victorian Scotland* (Aberdeen, 1986), pp.x, 26.

25. Lynch, *Scotland*, p.396, pp.404–05, p.419.

26. Donaldson, *Popular Literature*, pp.2–3.

27. Ibid., pp.145–8.

28. Lynch, *Scotland*, pp.360–61.

29. Donaldson, *Popular Literature*, pp.88–95, pp.106–8.

30. T.C. Smout, 'Problems of nationalism, identity and Improvement in later 18th-century Scotland', in T.M. Devine (ed.), *Improvement and Enlightenment* (Edinburgh, 1989), pp.1–21.

31. See C. Beveridge and R. Turnbull, *The Eclipse of Scottish Culture* (Edinburgh, 1989).

32. P.H. Scott, '"The last purely Scotch age"', in D. Gifford (ed.), *The History of Scottish Literature*, Vol.3, *The Nineteenth Century*, pp.13–15; Lynch, *Scotland*, pp.357–8.

33. I. Henderson, 'Pictish art and the Book of Kells', in D. Whitelock *et al* (eds.), *Ireland in Early Medieval Europe* (Cambridge, 1982), pp.79–105.

34. A. Smyth, *Warlords and Holy Men: Scotland AD80–1000* (London, 1984), pp.125–7.

35. I.B. Cowan and D.E. Easson (eds.), *Medieval Religious Houses: Scotland* (London, 1976).

36. D. McRoberts (ed.), *The Medieval Church of St Andrews* (Glasgow, 1976), pp.63–120.
37. G.W.S. Barrow, *Robert Bruce and the Scottish Identity* (Saltire Society, 1984).
38. Macfarlane, *Elphinstone*, pp.231–46.
39. Broadie, *Scottish Philosophy*, pp.75, 77.
40. Durkan, 'Education', pp.124–5.
41. D. McRoberts, 'The Fetternear Banner', *Innes Review*, vii (1956), pp.69–86; Lynch, *Scotland*, pp.107–9.
42. A.A. MacDonald, 'Catholic devotion into Protestant lyric: the case of the *Contemplacioun of Synnaris*', *Innes Review*, xxxv (1984), pp.58–87.
43. D. McRoberts, 'Scottish sacrament houses', *Trans. Scot. Eccles. Soc.*, xv, pt. iii (1965), pp.33–56; idem, 'The rosary in Scotland', *Innes Review*, xxiii (1972), pp.81–6.
44. N. Macdougall, *James IV* (Edinburgh, 1989), pp.282–312.
45. J. Durkan, 'The Observant Franciscan province in Scotland', *Innes Review*, xxxv (1984), pp.51–7.
46. Macmillan, *Scottish Art*, pp.18–22.
47. Cowan and Easson, *Religious Houses*, pp.213–30, lists collegiate churches.
48. Lynch, 'Renaissance and Reformation', p.30, p.33.
49. M. Steele, 'The "politick Christian": the theological background to the National Covenant', in J. Morrill (ed.), *The Scottish National Covenant in its British Context, 1638–51* (Edinburgh, 1990), pp.31–67.
50. See H.G. Aldis (ed.), *A List of Books printed in Scotland before 1700* (Edinburgh, 1970), under 1570 and 1571, when Robert Lekpreuik printed *Blind Harry and the Brus*; cf D. Duncan, *Thomas Ruddiman: a Study in Scottish Scholarship of the Eighteenth Century* (Edinburgh, 1965), pp.41–71.
51. See Allan, *Virtue*, esp. ch.2.
52. D. Reid (ed.), *The Party Coloured Mind: Prose relating to the Conflict of Church and State in Seventeenth-Century Scotland* (Edinburgh, 1982), pp.1–16.
53. C. McKean, *The Architecture of the Scottish Renaissance* (Edinburgh, 1990).
54. T.I. Rae, 'The origins of the Advocates' Library', in P. Cadell and A. Matheson (eds.), *For the Encouragement of Learning: Scotland's National Library, 1689–1989* (Edinburgh, 1989), pp.1–22.
55. C.M. Shepherd, 'Newtonianism in Scottish universities in the 17th century', and R.G. Cant, 'Origins of the Enlightenment in Scotland: the universities', in R.H. Campbell and A.S. Skinner (eds.), *The Origins and Nature of the Scottish Enlightenment* (Edinburgh, 1982), pp.65–85 and pp.42–64.
56. H. Meikle, *Some Aspects of Later Seventeenth-Century Scotland* (Glasgow, 1947).
57. Scott, 'Scotch age', p.20.
58. R.J. Morris and G. Morton, 'The re-making of Scotland: a nation within a nation, 1850–1920', in M. Lynch (ed.), *Scotland, 1850–1979: Society, Politics and the Union* (Historical Association, 1993).
59. Lynch, *Scotland*, p.398, pp.403–04.
60. Morris and Morton, 'The re-making of Scotland'.
61. Gifford, *History of Scottish Literature*, p.iii, p.11.
62. Macmillan, *Scottish Art*, p.309.
63. C. Craig (ed.), *The History of Scottish Literature*, Vol. 4, *The Twentieth Century* (Aberdeen, 1987), p.2.

64. C. Harvie, *No Gods and Precious Few Heroes: Scotland 1914–1980* (London, 1981), pp.122–3.
65. R.J. Finlay, '"For or against?": Scottish nationalists and the British Empire', *Scottish Historical Review*, lxxi (1992); S.J. Brown, '"Outside the Covenant": the Scottish presbyterian churches and Irish immigration, 1922–38', *Innes Review*, xlii (1991), pp.19–45.
66. Craig, *History of Scottish Literature*, pp.5–6.
67. D. McCrone, *Understanding Scotland: the Sociology of a Stateless Nation* (London, 1992), p.173.
68. McKean, *Architecture*.
69. Macmillan, *Scottish Art*, pp.16–17; M. Kemp and C. Farrow, 'Humanism and the visual arts, c.1530–1660', in MacQueen (ed.), *Humanism*, p.39.
70. Lynch, *Scotland*, p.260, p.261: Purser, *Scotland's Music*, p.66.
71. Ibid., pp.83–92.
72. Broadie, *Scottish Philosophy*, pp.2–3, p.26.
73. Sir Thomas Urquhart of Cromarty, *The Jewel*, ed. R.D.S. Jack and R.J. Lyall (Edinburgh, 1983), pp.152–62
74. *The History of The Union of England and Scotland by Sir John Clerk of Penicuik*, ed. D. Duncan (Scottish History Society, 1993).
75. Colley, *Britons*, pp.117–32; Lynch, *Scotland*, p.388.
76. Colley, *Britons*, p.129.
77. D.A. Dow, *The Influence of Scottish Medicine: an Historical Assessment of its International Impact* (Carnforth, 1988), p.39; J. Rendall, 'The influence of the Edinburgh Medical School on America in the 18th century', in R.G.W. Anderson and A.D.C. Simpson (eds.), *The Early Years of the Edinburgh Medical School* (Edinburgh, 1976), pp.95–124.
78. N. Phillipson, 'Culture and society in the 18th-century province: the case of Edinburgh and the Scottish Enlightenment', in L. Stone (ed.), *The University in Society* (Princeton, 1974), ii, pp.440–41.
79. See J. Boyes, 'Sir Robert Sibbald: a neglected scholar', in Anderson and Simpson (eds.), *Edinburgh Medical School*, pp.19–24.
80. I.G. Brown, 'Modern Rome and ancient Caledonia: the Union and the politics of Scottish culture', in Hook (ed.), *History of Scottish Literature*, pp.33–48; Purser, *Scotland's Music*, pp.164–72.
81. Brown, 'Modern Rome and ancient Caledonia', pp.34–5, p.43.

Books for Further Reading

D. Allan, *Virtue, Learning and the Scottish Enlightenment* (Edinburgh, 1993).
G. Barrow, *Kingship and Unity: Scotland, 1000–1306* (London, 1981).
I. Donnachie and C. Whatley (eds.), *The Manufacture of Scottish History* (Edinburgh, 1992).
A. Grant, *Independence and Nationhood: Scotland 1306–1469* (London, 1984).
C. Harvie, *Scotland and Nationalism* (London, 1977).
C. Harvie, *No Gods and Precious Few Heroes: Scotland 1914–1980* (London, 1981).
M. Lynch, *Scotland: a New History* (2nd ed., London, 1992).

R. Mitchison (ed.), *Why Scottish History Matters* (Saltire Society, 1991).

W.H. Fraser and R.J. Morris (eds.), *People and Society in Scotland, 1830–1914* (Edinburgh, 1990).

T.C. Smout, *A History of the Scottish People, 1560–1830* (London, 1969).

A. Smyth, *Warlords and Holy Men: Scotland AD80–1000* (London, 1984).

J. Wormald, *Court, Kirk and Community: Scotland 1470–1625* (London, 1981).

Culture and Religion

DONALD SMITH

Religion has played a central part in the development of culture in Scotland, influencing most aspects of intellectual, emotional and artistic life. This, however, has always been a two-way process in which religious institutions have been as much shaped by as they have shaped wider forces of social and cultural change.

Since the sixth century, the dominant religious force in Scotland has been Christianity; but Scottish Christianity has distinctive features by which it is internationally recognisable, not least in those areas of the world in which Scots have settled as emigrants and missionaries. To risk a paradigm, Scottish Christianity has in general been intellectually grounded and profoundly interested in metaphysical ideas. At the same time it has been intensely practical and engaged in social and political life. This is not the contradiction it might appear because activism and intellectualism are linked in Scottish Christianity by a commitment to principles formed on the basis of clear ideas such as 'society' and 'humanity' or even 'justice' and 'freedom'. Since the Celtic era the concepts of church and society have been closely interrelated in a conscious and deliberate way which has provoked both enthusiasm and resistance, depending on the shifting balance and on the commentator's viewpoint.

From one perspective, a close affinity between ecclesiastical institutions and society has been the great strength of Scottish Christianity and this affinity, bordering at times on identity, has been a central plank of a distinctive Scottish culture. From another viewpoint Christianity may have become so characterised by its Scottishness and so implicated in Scottish society as to have lost contact with its own distinctive sources of inspiration. This perception has been at the heart of successive reform movements in the medieval and modern periods. The same argument of an over-identification of Church and society has led to equally severe criticism from outwith the Church and attempts to roll back the frontiers of church influence in the name of individual liberty, artistic and intellectual freedom, or sexual liberation.

It is not possible to generalise in a worthwhile way about the relationship between Church and culture without examining its phases and mutations, and to this our attention should be turned. But I would like to flag an important marker of this exploration which is often neglected by ecclesiastical and cultural historians, operating from their respective remits.

A vital characteristic of a religious tradition is the way in which its inherent values are expressed. What qualities are reflected in the form as well as the content of the prayers, the patterns of worship, and credal statements of the tradition? What does the way in which religious values are communicated say about the religion and about its relationship to the culture in which it is placed? What is its spiritual aesthetic? This is often confused with the question of religious art for although the two are closely related the distinctive aesthetic of a religious tradition may be by definition anti-aesthetic, eschewing sensuous form or canons of beauty and good taste. Nonetheless, even such a puritan aesthetic may be of profound cultural significance and the forms through which it is expressed of great importance.

THE CELTIC CHURCH

The rapid spread of Christianity in Ireland and Scotland from the fourth to the seventh centuries AD with its distinctive monastic structures was seen by later writers, many of them monks, as explicitly miraculous. Saintly men triumphed because the power of the Holy Trinity was greater than the worldly might of the Celtic kings or the spiritual resources of traditional religion. Even defeats could be turned to triumphs through the redeeming power of martyrdom. Certainly there is a sense that a new moral and spiritual force had entered Celtic tribal society, and followers were attracted in sufficient numbers to allow an extensive network of monasteries and churches to be established in a remarkably short period of time.

This was not an isolated phenomenon but comparable to developments on mainland Europe and in the Mediterranean where asceticism and monasticism were already flourishing and the Christian Church was putting down institutional roots wherever political and economic circumstances allowed. When Ninian travelled back from Rome to found his church at Whithorn in 398 he stayed at Tours where St Martin was the focus of a flowering of Romano-Gallic Christianity and of the new monasticism. Columba is also credited with visiting Tours and, in the words of the *Old Irish Life*, he 'brought away the Gospel that had been on Martin's bosom one hundred years in the earth, and he left it in Derry'.[1] What was to distinguish Celtic Christianity, however, was the longevity of its institutions through a period in which Europe would be convulsed by migrations and invasions.

The hallmark of Celtic Christianity is the expression of its values through the forms, language and imagery of Celtic Culture. The Monymusk reliquary, for example, which dates from Columba's own lifetime, contains no explicitly Christian symbolism. The potent imagery of Celtic Christianity was developed through Celtic art rather than imposed upon it and the resultant fusion was an impressive cultural achievement which still speaks eloquently in the stone-carved Celtic crosses and illuminated manuscripts, which required disciplined and sustained schools of artistic activity.

Much harder to assess is the degree of rapprochement between the existing Druidic religion and Celtic Christianity. The Celtic emphasis on the power and beauty of God

8. The Monymusk Reliquary, eighth century. Also known as the Brecbennach of St Columba. Carried by the Scottish Army at the Battle of Bannockburn. (National Museums of Scotland)

in nature may well reflect earlier religious sensibilites, though it is to Christianity that an ethic of kindness to all living beings is ascribed. Celtic monasticism may also owe something to the precedent of the Druidic priesthood as well as to the general patterns of social organisation in Celtic society. But the characteristic asceticism of the Celtic saints is so clearly akin to that of the Desert Fathers and early European monasticism in general that emphasis must fall on the radical influence of a new spiritual ethos which was nonetheless expressed in characteristically Celtic forms.

The synergy of Celtic Christianity is as evident in language and in literature as it is in the visual arts. In Adamnan's *Life of Columba*, the saint is depicted in a memorable clash with Broichan the Druid, but he is also credited with saving the ancient order of the Bards from banishment at the Convention of Drumceatt in 575. In consequence, Dallan Forgaill, the chief bard, composed the *Amhra Columcille* in his honour. Columba may have been recognised as a bard in his own right and the *Old Irish Life* explicitly praises Columba as a poet in both Latin and Gaelic.[2]

Whatever Columba's personal contribution to Celtic literature, the key innovation of Celtic Christianity was the introduction of writing and manuscript records. All surviving lives of Columba testify to the amount of time which he spent transcribing. A special significance and even power was believed to rest in the written scriptures as is clear from the connection between Finian's psalter which Columba copied, apparently without permission, and the Battle of Culdreimhe in 563, and from the way in which the

Cathach (allegedly the same psalter) was carried into battle in a shrine.

The Cathach may date from approximately 600 and belongs in the early stages of a manuscript tradition which stretches with increasing complexity and artistic ambition to the *Book of Kells* (*c*.800) which was probably begun on Iona and then moved under the pressure of Viking raids to the relative safety of Ireland. (See Plate 3.) These illuminated manuscripts are, of course, celebrated as superb art works and a culmination of the visual achievements of Celtic culture, but they are also part of a new written culture which provided the means by which Early Irish and Gaelic found their literary form and new genres such as the Lives of the Saints came into being. It is often forgotten that Adamnan's *Life of Columba* and Ailred's *Life of Ninian* (to name only two better-known authors) are among the great achievements of early Scottish literature.

THE MEDIEVAL CHURCH

The marriage of Malcolm Canmore to the Saxon Princess Margaret in 1068 is a watershed in many areas of Scottish life, ushering in a period of English and European influence which was to radically alter the power structures of Scottish society. In religious terms, however, Margaret stands symbolically at the opening of the first of the major reform movements which were to be a recurrent feature of European and Scottish ecclesiastical life in the next centuries.

Although the systematic implementation of reform and the creation of the fabric and structures of the Scottish medieval Church belong to the reigns of Margaret's children and their successors, Margaret herself brought a re-injection of the spirituality which had been nurtured in the monasteries of Western Europe and which was reinvigorated by the Cluniac and Cistercian orders, both in themselves reforming offshoots of the main Benedictine stream.

It is unfair to depict Margaret's ecclesiastical example as anglicising in aim. There is ample evidence of her esteem for the Celtic anchorites or 'Friends of God', her devotion to the shrine of the national saint at St Andrews, and her desire to re-establish Iona as a place of prayer. It is natural that in seeking to reform the Scottish Church she should turn to the best contemporary models in devotional practice and spiritual endeavour. In the process Margaret moved the Scottish Church in the direction of the European mainstream and this instinct was to be vindicated and fulfilled in the remarkable renaissance of Scottish Christianity during the next two centuries. To this period belongs a succession of outstanding ecclesiastical foundations including Melrose, Holyrood, Cambuskenneth, Jedburgh, Kelso, Dryburgh, Dundrennan, Arbroath, Inchcolm and Sweetheart, not to mention the cathedrals of Glasgow, Elgin and Dunblane.

Given the ambition and scale of these buildings there is no doubting the comparable impact of their furnishings and art works, or the educational and social impact of the monks' activities in liturgy, music, manuscript production, medicine and agriculture. From the *Inchcolm Antiphoner* to the Hospital at Soutra, the surviving evidence is of a significance and quality as to imply the overall worth of what has been lost. It is also interesting to note that orders such as the Tironensians and Cluniacs who favoured artistic adornment and attracted artisans and craftsmen, as well as the more austerely inclined Cistercians, flourished in Scotland. There is no reason to think that the Scottish medieval Church was any less a patron of the arts than its sister churches in Europe, and much evidence to suggest that relative to its size and wealth Scotland's endowments were on generous scale.

It is tempting to comment that this wave of ecclesiastical activity did not in its early stages contribute to a distinctively Scottish Christianity but this would be to miss the main point. The development of the Scottish Church was the creation of a conscious and deliberate policy, the key architect of which was probably David I, the third of Margaret's sons to become King of Scotland. The aim of this policy was to establish the political, social and cultural structures of Anglo-Norman society in Scotland and the monastic movement was an integral part of the process. Perhaps the principal consequence of this policy in religious terms was to bring Church and society together in a structural symbiosis quite different in quality from the Celtic synergy. The Church would provide the administrative skills and the manpower required for royal policy, as well as the necessary spiritual superstructure. It was not so much a question of the Church influencing culture as the Church being culture or at least its dominant institutional expression. The fate of Church and nation became indissolubly linked, deeply implicating the Church in national instability after 1296, the Wars of Independence, and the weakness of the Scottish Crown after the death of Robert the Bruce in 1329. The foundations of a distinctive Scottish nationhood were laid at the Battle of Bannockburn in 1314 but a golden age of the medieval Church in Scotland had already drawn to a close.

The next surge of reforming activity in European Christianity was an urban missionary movement designed to reach people in the growing towns and cities. The principal instrument of this reform were the Franciscan and Dominican friars who, despite the relatively slow growth of the Scottish burghs and the economic uncertainties caused by war and weak monarchy, made steady progress in Scotland from the late thirteenth century, pioneering new forms of social care and stimulating the foundation of leper houses, almshouses, hospitals and hospices for travellers and pilgrims. The friars were also pioneers in preaching as a popular art form and should perhaps be credited with establishing what was to become one of Scotland's most widespread forms of oral literature. In devotional life they were assiduous confessors and promoters of pardons and pilgrimages, while producing from their ranks some notable educators and theologians, not least the Franciscan Duns Scotus. The friars' influence on medieval Scottish life should not be judged by the fact that so few of their town centre friaries have survived later urban development.

The success of the friars points to the increasing importance of the Scottish burghs and it is noteworthy that when church building began again in Scotland in the early fifteenth century, the burghs led the way with the construction of buildings such as St Michael's Linlithgow, the Kirk of the Holyrood at Stirling and St John the Baptist's in Perth. During the same period wealthy laymen began in significant numbers to found collegiate churches, chapels and chantries. These foundations brought increased artistic patronage in the shape of sculptures, stained glass, wood carving, vestments, manuscript illumination, sacramental vessels, choral music and drama. Although the main cultural influences of the late medieval Scottish Church are clearly Continental, particularly Flemish and French, native patronage assisted the development of craft industries in the Scottish burghs often under the initial leadership of immigrants from the Continent. The Western Highlands are, however, a major exception to this scenario since there the late medieval period saw a renaissance of the native Celtic traditions in a new medieval guise, under the patronage of the Lord of the Isles and of other Chiefs who retained their political and military independence from the Scottish kingdom.

Again the volume and quality of this second artistic renaissance, which stretches into the prosperous early decades of the sixteenth century, are impressive, with survivals including the rood-screen of Glasgow Cathedral, the choir stalls of King's College Chapel, Aberdeen, the carved ceiling of St Machar's Cathedral, the wall paintings in Fowlis Easter Church near Dundee, and the magnificent carved stone grave slabs in the Western Highlands. The Trinity College altarpiece, now in the National Gallery of Scotland, which was commissioned from the noted Flemish painter Hugo van der Goes, indicates the importance placed on the altarpiece as the essential backdrop to the Mass. (See Plate 22.) Every Scottish medieval church of significance must have had an impressive altarpiece but these images were among the most vulnerable items at the time of the Reformation.

The dramatic relationship between the altarpiece and the Mass is an apt reminder of the relationship between church buildings and what happened in them. One of the many contributions of Monsignor David McRoberts to the recovery of Scotland's medieval heritage is his painstaking cataloguing of liturgical manuscripts including psalters, missals, breviaries and books of hours. These reflect a rich liturgical life with a distinctively Scottish flavour, including a devotion to the Scottish saints which was to be recognised and catalogued in Bishop Elphinstone's *Aberdeen Breviary* of 1509–10. Some outstanding church music has also survived, though of the mysteries, passions and pageants of the Scottish burghs only a few titles and possible fragments remain.

Ecclesiastical historians have often represented the late medieval period as one in which the spiritual aesthetic of the European Church became over-elaborate, heavily dependent on the visual image and, in Christian terms at least, decadent. The Church therefore was ripe for reform and renewal. Although admittedly the evidence is incomplete, there is little to support the application of this cultural critique to Scotland, whatever other problems beset the late medieval Scottish Church. Scottish Humanism evolved gradually from the late medieval period and Scottish churchmen were at the forefront of the introduction of new literary, artistic and philosophical ideas. Any assessment of the late medieval Church must combine the fine surviving art work with the influence of Humanism's impressive commitment to education, learning and the concept of a humane culture.

HUMANISM, REFORM AND REVOLUTION

The most important cultural change in fifteenth-century Scotland was the growing significance of the towns and cities and of the emergent 'middling folk' who included lawyers and merchants as well as the clerics who still provided the skilled manpower for education and administration. As a class they were unimpressed by the courtly ideals of much medieval Scottish literature and fostered a new sense of realism and moral seriousness in cultural life. One of the finest embodiments of this spirit is Robert Henryson, priest, poet and schoolmaster, whose humanity and moral integrity pervade a poetic corpus blending the medieval Christian inheritance and classical influences in a distinctively Scottish achievement.

The movement for social, political and ecclesiastical reform predates the Reformation, and many of the aims of the Protestant reformers were shared by

Catholic reformers. At the turn of the fifteenth century the outstanding figure in Scottish Church life was Bishop Elphinstone of Aberdeen who combined close involvement in the political, legal and economic affairs of the realm with a devotion to the pastoral well-being of the Church and to its spiritual life. He is remembered today as the instigator of the *Aberdeen Breviary* and as the founder of Aberdeen University and King's College. Elphinstone's own training was rooted in medieval scholasticism but in his foundation at Aberdeen he reflected all that was best in the new Renaissance and Humanist ideas. Among the distinguished teachers Elphinstone brought to Aberdeen was Hector Boece who had been a friend of Erasmus and a colleague of another eminent Scots scholar, John Mair or Major, at the University of Paris. Boece was also an eminent early historian of Scotland, contributing to a tradition of historical writing which embraces Mair himself, George Buchanan the Protestant Humanist, and John Knox. The Humanist culture of the Scottish universities was also Christian, embracing the new classical learning, neoplatonism and the biblical scholarship of Erasmus.

The same Christian Humanism is apparent in the work of another important Scottish reformer, the poet, dramatist and diplomat, Sir David Lyndsay of the Mount. Lyndsay's monumental drama *Ane Satyre of the Thrie Estaitis* may also reflect Lutheran influence, but its aim is the reform of both Church and state to improve the well-being of society as a whole, not radical theological or political change. (See Plate 19.) The *Satyre* is a major linguistic achievement based on a confidence in the

IOANNES CNOXVS.

9. John Knox (c.1513–72). After Adrian Vanson.
From Theodore Beza's Icones, *(1580). (*National
Library of Scotland*)*

vernacular and on compassionate realism about social conditions in Scotland. In literary terms Lyndsay's work raises the drama beyond the Robin Hood folk-plays, and the popular pageants and festivals of the medieval mysteries. The Catholic Church in Scotland legislated against the popular dramas and their accompanying festivites in 1555, and the drive for increased public order and moral discipline was taken up by the General Assembly of the Reformed Church. In the same way Catholic reform of education, particularly of the clergy, was carried forward in a much more comprehensive way under the influence of the *First Book of Discipline*.

To this point it is clearly possible to identify a social and intellectual agenda which was common to Christian Humanism and Protestant Reform. The ethos was urban, morally serious and dedicated to improvements in culture and education based on the supremacy of language and texts, which were now more widely available than ever before due to technical improvements in printing. The impact of this change is most evident in the effect which the introduction by the reformers of the English Bible was to have on the long-term fate of the Scots language, though at the time this was more a matter of political and practical convenience than of conscious cultural design. In addition, Humanist reform, like Medieval reform before it, was a European cultural movement in which Scotland played an active part. But the Protestant Reformers also brought to bear a mix of radical politics and popular piety which could not be sustained within the existing power structures, and which laid a trail of revolutionary conflict which was to continue to explode periodically until 1745.

At the core of this conflict was the close identity of Church and state, espoused not only by medieval theorists but by most Protestant Reformers and by the career statesmen who were the architects of the rising national monarchies and to whom Church policy was a critical weapon in their armoury. That the ruler and the ruled should share one religion was taken for granted; the issue was which form of Christianity should apply. If the monarchy was to be sustained at the head of a Catholic realm then the authority of the Pope could be acknowledged and a new realistic concordat achieved, redistributing power between Church and state to the benefit of the latter. If, however, papal authority was to be dispensed with, then a new concept was needed to express and to channel the vital relationship between Church and state.

In general, ruling monarchs and the nobility, who had much to gain from annexation of Church property, saw no difficulty in simply subordinating the Church to the authority of the monarch or the monarch in parliament, though in the long run this view had to be buttressed by a quasi-sacerdotal view of monarchy as inherently sacred. In opposition to this secularising tendency the Protestants maintained the essentially medieval *Doctrine of the Two Kingdoms* — the Kingdom of Christ and the Kingdom of this World — which justified the Church's spiritual and often temporal independence on the grounds that Jesus Christ was the only true King and Head of the Church. But the reformers had no wish to separate Church and state, which they saw as mutually interdependent, and the lack of any institutional mediation for this relationship, such as the papacy had theoretically provided, left the Church exposed to every turn of state policy and led inevitably to conflict.

Had this conflict only been a matter of politics it would have been fierce enough, but the Reformation also accelerated a genuine shift towards a more internalised piety rooted in both personal emotion and individual conviction, which affected a much wider stratum of the population through education and the reform of the parish system. The political and ecclesiastical issues became intermixed with deeply nurtured religious emotion. However rapidly the initial Protestant Reformation was effected in 1560, these changes were not the work of a few months or even a few years, but they underlie the bitter struggles between Church and state and between competing models of Church authority which disrupted national life so severely and marked Scottish religion with the scars of ideological coercion and the stains of unjustifiable bloodshed, not least in the civil wars of the Covenanting period.

Despite the crescendo of polemic and disputation, however, cultural development continued. Humanist achievements in literature, architecture and music were not set aside but continued in the work of post-Reformation poets, scholars, portrait painters, bibliophiles, builders, ballad makers, and craftsmen. Artistic patronage was dealt a much greater blow by the removal of the Scottish Court to London in 1603 than by the Protestant Reformation of 1560, while many areas of intellectual endeavour, notably medicine, jurisprudence and mathematics, continued to advance throughout the seventeenth century. Nonetheless, the spiritual aesthetic had shifted decisively in favour of verbal expression within a restraining intellectual framework. There was a definite bias towards moral action, rather than divine contemplation, though devotional writers of as different theological persuasions as Robert Leighton, Bishop of Dunblane; Robert Bruce, minister of St Giles; the 'Aberdeen Doctor', John Forbes of Corse; and Thomas Boston, the Puritan Divine, continued to demonstrate that a religion which was not also of the heart and soul could only be an empty shell.

The new model had many admirable qualities, though its appropriateness to the religious needs of the whole population is perhaps questionable. The emotional outlets which were provided, particularly the congregational singing of psalms, were enthusiastically taken up and did much to establish the Protestant order in the affections of a significant proportion of the Scottish people. But even at the peak of seventeenth-century Puritanism, thoroughgoing austerity was never more than a minority taste in lowland Scotland, while in the Highlands Scottish Gaeldom continued to pursue a much more traditional cultural and religious agenda.

ENLIGHTENMENT AND DISRUPTION

If seventeenth-century Scotland was disproportionately affected by the political consequences of Calvinism and its antitheses, then the eighteenth century enjoyed some of its cultural fruits, in association with the Humanist tradition which had taken such firm root in Scottish education in the fifteenth and sixteenth centuries. It is hard to understand in retrospect how Calvinist orthodoxy and rational enlightenment could coexist in the Scottish universities but the educational system itself owed its development to the Protestant Reformers of the *First Book of Discipline*. In addition, scholastic Calvinism had by the early eighteenth century adopted much of the academic aridity of its medieval predecessors, and offered a secure and established system of background belief to progressive rational enquiry into the natural world, history, philosophy and the social sciences. The earnestness and moral commitment of William Robertson, Adam Ferguson, Hugh Blair and the other Enlightenment luminaries were in the Presbyterian tradition, though their tolerance of opposing viewpoints was less characteristic. In their devotion to humane and scholarly values they were also the direct heirs of the Christian Humanists.

Political circumstances contrived to create and sustain this alliance since the settlement of 1690, confirmed by the Treaty of Union in 1707, laid the foundations of a secure Calvinist establishment which steadily allied itself with conservative forces in Scottish society. The great age of Enlightenment was also an age of political management, and the ecclesiastical Moderates were firmly on the side of order and patronage. Political security was in its turn the basis of politeness, elegance and intellectual advance, though true ecclesiastical and religious unity continued to be elusive.

On the one side, the Episcopalian tradition remained politically disaffected and until the Battle of Culloden in 1746 the possibility of a return to an older order was a live one. The association of the Stewart cause with the Scottish Highlands and with Roman Catholicism as well as Episcopalianism did nothing to enhance its appeal in the towns of lowland Scotland, but the defeat of the Jacobite Rebellions sowed the seeds of a powerful imaginative appeal to a former era which was viewed by many as more spiritually and emotionally attractive than Calvinist realism. The Presbyterians had a number of good arguments on their side but they lacked effective imagery and colour.

On another side the Settlement of 1690 could not satisfy the radical Calvinism of the Covenanting period because it was necessarily based on a compromise between Church and state. A Church established by law could also be a church changed by law. From the beginning the Covenanting dissenters or Cameronians of the south-west refused to acknowledge the 1690 Settlement since it made no mention of the national Covenants. Furthermore, the worst fears of many seemed confirmed when, in 1712, the British Parliament re-imposed lay patronage on the Scottish Church, setting aside both the spirit and the letter of the Treaty of Union signed only five years before. The idea that a Scottish ecclesiastical settlement might qualify the sovereignty of the Westminster Parliament was not so much unacceptable to the majority as simply incomprehensible. The origins of a series of disruptive secessions from the Presbyterian establishment lie in the 1712 Act, even while that establishment was still in the making. The exclusion of Episcopalian nationalism was now complemented by the alienation of the radical, deeply emotional piety which, arguably, had sustained the Reformed Church through its darkest days and which continued to exert a strong grip on the popular imagination. Later criticism of the eighteenth-century Presbyterian Church as both secularising and Anglicising has its roots here, though it is hard to see how an established state Church could escape the dominant economic, social and political influences of the period as they affected Scotland within the Union.

The contribution made by a small northern European country to the philosophical, literary and scientific Enlightenment after 1750, and the important role played by the Church's ministers in that flowering, must provoke admiration. An outstanding example was the *Statistical Account*, edited by Sir John Sinclair and published in twenty-one volumes between 1791 and 1792. This was the first attempt anywhere to describe a country in detail and in all aspects, and it was written by the 938 ministers of all the parishes in Scotland. But if the purpose of religion is to promote a wholeness, health or 'salvation' in the human psyche and community, then the cultural influence of the Scottish Church in this period cannot be counted a complete success. As conformity to the Westminster Confession became a benchmark of social stability and a backcloth to rationalism, the creeds of the established Church ceased to be a framework for responsive religious development in the face of changing social and intellectual conditions, and this legacy was to dog the Protestant Church into the twentieth century. Likewise, the worship of the Church became static and, to the more enthusiastically inclined, positively arid as the century progressed.

Inevitably, reaction ensued with the growing influence of the Evangelical movement in religion, not least in the Scottish Highlands, and of Romanticism in literature and art. The links between an emotional and increasingly individualistic piety, with the influence of nature, the 'rediscovery' of the past and the cult of feeling, are well established across European culture, but the form which these developments took in Scotland was strongly affected by the fact that Presbyterian rationalism remained the dominant cultural ethos. Nearly four centuries of intellectual development were not to be so easily shaken off and the alliance between religious establishment and secular management survived until the upheavals between the Reform Act of 1832 and the Disruption in 1843.

Something of the uneasy division between heart and head which affected Scottish religion and culture in this period is reflected in the writings of Boswell, Scott and Hogg, but the contradictions are laid out with an engaging frankness in the Journals of Lord Cockburn. Cockburn's favourite author was Tacitus and by social standing, his legal profession, and ability, he belongs in the Enlightenment tradition. A Whig in politics, Cockburn drafted the Scottish Reform Bill but opposed radicalism and any further extension of the franchise beyond the respectable classes. At the same time Cockburn conducted a love affair with the countryside, felt deeply about the history of his country, defended the beauty and historic character of Edinburgh, and stretched his own personal finances to breaking-point by building a Gothic tower at the foot of the Pentland Hills. In religion, Cockburn was an orthodox believer in the eighteenth-century fashion who saw little connection between his rational faith and personal spiritual enthusiasm. By most counts Cockburn should have been a firm establishment man but he was a personal admirer of Thomas Chalmers and greatly moved by the Disruption as an expression of heroic national spirit.

Cockburn is one of our best witnesses for the conflict which led to the departure of one third of the ministers and congregations of the Church of Scotland to found the Free Church in 1843, because as a judge he sought unsuccessfully to temper the increasingly inflexible judgments of his colleagues which were pushing the Church into an intolerable corner in the dispute over who appointed its ministers. The Disruption commands admiration because its cause was clearly a principled one and because it reasserted the combination of self-sacrificing independence and intense piety which had characterised Calvinism in its heroic period and which many now claimed as an essential expression of 'Scottishness'. In reality, the Disruption unintentionally hastened the demise of most of what it stood for. The Disruption was not a secession but a defence of the establishment principle and a herculean attempt to recreate the Established Church anew. The practical consequence, however, was that no church any longer represented a social cohesion sufficient to sustain establishment on the old model, and within thirty years social care and education had been taken out of the control of the Church. The close identity of Church and state which had been sustained since the medieval era was never regained. A further irony is that Chalmers believed in financial support of the Church by the state, both through central funds and local church rates. But the astonishing growth of the Free Church was based entirely on voluntary contributions, so providing the most powerful example of a religious movement based on the free and individual choice of citizens to give or withhold their support.

Thomas Chalmers, the leader of the Disruption, combined the Calvinist orthodoxy, establishment principles and learning of the eighteenth century, with an intense evangelical piety and a reassertion of the primacy of conscience. He is an embodiment of three centuries of Scottish presbyterian culture; but, in a dramatic and largely unrealised way, the Disruption marked the beginning of a modern era, many of whose tendencies Chalmers would have vehemently disowned.

SPIRITUALITY AND SECULARISATION

Though the intellectual principles of the Disruption embodied the tenets of previous centuries, the phenomenal energy which created the institutional fabric of the Free Church reflected the activism of the Victorian era. From the 1830s onwards, Scotland witnessed industrialisation and urbanisation to a previously unthinkable degree, in addition to experiencing huge shifts of population including both emigration and immigration on a massive scale.

The Church mirrored these changes and it is questionable whether even at the height of the Covenanting period the Christian religion played such an extensive role in Scottish life as during the late Victorian era. The keynote now, however, was one of denominational diversity with the earlier secession Churches (later to become the United Presbyterian Church), the Free Church, the Church of Scotland, the Episcopalian Church and the Roman Catholic Church all enjoying expansion – and even that list excludes the independent Churches such as the Methodists and Baptists. It is hard to conceive of the sheer scale of this activity but the physical evidence is there for all to see, and a walk round the centre of Paisley, for example, reveals immediately the density and variety of Church presence at this period. In addition to this domestic energy many of the Scottish Churches were a powerhouse of overseas missionary endeavour and a century and a half later we are still grappling with the consequences of the way in which Western European trade and religion were zealously carried into every corner of the globe.

Since the nineteenth century, religious diversity and globalisation have increased hand in hand through the engines of imperialism, trade, cultural cross-fertilisation, improved communications and the movement of peoples. Lord Cockburn could not have forecast that by the late twentieth century the Jewish, Sikh, Buddhist, Hindu, Islamic and Bahai faiths would all have a place in Scottish life, though he did accurately predict the effective end of the Presbyterian establishment. The reunion of the largest Protestant denominations in the early twentieth century to form the present-day Church of Scotland was more a tactical recognition of the new situation than a recreation of a national Church in its previously understood sense.

On one level the process of secularisation dates from the effective division between Church and state in 1843. This might be described as political or governmental secularisation. But ever increasing prosperity brought a sociological secularisation in which the previous constraints and imperatives of religion were distanced from everyday existence by greater life expectancy and an improved quality of life. Religious faith became a matter of individual choice rather than communal necessity, even though considerable social sanctions were still exercised in the interests of the institutional Churches.

Most intriguing of all, however, was the process of intellectual secularisation in which the previous metaphysical presumptions were abandoned as the basis of all human cultural enterprise. This was perhaps a relatively simple step for the rationalist whose deistic separation of God from the world could move to the abandonment of God as a necessary first hypothesis. But even explicitly spiritual and imaginative thinkers such as Thomas Carlyle wished to shed the metaphysical framework of religious orthodoxy. Carlyle believed passionately in spiritual transcendence but his religion was based on a God immanent in the natural world and human culture rather than one expressed and institutionally guaranteed by the authority of religious tradition. Conversely, the Protestant Churches became increasingly uncomfortable with spiritual prophets, adapting instead to the pragmatic materialism of industrialised society. Only in the Scottish Highlands where Presbyterian evangelisation was a phenomenon of the eighteenth century, did an inherently religious culture survive in the way that the Disruption leaders had envisaged. In these areas religious culture, Protestant and Catholic, became a symbol and expression of the survival of economically hard-pressed and culturally marginalised Gaelic-speaking communities.

Given the rapidity of intellectual and social change in the late nineteenth and twentieth centuries, it is the resilience of the institutional Churches rather than their late twentieth-century decline which attracts notice. Both in the 1930s and again in the period of post-Second World War reconstruction, the Christian Churches showed their ability to contribute to the national well-being through social care, moral concern and community development. Culturally, too, the Churches have continued as patrons in architecture and in artistic commissions within their respective ecclesiastical traditions.

To this extent it could be argued that the spiritual aesthetic of twentieth-century Scotland has been diverse but no less influential than the dominant modes of the medieval Celtic and Protestant eras. Closer examination, however, reveals that the aesthetics of the Scottish Churches in the modern period have been largely based on the attempted revival of older styles and patterns and on the identification of Christianity with a historical ethos. It is perhaps unfair to criticise religious institutions for not embracing the discordant challenges and discontinuities of modernism in music, art and literature, though where the Church has taken up the challenge – as, for example, in St Giles Cathedral – the results have been impressive. Yet the clear implication is that the Scottish Churches have not wished to confront the radical problems of religious belief posed by a century in which Europe has torn itself apart in two gruelling world wars, created and implemented means of mass destruction, racial extermination and global degradation, and defied every confident hope that intellectual and moral progress implied each other. Religious aspiration and secular reality have rarely seemed so far apart and no twentieth-century theologian has succeeded in holding the two in a satisfying focus or tension. To many engaged in a twentieth-century spiritual search Scottish Christianity seems tainted by association with Western European culture, and alternative religious paradigms have been sought in South American or African Christianity, Buddhism or varieties of Nature worship. The late twentieth-century ecumenical movement may represent an attempt to share religious insights and to refashion Scottish Christianity in the light of secularism and pluralism.

If the Scottish Churches have shied away from the religious challenge of modernism, then the same cannot be said of twentieth-century Scottish artists, writers and musicians. The loss of the cohesion provided by shared religious values, the spiritual emptiness of much contemporary life, the moral, social and environmental consequences of industrialisation, and the search for a renewed spiritual reality, have been major preoccupations of Scottish culture since the time of Carlyle. The twentieth century has seen significant achievement in poetry, the novel, the visual arts, drama and music, but when critics try to characterise or interpret these achievements they turn constantly to phrases such as 'moral intensity', 'metaphysical concern', 'visionary awareness', 'collective memory', 'prophetic voice', 'social commitment', or 'mythic consciousness'. Many of these phrases equally apply to earlier phases of Scottish religious consciousness.

There is much in late twentieth-century Scotland to suggest that religion and culture are still closely related to each other, though the institutional basis of this relationship and its means of expression are constantly changing.

Notes

1. Wentworth Huyshe (ed.), *The Life of Saint Columba by Saint Adamnan xvii* (London, 1905).
2. ibid., pp.xxxvi–xxxvii. Of the surviving pieces ascribed to Columba, the Latin 'Altus Prosator' has perhaps the strongest claim to authenticity.
3. See N.M. de St Cameron (ed.), *Dictionary of Scottish Church History and Theology* (London, 1993) under relevant entries.

Books for Further Reading

S.J. Brown and M. Fry (eds.), *Scotland in the Age of the Disruption* (Edinburgh, 1993).
J.K. Cameron (ed.), *The First Book of Discipline* (Edinburgh, 1972).
A.C. Cheyne, *The Transforming of the Kirk* (Edinburgh, 1983).
C. Dawson, *Religion and the Rise of Western Culture* (London, 1950).
J. Durkan and A. Ross, *Early Scottish Libraries* (Glasgow, 1961).
I. Finlay, *Columba* (London, 1979).
F. Kaplan, *Thomas Carlyle* (Los Angeles, 1983).
I.D. MacFarlane, *Buchanan* (London, 1981).
L.J. MacFarlane, *William Elphinstone and the Kingdom of Scotland* (Aberdeen, 1985).
J. MacInnes, *The Evangelical Movement in the Highlands of Scotland 1688 to 1800* (Aberdeen, 1951).
D. Macmillan, *Painting in Scotland: the Golden Age* (Oxford, 1986).
J. MacQueen (ed.), *Humanism in Renaissance Scotland* (Edinburgh, 1990).
J. MacQueen, *Progress and Poetry: the Enlightenment and Scottish Literature* (Edinburgh, 1982).
D. McRoberts, *Catalogue of Scottish Medieval Liturgical Books and Fragments* (Glasgow, 1953).
D. McRoberts (ed.), *Essays on the Scottish Reformation* (Glasgow, 1962).
D. Martin, *A General Theory of Secularization* (Oxford, 1978).
W.L. Mathieson, *Politics and Religion* (Glasgow, 1902).
National Museum of Scotland, *Angels, Nobles and Unicorns* (Edinburgh, 1982).
S. Piggot, *The Druids* (London, 1968).
R.B. Sher, *Church and University in the Scottish Enlightenment* (Edinburgh, 1987).
T.C. Smout, *A Century of the Scottish People (1830–1950)* (London, 1986).
T.C. Smout, *A History of the Scottish People* (London, 1969).

A Nation of Philosophers

ALEXANDER BROADIE

INTRODUCTION: DRAMATIS PERSONAE

Scots have played a part in western philosophy for at least the past eight centuries. Few Scottish works remain from those earliest years, but they bespeak a formidable contribution, including, as they do, writings by Richard of St Victor (Ricardus de Sancto Victore Scotus, *d.*1173); and more spectacularly by John Duns Scotus (1266–1308) whose impact on Scottish philosophy lasted, arguably, at least until the middle of the nineteenth century. Those two philosophers were closely related, for Richard, who lived before the founding of the Order of Friars Minor – the Franciscans – had a great influence on the philosophical and theological stance of the Order, and Duns Scotus was one of the greatest of the Franciscan philosophers. Scotus quotes Richard, for example, on the nature of personhood, a topic in which the Church was naturally interested, and on which it was inclined to follow Boethius. On that matter Richard and Scotus submitted a minority report.

During that earliest period few Scottish philosophers, so far as we know, taught and wrote in Scotland, for there were then no Scottish universities. Thus, for example, Michael Scot (died *c.*1236),[1] who played a major role in the transmission of Aristotle's works from the Muslim world to the Christian west and also made Latin translations of Arabic commentaries on Aristotle, may well have done much of his philosophical work on the Continent. Though there is persuasive evidence that he worked for some time in Scotland we lack proof that he engaged in philosophical activity while in this country.

There were, however, great religious houses, such as the Border abbeys, in Scotland, and no doubt some philosophy was taught in them along with the theology instruction that was surely given. Adam Scot,[2] abbot of Dryburgh, a twelfth-century thinker many of whose works have come down to us, may have taught philosophy as well as theology at his abbey, for his theological writings include many philosophical insights. As regards Hugo de Scotia, whose *De otiositate hominis* appears to be his only extant work, we know as yet practically nothing. It is possible that the sole extant

10. John Mair lecturing at Paris (c.1505). From In Petri Hyspani Summulas Commentaria.

manuscript of the work was written during the author's lifetime, in which case he lived during the fourteenth century.

The first three universities in this country, at St Andrews, Glasgow and Aberdeen, were founded in the fifteenth century, and Edinburgh University followed in the late sixteenth. Once there were universities here, there was philosophy in abundance, and from the start it was taught by Scots whose works were widely read in the great intellectual centres of Europe. The first rector of the University of St Andrews (founded 1411/12), Lawrence of Lindores, a number of whose writings are extant, had a considerable reputation on the Continent, as did John Ireland (c.1440–95),[3] a graduate of St Andrews (1455) who was briefly rector of the University of Paris and subsequently chaplain and confessor to James III. John Ireland's *The Mirror of Wisdom* (completed 1490) was the first philosophical prose work in the Scots tongue. But it was not the first philosophy written in Scots; sixty years earlier James I (1394–1437) had written philosophy in his great poem *The Kingis Quair*. The poem, written shortly after James was released from eighteen years of English captivity, was heavily influenced by Boethius's *The Consolation of Philosophy*, a work written in prison. Both authors are concerned with the role of fortune and of divine providence in human lives. The place of *The Kingis Quair* in Scottish literature has been the subject of several studies, a recent judgment being that 'it is a complex, powerful and, above all, influential work of art',[4] but its place in the Scottish philosophical tradition has yet to be investigated.

A circle of Scottish philosopher-theologians, active on the Continent, as well as in Scotland, played a crucial part in the intellectual life of the country in the decades leading up to the Reformation. At the centre of the circle was John Mair or Major (c.1467–1550)[5] from Gleghornie near Haddington, the greatest of the pre-Reformation principals of Glasgow University and provost of St Salvator's College, St Andrews. Amongst other members of the circle were David Cranston (c.1479–1512), a priest of the Glasgow diocese, Gilbert Crab (c.1482–1522) of Aberdeen, George Lokert (c.1485–1547)[6] of Ayr, overseer of the Scots College in Paris and for thirteen years dean of Glasgow, William Manderston (c.1485–1522) of the diocese of St Andrews, successively rector of the Universities of Paris and St Andrews, and Robert Galbraith (c.1483–1544), a senator of the College of Justice in Edinburgh, all of whom taught at the University of Paris, and several of whom stayed at the College of Montaigu in Paris while Erasmus was in residence there.

We should add to this list of Scots who taught at Paris: Hector Boece (c.1465–c.1536, writing under the name Hector Boethius) of Dundee, logician and philosopher as well as historian, who left Paris in 1497 for the newly founded University of Aberdeen, rising shortly thereafter to become its first principal; and James Liddell (writing under the name Jacobus Ledelh, d. prob. after 1519) of Aberdeen, the first Scot to have a book printed and published during his lifetime. Given the centrality of philosophy within the Scottish cultural tradition it is appropriate that that first ever printed book was a philosophical work, on what we should now call semiotics. The book, *On concepts and signs*, appeared in 1495. Finally in this list of pre-Reformation Scots associated with Paris we should note Florence Wilson (d.1550s) from Moray, who studied under Hector Boece at Aberdeen before attending the University of Paris where he was a friend of George Buchanan.[7] His writings, especially the *Dialogue on the Tranquility of the Soul*, a work consciously modelled on Boethius' *Consolation of Philosophy*, reveal the deep influence of Italian Humanism.

Mair taught John Knox theology at the University of St Andrews, and in due course Knox was to refer to his teacher as 'an oracle on matters of religion'. The precise impact that Mair had on the leader of the Scottish Reformation, though an important subject, has never been investigated. But whatever the nature of that impact, it is easy to argue that the achievement of Mair and his circle in the fields of philosophy and logic constitutes a high point in the history of Scottish culture.[8]

Significant philosophical activity continued through the latter part of the sixteenth century and during the seventeenth, with works by men such as John Rutherford (writing under the name Joannes Retorfortis) of Jedburgh, a friend of George Buchanan and tutor in the Montaigne household, John Dempster (writing under the name Johannes Themistor) of Aberdeen, William Davidson, also of Aberdeen, whose brother John was the first Protestant principal of Glasgow University, and Robert Balfour (d.1625) from Tarrie in Angus, a man in the Rutherford mould whose aim was to understand the real Aristotle, that is, without the disadvantage of seeing him through the distorting lens provided by the medieval commentators. The work of these men was important in helping both to maintain the philosophical tradition in Scotland, and also to keep the country abreast of the humanist movement that was gradually forming the dominant ethos of the universities on the Continent. In the middle of the sixteenth century one of the greatest humanists of the age, Joseph Scaliger, declared: '*Les Escossois sont bons philosophes*',[9] and even as applied to the Scots of his own generation the judgment is entirely just. In the seventeenth century, among those whose work helped to prepare the country for the wonderful events that were to follow, were Samuel Rutherford (1600–61), Robert Leighton (1611–84), James Dalrymple later first Viscount Stair (1619–95), Thomas Forbes (c.1625–88), Henry Scougal, whose *Life of God in the Soul of Man* (1677) was a key text, Robert Sibbald (1641–1722), and Gilbert Burnet (1643–1715) of Aberdeen.

In the eighteenth century there occurred one of the most celebrated moments in the history of philosophy, the Scottish Enlightenment, a moment dominated by an extraordinary quartet of thinkers, Francis Hutcheson (1694–1746), David Hume (1711–76), Thomas Reid (1710–96), and Adam Smith (1723–90), though many others, such as Adam Ferguson (1723–1816), were major figures on the international philosophical scene. It can be demonstrated both that there are numerous similarities between the philosophy of the pre-Reformation thinkers and that of the Enlightenment, and also that the similarities are no mere coincidence but are to be explained in part in terms of the philosophy done in Scotland in the intervening period.

In the latter part of the Enlightenment Dugald Stewart (1753–1828) and others ensured that the common-sense philosophy of Thomas Reid would continue to have a strong influence in the Scottish universities well into the nineteenth century. Reid's system also proved highly exportable. It made a significant impact in Germany, and also in France, particularly through the work of Victor Cousin. It was also well received in northern Spain, where there arose a significant school of common-sense philosophy heavily influenced by Reid and subsequently by William Hamilton (1788–1856).

Of course philosophy has continued to be studied and written in Scotland. In the latter part of the nineteenth century there emerged a significant school of neo-Kantians and neo-Hegelians, including James Ferrier (1808–64), John Caird (1820–98), Edward Caird (1835–1908), John Watson (1847–1939) and others writing on Kantian and Hegelian ideas. And during the inter-war years perhaps the most important work being conducted anywhere on the philosophy of Immanuel Kant was being carried out by Norman Kemp Smith (1872–1958) in Edinburgh and H.J. Paton (1887–1969) in Glasgow.

It is perhaps too early to judge how philosophy conducted in Scotland during this century fits into the tradition of Scottish philosophy, and in what follows therefore I shall restrict myself to describing certain salient features of that tradition from its known beginnings up to the common-sense school which flourished until the middle of the nineteenth century. I believe that the Scottish philosophical tradition can be described largely in terms of an ongoing debate between two great schools of philosophy, the realists and the nominalists, and I shall therefore pay particular attention in what follows to the role that Scottish philosophers played in that debate. Close inspection reveals a marked tendency for Scottish philosophers to be realists, although undoubtedly there were some who were strongly in the opposing camp, that of the so-called nominalists. Indeed, the most significant nominalist in Scottish philosophy is one of the two greatest philosophers from this country, David Hume. The other of the two was Duns Scotus, a realist with a distinctive brand of realism. The opposition between the two men is the whole tradition of Scottish philosophy writ small.

SCHOLASTIC THOUGHT

It is characteristic of Franciscan thought concerning our spiritual life that it places emphasis on the will, and in particular assigns primacy to will over intellect. Duns Scotus made a major contribution to this feature of Franciscan thinking and since that contribution lies at the heart of his system it is upon that part that I shall here concentrate.

What is the relation between intellect and will? It is Scotus's view[10] that there is not a 'real distinction' between them; that is, they are not so distinct that they can exist separately from each other. In particular, will cannot exist without intellect, for we cannot will to perform a given act if our intellect has formed no concept of that act. To will blindly is a way of not willing. On the other hand, the distinction between intellect and will is not merely logical, a so-called 'distinction of reason'. In that sense the distinction is not just a matter of different ways of conceiving one and the same thing. What is required is something intermediate, a distinction between two things that are indeed two but are so closely related as to form an unbreakable metaphysical union. Between two things thus related there is a 'formal distinction' – Scotus's terminology – and the concept of a formal distinction is a major weapon in his armoury. With it he probes deeply into the nature of human freedom.

There had been a tendency among philosophers to over-intellectualise the will, and to approximate to a form of intellectual determinism. According to such a form of determinism, once the intellect has formed a concept of the most appropriate act for the will to will, there is no room for the will to manoeuvre; it must seek the instantiation of that concept. The alternative, it seems, is to say that the will wills randomly, in that it ignores the deliverances of intellect, and proceeds unaffected by anything we know or believe. However, these alternatives were equally unacceptable to Scotus. The will cannot be determined by the intellect, for a will thus determined is not free, and yet freedom is the essence of the will. On the other hand, a will that acts in total disregard of the deliverances of the intellect is not in an unbreakable metaphysical union with the intellect, contrary to Scotus's teaching on the 'formal distinction' between will and intellect. Scotus relies on an Augustinian principle, that nothing is so much in the power of the will as the will itself. It is true, Scotus argues, that the will cannot act without a prior act of intellect; but though the object presented by the intellect carries weight with the will and inclines it (*pondus est et inclinatio*), it does not compel it. Sometimes it may be difficult for the will not to give assent to the dictate of the intellect, but it is never impossible.

This position can be seen as a virtuous intermediary between two vices, on the one hand the vice of extreme voluntarism which leaves the intellect with no role to play in the acts of the will, and on the other hand the vice of extreme intellectualism which assigns to the intellect full responsibility for the will's acts.

In brief, that there is a close interdependence of acts of will and of intellect follows from Scotus's doctrine that there is a 'formal distinction' between them. What Scotus refuses to lose sight of, however, is that the metaphysical bond which holds will and intellect in an inseparable union is not such as to annihilate the freedom of the will. Without ever ignoring the objects provided by the intellect, the will is always free not to act in the way the intellect inclines it.

The formal distinction is deployed in the course also of Scotus's account of universals. Different members of a species share a common nature, and a major battle was fought in the Middle Ages over the location of the common nature. Some held that the nature cannot exist in each member of the species; if it is in one member there can be nothing left of it to be in another, in which case it would not be common to many individuals; instead it would be peculiar to the individual it was in. One alternative espoused by those who argued in this way is that the common nature is a concept under which can be brought all the individual members of the species. Thus that nature, the universal element ascribed to each member of the species, is located not in the individuals but in the mind which has the concept. That is a nominalist solution to the problem of universals.

But Scotus rejects that solution. In his view it is impossible that the common nature should be elsewhere than in each and every thing that has the nature. If something is a cat, it must be in virtue of a nature, cathood, that is both in that very cat and also in every other cat. For Scotus the cat is a metaphysical union of a *this* and a *what*, with the thisness individuating the whatness, the common nature. According to this account, which is a realist account of universals, the *this* and the *what* are not really distinct, for they are not really separable from each other – there can be no catness if there is no cat that has it, and there is no cat that does not have the common nature of a cat. Neither is the distinction merely logical, for it is not a matter of one and the same identical thing being brought under different concepts; the nature and the individuating principle cannot be identical if the nature is truly to be common. The distinction is, in Scotus's technical sense, 'formal'. A doctrine similar to this one duly re-emerges in Thomas Reid's philosophy, though realism about universals had strong support from Scottish philosophers much earlier than that, during the pre-Reformation period.

Not all Scottish philosophers in the century or so before the Reformation were realists, however. Lawrence of Lindores, for example, the first rector of St Andrews University, was firmly in the nominalist camp, to the extent that he was responsible for the banning, in 1418, of the teaching of the realism of Albert the Great, a ban that was revoked immediately upon Lawrence's departure in 1438. The very speed of the revocation suggests the presence, during his reign, of closet realists impatient to return to a more congenial doctrine. But nominalism retained its appeal, and in 1474 John Ireland was a member of a delegation in the University of Paris which sought from Louis XI repeal of a royal proclamation authorising the doctrines of a number of realists including Albert the Great and Duns Scotus, and banning the doctrines of a number of nominalists, including William of Ockham and John Buridan, two writers to whom Lawrence of Lindores had been philosophically close.

Ireland's *The Mirror of Wisdom* shows him as preoccupied as Scotus had been before him with problems concerning the will. Ireland's preoccupation is as much with God's will as with ours. He argues that the absolute freedom of God's will must be posited, for its denial leads to absurdity. If God created the world not freely but by necessity then the existence of created things is a necessary consequence of God's existence; which is to say that God had merely to exist for created things to exist. But God exists eternally, from which it follows that all created things must exist eternally also, which is absurd. Hence God must have created freely.

God is, however, not only free but also omniscient, and this latter fact about him might be thought to imply that God is not free. For if God knew from all eternity that he would create a given object, he could not then not create it, from which it follows that he was necessitated to create it. Ireland's solution to this problem is that God knew from all eternity not merely that he would create the object but that he would freely create it. His prescience therefore does not necessitate either his will or the object. If freely he does not create it then he knew from all eternity that it would not exist, and likewise if freely he does create it then he knew from all eternity that it would exist. God's freedom is therefore compatible with his omniscience.

Ireland is also concerned with the question of whether God's foreknowledge is compatible with the freedom of the human will. Once again the problem arises because God's foreknowledge of a supposedly free act seems to imply that the agent is not free not to perform it. For if he is free not to perform it then perhaps he will not perform it, in which case God's knowledge of the future act will turn out to be an error. Ireland resolves this problem by a move which places him firmly within the Thomist tradition.

If from all eternity God sees a person perform an act which lies in the future in relation to us now, then necessarily the person will perform that act. But what is necessary here is not the act but the inference. What is being said is this: necessarily if God foresees a given act then the act will be performed. But the act is not any the less free for God's knowing that it will be performed, just as an act that we are now looking at is not the less free for our knowing that it is now being performed.

In 1495, the year of John Ireland's death, John Mair became regent in arts at the University of Paris. He quickly rose to become a leading member of the academic community, with a considerable reputation as a philosopher and theologian, as a teacher, and as the leader of a team which produced a number of editions of the writings of earlier generations of thinkers. Significantly Mair himself edited one of the major works of Duns Scotus, the *Reportata Parisiensia*, 'significantly' because Mair, though always his own man, was in many ways a philosopher in the Scotist mould. He wrote on a wide range of topics, covering indeed practically all the traditional areas of logic, philosophy and theology. Knowledge, its nature and causes, was of particular interest to him. As a theologian he was interested in the extent to which we can know God, and in the relation between knowledge of God and faith in him. He wrote also on the nature and conditions of human knowledge, particularly of our perceptual knowledge of individual substances, and our scientific, and therefore universal, knowledge of the perceptual world. And several Scottish colleagues of Mair, in particular David Cranston, Gilbert Crab and George Lokert wrote treatises devoted to the study of human knowing.

All these philosophers had an interest in language, and two basic sorts were discussed, one a system of signs available for public inspection by which we can communicate our thoughts to others, and the other a language to which each individual alone has immediate access. As regards the former kind, emphasis was placed upon spoken and written language, language as a system of utterances and inscriptions. The distinction is made on the basis of the sensory modality involved. Spoken language is audible, written language visible. For this reason the system of nods that monks under a vow of silence employed to communicate with each other was classed as written language, and in that case written language might more perspicuously have been called visible language, just as speech might more perspicuously have been called audible language since an utterance (vox) is not necessarily made by the human voice – a bugle call (as opposed to simply playing the bugle) is a vox in this sense. It was pointed out that there could be other languages corresponding to the other sensory modalities, and indeed, braille would have been classed by our late-medieval Scots as a tactile language. All such languages are in the public domain, in that people other than the speaker or writer have immediate access to the sensory output. But these public languages were thought of as expressions of thought; and thought was regarded as a kind of language also, for when I utter a sentence consisting of nouns, verbs, and so on, there must be in my thought something corresponding to those different sorts of term. If there is not it follows that the sentence is not a true expression of my thought.

Central to this account is the concept of a 'notion' (notitia).[11] I look at a tree and in so doing form a notion of a tree. Likewise I look at the leaves and form a notion of the leaves. If I have not formed those notions I cannot know what the words mean when I hear or read them. The language of thought is composed of such notions, mental nouns, mental verbs, and so on, which can be combined to form mental sentences, which are duly made public in speech or writing. David Cranston, Mair's favourite pupil, is very clear about the fact that though our thinking is expressed in some conventional language, the thinking itself is not in the language in which the thought is duly expressed. That I express my thought in English does not imply that the thought itself is in English. Indeed, for reasons well appreciated by the philosophers I am discussing here, the thought could not be in English. People monolingual in English, French, Latin or Chinese, could all have exactly the same thought even though they could not express it in the same language, and hence the thought itself could not be in any of these languages.

A helpful way to grasp the concept of a notion, and of mental language as the language of which notions are the building blocks, is to think of the mental term and the mental sentence as an act of understanding – Mair calls it just that: *actus intelligendi*. I hear a sentence and understand it. The act of understanding the sentence is a notion and the act of understanding each term in the sentence is also a notion. It follows from this that terms in mental language cannot be spelled, for it does not make sense to speak about spelling an act.

It further follows that a mental term or notion cannot change its meaning for there is nothing to change. An utterance or inscription can change its meaning for we can decide to give it a new one; in medieval terminology we would 'impose a new signification' upon the string of letters or sounds. But since a notion is not composed of letters or sounds we cannot understand it in a different way. Indeed, the notion is the very act of understanding by which we grasp what others have said or written and by which we do the thinking which is or can be expressed by utterance or inscription. For outer terms to have a meaning is precisely for us to understand the terms in a certain way.

In the light of points noted earlier concerning Duns Scotus, it should be plain that the position just ascribed to Mair and Cranston can fairly be classed as a nominalist theory of meaning, one according to which meaning depends for its existence upon acts of mind. According to a current version of realism the sense of an expression has a life of its own independent of the temporal world in which the expression which has that sense exists. Cranston's position, which is also Mair's, is that not only is meaning mind dependent; it is also temporal. For there is meaning only while thoughts, inscriptions and utterances exist, and these are temporal things.

Before leaving this topic I should like to make a further point. Except in the special case of reflection upon our own mental acts, a notion is not itself the object which we apprehend but rather the mental act by which we apprehend the object. When I have a visual notion of a tree, the immediate object of apprehension is not in my mind but is the tree itself. Mair emphasises the fact that though perception of an external object requires intermediate stages such as changes in my brain, there is no internal object I have to apprehend through the grasp of which I am able to apprehend the external one. What Mair says on this matter seems common sense. And, as we shall see, the particular common-sensical point that he makes here links him directly with the Scottish common-sense school which flourished two and a half centuries later.

While at the University of Paris, Mair had students and colleagues from many nations. There was a large contingent of Spaniards there, and it was one of their number, Antonio Coronel, who referred to Mair as 'the prince of philosophers and theologians' at the university. Mair's ideas were taken to Spain, where they received wide acceptance and respect. He was quoted extensively by the great Spanish political theorist and philosopher Francisco Vitoria, and also by Suarez, and long after Mair had ceased to be studied in Scotland he was still an authoritative source of ideas in Spain.

No doubt part of the reason for the failure of Scottish thinkers to read Mair after the Reformation was the Reformation itself. Mair was a priest dedicated to the Old Faith, and the fact that his pupil John Knox evidently had deep respect for him was not sufficient to preserve his reputation when the Old Faith was marginalised, though not quite obliterated, in Scotland in 1560. In addition, Renaissance humanism, with a different conception of logic, one based on the idea of logic as a branch of rhetoric, the art of persuasion, became a dominant feature of the university scene. And that conception was very far removed from the scholastic logic of which Mair was in his day perhaps the most distinguished practitioner anywhere. And finally the dominant influence of John Calvin and of Andrew Melville militated against an early revival in interest in the kinds of things Mair had been saying.

Following the Reformation Scotland made a contribution to the Europe-wide project of retrieving the original texts of Aristotle. The study of Greek was fostered and, unlike the Middle Ages, when Aristotle was read in Latin, the post-Reformation period saw intense interest in the original texts. In the spirit of the times, the lectures on Aristotle by Robert Rollock, the first principal of Edinburgh University, were little more than a dictation of those newly edited Greek texts. But interest in the very old did not stifle interest in the very new. The new philosophy from the Continent was taught in the Scottish universities, Descartes especially. And Calvinist writers of the seventeenth century made a deep impact on the cultural ethos within which the philosophers wrote. But for all the intellectual vitality of seventeenth-century Scotland, nobody could have been prepared for the glorious philosophical flourish of the Scottish Enlightenment.

SCEPTICISM AND COMMON SENSE

The central concept of the Scottish Enlightenment was that of human nature, and it was studied in all its aspects. It is not an accident that the period in Scotland was a high point in portraiture, the investigation of human nature by way of a study of the infinitely revealing (and concealing) features of the human face. Philosophers too were in the business of portraiture, but they were doing it their way, analysing concepts rather than applying pigment. Francis Hutcheson made a pioneering study of the nature of value and of valuing, especially in the fields of morals and aesthetics. Hume's *A Treatise of Human Nature* was influenced in many ways by Hutcheson's work. The *Treatise* is an essay, unsurpassed in the history of philosophy, on the fundamental belief system of human beings. Thomas Reid's two great collections, *Essays on the Intellectual Powers of Man* and *Essays on the Active Powers of the Human Mind*, are a formidable anti-Humean attack on behalf of common sense. And Adam Smith's *The Theory of Moral Sentiments*, taking its starting point from the essential sociality of human beings and from our natural capacity to sympathise with others, is a profound study of duty, virtue, and the nature of moral judgment.

As indicated earlier, the work of all four philosophers has to be seen within the context of the ancient and ongoing debate between realists and nominalists, and I should like to defend this claim now with particular reference to Hume and Reid. We all live in what we like to think of as reality, a world of causally interacting objects which exist as much when we are not perceiving them as when we are. Hume affirms that such is his world too, but he asks questions of it, and provides answers which led Reid to doubt the truth of Hume's affirmation. The framework for Hume's philosophy, and the central target of Reid's attack, is the 'theory of ideas'. As expounded by Hume, the theory affirms that our perceptions fall under one or other of two headings: impressions and ideas. He says, optimistically: 'I believe it will not be very necessary to employ many words in explaining this distinction. Every one of himself will readily perceive the difference betwixt feeling and thinking.'[12] What he has in mind is this: we are angry and later think about the anger we suffered, we hear a voice and later form an auditory mental image of the voice, we see a person and later form a visual mental image of the person, and so on. In each of these pairs the first item is our having an impression and the second is our having an idea. Hume contends that it is impossible to have a simple,

11. *David Hume (1711–76). Portrait (1766) by Allan Ramsay (1713–84).* (Scottish National Portrait Gallery)

that is, a non-complex idea which does not resemble a preceding impression, though it is possible to have a complex idea which does not resemble a preceding complex impression.

This contention provides Hume with the basis of his methodology. A way to investigate a given idea is to examine the impression which the idea resembles. He examines several ideas by asking about the corresponding impression. One of the ideas is of the necessary connection linking a cause and its effect. Do we have an impression of a necessary connection?[13] Hume considers examples of causally related events, such as a billiard ball hitting a second ball which immediately begins to move while the first one stops. If we have no previous experience of a collision, and now for the first time are seeing one, we would not be able to say if the second ball moved because the first hit it. It might have been a coincidence. And if we thought it were, we would deny that ball 1 hitting ball 2 necessitated ball 2 moving. We do not, then, learn that there is a causal relation by observing a single sequence.

On the other hand, if we see a given sequence several times, that is, an A-type event always followed immediately by a contiguous B-type event, we will conclude that the A-type event is a cause of the B-type event. At the point at which we see the two as causally related we see them as necessarily related; we judge that A must be, not merely is, followed by B. Hume's puzzle is this: what do I perceive in the tenth or hundredth sequence which I do not perceive in the first which leads me to make the judgment concerning a necessary connection? The puzzle is fuelled by the fact that there is no difference between the first sequence and the hundredth beyond the fact that one is the first and the other is the hundredth – but why should *that* make a difference?

Hume's reply is that there is a habit or custom of the human mind to form beliefs in the light of repeated experience. Having for the hundredth time seen A immediately followed by B, and having never seen A not followed immediately by B, when I next see A I immediately form a lively idea of B, and that lively idea is a belief in the occurrence of B. This process does not involve making a logical inference from a premise about past sequences to a conclusion about a future sequence. The process is not rational; it occurs at the level of habit or custom. Having customarily seen A followed by B, I come by a natural process which is not rational to form an expectation of B whenever I perceive A. The expectation is projected, or read, into the world. I see the necessity as in the world linking A and B when strictly the necessity is in my imagination, as a lively idea that by habituation I form of B when I perceive A. Hence Hume is not saying that there are no necessary connections. He is saying that there are, but that they are not located where everyone thinks they are; they are not in the outer world, but in the imagination of the perceiver.

The outer world itself is a source of puzzlement to Hume.[14] I believe in continuing and distinct objects, objects which continue to exist whether they are being perceived or not, and which are distinct from me in the sense that they are external to and independent of me. But by what route do I reach this belief? It cannot be by my senses, for by definition they can inform me only of what is sensorily present to me. It cannot be my senses that tell me of the existence of things which are not present to my senses. Neither can it be my reason, for if it is reason then my belief in the existence of a continuing and distinct world must be the conclusion of a process of reasoning. But I do not know what the acceptable premises are whose conclusion is that there is a continuing and distinct world. And very unsophisticated people, who have not had the benefit of a university education, also believe in the existence of such a world, and what argument is it that they know that I do not, whose conclusion is that a continuing and distinct world exists?

The only faculty left to which Hume can plausibly turn is that of the imagination, and in pages of great brilliance he argues that the outer world is in large measure a product of our imagination. We have impressions and ideas, fleeting existents, dependent for their existence upon our awareness of them, and out of these the imagination builds a world which we cannot but interpret as continuing and distinct. We live in the world of things which seem in many ways alien to us. Yet we feel at home in the world and might wonder how we can do so. And the answer is that this world is by its nature ours. It is our home, for we have built it, though by a process of imaginative construction of which we are totally unaware while the process is under way. It is by a philosophical investigation of human nature that the process can be shown to exist, which is not to say that once a philosopher has pointed out that it does exist we are thereafter aware of the process whenever we look out upon the world.

Hume's discussions of necessary connection and of the continuing and distinct world show him to be firmly in the nominalist camp. Just as the nominalists argued that a common nature must exist in the mind for otherwise there was no way to account for the fact that it is common to many things, and just as a nominalist account of meaning states that meaning is an act of understanding and hence is essentially a mental phenomenon, so also Hume argues that the necessary connection between a cause and its effect in the world is in the mind as an expectation, and is projected into the world. Likewise, in so far as he argues that the continuity and distinctness of the world are read into the world but are due to an act of imagination he is again presenting a nominalist position.

But I mentioned earlier that there is a strong streak of realism in the Scottish philosophical tradition, and during the Enlightenment that streak was represented most especially by the school of common sense, whose first and greatest spokesman was Thomas Reid. Reid's prime target was the theory of ideas, for he saw that theory as underpinning a tendency to over-internalise the phenomena. Things which exist outside were said to be inside. Hume is the prime target, for he held that the necessary connection between a cause and its effect is 'really' inside the mind, being a product of the imagination, despite the fact that it must be outside, for a bond which binds external things must itself be external, and he also held that the outer world is 'really' a product of an act of imagination working upon our impressions and ideas. In other words for Hume the outer world is, to use his own term, a 'fiction'.

In Reid's view Hume's fundamental error is to regard impressions and ideas as the immediate objects of perception when in fact the immediate objects are the things that the impressions and ideas are impressions and ideas of. John Locke, the first great exponent of the theory of ideas in British philosophy, had held that ideas are the immediate objects of perception and that through these we perceive, though indirectly, the objects that the ideas are of. Hume had objected to this on the grounds that we can know nothing whatever about the object that the idea is an idea of. Locke can if he wishes say that the idea I have of my desk is caused by my desk, but how can we be sure that the idea is not caused by another idea? All I have to go on are my ideas, and once inside the world of ideas I must stay there. It is true that I believe in an outer world but that is a fiction of my imagination.

Reid believed Hume's position to be absurd, and since the position followed from the theory of ideas, he drew the conclusion that the theory of ideas must be absurd. Not that Reid denies that we can have ideas, but he maintains that ideas are to be thought of not as objects of acts of mind but rather as the acts themselves. Thus having an idea about X is thinking about X, conceiving, imagining, or remembering it, and so on.[15] We have here a major link between the pre-Reformation period and the Enlightenment, for the concept of an idea, as Reid uses the term, is identical to John Mair's concept of a notion. Just as Mair regards notions as operations or acts of the mind (*actus intelligendi*) so also does Reid regard ideas. Just as Mair leaves no room for an object of knowledge intermediate between the notion of X and the external object X, so also does Reid leave no room for an object of knowledge intermediate between an idea, considered as a mental operation, and the object of which the idea is an idea. And finally, just as Mair is not at all sceptical about the existence of outer objects of which he has a notion, neither is Reid sceptical about the existence of outer objects of which he has an idea.

It should be clear from the foregoing exposition that Reid would reduce Locke's three elements to two. Instead of there being the mental act plus the idea plus the object which the idea is an idea of, there are just two elements, the mental act and the object of that act. Hume likewise reduces Locke's list of three elements to two, but in Reid's view it is the outer object that Hume omits, leaving the idea as itself the object of the mental act.

It should be clear that Reid's attack on the theory of ideas is an attack on the whole programme of nominalism, and is mounted on behalf of a realism that Reid believes to be common sense, the default position of humankind. Hume's philosophy, as we have seen, was treated as a *reductio ad absurdum* of the theory of ideas, for it appeared to lead to a total scepticism about the real existence of a necessary connection between a cause and its effect, and even to a total scepticism about the existence of a continuing and distinct world. But there is a problem concerning the target of Hume's scepticism. In particular there is some plausibility in the claim that Reid misidentifies that target. Hume does not deny that there is an outer world. When at the start of the *Treatise* he says that 'every one of himself will readily perceive the difference betwixt feeling and thinking', he is signalling that he is not going to call in question the real existence of the outer objects we see and hear, and the emotions, pleasures and pains we feel. As regards the outer world, his position is stated plainly: 'We may well ask, *What causes induce us to believe in the existence of body?* but 'tis in vain to ask, *Whether there be body or not?* That is a point, which we must take for granted in all our reasonings.'[16] It is Hume's view that certain of our beliefs are an original feature of our nature. We are so constituted that it is impossible for us not to give assent to them. Among these beliefs are one in a continuing and distinct world containing objects which are causally and therefore necessarily related to each other. Hume conceives it his task not to rebut those beliefs but to provide clarification of them. Granted we all believe in a necessary connection between a cause and its effect, what is the mode of existence of that connection? Is it a physical thing, in which case by which of our sensory receptors do we know it? Do we see a necessary connection, or hear or touch it? And likewise granted that we all believe in a continuing and distinct world, what is the mode of its existence?

Hume's chief concern is to undermine claims that might be made on behalf of reason. We do have certain basic beliefs about ourselves and the world we inhabit, but reason cannot prove those beliefs, any more than our senses can. Indeed, they are not available for proof in any form. We possess the beliefs not because we have accepted a proof of them but because we are so constituted that we cannot reject them. Yet in what respect does this position differ from Reid's? Reid's common-sense philosophy consists fundamentally of an attack on the theory of ideas. According to that attack we are immediately aware of objects of perception, not merely mediately aware through the mediation of ideas. But how do we know that we are in immediate contact with the outer reality when we perceive things? Reid's answer is that the belief in the existence of those things is irresistible. Nature, as Reid says in a closely related context, requires us to believe upon her authority. Reid, then, accepts the existence of the external world as a matter of common sense. We believe it irresistibly because we are so constituted that we can do no other, and certainly we do not believe in the authority of reason. But this seems to be just what Hume says also. Nevertheless, there is a large difference. Hume would say that Reid is correct as far as he goes in the articulation of the principles of common sense, but that he does not go deep enough. In particular, Reid does not address the metaphysical question of the mode of existence of the things of which we claim to have impressions or at least ideas, such things as the necessary connection between cause and effect, and the continuing and distinct world. Hume on the other hand answers these questions concerning necessity and externality in such a way that he convinces Reid that he, Hume, does after all deny that there are such things as necessity and externality.

The difference between the two men, therefore, lies in their analysis of the metaphysical status of things in whose existence we have a natural and irresistible belief. Hume ascribes to the imagination a crucial role in the construction and maintenance of our world. Reid ascribes no such role to the imagination or to any other of our psychological faculties. He says that he believes the world to be thus and so, and that though he cannot provide a philosophical explanation of the fact that this is how the world is, that fact does not diminish his conviction that that is how the world is. Hume says that he believes the world to be thus and so, that he can give a philosophical explanation of the fact that that this is how the world is, and that his ability to give that account has no effect on the strength of his belief that that is how the world is. Faced with the full list of Reid's principles of common sense Hume would give assent to all of them, and would add that the philosophy starts after that assent.

I believe that for Reid not philosophy but theology starts after that. Reid was a son of the manse, a minister of the Kirk, and a theologian whose theology is the main subtext of the *Essays on the Intellectual Powers*. He appears to have held that the truth of common-sense beliefs is underpinned by a benevolent God who created us with such a nature as to find those beliefs irresistible. Reid's God would not give us an irresistible belief in falsehood, and especially where the beliefs in question are structuring principles of our cognitive constitution. For our lives would then be false all the way through.

Hume rarely replied to his critics, and if he ever penned a reply to Reid it has not come down to us. My account of how Hume might have defended himself is therefore just that, a 'might have'. This is not the place to say which of the two men won the argument, and indeed the argument is on-going.

In Scotland till the mid-nineteenth century Reid's star shone brightly in this country, thanks especially to the work of Dugald Stewart and William Hamilton. Neither man, however, was entirely uncritical of Reid. Hamilton in particular, though a member of the common-sense school, took issue with Reid on a number of matters, for example, the nature of consciousness.[17] It is understandable that philosophers should be deeply interested in consciousness and Reid indeed introduces it into his first principle of common sense, namely that I think, remember, reason, and in general really perform all the operations of mind of which I am conscious. He holds that it is only such inner things as present acts of the mind that are the objects of consciousness, as contrasted with perception which is directed outwards. Thus I can be conscious of my act of perceiving by which I know that my desk is in front of me, but according to Reid the mental act by which I am in immediate cognitive contact with the desk is not the act of consciousness but the perceiving.

This doctrine did not commend itself to Hamilton, however; he held, on the contrary, that it is impossible to be conscious of a mental act without also being conscious of the object to which the mental act is directed; I cannot be conscious of perceiving my desk and not be conscious of the desk. To say otherwise is to imply that I can know and not know the same object at the same time. There is room for dispute over whether Hamilton's criticism on this matter can be sustained, but this disagreement over the nature of consciousness (a disagreement which had large ramifications) shows that Hamilton was his own man, not simply a spokesman for Reid. Hamilton's philosophy in its turn came under sustained attack by John Stewart Mill, and his reputation has hardly recovered since then.

In recent years Reid has become a focus of research, especially by philosophers and psychologists working in the field of cognitive science.[18] His brand of realism is being investigated in the present age which is characterised by a vigorous debate on the relative merits of realism and nominalism, a debate which is being conducted in this country as in many others. The track record of Scottish philosophy suggests that it is from this area that we should expect the next major advance in philosophy in Scotland.

Notes

1. For details of his life and work see Lynn Thorndyke, *Michael Scot* (London, 1965).

2. For details of his life and work see James Bulloch, *Adam of Dryburgh* (London, 1958).

3. See especially J. Burns, 'John Ireland and "The Meroure of Wyssdome"', *Innes Review*, 1955, pp.77–98.

4. J. MacQueen in R.D.S. Jack (ed.), *The History of Scottish Literature* (Aberdeen, 1988) Vol. 1, p.55.

5. For details see A. Broadie, *The Circle of John Mair: Logic and Logicians in Pre-Reformation Scotland* (Oxford, 1985).

6. His career is described in A. Broadie, *George Lokert: Late-Scholastic Logician* (Edinburgh, 1983), ch.1.

7. For discussion of Buchanan's intellectual milieu see I.D. McFarlane, *Buchanan* (London, 1981).

8. Evidence for this claim is provided in A. Broadie, *The Tradition of Scottish Philosophy* (Edinburgh, 1990).

9. *Scaligeriana* (Cologne, 1667), p.236.

10. See Allan B. Wolter, *Duns Scotus on Will and Morality* (Washington DC, 1986).
11. For details see A. Broadie, *Notion and Object: Aspects of Late-Medieval Epistemology* (Oxford, 1990).
12. *A Treatise of Human Nature* (Oxford, 1978), pp.1–2.
13. *Treatise*, Bk.I, pt.III, sect.14.
14. *Treatise*, Bk.I, pt.IV, sect.2.
15. *Essays on the Intellectual Powers*, Essay II, ch.9, in William Hamilton (ed.), *The Works of Thomas Reid*, D.D, 6th edn (Edinburgh, 1863), Vol. 1, p.277.
16. *Treatise*, Bk.I, pt.IV, sect.2, p.187.
17. See William Hamilton in H.J. Mansel and J. Veitch (eds.), *Lectures on Metaphysics and Logic* (Edinburgh, 1869), Vol. 1, lectures 15–19, esp. lecture 15.
18. See, for example, Keith Lehrer, *Thomas Reid* (London, 1989).

Books for Further Reading

A. Broadie, *The Circle of John Mair: Logic and Logicians in Pre-Reformation Scotland* (Oxford, 1985).

A. Broadie, *The Tradition of Scottish Philosophy* (Edinburgh, 1990).

R.H. Campbell and A.H. Skinner, *The Origins and Nature of the Scottish Enlightenment* (Edinburgh, 1982).

George E. Davie, *The Democratic Intellect* (Edinburgh, 1961).

Duns Scotus *see* Allan B. Wolter.

S.A. Grave, *The Scottish Philosophy of Common Sense* (Oxford, 1960).

Vincent Hope (ed.), *Philosophers of the Scottish Enlightenment* (Edinburgh, 1984).

David Hume, *Enquiries Concerning Human Understanding and Concerning the Principles of Morals*, ed. L.A. Selbey-Bigge (Oxford, 1902); 3rd edn, revised with notes by P.H. Nidditch (Oxford, 1975).

David Hume, *A Treatise of Human Nature*, ed. L.A. Selbey-Bigge (Oxford, 1882); 2nd edn, with text revised by P.H. Nidditch (Oxford, 1978).

James McCosh, *The Scottish Philosophy* (London, 1875).

Thomas Reid, *The Works of Thomas Reid*, ed. William Hamilton, 2 vols., 6th edn. (Edinburgh, 1863).

William R. Scott, *Francis Hutcheson* (Cambridge, 1900).

Adam Smith, *The Theory of Moral Sentiments*, eds. D.D. Raphael and A.L. Macfie (Oxford, 1976).

Allan B. Wolter (tr.), *Duns Scotus on Will and Morality* (Washington DC, 1986).

The Literature of Lowland Scotland, 1350–1700

RODERICK J. LYALL

The thread from which the rich fabric of the Older Scots literary tradition was woven had three principal strands. The first, strongly visible from the outset and born out of the Wars of Independence, but sustained in the later sixteenth and seventeenth centuries by religious discord and civil war, was a confident assertion of the autonomy of Scottish culture. In the works of John Barbour and his contemporaries, this nationalist discourse is already interwoven with the shared culture of Western Christendom: in the currency of genres, in the practice of rhetoric, in the prevalence of certain styles, and in the specific influence of medieval texts in Latin and French, we can see constant evidence of the intellectual proximity of Scottish writers to those of Continental Europe. But these two strands were always in competition with a third: the influence of an English literary tradition which must have overlapped with native Scottish writing from the outset and which, with the enormously rich Chaucerian hegemony exerting its power from the turn of the fifteenth century, came to play an ever-greater role in Scotland, until the accession of a Scottish king to the English throne brought to an end the institution of a separate Scottish Court, which had provided a safe refuge for a Scots literature undermined by the growing prestige of the English language.

Although there is only fragmentary evidence for the existence of an indigenous literature in Scots before the composition of the first complete and substantial work, Barbour's *Brus* (1375–76), it is scarcely credible that this archdeacon of Aberdeen was not working within a lively and well-established vernacular tradition.[1] Even *The Brus* itself survives in only two complete manuscripts, both written more than a century after the poem; and it is impossible to determine what else, like the text entitled *The Stewartis Oryginale* attributed to Barbour by his younger contemporary Andrew Wyntoun – which apparently included a version of the Banquo story later to be taken up by Shakespeare – may have vanished completely. Barbour was probably born in the last years of the reign of Robert I, and his surviving work is a lively celebration of the Scots'

12. George Buchanan (1506–82). Portrait by an unknown artist, c.1580. Buchanan was a scholar of European reputation and was widely regarded as the finest poet in Latin since classical times. His plays were performed all over Europe for well over 100 years, and his De Jure Regni Apud Scotos *was a decisive influence on Scottish constitutional thought.* (Scottish National Portrait Gallery)

successful defence of their independence at the beginning of the fourteenth century and of the chivalric virtues their leaders displayed, informed in part by eye-witness accounts.

For Barbour, one of the most important characteristics of his poem was its 'suthfastnes', the historical accuracy of its narrative; and it is a tribute to his concern for truth that *The Brus* is still regarded as a valuable primary source by modern historians. But he also calls it a 'romanys', and it is important to recognise that in its diction, the rhetoric of its descriptions and battle scenes, and in the way in which its heroes are portrayed, *The Brus* has much in common with contemporary French and English chivalric romances. King Robert himself is likened to the great figures of romance tradition, and Barbour specifically balances one of his more spectacular feats against that of Tydeus, no doubt familiar to many of his audience from the *Roman de Thebes*. This episode appears to be greatly elaborated for literary effect; elsewhere, in great set-pieces like Bannockburn (which provides the central section of the poem) and the siege of Berwick, Barbour stays much closer to the historical events. He is capable of moments of great rhetorical fervour, as in the best-known of all the poem's more than 14,000 lines:

A! fredome is a noble thing!
Fredome mays man to haiff liking;

Fredome all solace to man giffis:
He levys at es that frely levys!   (I, 225–8)

But it is typical of Barbour's clerical manner that this stirring sentiment is immediately followed by the Aristotelian maxim that things are known through their opposites and a clear indication that for Barbour freedom must be defined in personal, feudal terms, reinforced by a canon lawyer's quibble about balancing one's obligation to one's lord and 'the dettis off wedding'. The vision of *The Brus* is essentially a moral one: the Scots are victorious because their just cause is endorsed by God, and because Robert and his trusted lieutenant, Sir James Douglas, manifest greater chivalric virtue than their English opponents.

Barbour's romance style is well adapted to the flowing structure of the four-stress couplets in which *The Brus* is composed; and the predominance of this verse-form is one of the most striking features of the earliest phase in the development of Older Scots poetry. At a period in which English poets display great formal diversity, with complex lyric stanzas, Chaucerian 'rhyme royal', various alliterative forms, and the 'tail-rhyme' stanza of popular romance all occupying significant positions in the stylistic system, Scots has the appearance of being extraordinarily univocal. The impression may partly be created by the accidents of loss and survival; but it is remarkable that the poets who compiled the anonymous *Saints' Lives*, the Scottish translator of the *Troy Book*, Andrew Wyntoun and the author of the subsumed verse chronicle of the reigns of David II and Robert II, all of whom probably wrote between 1375 and 1425, all chose (with varying degrees of accomplishment) to work in short couplets.[2] In the next quarter-century, the tradition is continued in *The Buik of Alexander* (1438) and the moral treatise *Ratis Raving*, but it was by this time past its heyday.

In most of these works, we can see a twofold preoccupation: with the adaptation into Scots of some of the most important contemporary literary forms, and with the assertion of Scottish national identity in the face of English claims to overlordship. The interweaving of these strands can take surprising forms. We might expect the Older Scots *Saints' Lives*, for example, which are largely translated from one of the most influential of medieval collections, the *Legenda aurea* of Jacobus de Voragine, to add two specifically Scottish saints: Machar (linking the collection quite firmly with Aberdeen) and Ninian. But it is more remarkable that the latter is elevated into a national patron, with a longish coda to his legend documenting three occasions on which he rescued endangered Scots from the clutches of the English. Andrew Wyntoun's enterprise in his *Oryginale Cronykil* is more substantial: not only is he seeking to produce a universal chronicle in vernacular verse – comparable to the *Cursor Mundi* written in northern England a century earlier – but he systematically locates the history of the Scots within this larger narrative. By reaffirming the legendary story of the Scots' origins (ii, 631–962) he naturally maintains the national myth in the face of the rival English version; but he goes further than his predecessors and contemporaries (such as John of Fordoun, whose *Chronica Gentis Scotorum* treats the same Scottish material in more detail) by setting Scottish history within the sacred text of universal history from Creation to Last Judgment – although Wyntoun actually stops with the campaign of the Earl of Mar in the Netherlands in 1408.[3]

Soon after the completion of Wyntoun's chronicle, in the mid-1420s, we find a radical break with the tradition of the four-stress couplet. *The Kingis Quair*, almost certainly written by James I in 1424 or 1425, marks a profound change in form, style and content: it is an allegorical poem in the Chaucerian manner, composed in rhyme-royal stanzas and dealing with personal rather than public issues. In just what sense the *Quair* is personal is a contentious issue, for the situation of the poem's narrator is close enough to James's own for the text to be interpreted in straightforward autobiographical terms. Such a reading is, however, too simple an approach to this richly allusive work: there are evident similarities between the narrator's eighteen-year imprisonment after his capture when 'nought ferre passit the state of innocence / Bot nere about the nowmer of yeris thre' (that is, at the age of ten) and James's own captivity in England between 1406 and 1424, but there is nothing in the poem to suggest that the protagonist is royal, and the basis of the action owes at least as much to Chaucer's *Knight's Tale* as it does to the final stages of James's imprisonment. The influence of English literary taste, and of Chaucerian poetic diction, is in fact one of the strongest arguments for James's authorship – whoever wrote *The Kingis Quair* was steeped in the work of the poets fashionable at the English Court in the first quarter of the fifteenth century, not only Chaucer himself, but Gower and Lydgate as well.

But the most important literary presence in the *Quair* is arguably not an Englishman at all, but Boethius, whose *Consolation of Philosophy* was one of the most widely known texts of the Middle Ages, translated into English at least three times between 1350 and 1425, including one version by Chaucer himself. It is the *Consolation* that James's narrator is reading at the beginning of the poem (an intertextual device with strong Chaucerian precedents!), and which provides the inspiration for his account of his own fortunes. The Scots poem, however, provides a revisionist version of Boethius's argument: whereas the *Consolation* shows us a man of mature years reflecting on his fall from political power, his imprisonment and impending death, and concluding that the only sure defence against the whims of Fortune is to disregard worldly concerns in favour of the certainties of the life beyond death, the youthful narrator-dreamer in *The Kingis Quair* elects to climb on to Fortune's wheel, accepting the vicissitudes of this world and being 'rewarded' with the love of the lady he has seen from his prison window. *The Kingis Quair* is a thoughtful modification of Boethian doctrine, and an eloquent testimony to the power of love to make the world seem a better place.

It is not clear what direct influence, if any, the *Quair* exerted on subsequent developments in Scottish verse: the only surviving copy of the poem is in a manuscript written two generations after its composition. But the previously ubiquitous short couplet now gives way to a greater diversity of poetic forms, used for a much greater variety of genres. From at least the middle of the century, there are examples of texts written in a thirteen-line, rhymed alliterative stanza which is a close relative of that earlier employed in northern England for, among other works, the masterly *Gawain and the Green Knight*. This is the form adopted by Richard Holland for his *Buke of the Howlat*, a complex amalgam of beast fable, chivalric panegyric and ecclesiastical satire, composed at Darnaway Castle around 1450 and addressed to Elizabeth Dunbar, Countess of Moray, and her husband, Archibald Douglas. Holland's poem is richly allusive, poking gentle fun at the Papal court, celebrating the Douglas family in a series of heraldic descriptions, and ultimately warning its noble readers that, as the owl (the 'howlat' of the title) learns to his cost, 'We cum pure, we gang pure, baith king and commoun'. The alliterative stanza is also used, a little later, for the anonymous *Golagros and Gawaine*, an Arthurian romance which is again given a political twist with its lesson about the dangers of internal strife. And then there is *Rauf Coilyear*, formally a romance but in some ways subversive of its genre, the story of a charcoal-burner whose brusque lessons in good manners so impress the incognito emperor Charlemagne that he elevates him to the post of Marshal of France. It may be significant that, like *Gawain and the Green Knight*, *Rauf Coilyear* is explicitly set at Christmas, for the poem's inversions of order (and a hilarious knock-about between the newly knighted Rauf and a Saracen whom he believes to be Roland, failing to notice that his antagonist is riding a camel) are in many ways reminiscent of the festivities of that season.[4]

In the hands of skilled poets such as these, the alliterative stanza is an extremely flexible form, ranging from densely patterned descriptions of knightly accoutrements to narrative passages in which the alliteration is scarcely evident at all, and covering with equal verve chivalric combat and knock-about farce, high-style description and undecorated moralisation. Other types of verse permitted even greater variation. The five-stress couplet, for example, which largely displaced its shorter sibling after mid-century, was employed for romances like Gilbert Hay's *Buik of King Alexander the Conquerour* and *The Wallace*, apparently composed by the mysterious Blind Harry, as well as for moral tales like *The Thre Prestis of Peblis* and *The Talis of the Fyve Bestes* and – one of the neglected gems of Older Scots tradition – the richly comic fabliau *The Freiris of Berwik*. The third form in general use, the rhyme-royal stanza, could be adapted to formal allegory like *King Hart*, to moral lyric, and to an extended piece of political advice like *The Buke of Gude Counsale*, apparently written for James II some time in the 1450s. In his reign and that of his son James III, then, the Scots tradition expands and matures, reflecting an audience sophisticated in its appreciation of the entire range of medieval genres from allegory and romance to moral instruction and bawdy farce, and well able to appreciate a subtle interplay of different genres within a single text.

Amidst these notable but generally anonymous achievements, the work of three great poets stands out as the central monument of the Older Scots tradition. The first of these is Robert Henryson (?c.1435–c.1505). Comparatively little is known about his career, but it is clear that he was legally qualified, a notary public and, if a sixteenth-century title is to be believed, master of the grammar school at Dunfermline. His reputation mainly rests on three long poems: *Orpheus and Erudices*, The *Morall Fabillis of Esope* and *The Testament of Cresseid*, and in particular upon the latter two. As a reworking of the Orpheus legend, *Orpheus and Erudices* owes as much to the spiritual allegorising of the fourteenth-century Dominican Nicholas Trivet, whose moral interpretation of the story as the failure of (male) reason in the face of (female) sensuality Henryson translates as a *moralitas*, as it does to the main narrative source, Book III, *metrum* 12 of Boethius's *Consolation of Philosophy*. The subtle interaction of narrative and *moralitas*, visible in miniature in *The Bludy Serk* and on a grand scale in the *Fabillis*, here has a touch of scholastic heavy-handedness, but there is great skill in managing the rhyme-royal stanza and the characteristic terseness, identified by A.C. Spearing as Henryson's 'high concise style', in such moments as Orpheus's loss of Erudices:

> Thus Orpheus, wyth inwart lufe replete,
> So blyndit was in grete affection,
> Pensif apon his wyf and lady suete,
> Remembrit noucht his hard condicion.
> Quhat will ye more? In schort conclusion,
> He blent bak-ward and Pluto come anone,
> And unto hell agayn with hir is gone.   (387–93)

If Henryson ultimately fails to resolve Boethian narrative and scholastic allegory into a satisfying vernacular poem in *Orpheus and Erudices*, the combination of a much wider and more complex range of elements in the *Morall Fabillis* is triumphant. The core text is a well-known version of Aesop in Latin hexameters, sometimes attributed (for no good reason) to a shadowy and probably non-existent 'Walter the Englishman'; this was a key grammar text in medieval schools, and Henryson was no doubt all too familiar with it. But he brings to his cycle of a prologue and thirteen fables other traditions of beast narrative as well: whereas the Aesopic fable is typically brief, narratively uncomplicated, and essentially generalised, Henryson draws on the equally widespread genre of the 'beast epic', represented by the French *Roman de Renart* and its Dutch and German analogues, and also on various 'hybrid' fables into which elements of the Renardian tradition had already been assimilated. He, however, goes further than his predecessors in blending the two forms, retaining, expanding or inventing moral interpretations for Renardian narratives while developing the comic and satiric possibilities of familiar Aesopic fables like 'The Twa Myis' and 'The Wolf and the Lamb'. The result is a comprehensive account of human sinfulness, constantly playing upon a delicate balance of the human and the animal to illustrate:

> How mony men in operatioun
> Ar like to beistis in conditioun.   (48–9)

This is, of course, the essential premise of the fable genre, but Henryson's art gives it sharper definition and, at times, greater social relevance.

Modern critical scholarship has only recently recognised the full subtlety of the design of Henryson's fable-cycle, integrating his narratives symmetrically according to their source-types and creating a master-narrative in which the tone progressively darkens as the lessons of the *moralitates* continue to be ignored.[5] There are other patterns of recurrence as well: the importance of social order and the prevalence of injustice are repeated themes, and the role of the narrator shifts and wavers, from confident preacher to engaged bystander or even, when Aesop himself appears in a vision, to an audience in his own right. But many of the pleasures of the *Morall Fabillis* are local to the individual texts, whether in the outrageous flattery of the wily Tod in 'Schir Chantecleir and the Foxe' (425–80), the hilarious mock-confession in 'The Fox and the Wolf' (691–732), or the self-delusion of the sheep impersonating a guard-dog in 'The Wolf and Wedder' (2,518–80). Nor are all the most memorable passages comic: it is difficult to forget the bitterness of the condemned Sheep in 'The Scheip and the Doig' (1,286–1,320), or the horror of the sudden violence at the end of 'The Preiching of the Swallow' (1,874–80) and 'The Paddok and the Mous' (2,896–2,906).

The bleak ending of the *Fabillis* with this latter tale has some affinity with the 'sore conclusioun' of *The Testament of Cresseid*, Henryson's response to Chaucer's *Troilus and Criseyde*. The *Testament* is in many ways a baffling poem: it seems to offer an unambiguous moral message, using the illness and death of the unfaithful Cresseid as a warning, specifically to a female audience, to 'ming not your lufe with fals deceptioun' (613), and yet we are constantly denied such certainty by other aspects of the text. Henryson develops Chaucer's own narrative persona, for example, into a more clearly dramatised voice, an ageing and probably unreliable narrator who, like his heroine, is a worshipper of Venus. This mediating presence, who questions Chaucer's narrative authority but bases his own poem upon 'ane uther quair' the very existence of which seems highly dubious, seems to condemn Cresseid for her betrayal of Troilus, yet simultaneously suggests that she bears no moral responsibility for her actions:

> Yit neuertheles, quhat euer men deme or say
> In scornefull langage of thy brukkilnes,
> I sall excuse als far furth as I may
> Thy womanheid, thy wisdome and fairnes,
> The quhilk fortoun hes put to sic distres
> As hir plesit, and nathing throw the gilt
> Of the – throw wickit langage to be spilt!   (85–91)

Cresseid is judged, and condemned to suffer from leprosy, by an assembly of the planetary gods, not for her infidelity, but for blasphemy against Venus and Cupid. The gods themselves are scarcely beyond reproach: they are merciless in their condemnation, and they are clearly seen to be judging Cresseid in their own interest. Cresseid's world, Henryson seems to be implying, is a forbidding and unforgiving one.

Yet the poem is not without its indications of hope. Slowly and painfully, Cresseid does achieve a regenerative kind of understanding, and while there is no hint of a Christian salvation, either in the testament in which she bequeaths her soul to the goddess of chastity, 'Diane, quhair scho dwellis / To walk with hir in waist woddis and wellis', or in the final stanzas in which first Troilus and then (perhaps) the narrator himself pronounce upon her tragedy, it does seem that she is morally wiser by the time she dies. A crucial factor in this moral growth is the powerful scene in which Troilus encounters Cresseid, who is now blind and so disfigured that he is unable to recognise her; he is nonetheless reminded of her, and gives her alms 'for knichtlie pietie and memoriall / of fair Cresseid'. This act of human charity, once she is told that it was Troilus, transforms Cresseid's understanding, bringing her to penitence. There can be little doubt that medieval 'anti-feminism', the conviction that women were less rational and more inclined to sensuality than men, is an influence on Henryson's representation of Cresseid; and yet she is the point of focus for our sympathy and engagement, and the gender assumptions of the *Testament* are as uncertain as everything else. Even in Cresseid's pagan world, the poem seems to be suggesting, charity – in the strong sense of Christian love – can transform the life of a sinner. The ultimate theme of the *Testament*, as it is of the *Morall Fabillis*, is grace.

If Henryson's poetry marks a new maturity in the Older Scots poetic tradition, John Ireland's *Meroure of Wysdome* (1490) represents a novel ambitiousness in expository prose. There is, it is true, a hint of a developing corpus of prose works earlier in the fifteenth century, the most notable of which are Sir Gilbert Hay's three translations of French chivalric works; but there is certainly nothing to rival the medieval English traditions of mystical, devotional and homiletic prose, or the great prose romances produced in France (and in England by Malory). *The Meroure of Wysdome*, alternatively titled *The ABC of Chrestianitie*, is a comprehensive theological primer in seven books, offering the young James IV instruction on the fundamentals of Christian doctrine, some serious philosophical discussion of the problem of free will, and a detailed treatment of a number of aspects of political theory. Ireland's sources are extremely varied: Laurent d'Orleans' *Somme le Roi*, a commentary by Aquinas on the Pater noster, several sermons by the Paris theologian Jean Gerson, and Chaucer's *Tale of Melibee* (or its French original) are among those which have so far been identified.

But what is remarkable about the *Meroure* is the very fact that Ireland tackles both theology and philosophy in the vernacular, trying to find equivalents for the complex, technical syntax and vocabulary of scholastic Latin. It cannot be said that he is consistently successful, but the sheer stylistic variety of his prose is impressive, and when he imitates the more natural expository and narrative rhythms of the sermon tradition he shows his capacity for a forceful and expressive Scots prose.

Robert Henryson seems to have died in or a little before 1505, by which time two younger writers had begun to extend the poetic capabilities of Scots beyond the stylistic range exploited by Henryson and his contemporaries. The locus for William Dunbar (*c*.1460–*c*.1513) and Gavin Douglas (1476–1522) was the Court of James IV, an environment which no doubt encouraged the linguistic display which characterises the work of both men. The Court infuses Dunbar's poetry, whether he is petitioning the King for preferment in the Church, or celebrating a royal marriage, or giving a light-hearted account of a household entertainment, or attacking a rival for the King's patronage. It has recently been suggested that he is in the same tradition as the *grands rhétoriqueurs* of the French and Burgundian Courts,[6] and it is certainly true that in his elaborate and highly skilled rhetoric and his pursuit of public themes Dunbar shows many affinities with this Continental school. Yet his poetry also has a firmly Scottish context, not only because it is rooted in the social behaviour of the Court but also because it helps to raise the Scots language on to a new plane of stylistic variation and richness.

The persona Dunbar projects through his court-centred poetry is sophisticated, knowing and on intimate terms with his audience; but it is dangerous to take the 'I' of his verse too much at face value. Even when he seems to give us firm autobiographical evidence, as in the anti-Franciscan satire 'How Dumbar wes desyrd to be ane freir' (later to form the basis for George Buchanan's *Franciscanus*), we cannot be sure that the persona's 'confession' of having been either a Franciscan novice or a pretended friar is more than a rhetorical ploy. The assumption of a mask, creating an ironic distance between the author and his poetic persona, is more clearly a consequence of the conditions of performance in Dunbar's case than in Henryson's, and his verse constantly reminds us that it was written for a close coterie well able to appreciate the comic and satirical possibilities of the gap. In 'Sir Jhon Sinclair begowthe to dance', for example, Dunbar introduces – in the third person – the character of 'Dunbar the mackar' among the participants in a dance 'in the quenis chalmer', asserting that his gyrations were motivated by his love for 'Maesteres Musgraeffe'. This revelation at his own expense may be no more than part of a courtly game, as the dance itself appears (at least according to one recent interpretation) to have been a form of morris dance.

Elsewhere, as in the two poems attacking the alchemist John Damien, whose unsuccessful attempt to fly from Stirling Castle in 1507 Dunbar lampoons mercilessly, or *The Dregy of Dunbar*, the irony is sharper, working against the pretensions of his rivals at Court or the materialism of the Court itself. Even when he is writing formal, celebratory verse, such as the epithalamium *The Thrissill and the Rois*, composed for the marriage of James IV and Margaret Tudor in 1503, Dunbar takes the opportunity to offer the king some gratuitous political advice, using the device of Nature's parliament to instruct James, not only on public policy but on sexual mores as well:

And sen thow art a king, thow be discreit;
Herb without vertew thow hald nocht of sic pryce

As herb of vertew and of odor sueit;
And lat no nettill vyle and full of vyce
Hir fallow to the gudly flour delyce,
Nor latt no wyld weid full of churlichenes
Compair hir till the lilleis nobilness . . .   (134–40)

The framework of dream allegory in this poem proves its continuing flexibility, for a complex series of shifts in the opening stanzas contrasts an idealised, literary version of a spring landscape with a contemporary reality in which 'few birdis . . . sing', leading eventually to the visionary scene in which Nature marks the arrival of the Rois (Margaret Tudor, for whose family the rose emblem held a strong political significance) by establishing a new, harmonious order. The potential importance of the alliance between Scotland and England seems to have been fully recognised by Dunbar, for whom the marriage heralds nothing less than a symbolic reconstitution of the state; the death of the bridegroom ten years later at the hands of the army of his brother-in-law, Henry VIII, was to be only the first of the historical ironies set in motion by the union of Thistle and Rose.

The special relationship Dunbar evidently enjoyed with his immediate audience makes him a difficult poet for the modern reader to assess: apart from the element of oral performance, so many of his meanings are encoded in subtle modulations of conventional imagery, as in the rewriting of the Chaucerian *Parliament of Foulys* as *The Thrissill and the Rois*, that we cannot always be sure when he is making a serious point and when he is 'merely' displaying his rhetorical prowess. *The Goldyn Targe* is a further case in point: the poem has been interpreted both as a work almost exclusively concerned with its own rhetoric and as a coherent moral allegory in the 'reason and sensuality' tradition. The truth may well be that both elements are skilfully combined into an effective whole, in which brilliant 'illuminat' language both works in its own elaborate terms *and* reveals an illusory world which is ultimately subverted by the allegorical argument.

Dunbar's most elaborate descriptive language is again deployed in the opening of *The Tretis of the Tua Mariit Wemen and the Wedo*, a poem which defeats our expectations of a courtly celebration, carefully set up by the idyllic landscape of the first twenty lines, presenting us instead with accounts of the horrors of marriage from the point of view of the three 'gay ladeis' identified in the title. After his ornate initial description, Dunbar switches into a flyting style which exploits to the full the phonaesthetic possibilities of Scots and of the alliterative long line, and the bitterness of the two wives is counterpointed by the cynicism of the Wedo (manifestly a lineal descendent of Chaucer's Wife of Bath), who holds herself up as a model of predatory sexuality, parodying the language of courtly love in the process. That the poem, with all its bawdy anti-feminism, was intended to entertain a court audience is perhaps implied by the way in which Dunbar throws a final, ironic question to his 'auditoris most honorable': 'Quhilk wald ye waill to your wif gif ye suld wed one?' The correct answer, presumably, is '(d) none of the above'!

Even in his religious verse, Dunbar extends the stylistic possibilities of Scots. By contrast with his many moral lyrics, written in the sparsest of plain styles, there is the heavily Latinate 'Ballat of Our Lady', in which the specialised register of Latin hymnody is adapted into Scots. Choosing a verse-form which demands great virtuosity in rhyming, Dunbar meets the challenge by combining native vocabulary and Latin borrowings in a display of inventiveness which is itself a kind of index of Marian devotion:

> Hale, sterne superne; hale, in eterne
>   In Godis sicht to schyne;
> Lucerne in derne for to discerne
>   Be glory and grace devyne;
> Hodiern, modern, sempitern,
>   Angelicall regyne;
> Our tern inferne for to dispern
>   Helpe, rialest rosyne.
>   *Ave Maria, gracia plena:*
>   Haile, fresche floure femynyne;
> Yerne us guberne, virgin matern
>   Of reuth baith rute and ryne.   (1–12)

There is, perhaps, greater subtlety in the Nativity hymn '*Et puer nobis natus est*', where the whole of Creation is called in to celebrate the birth of Christ, and more still in 'Done is a battell on the dragon blak', where tight management of syntax, rhythm and alliteration is combined with a traditional complex of images to produce a confident trumpet-blast of assurance in Christ's victory over Satan:

> Done is a battell on the dragon blak;
> Our campioun Chryst confoundit hes his force;
> The yettis of Hell ar brokin with a crak,
> The signe triumphall rasit is of the croce,
> The divillis trymmillis with hiddous voce,
> The saulis ar borrowit and to the blis can go,
> Chryst with his blud our ransonis dois indoce:
> *Surrexit Dominus de sepulchro.*   (1–8)

It is one of the tragedies of Scotland's cultural history that the combined forces of the Reformation and anglicisation should have caused such achievements of medieval devotion to have been lost to the traditions of the Scottish Church.

Ranging from the plain style of his petitions and moral lyrics to the aureate language of *The Golden Targe* and the abusive vulgar style of the *Tretis* and his *Flyting* with Walter Kennedy, Dunbar extends enormously the stylistic resources of Scots verse. He shares this enterprise with Gavin Douglas, whose *Palice of Honoure* (*c.*1501) rivals the *Targe* in its rhetorical inventiveness and may well predate it slightly. But by far the most important of Douglas's works (which almost certainly do *not* include the allegory *King Hart* formerly attributed to him) is his translation of Virgil's *Aeneid* (1512–13). This is a remarkable achievement, one of the earliest translations of a major Classical text into any European vernacular, and a work of such comprehensive scope and technical virtuosity that it certainly demands to be considered as a major work in its own right. It is, moreover, one of the earliest Scottish texts in which we can detect the influence of the humanist scholarship which was now revolutionising literary studies, and literature itself, throughout Europe.

As he makes clear in his Prologue to Book I, Douglas had a keen awareness of the difficulties inherent in poetic translation; but he was determined to do justice to the greatness of Virgil's Latin epic. As Priscilla Bawcutt has demonstrated,[7] he made expert use of the edition of the *Aeneid* published by the humanist scholar Josse Badius Ascensius in Paris in 1501, drawing on the elaborate commentaries provided by Ascensius to illuminate his understanding of the text. This scholarly approach contrasts strongly with the reception of Classical literature in the Middle Ages, and Douglas himself begins with a vigorous assault on the representation of Virgil in Caxton's English prose version ('It has na thing ado tharwith, God wait, / Ne na mair lyke than the Devill and Sanct Austyne'), and even on the account of the Dido story in Chaucer's *Legend of Good Women*.

> And netheles into sum place, quha kend it,
> My mastir Chauser gretly Virgill offendit:
> All thoch I be tobald hym to repreif,
> He was fer baldar, certis, by his leif,
> Sayand he followit Virgillis lantern toforn,
> Quhou Eneas to Dydo was forsworn.
> Was he forsworn? Than Eneas was fals –
> That he admittis, and callys hym traytour als.   (Prol. I, 410–16)

The problem Douglas faces here is in some ways a revealingly medieval one: how can Eneas be both a hero and a deceiver? For Douglas, both the morality and the aesthetics of Latin epic are mediated through the conventions of medieval romance, and he must therefore try to find a way of absolving Eneas of as much blame as possible for his treatment of Dido. Nor is this the only point at which his admiration for Virgil's great poem is in conflict with his moral and theological assumptions: he is also at some pains to distance himself from the pagan framework of his original, while remaining as true as possible to its spirit.

All things considered, Douglas's virtuosity in squaring this religious circle and in adapting the *Aeneid* into Scots verse is remarkable, and the *Eneados* deserves to be much better known than it is. It is also notable for the prologues which Douglas attaches to each of the thirteen Books (for his version includes the thirteenth Book which was added to Virgil's twelve by the Italian humanist Maffeo Vegio in the fifteenth century). Written in a wide variety of verse-forms and covering a variety of themes, these prologues assist in the process of assimilation of the Virgilian narrative into the Scots poetic tradition, and they also permit Douglas to show off his own rhetorical skill and the stylistic possibilities of Scots; they constitute a virtual sampler of vernacular style. They give us, too, a sense of the translator himself and of the progress of his work, for several of them refer explicitly to the passing of the seasons as the translation proceeds. As with Henryson and Dunbar, Douglas's literary persona owes much to his 'mastir Chauser': he is capable of being winningly ironic at his own expense, but he is equally in no doubt about the magnitude of his undertaking, or of his claim to a place in the 'palice of honoure'. The *Eneados* is, in some ways, the high-water mark of Older Scots poetry; completed on 22 July 1513, it coincides almost exactly with the end of what has been called 'the aureate age' of James IV. Exactly seven weeks later, the king and many of his magnates were to die on the field of Flodden.

During the succeeding period of James V's minority, between Douglas's *Eneados* and the earliest works of Sir David Lyndsay, there is little evidence of writing in the vernacular, as if the trauma of Flodden had silenced the voice of the nation. Yet these years saw the appearance of two important Latin histories of the Scots, both published in Paris, each attesting in its own way to the distinctive experience of Scotland for an international audience. In other respects, the two accounts could scarcely be more different. John Mair (or Major) was, as Professor Broadie argues elsewhere in these pages, one of the most distinguished of late medieval scholastic philosophers and theologians, while Hector Boece was a humanist of the school of Jean Standonck and Erasmus. Mair's *Historia Majoris Britannie* (1521) is no masterpiece of Latin style, but his analytical skills far outweigh those of Boece, whose fine Livy-esque prose cannot disguise the fact that his *Scotorum historiae* (1527) is much less critical in its treatment of sources and evidence. Yet Boece's mixture of traditional legend, contemporary folklore and moral advice, all with a strongly nationalist subtext, was evidently more acceptable to his fellow-countrymen than Mair's thoughtful proto-Unionism, and his work was translated into Scots three times within a generation of its first appearance, most notably in the version by John Bellenden (1533). Its subsequent literary influence would be even more significant, for as a source for Holinshed's *Chronicles* Boece's history had a profound if indirect effect on the shape of Shakespeare's *Macbeth*.

By the time the Court again became a locus for literary activity, at the end of the 1520s, Europe had begun to undergo a cultural revolution. The first signs that the Lutheran movement, which spread rapidly through northern Europe in the years after Martin Luther's decisive attack on the Church in 1517, had begun to penetrate Scotland are apparent by the mid-twenties, and the Lutheran Patrick Hamilton was burned as a heretic in St Andrews in February 1528. It is, however, as a reformer rather than as a Reformer that Sir David Lyndsay, a courtier with many years of service during the king's minority and earlier, began his literary career: his first surviving works, *The Dreme* (1528) and *The Complaynt* (1529), demonstrate considerable concern for the state of the 'commoun-weill', but they deal with ecclesiastical matters only incidentally. *The Testament and Complaynt of Our Soverane Lordis Papyngo* (1530) is both a more sophisticated work of art and a more explicit condemnation of the rapacity of the clergy. The pet parrot of the title begins as a symbol of the ambitious courtier, but once she is on the point of death she becomes a voice of moral authority, not only offering advice to her fellow-courtiers and to the king himself, but challenging the clerical birds, magpie, raven and kite, who gather around her ailing body. The final scene, in which she is torn to pieces by the rapacious, quarrelling churchmen is a powerful indictment, reminiscent of the ending of Henryson's 'Preiching of the Swallow' but much more sharply pointed:

> And be scho had *In manus tuas* said
> Extinctit wer hir naturall wyttis fyve;
> Hir hed full softlye on hir schulder laid,
> Syne yaild the spreit with panes pungityve.
> The Ravin began rudely to ruge and ryve,
> Full gormondlyke his emptie throte to feid.
> 'Eait softlye, brother,' said the gredy Gled.
>
> 'Quhill scho is hote, depart hir ewin amang ws.
> Tak thow one half, and reik to me ane uther;
> In tyll our rycht, I wat, no wycht dar wrang ws.'

The Pyote said: 'The Feinde resave the fouther!
Quhy mak ye me stepbarne, and I your brother?
Ye do me wrang, Schir Gled; I schrew your harte!
Tak thare,' said he, 'the puddyngis for thy parte.'   (1,144–57)

Lyndsay combined his literary commitments with work as a royal herald, for much of his later life serving as Lyon King of Arms, and we have relatively little from his pen during the 1530s and early 1540s. In the last eight years of his life, however, he was enormously productive, repeatedly adapting familiar genres for new purposes. *The Tragedie of the Cardinall* (1547) uses the 'fall of princes' motif with devastating effect, making the murdered Beaton declare his own crimes as an example of the vanity of worldly power; *Squyer Meldrum* (c.1550) presents the experience of a contemporary Fife gentleman in terms of romance convention, incidentally reflecting the inadequacy of such idealisations in the face of a more brutal modern reality; and *Ane Dialog betuix Experience and ane Courteour* (1553) adapts the medieval tradition of historiography to the demands of Protestant propaganda, devoting the latter half of his poem to the 'Spirituall and Papall Monarchie' and, in apocalyptic vein, the Last Judgment.

It is, however, *The Thrie Estaitis*, apparently first performed in Cupar in 1552, which assures Lyndsay of a central place in the Scottish canon.[8] (See Plate 19.) There had evidently been lively theatrical traditions in later medieval Scotland, both in the burghs and at Court, but the rigorous suppression of all such activity after the Reformation ensured that no texts survive. Lyndsay presumably knew and drew upon this material (he had himself been involved in plays at Court as early as 1511), but *The Thrie Estaitis* also has much in common with the traditions of the English morality plays and the French *farces* and *sotties*. Its two-part structure with an Interlude between risks fragmentariness, but is finally held together by the sheer intensity of its attack upon the ills of contemporary society, especially those attributable to corruption and materialism in the Church. The play's central figure, King Humanitie, represents both the royal function in society and the individual Christian; this balance is subtly maintained in Part I, but in Part II it is the political theme which predominates, the debate enacting the process of reform through Parliament. Such wordiness could become tedious (and the play needs judicious cutting for a modern audience), but Lyndsay demonstrates a notable command of theatrical effectiveness; and it must be remembered that the play was first performed in a period of gathering crisis, against a background of intermittent heresy trials.

For the political situation had deteriorated greatly between 1530 and 1552. The decades after the execution of Patrick Hamilton saw a steady trickle of Protestant *émigrés* leaving Scotland, and a growing volume of Protestant propaganda entering it. Among those who were forced to flee because of their views, one of the most significant was Alexander Allan (1500–65), christened Alesius ('the Wanderer') by his mentor Philip Melanchthon, an Augustinian canon in St Andrews who was radicalised by the experience of Hamilton's martyrdom and who subsequently taught in Wittenberg, Cambridge, Frankfurt-an-der-Oder and Leipzig, where he spent the last twenty-two years of his life. Alesius's Latin writings, mostly controversial works and Biblical commentaries, were better known on the Continent than in Scotland; but his early *Epistola contra Decretum quoddam Episcoporum in Scotia* (1533), an attack on the decision to prohibit the vernacular New Testament, was directed to James V, and drew a response from the Catholic propagandist Cochleus, to which Alesius in turn replied with a *Responsio* (1534), including a good deal of circumstantial information about his persecution in St Andrews and eventual escape. Alesius deserves greater recognition than he has received in both Germany and Scotland, but his works, and those of other expatriates like John Macalpine (Macchabeus) and John Fethy (Fidelis), probably had little direct influence on the development of the Scottish Reformation.

The same may well be true of John Gau's *Richt Vay to the Kingdome of Heuine*, based on works by the Danish Reformer Christian Pedersen and by Luther himself and published in Malmö in 1533, and John Johnstone's *Comfortable Exhortation* (1535); but the absence of Scottish copies of these treatises does not necessarily prove that they had no effect, since such pamphlets were equally likely to be confiscated and to be 'read to death' by a covert community of Scottish Lutherans. Such circumstances certainly seem to apply to the *Gude and Godlie Ballatis*, a Lutheran anthology of psalm translations, spiritualised secular songs and satirical poems, the earliest versions of which were perhaps compiled by the Wedderburn brothers in the 1540s: there is no surviving copy of any edition before that of 1565. In these Protestant texts, both in prose and in verse, we see the adoption of an austere plain style, altogether opposed to the more florid styles still favoured at Court; the origins of the plain style are in the moral lyric and instructional prose of the later Middle Ages, but with the emergence of a Protestant aesthetics, distrustful of ornate rhetoric as of other manifestations of 'Catholic' decoration, these stylistic considerations acquire ideological significance. In the lyric verse of Protestant writers such as the theologian Alexander Arbuthnot (1538–93), and even of less partisan moralists like Sir Richard Maitland of Lethington (1496–1586), we can clearly see the triumph of aesthetic principles which dominated throughout those parts of sixteenth-century Europe in which Protestantism gained the upper hand.

The plain style was also encouraged in Scotland by the Reformers' dependence on the English Bible: although at least one Scots copy was made of the older Wycliffite version of the New Testament,[9] it was the translations by Tyndale and Coverdale, first produced in Germany in the 1530s, and then the Calvinist Geneva Bible (1560) which were used among Protestants in both England and Scotland, and whose cadences began to infiltrate Scottish religious prose, and to a lesser extent verse as well. Nowhere is this process clearer than in the exegetical and theological writings of John Knox (1514–72), although his personal letters and *Historie of the Reformatioun in Scotland* (1559–67) demonstrate his capacity for producing a lively and idiomatic vernacular Scots. It is perhaps for this reason, as well as on account of its (for a modern reader) unacceptable ideological content, that the rhetoric of a work like *The First Blast of the Trumpet against the Monstruous Regement of Women* (1558) is less accessible than that of the *Historie*. This latter work is, it must be acknowledged, as coloured by political and sectarian prejudice as any of Knox's writings, and it is less an historical account in the modern sense than an attempt to show the Reformers as instruments of Divine retribution; but its partisanship is to a degree relieved – even as it is reinforced – by the liveliness of Knox's prose, and the 'merriness' with which he recounts some of the excesses of the pre-Reformation Church.

Linguistically as well as politically and theologically, then, the Reformation process which had its crisis in 1559–60 brought fundamental cultural change to Scotland. That more of the Older Scots tradition did not perish along the way is in considerable measure due to a small number of scribes and printers who brought together and preserved many works of their own day and of the previous century. One of these was Sir Richard Maitland, whose folio manuscript (now part of the library of

Magdalen College, Cambridge) includes part of an earlier anthology, and thus poems by Dunbar and others as well as those of Maitland and his contemporaries. But the most important Older Scots anthology is that made by the Edinburgh merchant George Bannatyne, written while its compiler was escaping an outbreak of plague in the capital and completed in 1568.[10] Bannatyne gives a comprehensive selection of many kinds of vernacular verse, and while he took liberties with some of his texts, he is solely responsible for our knowledge of much of the poetry produced in Scotland before the Reformation.

Of the courtier-poets represented in these manuscripts, by far the most important is Alexander Scott: all thirty-six poems known to be by him were copied by Bannatyne, and his work is otherwise known only from occasional occurrences in song-books. Scott was capable of writing in the full aureate style, as the opening of his *New Yeir Gift to the Quene Mary* (1562) illustrates, but the great majority of his pieces are amatory lyrics which employ a comparatively sparse rhetoric but which display an impressive command of complex stanza-structures. The conditions of Court performance are as important a constituent of Scott's poetry as of Dunbar's, and each lyric seems to present a persona in another pose, leaving uncertain the 'true' voice of Scott himself. There is a connection here with Wyatt, an English contemporary whose work seems to have been known to Scott and who similarly presents himself in constantly changing form through his verse; there is perhaps a connection too with that wider European current of Mannerism with which Wyatt has sometimes been associated. Occasionally, Scott appears to stop playing games. It is hard to know what to make of the idiomatic bitterness of 'To luve unluvit', said by Bannatyne to have been written by Scott 'quhen his wife left him':

> Quhattane a glaikit fule am I
> To slay myself with malancoly,
>   Sen weill I ken I may nocht get hir!
> Or quhat suld be the caus, and quhy,
>   To brek my hairt, and nocht the better?   (16–20)

But a more complex, uncertain note enters 'Up, helsum hairt', one of Scott's finest poems, in which the persona unusually insists upon his happiness and fulfilment in a truly reciprocal relationship, only to end on a much more equivocal note:

> In oxteris cloiss we kiss, and cossis hairtis,
>   Brint in desyre of amouris play and sport;
> Meittand our lustis, spreitles we twa depairtis.
>   Prolong with lasar, lord, I the exort,
>   Sic tyme that we may boith tak our confort,
> First for to sleip, syne walk withowt espyis.
>   I blame the cok, I plene the nicht is schort;
> Away I went, my wache the cuschett cryis,
>   Wissing all luvaris leill to haif sic chance,
>   That thay may haif ws in remembrance.   (31–40)

There are conventional elements here: the medieval tradition of the *aubade* or dawn-song, later to be exploited in different ways by Shakespeare in *Romeo and Juliet* and

Donne in 'The Sunne Rising', underlies Scott's complaint at having to leave his beloved, but there is a sharp sense, too, of real constraints around an illicit, and in some respects dangerous, sexual relationship. A more acute awareness of the political uncertainties which run through a courtier's existence, and hence influence the practice of courtly verse, is increasingly evident in sixteenth-century verse in Italy, France and England; here we find the first traces of it in Scotland as well.

As we noted in the aftermath of Flodden, the destruction of the Marian Court with the Queen's forced abdication in 1568 again removed the obvious centre of literary patronage. In the ensuing minority, which began with five years of civil war, courtly verse gave way to political propaganda, and the dominant voice of the decade is not that of Scott, but the shrill if effective polemics of Robert Sempill (1530–c.1595). Like Knox's prose and the moral verse of Arbuthnot, Maitland and William Lauder, Sempill's broadsides put propagandist clarity above the demands of a more 'literary' art and the limited perspective of topicality above any more universal engagement with moral values; provided they are read in such terms, they can be appreciated for their sharpness of focus and their unambiguous commitment to a partisan viewpoint, while Gregory Kratzmann has recently made a convincing case for a greater degree of rhetorical sophistication in such pieces as *The Lamentatioun of Lady Scotland* (1572).[11]

While literary activity within Scotland was increasingly polarised by the Reformation and its aftermath, Scots continued to make a notable contribution to cultural life on the Continent. Florence Wilson's *De animi tranquillitate* (1543) is one notable expression of the humanist circle which flourished in Lyons in the mid-sixteenth century; but by far the most important Scottish scholar of his generation was George Buchanan (1506–82), who taught at Paris, Bordeaux and Coimbra as well as at St Andrews. The circle of his friends and correspondents included almost every major intellectual figure of his age, and his Latin writings enjoyed an enormous influence. His Psalm paraphrases were continually reprinted, while his Latin dramas, both translations of Euripidean tragedies and his own *Jephthes* and *Baptistes*, also circulated widely. To these achievements must be added his numerous epigrams and other Latin poems (including the *Franciscanus*, a reworking of one of Dunbar's satirical pieces), the work of political theory *De iure regni apud Scotos* (1579), and his *Rerum Scoticanum Historia* (1582). Most of Buchanan's work was manifestly directed to a European audience, but after his final return to Scotland in 1569 even the bulk of his Latin works reflect more local concerns. Occasionally, and most notably in *The Chamaeleon* (1570), he demonstrates his command of a vivid, polemical Scots; and we may suspect that his influence on the young James VI, whose tutor he was through the 1570s, was considerable despite the king's subsequent antipathy towards him.

With the end of the 1570s, we reach another important turning point in the development of the Scots literary tradition. If the period of James VI's minority is marked by the absence of a Court culture, the young king quickly took steps to rectify that position once he emerged from the tutelage of Buchanan. There is clear evidence that this revival was anticipated by at least one member of his Court: in June 1579 Patrick Hume of Polwarth produced *The Promine*, a formal, celebratory poem which manifestly harks back to the stylistic norms of Dunbar, Douglas and the aureate Lyndsay. But this was no longer a wholly acceptable stylistic option, and Polwarth's efforts would soon be eclipsed by those of a more significant poet whose voice is characterised by the tones of more modern, French models. Alexander Montgomerie apparently arrived at Court towards the end of 1579, and his intentions are made clear in *The Navigatioun*, a skilfully ingratiating performance-piece possibly written for a

Christmas masque in 1579–80. Direct confrontation between such clear rivals for the king's patronage was perhaps inevitable: it would seem that the stakes were high when Montgomerie engaged Polwarth in a formal *Flyting*, and the former would later look back with some satisfaction on the way 'I chaist Polwart from the chimney nook', that is, from a privileged place by the king's fire.

Of the circle of poets who gathered around the young James in the early 1580s, Montgomerie deserves his title of 'maister poete'. A skilled lyricist, he produces some of the most beautiful songs of the later sixteenth century, and he also displays linguistic virtuosity in his use of the sonnet for amatory, theological, political and panegyric themes. His one attempt at an extended poem, the allegorical *Cherrie and the Slae*, is marred both by the choice of an inflexibly repetitive lyric stanza and a plot of remarkably thin significance; but many of his short poems are among the finest achievements of the Older Scots tradition. As a love poet, Montgomerie seldom takes his Petrarchist models wholly seriously: his work is marked both by a preoccupation with the anxieties of the lover and a fondness for hyperbolic excess which equally suggest a desire to redefine Petrarchist conventions in linguistically innovative terms and an awareness of extreme psychological precariousness.

There is, moreover, another side to Montgomerie's output, which sets him aside from his contemporaries. As a convert to Catholicism, he clearly relied heavily upon the king's support. There is almost no hint in his surviving poems of explicitly Catholic sentiments, although a contemporary Catholic panegyrist suggests that he 'attacked the Calvinists with warlike song' ('*Picarditas carmine Marte tremens*'). His relationship with the Court was, however, always an unusually precarious one; and a long-running dispute over a pension (from the revenues of Glasgow Cathedral) drew from him several short sequences of increasingly embittered sonnets. These poems are no less sophisticated rhetorically than those devoted to love, theology, or literary encomium, but there is a note of personal grievance which gives unusual force to the terse, alliterating, proverbial style:

> Alace, my Lords, hou long will ye delay
> To put the poets pensione out of plie?
> Yon shifting sophists hes no thing to say;
> Their feckles flyting is not worth a flie.

His religious lyrics are sometimes personal in another sense: most notably in the spiritualised love-song 'Come, my childrene dere drau nere me', Montgomerie draws together rhetorical elements from the Psalms and the Song of Songs to produce a powerful assertion of the nature of Divine love in language which has much in common with that of George Herbert:

> Vhill I did these words besyd me
>   With a secreit sigh confes,
> Lo! my Lord and Love espyd me
>   And dreu neir me vhair I wes;
>   Then a ring
>   Did he thring
> On my finger, that was fyne:
>   'Tak,' quod He,
>   'This to the,
> For a pledge that I am thyne.'   (31–40)

Beside Montgomerie, the poetic achievements of the other members of the king's circle are comparatively modest. James himself set the agenda for his 'Castalian Band' with his *Essayes of a Prentise in the Divine Art of Poesie* (1584), which included a treatise on 'Reulis and Cautelis to be observit and eschewit in Scottis poesie'. In this collection and in his *Poeticall Exercises at Vacant Houres* (1591), he shows himself to be a competent versifier, and his heroic poem *Lepanto*, celebrating the Spanish naval victory over the Turks in 1571, was highly enough regarded in its day to be translated into French by Salluste du Bartas. Usually, however, the traffic was in the other direction, and James himself and most of his circle translated a good deal from French and Italian: among the more important Castalian projects were versions of du Bartas's *Judith* by Thomas Hudson, of Ariostos's *Orlando furioso* by John Stewart of Baldynneis, and of Petrarch's *Trionfi* and Machiavelli's *Il Principe* by William Fowler.

The influence of French and Italian literature, moreover, was not confined to these translations of major works. The vogue for the sonnet which seems to have begun in the early 1580s, and is manifested in fine examples of the form in the work of Montgomerie, Stewart and Fowler, has its parallel in every vernacular in Western Europe; and everywhere it is the influence of Petrarch's *Rime*, directly or at second or third hand, which underpins the fashion. In Scotland as elsewhere, the result is often love poetry which is extreme in its portrayal of the lover's condition and highly Mannerist in its deployment of 'conceits' (that is, extended metaphors which provide the structural framework of the poem). Whether the Castalian Petrarchists are translating directly from such sources as Ronsard, Desportes or Tansillo, or developing their own variations on familiar themes, their sonnets are generally elegantly formed; the Scots display a particular fondness for the demanding *ababbcbccdcdee* rhyme-scheme which is known in England as 'Spenserian', but which may well have been derived by Spenser from the sonnets in James's *Essayes of a Prentise*.

It seems fairly clear that the Castalian project was an attempt to revive the more elaborate styles of Older Scots poetry, reversing the narrowing of the stylistic system which had resulted from the triumph of a Protestant aesthetic in mid-century. But the confident use of a full range of Scots achieved by Montgomerie, and to a lesser extent by James VI, Stewart, and their contemporaries, could not in the end prevail against the inexorable political and cultural forces which were drawing the king and his Court towards Westminster. Nor was the force of Protestant poetics much diminished: one of the most eloquent gestures of the period is the destruction by Alexander Hume (1557–1609) of his secular verse, choosing instead to publish those *Hymns and Sacred Songs* (1599) which are at their best splendid enough – especially the vivid 'Of the Day Estivall' – to make us sincerely regret the loss of his other work. By the later 1590s, however, the more courtly poets of James's circle were looking southwards as the reign of Elizabeth neared its end, and in 1603 the ambitious Sir William Alexander produced *Darius*, the first of his *Monarchicke Tragedies*, in a language carefully calculated to appeal to an English readership; even James would subsequently upbraid him in verse for his betrayal of the 'smoothly flowing fire' of the Castalian tradition.

Two contrasting poets of the early seventeenth century demonstrate, on the other hand, that the collision of the Scots and English poetic systems was not necessarily destructive. The earliest poetry of Sir Robert Ayton (1569–1638) was written in Scotland before 1603, but his subsequent career was at the Court in Westminster, where he evidently came into contact with the Metaphysical style of Donne and the more cynical wit of the Cavalier poets. While he is closer in some ways to the lyricism of Scott and Montgomerie, or of Campion, than to the spoken rhythms of Donne, Ayton *does* take on something of the Metaphysical approach to imagery, and he is capable, as in 'Upon his Unconstant Mistress' and 'The Valediction', and latterly in 'Upon Platonick Love' (apparently written in the reign of Charles I), of giving poetic metaphor that innovative sharpness of focus which marks Donne and his imitators off from their Petrarchist predecessors. And among all the literary celebrations of James's accession to the English throne, it is Ayton's which declares quite clearly that something is being lost as well:

> Faire famous flood, which sometyme did devyde
> But now conjoynes two diadems in one,
> Suspend thy pace and some more softly slyde,
> Since wee have made the trinchman of our mone;
> And since non's left but thy report alone
> To show the world our captaines last farewell,
> That courtesye I know when wee are gon,
> Perhapps your lord the sea will it reveale.

While Ayton, like most of his contemporaries with literary aspirations, migrated to Westminster with the king, William Drummond of Hawthornden chose to stay in Scotland, living a life of genteel and scholarly retirement on his estate near Lasswade. There he accumulated a notable library, including much contemporary writing in Italian, French, Spanish and Latin. His own works grew out of this bibliophily: in both prose and verse, Drummond carries imitation even further than many of his contemporaries, creating texts which are, like the prose meditation *A Cypresse Grove*, woven together from materials created by other hands. But Drummond was a thoughtful manipulator of the diverse resources at his disposal, and his sequence of *Poems* (1616) transcends the Petrarchism of sixteenth-century poets, rediscovering the spiritual basis of Petrarch's *Rime* in the narrative framework of the loss of the beloved through death. As with Petrarch's Laura, the death of Drummond's Auristella (almost certainly a fiction) poses for the persona the most fundamental questions about the meaning of life and death, and the capacity of the human spirit to overcome such loss. Only with a remarkable closing 'Song' in which Drummond reworks the conventions of medieval dream-allegory in a Neoplatonist form does the poet come to terms with the transience of human happiness, and the final group of 'Spiritual Poems' extols the superiority of Divine love to the human, sexual love which was apparently the subject of the sequence at the outset. The contradictions thus created are not really resolved; but one of the advantages of the sonnet-sequence was the openness of structure which the interaction of disparate elements permitted.

The cultural world of Ayton and Drummond was very different from that a generation earlier, and the changes did not all arise from the Union of the Crowns. Even in the last two decades of the sixteenth century, new cultural forms were being developed in Italy, Spain and France, as well as in England and Scotland. In literature as in the visual arts and music, the stylistic patterns which are often described as Mannerist – reflected in fragmentation of structural unity, the elaboration of decorative detail, and a constant sense of formal tension – were being reshaped in ways which we can recognise as characteristically 'Baroque': the poems of Marino in Italy, de Sponde, La

Ceppède and Malherbe in France, Quevedo and Góngora in Spain, Donne in England, all reflect in different ways a cultural crisis the fruits of which are equally apparent in the painting of Rubens and Velázquez, and the sculpture and architecture of Bernini and Borromini. The Baroque elements in Drummond have recently been noted;[12] and while Scotland cannot be said to have produced any major Baroque writer, it is important to recognise the ways in which such comparatively minor figures as Ayton, Alexander Craig and William Alexander reflect not only the disruption of Scottish cultural life effected by James's accession to the throne of England, but also the wider movements which were sweeping across the Europe of their day.

The loss of the Court as a cultural milieu and a source of patronage certainly caused irreversible damage to an autonomous Scottish literary system. Individual writers like Ayton and Drummond were, as we have seen, able to master some of the prevailing styles of the English Court, and the same is true to a lesser degree of Sir David Murray of Gorthie, Sir William Mure of Rowallan and Patrick Hannay, all of whom wrote accomplished if conventional verse during the first quarter of the seventeenth century. But the Court of Westminster, too, was doomed, at least temporarily, and the two most gifted writers of the next generation to be born in Scotland, James Graham, Marquis of Montrose (1612–50) and Sir Thomas Urquhart of Cromarty (1611–60), were both caught up in the civil turmoil which affected both England and Scotland between 1638 and 1660. The few verses by Montrose which survive reveal typical Cavalier grace and elegance; but Urquhart is a more extravagant figure. His translation of the first two books of Rabelais' *Gargantua and Pantagruel* (1653) indicates his 'logofascinated' preoccupation with language, and his contributions to the seventeenth-century discussion of the creation of a universal language, *The Jewel* (1651) and *Logopandecteision* (1653), strike a precarious balance between persecution mania, national pride, and an apparently half-serious determination to press his 'invention' of a perfect means of communication upon an unappreciative Commonwealth. *The Jewel*, in particular, is a succession of *tours de force*; but it is the work of a genius at odds with his world, and one of its most revealing features is the emphasis Urquhart places upon the achievements of Scots in exile. The diaspora was now a fact of Scottish life.

The lyrics of Montrose and the euphuistic prose of Urquhart are equally uncharacteristic of the literary scene created in Scotland by the Union of the Crowns and the political upheavals of mid-century. The dominant voices were now those of lawyers and divines, and it was the professions which would for some time be the epicentre of Scottish literary culture. In the piety of Zachary Boyd's *Garden of Zion* and the sermons and Biblical commentaries of Robert Leighton, for example, there is evidence of great religious energy; and at times it finds powerful literary expression. The same is true of more polemical works like Samuel Rutherford's *Lex Rex* (1644) or George Sinclair's *Satan's Invisible World Discovered* (1685), which address very different themes with equal fervour. But there is a huge gap between the priorities of such writers and the sensibilities of modern readers, and it is a relief to turn to the cooler judgments of Sir George Mackenzie of Rosehaugh (1636–91), the most accomplished and varied prose writer of the later seventeenth century. His novel *Aretina* (1660) is the earliest Scottish example of the genre, and his legal, moral and religious writings mark him out as a figure who looks forward to the Enlightenment even as he deals with the tumultuous events of his youth.

If prose writing (at least of certain kinds) thrived on the conflicts of the seventeenth century, the same cannot be said of poetry. There are, it is true, traces of a tradition of polemical verse in the line of Sempill's broadsides of the 1570s, and it was James and Robert Sempill, of Beltrees, who produced the anti-Catholic *Packman's Paternoster* (*c.*1640, revised 1669). Robert was to have a more lasting influence on Scots poetry, however: for his 'Epitaph of Habbie Simson', piper of Kilbarchan, he used a verse-form which would become known to the poets of the eighteenth-century vernacular revival as 'standard Habbie', and which would contribute its aphoristic alternation of tetrameter and dimeter lines to many of their finest pieces:

> Now who shall play 'The Day it Daws'?
> Or 'Hunt's Up', when the cock he craws?
> Or who can for our Kirk-town-cause
>   Stand up in stead?
> On bagpipes now no body blaws,
>   Sen Habbie's dead.   (7–12)

Sempill's poem is the tip of an iceberg, for beneath the surface of literate culture the vernacular Scots verse tradition of which it is an expression continued, alive and kicking. There are few texts of Scottish ballads before the eighteenth century, but we can be certain that they were being widely performed; while poems like 'Habbie Simson' also form part of a vigorous popular culture. In the Advocates' Library in Edinburgh, founded by Sir George Mackenzie, moreover, were the manuscripts and printed books which testified to the thriving literary traditions of Older Scots. When, at the beginning of the eighteenth century, these two lines were again brought into conjunction, the result would be a new beginning for the literature of Lowland Scotland.

Notes

1. For evidence of surviving fragments, see R.J. Lyall, 'The Lost Literature of Medieval Scotland', in J. Derrick McClure and Michael R.G. Spiller (eds.), *Bryght Lanternis: Essays on the Language and Literature of Medieval and Renaissance Scotland* (Aberdeen, 1989), pp.33–47.
2. The identity, and even the existence, of Wyntoun's claimed 'anonymous contributor' (*Oryginale Cronykil*, viii, 2,931–64, ix, 1,120–4) remains uncertain; for one possible explanation, see David F.C. Coldwell, 'Wyntoun's Anonymous Contributor', *JEGP* 58 (1959), pp.39–48.
3. Although the final section of the narrative breaks off in 1408, the eulogy to the duke of Albany (ix, 2,683–2,756) indicates that Wyntoun must still have been working on his poem as late as 1424, when Albany died.
4. For a discussion of the background to such Christmas festivities, see Sandra Billington, *Mock Kings in Medieval Society and Renaissance Drama* (Oxford, 1991), pp.30–54.
5. The arguments are well summarised by Denton Fox in his edition of Henryson's *Poems* (Oxford, 1981), pp.lxxv–lxxxi; cf. George D. Gopen, 'The Essential Seriousness of Robert Henryson's *Moral Fables*: A Study in Structure', *Studies in Philology* 82 (1985), pp.42–59.

6. Joanne Norman, 'William Dunbar: Grand Rhétoriqueur', in *Bryght Lanternis*, pp.179–93.

7. Priscilla Bawcutt, *Gavin Douglas: a Critical Study* (Edinburgh, 1976), pp.95–127.

8. For the case against identifying *The Thrie Estaitis* with the play performed in Linlithgow at Epiphany 1540, see Joanne S. Kantrowitz, *Dramatic Allegory: Lyndsay's Ane Satyre of the Thrie Estaitis* (Lincoln, Nebraska, 1975), pp.11–27; and my edition of Lyndsay's play (Edinburgh, 1989), pp.ix–xiv.

9. Murdoch Nisbet, *The New Testament in Scots*, ed. T.G. Law (3 vols., STS, Edinburgh, 1901–5).

10. The circumstances of the manuscript's production and its date are discussed in the facsimile edition, ed. Denton Fox and W.A. Ringler (London, 1980), pp.ix–xvi; cf. Joan Hughes and W.S. Ramson, *Poetry of the Stewart Court* (Canberra, 1982).

11. Gregory Kratzmann, 'Sixteenth-Century Secular Poetry', in *The History of Scottish Literature: Origins to 1660*, ed. R.D.S. Jack (Aberdeen, 1988), pp.105–24, at 116–8; and 'Political Satire and the Scottish Reformation', *SSL* 26 (1992), pp.423–37.

12. David W. Atkinson, 'William Drummond as a Baroque Poet', *SSL* 26 (1992), pp.394–409.

Books for Further Reading

Priscilla Bawcutt, *Gavin Dougas: A Critical Study* (Edinburgh, 1976)
Priscilla Bawcutt, *Dunbar the Makar* (Oxford, 1992)
David Daiches, *Literature and Gentility in Scotland* (Edinburgh, 1982)
Douglas Gray, *Robert Henryson* (Leiden, 1979)
Joan Hughes and W.S. Ramson, *Poetry of the Stewart Court* (Canberra, 1982)
R.D.S. Jack, *Alexander Montgomerie* (Edinburgh, 1985)
Gregory Kratzmann, *Anglo-Scots Literary Relations 1430–1550* (Cambridge, 1980)
Robert H. MacDonald, *The Library of Drummond of Hawthornden* (Edinburgh, 1971)
John MacQueen (ed.), *Humanism in Renaissance Scotland* (Edinburgh, 1990)
David MacRoberts (ed.), *Essays on the Scottish Reformation* (Glasgow, 1962)
Ian S. Ross, *William Dunbar* (Leiden, 1981)
Helena M. Shire, *Song, Dance and Poetry of the Court of Scotland under King James VI* (Cambridge, 1969)

Dialectics of 'Voice' and 'Place': Literature in Scots and English from 1700

RODERICK WATSON

National identity grows from the stories we tell to ourselves about ourselves, and indeed the nation itself can be seen as an 'imagined community'.[1] It is no surprise, then, that literature should play a large part in that imagining, and in fact the main 'state' left to a 'stateless nation' may well be its state of mind, and in that territory it is most certainly literature which maps the land. The story of Scottish literature from the eighteenth to the twentieth centuries is the story of two major literary revivals, both prompted by a sense of cultural, political and economic unease with respect to a more powerful neighbour to the south, but both drawing on long-standing and original native sources.

The Union of 1707 may have led to a period of prosperity and increased trade, as its apologists have always claimed, but the first forty years were not very propitious in this respect, and no less than three-quarters of the Scottish populace had been deeply opposed to it in the first place.[2] Guarantees had been made to ensure the continuance of a Scottish identity in both Church and law, but the people at large looked to more than the Westminster Confession and Viscount Stair's *Institutes* (1681) for a sense of who they were and what it was to be 'Scottish'.

What they sought was a revivified sense of what I will call 'voice' and 'place' as things that make us 'different' from the English, or which can claim their own special status among the cultures of the world at large. The aim of this essay is to explore manifestations of 'voice' and 'place' in Scottish literature from 1700 to the present day. The theme is a rich one, and there is still more to say about it than can be managed here, so there will be inevitable omissions in what follows. Even so, some sort of framing device must be chosen if we are to establish any kind of coherence in such a vast and varied field, and the best that one can ask of it is that it should help to clarify the most salient features of what is under review.

VOICE AND PLACE

By 'voice' I mean 'a characteristic mode of discourse – as if spoken'; and the most immediate manifestation of this in the eighteenth century would be in the role of Scots, and especially vernacular Scots, as a matter of personal, and then national identity. Of course, the oral tradition has frequently interacted with the literary tradition in Scottish cultural history, as Hamish Henderson makes clear later in this book. Yet I think that the concept of 'voice' in Scottish writing goes beyond matters of language or dialect, to focus on an even more telling cultural and national preference for the speech act (as a guarantee of some sort of authenticity) over the written text, even if that speech act is, paradoxically, written down. The preference for first person narrative goes back a long way in Scottish culture,[3] and its theoretical implications will be developed shortly. For the moment it will suffice to note that the concept of 'voice' received a special emphasis with the rise of vernacular expression in the rediscovery or reconstruction of national identity after the Union of 1707.

By 'place' I mean to focus on what might be taken to be a sense of communal identity through geography and history, or rather through how these factors have been re-imagined by successive creative writers from the eighteenth century to the present day. The best known of these writers was, of course, Sir Walter Scott, but historians also had a part to play, for Scottish culture has a long tradition of historical writing, and it is no coincidence that such study, and the use of historical perspectives, should have been particularly marked in the thinking of a nation which had just witnessed 'the end of ane auld sang'. By 1770, David Hume claimed to know of no less then eight historical works in progress, declaring 'this is the historical Age, and this the historical Nation'. Like the rediscovery of Scottish 'voice', the re-invention of Scottish 'place' and its associated past were to be crucial elements in how our literature was to develop.

VOICE IN THE EIGHTEENTH CENTURY

In fact the most distinctive cultural identifier in eighteenth-century Scotland was Gaelic, and indeed by the mid-eighteenth century Gaelic literature (most especially poetry) had entered a particularly creative and productive period, nor was that output exclusively oral. Alasdair MacMhaighstir Alasdair visited Edinburgh in 1751 and had a collection of his poems printed while he was there, while Duguld Buchanan's poems were published in 1767 and a collection of Duncan Bàn Macintyre's work appeared in 1768. Indeed Duncan Bàn was living in Edinburgh at this time as a member of the City Guard, and was supported in later years by the London Highland Society who held annual piping competitions in Falkirk. It would be wrong to suppose, therefore, that contemporary Gaelic culture was not present or represented in Lowland Scotland at this time. And yet it seems to have made absolutely no impression whatsoever on Lowland writers, editors or commentators, even at the height of their enthusiasm for Macpherson's *Ossian*. Highland customs, dress and accents are commented on or mocked – most notably in Fergusson's attacks on the 'black banditti' of the City Guard – but the sophisticated wealth of Gaelic oral culture went unnoticed, or passed without comment. In effect, the Gaidhealtachd had long been marginalised, if not suppressed, among cultural circles in Lowland Scotland, and so the national 'voice', for many of those who had entered into the new Union with England, came to mean Scots.

(Paradoxically, under the patronage of Sir Walter Scott, the Highlands were to do much better in the iconography of national identity when it came to 'place'.)

The first and most influential volume in the evolution of a Scottish voice was James Watson's ragbag anthology, *A Choice Collection of Comic and Serious Scots Poems both Ancient and Modern*, which was published in three parts between 1706 and 1711. Strongly opposed to the Union, Watson had already got into trouble for printing anti-English material against the Darien Scheme and the Union, so it seems very likely that he saw his *Choice Collection* as an equally patriotic project. Indeed, he claimed to be following the example of 'Collections of Miscellaneous Poems in our Neighbouring Kingdoms and States' and opined that his selection was 'the first of its nature which has been publish'd in our own Native SCOTS Dialect'.

Watson's volumes contain poems in English and Latin along with sophisticated courtly poems and older pieces such as *The Flyting betwixt Polwarth and Montgomerie* and *The Cherry and the Slae*. But it was his examples of the popular vernacular tradition which turned out to be most crucially influential – with older poems such as 'Christis Kirk of the Green'; the seriocomic elegy 'Habbie Simson'; and a contemporary mock elegy by William Hamilton of Gilbertfield, 'The Last Dying Words of Bonny Heck, a Famous Grey-Hound in the Shire of Fife'. The structure, voice and spirit of these poems was taken up by Allan Ramsay, the most influential author, editor and publisher of his day, and they set a pattern for how the Scottish character was to be understood, for better and for worse, over the next two hundred years.

Much impressed by 'Habbie Simson' and 'Bonny Heck', Allan Ramsay took up the vernacular cause in his own writing and publishing. Established as a master wigmaker in Edinburgh and a burgess of the town, but largely self-taught, Ramsay was one among many in an increasingly influential class of smaller merchants who felt that Scotland's cultural and economic status had not been helped by Union with England. Determined that culture and trade should keep pace with the southern neighbour, he espoused the neoclassical values of English Augustanism. Equally determined that the Scottish voice should be unique, he adapted the stanza form and the vernacular tradition of 'Habbie Simson' to a whole series of broadly comic elegies on local figures from Edinburgh's street life around 1718: 'Maggy Johnston' and 'Lucky Wood' kept alehouses; 'John Cowper' was a servant of the Kirk dedicated to the frustration of fornication; and 'Lucky Spence' kept a brothel at the lower end of the High Street.

There is a genuinely goliardic and colloquial energy in these poems, greatly advanced by the driving force of the stanza form with its sustained iambic tetrameter rhymes, checked by the rhythmic hitches of the shorter lines before the whole pattern starts over again, like the dance movements of a good-going reel.

> Fou close we us'd to drink and rang,
> Until we did baith glowre and gaunt,
> And pish and spew, and yesk and maunt,
>   Right swash I true;
> Then of auld stories we did cant
>   Whan we were fou.
>
> ('Elegy on Maggy Johnston')

The goliardic connection is not accidental, for the original 'Epitaph of Habbie Simson' related to a world of popular song and local festivals, and Sempill's poem had praised the 'Piper of Kilbarchan' for his musical contributions to sheep-shearings, the summer festival of Beltane, Clerk plays, horse races, weddings, dances, fairs, football matches and wappinschaws. In fact, the tradition goes further back still, to the so-called 'medieval brawl' poems of 'Christis Kirk of the Green' and 'Peblis to the Play' which recreate all the vulgar energy, the dancing, fighting, eating, drinking and wooing of a Kermess painted by Bruegel, and still further again to the grotesquerie of Dunbar's 'Dance in the Queen's Chamber' or 'The Dance of the Sevin Deidly Synnis'. (One of Ramsay's earliest publications was an edition of 'Christis Kirk of the Green' with some stanzas of his own at the end.)

Ramsay reinforced the 'Habbie' stanza's association with a world of lively social intercourse by using it for an exchange of verse epistles with William Hamilton of Gilbertfield, author of 'Bonny Heck', and indeed such verse epistles were to prove even more popular with Burns and his many imitators. What is at issue here is the evolution of Scots (developing from certain aspects of its previous history) as a natural literary vehicle for colloquial discourse, for generating the fluidity and the force of a living voice. The same expressive preference can be seen in the century's interest in character monologues – Ramsay's 'The Last Speech of a Wretched Miser' looks forward to Burns's 'Holy Willie's Prayer', for example – and especially in the many collections of songs and ballads which were made at the time, from Ramsay's *Tea Table Miscellany* and *The Evergreen*, to the more scholarly volumes of David Herd, or George Thomson's *Select Scottish Airs*, and of course Burns's own work for *The Scots Muscial Museum*.

In effect songs, ballads and especially 'Habbie Simson' and his many relatives, all belong to the world of communal festivity, and it is of crucial significance in the history of Scottish culture that the eighteenth-century vernacular revival should have chosen this voice in particular to regenerate a Scottish identity. As poems of carnival and celebration, the 'Christis Kirk' genre and variations on the Habbie Simson stanza were the models for Robert Fergusson's 'Hallow Fair' and 'Leith Races', and for Robert Burns's 'The Holy Fair'. Indeed the latter used the 'standard Habbie' verse form so often that it is sometimes known as 'the Burns stanza'.[4]

COMMUNITY, FESTIVITY AND SUBVERSION

The Russian literary critic Mikhail Bakhtin has written very effectively on the spirit of carnival in medieval times as an outpouring of energy through which the common folk could escape from the power structures of their world (at least for a spell) by engaging in parody, travesty, inversion, physical grotesquerie, licensed misrule and Rabelaisian excesses of appetite.[5] The proper places for such communal celebration were the main street, the market-place and the local fair, and Scottish poems from 'Christis Kirk' to 'Leith Races' offer immediately identifiable examples of this unruly democracy in action. Bakhtin went on to associate the release and the excess of the medieval carnival spirit with the classical genre of Menippean satire from the third to the first century BC in which fantastic adventures are mixed with vulgar realism, topical events, metaphysical speculation, scandalous behaviour and different literary styles:

> A very important characteristic of the Menippea is the organic combination within it
> of the free fantastic, the symbolic, at times even a mystical-religious element with an
> extreme and (from our point of view) crude *slum naturalism*. The adventures of truth

on earth take place on the high road, in brothels, in the dens of thieves, in taverns, market-places, prisons, in the erotic orgies of secret cults, and so forth. The man of the idea – the wise man – collides with worldly evil, depravity, baseness and vulgarity in their most extreme expression.[6]

This is indeed close to the 'Christis Kirk' spirit of Scottish literature, but its more metaphysical implications look forward to 'Tam o' Shanter' and 'The Jolly Beggars' and, ultimately, to *A Drunk Man Looks at the Thistle* and 'Under the Eildon Tree'.

Bakhtin makes the point that the many-faceted and chaotic freedom of carnival often mocks or undermines the conventional values and power structures of the Church and the ruling classes, and he finds the same subversive force to be present in the literary genres of comedy and parody which challenge the single-minded voice of authorial, and hence ultimately of state power:

> Parodic-travestying literature introduces the permanent corrective of laughter, of a critique on the one-sided seriousness of the lofty direct word, the corrective of reality that is always richer, more fundamental and most importantly *too contradictory and heteroglot* to be fit into a high and straightforward genre.[7]

Bakhtin proposed that part of this dialogical, 'double-voiced' awareness arose from a sense of 'polyglossia', that is from the co-existence of (at least) two languages interacting within a single cultural system. The models he pointed to were ancient Rome, when Latin writers were always aware of Greek culture and the Greek forms which had gone before them; and the Renaissance, when national languages and mores were demanding their own say against the monoglot international humanist voice of Latin (however 'unclassical' it had by then become).[8] There are very instructive parallels to be found here in the cultural and political relationships between Scotland and England, and the respective status of the Scots and English tongues.

The 'vernacularisation' of Scots in the eighteenth-century revival has sometimes been seen as a reductive process – a slide into genre literature – and certainly poems such as 'Bonny Heck' do little to dispel such an impression. On the other hand, the growing potency of the 'Christis Kirk' tradition can be seen as an upsurge of the old carnival spirit, comic and subversive, a 'reductive idiom'[9] full of oral energy and folk irreverence in the face of a political and linguistic agenda which was increasingly centralising and monological in its aspirations. (The Union of 1707, after all, marked the beginning of 'Great Britain' and the first steps towards the formal concept of a British Empire.) On the literary front, the prevailingly neoclassical values of 'good' writing in England emphasised lucidity, balance and universal applicability, not at all the same thing as a delight in energy and contradiction, or in mixing the resolutely local with high-flown idealism or metaphysical aspiration. (This is not to say that such energy cannot be found in English literature – in Swift, for example – but it was not adopted, as it plainly was in Scotland, as a national 'voice'.)

That voice has been heard in Scottish literature ever since. It was carried into the nineteenth century, and although bowdlerised by the Kailyard writers, it resurfaced in the modern Scottish Renaissance, enormously invigorated, in the work of Hugh MacDiarmid, Lewis Grassic Gibbon, Sydney Goodsir Smith and Robert Garioch; and then in more recent times in the writing of Alasdair Gray, and of James Kelman and a number of his younger contemporaries.

In the last analysis, beyond matters of 'English' versus 'Scottish' identity, I believe that one of the main driving forces behind this development was a dialectic between written and spoken discourse, with the Scots literary tradition tending to side, much more often than not, with the speed, flexibility and passion of spoken discourse (with its roots in vernacular Scots), as opposed to the more formal registers of written English. And that oral energy was even carried over into discourse in English – most notably, for example, in the eighteenth and early nineteenth-century prose of Boswell, Hogg, Galt and Carlyle.

PARADOXES AND PHILOSOPHICAL PARALLELS

Of course, there were also those who favoured a 'British' rather than a 'Scottish' voice, and this led to the position in which many figures of Enlightenment Scotland sought English models – or more properly the 'Augustan' models of English neoclassicism – in both their creative and discursive writing. Even Allan Ramsay sought respectability in this mode, for his best-known and most successful work, the verse play *The Gentle Shepherd* (1725), offered itself as a Pastoral comedy in which Scots (associated with the Doric dialect as used by Theocritus) was the most appropriate speech for common country folk whose sturdy good values act as a foil for the rest of us, without in the least upsetting our notionally more sophisticated values. There is not much subversion, and no signs of carnival excess, in the modest heroic couplets of *The Gentle Shepherd*'s tale of rustic wooing and hidden noble birth. And although its vivid accounts of witches and witchcraft on the stage must have had their own special *frisson* (given the history of Scottish witch trials during the seventeenth century), enlightenment and politeness prevail when Ramsay resolves the matter as no more than the 'silly notions' of a 'clouded mind/That is thro' want of education blind!'.

The leading figures of the Scottish Enlightenment were equally uncertain about the impolite vernacular force of literature in Scots, even although its satirical bent could be recruited as a 'Horatian' mode. Adam Smith proposed that it was the duty of a poet to 'write like a gentleman', while Hugh Blair, Professor of Rhetoric at Edinburgh, decried passages, even in Ramsay's *Gentle Shepherd*, as 'rustic' and 'not intelligible'. David Hume sought to adopt a wholly English prose style in his own writing and thought that John Home's *Douglas*, a high-flown blank verse tragedy in English, improved upon Shakespeare because it was 'refined' from the latter's 'unhappy barbarism'. Equally in the cause of 'refinement', James Beattie, professor of Moral Philosophy at Aberdeen, published a little book in 1787 warning against 'Scotticisms' in speech and writing, by which he meant Scottish idioms in English, for he took it for granted that 'broad Scotch words' were entirely beyond the pale and 'the necessity of avoiding them is obvious'. Yet Burns's Kilmarnock edition had appeared only the year before, to popular success and great acclaim in certain circles of the Edinburgh intelligentsia. Indeed, Henry Mackenzie could praise Burns for the delicacy of his feeling, while simultaneously expressing reservations that 'even in Scotland the provincial dialect which Ramsay and he have used is read with a difficulty which greatly damps the pleasure of the reader.'[10]

David Daiches called this state of affairs 'the paradox of Scottish culture' in a seminal study of that name.[11] But Daiches's paradox is still more marked when we consider that, even if they did choose an English 'voice', the Enlightenment thinkers of the time were nevertheless operating from very Scottish first principles. The philosophical and moral commitment to be found in Hume, Smith, Reid, Adam Ferguson and others can be seen to stem from a native intellectual tradition in which older European models had been supercharged by the particular democratic and doctrinal urgencies which were so typical of the Reformation in Scotland. Thus the professors of Moral Philosophy in Scotland's universities came to play as crucial a role as ever Burns did in defining new understandings of the connections between feeling and reason, virtue and learning, the individual and society.[12]

Key texts in this respect would include Francis Hutcheson's *Inquiry into the Original of our Ideas of Beauty and Virtue* (1725), Adam Ferguson's *Essay on the History of Civil Society* (1766), and Adam Smith's *Theory of Moral Sentiments* (1759), each of which recognises the constructed, relative nature of human society and the role of empathy as an experience, albeit subjective, which gives us a strong propensity towards moral behaviour and communally located democratic sympathies. The passionate egalitarianism of Burns and the sentimental sympathies of Henry Mackenzie's hugely successful novel *The Man of Feeling* (1771) are both rooted in this philosophical ground, and for all that there was a positive craze for weeping in public at Mackenzie's novel, this was never taken to be a less than properly serious and moral response, fully available to rational and even philosophical exposition.

At first sight, the Scottish Enlightenment's emphasis on 'reason' might seem to be completely at odds with the vernacular spirit of carnival, and poems such as Robert Fergusson's 'Hallow-Fair', with its market hucksters and its fisticuffs, sit poorly with Adam Smith's proposition that the rise of a prosperous and respectable bourgeoisie must go hand in hand with refinement and cultivation in the arts. (It is worth noting, all the same, how many of Fergusson's poems actually *do* celebrate the confidence and spending power, not to mention the drinking power, of a new class of small merchants and urban wage-earners.)

From another point of view, however, the vernacular energy of Fergusson's world is not, perhaps, so very far removed from the inner nature of Enlightenment thought which placed a special emphasis on both social accountability and out-and-out eloquence. David Allan has pointed out[13] that the Scottish intellectual tradition, with deep roots in the Church and the law, greatly favoured public disputation and rhetorical persuasion; and this is no less, after all, than the organised power of the impassioned voice. Scholars and philosophers, too, could be equally adept at arguing a public good, even if Scots lawyers were sometimes criticised for winning cases on the strength of their tropes rather than on the facts. Allan goes on to note that at least part of the Enlightenment infatuation with Macpherson's *Ossian* was due to this respect for eloquence in the service of the community, and to the notion that the figure of the bard was its most ancient and noble exponent.

The gulf between Enlightenment and vernacular values, and the apparent paradoxes of the Scottish cultural condition in the eighteenth century, may seem less pressing if the twin imperatives of 'voice' and community are taken into account in this way. Thus the openly goliardic side of Ramsay and the 'Christis Kirk' tradition has gained a more social focus in the poetry of Fergusson – although still energised by a comic, satirical and celebratory spirit – while Burns's work goes further still, to turn that spirit towards a more overtly moral or philosophical support for the common man who is capable of feeling 'Ae spark o' Nature's fire':

> What's a' your jargon o' your Schools,
> Your Latin names for horns and stools;
> If honest Nature made you fools,
>   What sairs your Grammars?

Ye'd better taen up spades and shools,
  Or knappin-hammers.

          . . .

But ye whom social pleasure charms,
Whose hearts the tide of kindness warms,
Who hold your being on the terms
  'Each aid the others,'
Come to the bowl, come to my arms,
  My friends, my brothers!

          ('Epistle to J. Lapraik')

For Robert Fergusson all human life, not to mention the inexhaustible comedy of the social whirl, was to be found in the streets and markets of his beloved Edinburgh, and he celebrated it with a will in poems such as 'Auld Reikie', 'The Daft Days', 'Hallow-Fair', 'Caller Oysters', 'Leith Races', 'Braid Claith' and many more. There is greater warmth and much greater technical skill in these poems than in Ramsay's earlier accounts of city life and, indeed, Fergusson's was the affirmative spirit which so stimulated Robert Burns to write his own Scots poetry, acknowledging the debt by calling him an 'elder brother in the muse' and by commissioning a headstone for the young poet's unmarked grave.

Fergusson continued the Scottish fascination with the colloquial voice engaged in direct public address, or indeed in disputation, by writing elegies and odes, and also dialogue poems such as the 'Mutual Complaint of Plainstanes and Causey', with its sly reflections on social class, which led Burns to write more openly on class in 'The Twa Dogs', and in the debate he imagined between 'The Brigs of Ayr'.

MOVEMENTS OF VOICE AND HEEDLESS BEING

The changing dynamics of the informal speaking voice were developed still further by Burns's use of the epistle mode which, according to Tom Crawford, includes some of his finest work in expressing '*conflicting* principles and feelings' and 'a plethora of moods together with the transitions between them'. Kenneth Simpson associates this chameleon-like ability, and the adoption of such roles, with the unstable nature of Scottish political, linguistic and cultural identity in the post-Union years,[14] and there is much truth to this. Nevertheless, the 'speaking voice' has always had this quicksilver quality – open-ended and undetermined – compared to the more formal registers of what is 'written', and at least part of the equation has to do with a positive cultural preference for the mobility of oral experience, even in published 'literature'. In the twentieth century MacDiarmid and Goodsir Smith were to revive this fluidity to great effect in poems of dramatic monologue and self-addressed debate.

While it is true that Fergusson provided models for many of Burns's best-known poems, the latter poet went on to develop a much more politically and socially conscious satirical force in his work, with poems such as 'The Twa Dogs' and 'To a Louse', and most notably of all in his dealings with Kirk excess in 'Address to the Unco Guid', 'The Holy Tulzie', 'The Ordination', 'Holy Willie's Prayer' and 'The Holy Fair'. The Habbie stanza reaches its zenith in the deadly precisions of 'Holy Willie',

13. Portrait of Robert Burns (1759–96) by Alexander Nasmyth
(1758–1840). Nasmyth was a man of great versatility whose
interests, apart from painting, ranged from engineering to poetry. He
was a friend of Robert Burns and shared his political views. (Scottish
National Portrait Gallery)

while the driving iambic tetrameters and trimeters of 'The Holy Fair' mark the furthest
evolution and the most telling development of the 'Christis Kirk' tradition, somewhere
between a dance and a rhythmic chant.

Burns's dedication to writing, collecting and refurbishing Scots songs speaks again
for the strength of the oral tradition at this time, and recent scholars have made a strong
case for the value of the poet's work in this genre. Nevertheless, Burns's dynamic art,
and the carnivalesque subversion which I have associated with the Scottish 'voice',
reaches its finest and most telling expression in 'Tam o' Shanter' and 'The Jolly
Beggars'. Both poems call the ordered world into question, not least accepted Christian
teaching about sexual morality. Kirk Alloway is as 'real' an experience as Poosie
Nansie's howff, not just because they are both realised in such vivid detail, but because
they go beyond matters of social and moral behaviour, to touch on the deepest well-
springs and drives of the human psyche.

The true purpose of 'Tam o' Shanter' is to tell us (even while ostensibly warning us against it) about Dionysian energy — dangerous, uncontrollable, subversive and thrilling. Here, as also in 'The Jolly Beggars', we encounter a force which is beyond mere matters of drink and fornication, or girls in cutty sarks, for alcohol and sex are only the keys to this domain and not the kingdom itself. That kingdom's origins are wholly primal, rooted deep in a principle of heedless being as something which can never be contained, which says both 'yea' and 'nay' with total disregard for the consequences, and certainly without a thought for the single-minded authority of Church and State, and the single-voiced utterances by which they rule. Burns's roots in the 'Christis Kirk' carnival tradition of colloquial Scots have given him access to this uncensored inner voice in a truly Romantic and Blakean inversion of conventional morality, which carries over even into the English diction of 'The Jolly Beggars' closing lines:

> A fig for those by LAW protected,
>   LIBERTY'S a glorious feast!
> COURTS for cowards were erected,
>   CHURCHES built to please the Priest.

Beyond all his regular and well-meant affirmations of sentimental egalitarianism, Burns speaks in these poems for the absolute spirit of carnival misrule and Menippean subversion, a spirit that was not to be matched again until the appearance of MacDiarmid's *A Drunk Man Looks at the Thistle*. It is little wonder that Hugh Blair made Burns leave 'The Jolly Beggars' out of the 1787 collection, but it is curious to reflect that the author himself claimed in later years to have forgotten the poem, and to have no copy of it.[15]

PROSE VOICES IN THE NINETEENTH CENTURY

The colloquial force of 'voice' in a Scottish literary identity was by no means confined to poetry, nor yet exclusively to writing in broad Scots. It is James Hogg who provides the most striking connection between literary discourse in prose and the oral force of popular tradition in songs, ballads and, of course, the telling of tales. Like so many of his contemporaries, Hogg was a collector of songs, and a maker of them too. It was his knowledge of ballads which had brought him into contact with Walter Scott and the *Border Minstrelsy*, and he published a collection of his own as *The Forest Minstrel* in 1810. Hogg tried his hand at longer narrative verse in *The Queen's Wake*, whose various sections purport to record a recital competition between bards, but his best remembered poem today is probably 'Kilmeny', which is a remarkable hybrid between narrative literary couplets, spiritual idealism and traditionally balladic elements of supernatural experience and abduction.

Despite being widely perceived as a rustic 'Ettrick Shepherd', and not above playing that role himself, Hogg produced wickedly funny parodies of Scott, Byron, Coleridge and Wordsworth which show that an early lack of formal education had not in any way limited his literary and critical acuity. His roots as a writer, all the same, were never far from the local tales and border ballads with which he grew up. These debts are quite clear when he began to write essays and tales in prose, at first for his own periodical *The Spy*, and later for *Blackwood's Magazine*. The oral bias of Hogg's writing is clear in tale after tale, for they deal with the stuff of local legend, most especially supernatural events or the sufferings of the Covenanters in the hills, or with a confusion between the two, as in his novel *The Brownie of Bodsbeck* (1818). And the veracity of such tales is always creatively insecure, as Hogg frequently reminds us with interventions such as 'But the tale is a very old one, and sorry am I to say that I cannot vouch for the truth of it.' ('The Witches of Traquair'.)

These insecurities are less naïve than they may at first seem, for they engage both 'history' and 'imagination' and recognise that both outer and inner experience have equal significance in our lives. Such tales invoke a fundamental tension between the undoubted existence of the subjective and non-rational world of the mind, and the post-Enlightenment social world of reason and editorial control. Indeed, these are the crucial poles by which Hogg generates the many psychological and social tensions – between characters, between the 'editor' and his texts, and between the reader and the text – which do so much to destabilise and energise his masterpiece *The Private Memoirs and Confessions of a Justified Sinner* (1824). The same palimpsest of 'documentary' evidence and unreliable first-person narration was to characterise those other key explorations of the Scottish psyche from Robert Louis Stevenson, namely *Dr Jekyll and Mr Hyde* and *The Master of Ballantrae*.

The overtly colloquial, fluid and ventriloquial nature of Hogg's prose can be seen again in texts such as 'The Brownie of the Black Haggs', or 'The Cameronian Preacher's Tale' which begins: 'Sit near me, my children, and come nigh, all ye who are not of my kindred, though of my flock; for my days and hours are numbered; death is with me dealing, and I have a sad and wonderful story to relate.' These lines are a perfect evocation of the Scottish tradition of social narration spiced with an eloquence whose roots are in the Church, public philosophical discourse and in the law.

J. Derrick McClure has commented on the unusually wide variety of linguistic and expressive registers which Hogg uses, especially in *Confessions* and in *The Three Perils of Man* which embraces:

> . . . not only several registers of standard literary Scots and English, but at least five local dialects and numerous personal idiosyncrasies in the speech of the various characters, to say nothing of pseudo-Middle Scots and (so to speak) equally pseudo-Middle English, in a linguistic gallimaufry as rich and flamboyant as the novel itself. Even poetry features quite prominently in the book . . .[16]

This mixture of dialects, voices and parodic stylisations exactly meets Bakhtin's definition of how the dialogic imagination works through 'double-voiced discourse' and 'heteroglossia', which he calls 'another's speech in another's language'.[17] No doubt it was the fate of Scots speakers to inhabit exactly this territory after the Union of 1707, but the prevailing perspective in this essay has been to suggest that such fluidity – double-voiced, pluralistic and irreverent – has more truly evolved from the older and more unstable realm of oral discourse, carnival subversion and colloquial energy.

On the matter of 'eloquence' Hogg could not agree with what he took to be Walter Scott's parody of the Covenanters in his novel *Old Mortality* (1816), which portrays both their names ('Habakkuk Mucklewrath', 'Poundtext', 'Kettledrummle') and the tones of their conviction as something merely comic, grotesque and even perverse. In this respect Hogg's native sympathies were with the 'martyrs' of the Killing Times, while Scott's Tory preferences inclined him towards the more Augustan values of balance, compromise and what he took to be (innocent of its ultimately ideological implications) the course of 'reason'. Nevertheless, *Old Mortality*, like so many of Scott's novels, is infused by an extraordinary colloquial force. Even if the distinction Sir Walter makes between diagetic narrative in English and mimetic character dialogue in Scots is a divisive one, it is still true that his Scots dialogue generates an enormously vivifying energy.

Scott does not go in for psychological analysis, and his characters seldom indulge in introspection, but the drama and pathos of their speech gives them presence and an almost Shakespearean roundness, not to mention the injection of a social and historical dimension to their being, drawn from motifs which Scott found in a native tradition of songs and tales. The list of such characters is a long one, but it would include Mause and Cuddie Headrigg from *Old Mortality*; Edie Ochiltree and old Elspeth from *The Antiquary*; Bailie Nicol Jarvie in *Rob Roy*; David and Jeanie Deans and Madge Wildfire in *The Heart of Midlothian*; Wandering Willie's tale in *Redgauntlet*, and many more. In this context it is interesting to note how effective some of these characters became when Scott's novels were translated to the stage, and it is tempting to propose that his novels lost something of this dynamic linguistic force when he set them furth of Scotland and the well-springs of colloquial energy which he knew best.

14. Portrait of Sir Walter Scott (1771–1832) by Sir Henry Raeburn (1756–1823). (Scottish National Portrait Gallery)

It is not far to seek something of the same voice – derived from an equally strong sense of social interaction and local conditions – in the writing of John Galt. Galt's use of Scots is much more marked by region and dialect, however, and his ventriloquial skill in first-person narrative goes much further than Scott, whose controlling, authorial, and 'reliable' presence is never in doubt. In this respect Galt is closer to Hogg and, indeed, he undertook the imaginative autobiography of *Ringan Gilhaize* as a specific rebuttal of what he took to be Scott's lampooning of the Covenanting voice in *Old Mortality*. It was through the eloquence of Ringan's biblical style (full of what Yeats was to see as a very ambiguous 'passionate intensity'), that Galt managed an extraordinary psychic 'transfusion' in his novel, although many contemporary readers did not understand the method. Galt preferred to call his books 'theoretical histories' and in all his major novels, such as the epistolary *The Ayrshire Legatees* (1820), and then *Annals of the Parish* (1821), *The Provost* (1822), and *The Entail* (1832), he used a first-person voice which did full justice to the fluidity, and the changing registers and insecurities of genuinely dynamic first-person experience and expression. It was not easy for genteel Scots or English readers to follow and many critics found his work 'provincial', 'peculiar' or 'vulgar'. Galt would have resisted the pejorative implications of such comments, but in a sense, of course, this was exactly his point, for he sought to catch the constantly changing flux of subjective response and local conditions from out of which autobiography and social history – not to mention troubling questions of personal and national identity – are generated.

Just these questions of personal identity, caught between inner doubt and outer arrogance, were at the heart of the poetic personae by which George Gordon, Lord Byron more or less defined his period's conception of the Romantic hero. Obscurely tormented and rebellious figures, such as Lara, or the evolving hero of *Childe Harold's Pilgrimage* (1812–18), are deeply private and yet paradoxically public in their behaviour. More than this, however, it is the fluidity of Byron's tone which conveys the truly double-voiced – many-voiced – flux of inner experience. In particular, *Don Juan* (1819–24) is a *tour de force* of expressive registers: moving from high to low to written to spoken and back again with quicksilver speed, Byron's voice is comedic, parodic, self-reflexive, evasive, ambivalent, diverse, unstable and always hilariously, iconoclastically, *alive*.

For John Galt, unlike Byron, the many registers of this 'living' voice were further reinforced by his access to Scots, for he had found Scots particularly suited to 'versatility of fancy' and the 'spontaneous flow of . . . conceptions',[18] but many readers, and his editors at Blackwood's too, found this fluidity too difficult, or were blind to it. The tastes of the day preferred the fixities of genre literature by which double-voiced colloquial force (and its human potential) could be reduced to the 'charm' of 'the Scotch dialect' in the mouths of stable, humorous 'characters'. In the last analysis, the ideological implications of 'taste' and 'gentility' are quite profound, for these terms, and stereotypes too, have always been an instrument of control in the face of whatever 'other' cannot be accommodated into prevailing and would-be monoglot cultural value systems.[19]

Never in any danger of being called either 'charming' or 'genteel', Thomas Carlyle burst upon the intellectual scene, firstly through his engagement with German literature and philosophy, and then with his radical, playful, passionate, parodic and challenging work *Sartor Resartus* (1833–34). This extraordinary book (its title means 'the tailor re-tailored') presented itself as a mock scholarly disquisition on the nature of clothes and appearances, but its true force lies in its recognition that 'no meanest object is insignificant; all objects are windows through which the philosophic eye looks on Infinitude itself.' This metaphysical bent, and especially the passionate conviction and the immediately personal and dramatic tone of Carlyle's writing, certainly derive from the Scottish engagement with eloquence and the double-voiced nature of inner experience. No Scottish minister ever felt himself more in touch with the energy of the universe or preached with more conviction than Carlyle. The same fascination with flux, energy and the changing spirit of the times marked his two-volume study *The French Revolution* (1837), whose rhetorical immediacy was created by his use of contemporary memoirs and a narrative couched in the present tense. Indeed, he saw speech itself as historical, and history too as a kind of narrative to do with the stories we tell ourselves – always open to interpretation, but never finally knowable or exhaustible.[20] It would be difficult to find a more vivid exponent of the flux of 'voice' as opposed to the apparent control of discursive prose – right down to his frequent use of dashes as an expressive and particularly mobile form of punctuation – soon to be amended by staider editors.

The same metaphysical drive allied to a kind of radical suprematism was to appear at the beginning of the next century in the poetry of John Davidson, who shared Carlyle's concern for how the industrial work ethic oppressed ordinary people, and something of his long-winded delight in scientific knowledge and abstract thinking, too. Poems such as Davidson's 'Thirty Bob a Week' influenced the way T.S. Eliot came to see the modern city experience, and his longer 'Testaments' look forward to the 'scientific' content of Hugh MacDiarmid's later world-language poems – a debt MacDiarmid was happy to acknowledge.

PLACE

Explorations of 'place' have been just as vital as those of 'voice' in the evolution of Scottish literary and national identity (if, perhaps, less complex), and with more space this aspect could be much further developed. Suffice to say that an engagement with place includes both geography *and* history, for no landscape in Scotland is innocent of its past. More than this, it should be stressed that colloquial, vernacular or dialect utterances cannot escape their own locations in both space and time, and indeed 'voice' and 'place' are inextricably and creatively interfused. This is all the more so when a sense of national identity is at stake, with its need for crucial signifiers of 'difference'. Hume's claim that his was 'the historical Nation' did not depend on post-Union anxieties about identity and language, but there is no doubt that such anxieties did play a large part in subsequent Scottish literary creation, from the quest for a noble past in Macpherson's *Ossian* (bardic, oral and race-centred), to Scott's 'invention' of the historical novel and the Scottish landscape, in which individuals are challenged by events larger than themselves, and taken to places stranger than they have ever known before – even if Scott's impulse was to ameliorate both 'challenge' and 'strangeness' through a variety of reconciliations at the end of his plots.

If Scottish 'Romanticism' has a particular characteristic at this time, it is in its tendency to locate itself in landscape and history, or in political and religious ideals – that is to say, with factors which have a less subjective and more communal application than is commonly expected of 'Romantic' modes. Even the theme of the divided self – a

15. Portrait of R.L. Stevenson (1850–94) by Girolino Nerli. (Scottish National Portrait Gallery)

central feature of Scottish writing in the late eighteenth and nineteenth century – takes its force from wider historical, moral or metaphysical issues. (This is seen most clearly in Hogg's *Confessions*, but the same issues are equally central to *The Master of Ballantrae* and *Dr Jekyll and Mr Hyde*.)

Compared to Hogg, Galt or even Scott, Robert Louis Stevenson makes little use of vernacular Scots in his writing, and yet the fluidity of 'voice' and its associated instabilities of identity are central to his understanding of character. Like Hogg's *Confessions* before it, *The Master of Ballantrae* comes to us through a mixture of documentation, testament and memoir, all presented by not entirely reliable narrators or editors (*Jekyll and Hyde* mixes these with a narrative voice); while *Kidnapped*, *Catriona*, *Treasure Island* and a significant number of the short stories and tales (most notably 'The Pavilion on the Links', 'The Merry Men' and 'The Beach of Falesá'), are told through first-person recollection. Of course, this is typical of how adventure stories generate immediacy, but Stevenson's subjective empathy greatly enhances the effect by evoking how moments of action seem to us, or remain vivid in our memories – recreating those lightning flashes of vivid detail and danger, or the atmospherics of mood, light and place, and always with an added element of moral difficulty or duplicity. For Stevenson, landscape is both the theatre of action and the objective correlative for these inner struggles, it is never – however exotic – merely a 'setting'. In this he was to be followed by the modern novelist, Robin Jenkins, whose work has been continuously engaged with the difficulties of identity, truth, morality and faith in both private experience and public action, and equally skilful in finding symbolically resonant landscapes, as in *The Cone-Gatherers* (1955), *A Would-be Saint* (1978), or *Fergus Lamont* (1979), to match his often pessimistic vision.

If Scott tended to resolve the conflicts between adventure and stability, or individual freedom and the social good by returning to the status quo at the end, Stevenson's conclusions (like Jenkins's after him) are much more haunted by what has gone before, ambiguous and even a little desolate. The true denouement of *Jekyll and Hyde* (1886), his best-known novel of the divided self, is that we are not really divided between simple categories of purity and depravity, but that there are many more 'selves' within us than this dualistic (essentially Calvinist) model can convey. It is significant that it is Mr Hyde who is the truly single-minded and pure persona in the book, as opposed to the 'imperfect and divided countenance, I had hitherto been accustomed to call mine'. In a passage prophetic of modernist and post-modernist flux, Jekyll sees beyond the twin poles of his own case to propose that 'man will be ultimately known for a mere polity of multifarious, incongruous and independent denizens'.

Many of the novels of Allan Massie (another modern writer in the spirit of Stevenson in this respect) also revolve around the puzzle of identity. Massie gives a specifically political and historical dimension to the issue by exploring the disparities between how we act in public life, and the different truths – sometimes better, sometimes appalling – of our inner experience. Thus *The Death of Men* (1980) deals with questions of culpability in the face of extremist politics in the Italy of the 1970s, while *A Question of Loyalties* (1990) looks at Vichy France from within, and *The Sins of the Father* (1992) with the uncovering of war crime and shared family guilts after the Holocaust.

Such inner complexities of testimony and action, however, were not forthcoming in the later nineteenth century, for the tendency of the times in the prose of David Moir and the 'Whistlebinkie' school of poetry, was to narrow character and utterance down to the predictable, popular, single-voiced confines of 'Scottish' stereotypes and 'hamely' speech. After the vernacular 'theoretical histories' of Galt and the psychological and moral ambiguities of Stevenson, the forces of voice and place were still further bowdlerised and sentimentalised by writers at the turn of the century such as 'Ian Maclaren' (John Watson), S.R. Crockett and James Barrie, who came to be known as the 'Kailyard' novelists. And yet even here, the old concerns with voice, place and a moral or metaphysical dimension to human life – however local, humble or 'provincial' the setting – can still be found, if in admittedly diminished form. In a time of great industrial, social and intellectual ferment, urban Scots and Scots abroad bought these books in their tens of thousands, seeking the stabilities of a simplified national character and a fixed and essentially rural past. Nor was the vernacular language forgotten, as William Donaldson has shown in his studies of the many popular Scottish newspapers in the late Victorian period which published stories and discursive articles in Scots.[21]

STABILITIES OF PLACE IN THE TWENTIETH CENTURY

After the First World War, Scottish identity was recast from a complex crucible of historical, economical and class forces. The trauma of 1914–18 (in which a disproportionate number of Scottish troops died, they were told, for the 'freedom' of 'little Belgium') was followed by an economic and industrial decline which was especially marked in the north. The Imperial adventure of Great Britain Incorporated was drawing to a close, and returning servicemen, disemployed workers, intellectuals and a disaffected middle class began to be moved by Liberal and nationalist leanings towards Home Rule, the call of international socialism, ILP republican separatism, and various manifestations of neo-Jacobite patriotism. Scottish national and cultural identity was at issue again with an urgency that had not been felt since 1707.

Hugh MacDiarmid's espousal of a 'Modern Literary Renaissance' set the agenda for difference on a linguistic level as we shall see, and as a matter of cultural politics this position favoured the rights of all 'small nations', each with their own unique contribution to make to a post-imperial and democratic world. Thus MacDiarmid held that Scotland should look to Norway, Belgium and Catalonia as models for the future. (Although he also supported Stalin's version of communism which had obliterated so many small nations and ethnic groups.) The poet went on to propose a collocation of 'Celtic' nations – Scotland, Ireland, Wales, Cornwall and Brittany – which might seem merely 'peripheral' to English eyes, but whose aboriginal values would be at odds with London's increasingly centralising power.

In this respect new interpretations of 'place' were to play a vital part in the literary discovery of modern Scottish identity. Having been brought up on remote island farms in Orkney, Edwin Muir saw his boyhood landscapes as symbolic of the ideal life, at one with the seasons and timelessly apart from the horrors of urban industrialism. The poet's family had moved to Glasgow when he was fourteen, and within four years both of his parents and two brothers had met premature deaths. It is not surprising, then, that Muir's poetry in the early 1940s was haunted by a sense of expulsion from Eden, as if he had suffered some obscure fall from grace, nor that his later work shows something of the unlocatable dread associated with Kafka – whose novels he indeed translated in partnership with his wife, Willa.

*16. Portrait of Christopher Murray Grieve (Hugh MacDiarmid) by Robert Heriot Westwater. (*Scottish National Portrait Gallery*)*

The poet George Mackay Brown, a fellow Orcadian and one-time pupil of Muir, has constructed a similar vision of value in a Scotland remote from the modern world, with Orkney in particular as a place of 'fishermen with ploughs' (the title of one of his collections from 1971). Like Muir before him, Brown feels that the Reformation in Scotland spoke for the triumph of the head over the heart, bringing only alienation and industrial and human exploitation in its wake. The mythic force and the appeal of this account should not be underestimated, for Brown writes in both poetry and prose with a sparing and epic control which is very far indeed from the confessional turbulence of much modern work. And yet, at least for those of us who don't live in Orkney, it is a crucially remote vision of how things are, reviving images of Scotland which, although much better realised, are still far removed from the ahistorical spirituality of William Sharp ('Fiona Macleod') and the 'Celtic Twilight' of the 1890s.

Norman MacCaig's engagement with 'place' is equally strong, but it is also enlivened by an ironic sense of contrast between the Assynt he loves so much and whose landscapes and animals he has celebrated in so many poems, and the urban confusions he finds and enjoys in Edinburgh where he lives for most of the year. By comparison, Iain Crichton Smith's Free Kirk upbringing in Lewis marked many of his early collections – *Thistles and Roses* (1961), *The Law and the Grace* (1965) – with an extraordinarily intense sense of moral and metaphysical anguish, closely associated with the bare physical landscapes and the penetrating, oceanic light of the Outer Hebrides. A recent study by Colin Nicholson has developed this point to trace in detail the centrality of 'place' in the work of no less than fourteen modern Scottish poets.[22]

Among the key novelists of the modern period, Neil Gunn is just as powerfully rooted in 'place' as Muir and Mackay Brown. Gunn drew on his own upbringing on the Caithness coast to create novels in which young people, or older and more disaffected individuals, have to seek maturity, understanding and wholeness within themselves. Yet these figures are not isolated, for landscape and community are integrated by a common web of history and recollection in Gunn's world, and that network can be accessed at any time, if only the characters' immaturity, dignity or arrogance will let them unbend. In historical novels such as *Sun Circle* (1933) about the ancient world, *Butcher's Broom* (1934) about the Clearances, and *The Silver Darlings* (1941) set in the early herring industry, Gunn evoked organic communities of traditional and essentially Celtic wisdom. In *Highland River* (1937), however, and especially in the political dystopia (somewhere between *Brave New World* and *1984*) of *The Green Isle of the Great Deep* (1944), Gunn had to bring that vision into contact with the worst that the modern world had to offer in two World Wars, with the slaughter of the First, and then the death camps and the Russian show trials of the Second. In this respect these books are Gunn's finest and most important achievement, for he persuades us that the values of his Celtic vision can meet the malaise of the twentieth century, without seeming in the least nostalgic or backward-looking. In the last analysis this is because Gunn finds a universal insight in his Highland rivers, with their straths and elusive sources so minutely and particularly realised in the clarity and the Zen-like intensities of his descriptive prose. This is both a metaphysical and a political, communal insight for our times, for Gunn believed that 'new conceptions of life and work are needed', which would be opposed to 'the tyranny of the machine and the predatory instincts of the go-getter'.[23]

> The small nation has always been humanity's last bulwark for the individual against that machine, for personal expression against impersonal tyranny, for the quick freedom of the spirit against the flattening steamroller of mass.[24]

'Place' plays an equally essential part in Lewis Grassic Gibbon's *Scots Quair* trilogy (1932–34), which charts the social changes undergone by settled rural communities in the north-east of Scotland during the First World War and the years of economic depression which followed it. Gibbon has a more troubling and problematic vision than Gunn, for each of his three novels takes us a step further away from traditional community and closer to the personal and political alienation of the industrial city. *Sunset Song*, the first in the series, is indeed about the 'sunset' of the old ways, even although the author has no illusions about the narrowness and harshness of country life. Young Chris Guthrie's life seems to follow the seasons, indeed, as suggested by the section headings of the first volume: 'Ploughing', 'Seedtime', 'Harvest', and so on. But by the time she and her son Ewan arrive at the factories and lodging-houses of Duncairn in the third volume, their lives are marked instead by the geological hardness of *Grey Granite*. Section headings such as 'Sphene', 'Apatite' and

'Zircon' reflect the suppression of feeling and the revolutionary harshness which Ewan chooses to adopt in his struggle against industrial capitalism, a cause for which he would gladly sacrifice everything and anybody in his drive to stoke 'the whooming furnace of history'.

Ewan's alienation is all the more striking at the end because the trilogy is a *tour de force* of 'voice' and 'place', both inextricably united in the flowing discourse of the text, which is largely based on the inner speech rhythms of Chris herself. Thus Gibbon uses the cadences of spoken north-east Scots (even with an English vocabulary) as his narrative mode, and the books are set as if they were extended inner meditations, mostly by Chris but sometimes by the community itself. This subjective colouring allows him to break down the diagetic gap between authorial voice (in English) and the mimesis of reported speech, and indeed he even avoids the use of inverted commas, preferring italics to indicate speech and unuttered inner voicings as well. This device can be seen as a crucial step in the emancipation of Scots, Scottish culture and new ways of writing English, and in formal terms it relates precisely to what Gunn understood by his phrase 'the quick freedom of the spirit'.

It is no accident that the central proponent of such freedom in *A Scots Quair* should be a woman, for Chris in her continuously evolving identities stands resolutely apart from all the single-minded ideologies of men, which she imagines to be no more than clouds sweeping 'through the Howe of the world, with men that took them for gods: just clouds, they passed and finished, dissolved and were done . . .' Hers is a hard-won independence and her experience was shared by many women in the years during and after the First War – she is widowed twice, after all. By the 1930s, however, when the books were written, Chris's emancipation from the illusions and prejudices of those around her had become a more overtly feminist issue as well, not least because of the overwhelmingly male-dominated nature of Scottish society.[25] These issues had been specifically raised with equal force by women writers such as Catherine Carswell, *Open the Door!* (1920); Nan Shepherd, especially *The Quarry Wood* (1928); by Willa Muir in *Imagined Corners* (1935); and by Naomi Mitchison in her many novels and short stories, not to mention her political and social work in support of family planning and intellectual emancipation in general. The female voice in these books has gained a critical new perspective on the ideologies of male power in Scottish society, and this marks a welcome break from its symbolic role as a signifier of sensitivity (frequently interpreted as weakness), in earlier novels such as Stevenson's *Weir of Hermiston* and George Douglas Brown's 'anti-Kailyard' novel *The House with the Green Shutters* (1901).

Voice and place, individual stories and communal history, become one and the same in Gibbon's narrative prose, which thus manages to combine the vernacular integrity of Hogg's tales with the psychological, cultural and political complexities of a more modern sensibility. These are nowhere more evident than in the final impasse between an ageing and weary Chris and the steely agitator who is her son, which he describes as 'the old fight which will never have a finish, whatever the names we give to it – the fight in the end between FREEDOM and GOD.' The point is that Chris, Ewan, and most likely the reader, too, will have different interpretations of this passage, but no one reading is specially privileged, and so Gibbon's trilogy ends on a divided and deeply ambivalent note which conjures up an eternal dialectic between double-voiced mobility and monological authority. If we are tempted to prefer Chris's point of view, seduced by the fluid power of that colloquial narrative voice, we should not forget that in Gibbon's hands at least, this is the eloquence of elegy, and elegies are sung for the dead.

Thus it has to be admitted that in some respects Gibbon's tone looks back to the spirit of the Kailyard, which was equally elegiac, for the voice of the community in places like Barrie's Thrums had long warned against visits to the city, preferring their own Edenic enclosures and sweetly sad sunset tunes. The same fatalism had characterised books such as Dean Ramsay's *Reminiscences of Scottish Life and Character* (1858) which purported to record a language and 'a phase of national manners which was fast passing away'.[26] Nevertheless, the Scots voice did manage to retain its iconoclastic and irreverent power in the modern period, for this was exactly what had first recommended it to Hugh MacDiarmid in the 1920s, and it is MacDiarmid's example which must be cited in opposition to the more conservative mythopoeic visions of Scotland held by Muir and Mackay Brown, and the fatalism which seems to mark *A Scots Quair* at the end, despite Gibbon's own belief in socialism and radical change

ICONOCLASTIC VOICES FOR OUR TIMES

MacDiarmid's first programme for the modern Scottish literary renaissance was to overthrow the static complacency of nineteenth-century Whistlebinkie 'hameliness' in order to bring the language into line with its 'unexplored possibilities' and the 'newest and truest tendencies of human thought'.[27] He associated these possibilities with the swift transitions of mood in colloquial Scots by which 'diverse attitudes of mind or shades of temper are telescoped into single words or phrases, investing the whole speech with subtle flavours of irony, commiseration, realism and humour which cannot be reproduced in English.'[28] It seems unlikely that English should be incapable of such effects, but the point to note here is MacDiarmid's emphasis on Scots as 'speech' that maintains its double-voiced fluidity, even when written down, as opposed to his conception of literary English (not without cause at the time) as a much more monological tongue.

MacDiarmid had developed his understanding of the Scots tradition's capacity for creative contradiction and the combination of opposites from Gregory Smith's 1919 study, *Scottish Literature: Character and Influence*, which had christened this effect 'the Caledonian antisyzygy'. Smith had defined antisyzygy as a national idiosyncrasy which delighted in the collision of realism and fantasy: he associated it with a 'medieval . . . freedom in passing from one mood to another', and identified it in 'Christis Kirk of the Green', 'Tam o' Shanter' and in the supernatural elements in Hogg and Scott.

In MacDiarmid's hands, however, antisyzygy was redefined as an essentially modernistic, expressionistic and constantly changing dynamic drive: a Nietzschean iconoclasm at odds with itself, metaphysical and vulgar in the same breath. Indeed breath, flow, utterance – in other words 'voice' – were central to his realisation. His early lyrics owe some of their most strikingly effective and apparently original metaphors to colloquial expressions which the poet found complete in Jamieson's Scottish Dictionary, and his modernistic masterpiece, *A Drunk Man Looks at the Thistle* (1926), is nothing less than an extended dramatic monologue, operating somewhere between lyric verse, rhetorical address, metaphysical speculation, satire and stream of consciousness.

In his book *Scott and Scotland* (1936), Edwin Muir looked back to the political and linguistic disjunctions of 1707, after which he thought that Scots were doomed to feel in Scots and to think in English. 'The curse of Scottish literature,' he wrote, 'is the lack of a whole language, which finally means the lack of a whole mind.'[29] He went on to propose that the great tradition of literary Scots had now sunk to the status of dialect, 'irresponsible' and 'irremediably immature', for 'dialect is to a homogeneous language what the babbling of children is to the speech of grown men and women'.[30] Much could be said on this topic, but the most significant indicator of Muir's position is to note how he groups together 'wholeness', 'singleness' and 'maturity' as superior and desirable indicators of national and cultural status.

No language works like this, and nobody thinks or feels in such unitary fashion. More disturbingly still, the implications behind the privileged status of 'homogeneous' English as opposed to the 'babbling of children', take us straight to the cultural and linguistic imperialism of the Victorian empire-builders. Modernism was what swept such monoglot certainties away, for who can separate 'thinking' and 'feeling' in *The Waste Land*, and who would propose that Eliot spoke with a 'whole language', or even a 'whole' mind? The debate has become even more telling in post-colonial times, with the rise of so many 'Englishes' both in our inner cities and in the world at large.

In literary and political terms, the modernistic and expressionist dynamic which MacDiarmid introduced to Scottish life and literature in 1926 was absolutely crucial to the reconstruction of a healthy culture which could find a place in the twentieth century, without assuming exclusively monological linguistic or cultural rights, and without always looking backwards to the bens and the glens of a romanticised and static past. But the roots of MacDiarmid's drive *can* be traced back, I believe, to the irreverent mobility of a vernacular tradition, carnivalesque, parodic, iconoclastic and double-voiced – everything that Muir wanted to suppress, in effect, as 'the babbling of children'.

The same unstable and goliardic voice characterises the verse of Sydney Goodsir Smith, and although he sometimes adopts a self-consciously theatrical poetic persona, his finest work, in *Under the Eildon Tree* (1948), can match the intensity and the potentially tragic perspectives of *A Drunk Man*. With a more humble persona, and in much more colloquial Scots, Robert Garioch wrote poems in which the street authenticity of the common man's voice acts as a satirical or critical foil to all proponents of cultural or political power – a perfect modern realisation of David Craig's 'reductive idiom'.[31]

The politico-cultural challenge to monoglot authority which was largely implied in Garioch's poetry, has become much more overtly realised in recent years through the verse of Tom Leonard, and in James Kelman's prose. Leonard makes specific attacks on a cultural establishment – English *and* Scottish – which sets the reading lists and decides on proper language usage. His poetry reproduces the phonetic force of spoken demotic language in order to challenge conventional notions of what 'literature' or 'Scots' might be, and beyond that, he challenges 'education' itself, and certainly 'educated' speech which he sees as no less than the instrument of middle-class privilege in maintaining its own influence and power.

> This is thi
> six a clock
> news thi

man said n
thi reason
a talk wia
BBC accent
iz coz yi
widny wahnt
mi ti talk
aboot thi
trooth wia
voice lik
wanna yoo
scruff. if
a toktaboot
thi trooth
lik wanna yoo
scruff yi
widny thingk
it wuz troo.

(*from* 'Unrelated Incidents 3')

Kelman's prose makes a similar attempt to deconstruct cultural and linguistic power relationships, by refusing to move outside the experiential sphere of his characters. Thus the author resists the temptation to offer a privileged insight into his creation, and furthermore he refuses to adopt a narrative voice whose cadences are in any significant way different from the demotic utterance of his characters. Thus Kelman's art is largely conducted through a free indirect discourse which is in step with his characters' 'voices' as their thoughts and words twist and turn and change direction and repeat themselves in the immediate and erratic present of an unspooling consciousness.[32] In this way, not unlike Grassic Gibbon before him, Kelman has managed to marry the autobiographical voice with narrative discourse, and to bridge the unhappy gulf across which Walter Scott's characters spoke Scots while he told us about them, from an authorial vantage point, in English. In this respect Kelman's prose has found the integrity, as well as an existential clarity and an expressive force, which allows him to write from within his habitual milieu of unemployment, urban decay and the humiliations of low-paid work, without a trace of imitation or condescension.

Younger authors such as Gordon Legge and Duncan McLean have developed the fiction of inner-city blight and broken-down housing estates by writing with a manic punkish energy which generates its own optimism out of what might otherwise be violence and despair. Through these and a significant number of other writers, contemporary Scottish literature has given a voice to the voiceless in a way that echoes current developments in England and elsewhere – especially among new young black writers – but the vernacular energy and the working-class base of this tendency in Scotland can claim a long-standing historical and cultural tradition which has never been far from the mainstream, and by which the mainstream has been vitally reinvigorated at regular intervals.[33]

The same demotic force has characterised recent developments in Scottish drama, whose roots in this context go back to the plays of Joe Corrie in the 1920s, reinvigorated by later writers such as Roddy MacMillan, Bill Bryden, Tom McGrath, John McGrath and the 7:84 theatre company, Hector Macmillan and Donald Campbell. Peter Macdougall has carried much of the energy and violence implicit in this writing into a number of memorable plays for television in the 1980s, while John Byrne's work for the same medium in the 1990s has added wit, pathos and considerable structural complexity to some of the most challenging and entertaining accounts of modern Scotland yet achieved in any genre.

Many more books than Kelman's can be cited as exemplars of city life and demotic prose, including William McIlvanney's *Docherty* (1975), *The Big Man* (1985) and *Strange Loyalties* (1991); Alan Spence's *Its Colours They Are Fine* (1977) and *The Magic Flute* (1990); Carl MacDougall's *Stone Over Water* (1989) and Janice Galloway's *The Trick is to Keep Breathing* (1991) and *Blood* (1992). Naturally, these writers are each different in their own ways, but they can all be said to have helped create a very influential genre of contemporary West of Scotland urban fiction. The widespread popularity of such writing is a potent reminder that the imperatives of 'place' and 'voice' are as strong as ever in Scottish culture – if now relocated away from the north or the Highland glens. Nevertheless, the marked bias of West of Scotland urban fiction towards realism should not obscure the fact that there are other and equally convincing modes through which the modern Scottish sensibility has expressed itself, not least in challenging the very conventions of 'realism' in prose, and 'lyricism' in poetry.

The most notable poetic challenge in this respect was made by MacDiarmid's world-language poetry in the later 1940s. These lengthy catalogue-like poems (such as *The Kind of Poetry I Want* and *In Memoriam James Joyce*) were generated with all the passion of Carlyle and the single-minded metaphysical intensity of John Davidson, but it is a now notorious fact that many passages in them were taken without acknowledgment from other and usually prose sources. Scientific texts, magazine articles, essays on philosophy and linguistics, ephemeral book reviews, or works of fiction themselves were all sampled and incorporated into MacDiarmid's vast and open-ended poems, dedicated to the cause of 'adventuring in dictionaries' and to the 'debris of all past literature/And raw material of all the literature to be'.

Such a poetics raises a number of complex critical issues. But the real challenge, which is to recognise that modernist and post-modernist experience completely realigns significant aspects of how we relate to the acts of writing and reading, has not yet been fully taken up by many established Scottish poets. Among the leading exceptions to this is Ian Hamilton Finlay, as well as the late W.S. Graham, whose work shows a mixture of scrupulous irony and terror in confronting the slipperiness of language and the blank snowfields of white paper which face every writer each morning. Edwin Morgan, too, has been quick to welcome a modern world of constant change and instability as an invitation to new kinds of freedom and new methods of expression; and Iain Crichton Smith has also produced a number of brilliant poems and short stories with a markedly dislocating and surreal tendency.

The same innovative spirit can be found in the prose of Alasdair Gray, a writer of international stature whose post-modern fictional devices simultaneously define and validate the mode, and yet whose energetic and idiosyncratic learning can be traced back to Sir Thomas Urquhart – who featured, indeed, in one of his short stories. Gray's genial games with the structural and typographical conventions of prose fiction do much to destabilise the 'suspension of disbelief' upon which conventional prose realism depends. But his is a powerfully political vision, too, for just as he undermines conventional narrative, so he lays bare the hidden power structures of commercial, industrial and scientific authority in an age where everything is 'information' and hence everything is infinitely malleable under the hands of those who have power to shape it. In this world bankers, novelists and God are all equally answerable to their creatures, for in the last analysis what they each deal in, or steal from us, is no less than our time on earth.[34]

The political and moral force of Gray's work cannot be overestimated, particularly in his two masterpieces, *Lanark* (1981) and *1982 Janine* (1984) which demonstrate the Scottish penchant for vivid demotic and urban realism, only to transcend it by invoking crucial instabilities through what would once have been classed as 'fantasy', 'science fiction', or 'avant-garde' techniques. In this respect Cairns Craig has noted very tellingly that 'the union of avant-garde experimentalism, folk culture and political commitment has meant that there has never been the division between serious writing and working-class writing in Scotland that has existed in English writing', and indeed Gray's work makes a particularly searching critique of the abuses of authority and feeling in society at large, not least by using his many voices to deconstruct the authorial role itself.[35]

The ramifications of voice and place can be traced still further in the work of many other contemporary Scottish writers. John Herdman and Ron Butlin, for example, both make use of first-person narrative from paranoid or unreliable sources, while the terrors of self and delusion figure very markedly in many of Iain Banks's novels, in the work of Janice Galloway, and in the estranged events and withheld information of Frederic Lindsay. Challenges of growth, identity and maturity are confronted in the subtle symbolic structures of recent novels by Andrew Greig and Alan Spence, while fiction from Brian McCabe and Dilys Rose is notable for its delicate evocation of the mystery of identity, especially with regard to adolescent and sexual tensions.

In one way or another all of these writers can be said to deal with the unstable self in its confrontations with the nature of personal, social or cultural being, and it seems likely that in this respect they all look back to the historical conditions of a Scottish identity which has been so much derived, at least since the eighteenth century, from the vernacular iconoclasm of its destabilised and destabilising voices. In this respect the energy, the fluidity and the iconoclastic spirit of 'Christis Kirk', 'Tam o' Shanter' and *A Drunk Man Looks at the Thistle*, are still vividly present in modern Scottish literature, intimately bound up with the many strands of 'voice' and 'place' which have been the subject of this essay.

Notes

1. See Benedict Anderson, *Imagined Communities* (London, 1983) and Ernest Gellner, *Nations and Nationalism* (Cambridge, 1983).
2. See Michael Lynch, *Scotland: a New History* (London, 1991), p.323.
3. Consider the narrator's framing of Cresseid's story in Henryson's great poem, or the tradition of flyting in Dunbar in which verbal attack and counter-attack are offered as what is, in effect, a dramatic dialogue for two voices. Consider the personal, colloquial, and wholly prejudiced expression of Blind Harry and John

Knox; the waywardly discursive and extravagant energy of Urquhart; the enormously influential 'medieval brawl' genre of 'Christis Kirk of the Green' and 'Peblis to the Play', not to mention the very strong, long-sustained and directly oral tradition of ballads and songs.

4. See Thomas Crawford, *Burns: a Study of the Poems and Songs* (Edinburgh, 1965), pp.69–71 for a discussion of these verse forms and further references; also Kenneth Simpson, *The Protean Scot* (Aberdeen, 1988), pp.199–202.

5. See Mikhail Bakhtin, *Rabelais and His World* (London, 1965) and 'From the Prehistory of Novelistic Discourse' in *The Dialogic Imagination* (Austin and London, 1981).

6. Mikhail Bakhtin, *Problems of Dostoevsky's Poetics*, ed. and tr. Caryl Emerson (Manchester, 1984), p.115.

7. *The Dialogic Imagination*, p.55, Bakhtin's emphasis.

8. Ibid., see pp.61–83.

9. Used in a slightly different context the phrase comes from David Craig's pioneering study *Scottish Literature and the Scottish People 1680–1830* (London, 1961).

10. *The Lounger*, 9 December 1786.

11. David Daiches, *The Paradox of Scottish Culture* (Oxford, 1964).

12. See George Elder Davie, *The Democratic Intellect* (Edinburgh, 1964); Anand Chitnis, *The Scottish Enlightenment* (London, 1976); David Allan, *Virtue, Learning and the Scottish Enlightenment* (Edinburgh, 1993).

13. See *Virtue, Learning and the Scottish Enlightenment*, especially Chapter 4.

14. See Crawford, p.104, and Simpson, pp.186–7.

15. See James Mackay, *Burns* (Edinburgh, 1993), p.271.

16. J. Derrick McClure, 'Language Varieties in *The Three Perils of Man*', in G. Hughes (ed.), *Papers Given at the Second James Hogg Society Conference* (Aberdeen, 1988), p.56.

17. See *The Dialogic Imagination*, pp.324–6.

18. Claimed for Scots in an essay on John Wilson, cited by Emma Letley in an excellent study of how the Scots language was used and perceived in nineteenth-century fiction, *From Galt to Douglas Brown* (Edinburgh, 1988).

19. This is not to say that writing and publishing in 'dialect' voices is not genuinely problematic, in both expressive and commercial terms, as Galt knew from his own practice and experience.

20. See Thomas Carlyle, 'On History'; also Roderick Watson, 'Carlyle: The World as Text and the Text as Voice', in D. Gifford (ed.), *The History of Scottish Literature*, Vol. 3 (Aberdeen, 1988).

21. See William Donaldson, *Popular Literature in Victorian Scotland: Language, Fiction and the Press* (Aberdeen, 1986) and *The Language of the People* (Aberdeen, 1989).

22. Colin Nicholson, *Poem, Purpose and Place: Shaping Identity in Modern Scottish Verse* (Edinburgh, 1992).

23. Neil M. Gunn, 'The Gael Will Come Again', in A. McCleery (ed.), *Landscape and Light* (Aberdeen, 1987), p.169.

24. 'Nationalism and Internationalism', ibid., p.179. Both these essays were written in 1931.

25. The same spirit had informed D.H. Lawrence's account of English society in *The Rainbow* (1915) and *Women in Love* (1920).

26. This must have struck a chord with the reading public for there were dozens of such volumes, and Ramsay's alone sold 87,000 copies in fourteen years.

27. C.M. Grieve, 'A Theory of Scots Letters', *The Scottish Chapbook*, 1, no. 7 (February 1923).

28. 'A Theory of Scots Letters', ibid., no. 8 (March 1923).

29. *Scott and Scotland* (Edinburgh, 1982), p.9. Muir's solution was to try to *feel* in English, although it's not clear why this should be any easier than trying to *think* in Scots.

30. Ibid., p.42.

31. See, for example, the Edinburgh sonnets, 'The Percipient Swan', 'Sisyphus', and the metaphysical aspect of his longer poems, 'The Wire' and 'The Muir', all published in the 1960s.

32. See *The Busconductor Hines* (1984), *A Disaffection* (1990) and, most notably, *A Chancer* (1985).

33. Another way of putting this would be to say that the cultural canon with its essentially middle-class values has fed (vampire-like) from this colloquial energy without relinquishing its hegemony.

34. See Chapter 38 of *Lanark* for a brilliant deconstruction of the consumer society by way of a reversal of the phrase 'time is money'.

35. Cairns Craig, 'Going Down to Hell is Easy' in Robert Crawford and Thom Nairn (eds.), *The Arts of Alasdair Gray* (Edinburgh, 1991), p.91. The instabilities of form and place in Gray's work are further discussed in equally illuminating essays by Randall Stevenson and Christopher Harvie.

Books for Further Reading

Cairns Craig (ed.), *The History of Scottish Literature*, vols. 2, 3 and 4 (Aberdeen, 1987–88)

David Craig, *Scottish Literature and the Scottish People 1680–1830* (London, 1961)

Thomas Crawford, *Society and the Lyric* (Edinburgh, 1979)

David Daiches, *The Paradox of Scottish Culture* (Oxford, 1964)

George Elder Davie, *The Democratic Intellect* (Edinburgh, 1964)

Francis Russell Hart, *The Scottish Novel* (London, 1978)

Emma Letley, *From Galt to Douglas Brown* (Edinburgh, 1988)

John MacQueen, *The Rise of the Historical Novel* (Edinburgh, 1989)

David McCrone, *Understanding Scotland: the Sociology of a Stateless Nation* (London, 1992)

Kenneth Simpson, *The Protean Scot* (Aberdeen, 1988)

Roderick Watson, *The Literature of Scotland* (London, 1984)

Gaelic Literature

DERICK THOMSON

If it were magically possible to recover the literature, written and oral, associated with Gaelic in Scotland, there is no doubt that we would find it existing from the earliest years of Gaelic settlement in the country, that is to say from the third to the fifth centuries AD. The literature would be oral at that stage, and the earliest written examples would perhaps date from the sixth and seventh centuries, when Columba may well have penned both Gaelic and Latin verses. Columba's biographer, Adamnan, is said to be the author of a Gaelic verse[1] on the death of Brude son of Bile (685 AD), and if this is a genuine record it is the oldest surviving Gaelic verse composed on Scottish soil. Welsh has had a more fortunate history of survival, with its heroic poem on the Gododdin having probably been originally composed in some form, in what we now call Scotland, in the later sixth century, though surviving in a much later recension.[2] It is thought also that an Iona chronicle dating from before 740 AD was the source of Scottish entries in the Irish Annals, and that the text *Senchus Fer nAlban* ('History of the Men of Scotland'), was originally compiled in Dalriada (basically Argyll) in the seventh century.[3] From c.1093 we have the *Duan Albanach* ('Scottish Lay'), a versified account of Scottish history and pseudo-history addressed by an Irish author to the 'learned ones of Alba', presumably his bardic or literary colleagues in Scotland. Another early survival is the Gaelic notes written on blank spaces and margins in the Book of Deer, recounting the origin legend of the monastery and the land grants of later benefactors. As in the case of twelfth-century English charters, these notices of grant can refer to impermanent features of the landscape, such as piles of stones.[4] These *notitiae* were written between c.1130 and c.1150, and may be regarded as the oldest manuscript survivals of contemporary Gaelic writings in Scotland.

It is only in a strained sense that most of these instances can be regarded as 'literature'. What they do suggest, very strongly, is that what we have are some chance survivals from times and places that must have produced a 'normal' literature for their times. When we take into account the much more prolific Gaelic survivals from Ireland, and later Scottish evidence, the suggestion is convincingly underpinned.

17. Chess pieces of walrus ivory, late twelfth century, found in 1831 at Uig, Isle of Lewis, in the Outer Hebrides. (National Museums of Scotland)

In the early centuries and to an important extent down to early modern times, literary products and their survival were fairly rigidly linked to the social system and its requirements. The art of writing, in Celtic as in many other European contexts, was originally practised under the aegis of the Christian Church which used Latin in the main, though monks and missionaries soon showed signs of literary humanism as well as acquaintance with the humanities. They could write about cats and wild nature in the midst of their grammatical and theological duties. But gradually writing came to have important applications in secular society, as the leaders of society came to use it for propaganda and record. And in between the theological and secular extremes the writing classes developed a wide range of literary interests, so that the early clergy recorded saga and legend, and embellished these, and the later literate classes recorded traditional law, history both real and invented, and genealogy, and wrote on geography, medicine, herbal lore and many other topics. From the mid-twelfth century, if not earlier, hereditary lines of literate experts can be distinguished, many of them attached to the 'courts' of chiefs or kings, and using what became a standard literary language fairly tightly governed by rules (many of which survive in rule-books). Some of these literate experts were employed mainly to promote and extol their patrons: they were PR men but with highly developed linguistic and metrical skills, using poetry more than prose. Others concentrated on medicine or genealogy or law or music.

Although the great bulk of the evidence for the above activity has survived in Irish rather than Scottish sources, the Scottish evidence is diverse enough, and sufficiently distributed in space and time, to show that Scotland had the same basic system. Thus we have surviving traces of a Gaelic legal system with its judges known as *britheamhan* or breves, a large number of Gaelic medical manuscripts written by members of the Beaton hereditary dynasty and others, hereditary families of harpers and sculptors and, perhaps most notably, poets.[5] Hereditary lines of clergymen also appear, and contribute to Gaelic literature also. Some of these professionals served Scottish kings (this is the case with the Beatons), but most were attached to the courts of powerful clan chiefs such as the chiefs of the MacDonalds, Campbells and MacLeods.

Only fragments of this literary activity survive: in the main, the medical manuscripts referred to already, occasional manuscripts containing genealogies and history (especially the history of the MacDonalds of the Isles), versions of sagas and heroic ballads, and bardic verse. As the social system which underpinned this literary and literate activity declined or decayed, there was both loss of literary records and a transfer of some of these to the oral tradition. As a result of this process we find, for example, fragments of ancient sagas such as the *Táin Bó Cuailnge* ('The Cattle-raid of Cooley' so-called) surfacing in oral tradition in the second half of the twentieth century, and a few of the heroic ballads still sung, while much historical fact and legend also found its haven in the oral memory. This has encouraged some facile commentators to pontificate to the effect that the Gaelic tradition was basically an oral one. The truth is that it had strong oral and literate components, with the balance swinging from one to the other according to the dictates of society (and these dictates were sometimes Gaelic, sometimes not).

THE PROFESSIONAL POETS

One of the best-attested literary traditions is that of the professional poets, though here, too, the survival of manuscripts is clearly patchy. The most remarkable hereditary family of poets was that of the MacMhuirichs, apparently descended from the Irish exile-poet of the early thirteenth century, Muireadhach Albanach Ó Dalaigh (Scottish Muireadhach, of the famous Irish bardic family of O'Dalys). He is said to have come to Scotland c.1215, and two of his poems addressed to Earls of Lennox survive. The Scottish bardic family of the MacMhuirichs traced their descent from him over eighteen generations (though not all the links were identifiable by 1800AD). Over the intervening five to six centuries we find members of the family appearing in the records, for example, inciting MacDonald warriors before the Battle of Harlaw in 1411, mourning the decline in MacDonald power in the 1490s, celebrating a MacLeod/MacDonald wedding in 1613, a MacDonald leader returning from an Irish war in the late 1640s, the Battle of Sherrifmuir and the death of a Clanranald chief in 1715.[6] The work of these MacMhuirich poets is seen against a wider background in a manuscript from the first half of the sixteenth century, the fortunately surviving *Book of the Dean of Lismore*. This was compiled by a Perthshire cleric and notary public, Dean James MacGregor. He evidently had access especially to MacNab, Campbell and MacDonald sources (and probably through the latter, or more specifically through MacMhuirich sources, to the work of the Irish O'Daly poets). In his anthology we find a good range of Scottish poems dating from *c.*1310 to *c.*1500, praising chiefs and clans, recording battles, lamenting the dead and sometimes commenting on the trivia of daily life. These poems have a predominantly Perthshire and Argyllshire provenance (the areas the Dean moved in) but occasionally touch other areas. And his collection also includes a large range of heroic, mainly 'Ossianic' ballads. It is the earliest extensive collection of such ballads, a genre that had been growing since the eleventh or twelfth century, and was to retain its popularity for long after the Dean's time.

The MacMhuirichs served various branches of the MacDonald clan. Similarly, the MacEwen bardic family served first the MacDougall chiefs and then the Campbells, and the Ó Muirgheasáin bards served the Macleans in Mull and then the MacLeods in Harris and Skye. The MacGregors in Perthshire had their own bards, as had the Macintoshes in Inverness-shire, and doubtless any powerful Gaelic chiefs had similar arrangements.

A good deal of this 'bardic' poetry is formulaic in that it uses praise stereos to describe the hero's or the patron's warlike qualities, or generosity, or hunting expertise, or cultural range, or piety. Often historical or legendary analogues are used to reinforce the praise, suggesting that the patron is a latter-day Cù Chulainn or whatever. We are told that the forces of Nature are in sympathy with the hero's fortunes, the sea-currents boiling in anger at his death, or the sun and the flowers welcoming his good fortune. The metrical structures are usually strictly controlled, using lines of preordained syllabic length, with alliteration, complicated rhyme and rhythmical ornamentation. A wide range of set phrases can be called on to buttress these metrical structures, sometimes at the expense of poetic sensitivity. Yet there are plenty examples of poetic felicity in this strongly controlled landscape: the poets of quality rise easily above the hacks. The MacMhuirichs feature prominently among the quality poets, from Muireadhach in the thirteenth century to Niall Mór and Cathal in the seventeenth.

Though much of this poetry that survives is praise-poetry of one sort or another, there are examples of satire, and love-poetry, and religious verse, sometimes by professional poets and sometimes by amateurs who had learnt the literary language and the verse techniques. Sir Duncan Campbell of Glenorchy, who died at Flodden in 1513, was one such, writing witty satire and bawdry; the wife of a fourteenth-century Earl of Argyll has some short love-poems ascribed to her; and a lady called Aithbhreac Inghean Coirceadail (who would now be named Effie MacCorquodale) has a delicate lament for her husband, a MacNeill of Gigha who died about 1470.[7]

THE SEVENTEENTH CENTURY

Poetry in the literary language (referred to as Classical Common Gaelic) ceased to be produced in the 1740s, but by then it was a survival from a social system which had largely collapsed. The winding-down of that system, and the approaching demise of the poetry, is already being mourned by Cathal MacMhuirich in the mid-seventeenth century, and for probably a hundred years before then some poets were using a watered-down version of the literary language, and basically the same metres. These poets belong to the 'lesser gentry' classes, examples being the clergyman John Stewart of Appin, MacLeod of Raasay, MacCulloch of Park (in Ross-shire) and the Mackenzie lairds of Achilty (Ross-shire also). Some poets who used this style are referred to as *Aos-dàna*, a term once used as a collective for 'men of art' but coming to be used as a title for a particular kind of poet. As the seventeenth century proceeds, the title *aos-dàna* is used in reference to poets who no longer use the old literary language or the syllabic metres, though they have inherited certain praise stereos, metaphors and clichés. One such was the poet known as Eachann Bacach an t-Aos-dàna ('Lame Hector the Aos-dàna'), who made a lament for Sir Lachlan Maclean (of Duart in Mull) who died in 1648, and three poems on his successor and the Maclean clan who suffered horrendous losses at the Battle of Inverkeithing in 1651. Some extracts from the 1648 poem illustrate his style, which owes a good deal to the bardic poets but has a quite different movement:

> It was no sapling or plantling,
> last year's nut that you grew from,
> no flower planted in Maytime,
> but growth of leaves and of branches –
> this top twig that has left us:
> send, Christ, more in the place of the dead.

He gives a series of word-pictures of Sir Lachlan's household and its activities:

> When the dusk began closing
> the harp would be plundered,
> no music was hoarded, the fingers disclosed it,
> the hands did not weary
> till the time came for sleeping in peace.

> The gamblers, quick-moving,
> shot the dice at backgammon,
> the chessmen were rattling,
> at cards, calling and trumping,
> Spanish dollars and testoons
> were being paid without anger at all.

And finally he addresses the new Maclean chief:

> If you take, son, this rudder, your traditional chiefship
> will incline you to prayer;
> let the Trinity crew her:
> put the Father at first there,
> let the Son be the helmsman,
> Holy Ghost take her in to the roads.

The poet here is using a strophic, rather than a syllabic metre, with stanzas of variable length (five to eight lines), with each line of the stanza rhyming, and with a two-syllable addendum to the final line of each stanza, carrying a rhyme that links the eighteen stanzas of the poem. A simpler three-line strophic stanza was widely used in the seventeenth century, but probably has much more ancient roots. This was the favourite measure of such poets as Màiri Nighean Alasdair Ruaidh (Mary MacLeod of Harris and Skye) and Iain Lom (John MacDonald of Keppoch). These poets, like a number of their contemporaries, are closely associated with particular clans and chiefs – Mary MacLeod with the MacLeods of Harris and Dunvegan, and Iain Lom with the MacDonalds, both of Keppoch and more generally. Mary MacLeod's is a more personal and intimate music; Iain Lom's a strongly political, partisan poetry which nevertheless has great intellectual vigour. He gives a vivid commentary on MacDonald/Campbell rivalries, on the wars of the century, and on the Union of the Parliaments in 1707. His authorship of the last-named poem has been questioned, but if he was not the author, we find in the poem a similar exceptional genius, especially in the use of colourful, somewhat bawdy description.

We can see, in the seventeenth century, the appearance of a range of poets who seem to take on the function of official clan poet or praise-poet to a chief, without having the training of the professional bards. The old habits die hard, however, for a good many aspects of the old poetry survive, many of the praise-stereos, and such ancient metaphors as that which calls the chief a tree, with spreading branches, a powerful trunk and so on. MacLeod of Dunvegan had such a bard, who was also a professional harper, Roderick Morrison or An Clàrsair Dall, 'The Blind Harper'. Iain Mac Ailein or John Maclean, who seems to have functioned as a family poet to the Macleans of Duart, lived on well into the eighteenth century, keeping old legends alive in his praise-poetry and his humorous verse and prose. There is a group of women poets also, in Mull and Tiree and Keppoch: the best known of these is Sìleas na Ceapaich (Cicely MacDonnell of Keppoch) whose work has an interesting range of praise, satire, bawdry and religion.[8]

In literary terms, as in social and political terms also, the seventeenth century in Gaelic Scotland was a time of continual change and adjustment. A new ecclesiastical and religious landscape was emerging, with its Presbyterian and Episcopalian and revived Catholic vistas, with occasional surfacing of an indigenous paganism and the beginnings of an evangelicalism that was to become severely limiting in some senses. The Lowland ethos, distorted in its turn by religious extremism, was gradually imposing itself on the Gaelic areas, with pressure being brought to bear on chiefs to adjust to a non-Gaelic hegemony (as via the Statutes of Iona in 1609), and on the people more generally via the expanding schooling system, while the move of King and Court to London was eventually to lead to the Jacobite/Hanoverian confrontation that itself turned into a Gaelic/English one.

The literary changes and conflicts were not violent but they were widespread and significant. The beginnings of Gaelic evangelical verse, which was to become a strong and long-lasting tradition, can mostly be traced to the seventeenth century, with some influence flowing from the Continent via Highland mercenary soldiers. But native religious verse had been cultivated by the bardic poets, and other native traditions continue to show in the work of poets in the Fernaig Manuscript (late seventeenth century) such as Alexander Munro of Strathnaver and Duncan Macrae of Inverinate.[9] A tradition of somewhat urbane and conventional love poetry, some of it attributable to younger 'gentry' who had taken up military careers or become clergymen, begins to surface in the seventeenth century also, and continues in the eighteenth. We can see in it the influences of the new education, though its stronger roots are Gaelic. Even poets who are still anchored in the old poet-patron system make pungent criticisms of their patrons who are straying from the convention. The tradition of very localised humorous 'village' poetry begins to surface – eventually for many Gaels it was to become the only tradition that was appreciated. And finally, as some sort of bedrock for this varied landscape, there was the so-called 'folk poetry'. We can look at this in a little more detail.

EARLY SONG POETRY

Because of the dominant influence of the Gaelic literate community – including the professionals, the clergy, and the 'amateur' contingent from chiefs' families and 'lesser gentry' – there was little notice taken in manuscripts of work that did not emanate from that fraternity (or occasionally sorority). It was not until the influence of the professional writers was on the wane that the compositions of non-professionals began to be collected and written down. The Fernaig Manuscript, dating from c.1690, is one of the early instances of such collection, but they do not become common until the mid-eighteenth century, probably influenced by the publicity resulting from James Macpherson's 'Ossianic' publications. By then the sixteenth century was becoming ancient territory, and it is natural to find a great preponderance of eighteenth and seventeenth-century compositions in the collections. For all that, we can identify between forty and fifty items, some short, some longer, dating from before 1600, and can deduce, from the wide variety of topics, styles and metres, that the verse that surfaces from before 1600 represents merely the detritus of an old and varied tradition of 'non-professional' verse. This includes items such as a fragment of verse from the time of the first Battle of Inverlochy (1431), a poem by Hector Maclean, chief of the Macleans of Coll, probably dating from 1537 (this poet also wrote Latin verses), the famous lament of 1570 for a MacGregor chief ('Griogal Cridhe'), a rousing song in praise of a MacDonald hero of much the same time ('An Iorram Dharaich'), a song addressed to Seathan son of the King of Ireland, songs by nursemaids and so on. A wide range of metres is used in these, some showing affinity to the classical bardic metres, others with a strong rhythmical base, some having lines split by choruses, some maintaining end-rhyme throughout, others using paragraph-rhyme. Fortunately, there has been a significant survival of song-melodies and styles (now somewhat endangered by 'popular' bowdlerisation), so that the metrical forms are even more clearly distinguished.

This verse tradition, or these traditions, continue productively in the seventeenth century, building up the large corpus of song for which Scottish Gaelic is justly famous. Its ancient origins can sometimes be glimpsed in its themes and motifs as well as in its metrics. The 'heroic' society survives in it, with exaltation of the warrior-hunter, either as chief or as husband/lover; there are occasional pagan references as well as legendary ones, as in the 'lullaby' for Dòmhnall Gorm, a Sleat MacDonald chief of c.1600, whose galley is said to have

> a rudder of gold, three masts of willow,
> a well of wine down at her quarter,

and the maker of the song wishes Dòmhnall Gorm

> the might of the salmon headlong leaping,
> the might of Cù Chulainn in full war-gear ...

Songs dated to 1570, 1601 and the 1770s refer to the ancient motif of drinking the blood of a loved one, either in death or severely wounded. The wife or sweetheart of the dead Seathan lists the ransoms she would offer for his return: silver, gold, wine, beer, goats, sheep, cattle, pigs, salmon, trout, geldings. But many of the songs are pitched in a more homely and ordinary key, as where a girl complains to her lover: 'I did not get a snood or wedding linen from you though I was entitled to both of these'. In the nature of things, many of the songs record the loss, by death or otherwise, of sweethearts, and it seems that a significant majority of the songs were composed by women although more often than not they are anonymous.

A striking group of songs is connected with the MacGregors of Perthshire who existed precariously, persecuted by the Campbells and also by Government from the mid-sixteenth to the mid-seventeenth century. The lament for Gregor who was beheaded in 1570 is the earliest datable one of these songs, and others dating from the early seventeenth century give a sharp and detailed picture of their life on the run. One of these song-makers sits on his own hoping to see a fugitive who will give him news of his fellow-clansmen. He has heard that they are scattered between Loch Fyne and Dalmally. He complains that:

> this arrow from the field of battle
> has lodged in my hide.
>
> An arrow penetrated my thigh,
> a crooked shaft, badly fashioned,

as though he were ascribing crooked arrows as well as bent mouths to the Campbells (whose Gaelic surname, *Caimbeul*, suggests this unflattering origin). In another of these songs, 'MacGriogair à Ruadhshruth' (MacGregor of Roro, in Glen Lyon) the composer warns his clansmen to be exceedingly wary, to take their dram standing, and to take only one:

> Treat winter as though it were autumn
> and treat February like summer.
>
> Make your bed in the rocky nooks
> and sleep lightly.
>
> Scarce though the squirrels are
> a way can be found of catching them.
>
> Though the hawk is noble
> it is often captured by guile.

Other songs span a good range of themes, for example genuine lullabies, flyting songs between representatives of clans or islands, songs about battles (and later about the experiences of mercenaries in Europe), humorous or satirical songs about characters, nonsense songs, songs about fishing or smuggling, songs about fairies. But there can be little doubt that the love-songs have the edge, in their lyricism and the sharpness and depth of their perceptions. The period 1550–1700 can almost be regarded as the classic one for songs of this kind, though the genre certainly survived well beyond 1700.

EARLY PROSE WORKS

This account of Scottish Gaelic literature has been almost exclusively concerned with poetry up to now, and although that emphasis has its justification it is time to make some adjustment. The 'professional literates' did not neglect prose though they did not set a personal stamp on it as they tended to do with poetry. Such accounts as we have of the 'curriculum' of the bardic schools suggest that a wide acquaintance with prose saga was required, and the richness of manuscript sources, especially in Ireland, underlines the truth of this. The Scottish sources in this respect are scantier and more selective, but they include a good sample of prose writings: many medical manuscripts, frequent items of a religious or ecclesiastical kind (such as lives of saints, the law of Sunday, translations of Biblical passages), various historical and genealogical writings, fragments of astronomy, geography, lists of maxims and proverbs, and versions of sagas. There are some instances of identifiable Scottish scribes writing such manuscripts containing sagas, for example Ewen Maclean's manuscript of heroic tales, romances and poems written for Colin Campbell in 1690–91, or an eighteenth-century copy of the saga *Cath Fionntràgha* (The Battle of Ventry) in the hand of Alasdair Mac Mhaighstir Alasdair. Another late instance of a Scottish Gaelic manuscript containing much prose is the Black Book of Clanranald, which includes a fairly lengthy history (with legend) of the MacDonalds, the latter part apparently written in the late seventeenth century by the poet Niall MacMhuirich.

It is out of that tradition that the first printed book in Gaelic (either in Scotland or in Ireland) emerges: this is sometimes given the shorthand title of 'Carswell's Liturgy', and it was published in 1567; only three copies of it survive. The book is basically a translation of the Book of Common Order, itself a revision of the Geneva Book or 'John Knox's Liturgy' (1562). Carswell made various additions to this text, both in prose and verse, including a warning to readers against indulgence in secular Gaelic story-telling. John Carswell was parson of Kilmartin, held the Castle of Carnassery at least from 1559, and after the Reformation of 1560 became Superintendent of the district of Argyll and the Isles. His book is written in the Gaelic literary language, with various Scottish vernacular modifications. Clearly he must have studied this form of language, perhaps at the feet of a professional bard or scribe; he refers to himself as not fully skilled, but he uses the tricks of the trade skilfully, ornamenting his text with synonyms and alliterative pairings and runs.[10]

Literacy in Gaelic at this period was clearly associated with that professional literary register, and with its practitioners the bards, historians, and so on. But the overlap between that professional class and the clergy would have made it more natural for the clergy to adopt the literary standard for writing. Carswell's own choice may have influenced later ecclesiastical publications, and for the greater part of two centuries after 1567 such occasional Gaelic printed books as appeared tended to be church-related and to use varieties of the old literary language. The Gaelic translation of Calvin's larger Catechism was printed *c.*1630, and the translator is thought to be the professional poet Neil MacEwen. The Gaelic Shorter Catechism of 1653 has more vernacular usages. But the first secular Gaelic books to be printed were Alasdair Mac Mhaighstir Alasdair's *Vocabulary* in 1741 and his collection of poems in 1751. A Gaelic translation of Richard Baxter's *Call to the Unconverted* appeared in 1750, and a long series of religious prose works, mostly translations, followed for the next century. This use of Gaelic for prose was greatly stimulated by the translation of the Bible, mainly by a father and son, James Stewart minister of Killin, who published the Gaelic New Testament in 1767, and his son John, who was largely responsible for the translation of the Old Testament, completed in 1801. The Stewarts were influenced by the existing Irish translations, but set their own Argyll and Perthshire stamp on the language, while to an important extent establishing the conventions of orthography and grammar that were to last into modern times.

It is extraordinary how dominant religious themes are in Gaelic prose writings of these times. It was not until post-1830 that a significant flow of secular Gaelic prose began. The saga tradition remained oral until even later, despite its earlier literate tradition. And although clergymen were prominently involved, from the eighteenth century on, in collecting, and sometimes printing, Gaelic verse, they took little interest in secular prose. Yet in retrospect we can see that prose-writing in the second half of the eighteenth century, and especially the translation of the Bible, provided a foundation for later developments. The contrast between Gaelic and Scots here is instructive, for Scots still has great difficulty in re-establishing itself as a natural prose medium.

THE EIGHTEENTH CENTURY

Gaelic poetry reaches new peaks in the eighteenth century, both building on existing tradition and taking new directions. The classical bardic tradition was in its final phase in the early decades of the century, and its successor in the sphere of praise-poetry was still fertile but becoming less dominant. Most of the poets go through the motions of praise-poetry but show more positive and interesting developments in other directions. Duncan Bàn Macintyre praises Campbell chiefs and prominent men very competently, but comes into his own with praise of deer and wild Nature. Rob Donn praises his patron-friend Iain Mac Eachainn, but fun and satire and social commentary are his true strengths. William Ross can ply the conventional phrases in praise of Sir Hector Mackenzie of Gairloch:

> 'S craobh mhullaich dhosrach àghmhor thu
> Dhe 'n abhall 's àirde spèis;
> Gur droighean ri do dhùsgadh thu,
> Gur seobhac sùil-ghorm treun;
> Gur leòghann nach gabh mùiseag thu ...

Sir Hector is described here as a tall branching apple-tree, a thorn-tree when aroused, a blue-eyed hawk and a fearless lion. But Ross's reputation rests on his love-songs and satires. John MacCodrum of North Uist has a number of praise-poems for MacDonalds, but humour and satire, and topics from his local community, are more central to his work. Dugald Buchanan's surviving work shows us only his evangelical output, which was strongly influenced by current English poetry, but he laces that influence with the powerful lexical legacy of earlier Gaelic verse. Alasdair Mac Mhaighstir Alasdair has only one, rather perfunctory praise-poem for a chief (the perhaps cynical praise of Lord Lovat), allowing his Muse to follow various unconventional interests.

He and Donnchadh Bàn Macintyre are usually regarded as the leading Gaelic poets of the time. The case for Donnchadh Bàn is the less easy to sustain; perhaps a more convincing one could be made for Rob Donn, since there is no comparable body of close critical and amusing commentary on the society both high and low of his time. Donnchadh Bàn, however, occupies one peak of his own, with the long and detailed, eloquent and varied poem 'Moladh Beinn Dòbhrain' (In Praise of Ben Doran), which explores the life of that mountain and its vicinity, achieving an extraordinary empathy with all the ages and varieties of deer that frequent it. Iain Crichton Smith produced a fine translation of this poem, *Duncan Bàn Macintyre's Ben Dorain*.[11]

Alasdair Mac Mhaighstir Alasdair must be regarded as the leading genius of the Gaelic poetry revival of the eighteenth century. His work dates mainly from c.1720 to c.1760, but with a large and probably distorting emphasis on the short period c.1744– c.1749, when he was intimately involved in the '45 Rising and its aftermath. His poetry ranges from quite formal pieces such as his address to the Muses (probably from the 1720s) to ferocious satires which have a strong admixture of bawdry. In between there are detailed and evocative descriptions of Nature and landscape, erotic poetry, political and campaigning verse, and his mini-epic 'The Birlinn/Galley of Clanranald'. He set the fashion for poems on the seasons, taking a hint from Thomson's *Seasons* but making his own exclusive model, copied by most succeeding eighteenth-century Gaelic poets. His 'Moladh Mòraig' (Praise of Morag), using an inventive metre influenced by classical pipe-music (ceòl-mòr), is an entertaining medley of description, eroticism and fantasy. His political verse has some historical and philosophical depth, allied to fervent commitment, his satire is marked by prurience and linguistic exuberance, and his 'Birlinn' poem combines careful structure and a free imagination. Throughout there is evidence of an extremely rich and inventive linguistic drive. Unable to do justice to this work in the space available, we may leave it with a short quotation from the end of the Morag poem:

> My head is full of swarming bees
> since parting from your fondling;
> my nose is stuffed with hellebore,
> aflame with lust's indulgence;
> my eyes are so deficient
> I can't see without a telescope,
> and though a thing were mountainous
> it seemed to me a fleshmite.
> All my body's attributes
> were injured in my dreaming,
> I thought good luck had come to me
> there on my pillow snoring;
> on waking from that ecstasy
> I found there but the shade of it
> instead of all the glittzy wealth
> experienced seven times over.[12]

One literary event drew enormous attention to the Highlands in the eighteenth century. This was James Macpherson's series of publications from 1760 to 1763, purporting to be translations from the ancient poetry of Ossian. His *Fragments* of 1760 were followed in 1761–62 by his epic *Fingal*, and by a second epic, *Temora*, in 1763. After the first of these he was encouraged to tour the Highlands in search of more ancient poetry. He undoubtedly came back with Gaelic heroic ballads and Gaelic manuscripts, used some of this material and liberally invented the greater part of his epics.[13] The ensuing controversy brought Gaelic Scotland to the attention of Europe, catching the interest of Goethe, Napoleon and many writers and artists, of Walter Scott in due course, but also of contemporary Gaels who were stimulated to make their own collections of Gaelic verse. Among these were clergymen such as James McLagan, Donald MacNicol and Ewen MacDiarmid. Some of these collections still await full editing, but a succession of books began to appear, an early one being from John Gillies of Perth in 1780. This process, both of collection and publication, has continued ever since, with such nineteenth-century highlights as J.F. Campbell's *Leabhar na Fèinne* (1872), a massive collection of heroic ballads, and Alexander Carmichael's *Carmina Gadelica* (1900 and later).

The eighteenth century saw the build-up of a network of Highland schools by the Scottish Society for the Propagation of Christian Knowledge. This society was originally strongly opposed to Gaelic, but had to modify this stance somewhat. From the early nineteenth century a new network, promoted by the Gaelic Schools Societies, had a more positive Gaelic impetus, and this led to more widespread Gaelic literacy and a minor surge in Gaelic book publication. The nineteenth century also saw the founding of a series of Gaelic and bilingual periodicals, the earlier ones by the Revd Norman MacLeod or Caraid nan Gaidheal (Friend of the Gaels). These had the effect of widening the range of Gaelic prose-writing, bringing in current affairs, history and many other topics. (A short selection from an 1830 periodical includes the management of bees, treatment for burns and scalds, the condemnation of cock-fighting, a conversation on smuggling between a fox-hunter and a schoolmaster, Indian superstition, and so on.) Fiction also began to appear in these periodicals, often heavily influenced by the style and range of folk fiction. Folk-tales were also being extensively collected, especially by J.F. Campbell, whose *Popular Tales of the West Highlands* were published in 1860–62.

THE NINETEENTH CENTURY

The creation of a popular periodical literature is one of the main Gaelic literary achievements of this period, and it has a partial parallel in popular Scots fiction. In poetry the general level of achievement did not rival the creative burst of the eighteenth century. To match the massive migration and emigration that was drawing Highlanders to the Central Belt and overseas to Canada, America and the Antipodes, there was a flow of nostalgic verse, bidding farewell to islands and localities, recalling them repeatedly, and occasionally praising or making fun of the new places of settlement. Some watering-down occurs in language, style and metrics, with the simpler measures of hymns or music-halls becoming pervasive. This style was very popular, with Neil MacLeod of Skye and Edinburgh a great favourite. There was another perspective to migration, known as 'clearance', and this inspired some much tougher verse from campaigners such as Mary Macpherson or Màiri Mhòr nan Oran, and especially two poets from opposite ends of Gaeldom, William Livingston of Islay and John Smith of Lewis. For them, nostalgia is ejected by a bitter, sometimes intellectual anger directed against landlords and their lackeys. The literary campaign was not isolated, and political action produced some significant reform in the 1880s, with the setting up of the Crofters' Commission.

There seems also to have been a growth in the production of popular local verse, and certainly more publication of such verse, sometimes in the form of district and island anthologies. This trend continued into the twentieth century. The steady growth of Highland communities in the cities, especially Glasgow, created a localised Gaelic verse there, as an outcrop of the society which organised its own media for debate, entertainment and worship. The existence of such communities opened a way to increased book publishing in Gaelic, with such firms as Archibald Sinclair and Alexander MacLaren becoming the leading Gaelic publishers. In 1891 An Comunn Gaidhealach was founded in Oban, and soon became a national organisation, promoting music and language through its Mods and publications. A Gaelic choral tradition had started in Glasgow some years earlier, and choral competitions became an important part of the Mod.

The 1872 Scottish Education Act made no provision for teaching Gaelic in schools, and soon the old Gaelic Schools were supplanted. But a Gaelic agenda was sufficiently strong to arouse clear opposition to the new régime, though it was hard to undermine it. Gradually Gaelic teaching re-entered the school system, more notably in secondary schools (from 1905 onwards). Gaelic had got into some university curricula in the 1880s and 1890s. But it was not until the 1980s that an effective and growing demand for Gaelic-medium education got some response.

TWENTIETH-CENTURY RENAISSANCE

Not surprisingly perhaps, writers have usually been far in advance of public or official opinion in seeing the need for reform. There are good instances of such foresight in the early years of the twentieth century, when Ruaraidh Erskine of Mar founded and ran a series of Gaelic and bilingual periodicals which had a strong Nationalist and later a leftist emphasis. The longest-lived and most influential of these was *Guth na Bliadhna* (The Year's Voice) which ran from 1904 to 1925. Erskine ran shorter-lived periodicals concentrating on poetry and fiction. The first attempts at writing Gaelic novels date from this period, with Angus Robertson and John MacFadyen producing the earliest ones. Donald Sinclair wrote plays at this time also, and one-act plays were popular in the 1920s–1940s. An Comunn Gaidhealach ran a monthly periodical throughout this whole period, but did not have much room for literary items. An Comunn also published a great deal of Gaelic song, and further collections of local song and poetry appeared. The Gaelic Society of Inverness had been publishing its *Transactions* ever since 1872, with a wide variety of literary, historical, linguistic, folkloristic and other items. The range of Gaelic and Gaelic-related publications had been expanding from the early years of the nineteenth century, with noticeable growth from the end of the century and into the present one. It was partly on that foundation, partly on new and contemporary ones, that the revival of Gaelic writing in the twentieth century was based. It was, if we can trust near-sight, to be quite an impressive revival.

18. Portrait of Sorley MacLean (Somhairle MacGill-Eain) (1911–   ) by Sandy Moffat, 1978. (Scottish Arts Council and the artist)

The greatest and most sustained revolution took place in poetry, and was clearly influenced by the new developments in English and European poetry. The Gaelic poets concerned were all involved in some degree with these. One of the earliest to respond was John Munro, who wrote poetry at the time of the First World War, and died in it. In one poem in particular we can see his movement from one style to another: from conventional praise of the Highland landscape to sensitive, subtly-rhythmed reflections on his fellow-soldiers who had died in France. But it was in the 1930s, 1940s and 1950s that a body of work was written that dramatically changed the face of Gaelic poetry. Five poets are especially associated with the new verse: Somhairle MacGill-Eain, Deòrsa Caimbeul Hay, Ruaraidh MacThòmais, Iain Mac a' Ghobhainn and Dòmhnall MacAmhlaigh. The first two of these began to publish in the late 1930s, the third in the early 1940s, the fourth and fifth in the 1950s. We can see clearly now that the movement had a cumulative effect, with a series of developments – in choice of subjects, authorial stances including introspective explorations, structural and rhythmical and other metrical choices – taking place progressively, and extending into the 1960s and beyond. The main work of MacGill-Eain and Hay dates from the later 1930s and the 1940s (though Hay's most considerable poem was not *published* until much later), MacAmhlaigh's from the 1950s and 1960s, while MacThòmais and Mac a' Ghobhainn have continued to produce new work up to the present.

Many individual influences surface in this body of poetry, with W.B. Yeats probably the stongest of these, but MacDiarmid, Eliot, Pound and Lowell have all had some effect, as have more general movements towards symbolism and also towards freer metrical structures. These metrical innovations date mainly from the two post-war decades. A significant proportion of this poetry belongs to the cosmopolitan world of poetry rather than to a specialised Gaelic world, in spite of its frequent preoccupation with the Gaelic world. Yet it still relies to an important extent on Gaelic harmonies of thought and sound and its subtleties can defy translation, or at least need a knowledge of the Gaelic poetic tradition for adequate appreciation. Tendencies to type-cast this poetry, as either leftist or Nationalist, serve to distort its significance, and it will probably be in the twenty-first century that some balanced and objective assessment of it is achieved.[14]

This poetic revolution was specifically fostered by the quarterly periodical *Gairm*, which began to appear in 1952, and this has led to the publication of a further succession of new poets, most of them writing in the new styles. There was some controversy, especially in the 1950s, between the old and the new schools, and a smaller body of traditional verse still continues to be written. Several of the later new-style poets have published collections, for example Fearghas MacFhionnlaigh, Aonghas MacNeacail, Maoilios Caimbeul, Màiri NicGumaraid and Meg Bateman, while still younger poets such as Anna Frater and Peadar Morgan have a growing output. Several poets who are not native speakers have joined Fearghas MacFhionnlaigh: one of these, Crìsdean Whyte, has published a collection and an anthology of the younger poets.[15]

Another signal contribution to literary development was made by *Gairm*, in the publishing of an extensive body of short stories: close on five hundred in the magazine and many more in collections. Some of these have traditional folk-tale characteristics, but contemporary styles have become the norm, three of the most interesting writers being Iain Mac a' Ghobhainn (better known by his English name Iain Crichton Smith), Iain Moireach and Dòmhnall Iain MacIomhair. The first and last of these have written Gaelic novels too, as have Iain MacLeòid, Calum MacMhaoilein and several other writers. It is more difficult to develop the novel in Gaelic, partly because of the small market and the accessibility of English fiction.

Drama is something of a neglected member of the Gaelic literary family, and is sustained mainly by amateur drama festivals. Radio and television have not been greatly supportive, though the soapy variety of drama is currently receiving a boost.

The 'near-view' suggests at the moment that the twentieth century will be remembered in Gaelic literature as the age of the 'new poetry', and that it will rank alongside the eighteenth century in that area, but that it will also be notable for an unexpected breakthrough in the art of the short story.

Notes

1. See A.O. and M.O. Anderson, *Adomnan's Life of Columba* (Edinburgh, 1961), pp.96–7.
2. See K.H. Jackson, *The Gododdin, the Earliest Scottish Poem* (Edinburgh, 1969).
3. See John Bannerman, *Studies in the History of Dalriada* (Edinburgh, 1974).
4. See for comparison M.T. Clancy, *From Memory to Written Record* (Oxford, 1993).
5. See D.S. Thomson, 'Gaelic Learned Orders and Literati in Medieval Scotland', in *Scottish Studies*, 12 (Edinburgh, 1968).
6. See D.S. Thomson, 'The MacMhuirich Bardic Family', in *Trans, Gael. Soc. Inv.* 43 (Inverness, 1966).
7. For further examples and quotations, see D.S. Thomson, *An Introduction to Gaelic Poetry* (Edinburgh, 1989).
8. See Colm Ó Baoill, *Bàrdachd Shìlis na Ceapaich* (Edinburgh, 1972).
9. See John Macinnes, 'Gaelic Spiritual Verse', in *Trans. Gael. Soc. Inv.*, 46 (Inverness, 1971); and K.D. MacDonald, 'Religious Verse', in D.S. Thomson (ed.), *The Companion to Gaelic Scotland* (Oxford, 1983).
10. For further discussion, see R.L. Thomson, *Foirm na n-Urrnuidheadh* (Edinburgh, 1970).
11. See also Angus MacLeod, *The Songs of Duncan Bàn Macintyre* (Edinburgh, 1952).
12. See A. and A. MacDonald, *The Poems of Alexander MacDonald* (Inverness, 1924); D.S. Thomson, 'Mac Mhaighstir Alasdair's Nature Poetry and its Sources', in *Gaelic and Scots in Harmony* (Glasgow, 1990); and D.S. Thomson, *Alasdair Mac Mhaighstir Alasdair: His Political Poetry* (Inverness, 1991).
13. For detailed discussion, see D.S. Thomson, *The Gaelic Sources of Macpherson's 'Ossian'* (Edinburgh, 1952); and D.S. Thomson, 'Macpherson's *Ossian*: Ballads to Epics' in B. Almqvist *et al.*, *The Heroic Process* (Dun Laoghaire, 1987).
14. For further comment on individual poets, see D.S. Thomson, *The New Verse in Scottish Gaelic: a Structural Analysis* (Dublin, 1974); and D.S. Thomson, *An Introduction to Gaelic Poetry* (Edinburgh, 1989).
15. See Christopher Whyte, *An Aghaidh na Sìorraidheachd/In the Face of Eternity* (Edinburgh, 1991).

Books for Further Reading

A.O. and M.O. Anderson, *Adomnan's Life of Columba* (Edinburgh, 1961)

John Bannerman, *Studies in the History of Dalriada* (Edinburgh, 1974)

M.T. Clancy, *From Memory to Written Record* (Oxford, 1993)

Deòrsa Caimbeul Hay, *Mochtar is Dùghall* (Glasgow, 1982)

K.H. Jackson, *The Gododdin, the Earliest Scottish Poem* (Edinburgh, 1969)

Iain Mac a' Ghobhainn, *Bìobuill is Sanasan-reice* (Glasgow, 1965)

Iain Mac a' Ghobhainn, *An t-Eilean agus an Cànan* (Glasgow, 1987)

Dòmhnall MacAmhlaigh, *Seòbhrach às a' Chlaich* (Glasgow, 1967)

Dòmhnall MacAmhlaigh, *Modern Scottish Gaelic Poems* (Edinburgh, 1976)

A. and A. MacDonald, *The Poems of Alexander MacDonald* (Inverness, 1924)

Somhairle MacGill-Eain, *O Choille gu Bearradh/From Wood to Ridge* (Collected Poems) (Manchester, 1989)

John Macinnes, 'Gaelic Spiritual Verse', in *Trans. Gael. Soc. Inv.*, 46, (Inverness, 1971)

Angus MacLeod, *The Songs of Duncan Bàn Macintyre* (Edinburgh, 1952)

Ruaraidh MacThòmais, *Creachadh na Clàrsaich/Plundering the Harp* (Collected Poems) (Edinburgh, 1982)

Ruaraidh MacThòmais, *Smeur an Dòchais/Bramble of Hope* (Edinburgh, 1992)

Colm Ó Baoill, *Bàrdachd Shìlis na Ceapaich* (Edinburgh, 1972)

Iain Crichton Smith, *Ben Dorain* (Newcastle, 1969, 1988)

D.S. Thomson, *The Gaelic Sources of Macpherson's 'Ossian'* (Edinburgh, 1952)

D.S. Thomson, 'The MacMhuirich Bardic Family', in *Trans. Gael. Soc. Inv.*, 43 (Inverness, 1966)

D.S. Thomson, 'Gaelic Learned Orders and Literati in Medieval Scotland', in *Scottish Studies*, 12 (Edinburgh, 1968)

D.S. Thomson, *The New Verse in Scottish Gaelic: a Structural Analysis* (Dublin, 1974)

D.S. Thomson (ed.), *The Companion to Gaelic Scotland* (Oxford, 1983)

D.S. Thomson, 'Macpherson's *Ossian*: Ballads to Epics', in B. Almqvist *et al.*, *The Heroic Process* (Dun Laoghaire, 1987)

D.S. Thomson, *An Introduction to Gaelic Poetry* (Edinburgh, 1989)

D.S. Thomson, 'Mac Mhaighstir Alasdair's Nature Poetry and its Sources', in *Gaelic and Scots in Harmony* (Glasgow, 1990)

D.S. Thomson, *Alasdair Mac Mhaighstir Alasdair: His Political Poetry* (Inverness, 1991)

R.L. Thomson, *Foirm na n-Urrnuidheadh* (Edinburgh, 1970)

W.J. Watson, *Scottish Verse from the Book of the Dean of Lismore* (Edinburgh, 1937)

Christopher Whyte, *An Aghaidh na Sìorraidheachd/In the Face of Eternity* (Edinburgh, 1991)

Theatre in Scotland: 1214 to the Present

ALASDAIR CAMERON

We live in a country which, we are told, was for centuries inimical to drama and the organised theatre. As early as 1225, the religious authorities, then the Catholic Church, issued an edict against folk-plays. After the Reformation, we suffered, like the Dutch, from religious fanatics who selectively distorted the Bible to prove that plays and actors were sinful and that the theatre was the abode of the devil. As late as 1764, Glasgow's first theatre was burned down by a mob of the unco guid. Even after the hostility of the Church had abated, Scotland's small and scattered population did not prove very fruitful soil for theatre companies to put down roots, and only when urbanisation had created larger towns were they able to establish themselves. But somehow actors, the drama and a public taste for all kinds of theatre survived condemnation and neglect, and by piecing together evidence from a wide variety of sources, a coherent history of theatre in Scotland in all its manifestations begins to emerge.

It is not, however, a theatre history like that of Ireland, which is a litany of great plays and playwrights. It is, rather, the history of a social institution with several sometimes conflicting traditions. It is a history which includes fairgrounds and pantomimes, club theatres and opera houses, fit-up companies and prestigious tours; which covers great writers and dramatic hacks; which encompasses periods of intense national pride in the stage and periods when any mention of Scottish drama was the cue for an embarrassed silence; periods when theatre in Scots or about Scotland only existed because of Englishmen or the efforts of amateur actors, and periods when Scotland had a vibrant, indigenous, professional theatre culture.

Written evidence of this history begins with a proclamation, issued by Alexander II forbidding plays and banquets at Court after the death of his father in 1214, which is evidence that dramatic entertainment played a significant enough part in Court life for it to be an appropriate mark of respect to ban it. Indeed, until the removal of the Court to London in 1603, it is the royal household which provides the most consistent

19. Edinburgh International Festival production (1984) of Ane Satyre of the Thrie Estaites *by Sir David Lyndsay of the Mount. Scottish Theatre Company, directed by Tom Fleming. Three vices – Flatterie, Falsehood and Deceit – played by John Grieve, Walter Carr and Gregor Fisher. (*Edinburgh International Festival*)*

evidence of early theatrical performances in Scotland, including the first performance of *Ane Satyre of the Thrie Estaitis*, Sir David Lyndsay's great 'state of the nation' play, presented at the Palace of Linlithgow in 1540. Since it was first revived in 1948 at the Edinburgh Festival in Robert Kemp's shortened version, *Ane Satyre of the Thrie Estaitis* has almost assumed the role of the flagship of Scottish theatre. The first, innovative, thrust-stage production, directed by Sir Tyrone Guthrie in the Assembly Hall has been followed by many more, including the first modern performance of the complete text directed by Professor James Arnott in the Bute Hall of Glasgow University and a production by the Scottish Theatre Company, directed by Tom Fleming, which was much-praised when it visited Warsaw in 1986.

Theatrical performance in Scotland before the Cromwellian invasion can be grouped into four distinct types. As well as performances at Court, there were those which were part of state and national celebrations, like the lavish theatrical Entrances and entertainments which welcomed Margaret of England and Mary, Queen of Scots to Edinburgh, and those which were controlled by the Church and were part of national religious observance such as the Corpus Christi processions in Perth. There were also the folk-plays, linked to the natural cycles of rural and urban life, like the Robin Hood plays which the Catholic Church tried but failed to root out and which the Reformed Church spent much time banning from churchyards, from performing on Sundays and from causing too much public nuisance.

Performances at Court were both a recreation and entertainment for the royal courtiers and often served a diplomatic function. Maskings, when disguised strangers entered the Banqueting Hall and entertained the feasters, were a way of presenting gifts and paying compliments, but at state banquets something more elaborate could be produced, such as the appearance of various emblems; bowers, clouds and ships, for example, with dancers and singers in elaborate costumes praising the virtues of the king or queen and their guests, and perhaps including a coded political message in the midst of the elaborate sugared conceits.

The medieval Church in Scotland, like any other branch of Catholic Christendom, encouraged plays and performances of a devotional nature. Records of these, however, are thinner on the ground in Scotland than elsewhere in Europe, either because the Scottish Protestant iconoclasts did a more thorough job, or because religious plays in Scotland were processions and tableaux vivants, rather than fully developed dramatic cycles like those of York or Chester. Around the Reformation, crypto-Protestants used theatre and drama as a way of spreading a message about the need for reform and reconstruction of the Church and the nation's religious life. Some dramatists, like the hapless Friar Kilgour at Stirling, perished for their efforts; some, like Alexander Wedderburn and George Buchanan – who had also supplied many Latin texts for Court entertainments – were forced to flee; and others like Sir David Lyndsay saw their efforts go unheeded. Buchanan's period in exile was, however, extremely fruitful, as he consolidated his reputation as a scholar of European renown and his plays, in particular the Latin biblical dramas *Baptistes* and *Jephthes*, were taught and performed across the Continent well into the seventeenth century.

Even after the Reformation performances of folk-plays were tolerated. What was banned was any echo in them of Catholic doctrine, the tradition of performing these plays on a Sunday and the heinous custom of playing them in the kirkyard, a space flat, green and central which had become the favoured spot for town and village dramatics. Later, some more fanatical elements in the Church tried to weed out all such plays, but the early fathers of the Reformation, like Knox, often enjoyed a post-prandial theatrical performance – especially if it had an edifying religious or political theme.

State performances were the most lavish and the most public theatrical display in Scotland. Some of these, like the entry of Mary, Queen of Scots into Edinburgh in 1561 or the visit of Charles I in 1633, are famous and carefully – though occasionally conflictingly – recorded. Such entries involved elaborate planning and wholesale reconstruction of the city and its principal architectural features. A famous description of Mary's first encounter with her capital is quoted in Anna Jean Mill's study, *Mediaeval Plays in Scotland:*

> quhen sho was rydand down the castllehill, thair met hir hienes ane convoy of the
> young mene of the said burgh, to the nomber of fyftie, or thairby, thair bodeis and
> theis coveit with yeallow taffateis, thair armes and leggs fra the kne doun bair, cullorit
> with blak, in maner of Moris, upon thair heeiddis blak hattis, and on thair faces blak
> visouris, in thair mowthis rings, garnesit with inntellable precious staneis, about thair

neckkis, leggis and armes infynit chenis of gold; ... [At the butter tron] thair was ane
port made of tymber in maist honourable maner, cullorit with fyne cullouris, hungin
with syndrie armes; upon the quhilk port wes singand certane barneis in the maist
hevinlie wyis; under the quhilk port thair wes ane cloud opynnand with four levis in
the quhilk was put ane bony barne. And quhen the quenes hienes was cumand throw
the said port, the said cloude opynnit, and the barne discendit doun as it had bene ane
angell, and deliuerit to hir hienes the keyis of the toun, togidder with ane bybill and
ane psalme buik, coverit with fyne purpourit veluot ...

All the theatrical activity so far described was the province of amateurs and
important for the social collaborations such work entails but, just before the removal of
the Court to London, there were the beginnings of a professional theatre in Edinburgh.
A company of English players had set up a makeshift theatre in a close off the Royal
Mile under the protection of James VI. This was a company, led by Laurence Fletcher,
which, so Victorian antiquaries insisted, included Shakespeare himself on a trip to
Scotland to conduct some on-the-spot research around Glamis Castle for *Macbeth*.

In 1603 James and the other protectors of the theatre and drama at the Court left
Holyrood for Whitehall and, incidentally, to revolutionise the appearance of the British
theatre with the introduction of the Italian proscenium arch into Court entertainments.
The increasing hostility of the dominant party in the Church to any form of theatre,
paralleled by that of the Puritans in England, heralded a period of eclipse for the
organised theatre in Scotland. Before theatrical diversions were banned in all parts of
the British Isles in 1640, however, the Scottish nobility and institutions of learning
organised theatrical entertainments in private, and the folk plays – though coming
under renewed pressure – continued to exist in rural Lowland areas. Groups of actors
still toured, but the bulk of theatre was provided at fairs and hirings by puppeteers,
jugglers, acrobats and by touring mountebanks like John Pontus who was famous for
his attempts to sell patent medicines in the Royal Mile.

After 1660, with the return of Charles II, the climate changed and one of the first
and most public manifestations of the break with the previous régime was the
reopening of the theatres. In fact, theatres almost had to be reinvented. The model of
Elizabethan and Jacobean public playhouse was felt to be unsuitable and new theatres
following the French model were built within the walls of, in the main, royal tennis
courts. Edinburgh's theatre opened in 1662 in the tennis court of Holyroodhouse and
immediately attracted the nobility and gentry of the city. One Scottish aristocrat, Sir
John Foulis of Ravelstane, noted in his account book that he saw various plays at the
theatre including what was possibly the first production in Scotland of *Macbeth*. His
visits were very social occasions and involved much buying of fruit and sweetmeats for
the ladies of his party. Foulis also spent money on less weighty amusements like a
puppet show, a contortionist and a glimpse of an elephant which was brought to a close
off the Royal Mile.

Towards the end of the seventeenth century Scotland's continuing political and
religious strife meant that there were no longer the settled social circumstances which
make regular, professional theatre possible. Without the continued patronage of an
affluent and confident middle and upper class, companies of professional actors,
performing in specially designed theatre buildings, could not exist. Scotland was,
however, served by touring companies from the south and her writers like Archibald
Pitcairne wrote closet dramas which had little hope of performance. Indeed, Pitcairne's

play, *The Assembly*, a satire on the excesses of Presbyterianism written in 1692, was considered so inflammatory that it was not even published until well into the next century.

Amateur theatre and folk theatre continued, however, as did the tradition especially in the east of the country, of school plays in Latin. It was only after the Union and the upheavals which surrounded it had died down, that a semi-permanent theatre was opened in Edinburgh in 1715 by Signora Violante who had come over from Dublin to exhibit her acrobatic abilities. She was followed by various other theatrical entrepreneurs, like the comedian Tony Aston who, in 1725, embarked on a legal fight with the Presbytery of Edinburgh and won the right to perform within the city. From then on, the surviving records of the Scottish stage run in a virtually unbroken line.

Although Scotland contributed little to the European stage of the eighteenth century, the country's dramatists provided two of the most performed plays in English, Allan Ramsay's *The Gentle Shepherd* and John Home's *Douglas*. Ramsay's play was written in 1728 for some gentlemen amateurs of Haddington, and Home's in 1756 for a professional and predominantly Anglo-Irish company based in the Concert Hall in the Royal Mile. Home is often criticised for this company and for his ambitions on the London stage, but, in 1756, there were no legal, licensed theatres outside London and his most famous play, having been rejected by Garrick and Drury Lane Theatre, was produced 'gratis', at the end of a concert of music in Edinburgh. *Douglas* is important in Scottish theatre history, as the ridicule heaped on the fanatics in the Church over the commotion they raised about Home's authorship of a play and the perceived incompatibility with his profession as minister of the Kirk, led to a loosening of religious objections to the theatre in general and paved the way for the opening of the Edinburgh Theatre Royal in 1767. Seventeen years later, when this Royal Patent theatre was well established at the foot of the North Bridge opposite Register House, Mrs Siddons completed the victory of stage over pulpit with her first appearance in the city, in various roles including Lady Randolph in *Douglas*. Her performances, it is claimed, led to the cancellation and rescheduling of some of that year's meetings of the General Assembly of the Church of Scotland, so anxious were the younger ministers to avail themselves of Mrs Siddons' example in declamation.

The Gentle Shepherd remained in the repertoire of many theatre companies until well into the nineteenth century. Ramsay's play was enjoyed on many levels: for its use of Scots song; for the charm of the verse; and for the joyful experience for Scottish audiences of listening to English actors mangling the texts in their efforts to speak Scots. In addition to its popularity on stage, the play was performed communally, at least until the end of the nineteenth century, by villagers in the Pentland Hills where the play is set. Its tremendous popularity was probably enhanced by the scores of editions of the play which were printed, from finely bound and illustrated Folio volumes to cheap, roughly produced but widely available Chapbooks.

Edinburgh dominated Scottish theatre until well into the nineteenth century but gradually the taste for professional theatre and communities willing to support it became more widespread. The godfather of the eighteenth-century theatre in Scotland was John Jackson who, around 1785, owned the theatres in Glasgow, Edinburgh, Dundee and Aberdeen. Theatres also appeared in Perth, Ayr, Paisley, Montrose and Dumfries, but most of these were seasonal and depended on players from the larger theatres, like Edinburgh, touring at times when the Theatres Royal were closed. Touring companies travelled far and wide in Scotland and penetrated as far north as

Inverness and Elgin on the new Wade roads. These travelling players often had a miserable life, sometimes reduced to stealing turnips from fields and eating them in order to survive. There are records, too, of a company of actors, travelling on foot, who lost their way in a snowstorm and some days later were discovered dead in a ditch.

The pattern of theatre building in Scotland followed population movements and throughout the early nineteenth century, theatres catering for the new urban working class were established alongside the Theatres Royal (which in the main catered for the middle classes). Only a Theatre Royal with letters-patent from the government could produce spoken drama, so their sister theatres concentrated on musical theatre. These 'entertainments' were liberally interspersed with favourite national airs and dances, and often featured Highlanders, bagpipes and tartan. All this was as much in the service of national sentiment as the picturesque, and gradually plays with a 'national' element, or something recognisably Scottish in them, came to dominate the repertoire of both what were termed the legitimate and illegitimate stages. Coincidently, the taste of London audiences at the turn of the nineteenth century was for wild romantic plays set in wild romantic landscapes – and Scotland fitted the bill. From the early versions of vampire legends set on Staffa, with Fingal's Cave providing the noble natural setting for the vampire's lair, to the endless versions of the novels of Walter Scott – chief among them *Rob Roy* – with miles of painted canvas representing Aberfoyle and various lonely moors and lochs, the appetite of London and Edinburgh for Scotland on stage was rivalled only by their appetite for the works of the Bard of Avon.

Edinburgh's, and indeed Scotland's, contribution to an endless stream of national dramas was centred round the tenure of William Murray and his sister Harriet Siddons at the Theatre Royal. From 1815 to 1839 Murray not only produced adaptations of Scott's novels – some, like *Guy Mannering*, appearing on the stage simultaneously with their appearance in the bookshops – but he also wrote his own plays, versions of Scott's tales and episodes from Scots history, and his works, particularly *Cramond Brig* and *Gilderoy*, were constantly revived as curtain-raisers throughout the century. Murray and Siddons created what amounted to a national theatre in which all Scottish actors of the time wanted to appear. Indeed, many of the best actors of the day would rather have appeared there than in the 'wildernesses' of Drury Lane and Covent Garden.

Murray's theatre provided a blueprint for theatres all over the country and their dependence on the national repertoire allowed it to flourish and a Scottish acting profession to grow up. Actors no longer had to depend, as had Henry Johnston in the previous century, on making their name in London, but could now, like Charles Mackay, have a long and lucrative career playing only north of the border and in their own native accent. However, the nineteenth century ended with no indigenous spoken drama and the sad fact that Scotsmen who wanted to act or, like J.M. Barrie, to write plays, had to head for London rather than Edinburgh or Glasgow. The change came about primarily because of the spread of the railways and a change of fashion in London, first to Irish plays and then to society dramas. Each London production was replicated by numerous touring companies which were sent to the prestigious theatres in Scotland by the London-based syndicates who owned them, to provide Scotland's staple dramatic fare for the nation.

Scots actors who could not adapt to London or make their name in England had two options. One was to play with the fit-up companies who toured the rural and working-class areas of Scotland with portable theatres known as 'geggies'. The other was to take to the stages of the music-halls which were springing up in the crowded immigrant and impoverished areas of the Scottish cities. This led to a dichotomy between the prestigious and lavishly appointed city centre theatres which catered for Scotland's middle classes with an almost unvaried diet of what happened to be fashionable on the London stage, and the theatrical fare of the working classes in the towns and countryside, usually plays and entertainments in their own language and accents, using Scottish music, songs and dances. There was some crossover, but generally speaking, Scottish plays – which at the start of the century were the apotheosis of national theatrical pride and were presented on the most prestigious stages in the country – ended the century on the margins of society seen only as fodder fit for social inferiors.

The rise of the music-halls and later the variety theatres in Scotland was the most significant development in late nineteenth-century Scottish theatre, as these paved the way for the parallel traditions of Scottish pantomime and variety which have now become one of the most interesting features of Scottish theatre. It has, however, taken most of this century to stop apologising and feeling ashamed of this. In many ways the typical contemporary Scottish play, if such a thing exists, will ramble, be based round songs, sketches and direct audience address and owe more to the national dramas of the early nineteenth century than to Chekhov, Brecht or Pinter. This tradition also allowed working-class playwrights in the twentieth century to develop a unique and distinctive style, unencumbered by any notion of the well-made play which was to be such a burden for James Bridie in his attempts to please the West End.

Because Scotland has had in effect to reinvent its mainstream theatre in the past fifty years, having depended on amateur companies to keep it alive from 1920 to 1940, the history of Scottish theatre in the twentieth century is worth close scrutiny. At the start of the century the problem for Scotland was perceived to be the same triple blight inherited from the Victorian stage by all theatre in the British Isles outside London: the long run, the trivial play and the theatrical tour. For us it was the tour which was felt to be most damaging as, by 1909, most people equated 'real' theatre with productions sent out from London which arrived by train one Sunday and left by train the next. The first person who attempted to change this was an Englishman, Alfred Wareing. In 1909 he founded the Glasgow Repertory Theatre to 'make Scotland independent of London for her theatrical supplies'.

Influenced by the Abbey Theatre in Dublin and by an old Scottish actor, William Mackintosh, Wareing was convinced that only settled local theatre companies producing challenging plays could save the British theatre. Accordingly, he rented the prestigious Royalty Theatre in Sauchiehall Street to give a veneer of sophistication to his enterprise and recruited a company of seasoned professional actors whose repertoire included the first production of a play by Chekhov in Britain (*The Seagull*, November 1909) and the first production of J.A. Fergusson's *Campbell of Kilmohr*, the prototype for many a Scottish play of the next thirty years. The company also premièred around thirty other new Scottish plays which were performed alongside British and European writers, including Shaw, Galsworthy and Gorky. Its greatest popular successes were – perhaps inevitably, given the perennial taste of Glasgow – an adaptation of J.J. Bell's *Wee MacGreegor* and *Macpherson*, based on one of Neil Munro's popular characters. Wareing's enterprise suffered from being under-capitalised, from the stigma of being thought amateur as the actors actually lived in the city, and of being considered too

English in spite of its creditable record in producing new Scots plays and employing Scottish actors. The enterprise ended in 1914 at the start of a war in which many of its most promising writers were killed.

Wareing's overall aims for the Glasgow Repertory Theatre had been to provide first a civic theatre for Glasgow and then a prototype for a Scottish national theatre. With the demise of his enterprise, the torch of the indigenous drama was passed at the end of the war to the Scottish National Players, an amateur group attached to the St Andrew's Society. The Players became the most influential theatrical group in the 1920s. Not only did they tour the whole country with their plays, drawing their best audiences outside the cities, but they also influenced the development of broadcasting in Scotland by dint of the number of their members who joined the fledgling BBC Scotland. Their success and example also gave an impetus to the growing interest in amateur dramatics, and led, if not to the founding of the Scottish Community Drama Association, then to its rapid development from a handful of clubs in 1926 to over a thousand a decade later.

The Players also provided, albeit unwittingly, a forum for a debate about the kind of theatre modern Scotland wanted. A group in the company (including one of its directors, James Bridie) rejected Joe Corrie's *In Time o' Strife*, a play about the 1926 miners' strike which ended with the playing of 'The Red Flag'. Their tastes lay more with Neil Gunn and his play *The Ancient Fire*, which explored the Pictish and pagan rhythms which underlie the experience of every 'true' Scot. This split between the urban industrial experience of the country, which the Players chose not to explore (perhaps wisely as it would have been beyond their artistic powers to make much of the play, and Corrie himself toured it very successfully), and Gunn's vision of the 'real' Scotland – one of the moor, the deer hunt and the eternal verities of the Highlands – led them to reinforce this latter vision of Scotland as the one they favoured. This was further reflected in, for example, the pictures of Scotland presented in radio drama, which were almost entirely historical and rural.

The urban and industrial experience of Scotland was kept alive by another kind of amateur, the Labour player who worked through his or her trade union or co-operative to produce plays both didactic and artistic. God of these actors and indeed of the whole Scottish amateur movement before the war was Joe Corrie, the Fife miner playwright, whose one-act comedies and other more thoughtful pieces appeared constantly in the lists of plays which won SCDA competitions in the 1930s. Though he is best known for his lighter plays, Corrie was a very serious writer who sometimes found it difficult to work outside the jurisdiction of the Lord Chamberlain; he saw his satire *And So to War* censored in the mid-1930s and his play *Dawn* banned at the start of the Second World War.

Alongside the Labour players, Scots who wanted to act seriously and who for family and financial reasons could not take the risk of going on stage, joined groups like R.F. Pollock's Tron Players who were dedicated to exploring the theories of Stanislavsky. Other potential professionals – like Molly Urquhart, who refused to distort her voice by learning to speak 'proper' RP which would have enabled her to have a career on the English stage – started their own companies. In 1933 Urquhart was one of the founders of the Curtain theatre in Glasgow which aimed 'to give the Scottish writer and actor a platform' and introduced the Scots plays of Robert McLellan, most memorably *Jamie the Saxt*, with Duncan Macrae as Jamie. Later, in 1939, Urquhart started her own semi-professional theatre, the MSU, in Rutherglen. When that had to be wound up, due to wartime stringencies, she joined the new Citizens' company and became, with Macrae, one of the first Scottish professional actors to be based in Scotland for almost a hundred years. What those actors found was that, to make their living in Scotland, it was necessary to perform in a number of different theatrical environments principally in pantomime and variety as well as in more traditional plays at theatres like the Citizens'. This gave them a versatility which was enviable, but also made it more difficult for them to work in an ensemble, a problem which still plagues many Scottish actors.

Bridie hoped that the Citizens', founded in 1943 and the first theatre in Scotland to receive a government subsidy, would again fulfil the role of a true national theatre and become more than what he called 'the national theatre of the Gorbals'. The theatre gained international recognition with its contribution to the early Edinburgh Festivals, and might well have gone on to become a national theatre but for Bridie's untimely death just when he had helped to found Scotland's own dramatic conservatoire at the Royal Scottish Academy of Music and Drama.

The Citizens' had a rival in the shape of Glasgow Unity, one of the most successful companies in that miraculous decade for Scottish theatre, the 1940s. Unity had been founded at the start of the war by the amalgamation of a number of predominantly left-wing amateur theatre companies – the Glasgow Workers Theatre Group, the Clarion Players, the Jewish Institute Players and the Glasgow Transport Players. Unity was initially dominated by the Jewish Players and their international repertoire, but, gradually, Scottish plays entered their repertoire and by 1950 they had created successful productions of Ena Lamont Stewart's *Starched Aprons* and *Men Should Weep* and toured to the West End with Robert Macleish's *The Gorbal's Story* and Benedict Scott's *The Lambs of God*. Unity's huge popular following and their aim to create a 'Scottish people's theatre', must have made them seem a dangerous rival to the fledgling Citizens'. Their appearance at (and, indeed, creation of) the first Fringe Festival in Edinburgh in 1947, at a time when the Citizens' was not felt to be ready to appear on the official Festival programme, furthered increased tensions between the two organisations. But a mixture of internecine strife in Unity and the political and financial clout which Arts Council backing gave it, meant that by 1950 the Citizens' was the better established and with their pantomime that year, *The Tintock Cup* – which introduced actors like Stanley Baxter to the Scottish public and ran for four months – their reputation was assured and they became the touchstone by which Scottish theatre was measured until the mid-1960s.

In the 1950s the centre of theatre in Scotland was still London where all the prestigious television, film and theatre companies were based and whither Scottish actors, directors and designers would gravitate to find continuous lucrative work. After the death of Bridie in 1951, the Citizens' came to be seen as an important British repertory theatre and a stepping stone to the West End for actors and playwrights. Alongside this, however, the Citizens' made a policy of producing plays in Scots such as Alexander Reid's *The Warld's Wonder* and *The Lass Wi' the Muckle Moo*. These plays, though interesting linguistically and theatrically, must have seemed to have little relevance to the era of the atom bomb and the Cold War. Their recent revival by Theatre Alba, however, has revealed plays which are richly textured poetic parables which comment on the madness of man's race towards self-destruction.

Edinburgh's civic theatre, the Gateway, kept the emphasis of their company on Scotland, on new writing, and on developing a pool of Scottish actors, most prominent among whom were Lennox Milne and Tom Fleming. The theatre took advantage of their annual contribution to the Edinburgh Festival to revive or commission an important Scottish play every August. The Gateway's house dramatist was Robert Kemp who contributed many plays of Scottish life and character – such as his study of Burns, *That Other Dear Charmer* – to the company's repertoire. After twelve years of interesting programming, the Gateway was closed in 1965, when the Lyceum Theatre was bought by Edinburgh Corporation as the city's new theatre.

The Edinburgh Festival was also the catalyst which led to the founding of the Traverse Theatre Club in 1962. It was hoped that this theatre would keep alive the spirit of the Festival in the city throughout the year, and to do so, it presented some Scottish theatre, but concentrated on the plays of the international avant-garde. The Traverse gave Edinburgh an edge that Glasgow could not match until the Close Theatre Club was founded there in 1965. Both theatres fitfully explored new Scottish writing, but were better known for their exciting productions and daring challenges to the writ of the Lord Chamberlain in the years before censorship of theatre in Britain ended in 1968. Outside these two cities, however, theatre was more sedate and repertory was thriving in Pitlochry, Perth, St Andrews and Dundee. But in the 1950s and early 1960s, television was in the ascendancy and theatres, variety theatres and music-halls closed down all over the country. In its infancy Scottish television leeched as much on live theatre of all types as radio had done when it began in the early 1920s, and while audiences seemed to prefer to watch Scottish variety shows from the comfort of their armchairs rather than make the trip to the city centres, it was estimated that in 1959 some 450,000 people saw that year's *Five Past Eight Show* at Glasgow's Alhambra and in 1960, over 200,000 pantomime-goers saw *A Wish For Jamie*. But gradually, as the 1960s progressed, the attendance at all types of theatre dwindled and audiences, even those bastions of Scottish theatre, the summer variety show and the Christmas pantomime, shrank drastically.

Throughout the 1950s and 1960s, Scotland often seemed unsure whether it wanted any sort of distinctive theatre at all, but by the early 1970s, with the gradual upgrading and expansion of Scotland's media industry and a change in political, financial and cultural confidence, Scottish theatre once more seemed to be a source of pride. Two models of civic theatre vied for attention in Edinburgh and Glasgow. At the Royal Lyceum was a macho acting company of seasoned Scots actors directed by Clive Perry and Bill Bryden, which produced gritty plays about the working-class experience. At the Citizens', there was a design-led, visceral theatre of European classics aimed at a young audience. The Citizens' productions may have had little Scottish flavour, but they had a European reputation and a large and devoted audience. In 1973 these two theatres were joined by a touring model, 7:84 Theatre Company, who provided with *The Cheviot, the Stag and the Black Black Oil* the archetype of the touring political play which tried to unite the experience of the nation. Their use of popular theatre techniques, though it might have seemed ironic that a nakedly commercial and unanalytic art-form was now being exploited for socialist analysis and propaganda, alerted those who had forgotten about it, to Scotland's popular theatre heritage, still at that time struggling to survive outside the Christmas season. These techniques were also used to great advantage by Wildcat Theatre, an offshoot of 7:84, whose long run of successful and popular productions began in 1978.

The 1970s was a decade which saw an expansion in the number of theatre companies and theatre buildings. There was also a parallel profusion of new plays which, taken together, provided the basis of an exciting Scottish repertoire. Plays like *The Bevellers*, *The Hardman*, *The Sash* and *The Slab Boys Trilogy*, dealt with the male, Scottish, working-class, workplace experience. Their tone was already retrospective and elegiac and, though many of them came from the club theatre confines of the Traverse, the plays garnered large and loyal audiences by using techniques which would be familiar to habitués of the Pavilion in Glasgow or the Palladium in Edinburgh. The crossover between theatre forms is a reminder that in a small country all aspects of a profession as specialised as the theatre are interdependent. Neither do audiences go exclusively to see one kind of play: like actors who are willing to experience every kind of theatre and writers who will draw on any technique to make their plays work, Scottish audiences are famously eclectic and will happily absorb political propaganda in their community hall, Peter Brook at Tramway, Shakespeare at the Lyceum and *The Steamie* or *Rab C. Nesbitt* at the King's.

The 1980s began rather gloomily with Cassandra-like warnings that the impetus of the 1970s could never be kept up. However, even the improvements in theatrical provision and infrastructure which the 1970s brought was more than matched in the 1980s. New theatre spaces like Tramway and The Lemon Tree in Aberdeen opened; existing theatres like the Citizens' and Perth were refurbished; new theatres were built at Pitlochry and Dundee and for the Traverse in Edinburgh; exciting new dramatists like Liz Lochhead, Ian Heggie, Sue Glover, Chris Hannan, Peter Arnott and John Binnie came to prominence; and new theatre groups with staying power like Communicado, Fifth Estate and Clyde Unity were founded.

The decade also saw the rise and fall of the latest theatre company to take on the mantle of a national theatre, the Scottish Theatre Company. They revived a number of Scottish classics including Barrie's *What Every Woman Knows* with Una MacLean, Robert Kemp's *Let Wives Tak Tent* with Rikki Fulton, Robert McLellan's *Jamie the Saxt*, with Ron Bain and, most successfully, Lyndsay's *Ane Satyre of the Thrie Estaitis*. They also commissioned a number of new plays including Bill Bryden's *Civilians*, and revived recent Scottish plays, such as Marcella Evaristi's *Commedia*. The Scottish Theatre Company's idealism outstripped its meagre funding, but its bankruptcy and subsequent closure led to renewed calls for a national theatre to be established; and after a well-attended conference on the subject, organised by the Advisory Council for the Arts in Scotland (AdCAS) in May 1987, a working-party was set up to consider the various ways in which this might be achieved.

Much of the optimism of the 1980s came from the renewed energy and vigour with which the Scottish Arts Council and local authorities funded and planned for the theatre in particular and culture in general. In Glasgow there was the added bonus of the city's tenure as European City of Culture 1990. The preparations for this and the extra money which was available for the city to achieve the highest standards of production seemed to insulate Scottish theatre as a whole from the rude winds which blighted theatre in England. The international attention which the City of Culture brought to Scotland also gave an international focus to Scottish theatre which matched the continuing enterprise of the Edinburgh Festival. Much of this new attention was focused on the Third Eye Centre and Tramway where two producers, Nikki Milican and Neil Wallace, nurtured companies and presented some of the most exciting and imaginative theatre seen in Scotland. It was brought by such companies as the Maly Theatre of St

20. The Communicado Theatre Company's production of Edwin Morgan's Scots translation of Cyrano de Bergerac, *directed by Gerry Mulgrew. Traverse Theatre, in the Edinburgh Festival Fringe, August 1992. Valvert (Malcolm Shields) challenges Cyrano de Bergerac (Tom Mannion).* (Communicado Theatre Company)

Petersburg and Peter Brook's from the Bouffes du Nord in Paris. Robert Lepage from Quebec furthered this process by working with Scottish and Canadian actors in *Tectonic Plates*, to explore the connections between Scotland and Canada, while DV8 and Gloria worked at the Third Eye Centre and with other Scottish theatres such as the Traverse to expand the horizons and definitions of performance and theatre.

Through such enterprises Scotland took on a leading role at the cutting edge of British theatre. The only qualm felt by some was that in the 1970s, when this position was held by the Citizens' under the leadership of Giles Havergal, Philip Prowse and Robert David MacDonald, there was also an artistic product being exported. Companies such as Communicado, with much-praised productions like Edwin Morgan's Scots version of *Cyrano de Bergerac* or the Tron Theatre Company's productions of the plays of Michel Trembley, also translated into Scots, might fill this role, but there is also a perceived need to ensure that the exciting theatre artists who visit the country are able to share their skills and experience and that Scottish companies are sufficiently funded to allow the level of rehearsal, experimentation and innovation needed to create great theatre. It also seems vital that Scottish theatre practitioners use the experience of the prestigious and inventive visiting companies to recreate and replenish their own theatre. Otherwise the litany of those who have been here – Ninagawa, Robert Wilson, Peter Stein, the Wooster Group, the Rustavelli Company, Nuria Espert and so on – dwindles to a string of rather dusty theatre-goers' memories.

There are signs that this process of cross-fertilisation has begun. Noel Greig and Ian Reekie of 7:84 (Scotland) have used the techniques of Robert Lepage and the Theatre Repere from Quebec to explore the legacy of the Massacre of Glencoe. Links with Quebec have been further strengthened by a series of translations into Scots by Bill Findlay and Martin Bowman of plays by Michel Trembley, the Tron's production of *The Guid Sisters* being so far perhaps the most successful. Groups like TAG Theatre Company expanded the limits within which they worked during Glasgow's year as City of Culture when, having once been given resources which enabled them to work on a scale they could never before afford, they went on to produce a version of Lewis Grassic Gibbon's *A Scots Quair*. This was performed in the Assembly Hall at the Edinburgh Festival in 1993 and was felt by many to have assumed the status of a *Thrie Estaitis*, as a benchmark for Scottish theatre.

All these are vital developments for a theatre still too often casting its eyes south for the approval of the metropolis, rather than looking further afield or, better still, 'far ben into the national soul' as the Scottish National Players put it. The recent Scottish Arts Council document, *A Charter for The Arts in Scotland*, attempts to map the way forward for Scottish theatre by initiating discussions on the need for some kind of national theatre and the recognition of ethnic and linguistic minorities. If a Scottish national theatre is founded, it will have a wealth of theatrical experience to draw on. There may be less of a library of imperishable, internationally famous masterpieces of the written drama to fuel its repertoire than there is in Ireland, but dramatic genius is something for which you cannot legislate. It might, however, grow from a greater knowledge, understanding and recognition of a theatrical and dramatic heritage which is there waiting to be explored. Starting from new definitions of theatre, new ideas about what it could be and moving away from the equation of theatre with drama, Scottish theatre has no need to feel that it is either without heritage and traditions or that those it has are in any way inferior.

Books for Further Reading

Peter Baxter, *The Drama in Perth* (Perth, 1874)
Walter Baynham, *The Glasgow Stage* (Glasgow, 1892)
Frank Boyd, *The Dundee Stage* (Dundee, 1886)
Alasdair Cameron, *A Study Guide to Twentieth-Century Scottish Theatre and Drama* (Glasgow, 1989 and 1993)
Vivien Devlin, *Kings, Queens and People's Palaces* (Edinburgh, 1991)
James C. Dibdin, *Annals of the Edinburgh Stage* (Edinburgh, 1889)
Brian Hayward, *The Scottish Folk Play* (Edinburgh, 1992)
David Hutchison, *Modern Scottish Theatre* (Glasgow, 1977)

Robb Lawson, *The Scots Stage* (Paisley, 1917)
Anna Jean Mill, *Medieval Plays in Scotland* (London, 1924; reprinted New York, 1960)
Terence Tobin, *Plays by Scots* (Iowa, 1974)

Recent anthologies of Scottish plays include *A Decade's Drama* (1979) and *Scot Free* (1990). The Scottish Theatre Archive, which contains a wide variety of material mainly on twentieth-century Scottish theatre, is housed in the University of Glasgow Library and is open to the public for consultation.

The Oral Tradition

HAMISH HENDERSON

In 1951 the renowned American folklorist Alan Lomax, who had been commissioned by Columbia Records to make a series of LPs covering the folk music of the world, carried out two energetic recording tours in Scotland – first in the north-east, and later in the Hebrides. He came to this task with what seems in retrospect a definite advantage: the folk scene he was about to survey was totally new to him, and although he could draw on the help and expertise of scholars like the late Calum Maclean, he approached everything he found without the preconceptions which acquaintance with earlier studies might have implanted in him. The result was an entirely fresh approach to the field he proposed to document, and when he came to write up his findings for the notes to the Scottish LP – Vol. VI in the *World Library of Folk and Primitive Music* – he set down some valuable novel insights into the nature and reality of Scottish folk culture:

> The Scots have the liveliest folk tradition of the British Isles, but, paradoxically, it is the most bookish. Everywhere in Scotland I collected songs of written or bookish origin from country singers, and, on the other hand, I constantly encountered bookish Scotsmen who had good traditional versions of the finest folk songs. For this reason I have published songs which show every degree and kind of literary influence. Yet in this district there still lives the finest tradition of work-song singing in Western Europe.

It is customary to attribute the Scottish respect for book learning to the desire of the Protestant reformers to enable the people to read the Scriptures in their own tongue – or at any rate in a tongue reasonably close to their own. Be that as it may, the evidence of a reverence for the written word co-existing with a strong and resilient oral tradition is abundant in our history, and indeed this at first sight contradictory and puzzling phenomenon was regarded by Lomax – who had gathered evidence in many countries – as the main distinguishing feature of Scottish folk culture, both Highland and Lowland.

Certainly, on the Gaelic side, the evidence for an exceedingly tenacious and resilient oral tradition little if at all affected by written influences is indisputable. Francis Collinson lists, among the class of songs he defines as 'traditional', the 'labour songs and lilts of the Hebrides – waulking songs for the shrinking of the cloth, rowing songs, milking, churning, reaping, corn grinding, spinning and dandling songs as well as the laments and love-songs, the pibroch songs and fairy songs and sung "ports" for dancing'. Although one cannot exclude the possibility of the occasional text from print getting caught up and swirled around in this maelstrom of song, it is probably safe enough to regard the texts of these songs as – in an overwhelming majority of cases – stemming from an orally composed or communally created (and recreated) original. Furthermore, it must be remembered that the song-poems of even such famous eighteenth-century bards as Duncan Macintyre (Donnchadh Bàn) and Robert Mackay (Rob Donn) were composed orally, for the poets in question were non-literate – as, indeed, were the vast majority of *baird bhaile* (local or 'township' poets) who for centuries served as chroniclers and remembrancers for their respective communities, and made their presence felt far and wide through the much feared power of satire.

The very ancient heroic ballads, which died out in Ireland many years ago, have lived on into the present decade in the Outer Hebrides. One of these heroic lays provides a link between the early Welsh (P-Celtic) world and the Gaelic (Q-Celtic): it is '*Am Bròn Binn*' ('The Sweet Sorrow'), which undoubtedly owes its origin to the Arthurian cycle of romances. The King of Britain (*Rìgh Breatainn*) sees in a dream a most beautiful woman, and one of his knights offers to go in search of her. He finds her in a castle whose lord is the *Fear Mór* (the big man); she kills the giant when he is asleep and escapes with her rescuer (identified as Gawain). This ballad – the subject of an outstanding monograph by Linda Gowans – has been collected four times in this century: three times in the Hebrides by John Lorne Campbell and Calum Maclean, and once, by the present writer, in Sutherland, from a travelling tinsmith, Aili Dall (blind Alec Stewart of Lairg) who got it from his mother, Susie.

The origin of '*Am Bròn Binn*' – literary or oral – has been debated by several scholars; William Gillies has suggested that the archetype may have been a manuscript in Gaelic script composed by an author with access to the medieval Irish manuscripts replete with Arthurian motifs; John MacInnes, on the other hand, concludes from the available evidence that '*Am Bròn Binn*' has no literary origin. Whatever the truth of this, it is clear that – in the case of Aili Dall at least – the ballad has been carried forward among the 'summer walkers' (as the local crofters call the travellers) exclusively by oral transmission, for at least three centuries and possibly for far longer.

Aili Dall sang the ballad – and told the many folk-tales he had inherited from his people – in Sutherland Gaelic, but he could also speak the Highland tinkers' cant, the *Beurla-reagad* which is related to *bearlagar nan saor*, one of the seven secret languages of Ireland. *Beurla-reagad* is a sort of compression of *beurla nan ceard*, lingo of the cairds or craftsmen; like all such covert tongues, it protected the secrets of a privileged caste, probably in earlier times of quite high status in clan society.

The basic principle of the *beurla-reagad*, like Cockney backslang, is the rearrangement of consonants, but it is considerably more involved than the cants based on English; initial consonants are not only brought to the end of words, but also frequently changed into other consonants in the process; for example, *moine* (peat) becomes *noip*. Furthermore, some of the words which the *beurla-reagad* systematically deforms are themselves archaic Gaelic, so a double smoke-screen of obfuscation is laid down in the path of the innocent non-cant speaker.

21. *Jeannie Robertson (1908–75), who has been described as the greatest ballad singer of the twentieth century, was discovered in 1953 by Hamish Henderson. Photographed in the garden of the School of Scottish Studies, Edinburgh University, in about 1960. (*School of Scottish Studies*)*

In the Lowlands the travellers' cant is related to the Elizabethan 'thieves' slang' put on record by Thomas Harman in *A Caveat for Common Cursitors* (1566), but it has developed over the years into an identifiable separate covert tongue. The arrival of the gypsies in the British Isles at the beginning of the sixteenth century led in places to an infusion of Romany into the native cant: examples are *manishi* ('woman'), *gadgie* ('man' or 'outsider'), *choring* ('stealing') and *vardo* ('living waggon').

Needless to say, these covert tongues are passed down orally in the fraternity from one generation to another, but brilliant artistic use of the Lowland cant has recently been made by a gifted (and highly literate) traveller tradition-bearer, Stanley Robertson, nephew of the great ballad singer Jeannie Robertson. His attractive book of folk-tales, *Exodus to Alford*, is packed with expressions like *bing avree* ('go away'), *ker* ('house'), *mang* ('talk'), *peeve* ('drink'), *kinchens* ('children') and *mort* ('woman'). Here is a short passage from *The Mither's Tale*, describing a visit to Hoddie (the devil) by one of his (the devil's) aunties:

> When she gangs in, Hoddie is pleased to see her, as auld Sissie is his favourite auntie. She looks at him and says, 'Whit the deil ill ails ye, cos ye look awfy distraught.'
>   'Oh,' says he, 'I seem tae hae some pullichers o' hell in between my horns, and they are pittin me divvi.'
>   'Oh sit doon' cries Sissie, 'an I'll look yer heid for ony parries.'

Here the racy Lallan dialect is given colourful colloquial vigour by the use, in conversation, of cant words like *pullichers* ('fleas'), *divvi* ('crazy') and *parries* ('lice').

Stanley's own Auntie Jeannie, although justly famous as the most acclaimed classic ballad singer of modern times, was also a notable storyteller. Indeed, it was in her wee house (now demolished) in Causewayend, Aberdeen, that the tremendous wealth of folk-tales among the north-east travellers became apparent. These included international *Märchen* (wonder tales) like 'The Dragon Slayer', which is no. 303 in the voluminous compendium, *The Types of the Folktale*, begun by the Finnish scholar Antii Aarne and continued by the American Stith Thompson; and 'The Girl as Helper in the Hero's Flight' (AT 313). Both of these tale types have been recorded all over the world, but in Aberdeenshire have become so completely assimilated into the local landscape and idiom that anyone hearing them for the first time could easily be persuaded that they originated in Fetterangus or Inverurie.

Here is a dialogue passage from *The Green Man of Knowledge* – a version of the second of the tale types mentioned above – which is from the repertoire of Geordie Stewart, a traveller now settled in Banff:

> He lands at the banks o the river. And now, as the blacksmith telt him to hide hissel, so Jack hides hissel . . . just aside the bridge, and he sees this three lovely maidens comin ower, and they were bonnie lassies. But the littlest one was the slenderest, and the most graceful o the lot, you would have thought, you know? So they come trippin ower the bridge and undress, and into the water. And whenever they touch the water, the two oldest ones turned til a black swan, and they swum fast an away. And this youngest one undresses; and he watched where she pits her clothes, and ye ken what like Jack, I mean a fairm servant, never seen a woman in his life hardly, says, 'Lord, this is fine!' They're into the water, and they're away swimming. So he's awa up wi her claes, up every stitch o claes she had, everything, even the very ribbons, and hides them.

So the two oldest ones comes out and dresses, and across the bridge and away. And she's up and doon this side, and she says, 'Where are you, Jack?'

He says, 'I'm here.'

She says, 'My clothes, please, Jack.'

'Ah na na, I'm nae giein ye nae claes,' he says. 'I was weel warned aboot ye.'

She says, 'Jack, please, my clothes. Are you a gentleman?'

'Na, na,' he says, 'I'm just Jack the Feel. I'm nae gentleman.'

She says, 'What have I to do, Jack?'

'Well,' he says, 'it's a cruel thing to ask, but you must help me across this river on your back.'

She says, 'Oh Jack, you'd break my slender back.'

'Ah,' he says, 'the old smith's nae feel. Ye're nae sae slender.' He says, 'Ye'll take me across the river.'

She says, 'Well Jack, step on my back, but whatever you do, on the peril of my life and your life, don't tell how ye got across.'

He says, 'Okay.'

So he jumps on her back, and she takes him across, and he steps up on the bank.

Before a gallus corps of virtuoso Lallan storytellers began to record their repertoires for the School of Scottish Studies in the early 1950s, it had been generally assumed that storytelling had more or less died out south of the Highland line. It is true that in the early nineteenth century the maverick Peterhead printer-antiquary, Peter Buchan, had put together a collection of stories – nearly all identifiable international *Märchen* – which he claimed to have collected 'from the recitation of the Aged Sybils of the North Countrie'. Presumably these ladies had originally told them in one or other dialect of north-east Doric, but Peter had translated them into English – and a rather high-falutin English at that – so that when John Francis Campbell of Islay came to examine the as yet unpublished manuscript thirty years later, he gave it as his opinion that these must be stories, originally told in Gaelic, which had somehow found their way into the linguistic borderland of the north-east.

One can readily understand why Campbell came to what must now seem an untenable conclusion, because he and his helpers were in the process of amassing a vast collection of wonder-tales in Gaelic, and the sheer bulk of his marvellous collection – as compared with poor Peter's thin volume – must have seemed to clinch matters. However, the collections of tales told in Lowland Scots made by staff members of the School of Scottish Studies since its foundation in 1951 throw a very different light on the matter. (And one must add that one of the outstanding cultural debts Scotland owes to the travelling people is the preservation of this enormous *Märchengut* thanks to their own oral tradition.)

Needless to say these traveller tradition-bearers were overwhelmingly non-literate, and their tales were transmitted orally right up to the coming of the tape-recorder. The arrival of the latter engendered some odd paradoxes. In 1960 I wanted to record a story from a 'settled' travelling woman in Huntly, but after my first two visits her husband – who was not a traveller – began to suspect that my intentions were not purely folkloristic. When I called round to see her for the third time, she warned me that he would soon be home, and then pressed into my hand the story I had come to record. She had just taped it herself on her own tape-recorder!

The Gaelic folktales Campbell had collected and published in 1860 under the title

Popular Tales of the West Highlands include stories of Fionn Mac Cumhail and the Fingalian (or Fenian) heroes, which must be among some of the earliest of such stories in Europe. Some of these have been carried forward into this century, and recordings made by Calum Maclean and others for the School of Scottish Studies attest the strength and integrity of Hebridean tradition (called by Alan Lomax 'the finest flower of western Europe').

On the north Highland mainland, it was still possible in the 1950s – as we have seen with reference to the lay '*Am Bròn Binn*' – to come upon some precious orally transmitted records of the Celtic heroic age. The same traveller storyteller, Aili Dall, whose forebears had roamed through Wester Ross and Sutherland for centuries, turned out to have a version of *Oisein a's déigh na Feinne* (Oisin after the Feinne: the story of Oisin as an old blind man, and his meeting with St Patrick); he also had variants of international tales like AT 530 ('The Princess on the Glass Mountain'); AT 953 ('The Old Robber relates Three Adventures'), which is No. 191 in the *Kinder u. Hausmärchen* of the Brothers Grimm, and AT 910B ('The Servants' Good Counsels') – these titles are, of course, the 'model' titles given to the numbered tale types. Aili had his own Gaelic titles, namely '*Loircean*', '*Bonna Geal*', and '*Na Tri Comhairlean*'. His daughter, Mary, had a version of AT 503 ('The Gifts of the Little People') for which her title was '*Da Croit*' ('The Two Humphies'). These Sutherland Stewarts were also naturally the carriers of numerous local anecdotes and legends.

A present-day examination by the historic-geographic method of the many international wonder-tales which are to be found both among the Lowland travellers and their Highland compeers suggests a very different picture from that adumbrated 130 years ago by Campbell of Islay. If one takes as a representative specimen AT 530 (Aili's '*Loircean*') and looks at the variants collected across Europe, one finds this tale type on record in Finnish, Swedish, Estonian, Lithuanian, Norwegian, Danish, French, Flemish, German, Polish, Russian and Albanian; furthermore, it can be traced east into the Caucasus and Arabia, and yet further into India which seems to be the deep heartland of this and many other fantastic wonder-tales. Therefore, although the Celtic world became the repository of so many story types created by the Indo-European imagination, it seems highly likely that the bulk of these travelled from east to west, rather than vice versa. In any case, they certainly found a congenial realm to colonise in the far-flung Celtic redoubts.

This applies, naturally, not only to the wonder-tales but also to the usually shorter 'merry tales' (*Schwänke*) which likewise crisscrossed Europe. Jeannie Robertson had from her people a highly entertaining *Schwänk* ('Silly Jack and the Factor'), which in the Aarne Thompson index is numbered 1600, and given the catch-all title, 'The Fool as Murderer'. A poor widow woman has a silly son called Jack. She leaves him to guard the cottage while she gathers firewood. A factor comes to collect the rent, and goes to sleep beside the fire. A fly lights on the factor's brow, and Jack kills it with an axe – also, of course, killing the factor. When his mother returns, she and Jack bury the factor – but afterwards the mother removes his corpse to another grave, and then kills a billy goat and puts it into the first grave. When the police arrive, Jack directs them to this grave where they dig up the billy goat. Jack is astonished: 'Lord, he's grown whiskers and horns since we buried him here'.

This anecdote, as Jeannie told it, is localised so artfully in the Scottish north-east that it almost smells of the local countryside; however, it has been collected in almost as many places as AT 530, and can also be traced back to India. The indefatigable workers of the Irish Folklore Commission (now incorporated in the Folklore Department of

University College, Dublin) have over the years recorded over 150 versions, in both Irish and English.

Except in a tiny minority of cases, where orally transmitted tales seem to have been influenced by printed texts, such as popular editions of Grimms' fairy-tales in translation, this vast folk-tale treasury belongs exclusively to oral culture. The same cannot be said of the Scots classic (or Child) ballads, some of the most famous versions of which seem a blend of literary and oral provenance; indeed, as we have seen, Alan Lomax regards this philo-progenitive fusion as the most characteristic feature of Scottish folk poetry. The version of 'Edward' (No. 13 in F.J. Child's *English and Scottish Popular Ballads*), which Child made his B text, was communicated to Bishop Percy for his *Reliques* by Sir David Dalrymple (later elevated to the Bench as Lord Hailes), and is probably now the most celebrated ballad text in the world:

> 'Why dois your brand sae drap wi bluid,
>   Edward, Edward
> Why dois your brand sae drap wi bluid,
>   And why sae sad gang yee o?'
> 'O I hae killed my hauke sae guid,
>   Mither, mither,
> O I hae killed my hauke sae guid,
>   And I had nae mair bot hee O.'

Couched in a rather suspicious-looking 'auld farrant' Scots, Edward makes the impression of being a most accomplished poetic rewrite of something that has come to the author by oral transmission. The American scholar, Archer Taylor, called it 'a revision of a folk-song, a rewriting which may justly compare with Goethe's *Heidenröslein*'. As for the language, T.F. Henderson referred to it as 'a quite admirable example of the non-vulgarised Scots of the seventeenth and later centuries'. All commentators agree that, whatever this text *is*, it is *not* an unrevised traditional version.

In Child's A variant, the hero's name is not Edward – rather an unfortunate name, anyway, for a Scottish ballad hero in view of its better-known connection with 'oppressions woes and pains' – but the familiar Scots Davie. This was collected by William Motherwell in Kilbarchan, Renfrewshire, fifty years after Edward was printed in the *Reliques*, but it had no tune until Jeannie Robertson, the great Aberdeen ballad singer, provided one in 1953. Jeannie's version, now world-famous, is in an idiom which is unmistakable demotic ballad Scots, and yet shares with the older Scottish variants a stately 'aristocratic' milieu:

> 'Oh, what's the blood 'ats on your sword
> My son David, ho son David?
> What's that blood 'ats on your sword?
> Come, promise, tell me true.'
> 'Oh, that's the blood of my grey meir,
> Hey, lady Mother, ho, lady Mother,
> That's the blood of my grey meir,
> Because it wadnae rule by me.'

The development of stilted and prosaic broadside ballad texts into strong poetry, by virtue of oral transmission, is nowhere better exemplified than in the case of 'James

Harris', alias 'The Daemon Lover' (Child 243). The earliest version of this on record is an English broadside, printed in 1685, with stanzas like these:

> When he had told her these fair tales,
>   To love him she began,
> Because he was in human shape,
>   Much like unto a man.
>
> And so together away they went
>   From off the English shore,
> And since that time the woman-kind
>   Was never seen no more.

In the version in Scott's *Minstrelsy* ('taken down from the recitation of Walter Grieve by William Laidlaw'), the equivalent passage goes as follows:

> 'O hold your tongue of your weeping,' says he,
>   'Of your weeping now let me be;
> I will shew you how the lilies grow
>   On the banks of Italy.'
>
> 'O what hills are yon, yon pleasant hills,
>   That the sun shines sweetly on?'
> 'O yon are the hills of heaven,' he said,
>   'Where you will never win.'
>
> 'O whaten a mountain is yon,' she said,
>   'All so dreary wi frost and snow?'
> 'O yon is the mountain of hell,' he cried,
>   'Where you and I will go.'

Similarly, 'The Famous Flower of Serving Men' (Child 106) first makes its appearance on a seventeenth-century broadside in sedate English:

> You beauteous ladies, great and small,
> I write unto you one and all,
> Whereby that you may understand
> What I have suffered in this land.
>
> I was by birth a lady fair,
> My father's chief and only heir,
> But when my good old father dy'd,
> Then was I made a young knight's bride.
>
> And then my love built me a bower,
> Bedeckt with many a fragrant flower;
> A braver bower you never did see
> Then my true-love did build for me.

At some point it has been transformed into 'The Lament of the Border Widow' – which Scott claimed to have obtained from recitation in the forest of Ettrick, adding that it 'is said to relate to the execution of Cockburne of Henderland, a Border freebooter'. In his head-note to this ballad, Child referred somewhat scathingly to 'Scott's random inventions', and there is no doubt he got this fragment from James Hogg (who may well have recognised its actual provenance), but few will deny that as poetry it is far superior to the broadside from which it descended:

> My love he built me a bonny bower,
> And clad it a' wi' lilye flour;
> A brawer bower ye ne'er did see,
> Than my true love he built for me.
>
> There came a man, by middle day,
> He spied his sport, and went away;
> And brought the King that very night,
> Who brake my bower, and slew my knight.
>
> He slew my knight, to me sae dear;
> He slew my knight, and poin'd his gear;
> My servants all for life did flee,
> And left me in extremitie.
>
> . . .
>
> Nae living man I'll love again,
> Since that my lovely knight is slain;
> Wi' ae lock of his yellow hair
> I'll chain my heart for evermair.

The folk-songs which historically have less connection with print than any others are naturally the bawdy ballads – the songs of sexual comedy – which we in Scotland have in plentiful exuberance. The collection Burns made for the drinking and singing club, the Crochallan Fencibles (*The Merry Muses of Caledonia*), is the most famous; less well known is Peter Buchan's *The Secret Songs of Silence*, the manuscript of which is in the library of Harvard. The student of the techniques of oral composition can find delectable source material in some of Buchan's finds; the text of one of the bonniest of these – 'The Wanton Trooper' – can be found in *The People's Past*. Other examples of the *musa proterva* are preserved on tape in the archives of the School of Scottish Studies.

Many of these 'blue songs' may well have been composed by 'bookish Scotsmen' – to use Lomax's phrase, already quoted – but not necessarily written down and the same no doubt applies to some versions of the classic ballads themselves. One has the impression that many ballads which now exist in numerous variants must have stemmed from original versions composed by craftsmen-balladeers who took the inherited skills of their art very seriously indeed. In the case of some of the historical ballads – songs like 'Drumclog' (Child 205) and 'Bothwell Bridge' (Child 206) which deal with events of which the exact date is known – it may not be too sanguine to postulate an original song-poem by an unknown folksinger who was a virtuoso in the techniques of his craft, and also – quite possibly – a literate man, familiar with some at least of his country's written poetry. Ballads dealing with events like these, events which could excite high emotions among the listeners, may easily have existed orally for generations; Scott got 'Bothwell Bridge' 'from recitation'.

'O billie, billie, bonny billie,
    Will ye go to the wood wi me?
We'll ca' our horse hame masterless,
    An gar them trow slain men are we.'

'O no, O no!' says Earlstoun,
    For that's the thing that mauna be;
For I am sworn to Bothwell Hill,
    Where I maun either gae or die.'

. . .

Alang the brae beyond the brig,
    Mony brave man lies cauld and still;
But lang we'll mind, and sair we'll rue,
    The bloody battle of Bothwell Hill.

The modern folk revival has seen a resumption of this oral impetus in, for example, the songs of the brilliant Glasgow balladeer, the late Matt McGinn, and his Edinburgh mate, Bob Bertram. Thanks to the folk clubs which began to proliferate in the 1960s, songs like Matt's 'Dundee Ghost' and Bob's 'Buckie Wife' were picked up by direct oral transmission before they ever saw print. But what really caused a kind of explosion of oral song making was the arrival in the Holy Loch in 1961 of the depot ship *Proteus*, ready to service the Polaris-equipped submarines sent to save the western world. The most potent agent of resistance through song was the late Morris Blythman (Thurso Berwick) some of whose most pungent items were workshopped at the sit-downs at Ardnadam pier. As is usually the case, many were parodies of existing ditties – some unashamedly scatological:

Doon at Ardnadam, sitting at the pier,
When ah heard a polis shout: 'Ye'll no sit here!'
    Chorus:
    Ay, but ah wull sit here!
    Naw, but ye'll no sit here!
    Ay, but ah wull! Naw, but ye'll no!
    Ay, but ah wull sit here.
'Twis Chief Inspector Runcie, enhancin' his career,
Prancin up an doon the road like Yogi Bear
He caa'd for help tae Glesca, they nearly chowed his ear,
'We've got the 'Gers an Celtic demonstrators here.'
He telephoned the sodgers, but didnae mak it clear;
The sodgers sent doon Andy Stewart tae volunteer.
He radioed the White Hoose, but aa that he could hear,
Wiz ... two ... one ... zero – an the set went queer.
For Jack had drappt an H-bomb an gied his-sel a shroud,
An he met wi Billy Graham on a wee white cloud.

The booklets, *Ding Dong Dollar* and *Rebels Ceilidh Song Book No. 2*, put some of these anti-Polaris songs, and the songs that had sprung up alongside them, into print – acknowledging authorship by (among others) Jim Maclean ('We dinnae want Polaris'),

Johnnie McEvoy ('The Wee Magic Stane'), Roddy Macmillan ('Yuri Gagarin'), Ewen McColl ('The Banks they are Rosy'), Adam McNaughtan ('They're pullin doon the Buildings next tae oor's'), T.S. Law ('The Glesca Eskimos') and Dominic Behan ('The Patriot Game'). However, the two which have maintained a foothold in folk clubs both north and south of the Border were both by John Mack: 'The Misguided Missile and the Misguided Miss' (which has an excellent tune of its own), and the song which – for Pete Seeger – said it all: 'Ding Dong Dollar':

> O, ye canny spend a dollar when ye're deid
> O, ye canny spend a dollar when ye're deid
> Singing Ding Ding Dollar, everybody holler;
> Ye canny spend a dollar when ye're deid.
>
> Now the Yankees they drappt anchor at Dunoon,
> And they got a civic welcome frae the toon.
> As they cam up the measured mile
> Bonnie Mary o' Argyll
> Was wearin spangled drawers ablow her goon.

The tune of this one is 'Ye canny shove yer Grannie aff a Bus'.

At first the Scottish BBC was understandably gey sweir to broadcast this blatantly non-genteel material, but the pressure on it to present folk-song gradually became overwhelming, and when the floodgates opened, it became clear that the folk revival was going to command a lot of radio listener attention, and that the oral tradition had claimed a new and very broad channel to operate in. It was not long before record companies – first in the USA, and then in Britain – began to bring out 'folk' LPs, and soon, thanks to the technological revolution, performers in folk clubs were singing items they had learnt from such records, without benefit of mediation via the printed page. With the arrival of video tapes and CDs there seems little doubt that this tendency towards a new type of oral transmission will intensify.

By the same token, the fruitful cross-fertilisation in the fields of literary and 'folk' poetry – a permanent feature of Scottish creative work – will no doubt be again in evidence. It can look for models not only in the marvellous eighteenth-century anonyms like 'Edward', and songs with known authors like the Revd John Skinner's 'Tullochgorm', (which was a favourite of Jeannie Robertson's) but also in the writings of established poets of this century – including the great Hugh MacDiarmid, many of whose lyrics embedded in *A Drunk Man Looks at the Thistle* strike the same unmistakable note, which one might dub 'the scholar's ballad-Scots'. It is there, too, in Second Hymn to Lenin:

> Black in the pit the miner is,
> The shepherd reid on the hill,
> And I'm wi' them baith until
> The end of mankind, I wis.

The finest twentieth-century achievement in the old high ballad-Scots style is (for me) Lewis Spence's 'Capernaum', to which the modern 'Revival' singer, Ed Miller, has set a tune. The recurrent use of the place-name Embro at once recalls a version of 'The Twa Sisters' (Child No. 10) which Mrs Brown of Falkland, 'the Jeannie Robertson of the eighteenth century') gave to Jamieson, and for which the young Bob Scott (later Professor of Moral Philosophy at King's College, Aberdeen) painstakingly noted down a tune from her singing:

> There was twa sisters in a bowr,
>   Edinburgh, Edinburgh,
> There was twa sisters in a bowr,
>   Stirling for ay
> There was twa sisters in a bowr,
> There came a knight to be their wooer,
>   Bonny Saint Johnston stands upon Tay.

So here to conclude is Spence's superb 'Capernaum', a worthy heir to this tradition, which I quote in full.

> If a' the bluid shed at thy Tron.
>   Embro', Embro';
> If a' the bluid shed at thy Tron
>   Were sped into a river,
> It wad ca' the mills o' Bonnington,
>   Embro', Embro',
> It wad ca' the mills o' Bonnington
>   For ever and for ever.
>
> If a' the tears that thou has grat,
>   Embro', Embro'
> If a' the tears that thou has grat
>   Were shed into the sea,
> Whaur wad ye find an Ararat,
>   Embro', Embro',
> Whaur wad ye find an Ararat,
>   Frae that fell flude to flee?
>
> If a' the psalms sung in thy kirks,
>   Embro', Embro',
> If a' the psalms sung in thy kirks
>   Were gaithered in a wind,
> It wad shog the taps o' Roslin birks
>   Embro', Embro,
> It wad shog the taps o' Roslin birks
>   Till time was oot o' mind.
>
> If a' the broken herts o' thee
>   Embro', Embro',
> If a' the broken herts o' thee
>   Were heapit in a howe,
> There wad be neither land nor sea,
>   Embro', Embro',
> There wad be neither land nor sea,
>   But yon red brae – and thou!

Books for Further Reading

C.M. Bowra, *Primitive Song* (London, 1962)

David Buchan, *The Ballad and the Folk* (London, 1972)

David Buchan (ed.), *The Scottish Ballad Book* (London, 1973)

J.F. Campbell, *Leabhar na Feinne* (London, 1872)

J.F. Campbell, *Popular Tales of the West Highlands*, 4 vols. (Edinburgh, 1860; reprinted 1983)

J.L. Campbell, *Highland Songs of the Forty-Five* (Edinburgh, 1933)

J.L. Campbell and Francis Collinson, *Hebridean Folksongs* (Oxford, 1969)

Alexander Carmichael, *Carmina Gadelica*, 5 vols. (Edinburgh, 1928–54)

Thomas Crawford, *Society and the Lyric* (Edinburgh, 1979)

E.J. Cowan (ed.), *The People's Past* (Edinburgh, 1980)

Sheila Douglas, *The Sang's the Thing* (Edinburgh, 1992)

Josh Dunson, *Freedom in the Air* (New York, 1965)

M.J.C. Hodgart, *The Ballads* (London, 1950)

Albert B. Lord, *The Singer of Tales* (Cambridge, Mass., 1960)

Max Luthi, *The European Folktale: Form and Nature*, tr. John D. Niles (Philadelphia, 1982)

Ewan MacColl and Peggy Seeger, *Till Doomsday in the Afternoon* (Manchester, 1986)

Andrew McCormick, *The Tinkler Gypsies of Galloway* (Dumfries, 1905)

Ailie Munro, *The Folk Music Revival in Scotland* (London, 1980)

James Reed, *The Border Ballads* (London, 1973)

Stanley Robertson, *Exodus to Alford* (1988)

Margaret Fay Shaw, *Folksongs and Folklore of South Uist* (Oxford, 1977)

Leslie Shepard, *The Broadside Ballad* (London, 1962)

Music

JOHN PURSER

INTRODUCTION

The depth and breadth of Scottish music in terms of place, time, language and cultural diversity is only beginning to be fully appreciated. The political definition of the country, with the exception of the Western and Northern Isles which were ceded to Scotland in the thirteenth and fifteenth centuries respectively, has remained essentially unchanged since the early eleventh century, but the geography of the country has imposed its own clear definitions for very much longer, and these are still reflected in the variety of musical idiom. The oceanic west coast shares much of its culture with that of Ireland; the Northern Isles are proud of their Nordic inheritance; the central and eastern Lowlands support the whole range of European classical music, but at the same time have held on to ballad traditions in Scots which date back to medieval times. As for the music of Christianity, it varies from the most complex renaissance part-music to a style of psalm-singing in Gaelic with its roots in the Middle East and possibly as old as Christianity itself.

The impact of other cultures on Scotland's music has not been one of conquest so much as absorption. Romans, Scots (from the north of Ireland), Angles, Vikings, Normans and English have all invaded and left their marks; but at no time has there been recorded a complete conquest, with the result that many musical traditions have survived even from the pre-Christian era.

Though the oldest surviving musical artefact is dated to the eighth century BC, organological and manuscript evidence is very patchy: however, taken along with ancillary evidence from carvings and written accounts, it suggests a continuous preoccupation with music as a central part of the culture, as well as a determination that it should not lose touch with the various traditions from which it sprung, in many of which the influence of nature and the beauty of the land and seascape are seminal.

The Scots still sing regularly in three languages – Scots, Gaelic and English. The

22. *One of the panels of the Trinity College Altarpiece. Late 1470s.*
Hugo van der Goes. (The Royal Collection, Her Majesty the Queen)

latter, though the dominant spoken language, is the least favoured in song. Traces of Norn survive in ballads from the Northern Isles; and Latin was once sung in a secular as well as a sacred context. From the earliest peoples for whom we have linguistic evidence – the Picts, and the North British whose culture primarily survives in Wales – we have no songs. But the Picts have left carvings of many musicians, and the influence of the North British culture is evident in an heroic lay in Gaelic and medieval chants in Latin.

FOREIGN INFLUENCES

Foreign influences have been stongly felt at different periods. The Notre Dame school finds its earliest substantial record in a Scottish manuscript of the thirteenth century, and the long-standing political and marriage alliances with the French made a strong impact on music of Court and castle from the fifteenth to the seventeenth centuries. The sacred music of the Low Countries was influential in the early sixteenth century; and in the late seventeenth and early eighteenth centuries, Italian styles were interbred with the native idiom.

The growth of the classical system of harmony, modulation and large-scale forms was at first antipathetic to the Scots. An aesthetic movement in the eighteenth century outlined its objections and was paralleled by an increasing interest in collecting and preserving traditional music: but in the nineteenth and early twentieth century a group of Scottish composers succeeded in mastering this expanding harmonic landscape while remaining true to their native instincts and acting as seminal figures in the rebirth of classical music in Britain as a whole. The twentieth century has witnessed the expansion of this influence to such an extent that a conscious movement to protect, sustain and revive the native styles, again developed and took firm root. At the same time a considerable amount of musical talent was drawn to the American-influenced pop and rock music, as well as to jazz; and in these areas Scots have made notable contributions, on occasion identifying their musical nationality within the broader international idiom.

The country at present sustains an almost bewildering diversity of musical enterprise in which many different idioms are cross-fertilising. Traditional musicians are beginning to make an impact on performance styles of medieval and renaissance music. Classical composers are working in close community with the tradition as well as with jazz and rock musicians. Electronic music studios are paralleled by the reconstruction and revival of early types of bagpipe, harp and horn; and a number of distinguished composers are able to sustain themselves in their own country where earlier generations were obliged to emigrate.

SCOTTISH IDIOM

Despite this variety, there is still a readily identifiable Scottish style of music, by no means confined to bagpipes or fiddles and accordions, but influencing music in every conceivable genre. A preference for certain types of gapped scale; a predilection for melodic and harmonic patterns based on chords a tone apart and known as the 'double tonic'; a use of dotted rhythms, especially the 'Scotch snap'; a remarkable use of complex embellishment in bagpipe music and in Gaelic singing which has influenced other media: these are the more obvious indicators. But there are many other qualities less easy to define but adding to the variety of idiom available. The running quavers of a reel; certain unorthodox patterns of breaking up chords; characteristic forms of chorus and refrain songs, often work-related; a contrast between songs and ballads of remarkable vocal range (frequently employing octave leaps), and Fenian lays and protective chants and lullabies of narrow compass. To these may be added a variety of performance styles too complex to enter into here, but particularly associated with traditional music and varying markedly with the geography of the country.

INSTITUTIONS

The main musical institutions include the Royal Scottish Academy of Music and Drama, and two university music faculties and two specialist music schools at Edinburgh and Glasgow. Music is taught in schools but has only recently offered courses and examinations in Scottish music. Peripatetic instrumental teachers provide instruction in many schools in both classical and traditional styles. The School of Scottish Studies in Edinburgh includes traditional music in its archives, teaching and research; and the Scottish Music Information Centre in Glasgow provides library, archive, reproduction and information services covering the entire history of Scottish music. Performing institutions include Scottish Opera, Scottish Ballet, the Royal Scottish National Orchestra, the BBC Scottish Symphony Orchestra, the Scottish Chamber Orchestra, and a number of specialist ensembles. Funding for all these institutions comes from a variety of sources of which the principal one is the Scottish Arts Council, itself funded (from 1 April 1994) by the Scottish Office.

There are many musical societies, ranging from large-scale choral societies to local music clubs. Specific instruments and styles are catered for by such as the Piobaireachd, Clarsach, and fiddle societies, and the Traditional Music Association. Festivals with a strong or exclusively musical content range from the Edinburgh International Festival, the Glasgow Mayfest, and the Perth Festival; to jazz and folk festivals throughout the country, including Gaelic 'mods', both local and national, and piping and other events devoted to competitive performance.

OLDEST INSTRUMENTS

Possibly the oldest surviving musical instruments in Scotland are the ringing rocks, some of which are credited with antiquity by tradition, and have markings which may be very ancient. However, it is impossible to date the markings securely, so the honour of antiquity goes to a human artefact – a fragment of a cast bronze side-blown horn, dating from the eighth century BC and similar to many such horns found in Ireland, both side and end-blown, ritually 'drowned' with bronze rattles. The tone of these horns is rich and powerful, but they do not readily overblow and their mouthpieces are best adapted to circular breathing and to performance styles close to that of the didgeridoo, in the case of the end-blown horns; and the ivory horns of Africa, in the case of the side-blown horns.

The Caprington horn, also made of cast bronze, is the next survivor and dates from sometime around the birth of Christ, its nearest equivalents being Continental Celtic.

Its integrally cast mouthpiece is 'choked' and this encourages rapid tonguing and articulation, well suited to an instrument almost certainly used for signalling by Celtic cavalrymen.

Finest by far of these instruments is, however, the carnyx. Known throughout Celtic Europe, this magnificent beaten bronze trumpet was at least five feet long, was held vertically, and ended with a stylised realisation of a boar's head, issuing the sound from a good ten feet above the ground. The most important and complete surviving part of a carnyx comes from north-east Scotland and shows distinctive local design elements. It consists of the head, superbly realised in repoussé work with enamelled eyes, and (with the hinged jaw and sprung wooden tongue) acting as a sound modifier and acoustic chamber at the 'bell' end of the instrument. A recent reconstruction shows that this instrument was as powerful as a modern trombone and can produce a number of partials, capable of a rounded beauty of sound as well as of a brassy insistence. The instrument was played in consort and used in ritual, as well as carried by cavalrymen and sounded in anger.

From the eighth to the eleventh centuries AD the evidence for musical instruments depends virtually entirely on the Pictish stone carvings. These clearly indicate a variety of triangular-framed harps, some small and portable, others large enough to require the player to sit (usually on a zoomorphic chair). Straight and curved fore-pillars and various sizes of soundbox are also featured. The earliest of these carvings are also the earliest evidence for triangular-framed harps in the world, and the number and variety of the instruments and their gradual distribution from eastern Scotland to the south and west and thence to Wales and Ireland, strongly suggest that the introduction of the forepillar was a Pictish innovation. Other instruments appearing on the Pictish stones include triple pipes, a barrel drum, and short and long trumpets, depicted in battle and hunting scenes.

EARLY VOCAL MUSIC

Descriptions of a wide variety of vocal techniques (solo, choral and polyphonic) survive in early Gaelic manuscripts, but though attempts have been made to decipher some oghams and unorthodox knotwork designs as concealed musical notation, they have yet to find acceptance. However, a number of chants surviving in the oral tradition can be said to have their roots in pre-Christian culture. These include the 'Pi-li-li-liu', the refrain of a lament, based on the call of the redshank, and held in common with Irish tradition. A number of chants of protection, lullabies and worksongs of narrow compass and repetitive structure, though subsequently Christianised, are generally thought to reflect an earlier culture. Some of the meaningless vowel sounds, exclusively found in the choruses of Gaelic worksongs, are otherwise unknown in Gaelic and may reflect remnants of Pictish speech preferences.

The elaborate decorative singing and free heterophony of the Gaelic psalm singing finds its nearest parallels in Ethiopian Coptic chanting. The underlying melodies are post-Reformation, but the style of singing so transforms them that they are scarcely recognisable. It is widely accepted that this style is as old as Christianity itself, possibly related to early Coptic influences on manuscript illumination and liturgical practice in western Scotland and Northern Ireland.

THE FIRST MUSIC MANUSCRIPTS

The earliest period of religious and heroic music includes chants in Latin in honour of Celtic saints, as well as distinctive Scottish additions to the Notre Dame repertoire in the thirteenth century. The late thirteenth-century *Inchcolm Antiphoner*, with a number of unique chants in honour of St Columba, contains settings of texts in an elaborate early Celtic style, and in some cases both music and text may be reasonably assigned to the seventh or eighth centuries, the highly assonantal syllabic verse being structurally matched by the music. The Sprouston Breviary (also late thirteenth-century) contains a complete set of services for St Kentigern, but this material has yet to be fully analysed. The clarsach (or Celtic harp) was commonly used to accompany chanting, both Christian and heroic.

That the theory of music was well developed in Scotland is suggested by the works of Aaron Scotus (eleventh century) and Simon Tailler (thirteenth century); but as the titles of their various treatises are all that survive, we can only guess at their influence.

The earliest Scottish manuscript with polyphonic music is the famous mid-thirteenth-century *St Andrews Music Book* (known to scholars as 'W1'), compiled for and probably in St Andrews about the time of Bishop Bernham, whose partly noted pontifical survives in Paris. While the bulk of the *St Andrews Music Book* contains some of the earliest evidence of the music of the late twelfth-century school of Notre Dame, the ends of the fascicles, and the whole of the eleventh fascicle, have additional material, mostly unique and, in some cases, with unique cantus firmi. This music includes some of the most elaborately decorative solo tropes ever written, as well as a number of beautiful two-part tropes which display distinctive melodic and harmonic features, with a tendency to greater acceptance of the major third – a characteristic thought to typify early Northern European polyphony and exemplified by the famous *Hymn to St Magnus*, probably composed in Orkney some time after the martyrdom of St Magnus in the twelfth century.

While most of the *St Andrews Music Book* is devoted to two-part music, there are a number of three-part items, and the Arbroath fragments (W3) indicate that three-part singing was well developed in Scotland in the thirteenth century.

THE AGE OF THE BARDS

The early medieval period was, from the evidence of literature, land grants and other documents, rich in secular music, of which some survives in the oral tradition. The Fenian lays of the Gaelic culture were still sung in this century, though probably in a far less formal manner than their originals. Archive recordings and late eighteenth-century manuscripts and commentaries indicate styles varying from relatively monotonous intoning influenced strongly by speech rhythms, to more obviously melodically and rhythmically structured presentation. Early seventeenth-century transcriptions of clarsach (Celtic harp) music for lute, combined with eighteenth-century publications and manuscripts of music for the clarsach, give some idea of the simple harmonic style of accompaniment as well as the more elaborate variations which were purely instrumental; but the evidence is scanty and, judging by the medieval descriptions of harp-playing among the Celts, does little justice to the highly developed skills of the

23. *The Queen Mary Harp, c.1450. West Highland, hornbeam. Said
to have belonged to Mary, Queen of Scots. (*National Museums of
Scotland*)*

musicians, passed down through centuries from father to son – skills which entitled
them to hereditary lands, often adjacent to those held by bards and, later, by pipers.
Two beautifully made clarsachs survive from the fifteenth century, both probably
strung with metal and plucked with the fingernails, though gut and horsehair-strung
harps plucked with the flesh were equally common.

The medieval ballads sung in Scots have survived in profusion. These seem to have
passed freely between Court and commoner and in this century have been retrieved
mostly from the vast repertoire of the travelling people, whose singing styles may well
reflect an unbroken tradition of performance. The more declamatory epics and ballads
in both Gaelic and Scots often involve octave laps and require wide-ranging voices.

Apart from the exquisite sequence composed in the late thirteenth century for the
wedding of Margaret of Scotland to Eric II of Norway, which bestrides the sacred and
secular divide, we have two remarkable secular partsongs from the late medieval
period; the medley *Trip and Go, Hey* and *The Pleugh Sang* – a three-part work sung

and acted out at the annual plough festivals and the only surviving music for what was once a widespread European folk custom. A lovely Christmas medley, *All Sons Of Adam*, is also late medieval in character.

THE RENAISSANCE

The documentary evidence for music associated with the Scottish Court culminates in a small but highly distinguished body of sacred and secular music from the early sixteenth and seventeenth centuries. The chief figures are Robert Carver, Robert Johnston and David Peebles for sacred music; and William Kinloch and Tobias Hume for secular music: but there are many anonymous works of distinction, particularly in French-influenced partsongs. The Scottish lute repertoire of this period is remarkable for its beauty and simplicity.

Sacred Music: No fifteenth-century sacred music survives (unless Walter Frye is proven to be a Scot, or the compositions of James I are eventually discovered), but the quality of the music in the *Carver Choirbook* and the Thomas Wode partbooks (the main sources for the sacred music of the sixteenth century) and the evidence of provision for music in the cathedrals, abbeys and collegiate churches, suggest that high standards must have been maintained. Besides Carver's own music and a number of anonymous works, the *Carver Choirbook* contains music of the Eton Choir School and a mass by Dufay, and Carver's own music has absorbed both English and Flemish styles. The variety of his five masses and two motets, the virtuosity of his vocal writing, and the depth of feeling (especially in the great nineteen-part motet *O Bone Jesu* and the five-part *Fera Pessima* Mass) exhibit the hand of a master. Carver (?1485–post-1568) uses elaborate and distinctive ornaments (see the *Missa L'Homme Armee*), contrasted with passages of imitation or of vast chordal effects often employing a technique similar to that of the 'double tonic' of Scottish tradition, notably in the great ten-part mass *Dum Sacrum Mysterium*. His harmonic daring takes him into remote 'keys' (the motet *Gaude Flore* is a good example) and he enjoys the effect of passing dissonances, as well as exploring a wide variety of texture. While it is thought that Carver's music was primarily composed for the Chapel Royal choir, it is clear that there were many other choirs of high standard in the various Sang Schules, notably Dunkeld, Glasgow, Aberdeen and St Andrews.

More modest in his requirements, smoother in his vocal lines and harmonies, but subtle, refined and seductive in his music, is Robert Johnston (*c*.1500–*c*.1560), who fled to England before the Reformation, accused of heresy. His style reflects a gradual move towards simplicity in both word-setting (English as well as Latin) and part writing, but he did not disavow his earlier High Renaissance compositions. David Peebles displays a similarly sensitive use of close imitation, struggling to retain a sophisticated style against the backdrop of Reformation ideals which demanded increasing simplicity, notably in Robert Richardson's proposed reforms of the Augustinians (Paris 1530), though *The Art Of Musick* (a Scottish treatise from the 1580s) is less rigid and strives to retain something of pre-Reformation complexity, being in places decidedly arcane.

However, the Reformation (finally secured in 1560) did great damage to music in general, and the Union of the Crowns of Scotland and England under James VI and I in 1603 had a serious effect on secular music, as the Royal Court moved south to London.

Secular Music: The music of the Stewart courts from the fifteenth to the sixteenth centuries was rich and varied. Court trumpeters (both Italian and Scottish) and drummers (Scottish, Swiss and Moorish) provided the ceremonial music: clarsachs and harps and voices offered aristocratic music from the Gaelic culture (James IV spoke Gaelic, played the clarsach and was an accomplished all-round musician), and Highland bagpipes were in use for military purposes (and probably for Salutes and Laments) by the late fifteenth century. Professional violers, lutenists and shawm players were also on the regular pay-roll, and innumerable visiting musicians were regularly patronised by the Court which, on one occasion, records payments to over sixty musicians and which regularly maintained twenty to thirty liveried musicians. Organs and other keyboard instruments were carried about as the Court toured the country, and fiddlers and singers were often rewarded for special performances such as that of the great epic *Greysteil*, sung to James IV.

A number of exquisite partsongs and dances (often French-influenced) survive from this period, culminating in the vocal works of Scott and others in their settings of Montgomery and other Scottish poets. Many of these songs were danced to, either when sung or in arrangements for instrumental consorts. The musical traffic with France was two-way. The personal bodyguard of the French monarchs had been Scottish from the time of Joan of Arc, and the famous march tune used by Burns for *Scots Wha Hae Wi Wallace Bled* is still played by the French army, as it is reputed to have been when Joan of Arc entered Orleans, whose gates were opened to her by its

24. *Musicians in part of the painted ceiling of Crathes Castle, Aberdeenshire, c.1599.*
(National Trust for Scotland)

Scottish bishop, Kirkpatrick. Scottish versions of the branle were also known in France, where, according to Arbeau, there appear to have been Scottish musicians to perform them, and the pavan and galliard were cultivated in Scotland alongside the jig which may be of native origin.

However, the late sixteenth-century keyboard music of William Kinloch (fl.1585), James Lauder and Duncan Burnett is more closely allied to the great English keyboard masters such as Byrd and Morley. Indeed, Kinloch's superb Pasmessour and Quadran Pavans with their Galliards, are on a scale and ambition to vie with Byrd, and his astonishing *Battel of Pavie* outdoes Byrd's more fragmentary *Battel*. Kinloch's music covers a wide range of mood and technique, from exuberant bravura to growling menace. His style is marked by clarity of line and form, in which he occasionally incorporates passages of contrapuntal subtlety, though there is no vocal or sacred influence such as is found in Byrd. Kinloch's *Ground* (based on the English *Huntis Up*) is another powerful work, and his *Fantasie* is a skittish piece which appears to have been conceived for a two-manual instrument. By comparison, the works attributed to Burnett are more sombre and thoughtful, closer in mood to Lauder's outstanding *Golden Pavan*, his sole surviving work.

We rely for all the above on a mere handful of manuscripts, but the dearth of purely instrumental music from the late sixteenth century cannot truly reflect the reality. When Tobias Hume (c.1569–1645) arrived in England shortly after the Union of the Crowns, he was ready to publish (in 1605 and 1607) his adventurous and accomplished compositions for bass viol and for mixed consort. Previously thought of as English, he first appears described as a 'Scottish musician' in the papers of Queen Anne, wife of James VI and I. Such is the quality and technical brilliance of Hume's finest works (notably the great Pavans, his *Lamentations* and the much-loved *Cease Leaden Slumbers*) that he must have developed his skills over a considerable period. It is unlikely he would have been able to do more than nurture them during his previous years as a mercenary on the Continent, so we must look to Scotland as the source of his unprecedented development of the bass viol as an harmonic as well as melodic instrument, possibly tutored by the Hudson family of violers whom James VI had earlier imported from England.

The lute manuscripts of the early seventeenth century provide us with a repertoire which is frequently unequivocally Scottish. Pentatonic tunes, simply harmonised, but subtle and expressive, abound. Many of these are almost certainly transcriptions from the clarsach repertoire, especially tunes such as *Give Me Your Hand* and others in the flexibly-phrased genre known as *Port*. Later in the seventeenth century this repertoire of tunes tends to develop additional sections, and the Balcarres Lute Book of the late seventeenth century also includes a large body of French lute music.

THE SEVENTEENTH CENTURY

Religious music made a steady decline following the Reformation, despite the publication of fine psalm tunes, some of them given a cantus firmus treatment, others 'in reports' in which each phrase of the psalm started with imitative part writing. This decline continued into the eighteenth century, by which time the native predilection for embellishment and the slow nasal style of singing had become established. In the Gaelic community this style has survived in the form of free heterophony with powerful and inspiring effect (see above), but it did not suit the greater regularity of the psalms in Scots, and gradually choir masters (and the return of the organ to many of the churches from which the Reformation had evicted it) re-established more conventional congregational and choir singing.

The absence of Court music and Church music was, however, balanced by a steady growth of material from the Gaelic and Scots traditions. The Highland bagpipes established themselves with a sophisticated music (piobaireachd) uniquely adapted to their needs, involving sets of variations of increasing complexity. Pipers were given grants of land by chieftains to whom they were attached, and their skills were passed down from father to son, notably among the McCrimmons, MacKays and MacArthurs. The clarsach still maintained its place in aristocratic Gaelic society, and Gaelic singing continued with a growing repertoire in new genres influenced by metrical rather than syllabic verse. Satire and panegyric still featured and older material in the form of heroic lays and working songs survived alongside the new material. The complex relationship between vocal music and the bagpipe repertoire (which used a sung and written syllabic notation known as canntaireachd) culminated in the composition of extended poems designed to be sung to specific piobaireachd, requiring, and obtaining, remarkable vocal expertise. At the same time, the violin began a successful challenge for a place in this repertoire, imitating piobaireachd and clarsach variation forms and establishing itself as the instrument most used for dance, both in jig and in the newly developing Scottish dance forms of reel and strathspey.

Although it is during the seventeenth century that the Highland bagpipes appear to have come into their own, it should be emphasised that there were many different kinds of bagpipe in use in Scotland well into the eighteenth century, and now revived in the late twentieth century, and these employed a wide repertoire of lyric and dance tunes as well as employing variation techniques. The development of Scottish song, alongside the continuing and ever-expanding ballad repertoire, must have been taking place at this time, for in the early eighteenth century a substantial body of songs began to be published (see below); but as far as classical music was concerned, the difficulty of foreign travel occasioned by religious wars at home and abroad, left a barren field until the emergence of two remarkable men – John Abell of Aberdeen (c.1650–c.1724) and John Clerk of Penicuik (1676–1753), both of whom travelled extensively, in particular to Italy.

Abell is chiefly remembered for his remarkable male soprano voice, his extravagant lifestyle and mixed fortunes. A Roman Catholic, in 1688 he was forced to leave his position of high favour in the English Chapel Royal. He busked his way round Europe, playing the lute and singing to various monarchs, including William of Orange into whose favours Abell found a way by dedicating a number of his compositions to the king, including a splendid but obsequious cantata, celebrating the defeat of the Stewart and Roman Catholic cause at the Battle of the Boyne! While something of the plain vigour of Purcell can be heard in this music, there is an exuberance in the vocal writing and a melodic gift which is Abell's own. An extended work probably composed by Abell for the celebration of Queen Anne's birthday in Dublin (where he was composer to the Viceroy in the early eighteenth century), that shows Abell at his most sophisticated. Italian influences predominate and he makes effective use of contrasted scoring, using seven solo voices, flutes, oboes, recorders, lutes and bassoon as well as strings (Abell was also an accomplished violinist).

Though Clerk was later to visit England, his musical background is Scottish,

25. *A concert party in the home of Kenneth Mackenzie, Lord Fortrose, in Naples, 1770. Painted by Pietro Fabris (fl. 1768–78). The viola player on the left is Sir William Hamilton, the British envoy, and the two keyboard players are Wolfgang Amadeus Mozart and his father, Leopold. The picture, with its evidence of interest in literature, classical archaeology and painting, as well as music, suggests the width of taste of at least some of the Scots who visited Italy on the Grand Tour in the eighteenth century. (*Scottish National Portrait Gallery*)*

Dutch and Italian. His contribution as a composer (he was a leading lawyer, architect, landscape gardener and financier) is small but outstanding. The Scottish idiom is only noticeable in his *Sonata for Violin*; his other works consisting of two sacred and three secular cantatas, of which three are settings of Latin texts especially composed by his friend, the Dutch physician, Hermann Booerhaave.

Having studied in Leyden with Kremberg and von Zumbach, he travelled to Vienna but, dissatisfied with musical standards outside the Court, moved to Rome where he became a composition pupil of Corelli's. Corelli must have thought highly of him, for he played at the première of Clerk's only Italian cantata, *Odo Di Mesto Intorno* at Frascati. The work was composed for the departure of Lord Tavistock, and combines sorrow at leave-taking with anticipation of nuptial joys, the cantata being clearly intended to sweeten his lordship's marriage-bed. The sophisticated variety of emotions, ranging from sorrow through mock-strife to unequivocal sensuality, is superbly realised in Clerk's handling of the voice. The sombre maturity of outlook in *Eheu Eheu*, a sacred cantata confronting illness and death; and the mock agony of *Dic Mihi Saeve Puer* (a complaint to Cupid) display the subtleties of Clerk's refined understanding of mood. The latter cantata also exhibits Clerk's great interest in form, all the thematic material being developed from one germ motif. His five-part sacred cantata still awaits revival.

THE ENLIGHTENMENT

The Union of the Parliaments of Scotland and England in 1707 increased the gravitational pull of London still further, and Scottish musicians such as James Oswald (1710–69) and Robert Bremner (c.1713–89) moved their publishing businesses south, Oswald rising to be chamber composer to George III. William McGibbon (c.1690–1756) studied in London and the Earl of Kelly (1732–81) was also an influential figure in the English capital – but all four retained close ties with Scotland (McGibbon worked in Edinburgh) and in much of their music displayed distinctive Scottish characteristics. McGibbon on the one hand wrote sonatas in imitation of Corelli, and on the other published arrangements of Scottish airs.

The growth in popularity of the violin at all levels of society and in all parts of the country, created a musical tension in which unique forms were devised to accommodate Scottish and Italian styles in the one piece – variation sonatas, by McLean and Monro in particular; remarkable piobaireachd imitations for unaccompanied violin; and arrangements. A high point, in terms of dance music and slow airs, was reached in the work of the Gow family (late eighteenth to early nineteenth centuries) and of William Marshall (nineteenth century). The Gows and Marshall were essentially traditional musicians who found favour with the aristocracy, but the scale of their work is restricted by the genres they used, which include brilliant handling of the Scottish dance forms of reel and strathspey.

The music of James Oswald (who started his career as a dancing master and teacher of cello and violin) is also small scale. But Oswald created massive structures by linking his compositions. His *Airs For The Seasons* consists of ninety-six sonatas, grouped in two sets of twelve for each season, each sonata named after a different plant, and frequently evoking its physical, medical or mythological characteristics. His *Colin's Kisses*, also composed in the 1740s, probably constitutes the first true song-cycle, and his sets of Divertimenti and Lessons for English guitar cultivate a naive charm that is counterbalanced by the biting wit of his satirical cantatas and songs, and the deliberately old-fashioned solemnity of his Masonic music, published as early as 1742. Oswald's skill in blending Scottish and Italian styles is underpinned by his active melodic bass lines (he was a cellist), and by his overall melodic invention which is derived from the beauty of the line rather than by manipulating patterns of scale and arpeggio.

A fellow Freemason, but of aristocratic background, was the sixth Earl of Kelly, whose brilliant symphonies and sonatas were the first to bring the Mannheim style to the British Isles. Kelly studied under the elder Stamitz and his music is characterised by rhythmic energy and dynamic variety, though he is capable of lyrical and thoughtful passages and was also a master of the minuet form, of which he wrote several, particularly those heard at the *fête-champêtre* at The Oaks in Epsom in 1774.

Like McGibbon, Kelly was an outstanding violinist, but his writing for wind instruments is adventurous for the time. The beautiful concert aria, *Death is Now My only Treasure*, anticipates Mozart in its combination of lyric beauty and Masonic philosophy.

In the nation as a whole, however, there was resistance to the new sophisticated harmonic language developing in Europe and demanding use of modulation based on firmly established keys. This development was antipathetic to the national tradition, whether Scots or Gaelic, and a musical aesthetic and theory was evolved to justify these national instincts, Baillie, Mollinson and Tytler all writing in favour of what they conceived to be the ideal of beauty which resided in the native air.

This aesthetic was supported by the gathering of traditional music for publication dating from the early eighteenth century, although it is only a natural continuation of the manuscript tradition of the previous century. Thomson, Ramsay, Oswald, Burns and Johnson and many others published major collections, and by the end of the eighteenth century the popularity of Scottish music and culture in general was spreading beyond the amused curiosity of the English to the wild enthusiasm of the Continent. MacPherson, Burns, Scott and Byron had a profound influence on the development of the Romantic movement: but though Haydn, Beethoven, Pleyel, Kozeluth and Weber all harmonised Scottish songs, adding introductions and codas, for the enterprising publisher, George Thomson, not one of them was able to make a truly convincing marriage of traditional and classical idioms. Indeed, their efforts compare mostly unfavourably with those of Oswald before them.

However, the very traditions which were so romanticised were themselves under threat. The aftermath of the 1745 Rising left the Highlands devastated, and the break-up of the clan system brought to a virtual end the great aristocratic musical traditions of the Gaelic-speaking community. The clarsach died out; the more arcane forms of bardic eulogy were lost for ever; and the bagpipes were absorbed into the military system where their tradition fortunately survived, taking on a new role in providing dance music (ceol beg), but, it is thought, losing much of the creative spontaneity which would have been an integral part of performing piobaireachd. An evangelical revival gave sustenance to the richly embellished style of singing in Gaelic, but in other parts of the country it found later expression in gospel-hall hymnology, frequently accompanied by accordion and influenced by American as well as Scottish idioms.

Military music meanwhile evolved from sixteenth-century trumpets, fife and drum or solo bagpipes, to pipe bands in which the drummers became almost wholly integrated, developing skills which in the twentieth century were combined with renewed Swiss influence to produce standards of unparalleled virtuosity. The international spread of Scottish styles of music relates closely to the involvement of Scots troops in the building of the British Empire, as well as to the vast movement of people to North America and the Antipodes during the Highland Clearances.

The Highland Clearances and the development of new farming techniques led to many songs of sorrow and regret on the one hand, and to a new and lively kind of communal music-making in the form of 'bothy bands' on the other. In these the accordion joined the fiddle, bagpipes and voice, along with jew's harp, whistle, and other instruments. Highland and Lowland instruments and styles met in these bands, which were popular for dances. Their natural successors are the dance, ceilidh and folk groups of today.

The study of folklore by Frazer and Laing, and the continuing publication of annotated Scots songs by such as Motherwell and Greig-Duncan, was paralleled by first publications of Gaelic music and song by Daniel Dow, Simon Fraser, the MacDonald brothers, Patrick Macdonald, Campbell and others.

THE NINETEENTH CENTURY

As far as classical music was concerned, there was a hiatus. The Broadwood family were Scottish and played a major role in the development of the pianoforte, but the only significant works composed by Scots for that instrument over a period of one hundred years were by John Thomson and John Donaldson, the only two Scots ever to hold the chair of music in Edinburgh founded by the flautist and composer, General John Reid in 1840.

Thomson (1805–41) was a composer of outstanding gifts. His Weberesque overture *Hermann* is dramatic and brooding, as is the G minor *Piano Trio*; whereas the warm intimacy of the five-part glee *When Whispering Winds*, and the subtle refinement of the *Drei Lieder* (Leipzig 1838) display a completely different side to his musical character. His compositions were admired by his younger contemporary, Mendelssohn, but his two operas, the flute concerto and a number of other important works, remain unperformed in modern times. He died tragically young after holding the chair at Edinburgh for less than a year.

Alexander MacKenzie (1847–1935) could fairly be described as the father of British music. His influence as composer, conductor, administrator and teacher was seminal. He reorganised the Royal Academy of Music of which he was principal for thirty-six years (succeeded by John Blackwood McEwen); he established the Associated Board exam system; and, above all, he was an outstanding composer. His roots in Scottish traditional music combined with his early experience in Germany (where he was a professional violinist at the age of eleven) gave his style a breadth insufficiently appreciated today. His realisation of Scottish aesthetic ideals – wit and sentiment without pretension – was achieved with the huge forces of the late nineteenth century. The *Scottish Concerto* (premièred by Paderewski) and the *Violin Concerto* and *Pibroch Suite* (both composed for Sarasate) are fine examples of his achievements as an early promoter of musical nationalism; but he was no slave to this ideal, and his beautiful *Piano Quartet* and the ravishing sensuality of his great oratorio *The Rose Of Sharon*, have no hint of Scotland in them, but are wholly his own.

MacKenzie's output was considerable and includes several operas and oratorios, and a number of outstanding overtures of which *Britannia* is a particularly witty example. The best of his songs are very fine and the *Benedictus*, whether in its original form for violin and piano or arranged for small orchestra, is one of the loveliest works of the period, its extended lyrical but intense melodic line being matched by perfectly judged harmonic textures. His music deserves far wider attention, as does that of his natural successor, Hamish MacCunn (1868–1916), whose opera *Jeannie Deans* is a work of major significance.

Besides a number of fine overtures of which *Land Of The Mountain And The Flood* is the favourite, MacCunn composed several oratorios and dramatic cantatas; and from over 115 songs, there are many of beauty and distinction. MacCunn continued MacKenzie's introduction of Scottish idioms into works for the concert hall and was supported by William Wallace and Learmond Drysdale and succeeded by McEwen. Pressures of overwork on MacKenzie, MacCunn and McEwen (from which all three fell seriously ill) reflect the enormous responsibilities they undertook in reviving British music, MacKenzie and McEwen setting the Royal Academy of Music on its feet and MacCunn establishing opera on a regular basis, and McEwen working for the recognition and support of contemporary British composers.

At this time a number of fine Scottish performers began to find a place on the international stage. Amongst these were Frederick Lamond (1868–1948) – a pupil of Liszt and noted interpreter of Beethoven's piano works as well as a composer – and Mary Garden (1874–1967) who created the part of Melisande for Debussy's opera *Pelléas et Mélisande* and later became director of the Chicago Grand Opera. The tenor

Joseph Hislop was another leading singer, and Scotland might reasonably claim credit for Helen Porter Mitchell whose parents were both born and bred in Scotland, but who changed her name to Nellie Melba. Another Scottish singer who toured the world with considerable success was Marjorie Kennedy-Fraser (1857–1930). She was primarily an arranger of Gaelic song of skill, daring and imagination, and she has been unjustly castigated for this by scholars who confuse her publications and performances with her secondary work as a collector in which area she was one of the very first to make live recordings.

In a completely different sphere, but selling as many records as Melba, was the music-hall comedian and singer, Harry Lauder (1870–1950), who created a tartan image which has been bequeathed upon Scotland as something of a mixed blessing. He is paralleled by James Scott Skinner on the violin, though Skinner's blend of Scottish dance idiom, classical display and music-hall sentimentality is altogether more serious in intent and effect. However, this period at the turn of the century saw the rise of the modern dance band and the emergence of the accordion in preference to the fiddle,

THE TWENTIETH CENTURY

Whereas the main musical influences on MacKenzie, MacCunn and Wallace were Scottish and Germanic, McEwen's are Scottish and French. Some of his best works were written in Biscay and include the *Biscay Quartet*, and the remarkable group of piano pieces *On Southern Hills* show him to be a master of impressionism. His orchestral works have only recently been recorded and include the *Solway Symphony* and three fine *Border Ballads* of which *Grey Galloway* is best known. Here, too, the influence of impressionism is felt, with extensive use of whole-tone scales and colouristic harmonies and scoring. McEwen's major contribution is, however, to chamber music, particularly in his fifteen string quartets, of which *Biscay* and the *B Minor Quartet* are outstanding. His style, in the chamber works, is subtle and refined, but deeply rewarding for those who are prepared to do without drama.

In the world of song, the major contribution of F.G. Scott, particularly in his inspired settings of MacDiarmid, has been one of the most vital elements in the continuing tradition of national song. Scott (1880–1958) managed to bring together adventurous harmony, folk-like melody and a deep understanding of the poetry he set. Less successful but more ambitious in bringing traditional Scottish and twentieth-century idioms together was Erik Chisholm, whose efforts on behalf of new music brought leading composers such as Bartók to Scotland.

Following the Second World War, a new generation of composers wrestled with the twentieth century and serial technique in particular. Of these, Iain Hamilton and Thea Musgrave were the most radical and both emigrated to the USA and then to England. Hamilton has made his name chiefly through his operas, notably *The Catiline Conspiracy*, whereas Musgrave's *Horn Concerto* and *Clarinet Concerto* are good indicators of her skill in bringing drama into her concert works. Hamilton's style has at times been uncompromising and severe, but both he and Musgrave have lyrical gifts and hankerings after the Scottish idiom which have surfaced more than occasionally.

Ronald Stevenson and Thomas Wilson, on the other hand, have both chosen to live and work in Scotland. Stevenson is an eclectic with remarkable gifts and daring. His *Passacaglia on DSCH* is not only the longest piano composition in existence, but also an emotional and pianistic *tour de force* based entirely on a myriad of variations on a four-note motif. Wilson is, by comparison, more restrained and intellectual, the taut energies and lyrical intensities of his music being particularly impressive in the *Piano Concerto* as well as in a number of powerful religious works.

Newer generations have brought about yet another re-emergence of a Scottish idiom – Martin Dalby, Edward McGuire, John Geddes, William Sweeney, James MacMillan and Judith Weir all display a remarkable confidence in bringing international and Scottish idioms into contact with each other in a world in which stylistic norms are open to constant questioning. At the same time, the founding of the School of Scottish Studies, along with political and cultural motivation for the folk revival, has stimulated a vast outpouring of music in traditional styles, some directly derived from oral tradition or archive recordings, some marrying traditional folk material with contemporary idioms including those imported from North America. In all of this, a growing knowledge of the history of Scottish music, and access to scores and recordings, is of fundamental importance. Much of the material discussed above has only recently been brought to light, and it will be interesting to see whether a broader understanding of what it has meant to be a Scottish musician over the centuries has any effect on the future.

26. *James MacMillan (1959–   ). The programme of the 1993 Edinburgh International Festival included eighteen of his works, of which four were premières, a recognition never previously accorded to a living composer. (*Edinburgh International Festival*)*

Books for Further Reading

A Kinnaird and K. Sanger, *The Tree of Strings* (1992)
John Purser, *Scotland's Music* (Edinburgh, 1992)
D. James Ross, *Musick Fyne* (Edinburgh, 1993)

For a full discography and bibliography, see Purser, *Scotland's Music*; much of the music contained in *Scotland's Music* can be found on Linn Records CKD 008, CKC 008 and CKH 008

Scottish Rock Music, 1955–93

STEWART CRUICKSHANK

'There are only two types of music: rock and roll'

ALEX HARVEY

For some, the roots of Scottish rock music began with Alex Harvey. For others, Scottish rock music was and is epitomised by Alex Harvey. The truth, of course, is that there is no such thing as indigenous rock music in Scotland. Its beginnings lie in the pre-Harvey era, its influences are many and varied, the diversity of styles and approach infinite and the number of musicians who have contributed to its history incalculable. The roots of rock in Scotland lie in the ballrooms and folk clubs of the 1950s where American country, bluegrass, jazz and rhythm 'n' blues styles began to replace traditional Scottish music.

The influence of American roots music first crossed over into the mainstream via Glasgow-born Lonnie Donegan, whose skiffle group reached the Top Ten in 1956 with *Rock Island Line*. Donegan had recorded the song when he was a member of Chris Barber's Jazz Band. It had originally been attributed to Huddie Leadbetter (Leadbelly), the great black American folk artist who was discovered in a state penitentiary by song archivists John and Alan Lomax. Donegan later went on to become the leading light of the skiffle boom of the mid-1950s, though his career remained firmly based in London.

North of the border, groups of young Glaswegians increasingly began to spend their weekends camping on the banks of Loch Lomond. But taking the high road could not have been further from their minds. Instead they'd take their guitars and strum the songs of Woody Guthrie, Ramblin' Jack Elliot and Jimmie Rodgers. These young 'rogues of the road' included Bill Patrick, Jimmy Grimes and Alex Harvey. They would later play together in The Alex Harvey Big Soul Band and influence several generations of rock musicians.

Scotland was at first slow to accept the intrusion of rock music into the dancehalls, although the first professional rock 'n' roll band in Britain came from Glasgow. The Ricky Barnes All-Stars became regulars on the circuit, playing everywhere from village hops to Plazas and Locarnos. But in the main, the rise in rock's popularity began in rural centres. It was not uncommon for farmers in tackety boots to invade the stage at Strathpeffer and The Beatles made their first solo Scottish appearance in Elgin in 1963. Elgin's pre-eminence on the music map owed itself to Albert Bonici, concert promoter and owner of The Two Red Shoes. This historic venue is long closed, but in its day virtually every prominent British beat group appeared on its stage, inspiring local groups like Buckie's Johnny and The Copycats to make their own recordings.

Like The Beatles' native Liverpool, Glasgow became steeped in the transatlantic crossing of musical styles. In the early 1960s both cities were still major ports. Merchant sailors regularly arrived in Glasgow with the latest rhythm 'n' blues, rockabilly and Tamla Motown imports. Motown was a black music label from Detroit and its impact on young Scotland lasts to this day. Scottish beat groups like The Poets, The Beatstalkers, The Athenians and The Pathfinders specialised in covers of US r'n'b hits. Each group had its own screaming fans and a healthy regional scene developed throughout Scotland. Edinburgh had The Boston Dexters, Glasgow Dean Ford and The Gaylords, Aberdeen The Misfits, Dundee The Poor Souls, Dunfermline The Red Hawkes and Bathgate The Golden Crusaders.

Lulu and The Luvvers were the first to hit the charts – their cover of The Isley Brothers' 'Shout' was so raw that many fans thought they were an American band. The Poets from Glasgow were signed by Rolling Stones manager Andrew Loog Oldham and scored a ground-breaking hit in 1964 with 'Now We're Thru', an eerie self-penned ballad which signalled an avalanche of other Scots groups who would record their own material. The Poets' recordings are among the most innovative of their era and today are highly prized by music historians the world over.

The most legendary Scottish rock innovator of them all was Alex Harvey. He was among the first musicians to go to Hamburg in the late 1950s, his Big Soul Band became a top attraction in the 1960s and in the 1970s he formed The Sensational Alex Harvey Band. If ever a band lived up to their chosen name, SAHB were the one. Their mix of mime, vaudeville, hard rock, interpretations of Jacques Brel songs and use of the Scottish vernacular was unique and distinctive and their shows at the Glasgow Apollo in 1975 are still regarded as a pinnacle of live performance.

At the end of the 1960s, the mood of rock music got heavier in every sense. This was post-Vietnam and in Britain youth rebellion had nowhere to go. Developments in Scotland were in keeping with international trends – the music got heavier, as in louder, the songs became longer and the lyrics became heavier too: music, indeed, had a message. The Pathfinders mutated into White Trash and recorded 'The Road to Nowhere' for the Beatles' Apple label. This nerve-juddering masterpiece was the embodiment of late 1960s rock – a long, slow introduction, doom-laden lyrics, crashing guitars and a cavernous keyboard sound. Other chosen names told a tale too – groups like Tear Gas, Human Beast and Writing On The Wall played venues like Edinburgh's Middle Earth North and Glasgow's Electric Garden. But this new direction in sound all but killed dancing dead, particularly in Glasgow where many of the traditional venues closed down.

In contrast to Glasgow, the dance scene was very much alive in 1970s' Dundee. The city had long had close affinity to Stax, Atlantic, Stateside and other soul music labels. The Top Ten Club, run by Andy Lothian, was the principal venue for many years, and by the mid-1970s, Dundee had earned a reputation as Scotland's Soul City.

The Average White Band were anything but average. This Dundonian hard funk band contained world-class musicians and, like Lulu a decade before them, America thought they were black. That myth was exploded when their instrumental 'Pick up the Pieces' rocketed to No. 1 throughout the USA.

International success followed for other Scottish rock bands. Nazareth, The Bay City Rollers and Frankie Miller were all hugely successful worldwide. For Edinburgh's Rollers, success didn't equate with happiness and their career perhaps says something about the Scottish character – fight the world when you're down and continue to fight it when you rule it. And for a brief time The Bay City Rollers did rule the pop world. Hits like 'Bye Bye Baby' and 'Keep on Dancin'' sold millions, riots erupted at their concerts and eventually it all came to a sorry end when they split up in Japan, where their fans wore black to signify a state of mourning.

In part, The Rollers' untimely demise was due to another new music phenomenon – punk rock. The punk explosion in London and New York was initially a major shift away from established rock values. It encouraged a do-it-yourself approach to music-making and was quick to spread to Scotland which was soon awash with punk, thrash and new wave groups.

The Rezillos, The Skids, The Scars, The Jolt, The Valves and Johnny and The Self Abusers all made rough, rowdy and frequently witty records which swapped musical expertise for raw energy. The Self Abusers immortalised Glasgow venue Saints And Sinners in their first single, which was also the first recording by Jim Kerr and Charlie Burchill who soon went on to form Simple Minds. Simple Minds are Scotland's most consistently successful rock band. They reached No. 1 in the USA with 'Don't You (Forget about Me)', sold three million copies of their 1989 album *Street Fighting Years*, appeared at Live Aid and, in 1993, were again at No. 1 in the UK with their compilation *Glittering Prize*. Until the early 1990s Simple Minds were managed by Bruce Findlay whose career runs like a thread through Scottish rock music in different guises – from record-shop owner to label manager to broadcaster.

Simple Minds' success paved the way for other Glasgow bands to follow and by 1985 Glasgow was the record companies' first port of call in their search for new talent. Wet Wet Wet, Texas, The Big Dish, Horse, Deacon Blue, Love And Money, Hue And Cry and many others from the Greater Glasgow area signed major recording contracts, all with varying degrees of success. In particular, Wet Wet Wet have sustained a successful and continually evolving career. Their admiration for soul and black American music mirrors that of their 1960s' counterparts, and in vocalist Marti Pellow, they have a singer who speaks in a Clydebank brogue but who sings in a US soul style.

In rock music, rules only exist to be broken. The Blue Nile from Glasgow are the exception which proves the rule. Unlike their early 1980s' contemporaries, they have few discernible influences and their approach to releasing music is outwith the usual music industry conventions. Since their first single 'I Love this Life' in 1980, they have issued barely a handful of others and only two albums. Both, however, are universally regarded as classics. *A Walk Across the Rooftops* (1985) and *Hats* (1989) are dark, brooding and perfectly crafted records which evoke rainy nights in neon-lit cities and secret meetings on street corners. Paul Buchanan's voice is soulful in a way which bears little resemblance to Marti Pellow or other devotees of rhythm 'n' blues.

The Blue Nile have for some time lived abroad. Other notable Scottish successes have chosen to leave their native towns and cities. Annie Lennox and The Shamen have careers which have little to do with Aberdeen. Britain's most successful independent record label, Creation, owned by Alan McGee, is run not in Glasgow but in London.

All of which poses a question – is it possible that a vibrant, self-sustaining Scottish rock industry could become a reality?

So far this has failed to happen. In the boom-or-bust economy of the music industry, the lack of a suitable infrastructure for rock music in Scotland, properly funded and integrated, is as serious a drawback as it is for classical music. There are indeed good rock bands, recording studios and organisations such as MIST (the Music In Scotland Trust), all of which provide support or funding to the Scottish rock community. In 1990 New Music World, a major week-long event combining concerts, seminars and workshops, was staged in Glasgow. In 1991 The Scottish Chart was established in which the Top Twenty reflected the taste of the Scottish buying public rather than, essentially, that of England. This increasing sophistication of the Scottish market can do nothing but good for the future emergence of bands and of opportunities for them to develop musical styles which are not dictated by other markets.

But there are no major Scottish-owned record labels and no Scottish-based distributors capable of handling both mainstream and specialist rock products, so most profits from publishing and recording still flow south – just as they did twenty-five years ago.

So what hope is there for the future? In 1993 there are some encouraging signs that Scottish bands can have success abroad and remain based in Scotland. Bellshill bands Teenage Fanclub and The BMX Bandits, Glasgow's Del Amitri, Celtic rock band Runrig and others all have careers on the ascendent. Alan Horne, who founded the legendary independent Postcard Records in the 1980s, is back in Glasgow and staging events. Regular Music and Dance Factory are two of Britain's most successful concert promoters. And long-established folk label Iona has recently launched the Iona Gold subsidiary by signing singer-songwriter Carol Laula. And, in 1994, Glasgow will become host to Sound City, a huge event encompassing all forms of Scottish rock music.

The Proclaimers, from Edinburgh, mourned the demise of traditional Scottish industries in their song 'Letter from America'. Until June 1993, it looked as though The Proclaimers' career had hit the skids – no significant new songs or records for five years. Then, out of the blue, '(I'm Gonna Be) 500 Miles' was issued on the soundtrack to the film box-office hit *Benny and Joon*. Within weeks, it was in the US Top Three and The Proclaimers had reactivated their career and realised a dream – to take songs written in Scotland, make them successful in America and, in a small way, reverse the flow of musical influences across the Atlantic, when emigrants to the New World took with them Scottish music to the American continent.

Books for Further Reading

Brian Hogg, *All That Ever Mattered: Scottish Rock Music From 1955* (London, 1993)
John Purser, *Scotland's Music* (Edinburgh, 1992)
Jim Wilkie, *Blue Suede Brogans* (Edinburgh, 1991)

Other useful sources of information include back issues of *Cut*, *TLN*, *The List*, *Edinburgh City Lynx* and *242 Showbeat*.

Dance

ROBBIE SHEPHERD

Fiddlers! your pins in temper fix
And roset weel your fiddlesticks;
But banish vile Italian tricks
Frae out your quorum;
Nor fortes wi' pianos mix –
Gie's Tullochgorum

(from 'Daft Days' by Robert Fergusson)

That's fair comment on the music and dance of the fervent Scot of the eighteenth century. The original song of 'Tullochgorum' was written by the Revd John Skinner, pastor of the Episcopal Church in Longside, near Peterhead, and that was the Reverend's protest, along with many a kinsman at the time, against the Continental influences increasingly coming in to the Scottish folk music and dance scene. The Italian influence then was finding favour with the upper classes and both Fergusson and Robert Burns leapt to the defence, in published poetry, of 'Scottish' music.

The same passion exists today, though for many it is a subconscious feeling of a need to do something when Scottish dance music is being played – it could be auld granny tapping her fingers at the table as she listens to the radio, it could be young Douglas boisterously swinging his way through an eightsome reel, perhaps it's wee winsome Wilma on the platform at a Highland Games executing her first pas-de-bas in public. More than likely it's from folk all over the far corners of the earth as thousands of enthusiasts meet for a dance under the auspices of the Royal Scottish Country Dance Society. Aye, even folk with two left feet (self-styled) can get that special inner feeling which the music and the dance excites in us. Take away our music and dance, and part of our heritage is gone. What was it that is oft quoted on the Scot? – 'The best way to dish

27. *Highland Wedding at Blair Atholl, 1780, by David Allan (1792–1867). The fiddler is Niel Gow.* (National Gallery of Scotland)

out punishment to an enemy who is Scottish is to nail his boot to the floor and make him listen to a Jimmy Shand record.'

But in spite of Skinner's protestations on 'Tullochgorum', our dance is and, especially at the time of that song, always has been, influenced by other countries. Indeed, of all the many types of dance as perceived and performed today, only the reel and strathspey can be claimed to be truly indigenous to our native heath. Reels have from the early days of the Scot at leisure been popular, particularly in crofting communities since they could be executed anywhere – in the croft kitchen, perhaps, where an evening of jollification could have everyone dance the reel. A single dancer, a duo, a trio or a foursome could perform in the minimum of space but with the maximum of enthusiasm. The strathspey, of course, owes it origin to the valley of the Spey, and its popularity from the eighteenth century through the fiddle playing and the compositions of such as Niel Gow and, from Speyside itself, William Marshall of Fochabers.

I shall return to that era, which undoubtedly saw the greatest change in Scottish dance but evidence can be found of earlier influences on our traditional reel and similar steps. The combination of Scottish music and dance have always had a perfect marriage and, indeed, we find in our culture today remnants of the past with enthusiasts retaining the oral tradition in Gaelic circles of *Port a Beul* – 'mouth music', also known in the north-east of Scotland as 'diddling'. 'Give us the lilt and we will give you the dance' is the motto.

Elements of ritual dances, it is claimed, can be seen in the formation of some of our dances – for example, a circle dance as a worship to pagan gods, as the movement is usually clockwise in the direction of the sun symbolising, or hoping for, good luck. In the eleventh century, history tells us of an influence when an English princess,

Margaret, married Malcolm Canmore and that brought the introduction to the Court of guests from England and the Continent and with them their own music and instruments. James IV was a skilled musician and Mary Queen of Scots continued her dancing when she left the French Court at Versailles to come to Holyrood Palace. She who paid the piper called the tune.

The dances of the royal Court then were confined to mainly basse dances, branles and other titles which are so alien to the terms we now use for Scottish 'country' dances. The mistaken identity is in the word 'country' which has connotations of village-hall dances or rural mansion-hall balls. In fact, some say, the word came from *contrapassi*, a sort of figure dance devised by Italian dancing masters. Others say it came from *contre danse*, meaning to dance opposite each other. This practice came from the English country dance when the favourite dances were of the longwise variety suitable for the long halls and galleries of the great houses of the society circle. We would use the term 'set dance' today.

There can be little doubt that the start of the influx of more and more new dances of that type still popular now, took place in the mansion-halls up and down the country in the 1700s – a variation here and there created a new dance for the host, hostess or main guest of the evening. For example, from the books of the publications of the Royal Scottish Country Dance Society, we can pick out, at random, Captain MacDonald's Fancy (a reel first published in 1792), Lady Louisa Macdonald's Strathspey (Boag, 1797) and The Countess of Crawford's Reel (Caledonian Country Dances of 1754).

And to think that just a century before these dances were published, dancing certainly did not enjoy the popularity and social status it has now and, to a lesser degree, had then. The Church of Scotland frowned on such impropriety in the mid-seventeenth century – 'promiscuous dancing – the mere thought of it! Ladies dancing with men!!' The General Assembly passed an Act prohibiting this 'evil practice' in 1649 and again in 1701 so that dancing, at least publicly, was never seen. No doubt, though, the hoochs and reels were in full swing in the houses, behind closed doors.

Edinburgh appears to have been the main centre of the revolution and when the dancers came out of the closet, it was the upper classes who dared oppose the laws o' the Kirk. In spite of bible-thumping sermons, the dance scene became very fashionable with the gentry. At the start of the eighteenth century, regular public dances were taking place at the West Bow Assembly in the capital city. A popular dance tune at that time, as it is today, would have been 'Deil Stick Da Minister' – one in the eye with the fiddle bow for the poor old padre! From there, the Edinburgh Assembly, a private association, was formed in 1723, the purpose of which was to have musical evenings for the gentry; the object, though, was to raise money for the poor. More and more the new dances came in with different patterns and formations again taking in outside influences. It is astonishing how the dancers can remember all the different routines but the separate influences are there for all to see. The eightsome reel, for example, is danced with eight dancers in a circle, the Brouns reel with the couples facing each other in a straight line, and the complicated routines of the lancers and the quadrilles show most definitely the Continental influence.

That takes us back to the influence of the Gow family but there were many others at the time including 'Red Rob' MacIntosh, who was born in Tullymet about the time that Bonnie Prince Charlie was raising his standard at Glenfinnan. Amongst the tunes he wrote, which have that bounce that keeps dancers going to this day, is Lady Charlotte Campbell as a strathspey and then as a reel. But it was the Gows who had the

28. Portrait of Niel Gow (1727–1807) by Sir Henry Raeburn (1756–1823). Gow was a famous fiddler and a prolific composer of airs and dance tunes. (Scottish National Portrait Gallery)

influence in the days of revival after the Kirk's attempts to stop the dancing and society's determination to keep it going. Some say Niel Gow was lucky to be there at the right time but they forget that, like his contemporary and friend Robert Burns, he had the magic ingredient – it takes a genius to write and play as he did. Burns's poetry lives on and so do the tunes of Niel Gow. Hardly a Scottish country dance programme, be it in the halls or on the radio, gets by without a classic from the maestro or from his descendants (and particular mention must be made of Nathaniel, his youngest son). In the early days of publishing the music for a particular dance they and perhaps Robert Bremner (1713–89) deserve most credit for 'holding' the music as they played it or had heard it played.

Niel Gow, like Robert Burns, moved in society circles, and he was patronised by three Dukes of Atholl during his long life, but society would not have listened had he not had something special to offer. I feel, too, at this time that the dancing then was influenced by the 'upstairs-downstairs' syndrome of a mansion house and while the nobility enjoyed the music of the fiddle master, the servants from downstairs were aye eager to try out these new formations as they watched from afar – a new version of their own kitchen reel. There must be a connection, surely, of the sedate way of dancing an eightsome reel at formal occasions and the 'deil-may-care' approach of the lad in the village-hall.

> Warlocks and witches in a dance
> Nae cottillion brent new frae France
> But hornpipes, jigs, strathspeys and reels
> Pit life and mettle in their heels.

Robert Burns again, and I can picture the bard and Niel Gow over a glass of claret extolling the virtues of the Scottish dance.

Entertainment with the music galleries in the big houses was the height of fashion, and not only were minstrels required to play for the assembled guests but instructions in the art of dancing were also obviously necessary. This then, coming into the nineteenth century, saw the emergence of the artist as a solo dancer. It was male-orientated with the titles mainly round the battle scene. This laid the foundation for Highland dancing as we know it today, and again new dances had to be introduced like Wilt thou go the Barracks Johnnie, and the Sword Dance. The latter is not as old as might be thought and different versions of its inception abound. In some parts the dance is called The Ghillie Callum but that, in fact, is the tune to which it is traditionally danced, the tune being much older. Most observers agree that it is a dance of triumph in battle when the victor's sword is placed on top of that of the vanquished and the steps are executed over and round the crossed swords. Similarly, the Broad Swords depict a small unit returning in triumph raising their swords and letting them all fall to the ground. The steps are worked round that, the items of war picked up and off the visitors march for another sortie.

Highland dancing grew in popularity as Highland Games Societies were formed at the beginning of the nineteenth century, and it was quite a common occurrence for an athlete to compete in the heavy events as well as taking part in the dancing. Records of the Ballater Highland Games, who held their first gathering in 1864, show that the overall champion of the day was A. Grant of Birkhall who won the Heavy Stone, Light Stone, Heavy Hammer, Light Hammer, Long Race, Hurdle Race and High Leap. A crowd of seven hundred also saw him come first equal in dancing Highland reels.

The popular dance, 'The Reel of Tulloch', at Highland Gatherings today was thought to have come out of a small incident at the tiny church of Tulloch one Sunday morning when the minister was late and many of the congregation, frozen to the marrow, got up and danced to keep warm. Returning to the set dances we find one called The Eight Men of Moidart. It is suggested that when Bonnie Prince Charlie landed in Moidart in 1745 from crossing the Sound of Arisaig from Borrodale, eight local lads working at the peats, with prior warning of his arrival, got up and danced a reel of welcome.

It should be remembered that these were the days of the major changes in our country dances and inspiration in some instances came from the topical events of the day. In more modern times, in 1940 for example, prisoners of war in a German camp devised the Reel of the 51st Division which they originally called St Valery Reel. When the Royal Scottish Country Dance Society published the dance in their Victory Book of 1945 that title was dropped because of the painful memories it evoked in the many who lost family and friends. When Robert Burns wrote in scorn of the need to stop foreign dances coming in – 'nae cotillion brent new frae France' – he would not have been aware that further changes were in the offing, but which in retrospect have done nothing to impair their enjoyment: 'the pipers loud and louder blew – the dancers quick and quicker flew'.

As more and more people became aware of dancing as a pastime, so came the hey-day of the intinerant dancing masters. The start of this next period would be around the 1880s. Professional dance masters set up in business and were known as 'Dancie' followed by their surnames. These itinerant teachers taught country and Highland dancing, and also ballroom dancing which was just beginning to come into vogue. They travelled on foot, then on bicycle right up to the 1940s and 1950s when some had the comfort of the motor car. They were, of course, skilled musicians too – no gramophone to assist them. They played the fiddle, some the pipes, and they would teach the steps as they played. Such a dancing master was Dancie Reid of Newtyle who would think nothing of cycling ten or twenty miles a day to and from his classes which were scattered round his area of Angus. The strathspey king, James Scott Skinner of Banchory (1843–1927), was also for a time a professional dance master before he achieved international fame as a fiddle player. Skinner stopped teaching in 1885 but at his classes he would think nothing of hitting pupils over the head with his fiddle bow when he lost either their attention or his patience.

The dancing classes proved very popular and their cost was within reach of most of those interested though, of course, private lessons by the masters were still part of the society scene. The fee for twelve classes in the early 1900s would have been around six shillings and the venue would have been the village-hall or school, but if that was unavailable then a farm loft would suffice. Pupils were taught with the emphasis on deportment and etiquette. For a country lad of 'roch disposition' there was no suggestion of him being termed 'cissy' as he pursued his new hobby. The end result was important and, as well as being able to enjoy the dance, he aye had an eye for the bonnie lassie opposite. Dress was important, too, and these dance masters would ensure that patent leather shoes and white gloves were worn. Etiquette insisted upon the 'May I have the pleasure, please?' and the obligatory 'Thank you' before escorting the lady back to her seat. The ladies were taught to curtsey and the men and boys to bow. It appears, too, that the teachers weren't too fussy about attaining a high standard in technique and polish so long as the pupils got the rudiments of the figures of the dances and the correct steps. It was also the custom for ladies to carry small books of dance instructions in their handbags. The following is an example of what might be found in such a booklet – from *Allan's Ballroom Guide* – written in the nineteenth century:

> What place is so proper as the Ballroom to see the fashions and manners of the times,
> to study men and character, to be accustomed to receive flattery without regarding it,

to learn good breeding and politeness without affectation, to see grace without wantonness, gaiety without riot, air and dignity without haughtiness and freedom without levity.

All for the sake of a furl round the floor! The booklet then goes on to give instructions for eighty dances and there is evidence of more ballroom-type dances being introduced.

Foxtrots, Quicksteps and Modern Waltzes became fashionable at social dances but, by the nature of the music, we cannot take that into consideration here, and some of the popular dances of today danced to the real Scottish dance music came into being from outside of Scotland. Away from the set dances no programme would be complete without round-the-room numbers such as Gay Gordons, Boston Two Step, Eva Three Step or Highland Schottische.

The Boston Two Step was introduced in 1908 by Tom Walton and the Highland Schottische in 1855, known then as the Balmoral Schottische. The Eva Three Step was devised by Sydney Painter of Manchester for his daughter (hence the name). Sydney weighed around eighteen stone but as a dance master he was reputed to be as light as a feather on his feet. A lot of these round-the-room dances are variants of the ballroom dances originating in England, often with the addition of basic Scottish steps. At the time of the First World War Military Two Steps – quick marches – were very popular and from that scene emerged the Gay Gordons. It was attributed to the regiment of the north-east of Scotland, the Gordon Highlanders, and the original tune of the same title was actually given the name The Gordon Highlanders March by its composer James Scott Skinner, and dedicated to the Pipe Major, George S. MacLennan.

To go back to the set dances, there is no doubt that to a visitor, with the kilt the obligatory dress, these are the ones associated with the true meaning of dance in Scotland. The popularity of Scottish country dancing owes much to the Royal Scottish Country Dance Society, founded in 1923. In particular, the sheer dedication of its co-founder, Jean C. Milligan, must be acknowledged. From her firm base of strict tempo, proper dress and correct dancing steps, the attraction grew and there are now literally hundreds of branches of the main society and affiliated groups all over the world. The main interest is in Australia, Canada and the USA but groups are also found in Japan, Sweden and Kenya – aye, and with native-born dancers too! A mecca for these dancers from abroad is the annual summer school run by the Society in St Andrews with the emphasis on teaching. The tuition carries on every day of the course and for relaxation in the evening – what better than informal and formal dances!

The Royal Scottish Country Dance Society, since its inception as the Scottish Country Dance Society and now boasting over thirty thousand members, has periodically issued publications of dances, usually about twelve dances to a book and now they are up to book no. 37. Accompanying music on record or cassette is also available but there are literally thousands of country dances, and more and still more are being devised for special occasions. Among the most prolific of present-day devisers is John Drewery of Aberdeen.

Looking back over some of the older titles from the eighteenth century onwards it is fascinating to find out the stories behind the dances. The origin of the title of the Dashing White Sergeant, for instance, is not to be found in Scotland although it remains one of the most popular on the dance-floor. It comes from the theatrical lyric composed by General Burgoyne which tells the story of the young lass who dresses up as a soldier to follow the lad to the battlefields. Another popular dance, Deil Among the

Tailors, has as its title a game similar to miniature skittles which was played in pubs in the eighteenth and nineteenth centuries. The Wild Geese was a nickname for the Irish Jacobites who went over to the Continent with the exiled James VII – a wild goose chase.

Music, of course, as has been mentioned, plays a most important part in the popularity of Scottish country dancing and there have been many influences since the fiddle and cello days of the Gows, Marshall and Skinner. Not that these names and others of their era are allowed to die: the compositions – especially the strathspeys of Skinner – are heard at every dance venue to this day. In the 1920s, along with the fiddles and cornets a new sound was being introduced to the Scottish dance band scene. The melodeon of the farm bothies was gaining in popularity through the records of such as the Wyper brothers, Peter and Daniel of Hamilton.

Jimmy Shand holds a unique position in Scottish dance music and he made his first record in 1933 as a soloist before forming his band. His style, his mastery of the instrument and his job as a salesman with a music shop popularised the accordion as we know it today. He is still revered all over the world and has been honoured at the highest level as MBE, Honorary MA and Fellow of the British College of Accordionists. When asked to explain the unique Shand 'dunt' – the immaculate timing – he replied, 'I jist watch the feet o' the best dancers in the hall.' Such modesty, but it's right, of course, the dancer and the musician must be as one. Jimmy started his playing on the humble mouth-organ when he was but eight years old. He then graduated to the Double Ray melodeon favoured by the bothy lads of the day, in farming and mining areas alike. Later, when well established, he was invited to tour the Hohner factory in Germany and this led to the unique sound of the Shand Morino and today's musicians can vouch for his foresight in adapting the accordion for the Scottish idiom.

With the advent of the barn dance more pipe tunes were being adapted for the dance and Bobby MacLeod takes a great deal of credit for the introduction of the big 2/4 pipe marches from such great pipers and composers as John McColl, Willie Lawrie and George S. MacLennan. Other bands have developed over the years with Ian Powrie and his band having an influence on a lot of our leaders today; the basic ingredient is the ability to put a spring into the dancers' steps.

The dance in Scotland today is still very popular. As with the country dancing, Highland dancing has flourished abroad and you only have to attend Highland Gatherings to hear of the names and addresses of winners to determine that. Australia and Canada are the leading countries, and teachers such as Bobby Watson are continually on world trips passing on their skills. Over the past few decades, with many innovations into the teaching techniques and methods of handing down the skills, Highland dancing has been honed and polished into the artistic and bonnie spectacle we now see on those dancing platforms. The dress especially for the girls has improved, cutting out the old practice of wearing heavy kilts, jackets, sporrans and plaids, like the boys or indeed dancing soldiers, festooned with medals. A much lighter version of the kilt is worn now, and in 1952 the Aboyne Games Committee fashioned a light tartan skirt and plaid and the best-dressed lady dancer in the Aboyne dress is competed for each year now at these Games.

There is also a great revival in old-time dancing or what some term 'ceilidh' dancing. Jimmy Shand Junior has been running old-time dances for a few years now on a fortnightly basis and others have joined in with teaching coming back into favour.

This has resulted in more and more 'new' dances being incorporated such as Mississippi Dip and Swedish Masquerade — hardly Scottish names but they have a Scottish feel to them as you follow the steps with the traditional music.

Social dancing took a dip in popularity in the 1950s with the counter attractions of hotel lounges and pop groups and this led to a decline in the use of village-halls and thus indirectly to a threat to community life. There was, of course, still a great interest in the balls with such big sounds as Tim Wright and the Cavendish Band, but more and more the economics meant a reduction in personnel. Gradually the dances came back and this current revival includes young dancers who might not be expected to be part of the scene. The use of a caller to instruct in the dances is now commonplace and does much to stimulate interest. More and more young bands are coming forward and the breeding ground of accordion and fiddle clubs have helped in this respect. The music at some of these ceilidh dances tends to be racy but then the compositions have changed in style too. Like Jimmy Shand and his old-time dances, the music is there to suit the dancers.

The main thing, in all aspects of dance in Scotland as perceived by the visitor to our country, is a healthy glow and a vibrant feel to the scene. It adds greatly to our cultural vitality now as it did at the time of the revival in the eighteenth century. It is part of our tradition — the music and the dance go together and remains truly Scottish in texture.

To quote Moray McLaren in his book *The Scots* (1951):

> The traditional Scottish country dance (enjoyed quite as much in the towns as in the country) is one of the most truly popular of our pastimes, and it is as vigorously and unaffectedly national as any dance in Europe. It seems to me that in its passionate formality, in its blending of abandon and style, in its rhythm of colour and pattern it expresses the Scottish spirit as almost nothing else does. Were I to be asked to *show* Scotland to a foreigner for one evening I would show him the Scottish dance. But how, alas! can it be shown in writing.

Books for Further Reading

George S. Emmerson, *Scotland Through Her Country Dances* (Montreal, 1967)
George S. Emmerson, *A Social History of Scottish Dance* (Montreal, 1972)
J.P. Flett and J.M. Flett, *Traditional Dancing in Scotland* (London, 1964)
Robbie Shepherd, *Let's have a Ceilidh* (Edinburgh, 1992)
H.A. Thurston, *Scotland's Dances* (London, 1954)

More information can be found in the publications of the Royal Scottish Country Dance Society, Coates Crescent, Edinburgh.

29. Margaret Lyndsay, the Artist's Wife, c.*1758*, *by Allan Ramsay (1713–84).* (National Gallery of Scotland)

Scottish Art

DUNCAN MACMILLAN

In Scotland the iconoclasts of the Reformation were more thorough in their destruction than almost anywhere else. These losses were compounded with the destruction already caused by successive English invasions from the thirteenth to the sixteenth centuries. Much secular art was lost, too, as a consequence of the removal of the Scottish Court to England in 1603 and the political and social upheavals of the succeeding centuries. These facts and the consequent scarcity of art surviving from the pre-Reformation period have together conspired to present an image of Scotland as somehow disadvantaged in the visual arts. This is erroneous. Scotland is not some cold distant planet, dimly reflecting borrowed light at the outer edge of a solar system whose sun is France or Italy. This country gave as well as received in the exchange that has made Europe vital; and Europe is a nebula, a galaxy of stars, some larger and some smaller perhaps, but all contributing to the luminosity of the whole. What does survive from the early period of Scottish history is always interesting and is sometimes of outstanding quality. Nor in the later period were the visual arts extinguished by the Reformation, and they then went on to play an integral part in the Enlightenment when art as much as the other branches of Scottish thought made a vital contribution to the emergence of the modern consciousness. Since that time, too, Scotland has retained a rich, visual culture which has bred some of the most creative artists of their time in Britain as a whole.

In the early centuries of modern history, the art of the Picts, then the dominant people in eastern Scotland, was highly evolved, while western Scotland shared a common culture with Ireland of an equally high standard. Pictish art only survives in any quantity in the form of sculptured stones, probably dating from the seventh to the tenth centuries, but the quality of such surviving metalwork as the *Monymusk Reliquary* (see Plate 8), the *St Ninian's Treasure*, or the bells associated with the Celtic saints, such as *St Fillan's Bell*, makes it clear that, united, the traditions of Picto-Celtic art were not limited to such sculpture. The bells, though they are perhaps of a slightly later date, have a classic simplicity, but otherwise the decoration both of the stones and the metalwork is characterised by a fluent, linear style. It includes rich and complex, abstract and zoomorphic interlace, both secular (or pagan) and Christian imagery, and lively and naturalistic drawing, particularly of animals as in the magnificent *St Andrews Sarcophagus*.

This style can also be seen in the illumination of insular manuscripts and the tendency of Pictish sculptors to carve the whole surface of flat, roughly rectangular stones, as in the monumental *Hilton of Cadboll* stone, reinforces this similarity. In one of the earliest of the great, insular manuscripts, the seventh-century *Book of Durrow*, for instance, the animal forms are distinctly Pictish. Though much more modest, the *Book of Deer* seems to be Pictish, not only in style, but also in provenance, and it confirms the view of a distinctive style of Pictish illumination. In the west of Scotland, Iona was a major religious centre for both Scotland and Ireland and the great *Book of Kells* (see Plate 3) itself is most likely to have originated there.

In 843 Scotland was unified under Kenneth MacAlpin, King of the Scots, and in 1069 the marriage of St Margaret, daughter of Edward the Confessor, to King Malcolm Canmore brought the Celtic Church more closely into the sphere of influence of Rome. A book of *Gospels* associated with Margaret herself survives and is generally held to have been produced in Anglo-Saxon England, but until the Reformation, a great book given by Bishop Fothach who married Malcolm and Margaret was preserved in St Andrews Cathedral; and a contemporary psalter also associated with Margaret in the Scots-Irish style may preserve something of its character.

The Lewis chessmen are a witness to the importance of the Scandinavian links of northern Scotland and in the early medieval period, therefore, Scottish art reflected both the diverse character of the country's population and the range of its external contacts. The art of the Court and of the south and east belonged to the Gothic tradition shared with England, France and the Low Countries. It is seen in the beautiful seal matrices, such as the thirteenth-century seal of the Cathedral Chapter of Brechin, which preserve in miniature the high Gothic art of Scotland. The west and north, however, retained a common culture with Ireland until the sixteenth and even the seventeenth centuries. This is best seen in metalwork such as the magnificent *Kames Brooch* but also in the other applied arts such as the fifteenth-century clarsach, *Queen Mary's Harp* (see Plate 23), and in the grave slabs and carved stones of the West Highlands.

From the thirteenth century onwards, as church architecture became more ambitious, sculpture, wall painting and panel painting must have been common, but the only survivals of painting are fragments like the traces at Inchcolm and Dryburgh Abbeys. Fragments of sculpture are more plentiful, as at Elgin Cathedral for example, but they are nevertheless difficult to judge. Isolated objects like the twelfth-century *Guthrie Bell Shrine* (see Plate 2), or the fourteenth-century *Bute Maɀer*, do give us some idea of the kind of art that was produced in Scotland and how it was in step with developments elsewhere in Europe, but it is really only through illuminated manuscripts that it is possible to form any real assessment of the level and quality of contemporary art and patronage. The Scottish Church and aristocracy belonged to the cosmopolitan culture of Europe and the surviving manuscripts with Scottish associations reflect this. The *Iona Psalter*, for example, was probably made in Oxford between 1180 and 1220 for a nun of Iona. There are also other important books such as the very beautiful, thirteenth-century *Murthly Hours*, possibly produced in part in England and in part in France, but containing Scottish heraldry and certainly brought to Scotland by the later Middle Ages. Books of quality and undoubted Scottish production are rare, though there has always been a tendency to assume that anything of quality is imported. The fourteenth-century tomb of the Earl and Countess of Mentieth in Inchmaholme Priory on the Lake of Mentieth, however, in which the Earl and Countess are forever united in a gentle embrace, indicates that there was certainly imagination and not just rude mechanic skill to be found among the sculptors and so no doubt among the painters too, and secular tombs of similar quality, though they are not numerous, are to be found throughout Scotland.

By the mid-fifteenth century and the accession of James III, the rich and courtly art of the late Middle Ages was associated in Scotland with a new kind of self-consciousness that makes it meaningful to talk of the impact of the Renaissance here during the reigns of James, his son and his grandson, and to see this as a necessary precondition of the Reformation. By the mid-fifteenth century, the workshops of France and the Netherlands were providing high-quality goods in some quantity for Scottish patrons. The *Talbot Hours*, for instance, produced in France in the mid-fifteenth century, but containing the Scottish Royal Arms, is evidence of the kind of quality that members of the Scottish Court expected. There is also evidence of increasingly spectacular, individual patronage, such as the wonderful St Salvator's mace, made for Bishop Kennedy of St Andrews by a Paris goldsmith, Jean Mayelle, who was probably a Scot. Kennedy's tomb which survives, though ruined, in St Salvator's Chapel was once even more spectacular, but the *Book of Hours of Dean James Brown of Aberdeen*, made in Flanders in 1498, though probably finished in Aberdeen, shows too that patronage was not the exclusive province either of the very great or the foreign artist.

The existence of a lovely, illuminated *Virgil*, also produced in France for a member of the Scottish royal family in the mid-fifteenth century, demonstrates that culture was not only ecclesiastical, and a lively, illustrated copy of John of Fordun's *Scotichronicon* dating from *c.*1425 indicates that there were artists in Scotland capable of catering for this need, while something like its vitality is seen in a different medium in the contemporary, sculptural decoration of Melrose Abbey or Roslin Chapel.

Although books provide by far the most important evidence of the art of the period, James III's coinage provides evidence of how well he understood the value of the image. The groat that he produced with his portrait in three-quarter view is recognised as the first use of this device in a coin or medal outside of Italy. There is also a handful of surviving paintings on a larger scale, enough to make it clear that it is their survival that is exceptional, not their existence in the first place. The most important of these that was produced in Scotland is the painted rood-screen in the church of Foulis Easter, the work of an unknown painter in the late fifteenth century. Though now dismantled, its main element is a large painting of the Crucifixion which, though it is crude, is very spirited. Also in Foulis Easter there is stone-carving of a high quality similar to that seen in Trinity College Kirk, Edinburgh, and elsewhere. The sculptors may have been imported, but there is evidence of a distinctive style characterised by a kind of eloquent bluntness and this quality is recognisable later in work produced in the 1530s and 1540s suggesting the existence of a real and continuing school.

The most important surviving painting from the period is the *Trinity College Altarpiece* (see Plate 22) which was certainly imported. It was painted by Hugo van der Goes for James III in the late 1470s, but was commissioned through the agency of Edward Bonkil, provost of the church and a member of an Edinburgh merchant family with close links with the Netherlands, whose portrait appears on the altarpiece. Alone and definitely corporeal himself, he is kneeling in prayer to a transcendental vision of the Trinity and the explicit contrast between these two states seem to prefigure the direct, one-to-one relationship of man and God of the Protestant Church.

The only other surviving altarpiece made for a Scottish congregation also testifies to the importance of the Scottish trade links with northern Europe. This is the altarpiece painted and carved for the Scottish community in Elsinore, Denmark. Its centre contains the carved figures of Saints Ninian, James and Andrew and its wings show scenes from the life of St Ninian. Although it was not made in Scotland, these saints and a generous quantity of thistles in its decoration testify to the national self-consciousness of the Scots. It is also probably close in date to the Scottish *Calendar of Saints* prepared by Bishop Elphinstone at the very beginning of the sixteenth century.

The most important surviving work from the reign of James IV (reigned 1488–1513) is the beautiful *Hours of James IV and Margaret Tudor* (see Plate 5) that was James's wedding present to his queen in 1503. Amongst its many illuminations, this rich and beautiful manuscript contains much that is of specific Scottish interest, including the portrait of the king in prayer and the remarkable scene of a royal mass for the dead. Like the *Trinity Altarpiece*, it was commissioned in the Netherlands, probably from Simon Bening, who was Flemish, but whose father, Alexander Bening, may have been a Scottish painter. Alexander Bening was presented to the guild in Bruges by Hugo van der Goes himself.

Though they could not match this quality, illuminated manuscripts were also produced in Scotland at such abbeys as Culross, Lindores and Kinloss – the *Boswell or Kinloss Psalter* (c.1500), for example, or *Andrew Lundy's Primer* (c.1500). At the Court, Sir Thomas Galbraith, a clerk of the Chapel Royal, wrote and illuminated the treaty documents relating to James's marriage, the earliest works surviving by a named Scottish artist. He also produced several illuminated books for the king and there is some evidence that, as with music and poetry, James encouraged the development of a native school of art. As well as Galbraith, for instance, James had a Court painter, David Pratt (recorded 1496–1503), from whom he commissioned altar paintings for the Chapel Royal, and other individuals are known by name if not by any surviving works, though there are several portraits of both James IV and V. The finest of these, though only recorded in a seventeenth-century copy, shows James IV with a hawk on his wrist as a true Renaissance prince. From the 1530s we also have a record of a recognisably modern artistic temperament: the painter Andrew Bairhum, who worked for Robert Reid at Kinloss, is described by Ferrerius as 'outstanding in his craft, but . . . difficult to handle and cantankerous, struggling with a violent temper, no less than with a weak body and lame in both feet'.

A man of Reid's sophistication would not have put up with Bairhum's cantankerousness if he did not value the art that he got from him, evidently in some quantity. In time, he was halfway between Dunbar and David Lyndsay, and Ferrerius's account of Bairhum gives us a tantalising glimpse of the place that the painters may have taken as personalities in the vivid life of the Renaissance Court. No painting by Bairhum survives apart from a doubtful fragment at Pluscarden Abbey, but such works as the carved, wooden heads made for the great hall of Stirling Castle (see Plate 7) have a blunt forcefulness which suggests some strength of character in the artist who made them. Nor are they isolated and with the *Beaton panels* made for Arbroath Abbey or, a little earlier, the choir stalls of King's College, Aberdeen, they do seem to represent a distinct and self-conscious artistic tradition in which individualism was valued and which was continuous with that seen in the middle of the previous century. The bold, distinctive character of the architecture of the buildings for which such things were made, like Stirling Castle or Falkland Palace, (see Plate 39) supports this view. The Reformation was not the achievement of a community of pale, fawning courtiers, and something of the imaginative vigour that brought it about is surely reflected here.

The grandeur of these buildings also makes it clear that the level of patronage established by his father and grandfather continued in the reign of James V, even though no major work of art survives. Mary of Guise, too, had artists at her Court and her daughter, Mary, clearly understood the power of imagery. She is recorded in a number of paintings from her life-time, such as *Mary, Queen of Scots and Henry Darnley* (*c.*1565), and also posthumously, for example, the full-length *Blairs Memorial Portrait* (*c.*1604). The elegant restraint of the silver *Tulloch mazer* made by James Gray during the reign of Mary is an indication that the ideas of the Continental Renaissance were also appreciated and understood by Scottish craftsmen.

It was during James V's reign that the first episodes of iconoclasm are recorded, though it was not until 1560 that the Reformation was completed and the Kirk established. In the years that followed, the reformers carried out the systematic destruction of religious imagery and also of redundant churches and ecclesiastical buildings. This did not involve a blanket hostility to art, however, and it is in the 1580s and 1590s that several distinctive developments in the business of painting can be seen. It is in the reign of James VI, for instance, that it is for the first time possible to identify

*30. The Galloway Mazer. Made in 1569 by a Canongate goldsmith for an Edinburgh merchant. (*National Museums of Scotland*)*

known Court artists, Arnold Bronckhorst and Adrian Vanson, with surviving works. The uncompromising character of the Reformation leaders is personified in the fierce portrait of *Regent Morton* attributed to Bronckhorst. The only authentic portrait of John Knox is the woodcut after Vanson made for Beza's *Icones* (1580) (see Plate 9), and to match it there is an intriguingly psychological portrait of the king also by Vanson (1595) that hints at the kind of talents which the king needed to survive in such company. In the next generation, Adam de Colone (who may have been Vanson's son), though he only worked briefly in Scotland, produced some fine portraits such as the group of *George Seton and his Two Sons* (1625).

The painters also continued to play an important role in pageantry as they had done in the years before the Reformation, particularly the royal entries like that of James and his queen into Edinburgh in 1590. Their involvement in this kind of public spectacle was also reflected in the painters' association with heraldry, originally perhaps as mere providers of images as in such heraldic compilations as the *Seton Armorial* (c.1580) and the *Lyndsay Armorial* (c.1542), but increasingly, too, as heralds themselves, an important indication of their status.

It was during the latter part of the sixteenth century that the fashion for painted ceilings developed, producing a distinctive Scottish form of decoration. These survive in considerable quantity, though many have been damaged by restoration. Their production seems to have stopped abruptly with the outbreak of the Civil War, but they were also gradually replaced by the fashion for elaborate, plaster ceilings of the kind seen at Glamis or Craigievar castles. Ambitious painted ceilings are at Cullen House in Banff, The Palace in Culross, and Pinkie House, Midlothian. In the latter, the painter has made an attempt at a full-scale illusionistic ceiling. At St Mary's Kirk, Grandtully, and Provost Skene's House, Aberdeen, there is religious imagery in the ceilings which testifies to the tolerance of the early seventeenth century. Such tolerance did not extend to the king, however. When he proposed to introduce religious decoration into the chapel at Holyrood in preparation for his visit in 1617, he had to abandon the project though he had had sculptors sent specially from England.

Nevertheless, the painted ceilings together with the evidence for the use of colour on the outside of buildings suggest that Reformation Scotland was by no means as drab as subsequent, hostile propaganda would have us believe. Likewise, the number of tombstones in the graveyards of the period, their invention and variety and the kind of people that they commemorate, bear witness to the imagination and to the skill of the masons and to the emergence in the Reformation of a society in which individual pride and independence were no longer the exclusive prerogative of the rich and powerful. The period is also notable for a number of very grand tombs such as the Menzies memorial at Weem, Perthshire, or the Montgomery Aisle, Skelmorlie. This latter also has a very fine painted ceiling which is unusual in being signed (and dated 1638) by the artist, John Stalker of Edinburgh.

This new expression of individuality is personified both by and in the first artist for whom we can establish at all fully a distinct artistic personality: George Jamesone (1589/90–1644). His background was in decorative painting in Aberdeen, but he became a national figure. He was, for instance, brought to Edinburgh to orchestrate the decoration of the city for King Charles's entry in 1633. A series of over one hundred imaginary portraits of the king's ancestors that he painted for this occasion survives in part, though these remaining pictures were dispersed from Newbattle as recently as twenty years ago. It was the model for the better known series painted for Holyrood Palace by Jacob de Wet, fifty years later and still *in situ*. At Newbattle the remains of Jamesone's series were part of one of the first connoisseur's collections for whose origins we have evidence. It was begun by the Earl of Lothian in the 1640s with the help of John Clerk of Penicuik.

Jamesone's art is low key, almost tentative, but it does not lack subtlety. It is seen at its best in a gentle, half-length portrait like that of *Mary Erskine* (1626). He seems less at ease with the formality of the full-length portrait with its implication of rank, though his full-length of *Anne Erskine, Countess of Rothes with her Two Daughters* succeeds in being both charming and elegant. Jamesone painted several self-portraits, a fact that is itself indicative of his self-consciousness as an artist. The best of them is his *Self-Portrait with an Easel* (c.1637–40). It is both self-assured and introspective in a way that speaks to us directly of the complex self-awareness of the emerging Scottish professional class whose speaking voice is heard in the poetry of William Drummond of Hawthornden, Jamesone's collaborator on Charles's entry in 1633. Jamesone's most important pupil was John Michael Wright (1617–94) who seems to have come to Scotland to study with him before going on to be the most distinguished native portrait painter of the Restoration period in England.

Jamesone's death under the shadow of the Civil War marked a break in the continuity of painting, and many artists of the period went overseas to escape these upheavals. William Gouw Ferguson (1632/33–after 1695), for example, became well known as a still-life painter in the Netherlands. Partly as a result of this diaspora, in the years after the Restoration, although the native tradition was continued by painters like David Scougall (*fl.*1654–77), the principal artists were imported. In 1673 Jacob de Wet (1640–97) was brought from Holland by Sir William Bruce to work on the decoration of Holyrood, where he painted a number of ceilings and chimney-pieces in a rather wooden style. De Wet also worked elsewhere and he produced a small number of less formal paintings of which the most important is his *Highland Wedding*, the prototype for a tradition in painting and in literature that extends from Allan Ramsay to David Wilkie and beyond.

The most important painter of the later seventeenth century was John de Medina (1659–1710) who was born in Flanders and came to Scotland in 1693. It is a comment on the prosperity and self-awareness of the Scots that he had originally intended only to stay for a short time, but settled because of the volume of work that he found. Medina's work is found in all the older country houses. A good example of his energetic painting and lively characterisation is his portrait of *Sir John Clerk of Penicuik* (before 1701) but he also painted in a less formal idiom, as in his painting of the butler of Wemyss Castle, *David Ayton* (1702), and his double portrait of his own son and daughter is one of the most touchingly human paintings of its time. His biggest undertaking was a series of sixty portraits of the members of the Royal College of Surgeons to which he was invited to add his own self-portrait.

It is a further mark of the esteem in which Medina was held that he was knighted, and his success assisted the change in status of artists from a craft to a profession that had begun with Jamesone. They thus became members of the new intelligentsia that played such a key role in Scottish life in the Enlightenment. This is clearly seen in the initiative taken by such men as James Norie, William Adam and Allan Ramsay senior in 1729 to establish in Edinburgh Scotland's first art institution, the Academy of St Luke.

The craft tradition did not die, however, and the training of painters such as Alexander Runciman or Alexander Nasmyth as apprentices in the painter's trade was an important element in the distinctive character of Scottish art.

The first painters to develop these new ambitions successfully were William Aikman (1682–1731), who studied with Medina, John Smibert (1688–1751), who eventually settled in America, and John Alexander (1686–c.1766). All three studied in Italy, an important factor in the new sophistication of their painting. This is most striking in the case of Aikman whose art at its best – as in the portrait of George Watson (1718) – is characterised by naturalness tempered by a kind of austere simplicity which is ultimately classical in origin. Aikman and Smibert both use natural light in a way that also reflects an underlying continuity with Dutch art, which is seen more explicitly in Richard Waitt's outstanding *Still-Life with a Leg of Lamb* (1724). Indeed, no doubt for ideological reasons because of its association with Catholicism, the baroque is a rare style in Scotland in any art form. The restrained baroque of the ceilings painted by a pupil of the Dutch painter, Tidemans, at Hopetoun House (c.1709), or the marginally more convincing baroque of the *Pluto and Persephone* ceiling painted by John Alexander (who was a Catholic) for the Duke of Gordon a decade later, are both unusual. Like painting, architecture and the applied arts show a restrained combination of Dutch and classical inspiration, seen for instance in the austere simplicity of late seventeenth-century church plate.

Aikman was an important model for the naturalness of Allan Ramsay's early style, and in spite of their Italian experience, all these painters looked back to the empirical character of Dutch painting. The Union of the Parliaments in 1707 had a depressing effect on patronage, however. Though twenty years before Medina had stayed in Scotland because of the work available, both Aikman and Smibert were forced to leave because of the collapse of the market. Ramsay (1713–84) followed them, first to Italy and then to settle in London, but he remains a central figure in the development of Scottish art. One of the most interesting features of Ramsay's art is the close analogy that one can make between his own branch of the study of human nature by the empirical method and that of his friend David Hume. They both combined a commitment to perceived truth with a profound sense of humanity. In Ramsay's portraits, his analytical use of drawing and his handling of light, seen at their best in his portrait of *Hew Dalrymple, Lord Drummore* (1754) or even in a grand full-length portrait like the *Duke of Argyll* (1749), reflect this. Such pictures show how respect for the individual and for the observed truth, qualified by imagination expressed through sympathy, are the basis of his art. It is for this reason that Ramsay is at his best when most informal, as in such portraits as *Margaret Lyndsay* (c.1758–60) (see Plate 29) or *Martha, Countess of Elgin* (1766).

Ramsay was certainly influenced by the delicacy of contemporary French painting, and without compromising his commitment to truth, he created some of the loveliest, most subtle paintings of his period. Although based in London, he continued to work regularly in Scotland. His contemporaries there included several minor portrait painters amongst whom the most notable were his some-time assistant, David Martin (1737–97), William Mosman (c.1700–71), George Willison (1741–97), Thomas Seton (c.1735–c.1786) and Catherine Read (1723–78). Read was the first Scottish woman painter to train professionally and to establish a reputation. Anne Forbes followed her example to undertake a professional training in Italy, though her later career was less successful.

During the eighteenth century, links between painting and the other branches of contemporary Scottish thought – like those between Ramsay and Hume – are numerous. Perhaps in part their source lies in Francis Hutcheson's equation of moral and aesthetic sensibility. In Rome, before a European audience, Gavin Hamilton (1721–98), a pupil of Hutcheson, played an important part in the interpretation of the significance of such ideas for painting. For example, his *Death of Lucretia* (1766) is an essay in moral sentiment and perhaps on Adam Smith's idea of sympathy, and in a series of monumental pictures illustrating *The Iliad*, begun in 1759, Hamilton explored the implications of the new perception of Homer as a primitive poet, and therefore a poet of natural sensibility, that had been pioneered by Thomas Blackwell in his *Essay on the Life, Times and Writings of Homer* (London, 1735). His example had a far-reaching influence. Learning from Hogarth, he had his paintings engraved and thus they were circulated widely, but he also had an open studio and young painters of many nationalities gathered round him. Among these were Scots such as the Runciman brothers, John (1744–68/9) and Alexander (1736–85), John Brown (1749–87), Anne Forbes (1745–84) and David Allan (1744–96); and others from Switzerland, Ireland, Scandinavia and France – Henry Fuseli, James Barry, Nicholas Abildgaard, Tobias Serghells and, at a distance, J.–L. David.

Alexander Runciman's *Hall of Ossian*, painted in 1772 for Sir James Clerk of Penicuik, was the most dramatic product of this circle, but it combined Hamilton's inspiration with the more radical primitivism represented by Macpherson's *Ossian*, whose poetry was characterised by Hugh Blair as 'irregular and unpolished ..., but abounding in ... vehemence and fire.' Emulating these qualities, for the first time in modern art, spontaneity and freedom from convention were presented by Runciman as the objectives of painting. Runciman was friendly with David Herd, Thomas Mercer, Robert Fergusson and others in the Cape Club circle, and there is significant common ground between his painting and the contemporary revival of vernacular poetry and music. David Allan's illustrations to *The Gentle Shepherd* (1788) and his genre paintings, such as the *Highland Dance* (1780) (see Plate 27) and the *Penny Wedding* (1795) reflect this more clearly. It is not surprising therefore that Allan also collaborated with Burns, illustrating the songs that the poet was editing for George Thomson.

Alexander Runciman was also distinguished as the first native-born teacher in the Trustees Academy, a post that he took up in 1772 and in which David Allan succeeded him in 1786. The Academy was unusual in that it was founded to teach design, specifically pattern design for the linen industry. The Trustees of the Board of Manufacturers administered a fund paid by Westminster to Scotland in compensation for the acceptance by Scotland under the Treaty of Union of a share of the English National Debt. The fund was used to invest in the economy in a very modern way and the Trustees administering it made their main concerns the linen and the fishing industries. They recognised at an early date that design was an important part of the competitiveness of linen manufacture. Such an enterprise may perhaps have helped lay the foundations of the success of the weaving industry in the next century, but following the shift into cotton and wool, it would be difficult to prove.

From the start, the city of Edinburgh took an interest in the new Academy. They housed it in the university, for instance, as they had housed the St Luke's Academy before it, and it seems to have been the city that promoted the idea that it should also serve as a more conventional art school. The Academy's foundation in 1760 was preceded by that of the Foulis Academy in Glasgow in 1754, but unlike its rival which closed fifteen years later, the Trustees Academy flourished for a hundred years or more. After providing a start in life to many Scottish artists it was eventually absorbed into the Royal Scottish Academy schools. They in turn were absorbed into the new Edinburgh College of Art at the beginning of the twentieth century and so in a sense the history of the Trustees Academy has continued to the present

The mid-eighteenth century also saw the beginning of Scottish landscape painting. In the seventeenth century there had been occasional landscapes painted in Scotland by such visitors as Alexander Kierincx in the reign of Charles I, and in 1693 John Slezer published *Theatrum Scotiae* (see Plates 39, 40 and 41), a set of topographical prints covering the principal towns and houses of the country and one of the taxonomic undertakings that laid the Baconian foundations of the Enlightenment. In the eighteenth century James Norie (1684–1757) evolved a style of decorative landscape painting. It was developed by Charles Steuart (*fl.*1762–90), Alexander Runciman, Jacob More (1740–93) and Alexander Nasmyth (1758–1840), who were all linked by the apprentice system to the Norie firm, into an independent art, and it was Nasmyth, a close friend of Robert Burns, who really established the iconography of Scottish landscape. Looking at his work, however, one can see how this did not spring from some abstract idea of the beauty of nature, but from a recognition of the complexity of landscape as both a record of human history and a resource for the enquiries of natural science. The etchings of John Clerk of Eldin (1728–1812) of historic buildings reflect the interests of the antiquarian, but the drawings that he did for James Hutton's *Theory of the Earth* (1796) are a record of an inquiry pursued in collaboration between artist and scientist.

It is typical of this kind of convergence that Nasmyth himself was both a talented engineer and a landscape gardener. As an engineer, he pioneered several important ideas in the field of steel-bridge and shipbuilding, but in spite of this tradition and in spite of the Trustees Academy's function as a school of design, the interaction between the arts and the new industries seems to have been slight. It was in the traditional crafts of cabinetmaking, for instance, where Thomas Trotter was outstanding, or among the gold and silversmiths that the work that characterises the material life of the Enlightenment was produced. For a short time at the Carron ironworks, plaques and even items of furniture were produced of great neoclassical elegance, but this was an exception. It is really only in the pottery industry, itself a creation of the Industrial Revolution, that it is possible to see a continuity between the high standards of craft in the period of the Enlightenment and the commercial success of the developed industry at the height of the Industrial Revolution. Beginning on the east coast with cream ware in the late eighteenth century, by the mid-nineteenth century the potteries of Glasgow were competing worldwide with their transfer ware. Towards the end of the 1800s, notably in Fife, the development of sponge ware as a cheap form of decoration paradoxically reintroduced the inventiveness of the individual decorator into the methods of mass production and so established a new link with the artist-craftsman through the craft revival of the period that led to the creation of such potteries as Wemyss Ware in the 1920s.

Nasmyth was widely influential with painters of the younger generation, such as his own son, Patrick (1787–1831), John Knox (1778–1845), Hugh William Williams (1773–1829), Andrew Wilson (1780–1840) and others, including David Roberts (1796–1864) whose paintings of the Middle East have dominated the iconography of the region to the present day. Nasmyth's landscape painting was essentially neo-

31. Alexander Nasmyth (1758–1840). Princes Street with the Royal Institution Building under Construction (1825). (Photograph: Joe Rock). (National Gallery of Scotland)

classical, however. He represented a harmonious world in which man and nature, past and present all co-exist in a fruitful and mutually supportive relationship. This is seen in such lovely pictures as *Inveraray from the Sea* (*c.*1801), and in its most complex form in his paintings of Edinburgh such as *Edinburgh from Princes Street* and *Edinburgh from the Calton Hill* (both 1825), two deceptively simple paintings which between them present a whole vision of how the structure of society is reflected in the building of cities and how the proper balance of work and leisure is essential to that society's welfare.

In this way, Nasmyth's tranquil art is in marked contrast to the more subjective, even melodramatic approach developed by John Thomson of Duddingston (1778–1840) who was temperamentally closer to his friend Walter Scott and whose influence is still seen in the work of Horatio McCulloch (1805–67) and the painters of the mid-nineteenth century. Their work was not all melodrama, however. McCulloch himself, even though his best-known paintings such as *Glencoe* (1864) are of the grandeur of Highland scenery, also painted in a direct and naturalistic way, and this tradition was carried on by such younger artists as Alexander Fraser (1829–99) and Sam Bough (1822–78).

Richard Cooper (*c.*1695–1764), who settled in Scotland in 1720, established quality engraving in the country for the first time. His pupil, Robert Strange (1721–92), went on to become one of the most distinguished engravers of the later century. His engravings for William Hunter of the gravid human uterus are among the finest visual interpretations of scientific knowledge ever made. In the first half of the nineteenth century, in parallel with the publishing boom, engraving continued to flourish. William Lizars (1788–1859), for instance, produced work of the highest quality and, like Strange, was an outstanding medical engraver. Richard Cooper also contributed to the establishment of a tradition of artist printmakers. He taught the Runciman brothers who produced some remarkable etchings. David Allan also etched and his illustrations to *The Gentle Shepherd* are particularly important in his pioneering use of aquatint, whose secret he learnt from Paul Sandby. There were also important amateur etchers like John Clerk of Eldin and David Deuchar (1745–88) who, as an interpreter of the Dutch tradition, was an influence on both Raeburn and Wilkie.

Portrait painting maintained a central role in a society dedicated to the study of human nature and the greatest recorder of the people of that society was Henry Raeburn (1756–1823). Raeburn trained originally as a goldsmith. He was encouraged to turn to painting by Deuchar. He studied for a short time with Alexander Runciman and spontaneity remained the key characteristic of his style. He was influenced by Reynolds, but he also retained Allan Ramsay's respect for the individual, as in such forceful, direct, but also sympathetic portraits as *Baillie William Galloway* (1798) or *Mrs James Campbell* (c.1805), and even in the grand manner, *Sir John and Lady Clerk of Penicuik* (1792).

Unlike Ramsay, Raeburn never drew, but cultivated an informal and intuitive approach to painting. In his portrait of the fiddle player, *Niel Gow* (c.1793), for instance, one can see an analogy between his own painting and the simple, intuitive strength of Gow's playing. Such qualities closely parallel the theory of perception of Thomas Reid, and through the intermediary of Dugald Stewart it is possible to see Reid's influence in Raeburn's cultivation of a spontaneous and unpremeditated approach to the way that he records his perceptions in paint. Though in his later career Raeburn was influenced by the courtly style of Lawrence, he remained essentially loyal to the idea that a portrait as a human document should be true to the real presence of the individual recorded. It is perhaps because of Reid's subsequent influence in France that it is possible to see a real analogy between Raeburn's painting and the later development of Impressionism.

Raeburn's principal contemporaries in the field of portraiture were Archibald Skirving (1749–1819), who worked mainly in chalk, and George Watson (1767–1837). In the younger generation, several painters followed Raeburn's example: John Syme (1795–1861), Colvin Smith (1795–1875) and William Nicolson (1781–1844) were closest to him, but even D.O. Hill's calotypes of the 1840s clearly show his influence. Robert Scott Lauder (1803–69), who painted the most remarkable portraits of the two decades after Raeburn's death – for example *J.G. Lockhart and his Wife, Sophia Scott* (c.1844) – was less obviously indebted to him, but the most successul portrait painter of the mid-century, John Watson Gordon (1788–1864), started from Raeburn's inspiration and so carried his influence into the second half of the century.

It was really only in the later eighteenth century, following the professionalisation of painting, that sculpture was able to separate itself from the work of the masons. The greater formality of architecture from the late seventeenth century onwards had limited the scope for sculptural invention, but the quality of work in carved overmantels, for instance, indicates that the tradition of the mason-carver did not fade and it was from this background that the first artist-sculptors emerged. They worked mostly in the field of portrait sculpture and some among them – such as William Gowans, who may have been a pupil of Rysbrack (*fl.c.*1770), and Robert Burn (*fl.*1790–1816) – were distinguished. At least one sculptor, William Jeans, was studying in Rome in 1771, but he is only known by the figures of ancient Britons on the portico of Penicuik House. The most remarkable artist in the field of portrait sculpture was perhaps James Tassie

(1735–99) who specialised in small-scale profile portraits using vitreous paste. John Henning (1771–1851) also worked in miniature . He began making portrait sculpture, but after moving to London, he made his name with his miniature copies of the Elgin Marbles.

By the early nineteenth century, sculpture was established as a distinct profession. Leading practitioners were Laurence MacDonald (1799–1878) and Thomas Campbell (1790–1858), both of whom spent long periods in Rome and worked in an elegant neoclassical manner derived from Canova. Samuel Josephs (1791–1850) was an English artist who settled in Edinburgh. He had a very successful career as a portrait sculptor and by the mid-century there were a number of others working in this field, as the numerous portrait busts in the collections of the older Scottish institutions bear witness. It was, however, with Alexander Handyside Ritchie (1804–70), a pupil of Thorwaldson, and Sir John Steell (1804–91) that the sculptor's profession could be said finally to have been established. Steell was prolific and he established his reputation with the group *Alexander Taming Bucephalus* (1833), but his most ambitious work was the *Albert Memorial* (1876) in Charlotte Square, Edinburgh, which earned him his knighthood.

Raeburn had been the first Scottish artist to be knighted, when George IV visited Scotland in 1822. He was the first Scottish-born painter since Jamesone to establish such a reputation though staying in Scotland. His younger contemporary and friend, David Wilkie (1785–1841), however, had the greatest reputation and was the most influential of all Scottish painters. He settled in London, but his art closely reflects his Scottish background. Through his friendship with Nasmyth, who had been Ramsay's assistant, he inherited Ramsay's command of drawing. Like David Allan, too, for whom he retained a lifelong admiration, he took his principal inspiration from the Scots poets, especially Burns. Wilkie's paintings of common life are deceptively simple and he had close links with developments in philosophical thought, especially through his contact with the surgeon Charles Bell. Bell had been a pupil of David Allan and in his investigative surgery, drawing was a constant aid. Indeed, a collection of his painted studies of the pathology of wounds survives in the Royal College of Surgeons in Edinburgh. His *Anatomy of Expression* (1806), reflecting the two sides of his interests, was an important stage in the evolution of his ideas on the physiology of the brain and nervous system. There is a direct link partly through Bell between Wilkie, Géricault and the early history of psychiatric medicine in France.

Wilkie's social awareness is also reflected in his painting. *Distraining for Rent* (1815) and *The Penny Wedding* (1818) provided a commentary on social change and the human cost of the Agricultural and Industrial Revolutions. They are closely paralleled by John Galt in his novels, though in his approach to history in painting Wilkie was closer to Walter Scott, whose inspiration is clearly seen in his first true historical painting, *John Knox Preaching before the Lords of Congregation* (1832). It presented an approach to the psychological interpretation of history that was widely influential. In France, his example was followed by painters like Delacroix and Bonington.

In Scotland William Allan (1782–1850) was close to Wilkie, but others followed him at a greater distance to create a minor industry of historical painting. In part, as in the careful historical reconstructions of James Drummond (1816–77), this took its initial inspiration from Scott and contributed significantly to the historicism that dominated Scottish taste in the mid-nineteenth century, to reach its apogee (or nadir) in

32. The Letter of Introduction *(1813), by Sir David Wilkie (1785–1841). (*National Gallery of Scotland*)*

Balmoral. In implicit opposition to all of this, however, much of the work of painters like George Harvey (1806–76) and Thomas Duncan (1807–45) was religious and took its inspiration from the events leading up to the Disruption. Harvey made his name with paintings of the Covenanters such as the *Convenanter's Preaching* of 1830, while Duncan's painting of the *Death of John Brown of Priesthill* (1844), also a Covenanting subject, was one of the finest historical paintings produced in the years after the death of Wilkie.

The most striking response to the Disruption itself was the massive painting that D.O. Hill (1802–70) undertook to record it. The picture itself was a failure: it was not finished for more than two decades and in the end contained more than four hundred figures, all given equal prominence in proper democratic fashion. It is the calotypes that Hill undertook in partnership with Robert Adamson – originally in preparation for his painting in the four years between 1844 and Adamson's death in 1848 – that are enduring. They are amongst the very first art photographs and remain among the best.

Wilkie died two years before the Disruption, but the themes of such pictures as *Knox Preaching* and *The Cotter's Saturday Night* (1837) gave expression to the ideas at the centre of the developing religious crisis in Scotland. The shift in his work from the social to religious subjects paralleled the development of Thomas Chalmers' career. It is a reminder that the first half of the nineteenth century did not see a retreat into the comfort of religion, but a return to it in an attempt to draw anew on the moral and spiritual resources of the Reformation in order to deal with the Pandora's box of social change opened by the Enlightenment and industrialisation. It is this which explains why so much of the nation's moral capital was invested in the Disruption, an event which, far from being backward-looking, was prophetic of the social and moral concerns which have preoccupied western society since that time.

Wilkie also pioneered the attempt to find an appropriate style for modern history in major paintings like the colossal *Sir David Baird discovering the body of Sultaun Tippoo Sahib* (1838) and, though his early style is marked by high finish and complex compositions of small figures, he later imitated the breadth of handling of Rubens, Rembrandt and Velázquez in a way that influenced painters in the next generation such as John 'Spanish' Phillip (1817–67) and Robert Scott Lauder. In the 1850s, Lauder passed on Wilkie's influence, including his belief in the importance of drawing, to his pupils such as John Pettie (189–1893) and W.Q. Orchardson (1832–1910). It was thus maintained to the end of the century and beyond. Wilkie's earlier style of genre painting was also widely imitated in his lifetime by artists like Alexander Fraser (1786–1865), John Burnet (1784–1868) and Walter Geikie (1795–1837). Geikie's etchings and drawings are of particular interest because of the unaffected way that they record the lives and circumstances of ordinary people, but in subsequent generations this degenerated into the Kailyard imagery of painters like Tom Faed (1826–1900) and Erskine Nicol (1825–1904).

The end of the eighteenth century had seen a rapid increase in the number of artists working in Scotland. This was reflected, after a series of abortive attempts, in the establishment of the Scottish Academy in 1826, becoming the Royal Scottish Academy ten years later, and by the mid-nineteenth century there was a sufficient market to maintain a large and vigorous artistic community. To some extent this expansion was consumer-led and artists like Tom Faed or Joseph Noel Paton (1821–1901) pursued successful careers, providing the public with the kind of art that it wanted. Others, like David Scott (1806–49), Robert Scott Lauder and William Dyce (1806–64), worked to maintain the standards of seriousness of the older generation, even though it became increasingly difficult to do so. Dyce's painting, *Pegwell Bay, a Recollection of October 5th 1858*, for example, is a profound reflection on the struggle to maintain religious faith in the face of scientific progress. It is, above all, on human insignificance in the face of the new recognition of the enormity of time that he reflects. Time is present in the picture as geological time in the cliffs and as astronomical time in the comet in the sky whose presence is recorded in the specific date given in the title of the picture. In the movement of the tide on the shore, astronomy works on geology in the immense and continuing process of change first described by James Hutton and beneath which even such a landscape is eventually transient.

Dyce was for a brief period master of the Trustees Academy, and in 1837 moved south to take up a similar position with the Board of Trade and Council for Schools of Design in London with a view to setting up schools in England. He championed the idea of design in the modern sense, basing his arguments on a direct knowledge of the methods of modern industry, but it was typical of the nineteenth-century split between art and industry that he was frustrated by the universal insistence on the primacy of the fine art tradition. Nevertheless, as Prince Albert was a great admirer of his work, his ideas may have played some part in the development of the South Kensington museums. He also played an important role in the revival of mural painting and stained glass. In a century where sometimes it would seem art and the industry that sustained it existed on different planets, his was a voice, if not for a more radical, at least for a more rational view. In some respects he was a link between the Enlightenment tradition of convergent thought and the long history of the sometimes oblique attempts to reverse the nineteenth-century divergence of art and manufactures and which eventually led from William Morris to the Bauhaus.

With a similar concern for values in art, Scott Lauder passed on to his pupils ideas about truth in painting that Wilkie and even Ramsay would have endorsed. Scott Lauder's pupils were prominent as a group in both England and Scotland from the 1860s. Orchardson and Pettie were the two most prominent in the south. Close friends, they developed a kind of narrative genre that looked back to Wilkie and which in Orchardson's *Mariage de Convenance; After* (1888), for example, became as sophisticated and subtly understated a commentary on contemporary life as can be found in any of the fiction of the period.

William McTaggart (1835–1910) and George Paul Chalmers (1833–78) were the leaders of this group in the north. In their early careers, both worked in an idiom of cottage genre which looked back to Wilkie and which reached its highest expression in Chalmers' unfinished painting, *The Legend* (1864–79). Both were also inspired landscape painters and McTaggart eventually concentrated on landscape and especially seascape, developing a style of great, expressive freedom. This has links to contemporary Dutch painting, but also to Constable and Turner, and pictures like *The Storm* (1890) or *The Sailing of the Emigrant Ship* (1895) are really best understood in the tradition of the grand, romantic landscape. The first picture is a reflection on the impermanence of human life as fishermen struggle with the grand indifference of nature. McTaggart was a Highlander, and the latter picture is a more specific and tragic commentary on the destruction of the Highland way of life in the Clearances and forced emigration. The picture's force depends not on sentimental narrative as in Tom Faed's picture with the same theme, *The Last of the Clan* (1865), but on the dramatic dislocation and fragmentation of the means of representation itself. As such it is profoundly modern.

In Glasgow by the mid-century, the wealth and entrepreneurial spirit of the city was reflected in some quite adventurous collecting, some of whose results can still be seen in the city's collections. There were also regular exhibitions, and the Glasgow School of Art was established. This all helped to encourage a distinctive Glasgow point of view manifested in the emergence in the 1880s of the Glasgow Boys, a group that included James Guthrie (1859–1930), W.Y. MacGregor (1855–1923), E.A. Walton (1860–1922), James Paterson (1854–1932) and others. Because of their self-conscious identification with Glasgow, their work is usually seen as quite separate from the achievements of earlier Scottish artists. They did, in fact, have close links to painters of rural and agricultural subjects working in East Lothian and Berwickshire, like James

33. The Sailing of the Emigrant Ship *(1895), by William MacTaggart (1835–1910).*
*(*National Gallery of Scotland*)*

Campbell Noble (1846–1913), W.D. McKay (1844–1924), James Lawton Wingate (1846–1924) and especially Arthur Melville (1855–1904). Melville developed to be one of the most original painters of the period, especially in watercolour, and he provided an important example to the Glasgow Boys with whom he was on close terms – Guthrie, for instance, went to work alongside him in Cockburnspath in the early 1880s.

The Glasgow painters were also influenced by contemporary French and Dutch painting, and produced a series of dramatically direct and apparently matter-of-fact pictures such as Guthrie's *The Hind's Daughter* (1884) and W.Y. MacGregor's *The Vegetable Stall* (1884). Such pictures look back in part to the native Scottish tradition of painting rooted in experience, but they also helped to bring into British art the new, radical immediacy of Continental painting after Courbet.

These developments created tensions in the Royal Scottish Academy, resulting in the formation in 1891 of the Society of Scottish Artists as an alternative exhibiting society. This was probably also a reflection of the way in which in the later 1880s painters in Scotland, as elsewhere in Europe, went through a crisis of conscience as they saw how far their own concerns had drifted from those that shaped the lives of the majority of the society in which they lived. The leading Scottish spokesman in this was Patrick Geddes, champion of an organic view of society. As a social thinker, Geddes promoted art as necessary to the regeneration of society, but it was very much art in the service of the public that he had in mind. Thus, for instance, he saw mural painting as especially important. He was in close touch with the leaders of the Arts and Crafts movement, and in Edinburgh his ideas found interpreters in Phoebe Traquair (1852–1936), John Duncan (1866–1945), Robert Burns (1869–1941) and others. Phoebe Traquair's mural paintings in the St Mary's Song School (1889–92) and in the Catholic Apostolic Church, Edinburgh (begun immediately after the completion of the former though they took many years), are among the most distinguished of their kind, but she was also typical of the Arts and Crafts movement in the range of skills that she practised, producing superb work as bookbinder, enamellist and embroiderer as well as painter.

In Glasgow this view of the decorative – and therefore social – function of painting is reflected in the work of the younger Glasgow Boys such as George Henry (1858–1943) and E.A. Hornel (1864–1933). They followed the example of Arthur Melville to adopt a more formal, flatter style which also has obvious links to contemporary, Continental symbolism seen in Henry's *Galloway Landscape* of 1889, or a painting in which these two collaborated, *The Druids* of 1890. The most radical works of the period, however, were the symbolist watercolours of Charles Rennie Mackintosh (1868–1928) and the Macdonald sisters, Frances (1874–1922) and Margaret (1865–1933).

The Macdonalds were prominent among the women artists who were beginning to take advantage of the new opportunities offered them by art education, especially at Glasgow School of Art under its enlightened principal, Frances Newbery, but this whole group was typical of their generation in the way that, depending on the central discipline of architecture, they worked in a wide range of the applied arts. Mackintosh himself, for instance, designed not only all the decoration, but all the furniture and other equipment for Miss Cranston's several Glasgow tearooms. In his later career, Mackintosh worked exclusively as a watercolour painter, producing landscapes and flower paintings of great beauty.

There were also painters like Bessie MacNicol (1869–1904), Charles Mackie (1862–1920) and S.J. Peploe (1871–1935) who developed a less self-conscious way of painting that was in its own terms equally advanced. In the first years of the twentieth century, Peploe moved increasingly close to French painting. It was his friend J.D. Fergusson (1874–1961), however, who was most closely involved in the birth of the modern movement. His *Les Eus*, painted in Paris c.1912, is one of the most ambitious British paintings of its time. Like his contemporary painting, *Rhythm*, it reflects Fergusson's knowledge of Bergson's philosophy, giving it a utopian and so ultimately social interpretation, and so continuing the interaction between painting and the other branches of intellectual life. It is interesting and a reflection of their mutual interests that Fergusson and Mackintosh became close friends after Fergusson returned to Britain at the beginning of the First World War.

Peploe and Fergusson, together with two younger painters, F.C.B. Cadell (1883–1937) and Leslie Hunter (1879–1931), who painted in a somewhat similar way, have subsequently become known as the Scottish Colourists. Peploe's most distinguished works are his still-lifes which range from brilliant essays with the fluency of Manet around 1903, through Cubist-inspired, highly formal paintings around 1912, to austere, almost low-key paintings towards the end of his life. Of the four, Hunter was most closely influenced by Matisse, while Cadell, who worked first in an impressionist manner, developed a brilliant, formal way of painting that exploits intense colour (as in the *Orange Chair* of 1920). Working together on Iona in the 1920s, Cadell and Peploe produced some landscapes of rocks and sea that are of startlingly simple and luminous beauty. All four provided an important example to the younger generation of a free and adventurous kind of painting, though it was perhaps Fergusson – who was far more metaphysically inclined than the others – who had the most far-reaching influence, especially after 1939 when he settled in Glasgow.

At the end of the nineteenth century, following Whistler's lead, there was a dramatic revival in printmaking. The tradition of the artist's print had never completely died out. Wilkie, for example, made etchings as did Hugh William Williams, Walter Geikie and David Scott, but William Strang (1859–1921), D.Y. Cameron (1876–1953), Muirhead Bone (1865–1945), James McBey (1883–1959) and a number of others brought etching to a new level of achievement. Strang's etched portraits and Bone's powerful images such as *The Great Gantry, Charing Cross* (1906) are also outstanding in the period. The example of the printmakers of Muirhead Bone's generation was transmitted through E.S. Lumsden (1883–1948) and others to younger artists like Ian Fleming (*b*.1906) and William Wilson (1905–72) who were themselves the outstanding printmakers of the 1930s. Through their example in turn, the tradition carried on in the movement to found printmaking workshops in Aberdeen, Edinburgh and Glasgow in the late 1960s and early 1970s.

Bone's prints and drawings also reflect the commentaries of Geddes on the state of contemporary cities. His drawings of Glasgow published in 1911 are amongst the first sustained attempts to turn art to the direct contemplation of an industrial environment. Such drawings reflect Geddes's vision of the danger for society in the divergence between the human and the technical sciences, which he identified in *Dr Jekyll and Mr Hyde*. This prophecy was terribly fulfilled in the conflict of the First World War. It was Muirhead Bone, too, as the first official war artist, who produced the most appropriate response to its horrors in the terse drawings that he made on the Western Front. It was also the tragedy of the war that produced in the National War Memorial the fullest expression of the social and collaborative ideal of art. The memorial was designed by Robert Lorimer, but it was realised by a team of artists and craftsmen, and their co-operation commemorates not only those killed in battle, but also everyone who was involved, even the animals, and so in a profound way it is a communal expression. Among those who worked on it were the sculptors Pilkington Jackson (1887–1973), Alice Meredith Williams (*c*.1870–1934), Alexander Carrick (1882–1966) and Phyllis Bone (1894–1972), the stained-glass artist Douglas Strachan and the wood-carvers Alexander Clow (1861–1946) and his brother William (dates not known). Together this group played a vital role in the establishment of modern sculpture in Scotland.

The late nineteenth century had seen the art market in Scotland attain heights that it had not reached before or since. Several international dealers, such as Alexander Reid, worked from Scotland, especially in the climate offered by Glasgow in its heyday as Second City of the Empire. By the end of the First World War this boom had collapsed, and from that time forward it was and has remained the norm for artists to maintain themselves by teaching. William Johnstone, William Gillies and many others all taught throughout their lives. The market for portraits kept going rather longer and though on the whole it degenerated into the lifeless simulacra of boardroom portraiture, some painters, like James Gunn (1893–1964), who worked mostly in the south, and Alberto Morrocco (*b*.1917) and David Donaldson (*b*.1916) have kept alive an older, more honest tradition.

One of the most original painters in the 1920s and 1930s was James Cowie (1886–1956). His *Falling Leaves* (1934) is a complex, poetic study of the transition from child to adult that shows the influence of both Millais and Cézanne. In its subtlety it can be compared to Lewis Grassic Gibbon's contemporary novel, *Sunset Song*. In his later work Cowie created some of his most remarkable pictures under the influence of surrealism. A similar duality between symbolism and modernism is seen in the work of his contemporary, Eric Robertson (1887–1941), who was a pupil of John Duncan. Robertson was the leading figure in the Edinburgh group, a society that exhibited in the years immediately following the First World War. Cecile Walton (1891–1956) and Dorothy Johnstone (1892–1980) were also distinguished members of this group.

Other artists embraced the modernist aesthetic more directly. In the early 1920s, William McCance (1894–1970) produced some dramatic interpretations of the machine aesthetic. In alliance with Hugh MacDiarmid and influenced by J.D. Fergusson as well as by Wyndham Lewis, McCance also applied these ideas to the attempt to formulate an equivalent frame of reference for art to that evolved by MacDiarmid and others for literature in the Scots Renaissance. This was an idea first formulated by Geddes, and McCance, Fergusson and MacDiarmid all argued that such a movement should embrace the Scottish industrial tradition, too. They argued that the great ships of the Clyde, like the medieval cathedrals, represented the collective achievement of the nation's genius.

William Johnstone (1897–1981) provided the most convincing expression of this in a work of art of this kind of ambition in his major painting, *A Point in Time* (1929–33). It is a study in time and, using ideas derived from surrealism and contemporary American painting, it evokes the dynamic interaction of the present with the immemorial through the artist's own identification with the landscape of the Borders. It has close analogies not just with MacDiarmid's poetry but with the novels of Lewis Grassic Gibbon and Neil Gunn. This interaction with literature gave visual art a strength which was sustained in the work of the post-war generation to whom the example of both Johnstone and Fergusson was very important.

Johnstone's paintings in the 1930s were original, but were also recognisably part of contemporary developments in painting in Europe and America. Few of his contemporaries in Scotland were as adventurous, but in the 1930s and 1940s, William Gillies (1898–1973), William MacTaggart (1903–81), William Wilson (1905–72), John Maxwell (1905–62) and Anne Redpath (1895–1965) between them evolved a style that became identified with Edinburgh. Influenced by painters like Matisse, Braque, Chagall and Bonnard, and by the English painters of the St Ives school, it was strongly subjective, but at its best – as in some of Gillies's landscapes, for example – it was also capable of real poetry. Contemporary with this group were Robert Colquhoun (1914–62) and Robert McBryde (1913–66). From Glasgow, they made their reputation in the south during the war years where they became part of the English neo-romantic school.

In Glasgow a different influence was at work through the presence there of J.D. Fergusson, who provided an important link back, not only to early modernist Paris, but also to the perception of the function of art promoted at the turn of the century by Geddes and others. Fergusson therefore helped keep alive a sense of the essentially serious and social function of art that persists to this day as a distinctive characteristic of such major figures who came of age in the 1940s as Eduardo Paolozzi and Ian Hamilton Finlay. Fergusson founded the New Scottish Group, including painters like Donald Bain (1904–79) and Millie Frood (1900–88), and, helped by the presence in Glasgow of

34. Self-Portrait *(1941), by W.G. Gillies (1898–1973).* (Scottish National Gallery of Modern Art)

wartime refugees like Joseph Herman and Jankel Adler, he encouraged both a modernist and a politically radical approach.

In the late 1940s, for instance, Tom MacDonald (1914–85) and Bet Low (*b.*1924) worked together in Glasgow both to reflect contemporary life in their painting and to engage their art with the lives of ordinary people. The most important painter to emerge from this background was Joan Eardley (1921–63). At their best, her pictures of Glasgow children, such as *Andrew with a Comic* (*c.*1955), are unusual in the way that they combine this kind of social realist purpose with a real sense of individual dignity. Her later seascapes, though, are perhaps her outstanding achievement. They draw on the example of contemporary American abstract-expressionist painting, but they are never wholly abstract and so retain an essential tension between objective and subjective that links them to the long tradition of Romantic landscape painting. It is this which makes it possible to see her as a worthy successor to the elder McTaggart.

The Second World War, more than the First, disrupted the vital exchanges with the Continent which had been such an important inspiration to artists like Fergusson and Johnstone, but several Scottish artists found their way to Paris in the years immediately after the war. William Gear (*b*.1915) went straight from demobilisation in Germany to France and worked there alongside Asger Jorn, Karel Appel and other members of the Cobra group. Eduardo Paolozzi (*b*.1924) was in Paris at the same time and made contact with members of the Dada and surrealist movements. Gear and Paolozzi, together with Alan Davie (*b*.1920) and William Turnbull (*b*.1922), were pioneers in Britain of an approach to art that was more radical than anything that had been seen before, except in the work of William Johnstone. Johnstone, then head of the Central School in London, provided important support for several of these younger artists.

In the late 1940s, Paolozzi was already attacking the narrow definition of 'fine art' and was arguing instead that the art of our culture must embrace all its imagery, not just that which is defined as art. This was the perception that was eventually to give birth to the idea of pop art. Paolozzi developed from the art of collage – both in sculpture and printmaking – a metaphor for the experience of modern life, and his later work has become increasingly critical of the modernist aesthetic as irrelevant and distracting from the real issues that face contemporary society. His monumental bronze, *Monte*

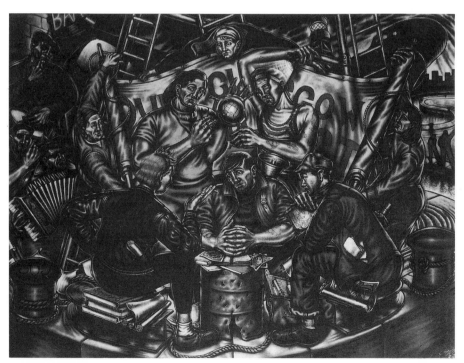

35. Young Glasgow Communists, *by Ken Currie (1960–   ) (from* The Glasgow Triptych*). (*With permission of Raab Boukamel Galleries and Ken Currie*)*

36. Panel from Spirit of Scotland *triptych (1986–87) by Peter Howson (1958–). (*Flowers East Gallery/Peter Howson*)*

Cassino, sited near his birthplace in Edinburgh, is one of the most ambitious pieces of public art to be installed in Scotland for many years and is worthy of the highest ideals for public art expressed by Geddes. In the 1950s and 1960s, working somewhat in parallel to Paolozzi, Alan Davie explored ways of achieving a truly spontaneous kind of painting. This ambition suggests links with French and American art, but also with the development of Johnstone's later work which is free and spontaneous and yet which he saw as still inspired by landscape.

In many ways Paolozzi's critique of modernism constituted the first step in the evolution of post-modernism, and though the example of Gillies and Maxwell remained a powerful influence, there can be no doubt that in the 1960s and 1970s there was an increasingly strong reaction generally against their aestheticism in favour of an art of greater commitment. Paolozzi's contemporary, Ian Hamilton Finlay (*b.*1925), has been a key figure in this. His most ambitious undertaking is his garden at Little Sparta. It is a metaphor in itself, created as it is on the edge of the tree-line and in its layout it is typical of Finlay in the way that with wit and irony it combines art, poetry and nature.

Also in the early 1960s John Bellany (*b.*1942) was one of a group that led a return both to figurative art and, drawing on his own background in a fishing community, to a kind of subject matter that was close to narrative. He was directly influenced by the tradition of the Scots Renaissance personified in MacDiarmid and he was in turn an important influence on his own contemporaries. The admiration for German art that Bellany shared with Sandy Moffat (*b.*1943) has, for instance, been echoed by a good many of the younger generation. Will Maclean (*b.*1941) has also continued the traditions of the Scots Renaissance. He has made fishing and the sea a source of rich metaphors in an art that is consciously rooted in Gaelic culture and which shows parallels with the novels of Neil Gunn and the poetry of Sorley MacLean.

One of the most significant developments of the post-war decades was the advent of direct state patronage through the formation of the Scottish Arts Council in 1964 and subsequently the increase in the number of small galleries. These two developments were an important factor in breaking the near monopoly of the exhibiting societies and so in encouraging greater diversity and experiment. Sculptors like Hew Lorimer (*b.*1907) and Eric Schilski (1898–1974) had remained loyal to older traditions of carving or modelling. Schilski had depended on teaching while Lorimer had depended on such architectural commissions as the decoration of the National Library, but in the 1970s – encouraged by this new source of support sculptors like Jake Harvey (*b.*1948), Doug Cocker (*b.*1945), Ainslie Yule (*b.*1941) and Gavin Scobie (*b.*1940) – began to explore the language of constructed, modernist sculpture. In the same way painters like John Houston (*b.*1930), Elizabeth Blackadder (*b.*1931), David McLure (*b.*1926) and David Michie (*b.*1928), and also younger artists like Duncan Shanks (*b.*1937) and Barbara Rae (*b.*1943), all developed in different ways from the tradition established by Gillies, Maxwell, Redpath and Eardley; but artists like Mark Boyle (*b.*1934) and Bruce McLean (*b.*1944) – like Bellany though with very different results – reacted against this tradition.

In Glasgow in the 1980s, a group of artists led by Steven Campbell (*b.*1954) pioneered a more radical approach to figurative painting which could also look back to the work of the painters of the 1940s in the city. In Campbell's work especially, some of the deeper insecurities of the late twentieth century are given expression in a way that has universal relevance. It is encouraging that since that time, there have been many new and even younger artists to maintain and extend the Scottish tradition of respecting the profound seriousness of art in this way.

Books for Further Reading

James Caw, *Scottish Painting Past and Present, 1620–1908* (Edinburgh, 1908)

Keith Hartley, *Scottish Art Since 1900* (Edinburgh, 1989)

David and Francina Irwin, *Scottish Painters at Home and Abroad, 1800–1900* (London, 1975)

Duncan Macmillan, *Painting in Scotland: the Golden Age, 1707–1843* (Oxford, 1986)

Duncan Macmillan, *Scottish Art 1460–1990* (Edinburgh, 1990)

Royal Scottish Museum, *Angels, Nobles and Unicorns* (Edinburgh, 1982)

The Scottishness of Scottish Architecture

CHARLES McKEAN

INTRODUCTION

If Architecture has national peculiarities impressed upon it, then it must be history —
the world's history written in stone.
C.R. MACKINTOSH, 1892

Building is messy, difficult and expensive; and not lightly undertaken. It therefore reflects the priorities of its time. A study of who has been building, what they have built, and why they built it is one of social history in stone. On the large scale, as Lewis Mumford put it, 'the great city is the best organ of memory man has created', just as it is on the scale of individual buildings, as Sir Robert Rowand Anderson explained in 1889:

> If you examine the plans of an old Scottish mansion, you can read it like a story-book from the foundations to the chimney-tops. You can distinguish the original tower that the family once lived in . . .. You will then notice an addition when the family became richer and times were less warlike . . .. It was never built solely to look picturesque or interesting . . .. It was built from time to time to suit the necessities of the day.[1]

A man of European predilections, tastes and stature, Anderson was unequivocal as to the value of his native culture. So necessary did he judge a deep understanding of Scotland's historic architecture to be, that he founded the National Art Survey both to record important Scots buildings and to train student architects in their detail; a method of learning he deemed equivalent to a medical student's study of anatomy. In 1915 he was instrumental in the foundation of the Royal Incorporation of Architects in Scotland to 'foster the national architecture of Scotland', of which he became first President.

37. Linlithgow Palace. There has probably been a royal palace on this site since the reign of David I, but the surviving buildings were mostly built in three phases between 1425 and 1620. Both James V and Mary, Queen of Scots were born here. The Palace was intact until 1746 when it was heavily damaged by fire, perhaps accidentally, when English troops were quartered in it after the second Battle of Falkirk. This view is from Scotland: The Tourist's Rambles in the Highlands *by Michael Bouquet, (Paris, c.1850). (*National Library of Scotland*)*

The Second World War brought the ensuing revival of architectural Scottishness (the third of its kind) to a premature close. Since then, the national architecture of Scotland has been subsumed as a variant – albeit obstreperous – of British architecture; our cultural Procrustes have trimmed architects as various as Charles Rennie Mackintosh, Robert Adam and Sir Robert Lorimer to fit. Scottishness in Scottish architecture was relegated to little short of kitsch – inappropriately plundered historic references exemplified in crowsteps: cultural amnesia produces some wilful creatures.

Historically, Scots have looked to outsiders for a corrective. English architects as various as Sir George Gilbert Scott, Philip Webb, W.R. Lethaby, Sir Edwin Lutyens and Oliver Hill, were inspired by Scots architecture to some truly outstanding creations. Indeed, Scott invented a Scottish style of his very own for Dundee's Albert Institute and Glasgow's University. Where Englishmen led, could Scots be far behind? Sir Robert Lorimer aspired for his House of Formakin that it should be the 'purest Scotch that I've done';[2] and in 1892 Charles Rennie Mackintosh, notwithstanding his European aspirations, suggested to the Glasgow literati that architects 'should be a little less cosmopolitan and rather more national in our architecture as we are with language'.[3] Robert Hurd, Basil Spence, Ian Lindsay and Sir Frank Mears, picking up the inter-war baton, sought an architecture fused from a combination of Renaissance Scotland and white Scandinavian modernism.

What was the genesis of such yearning? Although traditions inherited from Scottish Renaissance architecture lingered to the end of the eighteenth century and informed even the cosmopolitanism of Robert Adam, they were increasingly manifest in buildings down the social scale. By the early nineteenth century, the legacy had become imperceptible. The ensuing decades of cultural uncertainty were terminated by a self-conscious revival of Scots architecture inspired by the 1845–52 publication of beautifully crafted illustrations of old Scots architecture in *The Baronial and Ecclesiastical Antiquities of Scotland* by R.W. Billings. His volumes restored to Scots lairds a self-confidence in their native culture. Since then, belief in a national architecture has ebbed and flowed in line with broader Scottish cultural preoccupations.

The first revival came at a time when architects were glorying in the exploitation of iron framing; and when vastly improved rail communications reduced the traditional connection between a locality and its indigenous materials. Each subsequent revival also coincided with similarly dramatic technological innovation. Revivalism, therefore, may have been underpinned by the fear that untrammelled technology, devoid of any cultural roots or local reference, would lead to a deracinated Scotland – one, as John Buchan put it, 'with nothing distinctive to show to the world'.[4]

Another *fin de siecle*, and another re-examination of our roots after almost half a century of architectural amnesia. The focus is again upon what Robert Hurd christened the 'most national of Scottish architectural periods'[5] – that between 1530 and 1660. Scottish architecture is now receiving the systematic analysis – through study of plans, details, typologies, colour, massing and furnishing – that other cultures have long enjoyed. The architecture with which this country greeted the Renaissance had a vivid distinctiveness, proportion, colour and flamboyance. It is now possible to confirm the intuition of Billings and of C.R. Mackintosh that its creations were the work of architects rather than (weasel-word) *vernacular*. It was the essence of this period that each successive revival sought to recapture and retune for contemporary life.

*38. St Mungo's Cathedral, Glasgow, mainly thirteenth century. This is the only one of the great Gothic churches of the south of Scotland to have survived the devastation of repeated English invasion and the Reformation. (*RCAHMS*)*

Interpreted correctly, Scottish architectural history provides valuable historic documentation; misinterpreted, it is deployed to prop up the mythologies upon which so many of popular misconceptions about Scotland depend. Myth would have it that the country languished once James VI had left for London. The architecture implies a period of unprecedented mercantile confidence and affluence: when the Court style flourished, much of Edinburgh's High Street was recast in ashlar upon arcades, and the country lavished its substance upon Heriot's Hospital, the Tron Kirk, the Parliament House, substantial universities in Aberdeen, Glasgow and Edinburgh, and charitable hospitals in Glasgow, Edinburgh, Dundee and Inverness.

Myth presents the prevalence of gunlooped castles in Aberdeenshire as testimony to a primitive country bypassed by the Renaissance. They are, in reality, mock-military Renaissance country houses or châteaux of some swagger, whose restorers have occasionally been unaware of that fact. Over a hundred years after the Reformation is supposed to have spread a sad and drab conformity upon the land, the writhing and luminous skylines of Scots buildings proved otherwise.

It is time to retrieve Scottish architecture from its inappropriate position as an inconvenient footnote to British architectural history. (If Scottish architecture were to merit only the status of a footnote, it would be to European architectural history.)

This review falls into five sections: the fundamentals of Scottish architecture; the flourishing of the national architecture of Scotland, 1530–1700; assimilation (?) with England; the golden period of Scots urbanism, 1770–1840; and lastly, the period from 1845 to the present, characterised by architecture lurching between the attractions of the revivals and those of technical innovation.

FUNDAMENTALS OF A NATIONAL ARCHITECTURE

Sir Banister Fletcher propounded that the architecture of each country is the consequence of its geography, geology, culture, climate, politics, materials, religion and wealth. Scotland is the northern half of an island tipping off the north-west corner of Europe where – as Tacitus put it – the world and all things come to an end. It is only partially fertile, its climate adversely damp, and its rain is wind-driven – horizontally, if not upwards. By European standards, its sunlight is weak. In a climate such as that, Scots buildings are necessarily boxes to shelter human activity from the weather. When they become more than boxes, they become architecture.

Scotland is a country of stone: many various stones, but stone nonetheless. Its long span timber had mostly been burnt by the Middle Ages, save in localities like the Rothiemurchus, Drum or Cadzow forests. The absence of long span timber before seventeenth-century Baltic imports, led to Scottish buildings almost invariably the width of a stone vault: for that comprised their structure. It also proved wonderfully indestructible in times of turmoil. Rare amongst European and Baltic nations, Scotland had no tradition of framed structures.

The country's growing season is short with consequently fewer crops than its neighbours. It was thus often low in ready cash. It was, however, rich in men and materials, as Etienne Perlin reported to his Guise paymasters in 1553: 'nothing is short here save money'.[6] After the opening of the English wars, craftsmen came only rarely overland from the south; and their import over the North Sea was but sparingly

39. Falkland Palace. Construction probably started in the reign of James III, and it was completed by James V about 1537. This is John Slezer's drawing from Theatrum Scotiae *of 1693. (*National Library of Scotland*)*

afforded. The result was an indigenous architecture of unique plan form, geometry and mass. High craft decoration was sparse.

Scotland had many burghs, but few large towns or cities until required by agricultural and industrial expansion. The vast territory of Buchan, for example, was a seemingly empty land: in the seventeenth century it contained virtually no community of size save Turriff — a single street of houses with a church; and the newly feued fishing burghs of Peterhead, Fraserburgh, and Rosehearty were little more than a gaggle of fisher cottages. The Royal Burgh of Woodhead of Fyvie had fewer than thirty houses. Yet the quality and quantity of its châteaux reveals that seventeenth-century Buchan was prosperous; but the population inhabited dispersed settlements, fermtouns and kirktouns. Communication remained generally waterborne until the arrival of turnpike roads and railways in the nineteenth century; and settlements tended to follow river valleys or the coastline.

Scots Law was peculiarly important to the development of Scots architecture. Feuing favoured long-term enhancement as against short-term expediency, and that advantage may best be understood by comparison with the development of London's Regent's Park. When John Nash presented the Crown with his proposals for the construction of the Park, he justified expenditure on the landscaping, the lake and the tree-planting, thus: the houses were built to last only for their 99-year lease. Since the landscape would outlast the architecture, it would enhance the value of subsequent rebuilding. No comparable attitude existed in Scotland. Ownership in feu tenure gave the land proprietor perpetual rights to set building conditions; and yet the building's owner still owned. Both therefore had an interest in good-quality construction. Those with money to spend, spent more upon initial capital cost.

TOWARDS A NATIONAL ARCHITECTURE

Culdee, Celtic, Pictish and Norse buildings, such as they are known, seem to have taken the form of stone enclosures, generally circular, some thatched, some (like soutterrains) underground, and some (such as the brochs and duns) soaring upwards hugging rocky outcrops. Save for rare details like the door in the round tower of Brechin Cathedral, little survives of a deliberately architectonic nature.

The Celtic, principally West Highland, architecture of plain, undecorated enclosure, inherited from the brochs, reappeared in non-hierarchical curtain-walled castles that enclose rocky outcrops throughout the Highlands and islands (usually modified with later tower houses and palace blocks) as may be seen at Dunstaffnage, Tioram, Kilchurn, Duntrune, Dunvegan and Mingarry.

Norman influence in Scotland was partial, and followed great families like de Moravia, Comyn and de Vaux. They must have been accompanied by their craftsmen – particularly masons – since their castles have Norman plan forms and carving adapted to Scots construction techniques, climate and materials. In consequence they are plainer, taller, compressed, and deeper in mass and profile than their peers on the Continent or in England. That eschewing of detail and focus upon geometry, depth and mass became a native characteristic, which Sir Walter Scott was to expropriate with pride in his panegyric to Glasgow Cathedral: 'plain, weel-jointed mason work: none of your curly wurlies, open steeked hems ...'[7] The massing successfully conceals its diminutive scale: two Glasgow Cathedrals would fit inside that of Amiens.

Until the late thirteenth century, aspects of architecture could be accepted as variants upon English and French. Thereafter, only craftsmen accompanying the invaders (James of St George, Edward I's master architect, is known to have worked at Linlithgow) came overland. A new architectural identity was called into being: solid, usually plain and vertical, still to the width of a stone vault: now composed of plain, harled walls increasingly highlighted by dressed stone details and brilliantly gilt carvings.

Its most characteristic manifestation was the fortified house which, from the fourteenth century onwards, took the form of a tower, the living accommodation vertically disposed, the ground floor invariably kitchen and cellars. Generally sited for proximity to water rather than for fortification, passive defence was achieved through mass, limited entry point and defensive battlement. These buildings were houses not castles, and were usually accompanied by a walled livestock enclosure called a barmkin which, by the late fifteenth century, had begun to include structures of rather greater substance. Rarely less than two and a half storeys above the ground (cellar) floor, with their principal rooms or hall at first-floor level, these prominent tower houses were different in kind to the ground-hugging English manor-house, with its primary rooms on the ground floor.

Beyond the wealthier religious buildings or the greatest palaces, carved or dressed stone was deployed sparingly. From Paris came the master John Morvo (or Morrow) who may have been responsible for some of the most delightful decorative work in Melrose and Lincluden. Scottish churches came to adopt the structure, matched nowhere else, of a solid barrel vault with superimposed vault decoration. The somewhat thickset architecture that resulted may best be appreciated in conjunction with the distinctively Scots late medieval tracery in a fifteenth-century collegiate church such as Seton.

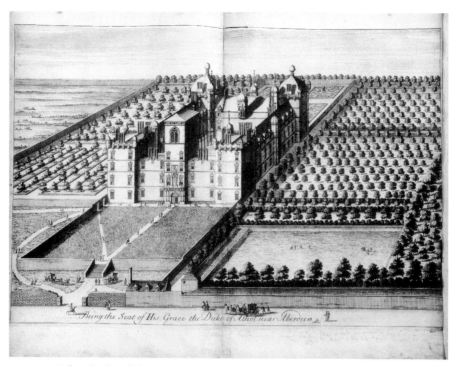

40. *Heriot's School, Edinburgh. Building started in 1628 by William Wallace and finished c.1700, to fulfil a legacy by George Heriot, the royal goldsmith and banker. This view is from John Slezer's* Theatrum Scotiae *(1693) (where it was incorrectly captioned.) (*NLS*)*

THE SCOTTISH RENAISSANCE

If architecture embodies the culture of its time, it would be absurd to suppose that the music of Robert Carver, the poems of Dunbar, Sir David Lyndsay or Gavin Douglas, the satires and tragedies of George Buchanan or the histories of Boece, Mair (or Major) or Bellenden would have been paralleled in architecture by primitive fortresses. Sixteenth-century Scotland enjoyed its role in the Northern European Renaissance: James IV (married to an English princess) and James V (married to two French ones) were notable patrons of architecture. James IV constructed the Great Hall at Stirling, and commissioned the splendid four-towered forework, the details of whose entrance may well have been inspired by a Roman arch.

James V, the greatest of Scottish building monarchs, squandered his own wealth – and that of the Church and his forfeited nobles – upon lavish construction. He appointed his friend, mentor and familiar Sir James Hamilton of Finnart to refit Linlithgow, refortify Blackness Castle and build a stunning Royal Pavilion of the finest stonework, Louis XII detail, and classical proportions within Stirling Castle. Finnart, head of the Hamilton family, soldier, ambassador, councillor, judge and probably inventor, was much preoccupied with military architecture. His palace at Craignethan represented a complete break with Scots tradition in plan and fortification. Probably associated with two manor houses, one other palace and twelve other properties,

Finnart was the first of a succession of lairds (followed by William Schaw of Sauchie, Sir James Murray of Kilbaberton and Sir William Bruce of Kinross) who approached architecture from the top down. They were complemented by those who earned their reputation through trade and craft: the Bel family, the French family, the Mylne family, Conn of Auchry, William Wallace and William Aytoun. The king's favourite hunting palace of Falkland, extended in the manner of Francois I, was in advance of anything in England of the time; and a tall, round-towered palace-lodging was added to his father's glittering Palace of Holyrood in Edinburgh, intending to balance it by another to the south.

The medieval mode of vertical living became transformed to horizontal: usually apartments of three rooms in processional sequence – an outer (or anti-) chamber, great chamber, and bedchamber. With the *corps de logis* flanked by a round bedroom tower at one corner and a staircase tower against the opposite, these houses shared a similar plan to their contemporaries lining the Loire. Construction remained the width of a stone-vault, the floor plan now widened to include a cross-vaulted service corridor.

French influence was strong. The temporary timber palace erected by the Earl of Athol for King James V near Pitlochry in 1531 had round towers in each corner, in a plan that closely resembled that of the Loire Château de Bury (now vanished). Pitscottie recorded how

> the Ambassador of the Pope, seeing this great banquet and triumph, which was made in a wilderness, where there was no town near by twenty miles, thought it a great marvel, that such a thing could be in Scotland considering that it was named *the arse of the world* by other countries.

The rippling walls at Thirlestane may be traced to the royal châteaux of the (old) Louvre and of Loches (south of the Loire); the first-floor arcaded gallery of Castle Gordon to Blois; and perhaps the Palace of Huntly, with its outsize round tower to the château of Amboise. However, Scandinavian, Hanseatic and Baltic countries, had greater influence in north-east Scotland; appropriately, in view of the Scots colonies that flourished with their trading staples, churches and colleges throughout the Baltic and the western edge of Europe. Moreover, architecture may have travelled in both directions – although a study of the Scottish churches and streets remains to be undertaken. (In later centuries, William Stark probably worked in Russia, and an unidentified Scot seems to have been involved in rebuilding Bergen.)

Courtyards, comprising the original tower, a new laird's lodging of the above type, a gallery, and offices, were not uncommon. Generally, courtyard houses were called 'places' or 'palaces'; freestanding houses by their own name; and large establishments by the title The House of (for example) Strathbogie. The seventeenth-century use of the word 'castle' was sparing and normally reserved for an overtly military or medieval structure.

The free-standing 'castle-wise houses of country gentlemen' as the English visitor Sir William Brereton put it,[9] standing tall in one corner of a courtyard, or walled garden, would be composed of laird and lady's apartments above each other. 'Castle-wise' may be translated into French as *château*; and it is châteaux like those of Fraser, Midmar, Kilcoy, Ballone, Glamis, Redcastle, Edzell and Muness – neither castles nor tower houses – that one can see almost every league.

The architecture was untamed to the point of fantasy. The notion of decorated structure was taken to its limit – seized and twisted any which way in an idiosyncratic if not perverse distension of geomerty. Cylinders are corbelled to square or octagonal (or octagonal to square); rectangular oriels corbelled over corners, superstructures in deconstructedly angular relationships with their plinths or adjacent wings, and wall planes patterned with corbel courses offering not a jot of added space within.

Rubble was invariably covered with harl or plaster, probably tinted with imported pigment. Much of the delight lies in counterpoint between monolithic wall and dressed stone detail – corner pilasters, turrets, superstructures, corbels, chamfers, string courses, octagonal chimneys, balconies, galleries, parapets, grand entrances and dormer windows – which were probably either painted or limewashed. Carved detail from France, Italy, Germany and Spain adorned superstructures, windows, doors, turrets and dormer windows. So the aesthetic of Renaissance architecture in Scotland was two-toned: part harl and part dressed stone. The harling or limewash had as much to do with design as with weather protection, although it was a useful method of concealing poor construction and loosely pinned rubble. Much of the superstructure – for both functional and aesthetic reasons – would have been in dressed stone, and perhaps what lies above the corbel course in houses like Fyvie, Craigston and Castle Fraser may yet prove to be dressed stone beneath later harl.

The best local artist was generally commissioned to paint the plaster walls within: and ceiling beams were vividly illuminated. A preference for deep encrusted plasterwork took hold in the early seventeenth century, and thereafter, mural painting was confined to panels within plaster or panelling (much as Robert Adam was to deploy).

Influence from Denmark and Holland was noticeable in the burghs – particularly those seafaring ones founded by James V – but peculiarly so in Glasgow, whose 1656 university had remarkable visual similarities to the Frederiksborg palace (see Plate 64). Edinburgh was a rock-grit European capital city more like Bohemia than England, whose similarity to Prague or to Salzburg, with its dense High Street crammed with arcaded merchants' lodgings, struck all visitors. Its brief spurt of immense mercantile wealth between 1600 and 1637 encouraged the growth of a distinctive Court style under the hand of Sir James Murray of Kilbaberton. Stately mansions, suburban villas, merchants' houses, courtyard U-plan *hôtels* such as Acheson House, the French Ambassador's residence in Edinburgh, or Argyll's Lodging in Stirling are testimony to the quality of the time: as are the national symbols of the Tron Kirk, the 1633 Parliament House, work within Holyrood and Linlithgow Palaces, and the Palace building within the Castle.

Arcaded tenements were to be found at the centre of most substantial towns, but nowhere so extensively as in the boom town of later seventeenth-century Scotland, Glasgow. Glasgow rebuilt its central four streets after a dreadful fire in 1652, and the resulting regularity of its arcades attracted the admiration of all visitors. To appreciate what the city must have been like you would now need to visit towns in southern Germany, Austria and northern Italy. Likewise, Scots towns were dominated by spires and towers: for most public buildings – its universities, charitable hospitals, its guildhalls, city gates and its huge tolbooths – were towered and capped with a flamboyance equal to that so evident in the châteaux.

The architecture of this 'most national' period was one of form and contrasting

41. Prestonfield House, Edinburgh. Built for Sir James Dick, Lord Provost of Edinburgh in 1689. (RIAS)

geometries in light enlivened by colour and fantasy: 'the masterly, correct and magnificent play of masses brought together in light', as Le Corbusier was to put it three hundred years later.

ASSIMILATION WITH ENGLAND?

After 1660, direct contact between Scotland and northern Europe began to wither and, after 1707, largely ceased. Instead, Scotland became susceptible to ideas emanating from the south as the nobility took to a Scottish version of baroque. Those who travelled abroad sought to recreate in Scotland an equivalent grandeur. The first architect of the Restoration – in every sense of the word – was Sir William Bruce, to be followed by James Smith, James Gibbs, Alexander McGill and William Adam. Scots architecture developed Janus characteristics: the wealthy European aspirant sought to adapt indigenous building traditions and plan forms to a Scots baroque, whereas the native Scots voice was relegated to providing houses for lairds. Bruce's first house, Balcaskie, was in the Scots tradition; his second, Kinross, in the English.

Later seventeenth-century Scots architecture derived from the U-plan noblemen's lodgings of the Jacobean Renaissance, retaining their geometry, harling contrasted with dressed stone, fine roofscape, sparingly applied decoration, and principal apartments upon the first floor or *piano nobile*. Some had the U-plan closed with a balustrade, as at Prestonfield House, Edinburgh, Methven, and Panmure; others took the form of a principal block with balancing square corner or flanking towers, as at Marchmont, Black Barony, and Gallery.

William Adam's baroque brandished dressed stone façades with applied pediment, columns and appropriate classical or baroque detail: yet much Scots inheritance remained. Adam's extravagant palace for Lord Braco by Banff, Duff House, has the plan of a compressed Heriot's Hospital or Drumlanrig, and its corner towers were paralleled in Floors, and Hamilton Palace. Adam's mansions protrude four square from the landscape in a manner not dissimilar to their predecessors; their room sequence perpetuates that of Holyrood and the old tradition, and their ground floor often remains stone vaulted. Their roofs remain prominent long after they have vanished behind a balustrade in England.

Small lairds' houses, mansions, and buildings like the manses of William Robertson in Buchan, remained four-square throughout the eighteenth century – their stairs in projecting drum towers (a motif to appear later in all three of Mackintosh's masterly houses – the Art Lover's House, Windyhill and the Hill House). Several larger mansions – like Moffat House by John Adam – are entered through a depressed ground floor of subsidiary rooms, and up a magnificent staircase into a *piano nobile* of statuesque proportions: much in the Continental manner. The aesthetic of contrasted harl and dressed stone assumed similarities to central European baroque in which poor stone is concealed beneath a smooth, coloured finish. Robert Mylne's Gaelic Church in Inveraray would not be out of place in Salzburg.

The dominant characteristic of quality rural architecture remained one of plain volume with limited surface decoration of which the small 1804 church at Scalasaig on Colonsay, a composition of white geometric mass (cube, cylinder and rectangle), is the purest example.

THE GOLDEN AGE OF SCOTTISH URBANISM 1770–1840

The Scots economy had stagnated in the interregnum between the Union and the '45 – and the towns showed it. Once 'the rage of faction in this country' (as Sir Gilbert Elliot of Minto's *Proposals* for Edinburgh put it in 1752) was over, Scots determined to profit. Investment in new construction would generate prosperity, but if the inconveniences of the capital were not tackled, Scots aristocrats would continue to prefer the sophistication of exile in London. The New Town planned for Edinburgh was grid-iron, based upon that devised in a 1767 competition by James Craig. It was essentially the same (although infinitely more sophisticated) as those of the new towns that lairds were sowing on uninhabited mosses the length and breadth of north-east Scotland. The New Town was conceived as an aristocratic housing estate on the model of a London square of terraced houses: professional people and all places of entertainment were to remain behind in the Old Town.

It did not transpire quite like that. The aristocrats remained in the south: the first new building of the New Town was a theatre, and its first inhabitants professional people. Principal streets and squares were of ashlar-faced terraced houses which offered the sophistication of private reception suites which heretofore had been the preserve of

42. *Register House, Edinburgh, designed by Robert Adam (1728–92) to house the public records of Scotland. Building began in 1774. (*RIAS*)*

the nobility. Their plain dignity was given unity by the consistency of the splendid blocks of dressed Craigleith ashlar with which the houses were built, and by the strict feu conditions which governed layout, height and scale. Tenements which infiltrated the New Town to populate the cross streets were tricked out in classic garb to resemble houses.

The rise of the New Town to its status as an icon of Enlightenment planning must be attributable to Robert Adam who, after his sojourn in Rome, had a conception of the grandeur to which his native capital should aspire. First, the houses. The discipline of the New Town had become frayed by decoration as it expanded west; and to Adam, Scotland owes the conception that dominated the next seventy years of an entire street block of terraced houses being marshalled within a unifying noble design, best emphasised by Charlotte Square (1792). To Adam, Edinburgh owes the notion of the stately public building closing a vista, as does Register House (1774), or punctuating the skyline, as was his plan for Edinburgh University (see Plate 63). A capital required suitably impressive noble entrances, and Adam responded with grandiose proposals for the southern and northern (both executed by lesser hands) and to the east to Calton Hill, realised to a degree twenty-five years later by Archibald Elliott.

Edinburgh's seventy years of classical development, emulated to one degree or another in most towns with aspirations, characterises the stone age of Scots architecture – cliffs and street walls of buildings, collectively much more important in their massing and layout than in their individuality. Even where its language became more sophisticated – almost baroque in James Gillespie Graham's layout of circus, oval and crescent for the Moray estate – essential elements of form, scale and enclosure remained consistent.

In adjacent fields whelped the suburban villa, an inheritor of both the Renaissance villa and Robert Adam's (of which Sunnyside, Liberton, was perhaps the apogee). By mid-century, stone-walled villadom had become expansive, and by the close of the century the suburban house had become the *desideratum* of the bourgeoisie.

Glasgow had followed an aberrant track. Colen Campbell's first house – the first Palladian villa in Britain – was the Shawfield mansion (1711) in Glasgow's Trongate: a

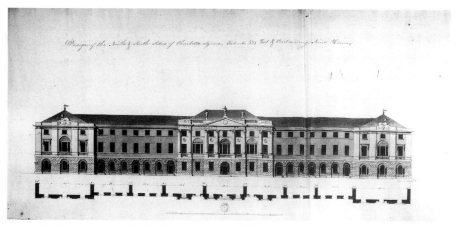

43. *Charlotte Square, Edinburgh, Robert Adam's design for the north and south sides of the square (1791). Building began in 1792, after Adam's death, and was completed by 1820.* (RCAHMS)

sign, perhaps, of how this entrepreneurial city was to dispose of the immense riches it was to earn from the tobacco trade. The Tobacco Lords espoused detached, steep-roofed, urned and pedimented classical villas with flanking pavilions, similar to those in Virginia in Maryland, in a suburban layout. The Glasgow Square, recalling the American custom of surrounding their courthouses, enfolded civic monuments (instead of the garden that was the norm in Europe), as in St Andrew's, St Enoch's, and Royal Exchange Squares. The wealth of the city purchased the skills of Robert Adam and Sir John Soane.

Early nineteenth-century Scotland is symbolised by proud neoclassical grammar schools, town halls, churches, hospitals and country houses, erected from one end of the country to the other in the form of a functionally useless (because theoretically windowless) Greek temple. Their details were deepened to compensate for the weak Scots sunlight. The most accomplished exponents were William Stark, William Playfair and David Hamilton, closely pursued by Archibald Simpson, John Smith, Thomas Hamilton, and William Burn. The legacy of Adam was that their monuments were of a scale and grandeur far in excess of the requirements of their sublunary purpose. The creators of the 'Athens of the North' had aspirations to eternity.

Siting and detailing was governed not by Attic reason but by its antithesis: romantic picturesqueness, of a kind inspired by artists such as Hugh 'Grecian' Williams. Within the walls of these sturdy, thickset and indomitable monuments burgeoned the wildest of Romantic revivals as the influence of the novels of Sir Walter Scott began to exercise the country's imagination.

Fifty years earlier, the *Ossian* controversy had transformed the idea of ancient Scotland from a land of inaccessible savages ill disposed to civilisation to a nation of Dark Age poetic heroes, with a primitive culture haunting heather-clad fastnesses. Travellers ventured north to emote at frightful waterfalls; and suitably ghastly grottoes, moss houses, hermitages, ancient springs, vista fillers and doocots were erected to satisfy the yearning. Inherited towers proved inadequate: Sir John Dalrymple, client of Robert Adam at Oxenfoord Castle in Midlothian, wrote to a friend: 'I have repaired a noble, old castle, and with the help of Bob Adams, *have really made it much older than it was*.[10] Adam's castle language was a composition of strong geometric form and picturesque skyline derivative of the Scots Renaissance.

In lesser hands, it was reduced to window dressing. Monzie, by Adam's chief draughtsman John Paterson, was described (and these are important words) as 'a pile of building highly suitable to the surrounding scenery. Mr Paterson has very judiciously introduced this style of house into those parts of Scotland which are on a grand and wild scale.'[11] Architecture had become a scenic adjunct.

Once English Gothic was preferred to a revived Scots Jacobean for Scone Palace (1802), Scots landowners embraced Englishness; and the Smirkes and the Atkinsons surged north in their smartly crocketted and buttressed neo-Elizabethan or neo-Tudor garb, uniting house and landscape in single concept. Copybook picturesqueness became fashionable, and when Abbotsford, Sir Walter Scott's house, seemed to have been built in this idiom, everybody wanted some. Scott himself regarded revivalism as a serious issue. In *The Pirate* he speculated that the Earl's Palace in Kirkwall might

> be selected ... as the model of a Gothic mansion, provided architects would be contented rather to imitate what is really beautiful in that species of building, than to make a medley of the caprices of the order, confounding the military, ecclesiastical and domestic styles of all ages at random with additional fantasies and combinations of their own device.[12]

Having been directly involved with the design of Abbotsford (more his than anybody else's), he would have rejected that charge against his own house, and was pleased that William Burn approved.

Schools and academies which had been housed in magnificent Doric temples to impart the most heavy instruction, fell prey to the seductive imagery of Oxbridge colleges. Their rationale was provided by Playfair, when explaining Donaldson's Hospital: 'I try hard to produce a building which, in the correctness of its parts, shall be worthy of comparison with the remains of Old English architecture.'[13] The revolution that occurred mid-century may best be understood by comparing old English Donaldson's to the maturely baronial Fettes College by David Bryce: two charitable schools split by the first Scottish revival. Whereas English architects had been happy to ape old Scots features in the illiterate manner condemned by Scott, prior to 1850, Scots were only rarely tempted – Playfair at Bonaly, Burn (reluctantly) at Laurieston and Bryce at Castle Menzies. North British lairds were terrified of being thought provincial. What was needed was an authoritative document to restore to Scots architecture its sense of *amour propre*.

THE RECOVERY OF A SCOTTISH VOICE

The revival of Scottish architecture may have been triggered by the tragic drowning of George Meikle Kemp in 1844, halfway through constructing his masterly medieval monument to Sir Walter Scott in Princes Street. Kemp, architecture's response to Thomas Chatterton, was steeped in old Scotland. He had designed restorations or completions for Glasgow Cathedral, Melrose Abbey and Roslin Chapel, and plans for several churches. He had also been preparing a tome of drawings intended to reveal ancient Scottish architecture, but his knowledge was lost with him.

44. The Library of Mellerstain. The two wings of the house were designed by William Adam for George Baillie, and building began in 1725. Robert Adam added the centre block in 1770 and designed the interior, including this magnificent library. Many Scottish country houses have fine libraries, but this is probably the most beautiful. (RCAHMS, Reproduced with permission from the Earl of Haddington)

The following year, William Burn and David Bryce brought to Scotland Robert William Billings, an English antiquarian, to carry out that task. By 1852 his four volumes of *The Baronial and Ecclesiastical Antiquities of Scotland* had achieved their purpose. Lairds seized them as pattern books. Amongst over 1,000 subscribers were those who ran or owned Scotland; and some 200 architects (150 from England and almost every member of the Architectural Institute of Scotland). A legitimate Scottish voice had been rediscovered; although, as at Fettes, it was quickly spiced with French.

Billings found it difficult to embrace what he had discovered within English terminology. Convinced that the buildings were the work of architects, and that they comprised a distinct national architecture, he devised the term 'baronial' to describe them — a term with as much meaning in Scotland as the phrase 'English manor house architecture' would have in England. However, it stuck — and soon devalued everything to which it was applied.

The short-lived *Building Chronicle*, which was published in 1854–58 to coincide with the Architectural Institute's Glasgow Architectural Exhibition, was troubled by the ensuing stylistic controversy:

> We would fain discover, in the present mania of fashions and conflict of styles, some symptoms of a principle which may hereafter be worked out in the ultimate production of a distinct national architecture.[14]

Mid-nineteenth-century architects devised their architecture according to function, and baronial was distinctly ill-suited to city offices (despite the furious attempt in Glasgow's Trongate by J.T. Rochead). Fantasist imagery was unbecoming to merchants.

Its power, rather, lay in country houses, schools, monuments and those symbols of ancient authority: town halls and sheriff courts. There was nothing incongruous in the manager of the sternest of classical banks retreating each night to a romantically turreted tower house in the country where he metamorphosed into a lairdling. Few would trust a romantic bank; but what a man did in his own time was his own affair. The *Chronicle* was tickled by Balmoral:

> Now, in north Britain, we have old Scottish, thanks to Burn and Billings 'baronial antiquities', taking its place, as *par excellence*, the style for nine-tenths of our domestic buildings. And oh! What oddities are being perpetrated in its name. The grim bastion towers of Caerlaverock and Craigmillar are being revived in the retreats of peaceable country gentlemen. Heavy battlements surround their doorways and loopholes command it; to sweep off marauders should they prefer that means of access to lifting the sash of the larder window.[15]

For the revival was generally a matter of the application of derived detail and massing to standard mid-century house plans.

The climax was J.T. Rochead's Wallace Monument (1859) on the Abbey Craig, Stirling, an extravagantly Scottish tower with ravenous masonry, that received adulation from European patriots like the Hungarian Kossuth and the Italian Garibaldi.

There was, however, another song. Mid-century Scotland was kind to the inheritors of the tradition of architecture as decorated structure; for, in 1854, Scotland had gained its first cast-iron office building in Glasgow's Jamaica Street. New possibilities were opened up with lightweight, framed structures, and battle was soon joined. Was structure the servant of architecture, or architecture decorated structure? Or could the two be fused? The *Chronicle* was on the side of the technocrats, although even-handed in its depiction of the cultural uncertainty displayed in the Glasgow Architectural Exhibition in Bath Street. For, within a design by Alexander Thomson, there were exhibition rooms in Italian, Greek, Gothic and Renaissance. Its organisers and funders were the leading new-wave architects in Scotland, including Thomson, Rochead, Charles Wilson, Burnet, Baird and Gildard. Thomson shared neither his colleagues' uncertainty nor Rochead's eclecticism. He sought to construct stone buildings with the transparency and explicit structure offered by cast-iron, thereby forging a new architectural language.

Mercantile Scotland generally preferred Italian and Renaissance models for their purpose-built business chambers, department stores, textile warehouses and hotels. It created in Glasgow an Italian hill-town at Park Circus, Venice's Ca d'oro or Golden House in cast-iron in Union Street, and Venice's Doge's Palace in polychromatic brickwork as a built advertisement for the international aspirations of Templeton's carpets at Glasgow Green.

Outside the bounds of the Ecclesiologists and purist Episcopalians, the English Gothic battle of styles had little resonance in Scotland, although, in the hands of James Gillespie Graham, Gothic offered a picturesquely pretty dress for Presbyterian God-boxes. Instead – almost as a form of marketing – the flowering of church building that

*45. Royal Scottish Museum, Edinburgh. The interior of the Great Hall. Built between 1861 and 1875 to the design of Francis Fowke. (*RIAS*)*

followed the 1843 Disruption reflected the various congregations. The most distinctive architecture belonged to the United Presbyterians, an intelligent, bourgeois, entrepreneurial, disputatious crowd which favoured Roman or Italianate temples rather than the mysteries of Gothic; and selected great architects like Baird, Burnet, Peddie and Kinnear and A.G. Thomson to provide them. F.T. Pilkington provided a touch of rare invention in his transformation of Presbyterian auditoria into European-Gothic extravagance.

THE SECOND REVIVAL

By the end of the century, Scotland's most distinctive and ubiquitous building form was the four-storeyed stone-fronted tenement within whose form vastly differing social classes could be accommodated: the bourgeois red sandstone tenements of Glasgow's Novar Drive were barely a mile from the single-ends of Partick. Architecturally, Glasgow and Dundee tenements were rationalist, whereas baronialism infected those of Edinburgh and Aberdeen.

The split between structure as the servant of architecture, and architecture as decorated construction, was nearly total. For in 1897, a new technology imposed itself upon Glasgow: the iron-framed (latterly steel-framed) tall office building served by a lift, usually faced with machine-cut red sandstone. Those architects happiest with what might be called the structural imperative – like Burnet and Boston and James Miller – were to rebuild much of central Glasgow on the American model, making it one of the few European cities with a recognisable 'downtown'.

In the countryside and in the burgeoning, railway-served suburbs, there grew a different aspiration which turned its back upon Scottish urbanism. The second revival, essentially Romantic, dominated the years to the end of the century, under the influence of Sir Robert Rowand Anderson and his pupils. That the time was propitious was signalled by the establishment of a Chair of Celtic Studies at Edinburgh University. This revival differed from the earlier in that it was based, not upon pictures, but upon an accurate recording and measuring of Scots buildings; and leavened with medieval French, Arts and Crafts and not a little baroque. It was often stunningly tactile, if not sensual. Moreover, the inspiration was of a different kind to Billings' *Baronial Antiquities*. The focus was now upon the middle-ranking houses – neither baronial nor vernacular – as may be gauged from the title of the series of books that accompanied it. *The Castellated and Domestic Architecture of Scotland* by David MacGibbon and Dr. Thomas Ross.

Anderson's practical attitude was revealed in his presidential address to the Architecture Section of the National Association for the Advancement of Arts in 1889:

> It is still too much the fashion to rely on the clever imitation of old work, without its reality and functional truth. I am told that many of the picturesque modern timber-framed houses in England have very little framing in them: it is all on the surface – a mere external show. How can any good come out of such work?[16]

It was for that reason that he encouraged drawing and measuring by the student: 'He was taught to dissect, to analyse, to work out for himself all the reasons that gave rise to various features he saw in buildings.'[17]

The coincident desire to reintegrate art and craft was promoted by Sir Patrick Geddes in his short-lived journal, *Evergreen*. He rejected the flight from the evils of industrialisation and urbanism into a suburban or rural retreat to the strains of a mythological past. Instead, he pioneered the reoccupation of Edinburgh's Royal Mile by the intelligentsia and the University.

That formed the context within which Robert Lorimer, Charles Rennie Mackintosh and their followers flourished. They were probably influenced by the pioneering work of James MacLaren's 1879 Kirkton Cottages and farmhouses in Glenlyon, amongst the first buildings of the new generation of Anderson-inspired

*46. Glasgow School of Art, built between 1897 and 1909 to the design of Charles Rennie Mackintosh. (*RCAHMS*)*

Scottishness to deploy the rational planning and simple massing from seventeenth-century Scotland. But the revivalists split. Those of the Anderson camp like Lorimer, Sidney Mitchell, Henry Kerr, Henbest Capper and A.N. Paterson, returned to seventeenth-century Scotland for inspiration; and – sentimentalists that they were – stayed there. Witness Lorimer's desire for Formakin to be seventeenth century. The others, despite sharing the nationalist sentiment, produced a radically different architecture. Of these, Charles Rennie Mackintosh was the best. He understood that Scots Renaissance architecture was the product of as yet unknown designers.[18] Unlike Lorimer, he derived inspiration from them to synthesise a new architecture, most magnificently exemplified in the Hill House (1904) and the Glasgow School of Art (1897–1909). The Hill House fuses a standard north-corridor Edwardian house with a family wing to one side, into a seventeenth-century Z-plan tower extended with an eighteenth-century wing: very like a reversed version of Crathes.

The exterior of his buildings reveal his tendency toward an abstraction which culminated in that totem for inter-war architects: the Willow Tearooms, with its white façade, oversailing flat roof, long strip window, and smaller windows deepset into a white façade. The interiors, following a different programme of different aesthetic origins (probably Japanese), comprise a series of light and frequently colourful magical spaces in contrast to the solidity of the exterior.

The architect that came closest to synthesising the nationalist ideal with new technology, fusing the structure and the art of architecture into a homogeneous whole, was Mackintosh's close friend, James Salmon. His Hatrack (1892) in St Vincent Street broadcast its modern plan and structure by its huge windows, but knitted them together with sensuously carved red stonework. More revolutionary yet was his Lion Chambers (1904), Hope Street, in which he stretched the structure of Hennebique concrete to its limit, in order to achieve a Scottish design.

THE TWENTIETH CENTURY

The inter-war period was dominated by the construction of some 350,000 houses, mostly municipal. The tenement was banned as anti-social in 1918, all future houses to be to the density of twelve houses to the acre with back drying-greens, to a sub arts and crafts aesthetic imported by Parker and Unwin to Rosyth in 1909. Country houses became scarce.

Scotland enjoyed a consumer boom in the uncontrolled sowing of bungalows, and, for the first time, the country was threatened with 'bungalurbia' on a wide scale. Until the tenement revival in 1934 (to a reduced height and grossly reduced specification) for economic reasons – with rare examples of Continentally inspired tenements in Aberdeen, Edinburgh and Renfrew – this vast construction boom failed to develop an urban form of its own; but irreparably damaged the coherent edge that Scots towns and cities had managed to retain until then.

During the 1920s, the Scots architectural profession was preoccupied with establishing its identity through the medium of the newly established Royal Incorporation of Architects in Scotland: and adapting itself to a new economy and altered client demand. Upon that, it founded a movement for a new architecture in the 1930s – one that was both Scottish and modern – a Caledonian response to the stirrings upon the Continent. They looked to Holland for efficiency, to Sweden for pragmatism,

47. Castle Fraser, Aberdeenshire. Begun about 1575, incorporating some earlier building, and completed in 1636.

*48. The Hill House, Helensburgh. Completed in 1904 for the Glasgow publisher, Walter Blackie, to the design – including internal decoration and furniture – of Charles Rennie Mackintosh (1868–1928). A comparison with Castle Fraser shows the striking combination of tradition and modernity in Mackintosh's work. (*Photographs by courtesy of the National Trust for Scotland, who own both buildings*)*

to Czechoslovakia for style, and to Finland for poetry; but most of all Sir Frank Mears, Robert Hurd, Ian Lindsay, Sir John Stirling Maxwell, Basil Spence and others looked for inspiration to Scotland of the period *c*.1600.

Sir Frank Mears wrote in the *RIBA Journal*:

> Buildings from the earliest to the latest, especially when they were faced with rough stone, harled and white-washed, have a certain monolithic character; they are definitely Cubic if not Cubist.[19]

Mackintosh was the master to be studied. Meanwhile, in central Glasgow, James Miller, E.G. Wylie and their colleagues were refining upon American practice in pursuit of 'architecture as decorated structure': an idea well suited to the offices and factories of the period.

Despite steel, timber, and poured concrete houses (and heavy marketing from Sweden), prefabrication failed to make much inroad. The proto-nationalists, who sought to adapt the Rowand Anderson revival to contemporary life, created an architecture of spare white geometry based equally on Nordic models, Mackintosh and Scots Renaissance châteaux. The synthesis came with Thomas Tait and his young Scots colleagues in the Empire Exhibition of 1938. Using the most advanced techniques of prefabricated panels hung upon timber or steel frames, they nonetheless managed (as had Salmon) to produce a largely homogeneous architecture of plain, if vivid, geometric forms – of cylinders, rectangles, cubes and skylines, which approximated to the new Scots architecture to which they aspired.

POST-WAR

After the Second World War, nationalism in architecture lost its appeal. New materials and methods developed during the war were to be devoted to the rehousing of half a million people, improving the nation's health, reducing densities in cities, and replanning the country for a new, car-driven age. The fascination with technology, that had been germinating in the Scottish psyche since the 1850s, now had its chance. As the programmatic and structural aspects of speedy construction took priority over the architectonic, architecture become a matter, not just of decorated structure, but of undecorated structure. An aesthetic of prefabrication and light-weight construction seemed in tune with comprehensive redevelopment, high-rise (usually system-built) flats, Hutchesontown, motorways and new towns.

It was not the whole story. The legacy of the 1930s revival persisted subcutaneously. Solid, spare, white, cubist-inspired geometry informed churches, houses in small burghs or the countryside, and rural factories, distilleries and schools. Such characteristics were also magnificently deployed in Sir William Kininmonth's Mary Erskine's School, Edinburgh, Sir Robert Matthew's Stirling University, Sir Basil Spence's Mortonhall Crematorium and Peter Womersley's last Scottish project, a doctor's surgery in Kelso.

Poetic spaces integrating light, mystery and the applied arts in the Mackintosh tradition (without the stylistic overtones) distinguished the buildings of Gillespie, Kidd and Coia; whose St Peter's College, Cardross, deserved its international acclaim.

In the boom post-war years, buildings of such quality were marginalised. Architectural hands were but little involved in high-rise housing; but Glasgow took especial pride that Sam Bunton had produced the tallest flats in Europe at Red Road, and that Basil Spence had tackled head-on the issue of the 'tall building artistically considered' in Hutchesontown (as also Jack Holmes at Anniesland and Shaw, Stewart and Perry in Leith Fort). Giving architectural form to high-rise buildings was a lonely task: too fussy for those interested only in housing units, not thorough enough for those considering the flats as architecture. Unaware of Scotland's cultural identity, theorists from England planned, through the Town and Country Planning Association, to eliminate the last tenement flat from the face of the country. They were considered in the same light as slum dwellings in Leeds: their ruins made good hardcore for roads.

Those days ended in January 1968, with the great gale. Glasgow was compelled to undertake remedial repairs to buildings destined for demolition. One thing led to another, assisted by a Housing Act of 1969. Community-led tenement rehabilitation was initiated in Govan in 1971 by Strathclyde University; and within ten years, the tenement had been rediscovered as central to Scottish life. Much coincided in the 1970s: tenement rehabilitation necessarily led to the rediscovery of the pleasures of inner-city living; conservation provided grants for repair, cleaning and re-use of redundant buildings; the Scottish Development Agency reclaimed derelict land; and a new community-based client emerged for architects. After decades of remote — if not Stalinist — clients, the emerging *user* client, the community-based housing association, or the partnership client conjoining public and private sectors, required more responsive and particular buildings from their architects.

Scotland's role in microchips was reflected in estates of high-tech factories (rechristened 'industrial units'), there was an office boom, and tourism provided the opportunity for pavilions, visitor centres, hotels and tat. Prefabrication had nearly exhausted itself as an aesthetic generator. Enduring cultural uncertainty was characterised by the import of 'name' architects (for Edinburgh's Maybury Park and Conference Centre); a rash of patterned brick façade concealing standard plan flats; and in pressure upon architects to design nothing that might affright dowagers.

A continuation of Scottish characteristics may be inferred from heavy modelling (the vertical expression of stair and service towers in the National Library extension), the patterning of heavy masses (Edinburgh's Tollcross fire station); the return of street walls of building (Ingram Square, Glassford Street and Craigen Court in Glasgow, and Sinderins in Dundee) and city block revival (the Italian Centre). Glasgow's downtown feels downtown once again.

The white geometric tradition which flickered in the Glasgow Garden Festival (hitherto preferred for non-urban housing) should gain great momentum for the Museum of Scotland in Edinburgh and the proposed Scottish Office in Leith.

A picturesque façade, however, is no substitute for architecture. Scottish architects are subject to international inspiration and an international palette of materials. The quality of their architecture will depend entirely upon how well they understand how Scottish architecture developed and how sensitive their clients are to our culture and to our particular climatic needs. International opportunity has to be married to the task of building in and for Scotland. The support which they receive from society at large will determine how well they do it.

Notes

1. Sir Robert Rowand Anderson, *Place of Architecture in the Domain of Art* (Edinburgh, 1889), p.24.
2. Peter Savage, *Lorimer and the Edinburgh Craft Designers* (Edinburgh, 1980), p.115.
3. Charles Rennie Mackintosh, *The Architectural Papers*, ed. Pamela Robertson (Glasgow, 1990), p.196.
4. John Buchan, *Speech to the House of Commons*, 1932.
5. Robert Hurd in J.R. Allan (ed.), *Scotland 1938* (Edinburgh, 1938), p.120.
6. Quoted in P. Hume Brown, *Early Travellers in Scotland* (Edinburgh, 1973), pp.72–79.
7. Sir Walter Scott, *Rob Roy* (Edinburgh, 1829), Vol. 2, p.29.
8. Robert Lindsay of Pitscottie, *History of Scotland* (Edinburgh, 1778), p.228.
9. Quoted in Brown, op.cit., p.148.
10. Quoted by Dr Alistair Rowan, 'Oxenfoord Castle', *Country Life* 156, 15 August 1974, pp.94–8.
11. James Fittler, *Scotia Depicta* (London, 1804), Plate XV.
12. Sir Walter Scott, *The Pirate* (Edinburgh, 1829), Vol. 2, p.175.
13. Quoted by Dr David Walker, *Essays in Honour of Howard Colvin*, Architectural History Vol. (London, 1982).
14. *The Building Chronicle*, no. 8, 9 November 1858, p.69.
15. 'Modern Old Scottish', in *The Building Chronicle*, no. 11, 1 February 1855, p.143.
16. Sir Rowand Anderson, *Place of Architecture in the Domain of Art*, p.39.
17. Quoted by Ian Gow, *Sir Rowand Anderson's National Art Survey in Architectural History*, Vol. 27 (London, 1984).
18. Charles Rennie Mackintosh, *The Architectural Papers*, p.52.
19. Sir Frank Mears, *RIBA Journal*, January 1938.

Books for Further Reading

Architectural Heritage 1 (Edinburgh, 1991)
Architectural Heritage 2 (Edinburgh, 1992)
John Dunbar, *The Historic Architecture of Scotland* (Edinburgh, 1966)
John Gifford, *The Architecture of William Adam* (Edinburgh, 1989)
Ian Gow, *The Scottish Interior* (Edinburgh, 1992)
David King, *The Works of Robert and James Adam* (London, 1992)
Charles McKean, *Architectural Contributions to Scottish Society 1840–1990* (Edinburgh, 1990)
RIAS, *The Architecture of the Scottish Renaissance* (Edinburgh, 1990)
Fiona Sinclair, *Scotstyle* (Edinburgh, 1984)
Audrey Sloan and Gordon Murray, *James Miller* (Edinburgh, 1993)
The *Buildings of Scotland* series (London, 1979 onwards)
RIAS/Landmark Trust Illustrated Architectural Guides to Scotland: Series (Edinburgh, 1982 onwards)

Photography

SARA STEVENSON

The history of photography in Scotland is an extraordinary confluence of the intellectual forces of science and aesthetics – fluidly dynamic and inventive in a manner difficult to chart with certainty. It saw the conjunction of research in the fields of physics, chemistry and the arts which led to a revolution in visual understanding and visual education.[1] Both scientifically and artistically Scotland made an outstanding contribution to the development of this new medium.

When the first notably impressive photographs were taken in Scotland – the calotypes of David Octavius Hill and Robert Adamson – Hugh Miller reported with astonishment that:

> Phrenomesmerism and the calotype have been introduced to the Edinburgh public about much the same time; but how very differently have they fared hitherto! A real invention, which bids fair to produce some of the greatest revolutions in the fine arts of which they have ever been the subject, has as yet attracted comparatively little notice; an invention which serves but to demonstrate that the present age, with all its boasted enlightenment, may yet not be very unfitted for the reception of superstitions, the most irrational and gross, is largely occupying the attention of the community, and filling column after column in our public prints.[2]

The first announcements of photography – Louis Jacques Mandé Daguerre's daguerreotype process and William Henry Fox Talbot's calotype process – in 1839, generated a flurry of public interest. But Miller's remarks underline a curious point about the early history of photography; for many people it was oddly unsurprising. The invention of photography was not a sudden dramatic breakthrough but the result of years of experimental chipping away and calculation. When it became a practical art in 1842, with the discovery of the latent image, which brought exposure times well down into minutes and sometimes seconds, photography fell into the hands of sophisticated and knowledgeable people.

One of the central figures in the beginnings of photography in Scotland was the physicist, Sir David Brewster.[3] He and his circle in St Andrews took up daguerreotype photography and, as a personal friend of Talbot, he was able also to attempt the calotype process. It was in St Andrews that Dr John Adamson (1809–70) succeeded in taking the first calotype portrait in Scotland, probably in May 1842. By November 1842, John and his brother, Robert Adamson, were able to send Talbot a little album, bound in tartan, of their successful calotypes.

One of the key figures in the early technology was the Edinburgh instrument-maker, Thomas Davidson (1798–1878). Davidson published his own improvements to the daguerreotype process and camera in a paper given on 9 November 1840 to the Royal Scottish Society of Arts.[4] He also translated Daguerre's treatise into English and published it in Edinburgh in 1841. He supplied the cameras for St Andrews and caught the interest of photographers in England and Wales: the Revd Calvert Jones, a skilful photographer, admired both Davidson's camera and lenses.[5] Davidson's contribution to the advance of photographic technology provides an interesting gloss on a legal side-issue; Scotland had a separate legal system from England and a separate patent was needed to cover inventions in both countries – inventors rarely bothered with a Scottish patent, and indeed, Sir David Brewster persuaded Talbot that it was not worth his while taking one out for the calotype. This was important, not so much from the point of view of economy, but because it enabled general experiment and the development of basic ideas. One of the many that Davidson worked with was the idea, originally used for telescopes, of employing a concave mirror rather than a lens to focus the image on to the photographic paper, and it was a large-scale camera of this kind that he made for David Octavius Hill and Robert Adamson in 1844.[6]

Interest in photography in the early years was substantially open in character. Experiments had a sociable basis – from country house meetings to discussions in the Royal Scottish Society of Arts – and information was freely exchanged. The early history, recalled at a later date, has an anecdotal vein, often inaccurate, which gives a sense of this sociable enthusiasm. The Revd Robert Graham's account of the arrival of the calotype process in Scotland (which gives the wholly confusing impression that the albumen process and stereoscopic photography were all invented in a short span of 'several weeks' at Rossie Priory) serves as an example:

> All available tubs, buckets, foot-pails, wash-hand basins, and every sort of vessel which would contain water, were laid hold of for the frequent washings and soakings which were required. Every room which could be darkened was needed for the drying in the dark. The region of every domestic in the household was invaded and servants were kept running perpetually with pails of hot and cold water, warm smoothing irons, &c. The whole establishment was turned topsy-turvy while its superiors were bent on photographic studies. Rossie Priory is one of the largest houses in Scotland, yet we have often seen it moved from one end to another, and all in it, from its noble owner to the humblest domestic, in a fever of excitement.[7]

At the Scottish Society of Arts, on 29 May 1839, one of the more extraordinary amateurs, Mungo Ponton (1801–80), read a paper on the use of bichromate of potash as a substitute for silver in the photographic process.[8] This was the basis of the carbon process which was not fully realised until the 1860s when it was patented by Joseph Swan. Ponton was a banker by profession, a wistful polymath by inclination. His interests ranged from patent bread to the transportation methods of angels and he has the rare distinction of having written the only known hymn to photography (with footnotes).[9] Less eccentric, but equally wide-ranging, was George Cundell (d.1882), agent for Patrick Maxwell Stuart and a close friend of James Nasmyth: 'George was known amongst us as "the worthy master". He was thoroughly versed in general science, and was moreover a keen politician. He had the most happy faculty of treating complex subjects, both in science and politics, in a thoroughly common-sense manner.'[10]

George Cundell and his brothers, Henry and Joseph, were amongst the early calotype photographers, taking small, engaging, peopled landscapes. George published a clear modification of Talbot's calotype process in May 1844.[11] In the opinion of Robert Hunt, 'Mr Cundell's process of manipulation is as good as any that can be adopted: and that gentleman certainly merits the thanks of all photographers.'[12]

Dr Andrew Fyfe (1792–1861), a lecturer in chemistry in Edinburgh, in 1839 and 1840 turned aside from his analyses of coal, electricity and steam to deliver papers on photography and the daguerreotype, including his own original experiments into silver and a discussion of photographic etching.[13] Fyfe's paper on photography was published also in the *Cornwall Chronicle* of Tasmania and was apparently the first published account of photography to appear in Australia.

Great advances were made in the amateur field and from this basis came the eminently professional partnership of David Octavius Hill (1802–70) and Robert Adamson (1821–48). In August 1842, Sir David Brewster wrote to Talbot, 'A brother of Dr Adamson who has been educating as an engineer is willing to practise the Calotype in Edinburgh as a Profession . . .. Mr Adamson has been well drilled in the art by his brother.'[14] With Talbot's agreement, Robert Adamson set up his studio in Rock House, the highest private house on Calton Hill in Edinburgh, in May of 1843.

By coincidence, Brewster was personally involved that month in the major Disruption of the annual assembly of the Church of Scotland and the consequent founding of the Free Church. This proved to be an impressive and emotive event, striking Scottish society with great force. The painter, David Octavius Hill, encouraged by Lord Cockburn's opinion that 'There has not been such a subject since the days of Knox – and not then!'[15] attended the meetings of the new Church and sketched out plans for a grand historical picture. Brewster met him and talked of using photography to capture the hundreds of portraits of ministers who would soon be scattered throughout Scotland. Hill, initially sceptical, went up to Rock House and within a few short weeks of experiment, he and Adamson were so impressed by the results that they entered into formal partnership. Brewster reported to Talbot: 'They have succeeded beyond their most sanguine expectations . . .. I think you will find that we have, in Scotland, found out the value of your invention not before yourself, but before those to whom you have given the privilege of using it.'[16]

Hill and Adamson's partnership lasted four years until Adamson's death in January 1848.[17] Their main period of activity seems to lie between June 1843 and the summer of 1846. The work is immediately remarkable for its phenomenal grasp both of the mechanics and the potential of photography. Robert Adamson's training with his brother and the alterations they had made to Talbot's original process enabled him to produce consistently rich prints – in 1845 Hill said, 'I believe Dr Adamson and his brother to be the fathers of many of these parts of the process which make it a valuable and practical art. I believe also from all I have seen that Robert Adamson is the most

49. D.O. Hill and Robert Adamson, Two Newhaven Fishwives, Mrs Elizabeth Johnstone Hall on the left, *Calotype photograph, taken between 1843 and 1846.* (Scottish National Portrait Gallery)

successful manipulator the art has yet seen . . . .'[18] The partnership employed at least one assistant, Miss Mann, characterised by the engineer, James Nasmyth, as 'thrice worthy Miss Mann that most skilful and zealous of assistants'.[19]

The partnership was led and directed by D.O. Hill. He was by profession a landscape and genre painter and his role as the organising secretary of the Royal Scottish Academy and effective curator of their annual exhibitions meant that he was closely familiar with the best of contemporary painting. Hill's circle of friends included the Nasmyth family, whose house acted in the 1820s and 1830s as a focus for wide-ranging discussion, both scientific and aesthetic. He himself took a considerable interest in practical and technical matters – he was, for example, one of the earliest to practise lithography, at the age of eighteen. Hill's skill as a painter was questioned by his friends, who felt that his talents and ideas were greater than his common performance. But this is not as uncomplimentary as it may seem. Hill was, in effect, a man overflowing with imaginative and poetic ideas who had difficulty in expressing himself in paint. Such

50. D.O. Hill and Robert Adamson, Revd Dr Thomas Chalmers and his Family in the Grounds of Merchiston Castle, *calotype photograph, taken in 1844.* (Scottish National Portrait Gallery)

paintings as his great historic picture of the Free Church (which was both helped and impaired by his use of the camera to record the faces of all the men involved) were thoroughly ambitious in concept; his failures should be measured by their ambition. He was also impressively social and sympathetic. This added up to an ability to estimate and exploit the new process, to understand what it could do physically and what it could be persuaded to do outwith its own rules; and, equally important, to consider and organise his subjects in a truthful manner.

Hill's skill as a photographer stemmed from his broad intelligence and readiness to examine the character of an invention – approaching it, not with set ideas, but with an open mind. His pleasure in the calotype was expressed as follows:

> The rough surface & unequal texture throughout of the paper is the main cause of the Calotype failing in details before the process of Daguerreotypes – & this is the very life of it. They look like the imperfect work of a man – and not the much diminished perfect work of God . . ..'[20]

Hill recognised the inherent, surreal paradox of photography that makes it an effective art form – the intriguing torque between its dynamic character as a truth-teller and its equally inherent poetic character for accident and untruth.

The bulk of Hill and Adamson's work, something over three thousand images, lies in portraiture. From June or July of 1843, they were substantially in control of their image-making and their 'experiments' are sophisticated. But with 1844, Hill's interest became greater. He moved into Rock House to work more closely with Adamson and in June they announced the publication of a series of photographic books: *The Fishermen and Women of the Firth of Forth*, *Highland Character and Costume*, *The Architectural Structures of Edinburgh*, *The Architectural Structures of Glasgow &c*, *Old Castles, Abbeys &c in Scotland* and *Portraits of Distinguished Scotchmen*. In the event, none of these were published, perhaps because of the expense. About 130 calotypes for the first of these publications, *The Fishermen and Women*, were taken and exist in the form of prints and unprinted negatives, so it is possible to reconstruct the plan.[21] This is certainly the most surprising of the photographic projects because it is closer to the twentieth-century idea of the documentary photo-essay than seems either practical or, in contemporary terms, logical; as a graphic idea, it was entirely new. The inspiration behind the series was a profound admiration of the fishing community, specifically at Newhaven, which was hard-working and culturally sophisticated. Hill's pictures of the people of Newhaven are a reflection of the beauty and confidence of the society and present that society as an ideal model. The photographs are layered in meaning – offering a simple visual pleasure backed by an understanding of wider truths. For example, the photograph of the two fishwives walking to market is an effective composition (Plate 49) but its conviction and truth derive from the true affectionate support the women offered each other in reality, which was the stability and mainstay of the community. As Hill remarked, 'I think you will find that the calotypes . . . will always be giving out new lights.'[22]

The Newhaven photographs are an effective illustration of Hill and Adamson's approach to the calotype process in another way. The calotype was a potentially beautiful process, but it was also limiting and faulty. Certain ideas were blocked by practical constraints – it was not possible to photograph movement, small children and animals were impractical sitters, photographing into the sun was impossible, the imperfection of lenses meant that it was advisable to keep the head of a sitter in the centre of the paper, and so on. The Newhaven photographs include pictures taken on board the boats, pictures of children, a group taken against the sun. They ignored the constraints in favour of coherence and truth and made considerable discoveries as a result. Similarly, the large camera commissioned from Davidson in 1844 proved difficult to handle but with it they took a few extraordinary pictures, including the family of Revd Thomas Chalmers in the grounds of Merchiston Castle School, which is radically interesting in its use of light and coarsely abstract focus (Plate 50).

The success of the Hill-Adamson partnership was not financial. Hill spent 'some hundreds of pounds and a huge cantle of my time in these Calotype freaks'.[23] They did, however, achieve considerable critical acclaim and established a phenomenal standard which dominated the aesthetic practice of photography in Scotland during the nineteenth century and was notably influential on international photography in the twentieth.

In 1847 Sir David Brewster publicly expressed dissatisfaction with the calotype process because of its lack of accurate detail. He himself designed a version of the stereoscopic camera to give photography the potential of two-eyed vision and he transferred his affections to the smoother and clearer albumen process, which could rival the miniature details of the daguerreotype process.

In the Great Exhibition of 1851, the work of Hill and Adamson was awarded only an Honourable Mention; a Council Medal was awarded to the lesser Scottish photographers (protégés of David Brewster), James Ross (*d*.1878) and John Thomson (*d.*1881), for their early success in the albumen process. The jury admired the 'beautiful and extreme delicacy and variety of tint' in their prints.[24] Ross and Thomson's work, at its best, bears comparison with the constructed photographs of O.G. Reijlander and Henry Peach Robinson. In general, their work consists of competent studio portraiture characteristic of the commercial world of photography from the mid-1850s, specialising in engaging studio properties – a little lake and boat, a rustic balcony, the rigging of a ship – which ensured their popularity. The detail of the albumen process allowed very small, carte-de-visite photographs to be produced cheaply and in quantity. It is from this time that photography became a public art in the sense that most people could afford to own photographs of their friends and family.

By the 1850s, photography was tending to divide into two opposed camps – the aesthetic and the scientific-technical. Roughly speaking, the first maintained an allegiance to the plain or uncoated paper processes: the calotype or the waxed paper process; and the second adopted the albumen process. The fascination with the rich possibilities of print-making in photography turns up in the work of two notable amateurs: John Muir Wood, working from the 1840s through into the 1850s,[25] and Thomas Keith, whose photographs were taken between 1852 and 1857.[26] Wood was a musician and entrepreneur working from Edinburgh and Glasgow but with a European sophistication. His experiments with the variant colours and effects given by different metals – gold, uranium, tin and copper – are often mysterious and beautiful, exploiting the results of accident for their pleasure. Wood was both a portrait and a landscape photographer; Thomas Keith was more selective and controlled in his work. His description of his handling of Gustave Le Gray's waxed paper process is precise and methodical, as befitted his professional career as a surgeon – he did not risk exposing a negative unless the light was perfect. His photographs of Scottish landscape and buildings, principally in Edinburgh and Iona (Plate 51), have a density and richness that gives them a signal authority, a handling of light, shade and texture that conveys a loving sense of both the beauty and the history in his subjects.

John Muir Wood's photographic experiments may well depend on the work of Charles John Burnett (1820–1907), published in *The British Journal of Photography* in the 1850s and 1860s, and in his *Photography in Colours* (1857) on the search for photographic permanence. Like Wood, Burnett was interested in uranium and he also conducted what may have been the earliest experiments with platinum. Burnett lived between Aberdeenshire and Edinburgh. In Glasgow, the most extraordinary experimental photographer was the engineer, John Kibble (1815–94). There remains of his photographic work an exceptionally large glass negative, 22 × 16 inches, of the Broomielaw in Glasgow, which was dwarfed by a 39 × 29-inch plate of Gourock. These were first exhibited at the meeting of the British Association for the Advancement of Science in Glasgow in 1854 and were referred to by Horatio Ross in 1857 as 'the greatest triumphs of photography that have yet been exhibited; immense in size, but perfect in detail'.[27] Kibble also achieved instantaneous photographs with the supposedly less sensitive dry collodion process, reviewed in 1859:

> 'Express Steamer' is a magnificent production, though the picture is small; it is taken
> in the fortieth part of a second, and developed in ninety hours: the rolling clouds are a
> beautiful transcript of nature. The steamer is running very quickly, leaving a deep
> furrow in the waste of water, heaving with agitation, as she is forced onwards by the
> propulsion of steam . . .. This is verily a triumph of instantaneous photography.[28]

51. Thomas Keith, Pillars of Iona Cathedral, *salt print from a waxed paper negative, 1856.*
(Scottish National Portrait Gallery)

In 1855, the young James Clerk Maxwell (1831–79) 'laid down the fundamental theory behind all subsequent systems of indirect colour photography'[29] – that is to say, that by filtering the light impression through the three principal colours of light a photograph can be taken which can be reconstructed in the true colours by projection through those same three colours. He demonstrated this to the Royal Institution in London in May 1861, appropriately, with a picture of a tartan ribbon. The work of Charles Piazzi Smyth (1819–1900) involved the scientific development and exploitation of photography in an extended field.[30] Smyth was the Astronomer Royal for Scotland and it is perhaps of marginal interest that he worked also on Calton Hill from 1845 and with the assistance of Miss Mann. While working previously at the Cape of Good Hope, he was able, with the practical assistance of Sir John Herschel and Robert

Hunt, to take the first photographs in the continent of Africa, probably in 1841 or 1842. Smyth used photography first in a public project in 1856 on an expedition to Tenerife to demonstrate the greater clarity of the atmosphere at high levels – an important astronomical consideration. He used stereoscopic photography to document the progress of the expedition and he and his wife, Jessica Duncan, were the first to publish a book illustrated with stereoscopic photographs.[31] He was very concerned with the accuracy of the photographic record and its practical use for measurement. Further expeditions to Russia and, in 1865, to the Great Pyramids extended his interests, in the use of small, accurate negatives, 'one inch square, or indeed only as large as one's thumb nail'[32] which could be enlarged, and in flash photography.

Exemplifying the commercial success of photography, three impressive photographic businesses were established in the 1850s: James Valentine (1815–80) in Dundee in 1851, George Washington Wilson (1823–93) in Aberdeen in 1852, and Thomas Annan (1829–87) in Glasgow in 1855. Both G.W. Wilson and Valentine developed a phenomenal trade, based on the tourist industry, for scenic views of Scotland.[33] Thomas Annan's main commercial interest was in the reproduction of works of art but his own personal work remained distinctive and important.[34] He is nowadays best known for his series of *The Old Closes and Streets of Glasgow*, taken between 1869 and 1871 – a survey of the condemned slums of the city which achieved a touching and sensitive beauty (Plate 52). Annan admired D.O. Hill both as a man and as an artist, and this emerges in his photographs in a poetic idea of landscape and an effective, broad approach to portraiture. His portrait of David Livingstone (1864) has a critical sympathy unequalled in the many other portraits of that sitter. Annan's work won him the high opinion of the photographic press: 'There is much beyond fine manipulation in the beautiful landscapes of Mr Annan, which are indicative of deep poetic feeling, and strong appreciation of the beautiful in the artist. The portraits by the same gentleman are also very fine, possessing rare softness and delicacy.'[35]

From the 1850s, Scottish photographers working abroad produced an impressive range of work, which can be said to have developed a Scottish tradition outside the country. Photographers like Robert Macpherson in Rome, William Carrick in St Petersburg, John Thomson in the Far East and Alexander Gardner in the United States were working in a manner recognisably related to their peers in Scotland and they maintained communication, exhibiting and publishing in Scotland.

After his brother's death, John Adamson encouraged the young chemist, Thomas Rodger (1833–83), to take up photography. Rodger became one of the country's leading portraitists. Adamson himself, despite his engulfing practice as a doctor, was noticeably encouraged in his turn by D.O. Hill and developed an appreciation of aesthetics. From the mid-1850s to the early 1860s, he took a number of strong, challenging portraits – impressive in their character and aesthetically independent rather than simply echoing Hill and Adamson's earlier work.

In numerical terms, photography was dominated from about 1860 by the professionals – the public at large were the audience and consumers. In the 1880s the trend was reversed in favour of the amateurs. One of the many amateur societies set up at this time was the Dundee and East of Scotland Photographic Association. Its first President was James Cox (1849–1901), the son of one of the leading jute manufacturers in Dundee.[36] Cox experimented with a range of technology and processes, working from a large plate to a snapshot camera, making albumen, gelatine, carbon and platinum prints. His most interesting photographs were taken in the fishing villages of

52. *Thomas Annan*, Close no.46, Saltmarket, Glasgow, *albumen print, 1868–71*. (Scottish National Portrait Gallery)

Auchmithie and West Haven and contrast with Hill and Adamson's Newhaven images in emphasising the hardness and bleakness of the life. This approach derived from the French realist school, demonstrably the paintings of Jules Bastien-Lepage which Cox seems to have encountered before the Scottish realist painters. It is a truthful reflection of the particular hardness of fishing life in the 1880s and has more conviction, albeit a less decorative character, than the comparable contemporary work of Frank Meadow Sutcliffe in Whitby. Cox's photography shows also an interest in the distortions of light and movement, which are particularly evident in bright seaside conditions, and here his photography links also with the painting of William MacTaggart.

Thomas Annan's son, J. Craig Annan (1864–1946),[37] was similarly involved with the work of painters and engravers, working in close association with D.Y. Cameron and William Strang. He worked mostly in photogravure which enabled him to manipulate his images in an immensely subtle but often extensive manner – exploiting both the dynamism of the speed of the new snapshot camera and the 'long-drawn-out pleasure' of etching the gravure plate. Neither his skills nor his choice of subject fall within a limited pattern and his images have an individual character, which is strongly personal. His *The Beach at Zandvoort* (1892) is a disconcerting, abstract signal of modernity, picking up the subject matter of the Hague school but giving it a radically new treatment, both unstaged and formal in construction. His photogravure, *The White Friars* (1894), taken in Venice, remains one of the most effective photographs of action, and was considered in its day to be 'one of the greatest pictures ever made by means of the camera'.[38] Annan's *Stirling Castle* (1906) (Plate 53) is a mysterious illustration of Cameron's opinion of his photographs: 'reticent, reserved, weird, and tenderly beautiful'. Annan's work remained remarkably variable and experimental. His skill was considerable and his understanding relaxed, with the simplicity of excellence: 'The aim of a picture is not to demonstrate any theory or fact, but is to excite a certain sensory pleasure.'[39]

Annan was the first major photographer based in Scotland to achieve a leading position in the international arena. He was responsible for the spectacularly successful exhibition of pictorial photography which was presented in the Glasgow International exhibition of 1901 and was seen by eleven and a half million visitors. He was a friend of the American photographer, Alfred Stieglitz, who regarded him as 'a true artist and a decidedly poetic one at that'. Through Stieglitz's journal, *Camera Work*, Annan's

53. James Craig Annan, Stirling Castle, *photogravure, 1906 (*Scottish National Portrait Gallery*)*

photogravures of his own work and of Hill and Adamson's calotypes were shown to the world and proved a significant influence on American and European photography in the twentieth century.

By the 1920s, significant photographic work was lessening in Scotland. The mid-century saw exponents of documentary photography, working mostly in the sympathetic tradition, coming in from outside. Much of this focused on a particular concern for Glasgow, as with the work of the *Picture Post* photographers, Humphrey Spender (*b*.1910), who visited Glasgow in 1939, and Bert Hardy and Bill Brandt who came in 1948. This tradition has remained lively in the hands of the Scottish photographers, Joseph McKenzie (*b*.1929) who is based in Dundee, and Oscar Marzaroli (1933–88), who worked principally in Glasgow. Photographers were in the main working in isolation until the 1980s. At this point, a revival of comprehensive interest has resulted in a resurgence of talent in which the art schools, the galleries and the photographers are finding considerable stimulation. Work comparably wide-ranging and independent in character is once more taking the Scottish art into an international field.

Notes

1. Research into the history of photography in Scotland is in progress, not by any means complete, and our understanding of the field continues to broaden. This essay is necessarily arbitrary in character and, for a wider idea of the subject, the reader is referred to S. Stevenson and A.D. Morrison-Low, *Scottish Photography: a Bibliography 1939–1989* (Edinburgh, 1990).
2. Hugh Miller, *The Witness*, 12 July 1843.
3. An idea of Brewster's position can be realised from the remaining album of his early collection, now in the Getty Museum. See Graham Smith, *Disciples of Light: Photographs in the Brewster Album* (Malibu, 1990).
4. Thomas Davidson, 'Description of the Process of Daguerreotype, and remarks on the Action of Light in that process, both in respect to Landscape and Miniature Portraits', in *Transactions of the Royal Scottish Society of Arts* (Edinburgh, 1941), Vol. 2. pp.21-25.
5. Letters from Jones to Talbot, 29 May 1841 and 1 October 1845, Fox Talbot Museum, LA 41034, LA 45-133.
6. Davidson described this in a letter to the Editor, *Liverpool Photographic Journal*, October 1859, p.264. The idea was patented in the United States and in England in 1840.
7. Robert Graham, 'The Early History of Photography', in *Good Words* (London, 1874), pp.450-53.
8. *Transactions of the Royal Scottish Society of Arts*, Edinburgh, I, 1839, pp.336-37.
9. Mungo Ponton, *Songs of the Soul* (Bristol, 1877), pp.8-10.
10. Samuel Smiles (ed.), *James Nasmyth, Engineer: an Autobiography* (London, 1902), p.149.
11. George S. Cundell, 'On the practice of the Calotype Process of Photography', *The London, Edinburgh and Dublin Philosophical Magazine*, May 1844, Vol.24, pp.321-32.

12. Robert Hunt, *A Manual of Photography* (London, 1957), p.62.

13. 'On Photography' and 'On the Daguerreotype', *Edinburgh New Philosophical Journal*, Vol.XXVII, 1839, pp.144–55 and Vol.XXVII, 1840, pp.205–11.

14. Letter from Brewster to Talbot, 15 August 1842, Science Museum, London.

15. Lord Cockburn, quoted in the prospectus for Thomas Annan's photographs of D.O. Hill's painting, *An Historical Picture Representing the Signing of the Deed of Demission . . .*, 1866, p.4.

16. Letter from Brewster to Talbot, 3 July 1843 (Science Museum collection).

17. For an account of their career see John Ward and Sara Stevenson, *Printed Light: the Scientific Art of William Henry Fox Talbot and David Octavius Hill with Robert Adamson* (Edinburgh, 1986).

18. Letter from Hill to David Roberts, 12 March 1845 (private collection).

19. Letter from Nasmyth to Hill, 27 March 1847.

20. Letter from Hill to Henry Bicknell, 17 January 1849 (George Eastman House).

21. Sara Stevenson, *Hill and Adamson's 'Fishermen and Women of the Firth of Forth'* (Edinburgh, 1991).

22. Letter from Hill to Henry Bicknell, quoted above, note 20.

23. Letter from Hill to David Roberts, 14 March 1845 (private collection).

24. *Exhibition of the Works of Industry of All Nations, 1851: Reports of the Juries* (London, 1852), p.278.

25. Sara Stevenson, Julie Lawson and Michael Grey, *John Muir Wood 1805–1892: an Accomplished Amateur* (Edinburgh, 1988).

26. John Hannavy, *Thomas Keith's Scotland* (Edinburgh, 1981).

27. *Photographic Notes* (1857), p.97.

28. *British Journal of Photography* (1859), p.8.

29. Brian Coe, *Colour Photography: the First Hundred Years 1840–1940* (London, 1978), p.28.

30. Larry Schaaf, 'Charles Piazzi Smyth, Photography, and the Disciples of Constable and Harding', *Photographic Collector*, Winter 1983, pp.314–331.

31. C. Piazzi Smyth, *Tenerife: An Astronomer's Experiment* (London, 1858).

32. C. Piazzi Smyth, *A Poor Man's Photography at the Great Pyramid . . .* (London, 1870).

33. Roger Taylor, *George Washington Wilson, Artist and Photographer 1923–93* (Aberdeen, 1981); Robert Smart, "Famous Throughout the World": Valentine and Sons, Dundee', *Review of Scottish Culture*, 4, 1988, pp.75–87.

34. Sara Stevenson, *Thomas Annan 1829–1887* (Edinburgh, 1990).

35. Review of the exhibition of the Photographic Society of Scotland, *The Photographic News*, 6 January 1865.

36. Sara Stevenson, *James Cox 1849–1901*, (Edinburgh, 1988).

37. William Buchanan, *The Art of the Photographer: J. Craig Annan* (Edinburgh, 1992).

38. Joseph Keily, 'Loan Exhibition', *Camera Notes*, April 1900, p.214.

39. 'Mr Craig Annan's Address at the Opening of the Exhibition of his Works at the Royal Photographic Society', *Amateur Photographer*, 2 February 1900, p.83.

Books for Further Reading

David Brittain and Sara Stevenson, *New Scottish Photography: a Critical Review of the Work of Seventeen Photographers* (Edinburgh, 1990)

Sara Stevenson, *David Octavius Hill and Robert Adamson: Catalogue of their calotypes taken between 1843 and 1847 in the collection of the Scottish National Portrait Gallery* (Edinburgh, 1981)

Sara Stevenson, *Hill and Adamson's Fishermen and Women of the Firth of Forth* (Edinburgh, 1991)

Sara Stevenson, *Thomas Annan 1829–1887* (Edinburgh, 1990)

Sara Stevenson, Julie Lawson and Michael Gray; *The Photography of John Muir Wood: an Accomplished Amateur 1805–1892* (Edinburgh, 1988)

Sara Stevenson and A.D. Morrison-Low, *Scottish Photography: a Bibliography, 1839–1989* (Edinburgh, 1990).

John Ward and Sara Stevenson, *Printed Light: the Scientific Art of William Henry Fox Talbot and David Octavius Hill with Robert Adamson* (Edinburgh, 1986)

The Cinema

FORSYTH HARDY

As it is not possible to go very far, in considering Scotland's contribution to the cinema, without encountering the financial factor, it would be better to take it on board at once. Now a hundred years old, the film is a mass medium of entertainment. A film can be seen by many millions of people across the world. It can make larger profits than any other form of entertainment. It therefore attracts massive investment in the main centre of production, Hollywood. No other country in the world can compete with American domination.

This affects the volume and nature of film-making outside Hollywood. Other countries can make films on a modest scale for audiences within their boundaries. Very occasionally a film from another country can reach a world audience comparable to that achieved by even the ordinary American film, by reason of the novelty of its subject or exceptional treatment. For example, in a Scottish context, *Whisky Galore!* and, more recently, *Local Hero*. This does not provide a basis for any substantial volume of film-making by a small country. Over the shouts of American movies it is difficult to hear the still small voice of Scottish films.

I put this forward so that any claims made in this essay can be kept in scale. For better or worse (and many would opt for worse) the picture of Scotland on the cinema screen has been painted in the main by producers outwith the country. In the earliest years of the century there were some short films (of a few minutes' duration) on such subjects as Highland dancing, Gretna Green and the bagpipe. The first of many films on Mary Stewart was made in France in 1908 and the first of many versions of *Macbeth* in the same year. Even in cinema's first decade it was clear that the bloodier elements in Scotland's story were going to be preferred.

In one sense the Scottish movie experience was not going to be different from that of other countries. The producers looked for subjects among published novels or theatre productions. The reason was obvious: someone else had selected and interpreted a theme and tried it out on the public. Scottish novelists and dramatists therefore were the main source, not only of the earliest Scottish films but also into contemporary practice. Before the First World War there were versions of Walter Scott's *Lochinvar, Kenilworth, The Bride of Lammermuir, Rob Roy* and *The Heart of Midlothian*. The cumulative effect of these films was to build up an image of Scotland as a wild, romantic country, rich in picturesque drama and blessed with magnificent scenery. It could have been worse.

J.M. Barrie was one of the other sources of this fictionalised Scotland. His was an altogether gentler view of Scottish life. The extraordinary popularity of his plays in the United States inevitably meant that film versions were made even before moving pictures found a voice. There was a version of *The Little Minister* as early as 1915, followed by *What Every Woman Knows* in 1917. Both were to reappear at regular intervals into the sound period. This essentially sentimental, rose-tinted conception of Scotland was to be found also in such films as *The Shepherd Lassie of Argyle* (1914) with Florence Turner, *Annie Laurie* (1916) with Alma Taylor, and *The Pride of the Clans* (1917) with Mary Pickford. Harry Lauder made a few short films and in *Auld Lang Syne* (1929) appeared as a Scots farmer visiting London to search for his son and daughter.

With the coming of sound to the cinema the selection of Scottish subjects became a little more diversified. A brave attempt was made by Herbert Wilcox to film *The Loves of Robert Burns* (1930) with the tenor, Joseph Hislop, as the poet: acceptable as long as he was singing 'Flow Gently Sweet Afton' or 'Comin' Thro' the Rye' but otherwise a stiff and stilted rendering. *The Flying Scotsman* (1930) had Moore Marriott as the engine driver and in *The Secret of the Loch* (1934) Seymour Hicks appeared as a scientist persuading London journalists that the Loch Ness Monster had been hatched from a prehistoric egg. Hollywood contributed *The Cohens and Kellys in Scotland* (1930) and *Bonnie Scotland* (1935) with Laurel and Hardy.

Beyond this picturesque periphery there were the first signs of a more realistic approach to the screen image of Scotland. Michael Powell, who was to produce several notable Scottish films, made *Red Ensign* (1934), based on a Clyde shipbuilding story he had written. Alfred Hitchcock directed *The Thirty-Nine Steps* (1935) from John Buchan's novel. Alastair Sim and Fay Compton appeared in *Wedding Group* (1936), directed by Alex Bryce, later to be involved in Walt Disney's Scottish films. René Clair accepted Alexander Korda's invitation to direct *The Ghost Goes West* (1936) and lent a light touch to its fantasy. On a lesser scale was *The Rugged Island* (1934), made by Jenny Brown in her native Shetland, modest but still significant as a genuine film of Scottish life. She was encouraged by John Grierson and made several other films in Shetland.

Grierson had founded the British documentary film movement with *Drifters* (1929), his film of the Scottish herring fleets. He was to have a major influence on Scottish cinema for the rest of his life. It surfaced first in the group of short films he made while he was film officer to the Empire Marketing Board. They included notably *O'er Hill and Dale* (1931) in which Basil Wright gave a hint of the poetic touch which was to distinguish his *Song of Ceylon*. Grierson's influence emerged again very strongly in the most memorable film produced during his régime at the GPO Film Unit, *Night Mail* (1936), in which he ensured that the postal train should travel north to Scotland and not the alternative journey south to the metropolis, as might have been expected. He had Benjamin Britten to compose the music and W.H. Auden to write the verse for the crossing the border sequence.

Grierson was also producer of a group of films on Scotland commissioned by the first Films of Scotland Committee for showing at the Empire Exhibition in Glasgow in 1938. Before the flood of documentary film-making released by television, this was the first considered and comprehensive record of the life of a country in film. Scotland was a small enough area for the films to look in some detail at the country's history, industry, agriculture, fishing, education, health and sport. The series earned many tributes. Ritchie Calder thought that the films would 'tell the world of the other side of Scotland, tear away the tartan curtain of romance and show a nation fighting for its existence', while Paul Rotha wrote later that 'the project was, and still is, unique in film history and was successful in every way'. Modest in scale, it was a beginning.

Documentary film-making continued in Scotland during the war. Inevitably the films had a propaganda purpose: digging for victory, health care, land reclamation, food rationing. Several of the films of the war or immediate post-war period ventured beyond that limitation. *Children of the City* (1944) bravely took child crime as its theme and even advanced solutions. *Crofters* (1944) looked to the far north-west to record a way of life as far from the battle fronts in Europe, North Africa and the Far East as could be imagined. The superb photography of this unique corner of Scotland ought by now to have inspired producers of fiction films. *North-East Corner* (1944) crossed to the other side of Scotland and, from a script by John R. Allan and Laurie Lee, made something memorable of the daily life of Aberdeenshire's fishermen and farmers. Matching these films was *Waverley Steps* (1947), a film of Edinburgh which earned many tributes including one from the critic Richard Winnington: 'a crisp, rhythmic film with brain and wit behind it'.

Michael Powell had not previously been in Scotland when he arrived to make *The Edge of the World* (1936–37). Powell had been fascinated by an account he had read of the evacuation of St Kilda and thought the dilemma of the islanders, faced with a choice between the hardships of their harsh island life and the amenities of the mainland would provide a promising theme for a film. He did not think of it as a documentary: it was too late for that. But the St Kilda story had a relevance for isolated communities anywhere in the world. Indeed the film was made not in St Kilda, whose use was withheld from him, but on Foula, west of Shetland, where conditions were similar, the cliffs as menacingly high and life was as hard for its small population.

The Edge of the World was important, not only because of its intrinsic qualities as a film but also because it demonstrated that films could be successfully made on natural locations. In a personal sense the film changed the course of Powell's life: he became an associate of Korda's and made some of the most ambitious films every produced in Britain. For Scotland it meant that he would return to make first *The Spy in Black* (1939) from a Storer Clouston story set in Orkney and, later, *I know where I'm Going* (1945) from a story by his associate, Emeric Pressburger, which for audiences throughout the world conveyed something of the enchantment of the Western Isles. Powell retained his affection for Scotland and had exciting ideas for other Scottish films, including an imaginative treatment of *Tam o' Shanter*. His influence on Scotland's story films was comparable to Grierson's on documentary.

The theatre was still a source for Scottish fiction films. *Storm in a Teacup* (1937) was adapted by James Bridie and, directed by Victor Saville, gave a lively account of life in a small Scottish town afflicted by bumbledom. *Marigold* (1938), from the play by Charles Garvice, had Sophie Stewart in what was described as 'the sweetest love story ever'. In contrast *Hatter's Castle* (1941), from the novel by A.J. Cronin, was as gloomy and doom-ridden as any film ever made. Much more successful as an adaptation was *The Shipbuilders* (1943) for which John Baxter had the guiding hand of George Blake. Together these fictional films began to build up a picture of Scotland, however patchy, which at best was recognisable.

The life of Mary, Queen of Scots had a seemingly irresistible appeal for film producers in several countries. Five versions were made in France between 1908 and 1913. Others were made in England and Germany. The best known, or most notorious, was *Mary of Scotland* (1936) from Maxwell Anderson's play, with Katharine Hepburn unhappily cast as Mary and Fredric March not much more at ease as Bothwell. John Ford, the masterly director of *The Grapes of Wrath*, found the subject beyond him and the result was ill-informed, confused and lacking in conviction. A later version, *Mary, Queen of Scots* (1972), had Vanessa Redgrave as Mary. Transplanting the story from the compact turreted Palace of Holyroodhouse to the spacious, restored battlements of Bamburgh Castle deprived the film of credibility. Among the directors attracted to the subject were Carl Dreyer of *The Passion of Joan of Arc*, whose preparations included visits to Edinburgh to select locations and the writing of a script; and Alexander Mackendrick who thought of telling the story of murder, abduction, conflict, escape, imprisonment and eventual beheading with graphic, headline urgency. His treatment still awaits production.

Matching Mary Stewart in appeal for the film-makers was Prince Charles Edward Stuart. Sir Alexander Korda had this in mind before the war as a companion film for *The Private Life of Henry VIII*. Leslie Howard was to play the Young Pretender. I recall him discussing the project with me at Denham Studios. He said he thought of the prince as 'the very embodiment of youthful idealism. I have always felt that the story of Charles Edward, with the lesson of unquestioning loyalty to an ideal, should be the real expression of undying Scottish national spirit.' Perhaps it might have worked. But Howard died in an air accident and when *Bonnie Prince Charlie* was put into production in 1947 his place was taken by David Niven, whose flair was for light comedy. Had it not been for this mis-casting the film might well have succeeded. Certainly Korda spared no effort and expense. Clemence Dane wrote the script and provided at least one sequence which helped to make the story understandable by audiences outwith Scotland: the confrontation at Derby between the prince, eager to press on to London, and the clan chiefs who knew that their men wanted to return to the Highlands. Despite the splendid photography, the elaborate sets and costumes, the acting of such stalwart Scots as Finlay Currie and the music of Ian Whyte, the film did not carry conviction. Although it lacked all this expensive elaboration, the film which Peter Watkins made of *Culloden* in 1964 had a much stronger emotional appeal. Audiences were moved to tears by the treatment of the Highlanders after the battle.

For a succession of film-makers over several decades, Shakespeare's *Macbeth* had an inescapable attraction. Silent versions were made in France, Italy, Germany and England. Orson Welles had long cherished the project but production companies were wary of the director of *Citizen Kane*. In 1948 he was at last able to persuade a minor Hollywood company, Republic Pictures, to finance the film, perhaps influenced by the help he had given with *Trouble in the Glen*. Welles had his own conception of Macbeth: 'He was a detestable man until he became king, and then once he is crowned he is doomed; but once he is doomed he becomes a great man.' He saw Macbeth's Scotland as a dark and dank land, inhabited by vicious, ruthless and superstitious warriors. His film was admired for his obvious determination to give the theme cinematic form, largely unhampered by Shakespeare's words. It had unmistakable power. In contrast, George Schaefer's *Macbeth* (1961) was an unexciting record of a stage performance, with Maurice Evans and Judith Anderson in parts they had created for the theatre. The version made by Roman Polanski in 1972 from a treatment written by Kenneth Tyman highlighted the violence in the theme, including off-stage action such as the murder of Lady Macduff and the decapitation of Macbeth. Polanski perversely shot exteriors for the film, not in and around Inverness, but in the Snowdonia National Park and at Lindisfarne and Bamburgh Castles, wrong in period and in style for Macbeth's Scotland.

Another borrowing from literature was the work of Robert Louis Stevenson. His short story, *Dr Jekyll and Mr Hyde*, became an impressive film, directed in Hollywood in 1932 by Rouben Mamoulian, with Fredric March and Miriam Hopkins in the leading parts. It is remembered for its on-camera facial transformation from doctor to villain rather than for its picture of contemporary Edinburgh. Another version was made in 1941, directed by Victor Fleming, with Spencer Tracy reluctant to convey the evil living within Dr Jekyll, and Ingrid Bergman insisting on playing the barmaid rather than the sweet-natured heroine. Several versions of the Burke and Hare story were also made. The earliest and most successful was *The Body Snatcher* (1945) with a cast headed by Boris Karloff, Henry Daniell and Bela Lugosi, a sinister trio. *The Flesh and the Fiends* (1950) had Peter Cushing as Dr Knox, Donald Pleasence as Hare and George Rose as Burke, with smaller parts for Renée Houston and John Cairney. *Burke and Hare* (1971), *Dr Jekyll and Sister Hyde* (1971) and *The Doctor and the Devils* (1985), however far they departed from Stevenson's original, demonstrated the fascination of the basic story. *The Doctor and the Devils* was presented as a stage play at the Edinburgh Festival. Dylan Thomas was commissioned to work on the screenplay by the film's producer, Donald Taylor.

Stevenson provided the inspiration for other films where the emphasis was on romantic adventure rather than colourful melodrama. *Kidnapped* with Warner Baxter and Freddie Bartholomew was filmed in Hollywood in 1938 and again in 1948 with Roddy McDowall and Dan O'Herlihy. The pursuit motive, yielding an abundance of lively and exciting incident, was not fully realised until Robert Stevenson directed a version for Walt Disney in 1959 with Peter Finch and James MacArthur and a cast which drew wisely on the strength of Scottish acting at the time. Cedric Thorpe Davie's music was directed by Muir Mathieson, two Scots whose names on a film meant an assurance of musical quality. The story was filmed again in Britain in 1971 with Michael Caine, Trevor Howard, Jack Hawkins and Gordon Jackson. A Stevenson adaptation which came near the spirit but certainly not the letter of the original was *The Master of Ballantrae* (1953), a spirited, fast-moving piece of adventure with Errol Flynn and Roger Livesey involved in exciting sword duels and hair's-breadth escapes. Jack Cardiff's photography of the western seaboard gave the film visual distinction.

In addition to *Kidnapped*, Walt Disney made several films at this period which drew on picturesque elements in Scottish life. His *Rob Roy* (1953) owed nothing to Scott: it was based on legendary adventures and, that parameter accepted, it was an accomplished piece of film-making with more authoritative acting than was usual in a film of this kind, with James Robertson Justice a commanding figure as Argyll. There was a gentler touch in *Greyfriars Bobby* (1960). Exteriors were to have been filmed in

Edinburgh until it was realised that the forest of television aerials on houses round the church made this impossible. As sentimental was *The Three Lives of Thomasina* (1963), adapted from the novel by Paul Gallico and set in Inveraray.

These and such others as *Brigadoon* (1954), Vincente Minnelli's version of Alan Jay Lerner's musical, presented a Scotland which stood at some distance from reality. There were some correctives. *The Brothers* (1947), adapted from the novel by L.A.G. Strong, was a powerful story of love and hate among the crofters and fishermen of the west coast. This was conflict in the raw, a feud between two families sustained with treachery and violence. The Scottish director, David Macdonald, made maximum dramatic use of the Skye background and drew on legend, as in the trial of strength of the Rowing, to give colour and character to his film. He also had a responsive cast, including Finlay Currie and Duncan Macrae, relishing demanding opportunities for acting which all too seldom came their way. Dilys Powell regarded it as 'another proof of the coming of age of the British cinema that we in this country are able to recreate so grim a poetic tragedy'. A film of stature.

Much lighter in touch was *Whisky Galore!* (1948) which had its origin in Sir Compton Mackenzie's novel about the wartime wreck of the S.S. *Politician* off the Isle of Eriskay and the salvaging of its cargo of whisky by the islanders. It had been strangely neglected by the film-makers until Monja Danischewsky brought it to the attention of Sir Michael Balcon, who agreed it could be made if it could be filmed on location away from the overcrowded Ealing Studios. Alexander (Sandy) Mackendrick was given the opportunity to direct this, his first film. Mackenzie insisted that it should be made on Barra. The players included Duncan Macrae, Gordon Jackson, James Robertson Justice and Joan Greenwood, and among the natives was the legendary Father John Macmillan. The film was an immediate success, not only in Britain but also in the United States (as *Tight Little Island*) and in France and Italy. It is remembered with affection by audiences all over the world.

The conflict between seemingly simple peasantry and officialdom in any shape set a pattern for Hebridean films. In *Laxdale Hall* (1952) it took the form of a refusal by Highlanders in a remote community to pay road fund licences when they had no usable roads. The source here was a treatment written by Eric Linklater for production at Ealing, acquired by Grierson when he was executive producer at Group 3, one of the enterprises initiated by the National Film Finance Corporation with the aim of encouraging young film-makers. It was shot in Applecross and the road over the hill from Kishorn was convincing justification for the film's theme. John Eldridge (of *Waverley Steps*) directed and the players included Roddy Macmillan, Fulton Mackay, Jameson Clark and Andrew Keir. If it did not achieve the worldwide success of *Whisky Galore!*, it attracted delighted audiences in Scotland for many years.

It was followed into the cinemas by another Hebridean comedy, *The Maggie* (1954). Neil Munro's tales of the puffers, the chunky little flat-bottomed boats plying between the Clyde and the Western Isles with cargoes of coal, had long seemed to invite film treatment. A linking narrative was needed to provide continuity and conflict. Sandy Mackendrick found it in the efforts of a hustling American businessman to have plumbing transported to his new home on a Hebridean island and the opportunity a puffer captain saw to earn enough from the commission to have his creaking craft repaired. Mackendrick was fortunate in his casting, setting the mounting exasperation of Paul Douglas's bluff American against the quietly stubborn scheming of Alexander Mackenzie's captain. John Grierson saw Neil Munro's 'Para Handy' stories as 'an

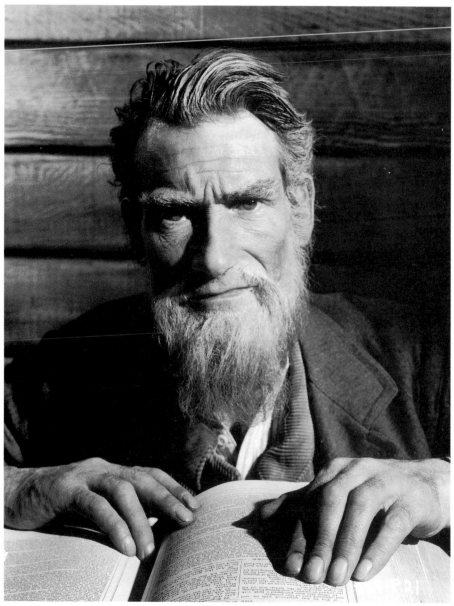

54. Duncan Macrae (1905–67) in the film, The Kidnappers *(1953), based on a story by Neil Paterson and directed by Phil Leacock at Pinewood. (*Scottish Film Archive*)*

Odyssey of the common man with all his prides and his humours, wandering through the little places and getting a terrific bash out of life wherever he goes'.

Into this group of films by way of Nova Scotia comes *The Kidnappers* (1953), adapted from a short story by Neil Paterson set in Cape Breton but filmed in Glen Affric. This study of a child's instinctive longing to love, or be loved, and of the resistance of an old man who has brought with him from Scotland a stern code of moral values, had been shaped by the author with a narrative skill honed in Hollywood. The strength of the film lay in the performance of Duncan Macrae as the unyielding grandfather who disapproves both of the desire of his grandsons to have a dog and of his daughter's romance with a Dutch settler. It was probably the actor's finest achievement in the cinema. Philip Leacock's interpretation of Paterson's story had the virtue of simple sincerity.

Much the strongest of the films with Scottish themes made at this period was *The Brave Don't Cry* (1952). Like *Laxdale Hall* this was a product of Group 3 under Grierson's direction and it reflected not only his conviction of the value of social documentary but also his personal experience of the life of the miner as he had seen it in his native Stirlingshire. Written by Montagu Slater, a writer with strong socialist sympathies, and the like-minded Scottish author Lyndsay Galloway, it was a reconstruction of the Knockshinnoch mine disaster and rescue: a story of bravery below ground, resource of the rescue teams and the reaction of the mining community. Philip Leacock, the director, achieved the right balance between the varying moods of the trapped miners and the quiet stoicism of their wives above ground. He had the understanding co-operation of players drawing in the main from the Glasgow Citizens' Theatre: Andrew Keir, Fulton Mackay, Archie Duncan, Jameson Clark, Meg Buchanan and Jean Anderson. If they were not acting themselves, said Grierson, they were acting their next-door neighbours. This was an example, a superb example, of the kind of film on which Scottish cinema could be built: a drama drawn directly from everyday life, owing nothing to other art forms. A film about fighting back.

There is some relevance in the Group 3 experience to the situation in Scotland today. The films had modest budgets, about 25 per cent of what was normal at the time, and by using regional story settings and acting sources like the Glasgow Citizens' Theatre, costs were restricted. Success for the films depended on distribution and this was denied by the major production-exhibition companies who were short-sightedly opposed to what they saw as government interference in their industry. With the exception of *Everest*, where exceptional circumstances applied, *The Brave Don't Cry* was the most successful of the twenty-two films produced by Group 3. It did find an audience despite the resistance of the big companies (and with *Laxdale Hall* was shown overseas). Scottish films could similarly be made with modest budgets, as indeed *That Sinking Feeling* was. Their producers would still have a struggle to find audiences. Much has changed but not that.

I am running ahead somewhat. In 1955, when Group 3 was closed down, the production of documentary films produced with government monies had also ended. At the Scottish Office there were enlightened civil servants, among them Sir Charles Cunningham and William M. Ballantine, who were concerned that no use was being made of this information medium. How to fill the vacuum? Their answer was to revive the organisation which had produced films for the 1938 Empire Exhibition in Glasgow – the Films of Scotland Committee. And so a group under the leadership of Sir Alexander King, Hugh Fraser (later Sir Hugh and Lord Fraser of Allander), John Grierson, Neil Paterson and George Singleton was formed, charged with stimulating the production of films projecting the life and achievement of Scotland. I was released (not seconded) from my post of Senior Press Officer at the Scottish Office to guide the fulfilling of this remit from the Secretary of State for Scotland.

It was in many respects an impossible task. An initial contribution of £10,000 from Hugh Fraser was the sum of the Committee's resources. There was no money from government sources; nothing for administration far less than for film production. The theory was that I should find in industry, local government and national organisations sponsors who would pay for the films in return for the assurance of distribution Sir Alexander King could provide, assuming that they were of sufficient merit and interest to go into the cinemas. Astonishingly, the theory worked and the films were distributed. It was believed by several members of the Committee that the discipline of finding an audience for films with something to say, even if it were muted to find acceptance by exhibitors and audiences, was a good one. Perhaps it was, in its day. It did not make for an easy life; but there were always the inspiration and encouragement of John Grierson, who had the similar experience of the GPO Film Unit and the National Film Board of Canada behind him, and the practical help of Sir Alexander King in persuading distributors to accept the films. As an attraction to potential sponsors there was also the outlet to overseas distribution through the Central Office of Information.

Looking back on the Films of Scotland experience, I find it remarkable to consider the degree of response. The effort began modestly enough with films on the Western Isles for Macbrayne's, Aberdeen Corporation and the Edinburgh International Festival. The range quickly increased with a film (the first of several) for the North of Scotland Hydro-Electric Board which Grierson, who wrote and spoke the commentary, wanted to call *Scotland Be Dammed* but which went out as *Rivers at Work* (1958). A film on Scottish country dancing was the first of a series on the arts and leisure activities which at its most ambitious was to include films on Charles Rennie Mackintosh, Robert Adam and contemporary Scottish painters. A film pattern of Scotland, from St Kilda to Berwick-upon-Tweed and from Shetland to Stranraer, was gradually built up. The introduction of the new towns was recorded as was the building of bridges over the Forth, the Tay and the Clyde at Erskine.

Industry was one of the main concerns. It was a time of expansion and the developments at Ravenscraig, Invergordon, Corpach and Cruachan were filmed. Carpet-making in Glasgow, tweed-making in Harris, wool in the Borders and whisky distilling in Speyside all had their films. The most successful as a film was *Seawards the Great Ships* (1960–61) on Clyde shipbuilding. There were twenty-three shipyards on the Clyde at that time and the Clyde Shipbuilders' Association was reluctant to have a film made on their craft as their order books were full. Grierson wrote the treatment; the direction was by a young American, Hilary Harris, whose work he had admired at the Brussels Film Festival; Templar Film Studios provided production facilities; every launching on the Clyde for a year was covered by Scotland's cameramen; Iain Hamilton composed the music; and Cliff Hanley wrote the commentary, spoken by Bryden Murdoch. Whatever the fate of shipbuilding on the Clyde the film was a triumph, a tribute by a new craft to a much older one. In 1961 it won the Oscar in Hollywood as the Best Documentary of the year.

When I was appointed Director I drew up a list of a hundred films which optimistically I thought we might make. When I resigned in 1975 we had made 150. Together the films represented the most complete documentation of the life and achievement of a country on record anywhere in the world. They were seen with pleasure at special performances in Edinburgh during the Festival and at the Royal Festival Hall in London as well as in cinemas all over the country. I took them on tours to Canada, the United States, Australia and New Zealand. They gave employment to Scottish film companies which grew in number from two in 1955 to a dozen or more twenty years later. The film-makers, restive over the comparatively limited nature of the documentaries, were ready to embark on the production of fiction films for the cinemas. Two experimental short fiction films made for Films of Scotland, *The Duna Bull* (1971) by IFA (Scotland) and *The Great Mill Race* (1975) by Edinburgh Film Productions, showed that the skills necessary for longer films were there. When the Committee ceased functioning its films and its funds passed to the Scottish Film Council and the Scottish Film Archive.

Before the Scottish documentary film-makers began making fiction films there were several major productions by London companies to note. *The Battle of the Sexes* (1959) had its origin in a short story by James Thurber, adapted by its enterprising producer, Monja Danischewsky, and placed in Edinburgh. It concerned the disturbing impact on an old-established tweed firm of a young American efficiency expert who found her ideas stubbornly opposed by a mild little middle-aged clerk. The performance of Peter Sellers in this part gave the film its character, and the director, Charles Crichton, used the Edinburgh setting successfully. Also set in Edinburgh was *The Prime of Miss Jean Brodie* (1968), derived from Muriel Spark's novel and the play by Jay Presson Allen, directed by Ronald Neame. The Edinburgh private school tradition and the discipline which was part of it were affectionately recognised, while Maggie Smith excelled in bringing the redoubtable Jean Brodie convincingly to life. Neame was also the director of *Tunes of Glory* (1960) from the novel by James Kennaway. This became a powerful depiction of personal conflict between John Mills's martinet of a commanding officer and his immediate predecessor, Alec Guinness's hard-drinking, easy-going character who had the loyalty of most of the members of the mess. In addition to the well-realised setting of Stirling Castle, the film enjoyed some memorable performances by its Scottish actors. Kennaway's death in a road accident was a damaging loss to Scottish film-making potential. David Puttnam's *Chariots of Fire* (1981) could scarcely be claimed as a Scottish film, its key action placed elsewhere, but it could not have been made but for the life and example of Eric Liddell who so unshakably upheld one of the characteristics of the Scot, a respect for the Sabbath.

Meanwhile, the Scottish film scene was significantly changing. Bill Douglas had begun what was to be a notable trilogy on his upbringing in the mining village of Newcraighall, south-east of Edinburgh. The picture he drew in *My Childhood* (1972), *My Ain Folk* (1973) and *My Way Home* (1978) was austere and uncompromising, relieved only by the light of the director's imagination. The trilogy drew high praise: one critic wrote that it would come to be regarded 'not just as a milestone, but as one of the heroic achievements of the British cinema'. The vein of Scottish life which Bill Forsyth was simultaneously exploring could not have presented a greater contrast: the pains and preoccupations of young people in Glasgow, growing up in deprived conditions but accepting their plight with cheerful good humour. This was the theme of his first film, *That Sinking Feeling* (1979), which marked him as a director with ideas and initiative. Something of the same spirit enlivened *Gregory's Girl* (1980), set in Cumbernauld and revealing what one critic described as 'a cutting edge, an affectionate delicacy, and a free-wheeling impulsive gaiety'. These films had been made on modest budgets, mainly funded by the director's own efforts. His determination and persuasive skills were altogether admirable.

With *Local Hero* (1983) Forsyth moved, with the help of David Puttnam, out of local film-making into the international arena. He had Burt Lancaster as a star, to give his film entry into the United States, and it moved expensively from location work there to shooting at Arisaig and the fishing village of Pennan in Banffshire. In Forsyth's words, the film was about 'what would happen to a small community if it suddenly became enormously rich' through an oil tycoon's proposal to site an oil refinery near a West Highland coastal village. Nothing in a film by Bill Forsyth is ever quite what it seems, and *Local Hero* held many diversionary elements in story and characterisation. It proved to be a commercial success: it cost over £3 million and on its first release made a profit of about £350,000. It was a more acceptable film than *Comfort and Joy* (1984), in which the elements in the theme did not fuse convincingly: an ice-cream war in Glasgow and the predicament of a disc jockey whose brief is to bring breakfast happiness into millions of homes and whose girlfriend deserts him. Bill Paterson, a highly accomplished actor, had this part but never looked comfortable in it.

Other directors began to emerge in this fruitful period, some influenced by the Forsyth approach, like Charlie Gormley in *Living Apart Together* (1983), others like John Mackenzie finding tougher themes in, for example, *A Sense of Freedon* (1981) based on the life of Jimmy Boyle, and *Just Another Saturday* (1975) on the religious tensions in Glasgow which erupt in violence. Outstanding as a film and as a portrayal of Scottish life was *Another Time, Another Place* (1983), an adaptation by Michael Radford of Jessie Kesson's novel about the impact of a group of Italian prisoners-of-war on a small farming community in the Black Isle. Everything about the film seemed to be right: the conflict of nationalities, enriched by its setting in a well-observed rendering of the farming year. This demonstrated that themes could be found outside the metropolitan setting of most films. A comparison with the films of Marcel Pagnol was not inappropriate.

Among the directors with a reputation for imaginative documentary was Murray Grigor who had made notable films on Charles Rennie Mackintosh, Robert Adam and the American architect, Frank Lloyd Wright. His *Sean Connery's Edinburgh* (1982) was an original and inventive treatment of a much filmed subject. *Scotch Myths* (1982) was an account of the abuse of Scottish emblems for commercial purposes, the theme of an exhibition he and Barbara Grigor had staged at the 1981 Edinburgh Festival. Much technical skill was employed in condemning the tartan preoccupation. More commendable was his ambition to make a film about R.B. Cunninghame Graham, a subject for a major work which could add to the stature of Scottish cinema.

Even given the limitations I described earlier, there are one or two encouraging developments to note as we approach cinema's centenary. The Scottish Office, having declined to provide finance for feature film-making during the Films of Scotland period, supported the setting up of a Scottish Film Production Fund to assist projects likely to contribute to the growth of a national cinema. Among them was *Venus Peter* (1989), an adaptation of a novel by Christopher Rush, filmed in Orkney and directed by Ian Sellar. The financial involvement of the Orkney Islands Council was an example of what another organisation, Scottish Screen Locations, hopes to achieve by persuading producers of feature films to locate them in Scotland. Allied with this constructive effort, either directly as in the *Take the High Road* and *Dr Finlay* series or contributing to the cost of independently made films, were Scottish Television and Channel 4. The Edinburgh International Film Festival could provide a prestigious launching platform, as it did for *That Sinking Feeling*.

Film-making in a small country cannot be easy, given the domination of Hollywood and the problem of finding outlets to provide an economic basis. It is being done today in the Scandinavian countries which together produce an average of fifty films a year. Given individual inspiration and determination it can be done. John Grierson with his broad vision of what might be once put the matter constructively:

> However small the country, however local the source of revelation, it is what is revealed in depth of what men have seen or felt or done that matters and, by and large, the language of revelation is a universal one, perhaps the only universal one. So I don't think we are engaging in small or provincial affairs when we take thought of our own small country, for they are not necessarily so. It is only we who in the smallness of our observation make them small . . . The arc of the sky over us is as wide as any, the land under has seen as much of the light of love as any.

Books for Further Reading

Eddie Dick (ed.), *From Limelight to Satelight: a Scottish Film Book* (London, 1990)

Forsyth Hardy (ed.), *Grierson on Documentary* (London, 1946; enlarged edn., London, 1966)

Forsyth Hardy (ed.), *Grierson on the Movies* (London, 1981)

Forsyth Hardy, *John Grierson: a Documentary Biography* (London, 1979)

Forsyth Hardy, *John Grierson's Scotland* (Edinburgh, 1979)

Forsyth Hardy, *The Real Picture: Films and the Post Office, 1933–93* (London, 1993)

Forsyth Hardy, *Scotland in Film* (Edinburgh, 1990)

Forsyth Hardy, *Slightly Mad and Full of Dangers: the Story of the Edinburgh Film Festival* (Edinburgh, 1992)

Michael Powell, *200,000 Feet on Foula: The Story of the Film* The Edge of the World (London, 1936)

Sport in Scotland

KEVIN McCARRA

In July 1993 the International Cricket Conference refused to allow Scotland to affiliate as an Associate Member. The fact that our team was therefore denied such fringe benefits as admission to the game's mini-World Cup did not produce uproar. The argument which underlay the ICC judgment was, however, far more shocking. Scotland was not a country, it decided, ignoring the fact that England, too, has just as sketchy a constitutional existence. It is a conclusion which would bewilder the average Scotsman, who has tended to believe that our independent sporting life was itself a touchstone of nationhood.

For many it is the athletes who make Scotland real. The football side in the World Cup, the rugby team in the Five Nations Championship, runners like Liz McColgan or a golfer of Sandy Lyle's stature give this land a cultural identity. For nationalists Scotland's intense emotional investment in sport can be a source of frustration. Ian Hamilton, one of those who removed the Stone of Destiny from Westminster Abbey in 1950, feels that eyes glued to *Scotsport* on television may also be averted from reality. In a 1988 article he wrote: 'Perhaps we need to be expelled from the International Federation of Football Associations on the grounds that we are no longer a nation to bring us to our senses.'

Yet it would be unsafe to assume that sport is necessarily a surrogate for more meaningful activity. The competitiveness which produces such surprising numbers of successful sportsmen may be another facet of the enterprise which has made so many Scots influential globetrotters. Both traits were, for example, combined in the nineteenth-century figure of Robert Cunningham who worked for the Donaldson Shipping Line and set up home in Valparaiso. After two years' residence there he was eligible to play for the national football team and won twenty-seven caps for Chile.

Our passion for games, it must be admitted, can also be unseemly. Those fans who ripped up the turf at Wembley in 1977 and smashed the crossbar had a lineage which could be traced back for centuries. English commanders guarding the border with

*55. The Revd Robert Walker Skating by Sir Henry Raeburn (1756–1823). (*National Gallery of Scotland*)*

Scotland in the sixteenth century were always alert when they heard of a football match taking place nearby. These games frequently served as the warm-up for a raid into England. The sport was also a source of domestic disorder and was viewed with disfavour by the Scottish kings. James I convened his Council at Scone in 1424 and issued an Act which said: 'It is statut and the king forbiddis that na man play at the fute ball.'

The rest of the fifteenth-century Scottish monarchs also tried to ban football. A welter of repetitive legislation, however, always suggests that the law is failing. It may be that even kings knew their place, for James IV was not wholly resistant to the game. His Lord High Treasurer's accounts for 1497 show two shillings being spent on footballs, presumably for Shrove Tuesday festivities. James IV also once attended a match arranged by noblemen for his benefit.

That was surely a fierce spectacle. The sixteenth-century poet Richard Maitland wittily gave thanks for old age since infirmity at least allowed him to be excused the game. The boisterous sport tenaciously held its place in society. Sir Walter Scott once told the American novelist Washington Irving that 'it was not always safe to have football matches between villages – the old clannish spirit was too apt to break out'. That sentiment, however, did not prevent Scott from taking a keen interest in games such as the one played before two thousand spectators at Carterhaugh in 1815.

It was also said of Scott that 'he would rather have seen his heir [play] gallantly at a football match on Carterhaugh, than heard that the boy had attained the highest honours of the first university in Europe'. Some care, though, must be taken in using the term 'football'. These rough games involved handling and there could be hundreds of men playing on each side. Football, as we understand it, was refined in a more unlikely setting. Ironically, the game which is so inextricably intertwined with working-class experience in Scotland really has its origins in England's public schools.

It is from the sports played there that both football and rugby in their recognisable modern forms spring. The process of properly codifying the game began with a meeting of fourteen ex-pupils of Eton, Harrow and Rugby at the University of Cambridge in 1848. In 1863 England's Football Association was formed. When the first Scottish club, Queen's Park, was established in 1867 they had no option but to seek advice from south of the border. A set of rules was obtained from the Nottinghamshire cricketer, James Lillywhite. Whereas a natural context for rugby swiftly developed among Edinburgh's public schools, football in Glasgow had a far more awkward upbringing.

The middle-class Queen's Park membership were forced at first to play matches amongst themselves (Smokers v Non-smokers, for example). Only in 1868 did another team, called Thistle (no relation to Partick) emerge to challenge them to a game. Queen's Park, however, had the brio and efficiency to develop the sport. They initiated and provided all the home players for the world's first genuine international football match, played between Scotland and England on 30 November (St Andrew's Day) 1872. There were no goals but the impressive crowd of four thousand gave the game a different form of abundance. Queen's Park made a weighty profit of thirty-three pounds.

Both the Scottish Football Association and the Scottish Cup were formed the following year. Queen's Park dominated the early decades, winning the Cup for the tenth and so far last time in 1893. The proper aim of their evangelising, however, was their own defeat, since only that could prove football was truly growing healthier in Scotland. Dunbartonshire's Vale of Leven gave them that sour satisfaction by taking the Cup three times in succession from 1877 to 1879. Idiosyncratic talents flourished in this era but it would be sentimental to suppose that football ever had an age of innocence.

The sport was far too popular. As soon as there were crowds, there were crowd invasions. In the first couple of decades disorder and wilful disruption of games were commonplace. The contemporary newspapers did not delude themselves. One journalist mocked any pretence of Corinthian standards: 'A vulgar cad, addicted to smoking and playing billiards, went into a blue jersey, and donning knickerbockers proved himself a true Scotsman with a genuine love of good manly exercise . . .'

The game was a market-place as much as a battleground. Scots were highly prized south of the border for their skill. Queen's Park twice reached English FA Cup finals (in 1884 and 1885), finding Scots in the ranks of the opposition on each occasion, England has lured talent south ever since but the game in Scotland was also quickly commercialised. Professionalism was rampant long before it was legalised in 1893. The large urban populations, eager for amusement on their Saturday half-day off, generated money.

Celtic were founded in 1887 for charitable purposes to assist the Irish poor in Glasgow, but were also ruthless in plundering their rivals to sign the best players. Rangers, formed in 1872, responded to that initiative to begin a rivalry which is often exhilarating, always lucrative for the clubs, and permanently disfigured by the sectarian interests which fuel it. It was obvious by the early twentieth century that football was a city game. Apart from Glasgow sides, Hearts, Hibs and Dundee were all trophy-winners by then.

By clinging to their amateurism Queen's Park had been left behind, but their building of the modern Hampden, opened in 1903, assured them of a central role, as host for the great matches, in Scottish football. In 1937 surviving European attendance records were set there for international matches (Scotland v England, 149,415) and club football (the Celtic v Aberdeen Scottish Cup final, 147,365). Grounds could not always contain such throngs or their passions. After the Old Firm drew the replay of their 1909 Scottish Cup final the crowd rioted, vexed by the absence of extra time. Spectators have themselves been in danger in Scotland's packed grounds.

There have been two disasters at Rangers' Ibrox Stadium. Twenty-five people died there in 1902 and sixty-six were killed in a stairway crush in 1971. For most Scots, though, football was an innocent and safe obsession. Large quantities of fine players emerged from this small nation. In 1928 the diminutive Scottish forward line spearheaded by the lethal Hughie Gallacher (thereafter to be known as the Wembley Wizards) dismantled England to win 5–1. Eight of that side, though, were playing for clubs south of the border. Few in Scotland could afford to keep their stars.

Rangers, managed from 1920 to 1954 by the intimidating Bill Struth, were the exception. In the 1920s they could hold a dazzling winger such as Alan Morton or beat off English competition to sign Bob McPhail, a fine inside-forward. Celtic were the principal source of opposition but even with mighty performers such as Patsy Gallacher and prolific goalscorer Jimmy McGrory, they more often mounted a challenge in the Cup rather than the League. It was the Scottish Cup which staved off monotony, even being won, in 1938, by Second Division East Fife. Clubs such as Motherwell, who took the League in 1932, were rarer.

Rangers continued to dominate after the war although there was a resurgence in Edinburgh football. Hibs had one of the game's most exalted forward lines, the 'Famous Five' in the early 1950s and took the League title three times. Hearts were stirred into responding. Their own deadly strike force, the 'Terrible Trio', made them champions later in the decade. Such achievements, though, tended to seem like interludes in the Rangers' supremacy. As well as characteristic, rugged performers such as John Greig they also fielded the arrogant, brilliant Jim Baxter in the early 1960s.

Celtic, lacking wealth, looked powerless, but the return to the club as manager of a former player, Jock Stein, made them the mightiest team in Scottish football history.

He took the talents he found on the staff – the passing skills of Bobby Murdoch, the intricate dribbling of Jimmy Johnstone – and fashioned a side which not only secured nine League championships in succession but also became the first British team to win the European Cup in 1967. The other European trophy to come to Scotland – the Cup-winners' Cup – was won by Rangers in 1972, when they beat Moscow Dynamo, and Aberdeen, victors over Real Madrid in 1983.

Football grew more outward-looking in the 1960s, with predatory Scottish forward Denis Law even playing in Italy for a time. The prime delirium, though, still came on any occasion we were able to defeat England at Wembley, as happened in 1963 and 1967. It has taken the string of five successive appearances in the World Cup finals from 1974 to 1990 to persuade us that there are, after all, greater issues and prizes. The fact that the England fixture has lapsed is sometimes blamed on hooliganism, but it has as much to do with Scotland's new awareness of the wider horizons. In this era, it has become possible for a great forward such as Kenny Dalglish to be honoured throughout the world.

Alex Ferguson, whose Aberdeen team commanded the 1980s, allied Scottish fervour to that cosmopolitan sensibility. Dundee United too were capable not only of winning the League title (in 1983) but also of reaching the 1987 UEFA Cup final. In 1993, though, the range of Scottish football is constricted. In the past smaller clubs like Partick Thistle, Morton, Airdrie, Falkirk, St Mirren and Clyde have won the Scottish Cup. In 1965, Kilmarnock even became League champions. Such heartening surprises are growing scarcer.

From 1986, when Graeme Souness was appointed as manager, Rangers have at last tapped all their potential and reversed the flow of a century by tempting top English players to Scotland. Their stadium is plush and their current manager, Walter Smith, astute. The club's owner since 1988, David Murray, has the acumen to ensure that cash continues to flow. In 1993 Rangers even broke the British transfer record by signing Duncan Ferguson from Dundee United for four million pounds. All of this endeavour has produced a team feared even in Europe, but the excitement of those exploits cannot hide the fact that their excellence is making football in Scotland monotonous. The future of the game in this country depends on the others finding the ingenuity to match Rangers.

Rugby, by contrast, is little influenced by monetary forces. In Scotland it is even something of an anomaly, being an amateur sport which can still command the interest of a population usually in thrall to professional contests. Rugby's resources are, in some senses, limited; the club scene is largely composed of the mainly fee-paying schools' former pupils teams (nowadays open to a wider membership) and sides from the Borders. The energies of the Scottish game, however, are carefully focused to create a few great occasions each year. Huge crowds, such as the 104,000 who saw Scotland play Wales in 1975, gather at Murrayfield, but attendances are small at club level. Conundrums abound. Rugby is regularly berated for its antiquated practices but in some respects it has been bold and experimental. Murrayfield, for example, has had undersoil heating since 1959. The magnificent rebuilding of the national stadium is now almost complete and football can only envy the speed and financial confidence of that project.

Funds were raised through a debenture scheme which demonstrated once again the primacy of the international games. The first recorded rugby match in Scotland was between Merchiston and the Royal High School in 1858 but international contests only arrived thirteen years later, when Scotland beat England at Raeburn Place. In that period Scotland were best known for the power of their forward play, but there was a deftness about their famed rushes with the ball dribbled at the feet.

Rugby, although played at varying levels throughout Scotland, did not really attempt to proselytise. The belief in amateur virtues caused the Scottish Rugby Union to frown upon competitions which might just have caught the public imagination. The ruling body, for example, was highly displeased by the formation in 1893 of the Border League. Lacking the population of England or the widespread rugby passion of Wales, Scotland has rarely been able to dominate the international arena.

Scotland won their first Grand Slam in 1925. The side still had famed forwards such as J.M. Bannerman but there was increasing flair too in the play of the backs. The title was clinched with a 14–11 victory over England on the day Murrayfield (formerly Edinburgh's polo grounds) was opened. Scotland were highly regarded throughout the 1920s but a further fifty-nine years passed before the Grand Slam feat was repeated. Stand-off Wilson Shaw was carried aloft from the field at Twickenham after Scotland had beaten England there in 1938 but it would be 1971 before the Scots won there again.

The years immediately following the Second World War were marked by particularly dismal standards and it was not until the 1950s that players who could genuinely be relished once more appeared. Winger Arthur Smith went on to captain the British Lions in 1962. The pre-eminent 1950s' figure, however, was Ken Scotland. Great players not only succeed but also alter the sport in which they play. Scotland demonstrated the creative possibilities of the full-back role.

His name is now bracketed with that of the inspirational 1970s' full-back Andy Irvine. In 1974 he kicked a huge penalty three minutes into injury time to beat England at Murrayfield. Irvine was part of a fine group who had the mishap of playing in the same era as an irresistible Welsh team. All the same, forwards Gordon Brown, Sandy Carmichael and Ian McLauchlan, as well as backs such as Jim Renwick, were vastly impressive.

A match with France in 1980 saw Irvine playing tamely as Scotland languished 14–4 behind with scarcely more than ten minutes remaining. In that period, Irvine discovered all his prowess, scored two tries, converted a pair of penalties and ran up the 16 points which swept aside the visitors. The arrival of so mercurial a figure can never be planned but the strength of Scottish rugby was bolstered by the creation of a national league system in 1974. It has achieved some of its objectives in raising standards but now requires an overhaul. Lions captain Gavin Hastings returned from the 1993 tour to New Zealand concerned about the adequacy of club rugby as a grounding for such tests. At present, Scottish sides meet only once a season and home advantage can thereby have an undue significance on the outcome of the League.

The benefits of the 1974 initiative, however, were apparent as the greatest period in Scottish rugby history took shape. The first hints of this potency were apparent in the 1982 trouncing of Wales in Cardiff. Two Grand Slams ensued in 1984 and 1990. The limited number of top-class players in Scotland at least allowed the development of a stable squad and they were expertly coached by Jim Telfer and, in 1990, Ian McGeechan.

Scotland found they possessed a startling calibre of forward. In the course of the past ten years men such as Colin Deans, David Leslie, Finlay Calder and John Jeffrey have given many of our sides an unprecedented degree of control. Two great half-back combinations have capitalised on that strength – Jim Rutherford and Roy Laidlaw in 1984, and Craig Chalmers and Gary Armstrong in 1990.

Zeal, though, has been at least as important as skill. England came to Murrayfield in

56. *A scene from the famous Five Nations Championship decider, when Scotland defeated England at Murrayfield by 13 points to 7 to clinch the 1990 Grand Slam.* (Herald *and* Evening Times *Picture Library*)

1990 confident that they would win the Grand Slam. Fine side though they were, the presumptuousness riled the Scots. David Sole led his men out in a slow, menacing march which proved to be anything but a gimmick. It truly reflected their mood. Scotland performed with obduracy, concentration, opportunism and no little skill to down England 13–7. The afternoon features high on any short leet of Scottish sporting achievements.

It is reasonable to ascribe a special role to this country in the history of football and rugby, but of the world's major games it is only golf which might be termed a Scottish invention. The Dutch derivation of the word should not delude us. The 'colf' game of the Low Countries seems to have borne more similarities to croquet. This may have been the version of golf played by the Scottish kings. As with football, the game prospered while it was being outlawed. James IV's parliament banned it in 1497 but the accounts for 1502 show him buying balls and clubs. Mary, Queen of Scots was criticised for playing golf at Seton House only a few days after the murder of Darnley in 1567.

By 1632 the game had assumed a form which we would recognise. A publication of that year makes reference to bunkers and such paraphernalia as irons. The sport had also established its appeal to all levels of society. An account of golf at Gullane tells us of local weavers playing there on a public holiday. Individual clubs may be bastions of privilege but the pastime itself remains unusually democratic in Scotland, as the vast and varied crowds who attend the Bell's Scottish Open each year demonstrate.

Scotland, with its seaside links courses, also provides some of golf's most extraordinary settings. Our landscape is a key player in the game. Britain's Open Championship is held in this country every second year and the world's golfers accept that their claims to genuine status will only be vindicated by success on Scotland's fiendishly undulating surfaces. The scene at Muirfield, St Andrews or Troon may appear outlandish to Americans but they have always applied themselves diligently. Much of the eminence of golfers such as Jack Nicklaus and Tom Watson was secured in these parts.

They do have a debt to repay. Emigrant Scots were influential in establishing golf on the eastern seaboard of the United States. Those pioneers had to be intrepid. In 1887 a Mr Lockhart from Dunfermline was arrested in New York for practising in sheep pastures in Central Park. Where golf is concerned, though, Scots have more often laid down the law than fallen foul of it. The Royal and Ancient club of St Andrews, dating from 1754, continues to be the arbiter of the rules of golf as well as the organiser of the Open. The codifying of the game actually began when the Gentleman Golfers of Leith set down thirteen laws in 1744. This body later became the Honourable Company of Edinburgh Golfers, based at Muirfield. They have a longer, documented history than any other club and may also be the world's snootiest golfing body.

It was, however, Prestwick who began the Open in 1860 by putting up a belt of red leather and silver to be played for. One family commanded the early years. Old Tom Morris won the competition on four occasions and his son, Young Tom, had three successive victories from 1868–70 and thereby took the belt outright. The tournament was put in abeyance before a new trophy, still in use today, was produced in 1872. Young Tom Morris won that year as well.

Scots were still prominent in the next generation. James Braid took the Open on five occasions but the talents of these men were not confined to simply playing the game. Willie Auchterlonie became champion on his twenty-first birthday in 1893 while playing with seven clubs he had made himself. He was later to establish the celebrated firm of manufacturers which bears his name. The success of the game throughout the world inevitably diluted the influence of the Scots but significant golfers have always appeared in this country.

Bernard Gallacher is the current Ryder Cup captain and Eric Brown was one of his predecessors in the role in the 1960s. As players, they were both redoubtable competitors on the European tour. In the present day Sam Torrance is also high on the money list and will be remembered as the man who holed the winning putt which clinched Europe's historic victory over the USA in the Ryder Cup of 1985. The progress of Colin Montgomerie and others demonstrates that the tradition persists in a country of well over four hundred courses.

Sandy Lyle, born in England but of Glaswegian parentage, must, however, be regarded as existing on a different plane of achievement from any other Scottish golfer. He took the 1985 Open at Sandwich but the languid giant achieved even greater celebrity by becoming the first British player to win the Masters. On the final hole at Augusta, Georgia, in 1988 he bunkered his tee shot at the par 4 eighteenth but remained untouched by dismay. Lyle played a 7-iron of uncanny accuracy from the sand and holed the troublesome downhill putt. He had won by a single stroke.

The emergence of a Scottish performer of the highest calibre, however, is not always a matter for simple celebration. Boxing has been a turbulent passion. The 1937 fight between Benny Lynch and Englishman Peter Kane at Shawfield stadium, then the home of Clyde FC, drew a record crowd of 40,000. In that period, though, the opponents of the violent sport were as impassioned as its adherents. Glasgow's city fathers frequently refused to license major fights in the city. Lynch himself took the world flyweight title against Jackie Brown in Manchester in 1935 only because permission for the fight was denied in his home town.

Lynch's life is remembered as much for its troubles as its triumphs. A talent for boxing and the wealth it brought proved an uncertain escape from the poverty of his background. Born in the Gorbals slums, he was still a child when his parents' marriage broke up. His skills as a fighter were uncovered in a boys' club and honed on the thriving local boxing scene in and around Glasgow. Although standing at only 5ft 3in Lynch generated tremendous power, particularly with his hooks to the body.

His career reached its peak when he defeated the American, Small Montana, in 1937. The decline was swift thereafter as Lynch's alcoholism took its toll. A year later, he emphatically failed to make the weight against another American, Jackie Jurich, and was stripped of his title although he won the fight. As Lynch's physical condition worsened he eventually found himself fighting in the savage world of the boxing booths before he died in 1946, aged thirty-three.

The biography of another Scottish champion is similarly dispiriting. Jackie Paterson became world flyweight champion by knocking out Peter Kane in 1943. Like Lynch, weight problems also dragged his career down. Paterson emigrated and went into business but was stabbed to death in South Africa in 1966. He was known to be an uncontrollable gambler.

The tale of Scottish boxing, though, is not always so ghastly. Dundee's magnificent amateur lightweight, Dick McTaggart, was suspicious of the professional game but his economical, leisurely style made him renowned throughout the world. He won the gold medal at the Melbourne Olympics of 1956. Of those in the paid ranks, Walter McGowan imitated the happier aspects of Lynch and Paterson's tradition, reclaiming the world flyweight title for Scotland by beating Salvatore Burruni in 1966.

Since then, this country's boxing has been distinguished by two great lightweights, Edinburgh's Ken Buchanan and Jim Watt of Glasgow. Buchanan, at his best, was the more impressive of the pair and performed superbly in hostile environments, beating Panama's Ishmael Laguna for the world crown in San Juan in 1970. America's boxing writers then voted him fighter of the year, ahead of Joe Frazier and Muhammad Ali.

Buchanan's record includes a 1973 win over Watt but the Glaswegian was to flourish later. When he came under the management of Terry Lawless in Romford, Essex, his style grew more commanding and Lawless had the connections to arrange major contests for Watt in Glasgow. The clever Watt, who thrives today as the most lucid of TV's boxing commentators, fought with great shrewdness to claim the world title against Colombian Alfredo Pitalua, and produced four successful defences before losing in 1981 to Alexis Arguello in London. Pat Clinton's brief tenure of the world flyweight title, which ended with defeat in 1993, brought a faint echo of past Scottish glories.

While football, rugby, golf and boxing can command mass spectator interest there are other sports which are deeply enmeshed in our culture. Shinty, a game whose origins lie over 1,500 years ago, sometimes even styles itself as Scotland's national sport. That may be a little fanciful but its vibrancy is not disputed. Newtonmore, Kyles Athletic and Kingussie have dominated since the formation of the Camanachd Association in 1893 but the sport's health was apparent when brand new winners of the Camanachd Cup, Skye and Fort William, appeared in 1990 and 1992 respectively. Kingussie, in dominating over the past ten years, have also brought new standards of fitness and tactical expertise to shinty.

Other sports such as curling are also quietly entrenched in Scottish life and there is a respectable case for saying that the sport originated in this icy country. Although now played in a wide variety of nations, Scottish teams, who are increasingly composed of young people, continue to be prominent in international contest. The Scots are also eager importers of games. Cricket is sometimes assumed to be quintessentially English but its Scottish adherents are tenacious. Mike Denness played with Ayr before going on to captain England in the 1970s. Another Scot, the prolific Essex batsman of the 1980s, Brian Hardie, learned his trade with Stenhousemuir. The English were also bemused, if entertained, by the sight of bagpipes and kilts at Lord's when Freuchie from Fife won the National Village Cup in 1985.

57. *The Curlers by Sir George Harvey (1806–76).* (National Gallery of Scotland)

The successful diversity of our sporting life brings pleasure even as it defies explanation. There seems to be little sense to Scotland's production of two great world champions of motor racing. Jim Clark, killed in a 1968 Formula 2 race at Hockenheim, and Jackie Stewart were both dominant figures and are among the most revered drivers in history. The variety of excellence which currently emerges from a population of some five million people is equally difficult to account for. There is little precedent or encouragement for the feats of Olympic medallists such as marksman Alister Allan or three-day eventer Ian Stark.

Few in this country were sufficiently versed in cycling matters to appreciate Robert Millar's feat in winning the Tour de France's King of the Mountains title in 1984. There is a proud obstinacy to Scottish inventiveness in adversity. In the summer of 1993 Graeme Obree was vying with Englishman Chris Boardman for the world one-hour record despite the disparity in equipment. Boardman's bike was a wonder of hi-tech engineering while Obree's included parts salvaged from a washing-machine. For all that, Obree gloriously won the 1993 World Pursuit title.

Football clubs fret over the fall in attendances since the war but that may also be an indication of wider health. Young Scots are conscious of a greater range of sporting opportunities than ever before. Stephen Hendry was inspired by television coverage to pursue the career which currently makes him the world's leading snooker player, and other youngsters who now watch his feats as world champion will strive to emulate him. The impact of Liz McColgan's achievement when she won the 10,000 metres title at the 1991 World Championships should also be intriguing, for Scotland has never before had quite so eminent a woman athlete.

Hers is an exacting example. Facilities remain inadequate and McColgan, who grew up in Dundee, might never have fulfilled her potential had she remained in this country. At sixteen she was working in a jute mill and the complete dedication athletics requires only became possible when she was offered a place at an American college in Idaho. She does, however, possess the innate ambition to take advantage of all opportunities. The 1991 New York Marathon was her first major race at that distance but she still won it. Others too have employed American resources to magnificent effect. David Wilkie, Olympic 200 metres breaststroke gold medallist in 1976, was also hardened in college competition.

There was a comparable intensity about Allan Wells, whose capabilities emerged slowly and awkwardly at first. He competed in triple jump and long jump before discovering his forte in sprinting. Wells' training methods, partly based on boxing practice with a speedball, built great upper body strength. There was a desperate, glorious power about the lunge which took him over the line marginally ahead of Cuba's Silvio Leonard in the 100 metres final at the Moscow Olympics in 1980.

For all the emotion of that occasion, it is the remote events of the 1924 Paris Olympics which dominate the history of Scottish athletics. Eric Liddell, born to Scottish missionary parents in Tientsin, China, was a sprinter who famously declined to participate in the 100 metres at the Paris Olympics of 1924 since the heats took place on a Sunday. There was consternation over Liddell's insistence on obeying the fourth commandment.

The film *Chariots of Fire* provides a deliciously syrupy account of these events but telescopes the chronology to heighten the drama. In the process, it ignores the precision of Liddell's preparations. He had known months before the Olympics that he would have to prepare himself to run the 400 metres. With the assistance of Hearts' trainer

Tom McKerchan he worked on his stamina throughout the winter and even sacrificed his career as an international rugby player in order to avoid distractions.

Liddell's explosive pace took him clear of the field in Paris and they were unable to close that gap as he set an Olympic record of 47.6 seconds. He went on to follow the same calling as his parents with the London Missionary Society, even if he did find time to win North China's 100 metres title in 1930. Liddell died in a Japanese internment camp during the Second World War.

The global success of *Chariots of Fire* was unprecedented but Scottish sportsmen do make headlines with impressive frequency. Our absorption in games can be mawkish but Scotland's role in shaping sport and providing its champions is a matter of plain, unsentimental fact.

Books for Further Reading

FOOTBALL

Bob Crampsey, *The Scottish Footballer* (Edinburgh, 1978)
Roddy Forsyth, *The Only Game* (Edinburgh, 1990)
Hugh Keevins and Kevin McCarra, *100 Cups* (Edinburgh, 1985)
Kevin McCarra, *Scottish Football* (Edinburgh, 1984)
John Rafferty, *One Hundred Years of Scottish Football* (London, 1973)
Andy Ward, *Scotland: The Team* (Derby, 1987)

RUGBY

Allan Massie, *A Portrait of Scottish Rugby* (Edinburgh, 1984)
Sandy Thorburn, *The History of Scottish Rugby* (London, 1980)
Sandy Thorburn, *The Scottish Rugby Union* (Glasgow, 1985)

GOLF

Peter Allis, *The Open* (London, 1984)
Bernard Darwin *et al*, *The History of Golf in Britain* (London,, 1952)
George Pottinger, *Muirfield and the Honourable Company* (Edinburgh, 1972)
Robert Price, *Scotland's Golf Courses* (Aberdeen, 1989)
Louis T. Stanley, *St Andrews* (London, 1986)

BOXING

Brian Donald, *The Fight Game in Scotland* (Edinburgh, 1988)

SHINTY

Roger Hutchinson, *Camanachd* (Edinburgh, 1989)
Hugh Dan MacLennan, *Shinty!* (Nairn, 1933)

ATHLETICS

John W. Keddie, *Scottish Athletics* (Edinburgh, 1983)

CURLING

David B. Smith, *Curling: an Illustrated History* (Edinburgh, 1981)

Mathematics and Science

JOHN LENIHAN

S ince the place of science in Scottish culture cannot be adequately reviewed in a few thousand words, this chapter will deal mainly with aspects of scientific thought and practice which can be related closely to the prevailing cultural background – educational, industrial, environmental and philosophical. These influences are most clearly to be seen in the two periods when Scottish science led the world – the mid-eighteenth century and the mid-nineteenth century.

THE ALCHEMISTS

Modern European science began in the seventeenth century. Before then there was a long tradition of speculation, associated in astrology (the precursor of astronomy) with observation of the heavens, and in alchemy (the precursor of chemistry) with experiments in the laboratory. The two disciplines were related by undertones of mysticism and, until their corruption by charlatanism, formed part of the intellectual equipment of many learned men.

One of these – the foremost scholar of Western Europe in the early thirteenth century – was Michael Scot, described by Pope Honorius III as 'singularly gifted in science among men of learning'. The *Liber Abaci* of Leonardo of Pisa, the greatest mathematician of medieval Europe, was dedicated to him. He died about 1236 and is said to have been buried in Melrose Abbey; the tradition that he was born in Balwearie, near Kirkcaldy, appears to be a nineteenth-century invention. Scot worked in Toledo and Bologna and later as astrologer and physician to Emperor Frederick II of Sicily. His translations (from Arabic into Latin) of many of Aristotle's scientific works made an important contribution to the recovery of Greek learning which had been lost to Western Europe after the decline of the Roman Empire. Scot's reputation – probably undeserved – as a magician led to his appearance in Dante's *Inferno*, Boccaccio's *Decameron* and Scott's *Lay of the Last Minstrel*.

Many of the early alchemists saw their work as a spiritual pilgrimage. The aim of their chemical experiments was to make the Philosopher's Stone, which would heal the imperfections of base metals, by elevating them to a higher state of perfection as gold. The associated Elixir of Life would cure all human diseases. The search for these powers was seen as an allegory of the ascent of man towards the ultimate purity of the soul. Some of the alchemists were serious scholars and ingenious experimenters. Before the seventeenth century there was nothing outrageous in the idea that one metal might be transmuted into another. Isaac Newton considered the process quite feasible and spent a lot of time in his alchemical laboratory. But there were many adventurers, tempted by the prospect of comfortable living at the expense of wealthy and gullible patrons.

James IV, King of Scotland, had a lively interest in science and medicine. His one-man health service, offering facilities for dentistry and minor surgery, had a unique financial structure: patients who submitted to the royal scalpel or pincers were handsomely paid. The king saw alchemy as a means of enhancing both the health of his people and the revenue of his country. To manage Scotland's first research laboratory, established in Stirling Castle about the year 1500, he recruited John Damian, a physician and alchemist, and endowed him with a sinecure appointment as Abbot of Tungland in Galloway. Damian, like Michael Scot, found a lasting place in literature; his pretensions inspired William Dunbar's satirical poem *The Fenyeit Freir of Tungland*.

MATHEMATICS

John Napier of Merchiston (1550–1617) was a minor alchemist, but gained more durable fame as the inventor of logarithms. This innovation involves the use of a table of numbers (derived from those that he calculated after twenty-five years of laborious effort) to reduce multiplication and division to mere addition and subtraction. Napier was also the first to introduce the decimal point in its familiar modern form. His invention of logarithms was the greatest achievement in mathematics between Euclid's geometry and Newton's calculus.

A major contributor to the development of calculus was James Gregory (1638–75). He was the son of John Gregory, minister of Drumoak near Aberdeen, and his wife, Janet, who founded a remarkable dynasty. During the succeeding two centuries, thirteen of their descendants served as regents or professors in Scottish universities. James Gregory, often claimed to be second only to Newton in seventeenth-century mathematics, was professor of mathematics in St Andrews from 1669 to 1675 and in Edinburgh for a short time before his death. He invented the reflecting (or Gregorian) telescope – a decisive advance on the earlier Galilean type, because it allowed great magnification to be obtained in an instrument of modest length. The basic principle is still used in the design of large telescopes. His nephew, David (1661–1708), professor of mathematics in Edinburgh from 1683 to 1691, was the first in Britain to teach Newtonian mathematics.

The work of Robert Simson (1687–1768), professor of mathematics in Glasgow from 1711 to 1761, had a remarkable influence on the development of British science. He restored many incomplete fragments of Greek geometry, but was better known for his *Elements of Euclid*, which was widely used for nearly two centuries. One of his first students in Glasgow was Colin Maclaurin (1698–1746) who was appointed professor of mathematics at Marischal College, Aberdeen, in 1717 and (supported by a testimonial from Isaac Newton) translated to Edinburgh in 1725. His preference for geometrical methods, rather than the more powerful algebraic analysis (in which he was also competent), was consistent with Scottish philosophical teaching of the time, but impeded the progress of mathematics in Britain for almost a century. He served his country well outwith the classroom. When the Edinburgh Medical Society fell into decline in 1735, he took it in hand, changing it into the Philosophical Society of Edinburgh, with a proportion of non-medical members. This was the forerunner of the Royal Society of Edinburgh, founded in 1783.

Maclaurin was conscious of the relevance of mathematics to society. He taught surveying, fortification and the theory of gunnery in addition to the more usual branches of his subject. His enthusiasm for military science was tested when he was charged with the defence of Edinburgh against the Jacobites in 1745. The city was captured and Maclaurin fled to York. Weakened by the hardships of the campaign, he died in the following year.

Maclaurin's friend, James Stirling (1692–1770), a distant relative of John Napier, was born at Garden in Stirlingshire and may have studied in Glasgow University before moving to Oxford and Venice. He developed proofs for some of the mathematical theorems that Newton had merely stated, and added some of his own, which are still useful. Unable, despite Newton's influence, to obtain an academic appointment in Scotland, he worked from 1835 until his death as manager of the mines at Leadhills in Lanarkshire. There he turned a loss-making company into a profitable enterprise. The lending library which he established in 1740, for the benefit of the workers, was one of the first in Britain.

SCIENCE AND THE ENLIGHTENMENT

Several influences helped to create an environment favourable to the advancement of science in eighteenth-century Scotland. By the beginning of the century, much progress had been made towards the fulfilment of Knox's vision of a primary school in every parish and a grammar school in every burgh. University education was also changing as the ideas of Descartes, Boyle and Newton were absorbed into the curriculum. Science became increasingly esteemed, both for its value in liberal education and for its promise of practical utility in the developing agricultural and chemical industries.

The accumulation of intellectual capital was accelerated by further changes in the universities, as the regents were replaced by (or converted into) specialist professors, each responsible for one subject. This policy, adopted in Edinburgh in 1708 and later in the other universities, had wider implications. Its benefits were not fully implemented in the short term, because many professors, largely dependent on students' fees for their income, chose to keep their options open by maintaining competence in a number of disciplines. In that way they could be candidates for more lucrative (or otherwise more congenial) chairs when vacancies occurred. In Edinburgh, Adam Ferguson was professor of natural philosophy from 1759 to 1764 and then of moral philosophy. In Glasgow, John Anderson was professor first of oriental languages and then of natural philosophy. The expert professors, active in scientific research and teaching, nevertheless grew in numbers during the eighteenth century. By opening their classes to interested members of the public, and by delivering courses of popular lectures, they hastened the recognition of science as an element of liberal education. They served the community in other ways too, by advising on problems of concern to industry.

CHEMISTRY BECOMES A SCIENCE

Major advances in chemistry, physics and geology were made. Until about the middle of the century, chemistry was sometimes seen as a development of alchemy or an appendage to medicine. Another school of thought clung to Newton's assertion: 'There are therefore agents in nature able to make the particles of bodies stick together by very strong attractions. And it is the business of experimental philosophy to find them out' – in other words, chemistry was an appendage of physics. By the end of the century chemistry emerged independent of both medicine and physics, as a discipline firmly based on experiment and with industrial connections.

The transformation was begun by William Cullen, the first teacher of chemistry in Glasgow University. Its later progress was dominated by Joseph Black, who was one of Cullen's students and laboratory assistants between 1749 and 1752; he then moved to Edinburgh to finish his medical education. Black's MD thesis was inspired by a practical problem – the treatment of stones in the bladder. This thesis is more often admired than read; an expanded version of its chemical content was published by the Philosophical Society of Edinburgh in 1756. Black was motivated first by the desire to find a remedy milder than the caustic alkalis then commonly used – and, no doubt, less nauseating than the concoction of soap and snails for which Mrs Joanna Stephens, a London quack, had received a reward of £5,000 from the government. The therapeutic problem soon gave way to a series of well-planned scientific experiments on magnesia alba (in modern terminology, basic magnesium carbonate). Black showed that this substance was a compound of 'a peculiar earth' and a gas, which he called fixed air; at that time it was believed that all gases were forms of air and that they did not take part in chemical reactions. Black went on to show that calcium carbonate, when roasted, lost more than half of its weight by the escape of fixed air, which could be restored by a series of chemical procedures. The idea of a gas as a chemical substance which could exist in combination in a solid – and could be weighed in that state – was revolutionary.

Black's work on magnesia alba established chemistry as a quantitative discipline. He did more, for he showed that fixed air (which we know as carbon dioxide) was present in the atmosphere and that it was produced both by respiration and by combustion. He came close to realising that respiration is combustion – a doctrine, asserted later by Adair Crawford (MD Glasgow 1780), which was essential for the development of physiology and biochemistry.

Black returned to Glasgow in 1756, serving as lecturer in chemistry, professor of anatomy and botany and later as professor of practice of medicine. His main interest was in chemistry, which he regarded as 'the study of the effects of heat and mixture on bodies and mixtures of bodies'. The conjunction was appropriate at a time when heat was regarded as a material substance which, though weightless and invisible, could enter into chemical reactions.

Black was the first to distinguish clearly between heat and temperature. He went on to develop the concept of specific heat – a measure of the relationship between the heat

58. James Watt (1736–1819), portrait by John Partridge (1796–1872), after Sir William Beechy (1753–1839). (SNPG)

absorbed by a substance and the resulting rise in temperature. Another major achievement arose from his study of phenomena which were commonplace in Scotland. Black often asked his students to consider why snow and ice did not melt suddenly on the first warm day in spring, or why water did not change violently into steam as soon as it was brought to boiling point. He also reminded them that in the making of whisky great amounts of cold water were needed to carry away heat from the vapours emerging out of the still into the condenser. Reflecting on these matters he was led, by a series of careful experiments, to the concept of latent heat. This is the heat which has to be supplied to change water at its boiling point into vapour, or ice at its melting point into water, without any rise in temperature. When water freezes, or steam condenses, this heat is given up.

JAMES WATT (1736–1819): THE SCIENCE OF STEAM

It is widely believed that James Watt, inspired by his mother's kettle, went on to become a mechanic and invented the steam engine. Another story tells that he was prevented by the Incorporation of Hammermen from practising his craft in Glasgow until the university gave him sanctuary. This story, though related with increasing adornment by many eminent authorities, is a myth. Watt's abilities were appreciated in the university before he was appointed as mathematical instrument-maker there in 1757. His mother's kinsman, George Muirhead, professor of humanity, had introduced him to Robert Dick, professor of natural philosophy; both had been impressed by his intelligence and enthusiasm. Watt opened a shop in the city in 1759, and another in 1763, without any objection from the Hammermen. But these legends are too secure to be dispelled merely because they are untrue.

Watt's work on steam engines is not always properly appreciated. It began when, during the winter of 1763–64, he was asked by the professor of natural philosophy, John Anderson, to overhaul a small model of a Newcomen engine, used in teaching students. Newcomen engines were widely used during the eighteenth century to pump water from flooded mines; coal was needed in growing amounts because of the demand from the iron industry for coke. In a typical design, a piston moving in a vertical cylinder was connected by chains to one end of a horizontal wooden beam, pivoted at its mid point and carrying at the other end a chain terminating in a pump rod and bucket. The weight of the pump rod was enough to bring it down into the water, so lifting the piston. As the piston slowly rose, steam was admitted to the cylinder from a boiler immediately below. When the piston reached the top of its travel, the steam supply was cut off and cold water was sprayed into the cylinder. The steam condensed, producing a partial vacuum. The pressure of the air above the piston then pushed it down quickly, raising the pump rod and lifting with it a quantity of water from the mine. When the bucket was emptied the pump rod descended and the cycle began again.

The Newcomen engine was wasteful – so much so that it sometimes used more coal (in heating the boiler) than could be won when the flooded pit had been dried out. Using steam merely to produce a vacuum, it relied on air pressure to do useful work. In modern terminology its efficiency – the ratio of energy output (as mechanical effort) to energy input (as heat) was only about 0.5 per cent. The university's model was even less efficient; its small boiler could keep it going for only a few strokes before needing to be refilled. Watt realised that the Newcomen engine was inherently inefficient because of the heat wasted in the repeated cooling of the cylinder. The problem was that the cylinder had to be kept hot during the first part of the working cycle, to avoid condensation while it was filling with steam, but had to be cooled during the second half of the cycle, so that the steam could be quickly condensed to produce the vacuum on which the working of the engine depended. During a Sunday walk on Glasgow Green in 1765 Watt saw that the way to escape from the dilemma was to add a separate condenser. As soon as the cylinder was filled with steam, it was connected to a neighbouring vessel, which had been evacuated by a simple air pump. The steam was condensed there, by a spray of water, and the cylinder stayed hot throughout the cycle.

A legend which obscured Watt's scientific brilliance for nearly two centuries claimed that he was able to invent the separate condenser only because Black had told him about latent heat. This belief is so easily refuted that its persistence is hard to understand. In puzzling over the model Newcomen engine, Watt made a series of well-planned experiments. In one of them he showed that the weight of water that had to be sprayed into the cylinder to condense the steam was many times greater than the weight of water evaporated in the boiler to produce the steam. In another investigation he passed steam into a flask of cold water until the contents started to boil. He found that the weight of water in the flask had increased by one sixth. This meant that the steam produced by boiling one volume of water contained enough heat to raise six volumes of water to boiling point. Watt discussed these observations with Black, who told him of his own work on latent heat; Watt had come upon the phenomenon independently. Black's discovery did not influence him, for the release of latent heat when the steam condensed did not impair the efficiency of the Newcomen engine; on the contrary, it helped to keep the cylinder hot while it was filling with steam. The real difficulty was that too much heat was being lost in alternate heating and cooling of the mass of metal in the cylinder; this was the problem solved by the invention of the separate condenser.

Watt made many more innovations, guided by scientific insight. He enclosed the top of the cylinder and used steam, instead of air, to push the piston down. He then had a genuine steam engine; Newcomen's was really an air engine. Realising that steam rushed from the cylinder to the condenser with considerable force, representing a waste of energy, he cut off the steam supply before the cylinder reached the end of its travel and allowed the expansion of the steam to finish the stroke. This innovation reduced the demand for steam from the boiler. By the end of the century, steam engines were working with an efficiency of about 4.5 per cent – an eightfold increase on the Newcomen engine.

Watt can now be appreciated as a pioneer of thermodynamics, nearly a century before the basic concepts were crystallised in mathematical shape. He realised that the source of the mechanical energy delivered by the steam engine was in the heat passing from the boiler to the condenser; the way to improve its efficiency was to reduce the amount of heat lost in the progress without doing useful work. This insight could not have emerged from the operation of the Newcomen engine, where atmospheric pressure appeared to do the work. Watt's engine, with a hot source and a cold condenser, provided the inspiration for the later work of Carnot and Kelvin.

PHILOSOPHERS AND SCIENTISTS

Moral and natural philosophy had always been closely related in the Scottish universities. The eighteenth-century moral philosophers, notably Francis Hutcheson, David Hume and Thomas Reid, were fascinated by the new ideas and achievements of science and by the possibility that scientific methods could be used in the study of the mind and of human nature. They admired particularly the structure of Euclidean geometry, based on axioms from which everything else followed by logical reasoning. The Common Sense philosophers, led by Reid (a member of the Gregory family) asserted that geometry was the purest form of mathematics. Algebraic methods, based on manipulation of symbols, were of no value in training the mind. All sciences, they believed, should, like Greek geometry, be based on first principles which needed no proof or justification.

The interchange of ideas between the philosophers and the scientists was very fruitful, because they shared a common body of knowledge. The scientists had been educated in the philosophically oriented curriculum and the philosophers were anxious to prescribe the principles of the scientific method. Thomas Reid taught mathematics and natural philosophy (as well as logic and ethics) when he was a regent in Aberdeen. Before he came to Glasgow in 1764 as professor of moral philosophy, he had discovered a system of geometry which did not depend on Euclid's axioms – some sixty years before non-Euclidean geometry became a major field of research among mathematicians. Reid attended Black's lectures on chemistry in Glasgow and acknowledged that he had been greatly influenced by the experience. In the Scottish universities, moral and natural philosophers were in daily contact and often belonged to the same clubs and societies. Since most of their discussions were not recorded, it is difficult now to know whether the speculations and experiments of the scientists were inspired by advice from philosophers or whether the teachings of the philosophers drew on ideas derived from contemporary scientific practice.

The long-running seminar influenced the course of Scottish science in a number of ways. Hume believed that utility was the only criterion by which the validity of scientific theories or philosophical propositions could be judged; both must have some relevance to future phenomena or behaviour. Reid and his followers cautioned against the use of hypotheses in scientific enquiry. Science must advance by induction – that is, by assembling facts, from observation or experience, studying similarities or regularities among them to establish laws and from these finding more general laws. Suspicion of hypotheses gave some anxiety to Rankine and Maxwell a century later, but was generally of more concern to philosophers than to scientists. Black did not approve of hypotheses or of theories – which he described as 'a mere waste of time and ingenuity'. But he did not need such aids; he proceeded, as did Watt, from one well-planned experiment to the next.

SCIENCE AND INDUSTRY

Cullen told his students that chemistry must be based on sound philosophical principles; truth and utility were the goals. He tried to put these ideas into practice in a number of projects, including the purification of sea salt and the enhancement of crop yields by use of fertilisers. The scientific principles needed for success in these exercises had not yet been discovered; Cullen's efforts were unsuccessful. Black and Cullen worked inconclusively in the search for a cheap and effective bleaching process, greatly needed in the manufacture of textiles. Watt had more success, though his methods were overtaken at the end of the century by Charles Tennant, whose invention of bleaching powder had an important influence on the growth of Glasgow's chemical industry in the nineteenth century.

In Glasgow, the work of John Anderson (1726–96) in popularising scientific and technical education had far-reaching consequences. His lectures in the university on natural philosophy were immensely popular among craftsmen, employers and the general public. His will proposed the foundation of a university governed by eighty-one trustees and thirty-six professors, all of whom he named. When his estate was wound up there was nothing left – indeed there was a deficit of fifty-five pounds – but the importance of his scheme was recognised. A public appeal raised enough money for the employment of one professor, to teach natural philosophy and chemistry. Thomas Garnett, who was appointed in 1796, left in 1799 to work at the Royal Institution in London, which was modelled on Anderson's plan. His successor, George Birkbeck, moved to London in 1804 and practised as a physician. In 1823 a breakaway group from Anderson's Institution (one professor did not make a university) founded the first Mechanics' Institution. Before long, Birkbeck established the concept in England, where it spread rapidly, creating new opportunities for higher education; the London Mechanics' Institution was the forerunner of Birkbeck College. Anderson's Institution survived many difficulties during the nineteenth century and eventually grew into the University of Strathclyde.

The eighteenth century was a period of enlightenment in agriculture as well as in science, letters and the arts. Landed gentry saw agricultural improvement as part of their responsibility to society. The Society of Improvers in the Knowledge of

Agriculture, founded in 1723, lasted only until 1745 but was the first of many organisations for the exchange of knowledge and experience. The achievements of the Dutch and English improvers were admired and imitated and, by the end of the eighteenth century, surpassed. Liming, drainage, introduction of novel crops such as potatoes and turnips, and development of better implements all contributed to increasing productivity and prosperity. Scientists, including Cullen and Black, were eager to help but their efforts were premature. Even the great advances in chemistry and biology during the nineteenth century did little more for agriculture than to explain the success of existing practices. In Scotland, as elsewhere in the developed world, agriculture became a science-based industry only after the 1930s. By then, progress was increasingly achieved by the new improvers — neither farmers nor landed gentry, but scientists working in laboratories and in the field.

KELVIN AND MAXWELL

Nineteenth-century science was dominated — and much of twentieth-century science decisively influenced — by the achievements of two Scots, Kelvin and Maxwell. Both were mathematical prodigies who studied in Scottish universities and in Cambridge. Both took second place in the Tripos and first place in the more demanding Smith's Prize competition. Both considered legal careers before returning to Scotland to teach natural philosophy and to make massively important contributions to almost every branch of physics. But their styles were different.

Kelvin could tackle a difficult scientific problem in furious haste, record his findings in a few pages and pass on to something else. He published 661 papers — sometimes more than twenty in a year — but often lacked the vision to see where his ideas might lead. His intellectual indiscipline was not apparent in his alter ego, the inventor and manufacturer. He was the first to establish an extensive and profitable relationship between industry and academe; his laboratory in the university — first in a disused wine cellar and later in purpose-built accommodation — became an annexe of the scientific instrument company in which he was a partner.

While still in his twenties Kelvin enunciated the foundations of thermodynamics (the science of energy) and discovered the clues which, exploited by others, led to radio communication and to the theory of the electromagnetic field. He went on to practical triumphs in the Atlantic cable project and other areas of technology guided by science. Throughout his long life, the importance of his work was immediately apparent to other scientists — and often to a wider public.

Maxwell, by contrast, was seldom in the public eye. He had only three short spells as a professor and did not produce inventions of immediate commercial value. His achievements were not widely appreciated during his lifetime, but his contributions to science have survived, while many of Kelvin's have been superseded. Maxwell is now recognised as the greatest scientist of nineteenth-century physics, providing a bridge between Newton and Einstein; his work is discussed in more detail below.

Kelvin (as he is generally known, though he was William Thomson until elevated to the peerage in 1892), was born in 1824 and educated at home before enrolling, at the age of ten, as a student at Glasgow University, where his father was professor of mathematics. In 1841 he moved to Cambridge to continue his studies. He published twelve papers before graduating in 1845 and ten more before his appointment to the

Glasgow chair of natural philosophy in 1846. His output of eighty-four papers during the succeeding ten years gave a display of virtuosity unequalled in the whole history of science. In 1847 he showed mathematically that electric and magnetic forces could be represented by strains travelling through an elastic solid. He did not appreciate the implications of his discovery; Maxwell did, and began an investigation which led to the electromagnetic theory of light and such else.

THERMODYNAMICS: HEAT AND WORK

Kelvin's greatest achievement was in the development of thermodynamics, perhaps the most elegant and fruitful of all scientific disciplines. It arose from attempts to put a scientific foundation under the abundantly successful technology of steam. As early as 1825, the French physicist Sadi Carnot (1796-1832) had been thinking about the properties of an idealised heat engine. This is an imaginary machine comprising a source of heat, a receiver to accept waste heat and a cylinder (containing air) with a movable piston. By a cyclic process involving alternate compression and expansion of the air, heat is transferred from the source to the receiver and the piston does work by moving up and down. The engine is reversible. If the heat supply is withdrawn and the piston is moved up and down (by external effort), heat is transferred from the receiver to the source; the engine then operates as a refrigerator. The efficiency of a Carnot engine – or indeed of a real-world steam engine – depends on the temperatures of the source and receiver. These ideas were neglected until Kelvin drew attention to them in 1848. He showed how Carnot's conception could be used to construct an absolute scale of temperature, independent of the properties of mercury or any other substance. Scientists still use the Kelvin scale.

As he reflected further, Kelvin was disturbed. In Carnot's account of his speculations, heat was regarded as an indestructible fluid. It did work in falling without loss from a high temperature source to a low temperature receiver, in much the same way as a waterfall could be used to turn a mill-wheel. But Kelvin's friend, James Prescott Joule, an English amateur scientist, had shown that heat and work were interconvertible and were in fact manifestations of the same thing. If heat was an indestructible fluid, how could it disappear and change into work? After a long period of indecision, eased by ideas from his colleague Rankine, professor of civil engineering and mechanics, Kelvin decided (as others had thought before him – including Carnot, whose notes on the matter were not found until 1878) that heat was a form of mechanical energy, residing in the motion or vibration of molecules. He went much further. Starting from Watt's insight that the source of the work done by a steam engine was the heat abstracted from the boiler fire, he concluded that some of this heat was converted to mechanical work and the rest was dumped in the condenser or discharged in to the air; unknown to him Rudolf Clausius in Germany had reached the same conclusion independently. Heat was not conserved, as Carnot had supposed; energy was conserved – not only in steam engines, but in all mechanical, chemical and electrical processes. The universe was, as we might say, a gigantic stock exchange, regulated by a fixed money supply. Kelvin was now on the threshold of the new world of thermodynamics (he coined the word) and he explored it vigorously.

THE END OF THE WORLD

Kelvin had achieved much by reflecting on Carnot's imaginary engine. But in the real world there are no truly reversible processes. Whenever energy is converted from one form to another, some is wasted – in friction or in exhaust gases, for example – and is not available for further use. So how, Kelvin asked, could energy be conserved? He resolved the difficulty by asserting that the total stock of energy in the universe is constant, but not all of it is available for use by man. These ideas were summarised in characteristically terse conclusions, delivered before the Royal Society of Edinburgh in 1852:

> There is at present in the material world a universal tendency to the dissipation of mechanical energy ... Within a finite period of time past the earth must have been, and within a finite period of time to come the earth must again be, unfit for the habitation of man as at present constituted, unless operations have been or are to be performed which are impossible under the laws to which the known operations going on at present in the material world are subject ...

Restrained by his Christian faith, Kelvin stopped short of the ultimate prediction. He agreed, in effect, that the operation of the laws of science might be pre-empted by miracles; otherwise, the universe must decline into a formless state, later to be described as heat death – still, silent and everywhere at the same temperature. This magisterial pronouncement, leaping from Watt's steam engine to the end of the world, might fittingly have crowned a lifetime of meditation and experiment; it was an extraordinary achievement for a man of twenty-seven. The doctrine that energy can be transformed but not destroyed constitutes the first law of thermodynamics. Kelvin's statement of the inevitable dissipation of energy is one version of the second law. His combination of mathematical ability and scientific insight in the development of thermodynamics represented his greatest intellectual achievement; but he might have done more.

GENIUS WITHOUT VISION?

In 1853 Kelvin showed that the discharge of a condenser through a conductor could, in certain circumstances, be oscillatory, generating an alternating current. This discovery provided the foundation for the development of radio communication, but Kelvin did not pursue the prospect; his imagination was soon to be diverted into triumphs of science-based technology – the Atlantic cable, the mariner's compass, the tide predictor, the design of electrical instruments.

In other matters he was involved in vigorous controversies. His views on the age of the earth caused concern among geologists and biologists. His calculations were quite sound on the basis of existing knowledge. The temperature of the earth increased with depth below the surface; so the earth must be losing heat (ultimately from its molten core) into space. Assuming that the earth began its life at the same temperature as the sun, how long had it been cooling to reach its present state? The answer changed from time to time, but eventually settled at 28 million years. Biologists and geologists wanted a billion years or more, but could not shake Kelvin's confidence. The problem was resolved in a way that could not have been foreseen.

Conscious as he often was of God looking over his shoulder, Kelvin had speculated, as early as 1862, that an additional source of heat might exist 'in the great storehouse of creation'. Before long it was found. Early in the present century, Ernest Rutherford and others showed that the heat produced in the decay of radium and other radioactive materials in the earth was enough to reconcile the difference between Kelvin's estimate and the geologists' requirements. Kelvin was not convinced. Indeed, he did not believe in radioactivity; radium, he insisted, was a compound of lead and helium.

It is beyond dispute that Kelvin dissipated his genius, jumping from one project to another without pursuing any of them to the limits that his great intellectual powers might have allowed. But he was more sensitive than Newton or Einstein to the impact of science and technology on the needs and opportunities of the age in which he lived. His achievements in the application of difficult and subtle scientific ideas to the formulation and solution of socially important practical problems were without parallel. Yet he was not satisfied. In 1896 he said: 'One word characterises the most strenuous efforts for the advancement of science that I have made perseveringly during fifty-five years. That word is failure.' He was referring to his ambition to create a comprehensive theory which would explain mechanics, heat, light, electricity and magnetism in terms of the behaviour of molecules or their relationship with the ether – that mysterious fluid supposed throughout the nineteenth century to permeate the universe. Maxwell had no such ambition. He did not seek a comprehensive theory of everything – but he came nearer to it than Kelvin.

A SCIENTIST FOR ALL TIME

James Clerk Maxwell was born in Edinburgh in 1831. His first mathematical paper, on oval curves, was read to the Royal Society of Edinburgh in 1846 by Professor J.D. Forbes – it was considered unseemly for a schoolboy to appear before the learned assembly. Maxwell spent three years at Edinburgh University before going to Cambridge, where he graduated in 1854. Two years later he was appointed professor of natural philosophy at Marischal College, one of the two universities in Aberdeen; the other was King's College. When they were amalgamated in 1860, one of the two professors in each discipline was made redundant – generally the older man, whose pension would terminate sooner. But in the natural philosophy department an exception was made in favour of the genial and undistinguished David Thomson of King's College. Maxwell was not upset, as he had already decided to move on. He found the Aberdonians lacking in humour and they thought him somewhat eccentric. He spent the next five years at King's College, London, before returning to the family estate in Scotland to write his celebrated textbook of electricity and magnetism.

When the chair of experimental physics was established in Cambridge in 1870, along with a new research laboratory named after William Cavendish, Duke of Devonshire (who paid the costs), Kelvin was the first choice of the electors. He declined the offer, as he was to do on two subsequent occasions. He was comfortably settled in Glasgow, where his lucrative industrial activities were centred. Hermann von Helmholtz, the next choice, was not interested. Amid fears that an undistinguished local candidate would be appointed, Maxwell was, with some difficulty, persuaded to take the job. The laboratory, built largely to his design, was opened in 1874 and soon occupied by a brilliant team of research students, including Donald MacAlister, senior wrangler in 1877 and later Principal of Glasgow University. Maxwell died in 1879, but his influence remained, contributing to the lasting eminence of Cambridge University in the world of science.

ELECTROMAGNETIC THEORY

Maxwell's greatest work was on the inter-relationship of electricity, magnetism and light. Starting in 1856, where Kelvin had left off, he developed a model of the ether in which electric and magnetic forces were represented as streamlines in a moving fluid. This concept was consistent with existing knowledge but had no predictive power. The next model, produced in 1862, was much more elaborate. The ether was seen as an elastic material, filled with rotating cylinders separated by electric particles arranged in rings, rather like ball-bearings. With this model Maxwell predicted that movement of the electric particles, first in one direction and then in the other (as we would say today, an alternating current in a wire) would produce a sequence of interlinked electric and magnetic changes travelling through the ether as a wave. Having next calculated the speed of this wave and found it to be approximately the speed of light, he declared that light was an electromagnetic wave. This was a bold speculation, since the existence of electromagnetic waves had not been proved experimentally. Conscious of the dislike of elaborate hypotheses among the Common Sense philosophers, whose ideas had fascinated him since his student days in Edinburgh, he made a fresh approach, using only known facts and skilful mathematical manipulations, without the need for a mechanical model. His achievement of the same result was an extraordinary demonstration of the power of mathematical analysis to explain and predict physical happenings.

Maxwell's statement of the properties of the electromagnetic field, in four equations which can be written on the back of a visiting card, constitute the nearest approach that science has made towards a theory of everything. It was acknowledged by Einstein as the origin of his theory of special relativity. But the electromagnetic theory of radiation was not generally accepted during Maxwell's lifetime. Kelvin never came to terms with it, even after the ideas in his 1853 paper led Hertz to produce radio waves in 1887. Maxwell made many other advances, notably in his kinetic theory of gases. There his use of statistical methods to explain and predict the behaviour of matter in bulk, by analysing the random movements of large numbers of particles, marked the beginning of statistical mechanics, a technique of the greatest significance in twentieth-century physics. He made important advances in the understanding of colour vision, took the first colour photograph and initiated the science of cybernetics. His mathematical analysis of stresses in structures was applied to the study of girder bridges, used by D'Arcy Thompson in his description of the mechanics of bone and, more recently, exemplified in the elegant domes designed by the American architect, Buckminster Fuller.

Newton saw the universe as a clockwork mechanism, set in motion by God and running for ever according to immutable laws of science. Kelvin's universe was a heat engine, moving slowly towards the ultimate lifeless chaos. Maxwell pointed the way to the twentieth-century perception of a universe designed, not by a watchmaker, nor by an engineer, but by a mathematical physicist.

THE HISTORY OF THE EARTH

Few small countries have such rich resources as Scotland for the observation and study of natural history. The landscape is an open-air museum of geology, exhibiting much of the earth's history. The Torridonian sandstones of the north-west are among the oldest rocks in Europe. While Black was creating the science of chemistry his friend James Hutton (1726–97) was doing the same for geology. Born in Edinburgh, he studied medicine there and in Leiden, where he graduated in 1749. He never practised medicine, but worked first on a Berwickshire farm which he inherited and then went to Norfolk to learn about advances in agriculture. After returning to Edinburgh he established a factory for the manufacture of ammonium chloride from soot; this material was used in tinning iron, brass and copper as well as in calico printing and pharmacy. The enterprise was so profitable that by 1768 Hutton was able to devote all of his time to research in geology.

The prevailing wisdom told that the earth was originally covered by water, which disappeared (as the result of an unexplained process) after the continents had been laid down by sedimentation and occasional catastrophes, including Noah's flood. Hutton asserted that the surface of the earth had been shaped by slow processes which were still going on. The centre of the earth was occupied by molten lava, which occasionally escaped – through volcanic action, for example. Material deposited on the sea-bed through erosion of rocks and soil was consolidated by heat and pressure and periodically uplifted to the surface. These and other processes continued endlessly in slow cycles. Hutton's theories, supported and extended by the work of two other Scottish amateurs – James Hall (1761–1832) and Charles Lyell (1797–1875) established geology as a science. His view of the earth as ageless was amended in the following century, but the broad outlines of his theories are still valid. The concept of slow changes in an earth of great antiquity appealed to Lyell's friend Charles Darwin and influenced his thoughts on biological evolution.

WEIGHING THE EARTH

The influence of Scottish scenery on music, literature and painting is well documented. Scottish mountains also inspired two great scientific achievements – the first experiment to weigh the earth and the invention of the cloud chamber. Although the size of the earth was estimated with reasonable accuracy by Eratosthenes in the third century BC, the idea of weighing it did not make sense until Newton's theory of gravitation postulated a force of attraction between any two objects. It then seemed possible that a plumb line held near a mountain would not hang vertically, because the earth would attract it downward and the mountain would pull it sideways. Newton was not optimistic of success in such an experiment. Discussing the attraction of large objects in comparison with that of the earth, he wrote: 'Nay, whole mountains will not be sufficient to produce any sensible effect'. He was wrong; a sizeable mountain will deflect a plumb line by a measurable amount.

After an inconclusive experiment made in 1735 by French scientists in Peru, nothing more was done until 1772, when the English Astronomer Royal, Nevil Maskelyne, suggested using a British mountain. Skiddaw and Helvellyn were found

59. James Hutton (1726–97). His book, A Theory of the Earth *(1785), formed the basis of modern geology. Portrait by Sir Henry Raeburn (1756–1823). (*Scottish National Portrait Gallery*)*

unsuitable and the choice fell on Schiehallion in Perthshire. The nearly conical shape of this mountain made it ideal for the purpose, since its volume could be estimated fairly easily. Knowing the density of the rocks, the mass of the mountain could be found and – by calculation based on the deflection of the plumb line – compared with the mass of the earth. Maskelyne made measurements in 1764 and concluded that the density of the earth was about five times the density of water; subsequent experiments (usually made indoors with much more sensitive instruments) have not greatly modified this result.

INSPIRATION IN THE CLOUDS

The development of nuclear physics – one of the greatest triumphs of modern science – was decisively influenced by an observation made on a Scottish mountain. C.T.R. Wilson (1869–1959), a farmer's son from Glencorse, near Edinburgh, studied physics in Cambridge and escaped to Scotland whenever he could. During the summer of 1894 he worked for a few weeks in the observatory which then existed on the summit of Ben Nevis. Fascinated by the clouds as they formed and faded in the sunshine, he tried to imitate some of these effects when he returned to the Cavendish Laboratory. Clouds could be made easily enough by cooling moist air – but only if it contained dust particles, on which water vapour could condense; this discovery had been made by John Aitken (1839–1919), a physicist born in Falkirk. After Roentgen's discovery in 1895, Wilson found that clouds could be formed in dust-free air after the passage of an X-ray beam; the water vapour was condensing on the ions (charged atoms) produced by collision of the X-rays with molecules in the air. Wilson worked hard at this experiment. By 1911 he had made the first cloud chamber, capable of showing the tracks of sub-atomic particles emitted from a radioactive source. For more than forty years the Wilson cloud chamber was invaluable in the study of cosmic rays, radioactive decay and nuclear reactions associated with high-energy accelerators. These investigations influenced the award of many Nobel prizes, including one for Wilson in 1927.

EXPLORING THE OCEANS

In the mid-Victorian era the deep oceans were as mysterious as outer space – remote and offering only a few tantalising clues to suggest what might be found by the first explorers. The foundations of oceanography as a modern science were largely created by three alumni of Edinburgh University – Edward Forbes (1814–54), Charles Wyville Thomson (1830–82) and John Murray (1841–1914). Although none of them took a degree, they all achieved distinction. Forbes and Thomson became professors; Thomson and Murray became Fellows of the Royal Society. Forbes spent much of his short life collecting and studying marine organisms. His suggestion that no life existed in the sea at depths below 600 metres was generally accepted, but posed a challenge to adventurous biologists. Wyville Thomson, supported by William Carpenter, vice-president of the Royal Society, pushed the limit further in a series of dredging expeditions in old ships borrowed from the Royal Navy. Their results were so exciting that the government was persuaded in 1872 to commission a comprehensive scientific study of the oceans.

The steam corvette HMS *Challenger* was provided by the navy, with a crew of 240. Thomson, by then professor of natural history in Edinburgh University, directed the scientific staff of three naturalists (including Murray) and a chemist. The expedition lasted for more than three years, covering almost 70,000 nautical miles, collecting specimens and making scientific measurements at 362 stations around the world. Depths were measured down to 8,000 metres. Samples of mud, water and animal life were dredged from the bottom and trawled from intermediate depths. These experiments produced the greatest additions ever made to biological knowledge by a single expedition; 715 new genera and 4,417 new species were identified. Samples dredged from the Pacific Ocean floor contained great amounts of manganese – a resource which has not yet been commercially exploited; manganese nodules were later found on the bed of Loch Fyne. Fragments of phosphate rock found off Java were recognised by Murray as having been formed on land. He returned to the scene later and, after a systematic search, found huge deposits of the material (which is a useful fertiliser), on Christmas Island, 250 miles south-west of Java. Britain took possession of the island and Murray established a company to mine the phosphate. The profits made him a rich man and the royalties paid to the government exceeded the whole cost of the *Challenger* expedition.

The report of the expedition, in fifty large volumes, was completed under Murray's direction (and eventually at his expense) in 1895; constant battles with the Treasury, which threatened to terminate the project, had undermined Thomson's health and contributed to his death in 1882. By then the achievements of the *Challenger* expedition were stimulating research in other countries, where better funding was available. Scotland's supremacy in marine science was lost as the focus moved to Scandinavia. Murray was instrumental in the foundation of the Granton Marine Station in 1884 and the transfer of its activities to the newly built Marine Station at Millport in 1897. Scottish research in marine science, now relevant to issues in oil exploration, pollution, meteorology, fish farming and traditional fisheries, has expanded in recent decades.

BIOLOGY BROADENED

The early growth of ecology – the study of relationships between living organisms and their environment – owed much to the seminal ideas of Patrick Geddes (1854–1932), professor of botany in University College, Dundee, between 1889 and 1919. The work of his associates, Marcel Hardy and Robert Smith, was influential in the development of plant ecology, first in Scotland and then in England. Geddes published little in plant ecology, but became famous for his application of ecological concepts to town planning. In animal ecology, the work of nineteenth-century naturalists provided a basis for the twentieth-century studies of Seton Gordon, Frank Fraser Darling and others.

Among Geddes's colleagues in University College, Dundee, was D'Arcy Thompson (1860–1948), a man whose aristocratic appearance was complemented by his intellectual distinction. His major work, *On Growth and Form*, introduced new concepts in biological thinking. For half a century before its appearance in 1917, British zoology had been concerned almost entirely with comparative anatomy and with the details of evolutionary descent. D'Arcy Thompson created a new approach, mobilising ideas of mathematics, chemistry and physics in a heroic attempt to harmonise structure and function at every level from the molecular to the macroscopic. Later developments, such as X-ray crystallography, electron microscopy and the genetic code, have enhanced the validity of his approach. He has been described as the first completely modern anatomist – but that is not the whole of his learning or his fame. His record of service as a professor – thirty-three years in Dundee, followed by thirty-one years in St Andrews – is without equal. His eminence as a Greek scholar was recognised in his appointments as president of the Classical Associations of Scotland and of England. His magnum opus – which he mischievously described as an essay, though it ran to half a million words – was written with an elegance and clarity unsurpassed by any scientist and by few men of letters.

THE END OF THE STORY?

By the early years of this century Scotland's pre-eminence in the world of science was declining. Cullen, Black, Kelvin and Maxwell had no successors of comparable distinction. The partnership of science and philosophy had been dissolved. But the contribution of science to the impact of Scottish culture on the rest of the world was not exhausted.

Kelvin's scientific judgment was faltering. He dismissed Maxwell's electromagnetic theory, radioactivity, the aeroplane and, for a while, alternating current power distribution. But on other issues he still showed masterly insight. In 1901 he was appointed chairman of the Royal Commission on Arsenical Poisoning. Six thousand people had been poisoned and more than seventy had died in England through drinking beer contaminated with arsenic. The commission pinpointed the cause and made recommendations which were – and still are – valid in a much wider context. The presence of arsenic in beer or food, they advised, could not be completely eliminated, but should be controlled by prescribing a maximum permissible concentration of approximately one part per million – the limit used in most countries today. This figure was justified on three grounds: it could be achieved by good manufacturing practice, could be monitored by readily available means and had been shown by experiment to do no harm to experimental animals. These are the principles used to this day in setting limits for radiation and for almost every hazardous chemical in food or the environment.

The recognition of isotopes – an event which had a distinctive impact on twentieth-century physics and chemistry – took place during a dinner party in Scotland in 1913. The scene was the home of Dr G.T. (afterwards Sir George) Beilby, an eminent chemical engineer. The diners included Beilby's daughter and her husband, Frederick Soddy (1871–1956), lecturer in physical chemistry at Glasgow University. Soddy was discussing a puzzling situation which had arisen during his work on radioactive elements, for which he later received the Nobel Prize. He had found that some places in the Periodic Table appeared to be occupied, not by single elements as chemists had long believed, but by as many as three or four elements, produced by different routes from the decay of uranium, thorium or other radioactive substances. One of the guests at the table was Dr Margaret Todd, a Glasgow physician who was well known for her novels, written under the name Graham Travers. She suggested that elements occupying the same place in the Periodic Table ought to be called 'isotopes'. Had she been a better scholar, she would have suggested 'homotopes' but the name stuck, greatly easing the acceptance of Soddy's novel idea.

SCOTTISH GENIUS – DECLINE OR DIFFUSION?

The sciences of chemistry, geology and oceanography, and many of the foundations of modern physics, were created by Scottish genius during a period of little more than a hundred years. No small nation – except ancient Greece – has ever achieved an intellectual and cultural breakthrough of this magnitude. The hope of a repeat performance must be tempered by the realisation that the world of science has greatly changed since Scotland was at its centre. Even in the nineteenth century, talented Scots

– in science as in many other professions – were attracted by better opportunities and rewards in other countries. One of the most eminent was Thomas Graham (1805–69), who studied at Glasgow University and served as professor of chemistry in Anderson's University between 1830 and 1837. His work on diffusion in gases was begun in Glasgow, but most of it was done after he moved to London as professor of chemistry at University College and later as Master of the Mint; he was the last scientist to hold that office, which since 1870 has been vested in the Chancellor of the Exchequer. His ideas – forgotten and rediscovered more than once – were important in the gaseous diffusion project used to separate the isotopes of uranium for the first atomic bomb. When he turned his mind to the motion of molecules in liquids, he discovered the principles of dialysis and osmosis, which made possible, many years later, the design of the artificial kidney.

Another celebrated scientist lost to Scotland was the botanist Robert Brown (1773–1858). Born in Montrose and educated at Edinburgh University, Brown spent many years exploring and collecting plants before settling in England. He was the first to recognise the cell nucleus and achieved lasting fame through his discovery of the random motion of pollen grains in water. The Brownian motion, later explained mathematically by Maxwell and by Einstein, is caused by collisions with water molecules; it provided the first visible demonstration of the existence of molecules.

Graham used only simple equipment. Brown's scientific studies needed no more apparatus than a microscope. Both could have done their work in Scotland, had they not found better opportunities elsewhere. During the present century the brain drain has increased, not only because of the worldwide growth of scientific activity, but also because the nature of that activity has changed. The progress of science now depends less on the achievements of individuals and more on the work of teams supported by costly equipment or other facilities. In many sciences it has become apparent that the great problems now demanding attention – in nuclear physics, genetics, and meteorology, for example – can be tackled effectively only in large and specialised institutions or, when the task is too great for any single country, in multinational efforts. So the achievements of scientists born and educated in Scotland are diffused through a larger community and contribute in a less obvious way to the perception of the national culture. This is not a new situation. In the early years of the seventeenth-century there were many Scots among the wandering scholars who studied and taught in the universities of France, Germany, Italy and Bohemia. Thomas Seget of Seton, near Edinburgh, was the first to tell Kepler of Galileo's revolutionary advances in astronomy. John Wedderburn of Dundee also helped to promote Galileo's reputation. Alexander Anderson of Aberdeen edited the works of François Viète, often regarded as the father of algebra. The work of these exiles had no apparent influence on the advancements which were to come during the eighteenth century. The progress of science is still unpredictable; the day may come when Scotland will again lead the world.

Books for Further Reading

R.H. Campbell and Andrew Skinner (eds.), *The Origins and Nature of the Scottish Enlightenment* (Edinburgh, 1982)

A.G. Clement and R.H.S. Robertson, *Scotland's Scientific Heritage* (Edinburgh and London, 1961)

J.G. Crowther, *Scientists of the Industrial Revolution* (London, 1961)

J.G. Crowther, *British Scientists of the Nineteenth Century* (London, 1935)

D.K.C. MacDonald, *Faraday, Maxwell and Kelvin* (London, 1965)

Engineering and Technology

JOHN R. HUME

The contribution made by Scots and non-Scots working in Scotland to technical change and industrial development, particularly since the mid-eighteenth century, has been of remarkable importance. Some of this contribution has been at such a level of principle as to be comprehended in the term 'science', which has been considered in a previous chapter, but much of it has been at a level of thought which crosses any arbitrary boundary between science and technology. The relative absence of class distinction in Scotland made it possible for industrialists to achieve high social standing, at least outside Edinburgh, and Scottish attitudes to intellectual excellence were also more liberal than those in English circles. Scottish trade with France in wine, tobacco and sugar, and with North America and the West Indies also encouraged openness to new ideas. The dialogues between Scottish chemists and civil engineers and their French counterparts were particularly notable. Links with Holland, Sweden and Russia were also significant. These European and North American links set the tone of Scotland's contribution to world technology, but it is certainly true that transfer of ideas from England, and to a lesser extent Wales, was also important, and in certain industries at certain times, dominant.

It is in the nature of industry and technology to be multifaceted and full of complex inter-relationships. This is an important reason why non-technical historians either eschew consideration of technical matters or give non-technical explanations of the timing of events in which the technical factor is paramount. The complexity of industrial and technical structures inevitably makes concise analysis of a whole country over a long period difficult. This is compounded by the paucity of detailed study of any other than a handful of industries and technologies, and by assertions of primacy in innovation and scale, which at this stage are difficult to judge. To make the subject reasonably coherent and manageable, the treatment in this chapter will be thematic, within a loose chronological framework.

60. *Locomotive number 52 of the Tharsis Railway, built by the North British Locomotive Company in 1955. The railway served mines owned by the Tharsis Sulphur and Copper Company, a Glasgow-based concern founded by Sir Charles Tennant of St Rollox to supply pyrites, a source of sulphur to British sulphuric acid manufacturers. The simplicity and balance of this locomotive design are characteristic of Scottish builders.*

Not much is known of Scottish industry before the mid-seventeenth century. The archaeological record suggests that a fairly wide range of craft industries was practised, including silver, gold, bronze, lead and ironworking, the last-named widely diffused at the level of the bloomery. Recent excavations at Whithorn suggest that large bloomeries of Roman pattern were in use. Extensive evidence of brooch-making has been unearthed at Dunadd, and both gold and silver were being obtained from native sources by the late medieval period. The heavy iron yetts and window grilles characteristic of the houses of royalty, the nobility and gentry in the sixteenth century, are surviving evidence of secondary ironworking, though it is possible that the iron bars used were imported from Sweden or Russia. The practices of woodturning, woodcarving and cabinetmaking are also well-attested, with excavation of Threave Castle producing quantities of turned ware, and some surviving furnishings. Wood panelling dating from the late sixteenth and early seventeenth century is not uncommon, with notable examples in Culross Palace, Newark Castle (Renfrewshire) and in the church roofs at Largs (Skelmorlie Aisle) and St Mary's Grandtully. The timber used was imported, quite probably in sawn form. Pottery appears to have been fairly generally made in central Scotland, with most castle excavations revealing quantities of green glazed ware, some of it inventive in form if not in production technique. Heavier ceramics are represented by church floor tiles and clay water-supply pipes at Glenluce Abbey, quite probably locally made. The most widely diffused skills were probably those of stoneworking, though the houses of the poor often used materials such as brushwood, clay, sods and various thatches. The more sophisticated stone building techniques seem to have been imported, perhaps from Scandinavia in northern Scotland, and certainly from England and France from the twelfth century onwards. Although native designs developed, some with a degree of refinement, as in many tower houses and in Court architecture, the constructional techniques used remained conservative. Stonecarving, however, became notable in the later Middle Ages, though again techniques were not particularly advanced.

It is in the nature of textiles that they are perishable, so only fragments of early Scottish textiles survive. It is likely, though, that both wool and linen textiles were generally made, and some of these were probably fairly sophisticated. The depiction of sheepshears, scissors, combs and cloth shears on grave slabs at Kilmory Knap in Argyll points to a developed woollen industry in that area in the fifteenth century, and it seems most unlikely that this was unique.

The extent to which the techniques of these, and other craft industries such as leather and bone working, developed independently or semi-dependently of European technology is difficult, and may ultimately prove impossible, to assess. The best hope for fundamental reinterpretation lies with technically aware archaeology.

By the middle and later seventeenth century the nature and function of industry was changing. The impression one has of the period before that is of craft industry, fairly widely dispersed, and probably serving very local markets. There were some industrial units that for technical or business reasons probably catered for larger markets, such as the coal mines of the Forth basin, and perhaps the larger potteries. At the specialist level the West Highland grave-slab industry seems to have had a large sea-borne sphere of influence, though the volume of output was not large. The minting of coinage by its very nature and purpose produced items widely circulated. Even allowing for this, however, it would seem that the discrete industrial unit, employing more than a handful of workers, and designed of itself to generate wealth rather than to satisfy need, was an anomaly until the later seventeenth century. The impetus to develop industrial businesses seems to have come from a range of sources. An apparent rise in living standards during the seventeenth century, obscured in most historical writing by the much more entertaining civil and religious conflicts of the period, was one factor. Another was the concept of mercantilism, the notion that a state should maximise its wealth in the form of bullion, which implied the manufacture of goods within the state in preference to importing them. A third reason was an apparent improvement in communication both by land and sea. Though one cannot yet point to made roads in a modern sense, it does seem to have become easier to move around, and some new bridges were being constructed. On the Continent and in England river navigations were being improved and canals constructed, and the 'fluit', an improved Dutch design of merchantman, was making longer-distance trade more attractive.

It is against this background that one can view both the establishment of new industry and the attempts to gain access to larger markets that characterised the Scottish economy between 1660 and 1700. A whole range of new industries was introduced, all based on the application of capital and new technology, and intended to supply large areas, perhaps including exports. These included sugar-boiling, using Dutch expertise, soap-making, salt-boiling, large-scale woollen manufacture, and glassmaking. All these used coal as a fuel, and this stimulated the coal-mining industry, which relied on

English expertise. Of these industries, the woollen trade proved ultimately unsuccessful, probably because of competition from the sophisticated English woollen trades. The others succeeded, and became woven into the fabric of Scotland's subsequent industrial development.

The pros and cons of the Union of the Parliaments in 1707 have been the subject of much debate during the intervening years, and convincing arguments can be constructed for both sides. Given the mercantilist philosophy of the period, however, there is little doubt that the Union, eventually and while the Empire lasted, had a beneficial effect on the development of Scottish industry, by opening up the English colonies in the West Indies and North America to Scottish merchants. The partnership of English and Scots in extending and consolidating not only the formal empire of directly governed territorials but also the informal empire of 'spheres of influence', had the most profound effect on Scottish industry both as to character and as to scale. Scotland's internal market was small; trade with Europe was very competitive unless Scottish merchants had privileged access to trade goods; and England was difficult both owing to competition and to duties on cross-border trader. Scottish industrial success was based on importing colonial produce and re-exporting it either unprocessed or after processing, and on manufacturing trade goods for the colonies. On this superstructure, and on the infrastructure of communications to sustain it, more broadly based industry could be developed, and the 'world trade' industries themselves generated an economy of such sophistication that it required industries to satisfy home demands.

This thesis may perhaps seem oversimplified, but is borne out by the experience of Scottish industry since 1914. The disruption of world trade that followed the First World War, and which was indeed one of the principal reasons for fighting it, coupled with the over-expansionist post-war euphoria, greatly weakened a Scottish economy that had been dynamic until 1914. The loss of empire after the Second World War, coupled with the British debt to the United States, meant that after the immediate post-war re-equipment boom, most of the surviving colonial-based industries withered.

So far as this essay is concerned the nature of the industries, and associated trade, generated by colonial orientation, and modified by English influence, is critical. Territorial expansion by exploration and conquest, the growing and processing of exotic materials and the wider distribution of effective demand were engines of change, and rapid change. This change might have been slowed by bottlenecks in production; but the problems which could have occurred were resolved by some inspired thinking, a good deal of common-sense, and, so far as Scotland is concerned, good sources of important raw materials, a reasonable climate, good natural internal communications, and a pivotal geographical position. The dynamic introduced by rapid change in access to markets, which were to some extent protected, and the mercantile ability of many Scots, created an exciting situation for inventors and entrepreneurs. Scotland's legal and banking systems – and the already mentioned low level of class distinction – facilitated the realisation of technical aspiration. A lively intellectual climate in which landowners, philosophers and practical men, such as merchants, industrialists and financial managers could not only meet on common ground, but even be the same people, certainly contributed. It is clearly possible to make too much of these factors, but it is otherwise quite difficult to explain the transition from a relatively poor country with some background of intellectual achievement – but nothing of note in industrial, and little of scientific thought – to a nation in the forefront of many kinds of intellectual activity, not least technico-economic, as Scotland was by the end of the eighteenth century.

And this is not just a flash in the pan. The inspired rationality that became a hallmark of Scottish thought in the late eighteenth century persists through the nineteenth century not just in individuals but in institutions. Concern for truth, virtue, 'rightness' and structure underpin the phenomenal success of shipbuilding, engineering, both fine and heavy textiles and a wide range both of chemical and processing industries. Quality, both technical and aesthetic, and reliability, became ingrained in the thinking of industrialists and technologists. Both the capacity to invent, and the willingness to innovate became endemic, and encouraged men of ability to settle in Scotland, or at least to seek markets for innovations.

Rather than produce a catalogue of people and inventions, the rest of this chapter will highlight a few industries, industrialists and inventions in which Scotland or Scotsmen have been particularly prominent, and attempt to explain their success. They will be grouped by sector, and roughly by period.

CHEMICAL AND RELATED INDUSTRIES

Today it is conventional to class as chemical those industries which produce relatively pure chemical compounds as a result of chemical change. In this section, however, the isolation of pure, naturally occurring compounds will be included. The oldest large-scale chemical industry in Scotland on this definition was the salt trade, extracting salt from seawater by evaporation using coal fires. Salt-boiling as a trade preceded the Union, but rose to prominence during the eighteenth century. Its greatest strongholds were in the Forth and Clyde estuaries, where, according to recent research, it was directly responsible for the opening up of coal pits. When Carron Iron Works was founded in 1759 one of its notable products was salt-pan sections. The techniques of crystallisation used to prepare salt of different qualities were transferable to other branches of chemical industry, and, from the residues after crystallisation, magnesia, and later bromides and iodides, could be recovered. The salt produced was used primarily for food preservation, but also for soap-making and dyeing (to throw the soap and dye out of solution). During the eighteenth century the Irish and English salt industries, using brine and rock salt, proved more economic, but the United Kingdom Parliament gave concessions on duty to even out prices. Eventually in 1825 the duties on salt were abolished, and salt-boiling quickly declined, though the last salt-pan in Scotland did not close until the 1950s. Scotland appears to have had by far the largest salt industry, employing artificial evaporation of sea salt.

A much less significant chemical industry, but one of unusual interest and implication, was the making of cudbear. This was a dye stuff made, like many others in the eighteenth and early nineteenth centuries, from a vegetable substance, in this case lichen. The process for making it was discovered by Cuthbert Gordon, who used it without much commercial success at Leith. The rights were then acquired by George Mackintosh, a Glasgow industrialist, who transferred manufacture to Glasgow, where it prospered. The process involved extracting the lichen with ammonia made from human urine. This was expensive to collect, so when the Glasgow Gas Company started in 1817 George Mackintosh's son, Charles, tried purifying the weak by-product, ammoniacal liquor, from its works. He succeeded, but in the distilling process the ammonia also produced a light oil (mainly benzene). He found that this would dissolve natural rubber, and that the sticky solution could be used to coat cloth. By sandwiching a rubber layer between two layers of cloth a durable waterproof could be made. Mackintosh took this process down to Manchester, abandoning cudbear, whose economic life was limited by shortage of lichen.

Charles Mackintosh was also involved in developing new mordants for calico printing. These were chemicals – iron, lead, aluminium, tin and copper salts – which reacted with dye stuffs to make insoluble, wash-fast colours. With a suitable choice of mordants a single dye stuff could produce a range of colours from black through red to orange. The invention of bleaching powder, ascribed to Charles Tennant, a Renfrewshire bleacher, who patented it in 1799, is said to have been partly due to Mackintosh. Bleaching powder was one of the critical chemical inventions of the Industrial Revolution, making it possible to use chlorine in bleaching without expensive equipment and undue personal hazard. Its large-scale manufacture made Glasgow home of what was claimed at the time (in the 1830s) to be the largest chemical works in the world, St Rollox Works. As is common in chemical manufacture, to make this single product, calcium hypochlorite, required other chemicals and produced usable by-products. Sulphuric acid salt and manganese dioxide were needed for producing chlorine, so the lead chamber process was used on a large scale. The by-product, sodium sulphate, could be used to make sodium carbonate (washing soda) using the French Leblanc process, and the by-product from that, calcium sulphide, an evil-smelling compound, could be treated to recover sulphur. Related sulphates, sulphites and hyposulphites (thio-sulphites) made up other aspects of the business. The St Rollox Works was followed by a large number of smaller works throughout west central Scotland making industrial acids, alkalis (soda and caustic soda) as well as bleaching powder. They called into being classes in industrial chemistry in various Glasgow institutions which proved very influential.

Taking the St Rollox story further, by the 1870s the main product at the works had become soda. When the Leblanc process was challenged by the less-energy-consuming Belgian Solvay process during the 1880s, Charles Tennant, owner of St Rollox, took the lead in forming a protective amalgamation of Leblanc soda producers. This, the United Alkali Company, was the British pioneer of such rationalisations in the chemical industry. In the post-First World War depression it was Sir Harry McGowan of Nobel Industries, another of Charles Tennant's concerns, who headed the amalgamation of major British chemical manufacturers which produced Imperial Chemical Industries, the largest chemical company outside Germany.

Finally in this section, the manufacture of coal-gas has been mentioned. This industry had strong Scottish connections and far-reaching implications. Archibald Cochrane, Lord Dundonald, was one of the first people to realise that the distillation of coal (which had been practised to make coke for iron-smelting since the early eighteenth century) could be made to yield useful by-products in the form of tar and a light oil which could dissolve resin to make varnish, both of which could be used to protect timber on ships. Dundonald built works at Culross, Muirkirk and in Coalbrookdale. The by-product gas was not used. William Murdoch, an Ayrshire man, moved south to work with James Watt, and while with Boulton & Watt devised a process for making a purified coal-gas which could be used for factory lighting. Though others developed the idea of public gas supply (the first public utility to be piped generally into the homes of consumers) Murdoch's basic process continued in use until coal-gas manufacture ceased in Britain in 1983. Most coke for iron-smelting continued to be made in ovens where the gas was not recovered until the end of the nineteenth century. From the 1830s, however, raw coal was used in Scottish blast furnaces, and in the 1880s low levels of profitability in iron-smelting and a demand for by-products led Scottish ironmasters to pioneer by-product recovery from blast-furnace gases. Coal-tar chemicals and ammonium sulphate sales did much to tide the industry over a very difficult period. More significantly, however, the destructive distillation of coal was an analogue for James Young's method of obtaining oil from cannel coal, later from shale. Young, like Murdoch, was faced with problems of purification: his resolution of these was transferred to American petroleum refining, and hence the world oil industry. Young's prime products were paraffin oil for lighting, mineral lubricating oils, and waxes used in candlemaking and for paper-coating. The quality standards he set did much to establish domestic oil lighting on a safe footing. Young was a philanthropist, and founded a chair of technical chemistry in the Andersonian University, Glasgow, which was the first of its kind.

Of the metal mining and smelting industries in Scotland, iron was unquestionably the most significant. Apart from the primitive bloomery hearths that produced small quantities of wrought-iron for local use in making implements and weapons, the earliest Scottish ironworks on a large scale appear to have been in Wester Ross, at Fasagh, Letterewe and near Poolewe. These sites, two of which at least were working in the seventeenth century, illustrate the transition from large bloomery (Fasagh) to semi-blast-furnace to fully-fledged blast-furnace. The latter two, owned by Sir George Hay, and exploiting a privilege granted by James VI, were built to use techniques developed in Europe from the fifteenth century. They were short-lived ventures, using locally produced charcoal and both local and imported ores. From the 1720s to the 1750s blast-furnace plants were set up in various parts of the Highlands to use similar materials, and were established by English and Irish entrepreneurs. The only sites to survive for any length of time were the Lorn and Argyll furnaces (Bonawe and Craleckan), the former operating for about 120 years. Only six years after Bonawe and four years after Craleckan, a major step forward took place in 1759 when the English entrepreneurs John Roebuck and Samuel Garbett, with William Cadell, partners in the Prestonpans Vitriol Works, founded the Carron Company which, with its four blast-furnaces and associated foundries, was the first large-scale integrated coke-smelting works in the world. Carron remained unique in Scotland in its degree of sophistication and integration, and attracted a stream of English and Scots innovators including John Smeaton, James Watt and Robert Adam. The ironworks at Wilsontown, Muirkirk, Clyde, Glenbuck and Shotts, founded from the 1770s to the early 1800s used similar blast-furnaces, but were both smaller in scale and less sophisticated. None had the carefully selected locational advantages of Carron, though they were not negligible in their influence, having strong links with iron forges and foundries. Glenbuck cast the tramplates for Scotland's first public railway, the Kilmarnock and Troon, in 1811–12, and it was at Muirkirk and Clyde that James Beaumont Neilson in the late 1820s developed the hot blast, which entirely altered the economics of iron-smelting in Scotland. The hot blast was particularly suited to the making of foundry-iron from the non-caking splint coals and hitherto difficult to smelt black band ironstones of central Scotland. The availability of excellent inexpensive foundry irons did much to encourage engineering and architectural iron-founding in Scotland, and generated important trade with the United States. The Bairds, who dominated this trade, were

Scots, as were Merry and Cunninghame; but William Dixon and the Houldsworths, other important players, were English. The rapid expansion of iron-smelting from the 1830s to the 1880s gave a boost to coal and ironstone-mining, and it was the Bairds who introduced one of the earliest successful coal-cutters.

Expansion of the iron-smelting trade was slowed from the 1870s by competition and by exhaustion of accessible mineral reserves, but by that time there was a significant trade in structural wrought-iron for engineering, boilermaking and shipbuilding, and this provided a basis upon which an acid open-hearth steel-making industry could be built from the 1880s. This interacted with the local iron shipbuilding and structural engineering industries most effectively, giving the Clyde an unbeatable advantage from then until 1914. Scots engineers appear to have been instrumental in developing the equipment for manipulating bulk quality steel.

The disruption introduced by the First World War created conditions in which the foundry-iron industry had little future, and the steel industry came under the control of shipbuilders. The catastrophic depression of 1931–34 began a process of concentration of ownership, led by Sir James Lithgow, which made Colvilles Ltd one of the largest and most cleverly integrated steel firms in Britain. Sir Andrew McCance was one of the technical leaders of this business and did much to form post-war steel policy which was, however, dominated by the politics of nationalisation, denationalisation, renationalisation and privatisation. Sir Monty Finniston's policy of concentrating steel-making on a small number of large plants on a British scale and European agreements on reduction of steel capacity have now shrunk Scotland's steel industry to a re-rolling function, and there are now no blast-furnaces working in the country for the first time since the early eighteenth century.

Apart from iron-smelting, its conversion to steel, and subsequent rolling or forging to produce semi-finished components for other industries, Scotland developed an international reputation for cast-iron goods. The architectural products of Walter Macfarlane's Saracen Foundry, George Smith's Sun Foundry, the Lion, Star and Grahamston foundries were shipped all over the world, and stoves from Smith & Wellstood and Lane & Girvan also had international customers. The ability of 'Scotch Number One' pig-iron to fill cleanly ornate moulds was at the root of this success, and it was the light castings expertise of central Scotland that attracted Singer's sewing-machine factory, the Kilbowie works becoming for a time the largest sewing-machine works in the world.

During the eighteenth century the scale of investment in civil engineering works increased markedly. Early Scots civil engineers included James Watt and Robert Mackell, who were involved in the construction of the Monkland and Forth and Clyde canals. English engineers such as John Smeaton, John Golborne and Robert Whitworth were, however, more influential. From the 1790s Scottish engineers began to dominate the profession. Thomas Telford was the greatest in terms of the number, scale and virtuosity of his commissions, but in their various ways John Rennie, Robert Stevenson and John Loudoun McAdam were also giants. Apart from work on canals, harbours and lighthouses their great contribution to the development of roads both north and south of the border. In the 1790s there were large areas of northern Scotland where wheeled vehicles were unknown. By 1840 there were good roads throughout the country. Both Telford and Stevenson were ahead of their time in the railways they designed, and it was John Miller who emerged as the greatest of the early Scottish

61. Girdle Ness Lighthouse, south of Aberdeen, designed by Robert Stevenson and built in 1833. Uniquely among Scottish lights, it was fitted with a low-level lantern to aid recognition. This, now disused, retains its original square panes. The principal lantern is of the triangular-paned type devised to reduce interference with the light beam by Alan Stevenson, Robert's son, in 1849.

railway engineers, and probably the finest designer of masonry viaducts of all time. Robert Stevenson was most famous as a lighthouse engineer, and founded a dynasty that built most of the Scottish lighthouses and developed designs that were internationally influential.

The range of projects undertaken by civil engineers widened greatly in the course of the nineteenth century, and the role of individual engineers became less public. Scottish firms of consulting engineers developed which retain international reputations today. A characteristic of the later nineteenth century was the emergence of the large contracting company. Sir Alexander Gibb & Partners, Sir William Arrol & Co and Sir Robert McAlpine & Co are notable examples. Arrols' involvement in the Tay and Forth railway bridges and in Tower Bridge, London, made them legendary. Scottish structural engineering manufacturers were also internationally notable, including P. &

62. *The Inman International Line's* City of New York, *one of a revolutionary pair of liners built by J. & G. Thompson at Clydebank in 1888–89. They were the first transatlantic liners with twin screws, and their accommodation set new standards of comfort. This photograph was taken when the vessel was passing Bowling on the Clyde soon after she was completed.*

W. MacLellan and the Motherwell Bridge & Engineering Co. In all of this the Scots characteristics of rationality and integrity are clearly evident.

Between 1840 and the 1960s Scotland's shipbuilding industry was a leading force in the industrial development of the country, but the seeds of this were sown in the second decade of the nineteenth century. Henry Bell's *Comet*, an inspired synthesis of Glasgow-made engine and boiler with Port Glasgow-built hull was enough of a commercial success to stimulate the rapid development of estuarial steam navigation. Of the pioneers, David Napier was the most scientific in his approach to hull and engine design, and was instrumental in extending the range of steamships to coastal and cross-channel trades. His cousin, Robert Napier, a better businessman who drew on the design skills of David Elder, was the most successful steamship builder of his day, and founder of the Clyde's reputation for quality and reliability. Tod & McGregor, at about the same time, were introducing iron hulls and screw propulsion. The skills of marine engineering, boilermaking and iron hull construction developed on the Clyde between 1812 and 1850, together with links with shipowners, created a culture of quality, integrity and sophistication which was sustained at least until 1914. Within this culture, competition and the transfer of both manual and intellectual skills flourished, and because the Clyde built for the best British – and often foreign – shipping lines, Clyde yards found it essential to be in the forefront of innovation: compound, triple and quadruple expansion; high-pressure boilers; forced draught; steel-hull construction; tank testing of merchant ship hulls; turbines, both direct drive and geared; the first British use of diesel engines for large vessels. Underpinning the practical, if not always financial, success of these innovations was a keen interest in scientific analysis. W.J. McQuorn Rankine and Sir John Biles stand out as academics who made major contributions to ship and engine design.

Though the Clyde became the dominant area for ship construction Dundee, Aberdeen and Leith were also in their day notable, and the Aberdeen clippers among the fastest. The émigré Scots should not be forgotten, either, as John Scott Russell, builder of Brunel's giant *Great Eastern* on the Thames, and the founder of what is now Vickers' yard at Barrow were Scots.

The expertise which developed in Scotland in construction of ships, boilers and marine engines was transferable to other products. Locomotives, land engines of various kinds, sugar machinery, plant for collieries, and iron and steelworks all required machine-tools, handcrafts and foundry skills comparable in quality if not in scale. High levels of reliability were required in all these types of machinery, as breakdowns could affect the employment or even the lives of large numbers of people. This was also true to some extent of the specialised machine-tools used in making large precision parts and for working plates and sections. The careful manufacture of such machinery and plant engendered a spirit of pride in work and a quality of design – both aesthetic and functional – which was generally unequalled. Scots locomotive engineers, for example, were highly influential in United Kingdom terms, and their products were generally not only efficient but demonstrated a simple and elegant approach to engineering aesthetics. The Drummonds (Dugald and Peter), the Stirlings (Patrick and James) and their schools were particularly notable. In driving engines, Fullerton Hodgart & Barclay and Douglas & Grant were notable; in sugar machinery, Mirrlees Watson and its predecessors A & W Smith led the way; in machine tools, Shanks & Lang, Craig & Donald, Bennie, Hugh Smith were outstanding; and in marine auxiliaries G & J Weir and, on a smaller scale, Dawson & Downie must be mentioned. These firms, and others of similar excellence in fields such as textile engineering, were successful partly because of their open-mindedness to innovation. Some generated their own patented improvements and few were reluctant to buy in good ideas.

The heavy and medium engineering trades are so generally linked with central Scotland that one can forget the importance of lighter engineering products. From the 1860s the Glasgow area nurtured sewing-machine, bicycle, motor car and agricultural machinery manufacture. The Singer factories, first in Bridgeton and later in Clydebank, were not just branches of an American parent but generated new designs of machine, and the brief flowering of car manufacture in Scotland before the First World War produced many innovations. Both Singer's Clydebank factory and the Argyll Motor Works in Alexandria were large by world standards – indeed Singer's was the largest sewing-machine works in the world. Alexander Govan's entrepreneurial flair was central to the success of the Argyll Works, as his untimely death proved; the mélange of ideas represented by the sewing-machine made individual contributions hard to disentangle.

The textile industries in Scotland developed after the early chemical and iron industries, and before large-scale shipbuilding. Attempts to make both coarse and fine woollens in the seventeenth century and fine linens in the early eighteenth century were not notably successful. After the Union of the Parliaments in 1707 woollen manufacturing was discouraged, but linen manufacture was promoted, particularly by a Board of Trustees for the encouragement of manufacturers which was set up in 1726. At first the fibre preparation techniques of spinning, weaving and finishing were based on ideas derived from the Continent, but Scots made notable advances in bleaching. It was, however, in the new machine-spinning of cotton that Scots entrepreneurs and inventors were most successful. By the 1790s the Scots were rivalling the English cotton districts, and New Lanark was at once the largest and probably the most innovative mill complex in Britain. Scots spinning continued to flourish until the 1840s, but by this time innovation was most marked in weaving, where the west of Scotland manufacturers took a commanding lead over their English rivals in the 1820s and 1830s. The wiper loom was in its day much more satisfactory than its crank-operated cousin, producing calicos for the textile-printing trade. It is perfectly possible that in other circumstances the west of Scotland cotton industry could have continued to grow and rival the Lancashire industry, but it seems probable that better return on capital could be had from the iron and engineering industries, as the Houldsworth family investment decisions illustrate.

By the time the pace of investment in cotton was slacking in the west, the linen trade of Dundee and district was beginning to dominate British trade. The sailcloths of Dundee and Arbroath were the quality products, making the reputation of the Cox, Baxter and Grimond families, but other heavy linens were in demand for sacking and bagging. The substitution of hemp and then jute for expensive flax in the heavy end of the trade was a Dundee achievement, opening up new markets for grain and coal sacks, and in wartime for sandbags. By the 1860s Dundee's linen industry was the largest in Britain. Cox's Camperdown Works was the world's largest jute mill, and Baxter Brother's Dens Works the largest linen factory in the world.

There were other major textile trades in which Scotland excelled. These included the making of tweed, of hosiery, and of carpets. Tweeds and related fine woollens and worsteds were not only made in the Borders, but in Dumfriesshire and in the Forth valley. In quality these were unsurpassed, and became high-fashion fabrics for international markets. Hosiery, too, for the late nineteenth century, became a high-fashion product, a status it still retains though the scale of hosiery manufacture is much less than it was. Carpet-weaving was largely a west of Scotland trade, and its practitioners in Glasgow and Kilmarnock were both inventive and innovative. In all these manufactures – as in tambouring (embroidery popular in the 1840s and 1850s), Paisley shawl-weaving, fancy muslin-weaving, linen damask-weaving, machine lacemaking and calico-printing – quality of design, as well as skill and cost-effectiveness in manufacture, was an essential component of success, as it remains in surviving businesses.

In the field of food and drink there were few distinctively Scottish manufactures. Scotch whisky is a clear example, though much of its technology can be paralleled in, for example, rum and brandy distilling, and in gin manufacture. The most distinctive contribution of the whisky industry was in marketing and organisation. The success of the big blenders' operations, such as William Usher, Alexander Walker and John Dewar, was based on flamboyant marketing styles as well as on the quality of their products. A tendency towards overproduction and consequent price depression in the manufacture of grain spirit led in 1876 to the formation of The Distillers' Company, a model for later defensive amalgamations. William Ross, chairman of the DCL from 1925 to 1935, pursued a policy of amalgamation of blending houses and of takeover of redundant malt whisky distilleries, creating a dominant grouping in Scotch whisky production. On a smaller scale Highland Distilleries carved out a similar niche from the 1880s. In the 1930s Joseph Hobbs, acting for the American National Distillers, and Hiram Walker (UK) Ltd, subsidiary of a Canadian distilling company, put together comparable operations.

The excellence of Scottish beers and their penetration of export trades was notable, with the Younger, Usher and Tennent families particularly outstanding. Tennents pioneered the brewing of lager in Britain. Oatmeal mills, common in Scotland though rare in England, have their parallels in Wales and Ireland. The Scots flour millers were pioneers of roller milling of imported hard wheat, and mechanised bread-baking appears to have been initiated in Glasgow. Certainly Glasgow's mechanised bakeries were early, large and numerous. Biscuit-baking, too, was very much a Scottish industry, based both in Glasgow and in Edinburgh. McFarlane Lang, Gray Dunn and McVitie & Price were among the leaders.

The contribution made by Scottish innovators and inventors as outlined in this chapter is characterised by a high level of thought and organisation. Scottish industry from the middle of the eighteenth century, though varied in character, has running through it a thread of serious thought which can be matched in England by the Quaker entrepreneurs and a few visionaries, frequently non-conformists, like Richard Arkwright and Titus Salt. In England the entrepreneurial stratum of society sat uneasily between the landed classes (and those with pretensions to ape or join them), and the working classes, who accepted a position of inferiority and indeed at times revelled in it. In Scotland there were indubitably some parallels to that situation, but the greater openness of society (especially outside Edinburgh) made it possible for gifted industrialists to make their way socially and politically into accepted positions without having to use wealth as the overt key. The universities, especially Glasgow, were part of this open structure, and the senior technical colleges enjoyed a standing much superior to that of most equivalent institutions in England. Religion was also important. Though industrialists tended to favour the free Churches, the social gap between the major free denominations and the rump of the established Churches was not extreme, and the association of membership of secession Churches with intellectual issues tended to keep differences at that level. The fact that religion was at the forefront of the minds of educated people created a generally high moral tone, and though there were men with double standards in social terms, on the whole intellectual values were prized throughout Scottish society.

The practical effect of this set of intellectual and (dare one say it) spiritual preoccupations can be seen both in the nature and the quality of the distinctively Scottish trades. While accepting that geographical disadvantage would predispose Scots businessmen to move up-market, the quality trades of mechanical engineering, shipbuilding, fine textiles (and, paradoxically, heavy textiles), Scotch whisky distilling and blending, and other food and drink trades designed primarily for export, had such a strong grip on the Scottish economy as a whole that they set a tone that became pervasive. A culture of intellectual enterprise was the consequence. Pride in work was common, and there was a wide desire to become educated. There were opportunities, too, for men to use expertise gained in employment to set up in competition with their employers, that competition stimulating excellence in design and construction and forcing innovation, often at the expense of profits. In mechanical engineering and shipbuilding these phenomena were particularly well displayed, with the Clyde shipbuilding dominated by firms founded by their Napier cousins and their former employees.

Though remarkable, the Scottish pursuit of quality was not without its weaknesses. It led to the production of goods of unusual durability, restricting the market for replacement. It relied heavily on individual skill and expertise, and was thus vulnerable to change in technique resulting in minimising skill. Most significantly, it introduced a kind of rigidity into the economic structure, a rigidity not borne of the inflexibility of individual units, but of the complex interlinking between them, and between businesses and their customers. Belief in inherent superiority, too, could be crippling, blinding firms to the value of ideas from other areas, though this was true more of the decline in British economic standing in the period after 1945 than it was earlier.

In a number of trades, all involving high levels of expertise and of intellectual input in organisation and implementation Scots have played a major role, at least since the mid-eighteenth century. Today their role is less public but still pervasive. Though quality, integrity and clarity of thought are perhaps less obviously valued today than they once were, they are clear aspects of 'Scottishness' and certainly form significant factors in determining both the industries in which Scotland excelled and also the extent to which Scots were successful in world markets and are successful in today's multinational businesses.

Books for Further Reading

Much of this article is based on research in contemporary sources. The following books either expand on ideas raised in the article or present alternative perspectives.

R.H. Campbell, *Carron Company* (Edinburgh, 1961)

R.H. Campbell, *Scotland Since 1707* (Oxford, 1965)

R.H. Campbell, *The Rise and Fall of Scottish Industry* (Edinburgh)

S.G.E. Checkland, *The Upas Tree* (Glasgow)

A. and N.L. Clow, *The Chemical Revolution* (London, 1952)

N. Crathorne, *Tennant's Stalk* (London, 1973)

Sir A. Gibb, *The Story of Telford* (London, 1935)

J.R. Hume and M.S. Moss, *Clyde Shipbuilding from Old Photographs* (London, 1975)

M.S. Moss and J.R. Hume, *The Workshop of the British Empire* (London, 1977)

M.S. Moss and J.R. Hume, *The Making of Scotch Whisky* (Edinburgh, 1981)

R.W. Munro, *Scottish Lighthouses* (Stornoway, 1979)

P.L. Payne, *Colvilles and the Scottish Steel Industry* (London, 1979)

A. Slaven, and S.G.E. Checkland (eds.), *Dictionary of Scottish Business Biography*, *1860–1960*, 2 vols (1986, 1990)

Extends 200 feet

The North Front *of the* Royal Infirmary *facing the* City *of* Edinburgh

ul. Adam inv. et delin   *R. Cooper Sculp.*

63. *Edinburgh Royal Infirmary. The design by William Adam (1689–1748) for the original building of 1738, which was largely demolished in 1882 to allow for extension. This drawing is from William Adam's* Vitruvius Scoticus, *published posthumously in 1812. (*RIAS*)*

Medicine

MALCOLM NICOLSON

In the Middle Ages, the most fully developed form of medical practice in Scotland was undoubtedly that of the physicians of the Gaelic-speaking community, with its strongholds in the Highlands and islands. The practitioners of Gaelic medicine formed an integral part of the professional learned orders that were a very distinctive feature of the traditional kin-based society. Physicians enjoyed high social status and noble patronage, ranking with the bards and the interpreters of the law. The office of physician seems largely to have been a hereditary one, the outstanding example of a medical kindred being the Clan MacBeth or Beatons. No less than seventy-six individual Beaton physicians have been identified as practising medicine in the Gaidhealtachd, the Gaelic-speaking region, between 1300 and 1700. Medicine was taught by the kindred in organised schools, with long periods of training and high standards of literacy being required of the aspiring physician.

The medical texts owned and used by the Beatons show them to have been firmly in the mainstream of European medieval medicine. For example, a widely used text was the *Lilium Medicinae*, a guide to medical practice written by Bernard Gordon, who taught at Montpellier in the late thirteenth century. Gordon's *Lilium Medicinae* was a very typical medieval production, embodying the legacy of classical Greek medicine, as extensively modified and developed by later Islamic and Scholastic commentators. Several Gaelic translations of this text are extant. Indeed, the extent to which major medical texts were being translated from Latin into Gaelic, while by no means unique in the wider European context, was well in advance of any equivalent English practice at this time. These translations, written in the Classical Gaelic script, also display the communality of culture between Celtic Scotland and Ireland, and indicate something of the extent to which Scotland was a beneficiary of the maintenance of scholarship in Ireland during the Dark Ages.

Apart from the scholarly Graeco-Arabist tradition, a more indigenous herbal medicine was also in use in the Celtic lands. This can be traced, in Ireland, back to the seventh century. The Beatons undoubtedly drew upon this native botanical knowledge; one branch of the kindred established a substantial herb garden at Pennycross in Mull. The learned Gaelic physicians also practised surgery to an extent, and there is evidence that their services were in demand outwith the Gaelic-speaking areas. By the sixteenth century, however, Gaelic medicine, reflecting the intense conservatism of the kin-based society from which it had sprung, was markedly unresponsive to the new developments taking place on the Continent. The patronage of the increasingly Anglicised Highland nobility gradually but irreversibly switched to university-trained physicians. By the middle of the seventeenth century, the traditionally trained Gaelic physician had disappeared, together with the other members of the old learned orders. From then on, in medicine as in other aspects of life in the Gaidhealtachd, hegemony would rest with the institutions of the mercantile Anglophone society.

Other strands of the early history of medicine in Scotland were associated with the Church. In the early Christian period, forms of medicine were developed within the monastic settlements. Early monastic medicine was a mixture of natural, generally herbal but also sometimes surgical, remedies, with supernatural elements, usually associated with the miraculous powers of the founding saints. Many wells and streams came to be associated with the names of saints and their waters were popularly credited with restorative properties. This ascription of healing virtues to particular sources of water was undoubtedly a continuation in a Christian guise of earlier pagan practices. The use of healing wells remained an important aspect of Scottish folk medicine into the twentieth century.

The advent of a Normanising influence in the southern part of Scotland, in the eleventh and twelfth centuries, produced a considerable expansion in the size and importance of the ecclesiastical institutions. The newly founded abbeys and monasteries of the Lowlands and the Borders further developed the monastic tradition of providing health care, both for the members of the institutions and, to some extent, for the outside community, for pilgrims, for the nobility, as acts of charity, and so on. Thus, in 1298, Edward I, injured before the battle of Falkirk, was taken to Torphichen Priory to benefit from the medical and nursing expertise to be found there.

The developing Scottish Church fostered fresh links with the learned culture of Europe. Academic medical learning was, at this time, confined largely to churchmen, because the Church was the major cultural and educational institution of the time and because a sufficient supply of medical texts could only be found in the libraries of the great religious houses. Thus, from the twelfth century, Scotland began to produce learned clerical physicians, of a type that were characteristic of European medicine as a whole throughout the Middle Ages. The career of Michael Scot, born about 1175 in the Borders – a translator of Aristotle, a writer on alchemy and physiognomy, a tutor of Frederick II of Hohenstaufen (King of Sicily and later Holy Roman Emperor), and supposedly a teacher at the medical school of Salerno – may be said to be largely lost in the mists of legend. But the pattern he presents of an academic physician, trained in theology, Scholastic philosophy and Graeco-Arabic medicine, able to move readily within a European learned community, united by common institutions and by a common scholarly language, is one we can discern repeated many times in the next three or four centuries.

William Schevez, born in Fife c.1428, might be cited as an important example. Schevez studied first at the newly founded University of St Andrews and then at the

University of Louvain, an important centre of medical learning. He returned to Scotland and, for a time, practised physic at the Court of James III. He later pursued his clerical career, rising to become Archbishop of St Andrews. Nor did the medical traffic consist only of Scots going abroad. Continental physicians might travel to Scotland to be consulted, at the behest of noble or ecclesiastical clients.

Within the social structure of medieval feudalism, a rigid distinction was made between academic learning, on the one hand, and practically oriented craft skill, on the other. Hence the academic physician, who did not undertake manual procedures, who worked with his mind rather than his hands, enjoyed higher social status than the surgeon, who bled, bandaged wounds, lanced swellings and undertook a small variety of operative procedures, often combining these activities with barbering. This is not to say, however, that surgeons and barber-surgeons did not prosper in Scotland in the Middle Ages. From the fourteenth century onwards, guilds of craftsmen began to be established in the Scottish towns, under the direct patronage of the Crown. A guild of barbers is known to have been in existence in Edinburgh in 1451 and, in 1505, the Town Council granted a Seal of Cause to the Barbers and Surgeons. This was ratified in the following year by James IV, who took a strong personal interest in matters scholarly, medical and alchemical. The Incorporation of Surgeons was represented on the Town Council and its Deacon sometimes sat in the Scottish Parliament. This may have been one of the reasons why surgeons seem to have enjoyed higher status in Edinburgh, and indeed throughout Scotland, than was the case in, for instance, London.

The considerable political power of the Edinburgh Incorporation of Surgeons had important consequences for the development of Scottish medical education. The surgeons were able to prevent the College of Physicians, when it was founded in 1681, from undertaking medical teaching. This had left the field open for the later establishment, with the support of the Incorporation, of a medical school under the auspices of the university.

Surgeons were, moreover, more numerous than physicians and they provided, despite notional legal restrictions on the extent of their practice, a generalised form of care for their patients. Like the apothecaries, the surgeons received their training in the form of apprenticeships, with supplementary lectures in anatomy being provided, albeit irregularly, by the Incorporation. The numbers of physicians were kept low by their need for a long expensive university education and by their preference for an upper-class clientele. Although universities had been founded in Scotland, at St Andrews, Glasgow and Aberdeen, in the fifteenth century, the early attempts at establishing medical teaching in these centres were not successful. Up to the beginning of the eighteenth century, medical education for the physician hardly existed in Scotland. Accordingly, aspiring physicians travelled to the Continent to study, the most-favoured venue for Scots being the Dutch university of Leyden. Not only was Leyden, by the late seventeenth century, the foremost medical school in Europe, it had the advantages of relative geographical proximity and, for post-Reformation Scots, a Protestant ethos. Its curriculum also reflected the fact that, in Northern Europe, physic had, by this time, become predominately a secular profession.

The University of Edinburgh was established in 1582. Unlike the three earlier foundations, Edinburgh's Town's College, as it was called, came under the auspices of the Town Council who remained largely responsible for the content of the curriculum and the appointment of the professoriate. The burghers of Edinburgh regarded the yearly exodus of young men abroad in search of education as both a poor reflection on the status of Scotland's capital and a lost commercial opportunity. Much better if they could be persuaded to stay and spend their money at home; better still if students from furth of Scotland could be attracted to come to Edinburgh to study. Accordingly, from 1685 onwards, the Town Council made a series of moves aimed toward the setting up of a medical school in Edinburgh. These did not, however, bear real fruit until 1724 when a grand total of six young medical professors were appointed to the Town's College and the medical school firmly established.

One of the main architects of the renewed initiative in medical education was George Drummond, the most influential of Edinburgh's eighteenth-century provosts. Drummond was also the prime mover behind the planning of the New Town. The inception of the medical school formed an integral part of a strategy to enhance the status of Scotland's capital, in the wake of the loss of the Parliament in 1707. The broadly based curriculum of the medical school must therefore be seen as complementing the wide streets, elegant terraces and bold bridges of the city's eighteenth-century physical renewal.

The rise to prominence of its medical school was, of course, roughly contemporaneous with Edinburgh's own ascent toward being the 'Athens of the North' – the principal locus of the remarkable social, intellectual and cultural developments now referred to as the Scottish Enlightenment. Undoubtedly the medical school both benefited from and contributed to the general cultural prestige of the city in the later half of the eighteenth century. The teachings of the medical professors reflected many of the scientific and educational ideas characteristic of the Scottish Enlightenment.

All six of the founding professors had received at least part of their training at Leyden and initially they largely followed the iatromechanical teachings of the great Dutch professor and medical systematist, Hermann Boerhaave. In doing so they were also being consistent with an older tradition of Scottish medical Newtonianism, as developed in, for example, the work of Archibald Pitcairne. In the 1740s and 1750s, with the appointment of a new generation of professors, notably William Cullen and Robert Whytt, however, a novel conception of how the human body worked was developed. Cullen, Whytt and their colleagues accorded a central importance to the nervous system in the overall integration of bodily functions. They held that the nerves were imbued with a 'sentient principle' which bridged the Cartesian divide between mind and body. Moreover, the nervous system not only communicated feeling from one organ of the body to another, but also responded to environmental circumstances. One's feelings, one's sensitivity, were thus a function of where and how one lived. In other words, this distinctively Scottish physiological theory laid particular stress upon organic integration and upon an intimate relation between man's moral qualities and the physical and social conditions of existence. It is interesting that the moral and social philosophers of the Scottish Enlightenment also stressed the importance of social cohesion and integration. Indeed Adam Smith, Adam Ferguson and David Hume all invoked aspects of the Edinburgh theory of nerve function to support the emphasis that they placed upon social solidarity and to legitimise the central role they accorded to 'men of feeling' as the natural leaders of a civilised and progressive society.

By the late eighteenth century the Town Council's scheme for the improvement of Edinburgh through the development of medical teaching had succeeded magnificently. Edinburgh had displaced Leyden as the foremost medical school in Europe. Most Scottish medical students now chose to study at home and large numbers of aspiring physicians were attracted from outwith Scotland, as the Council had hoped. Many came from England and from Ireland, especially Presbyterians and Non-Conformists, who were excluded from their home colleges of Oxford, Cambridge and Trinity College, Dublin. Significant numbers also came from Continental Europe and the Americas.

One may point to several reasons why Edinburgh Town Council's initiative in setting up its medical school was so remarkably successful. Glasgow and St Andrews Universities both made attempts to establish medical teaching at around this time but Edinburgh's faculty, although not always sustained at its original number, remained much more substantial than its rivals. The Council had, moreover, been sensible enough to appoint as professors young men who were not distracted by the need to teach other subjects nor unduly occupied with the demands of their medical practices. The initiative also had the important political support of the Incorporation of Surgeons. Alexander Monro, who already taught apprentices at Surgeons' Hall, transferred to the university as its professor of anatomy. The teachers were not salaried and were thus dependent on the class fees they received from their students. This circumstance encouraged them to take pedagogy seriously and to be sensitive to the needs of their students. Many of the original appointees were men of genuine ability and, with the later appointments of the calibre of, for example, William Cullen, Joseph Black, Robert Whytt, and Alexander Monro *secundus*, Edinburgh assembled an array of talent to equal, indeed to surpass, most of the medical faculties of Europe.

Another important factor in Edinburgh's popularity was that the Edinburgh professors, led by William Cullen in 1757, greatly enhanced the attractiveness and accessibility of their courses by adopting English rather than Latin as the language of instruction. Edinburgh was also a relatively cheap place at which to study. The students did not live in colleges but found their own accommodation, at whatever price they could afford, in the town. They were free to organise societies for mutual support and the encouragement of study. Unless they wished to graduate, and many did not, they could choose to attend only those classes they were particularly interested in. The class fees, while significant, were not prohibitive to those from a 'middling station' in society. Indeed, the relative inexpensiveness and accessibility of a Scottish medical education was one of the reasons why, from the late eighteenth century onwards, the profession of physic gradually ceased to be the domain of the younger sons of aristocracy and the scions of the landed gentry and became predominately a middle-class occupation.

From the 1760s, the Edinburgh curriculum came to reflect the need to provide a medical education which was accessible and appropriate to a new generation of students, whose attitudes were more business-like and whose pace of study less leisured than their predecessors' had been. The sixteenth and seventeenth centuries had produced a number of important scientific discoveries, notably the circulation of the blood, and a major enhancement of the understanding of human anatomy. But, at the beginning of the eighteenth century, the medical textbooks were still largely characterised by the complex and arcane niceties of the Scholastic tradition. It might indeed be fairly said of William Cullen that he 'did not add a single new fact to medical science' but his importance lies in his role in the reorganisation and transformation of medical knowledge and pedagogy.

Cullen was very interested in the classification of diseases, applying to medical phenomena the exemplar of the Swedish naturalist, Carl Linnaeus, who had successfully ordered botanical taxonomy and nomenclature. Cumbersome and pedantic as Cullen's nosology may seem to the modern reader, it represented to his contemporaries a major attempt to organise and, thus, to simplify medical knowledge. Such reorganisation had the important effect of making the principles of medical theory and practice more plainly taught, more easily learned and more readily applied than had previously been the case. The popularity of Cullen's own textbook *First Lines of the Practice of Physic*, first published in 1776, lies largely in the extent to which it served the distinctive needs of the Edinburgh student body, who were eager to learn but who demanded a quick return on their investments of time and money. *First Lines* went through several editions and was not wholly superseded until well into the nineteenth century.

The tendency of the Edinburgh teachers to simplify the medical curriculum might be said to have come to its apotheosis in the hands of John Brown, Cullen's pupil and later his bitter rival. Brown attributed all disease to two pathological processes – either the tissues were in too excited a state or they were not excited enough. Therapeutics was thus reduced to the provision of either stimulating or soothing agents. In remarkable contrast to the complex polypharmacy of orthodox physic, Brown favoured only two simple remedies – laudanum for stimulation, alcohol where sedation was required. The 'Brunonian System', as it became known, attracted many followers in Edinburgh, in Europe and in the Americas. Support for it was, however, short-lived.

Another reaction to the complexity and over-elaboration of eighteenth-century orthodox physic may be seen in the work of William Buchan, whose *Domestic Medicine* was published in 1769. Buchan's intention was to make the theory and practice of physic fully accessible to the general reader. His book was an outstanding success, in Scotland and internationally, going through many editions and being translated into several languages. It was said that *Domestic Medicine* and the Bible were the two books to be found in every croft and farmhouse in Scotland. While Buchan was broadly true to the received principles, if not the established practice, of orthodox regimen and therapy, *Domestic Medicine* may be regarded as a significant meeting point between the academic and the folk medical traditions.

Undoubtedly another major reason for the success of the Edinburgh Medical School was its association with the Edinburgh Royal Infirmary, which was founded in 1729 (see Plate 63). One of the self-conscious aims of the founders was to emulate the philanthropic institutions of London, to display that Edinburgh could look after its sick poor as well as the English capital. In 1738 the Infirmary was provided with new premises, built to a plan worthy of the grandest of aristocratic town houses. Like the medical school and the New Town, the Edinburgh Royal Infirmary was an expression of pride in, and aspiration for, the city and its institutions. Moreover, like the Scottish Enlightenment itself, the Infirmary reflected the characteristic eighteenth-century notion of social improvement. To the city fathers the cost of building a hospital could be justified on the grounds that adequate medical care, by restoring the sick to health, would thus equip them for useful and gainful employment, aiding the economy and reducing welfare expenditure. It is no coincidence, moreover, that many of the early patients of the Infirmary were domestic servants, often indeed the servants of the governors and sponsors of the hospital. The Infirmary, therefore, was focus of medical charity, enlightened economic self-interest, and civic pride – and not necessarily in that order of priority.

Edinburgh Royal Infirmary also functioned, from very early in its history, as a major educational resource. In 1738 its managers began to issue student passes which, at the cost of two guineas, granted the holder permission to enter the wards during certain hours of the day, to follow attending staff on their rounds, to observe surgical operations, and to refer to the case records kept by the clinical clerks. In 1748, John Rutherford, professor of the practice of medicine at the university, was granted permission by the managers to organise a formal course of clinical lectures in the Infirmary. These classes, designed to supplement and enlarge the instruction already given at the bedside, were given in the hospital's amphitheatre, to allow the attendance of large numbers of auditors.

By 1750, the success of Rutherford's initiative had persuaded the managers to set aside a ten-bed ward especially for clinical teaching. This clinical ward would be open throughout the academic year and would be occupied by patients individually selected by the professor. In 1756 Rutherford, Alexander Monro *secundus*, William Cullen and Robert Whytt agreed to teach the clinical classes in rotation. The capacity of the clinical wards was expanded first to twenty and eventually to one hundred patients. The roots of the managers' enthusiasm for clinical teaching lay in the fees that the medical students were willing to pay for access to it. In the last decades of the century, receipts from student tickets were the hospital's single largest source of revenue.

The scale and authority of its clinical teaching set the seal on the success of Edinburgh Medical School in the late eighteenth century. In beginning his clinical lecturing, Rutherford was following a Dutch model of hospital-based teaching of physic. A hospital the size of the Edinburgh Royal Infirmary, however, was able to provide a much wider range of clinical material, and thus a better clinical course, than could the twelve-bed institution available to the professors in Leyden. Moreover, the surgeons had been able, albeit after much political manoeuvring, to ensure that they were not excluded from teaching in the Infirmary. Thus surgery was side by side with physic – a circumstance which helped gradually to erode the distinction between the two branches of medicine.

The fact that clinical teaching was organised effectively and on a considerable scale in the Infirmary is often cited as one of the glories of the Edinburgh Medical School and one of its principal claims to historical distinction. This assessment is not entirely mistaken. The character of Edinburgh's clinical teaching needs to be put into careful perspective, however. It should be noted firstly that, in accepting the need for an element of bedside training for their students, the physicians were only imitating the routine and long-established practices of surgeons. Secondly, the teaching provided in the Edinburgh Royal Infirmary in the eighteenth century was very different from what came to be regarded, in the nineteenth century, as an adequate clinical education. The instruction was purely verbal. Indeed, Edinburgh clinical teaching has been characterised as 'stentorian'. The numbers of students were so large that the teacher had to shout to make himself heard. Students were not directly trained, other than informally by example, in the practical tasks of diagnosis and therapy. Many students regarded the privilege of reading and copying the physicians' and surgeons' case journals as being the most valuable return that they received for their investment in an admission ticket.

It should also be noted that many aspiring physicians, having graduated from Edinburgh, felt the need to augment their education by further periods of study elsewhere. The Edinburgh curriculum was often identified by contemporaries as being weak in its provision of both clinical experience and practical anatomical dissection. Walking the wards of the large London hospitals was the accepted way of remedying the first deficiency. It has recently been recognised by historians of medicine that, as far as eighteenth-century clinical teaching is concerned, the London hospitals collectively must be regarded as the major teaching centre, even although the metropolis did not, at that time, have a university medical school.

The second deficiency could be effectively addressed by undertaking a course of study at one of the London private schools of anatomy, the most famous of which being that of Great Windmill Street, run by the Scottish obstetrician and anatomist, William Hunter. These schools were also attended by trainee surgeons. It was in his brother's school that the great Scottish surgeon, John Hunter, received his anatomical training. Another Scotsman, William Smellie, gave private instruction in obstetrics, an area of practice into which male surgeons and physicians were only beginning to intrude. In the metropolitan success of men like Smellie and the Hunters, one also sees another aspect of the cultural significance of medicine to Scotland – namely that a medical qualification, whether in surgery or in physic, allowed its sons, and later its daughters, to take the high road south to seek their fame and fortune. In the late eighteenth and nineteenth centuries, this large-scale emigration of medically trained personnel was, to a large extent, itself a product of the success of the Edinburgh School, which resulted in a large surplus in the supply of doctors. However, the London College of Physicians, which subscribed to a more traditional model of the physician as a man of ornamental learning and social distinction and which effectively recognised only the degrees of Oxford and Cambridge, exerted itself to exclude the Scottish graduates from the most lucrative and prestigious forms of practice in the metropolis.

The Edinburgh-trained physician might also, if he could afford it, embark on a medical Grand Tour of Continental Europe. In the 1790s, for example, Andrew Duncan junior, son of the professor of the institutes of medicine, visited a number of medical schools and hospitals in The Netherlands, Germany, Austria-Hungary and Italy. Duncan junior was being groomed for greatness by his father – he later became professor of materia medica and one of the leading members of the early nineteenth-century medical school. Duncan's tour served him both as post-graduate study and as finishing school. He went to learn about European methods of medical practice and to make the acquaintance of the learned in each country. But he also thought it important, as he wrote to tell his father, 'to keep company with genteel people . . . it will in the end be more to my advantage by improving my manners and knowledge of the world, articles essential to success in my profession'. Thus, the élite eighteenth-century Edinburgh physician still cultivated social graces and literary and ornamental learning, as well as technical knowledge and skill. He wished to be a gentleman, or as near a one as his financial circumstances permitted. Physic remained, in other words, part of a wider humanistic culture.

Not every Edinburgh graduate had either the ambition or the funds to aspire to an academic career or a practice with an upper-class clientele. Many were happy to settle as general practitioners in provincial towns. Even that career plan required capital, however, and many newly qualified physicians had exhausted their resources in gaining their education. For them, a salaried post in the army, navy or East India Company medical service was often the best option. Such was the volume of this recruitment that a popular song of the period noted that the chief exports of the port of Leith were 'red herrings for the Colonies, surgeons' mates for the Navy'.

As has been noted above, the official curriculum in Edinburgh was regarded even by contemporaries as being deficient in certain respects. Before the medical school had been founded, the Incorporation of Surgeons had organised anatomical demonstrations. But, from the 1720s, the university had a monopoly of anatomical teaching. Alexander Monro *secundus* was, however, a consulting physician and in the hands of the successive members of the Monro dynasty, anatomy was taught in an academic and systematic manner. The Edinburgh surgeon, John Bell, vividly characterised the practical deficiencies of this approach:

> In Dr Monro's class, unless there be a fortunate series of bloody murders, not three subjects are dissected in the year. On the remains of a subject fished up from the bottom of a tub of spirits, are demonstrated those delicate nerves which are to be avoided or divided in our operations; and these are demonstrated once at the distance of 100 feet! – nerves and arteries which the surgeon has to dissect, at the peril of his patient's life.

Accordingly, in the 1780s, John Bell began to offer private lectures on surgical anatomy. He built an anatomical school and was so successful that members of the medical school organised against him. Edinburgh's learned élite were often riven by vigorous disputes but this one was of especial vehemence. Bell was forced to abandon his teaching, which was taken over for a time by his brother, Charles.

The Bells' school was only one of a number of establishments in late eighteenth and nineteenth-century Edinburgh which offered medical instruction complementary to the official curriculum. These extra-mural schools were collectively a very important component of the teaching of medicine in the city. The most famous, or rather notorious, extra-mural teacher was probably Robert Knox, whose anatomical classes, at the height of their popularity, attracted more than five hundred students. His reputation was, however, destroyed by his involvement in the Burke and Hare affair of 1828.

Public disquiet over the practices which the Burke trial revealed resulted in the passage of the Anatomy Act of 1832. This provided teachers of anatomy with a legal supply of bodies. It should be remembered that, enlightened as this legislation might have been in the support it expressed for education and research, the bodies it allocated for dissection were those of the inmates of the workhouses who were unfortunate enough to die without means or family to provide them with a burial. The provisions of the Anatomy Act were thus hated and feared by the urban poor, a circumstance which adversely affected popular attitudes towards academic medicine.

Another important innovation in which Scotland played a major part was the establishment of a medical periodical press. The first such journal to be published in Scotland, *Medical Essays and Observations*, appeared in 1731 and ran for six volumes. Continuous publication of a medical periodical in Edinburgh dates from 1773 with the initiation of *Medical and Philosophical Commentaries*. This was followed in 1796 by *Annals of Medicine* and then, in 1805, by the *Edinburgh Medical and Surgical Journal*. As was the custom at the time, *Medical and Philosophical Commentaries* and *Annals of Medicine* were run by Andrew Duncan senior as a private business. He was later assisted by his son who eventually became the editor-in-chief of the *Edinburgh Medical and Surgical Journal*. With his wide acquaintance among the leading medical men of Britain and Europe, and his working knowledge of more than one European language, Andrew Duncan junior was well qualified to be the editor of a medical journal. Under his guidance the *Edinburgh Medical and Surgical Journal* became the leading British medical periodical, publishing a wide variety of research papers and providing authoritative reviews of the latest scientific and clinical developments taking place in Britain and Europe.

Such an information service was very much required in the early nineteenth century for the pace of medical and scientific research was quickening. Moreover, with the rise of the Paris School, Edinburgh had been displaced as the foremost European centre for medical education. Much has been written about the causes of the decline of the city's medical school from its pre-eminent greatness in the eighteenth century. It is certainly true that the tendency to allow sons to inherit their fathers' chairs sometimes filled key posts with undistinguished individuals. Also, the fact that the professors' salaries were directly dependent upon the numbers of students they taught meant that the established faculty tended to oppose the setting-up of new chairs. Thus the school was slow to respond to the greater degree of specialisation which the expansion of medical knowledge in the nineteenth century demanded.

It must be acknowledged that, just as the last glimmerings of Edinburgh as the 'Athens of the North' were extinguished with the demise of Sir Walter Scott, so the decline of Edinburgh's medical school was largely inevitable. The medical faculty of a provincial city, for that was what Scotland's capital had now become, could not hope forever to enjoy dominance over larger, more politically important, centres. The historical trend toward centralisation of cultural and scientific leadership in the metropolis would, sooner or later, have undermined Edinburgh's pre-eminence in medicine, whatever the success of local initiatives. It should be noted, however, that the majority of the staff who established the reputations of the new medical schools in London, and in Dublin, were trained in Edinburgh. Thomas Hodgkin, Thomas Addison, Richard Bright, Dominic Corrigan and William Stokes might be cited as examples. Similarly, Edinburgh-trained doctors played a major role in the foundation of many of the medical schools of North America.

In the wider European context, medicine in France had, by this time, received a major stimulus with the educational and organisational reforms which followed the French Revolution. Another important factor in the development of French medicine was that the enormous hospitals of Paris could supply clinical and research material on a scale quite unattainable in Scotland. Later in the century, the rapid development in Germany of organic chemistry and a wide variety of technologies, consequent upon intensive industrialisation, coupled with a radical reform of higher education and a degree of state support for science, established the indisputable international supremacy of German science. Many German scientific and industrial advances had medical implications, particularly in the fields of pharmacology and medical instrumentation. It would be a long time before Britain as a whole, far less Scotland, could challenge German dominance in these areas. Furthermore, the introduction of salaried teaching posts in the German medical schools encouraged the development of clinical and scientific specialisations and of formal post-graduate education.

It could, however, be argued that Edinburgh's decline was only a relative one. The Edinburgh professors may not have been able to set the agenda in medicine in the 1820s as they had done in the 1780s, but the medical school could still reasonably aspire to excellence, if no longer to supremacy. There was certainly some dead wood on the faculty but several of the academic Edinburgh physicians did attend carefully to the new work of the Paris School. Andrew Duncan junior was prominent among those who endeavoured to undertake investigations in pathological anatomy, for instance, with a rigour and precision not seen among their eighteenth-century counterparts. The experience gained in the dissection room also prepared Duncan and his colleagues to appreciate the possibilities of 'anatomising the living' which were offered by the newly developed physical methods of diagnosis. Stethoscopy, for example, which had been invented in Paris in 1817, was more quickly taken up in Edinburgh than elsewhere in Britain. The stethoscope was in routine use in the Edinburgh Royal Infirmary by 1830, a full decade or more before the staff of the London hospitals arrived at a complete consensus as to its value. Undoubtedly, the Scottish tradition of clinical teaching – however inadequate subsequent developments might have made it seem – helped prepare students to benefit from visits to the Paris hospitals. It is also possible that Scotland's traditionally stronger cultural links with France were a factor in promoting a more positive attitude to the Parisian innovation in Edinburgh than in London. In the period immediately after the Napoleonic Wars the Scots were probably more receptive to French developments in scholarship and science than were the English. Even in the late 1820s there was a conspicuous element of Francophobia in some of the pronouncements made about the stethoscope by older London physicians. The instrument was called a 'French bauble' and an 'insult to John Bull'. Such sentiments are absent from the record of events in Edinburgh.

The nineteenth century also saw the rise of medical education in other Scottish centres. As we have noted above, Glasgow University had made attempts to establish medical teaching in the early eighteenth century. At this time it was still largely dominated by its major role in training ministers for the Scottish Church. The clerical academics were not particularly impressed by Continental secular learning but sought rather to revive and purify Calvinism in Scotland. Moreover, the Glasgow Faculty of Physicians and Surgeons, which had been founded in 1599, opposed the establishment of a medical school in the university fearing interference with its own teaching and licensing prerogatives. In 1746, however, William Cullen began successfully to lecture on medicine under the auspices of the university and in 1751, he was appointed to the chair of medicine. Continuous teaching of medicine in Glasgow dates from this period. But, in 1755, Cullen was attracted to a more lucrative post at Edinburgh University as, in 1766, was the chemist, Joseph Black. Their successors continued teaching but tended to have divided loyalties, being preoccupied by their medical practices and identifying more strongly with the Faculty of Physicians and Surgeons than with the university. Crucially, moreover, Glasgow did not have a large voluntary hospital to provide clinical instruction. Nevertheless the numbers of students in Glasgow gradually increased, from twenty in 1750 to nearly a hundred by 1800. While Edinburgh, by contrast, had more than six hundred medical students by this time, it should be noted that, in the wider British or indeed the European contemporary context, Glasgow University's production of doctors was by no means insignificant.

The enormous expansion of the population of Glasgow, as it was transformed into a major industrial city in the late eighteenth and early nineteenth centuries, led to the foundation of large voluntary hospitals which supplied the medical school with essential facilities for clinical instruction and research. In this period, however, the development of Glasgow's medical teaching was further handicapped by an acrimonious dispute between the university and the Faculty of Physicians and Surgeons, which refused to allow Glasgow graduates to practise medicine in the city until they had been further examined by the Faculty. This dispute seriously drained the energies and the funds of the medical professors and was not finally resolved until the passing of the Medical Reform Act in 1858.

The educational reforms imposed upon the Scottish universities, also in 1858, following the Royal Commission of 1831, introduced a more professional (if perhaps less distinctively Scottish) character to teaching throughout all the Scottish medical schools. Moreover, the strong links which Glasgow University forged with local industry stimulated the development of science and technology generally within the university. As in Edinburgh, a number of extra-mural schools developed, supplementing the teaching of the university faculty – the most famous of these, Anderson's College, remained in existence until after the Second World War. By the last decades of the nineteenth century, Glasgow's medical school, while still numerically smaller than Edinburgh's, could legitimately regard itself as having attained equality of status and prestige. Relations between the two centres have been characterised by more or less friendly rivalry and emulation up to the present day. By the 1890s, moreover, substantial and important medical faculties had become established in the Universities of Aberdeen and St Andrews.

The Medical Reform Act removed all geographical limitations to medical practice in Britain. It thus had the very important effect of freeing Scottish graduates practising in England from the restrictions and limitations which the London College of Physicians and the Society of Apothecaries had for long attempted to impose upon them. The Act fully established throughout Britain the legality of the general practice of medicine and thus finally fully legitimised the form of medical training received at the Scottish universities. Pressure from Scottish graduates and from the Edinburgh Royal Colleges played a large part in persuading Parliament to pass this legislation.

As has been noted above, however, in the nineteenth century Scottish medical education and practice was no longer as distinctive as it had been. The standard by which the quality of Scottish medicine as a whole would be now judged was the extent to which the internationally accepted exemplars of clinical practice and scientific research were adopted and utilised. As far as clinical innovation is concerned, Scottish surgeons were now more prominent than physicians. Surgery had, by this time, been fully accepted into the sphere of academic medicine – Edinburgh University finally establishing a chair of 'systematic' surgery in 1831. James Syme, Edinburgh's Professor of Clinical Surgery, was a major operative innovator, as were Robert Liston, also in Edinburgh, and John Burns in Glasgow. James Young Simpson, Professor of Midwifery in Edinburgh, was an important pioneer of anaesthesia.

The most famous Scottish-based surgeon of the nineteenth century was Joseph Lister, who held surgical chairs in both Glasgow and Edinburgh. Lister closely followed the work of the French chemist, Louis Pasteur, on the spoiling of wine and beer and was thus inspired to apply the principles of the newly developed Germ Theory to the problem of the septic infection of surgical wounds. Surgical sepsis was a major problem in the Glasgow Royal Infirmary, where Lister worked in the 1860s. This line of research led to the development of the so-called 'antiseptic' technique. After considerable controversy, the Listerian reforms came eventually to be regarded as the dawn of a new age of operative and scientific innovation in surgery. Lister was the first medical man to be raised to the peerage – a potent symbol of the complete emancipation of surgery from its origins as a lowly craft.

It is possible to argue that many of Lister's procedures were impractical and that they were based on the faulty premise that sepsis is primarily a result of contamination by air-borne pathogens. Perhaps the real historical importance of Listerian antisepsis – apart, that is, from its symbolic significance for the social and professional status of surgeons – lies in its role as the precursor of 'aseptic' surgery. The aseptic technique, rather than attempting to prevent the access of air to the wound, endeavoured to ensure that surgery took place in a sterile environment. One of the principal pioneers of asepsis was the pre-eminent Glasgow professor of surgery, Sir William Macewen.

As already noted, the industrial growth of Glasgow in the early part of the nineteenth century produced a very rapid increase in the city's population. The supply of housing did not keep up with the expansion, nor did the sanitary provisions of water and sewerage. The result was severe overcrowding and squalor. There were parts of Glasgow in which occupancy rates of fourteen person per room were not uncommon. Problems of poor housing and inadequate sanitation were compounded by poverty. Glasgow, in the mid-nineteenth century, for all its industrial wealth, was still, for many working-class people, a low-wage economy. The effectiveness of the old Poor Law, intended as a support for the destitute of individual parishes, was blunted by the new mobility of the workforce and by the sheer intensity of industrial urbanisation. The combination of poverty and squalor imposed a great burden of disease upon the community. Endemic diseases like tuberculosis, rickets, syphilis, alcoholism, and drug addiction flourished. And so did epidemic diseases such as typhoid and, most feared of all, cholera. There were outbreaks of cholera in Glasgow in 1832, 1848 and 1853. Typhus was both endemic and epidemic. In other words, Glasgow and its surrounding towns faced a major problem of public health. The situation in parts of Edinburgh and Dundee, and even in smaller towns like Stirling and Forfar, was very nearly as bad.

The first Scottish Medical Officer of Health, Henry Littlejohn, took up his post in Edinburgh in 1861. Glasgow followed suit with the appointment of William Tennant Gairdner in 1863 and James Russell in 1871. Medical officers of health had wide powers and could deal with problems of overcrowding, adulteration of food and drink and the control of infectious disease. But the real answer to the health problems of the cities lay with the legislator, the town planner and the civil engineer rather than with the medical profession directly. The most effective action of the medical officer of health often consisted of convincing his political masters of the need for legislative or executive action.

One of the major important improvements in the health of Glasgow came with the completion, in 1859, of a scheme to provide the city with a sufficient quantity of clean water. Improved water supply was almost certainly the reason why Glasgow escaped the cholera epidemic of 1866. Moreover, rather like the Edinburgh Royal Infirmary in the eighteenth century, the Loch Katrine scheme served a dual purpose. If one follows the course of the supply, from the dams of the loch, along mighty pipelines, through the elegantly laid-out cascades and holding ponds in Mugdock, to the grandly ornate fountains of Kelvingrove Park, officially opened by Queen Victoria, one sees a magnificent expression both of Scottish engineering skill and of the pride and confidence of Glasgow's Victorian city fathers. The Loch Katrine scheme thus functioned both to improve the health of the citizens of Glasgow and to provide a civic monument, an emblem of Glasgow's acquired status as the second city of the British Empire.

The requirements of public health medicine encouraged the introduction into Scotland of the newly developed science of microbiology. The Laboratory of the Royal College of Physicians of Edinburgh was established in 1887 and was the first institution of its kind in Britain. One of its chief functions was the routine analysis of samples and specimens for public health doctors. The laboratory also undertook research in physiological chemistry, physiology, nutrition and environmental health. The value of microbiology for Edinburgh's brewing industry persuaded a local brewer to endow the university with the John Usher Institute of Public Health, which also provided an important institutional focus for the new sciences in Scotland.

Overall, however, the Scottish universities were relatively slow to exploit the full potential of the new disciplines of scientific medicine. Edinburgh University, for example, did not appoint a professor of microbiology until 1913. This tardiness was, in part, due to the distinctive character of the Scottish medical schools. Strong commitments to medical education and clinical treatment produced an ethos which discouraged physiologists and biochemists from pursuing research projects which did not carry an immediate clinical implication. By contrast, the new departments of physiology and biochemistry at the University of Cambridge, for example, were always relatively independent of such utilitarian concerns and so were able to develop more autonomous and more successful programmes of research. It was to be some time before the Scottish medical faculties fully resolved the problem of accommodating laboratory science within institutional structures in which clinical priorities were necessarily dominant.

Another important innovation of the late nineteenth century was the entry of women into the medical profession. In 1869 Edinburgh University allowed Sophia Jex-Blake to begin a medical course and thus became the first British medical school to admit a woman. Many obstacles were put in her way by both professors and students, however, and she did not complete her studies in Edinburgh. An extra-mural school for women opened in Edinburgh in 1886, with clinical teaching at Leith Hospital. The Universities Act of 1889 finally clarified the legal situation and allowed women access to medical education.

The later half of the nineteenth century saw a general rise in the status and prosperity of the newly unified and legally recognised medical profession. Over-production of doctors continued and competition among new recruits to the profession was fierce. But even in quite small country towns the patronage of the affluent merchant and professional middle classes meant that a practitioner could make a comfortable living, if only he could establish his reputation. In some rural areas, however, and especially in large parts of the Highlands and islands, private practice was not economically viable due to the large distances to be covered and the sparseness and relative poverty of the population. Awareness that the inhabitants of the Highlands and islands did not have adequate access to medical assistance led to the setting up, in 1914, of the Highlands and Islands Medical Scheme, which provided for the first time Treasury support for doctors' salaries and equipment. The Scheme was, thus, an important precursor of the National Health Service, which provided general state support for Scotland's hospitals and medical practitioners from 1948.

With the decline of the great epidemic diseases of the nineteenth century and an enormous improvement in living conditions, the population of Scotland was probably healthier by 1950 than it had ever been previously. In the post-war period, however, Scotland's mortality and morbidity rates have not improved as fast as those of our Continental neighbours. In Scotland, moreover, the patterns of increased mortality and chronic morbidity among the urban working class which became established in the nineteenth century are still evident. The rate of infant mortality, for instance, among the working class has certainly shown a great diminution but it has still not fallen as far as that of the middle classes. Geographical inequalities of health, largely associated with class and income, still strongly characterise the medical map of Scotland – even although tuberculosis and syphilis have been replaced by cancer and heart disease as the major causes of serious ill-health among adults. The new threat of AIDS has developed a similar social geography. It is an abiding paradox of the medical culture of Glasgow, for example, that a medical school internationally famous for both clinical and public health medicine should be situated in one of the most unhealthy cities in Western Europe.

The Scottish medical profession enjoys considerable status and respect, partly due to its perceived efficacy, partly due to skilful public relations, partly due to the value the Scots have traditionally placed on education and professional expertise. There can be no doubt that orthodox medical practice has achieved overwhelming popular legitimacy in Scotland. But there has also long been a strand in Scots literature which has expressed scepticism as to the pretensions of medical art and science. Robert Henryson, in the fifteenth century, poked fun at the self-serving obscurantism of physicians and apothecaries. William Dunbar fearfully noted the impotency of physic in the face of human mortality. In his great poem 'Death and Dr Hornbook', Robert Burns vividly delineated the terrible ambiguities of medical power. The learned and resourceful Dr Hornbook is able to frustrate Death with his 'doctor's saws and whittles, of a' dimensions, shapes, an' mettles'. But his powerful drugs and vigorous interventions kill as many as they cure:

A bonie lass, ye ken her name,
Some ill-brewn drink had hov'd her wame;
She trusts hersel, to hide the shame,
    In Hornbook's care;
Horn sent her aff to her lang hame
    To hide it there.

Hugh MacDiarmid, in the twentieth century, argued many times that scientific advancement could not, by itself, produce social justice.

The purpose of this essay has been to show how medicine has always been an integral and, to a considerable extent a distinctive, aspect of Scottish cultural life. Scotland's medicine links the nation's culture to a common European heritage as surely as does its poetry or its law.

Books for Further Reading

John Bannerman, *The Beatons: a Medical Kindred in the Classical Gaelic Tradition* (Edinburgh, 1986)

John D. Comrie, *History of Scottish Medicine*, 2 vols. (London, 1932)

David Hamilton, *The Healers: a History of Medicine in Scotland* (Edinburgh, 1981)

Christopher Lawrence, 'The nervous system and society in the Scottish Enlightenment' in Barry Barnes and Steven Shapin (eds.), *Natural Order: Historical Studies of Scientific Culture* (Beverly Hills and London, 1979)

Gordon McLachlan (ed.), *Improving the Common Weal: Aspects of Scottish Health Services 1900–1984* (Edinburgh, 1987)

J.B. Morrell, 'The University of Edinburgh in the late eighteenth century: its scientific eminence and academic structure', *Isis 62* (1971)

Malcolm Nicolson, 'The introduction of percussion and stethoscopy to early nineteenth-century Edinburgh' in W.F. Bynum and R. Porter, *The Five Senses in Medicine* (Cambridge and London, 1992)

Gunther R. Risse, *Hospital Life in Enlightenment Scotland: Care and Teaching at the Royal Infirmary of Edinburgh* (Cambridge and London, 1986)

Lisa Rosner, *Medical Education in the Age of Improvement: Edinburgh Students and Apprentices* (Edinburgh, 1991)

Law

NEIL MACCORMICK

I t is possible to capture some of Scotland's character as a cultural entity just by allusion to a few books and documents: *The Declaration of Arbroath*, stating the right of the Scots to their kingdom; the *First Book of Discipline*, revolutionising Church, state and society; the *Thrie Estatis*, exalting John the Commonweal and the right of the poor man to get law; Burns's poems, uniting popular song with high art; Scott's *Waverley*, which, like his own *Lady of the Lake* in verse, re-bonded Lowland and Highland Scotland together in popular imagination, capturing also the European romantic imagination; Duncan Ban MacIntyre's poetry, *Sunset Song* by Gibbon and *The Silver Darlings* by Gunn. The present essay adds another, perhaps less generally known than these, but fully their match in cultural importance: James Viscount Stair's *Institutions of the Law of Scotland*, first published in 1681, with a second authoritative edition in 1693.

Scotland, like Switzerland, is a country without a single national language; crucial though the Church of Scotland and other Presbyterian reformed churches are and have been in forming the modern character of the people, there is no longer a unity of religion in the land; for nearly three hundred years, there has been no Parliament or independent government of Scotland. What then makes Scotland Scotland, what objective correlative is there for that widespread and obvious subjective sense of identity that makes Scotland so unquestionably a nation, not a mere region?

Scots law is at the heart of the answer to that question. We are apt to say that Scotland is not, or lacks, a state; but Scotland does in fact retain certain great offices and institutions of state, and has done so in unbroken historic descent over a remarkable period. The offices of Lord President of the Court of Session and Lord Justice General; Lord Clerk Register; Lord Justice Clerk; Lord Advocate; Lord Lyon, King of Arms; Dean of the Faculty of Advocates; Deputy Keeper of the Signet; the presidencies of local Faculties of Procurators and Societies of Solicitors and Advocates, and in modern times the Presidency of the Law Society of Scotland; these, and the two supreme courts

– the Court of Session in civil matters and the High Court of Justiciary in criminal –
furnish in complete panoply one of the three branches of state, the judicial. Moreover,
their existence was given a constitutional guarantee in the foundation instrument of the
United Kingdom, the Articles of Union that took effect in 1707 through Acts of Union
passed in 1706–7 by the two uniting Parliaments, that of England and that of Scotland.
(That there were two Acts makes it inept to refer, as is sometimes done, especially in
English accounts of the constitution, to 'The Act [*sic*] of Union'.)

Even this foundational guarantee of Scots law's special status can, according to one
view of constitutional law, be revoked by ordinary legislation of the British Parliament.
That Parliament has technically the power to do so is denied by many Scots lawyers,
including some of the highest authority. In any event, so revolutionary a step would be
fraught with such risks that it is most unlikely ever to be contemplated politically.
Whenever steps of that sort have been considered in the past as a part of broader
schemes for judicial reform, they have been rather speedily abandoned once attention
has been drawn to their constitutional and political implications.

The Scottish courts and the law they administer are thus a fundamental part of the
constitution of the realm. Scotland as an entity has a distinct legal existence and
character. This is either an assumed background to, or even a conscious part of, as well
as a security for, the people's cultural self-definition. Scots law accordingly has
profound significance for Scotland. The character of the country can in some measure
be read from the books of its laws. Without the independence of the legal system, who
can say what would have become of Scotland these last three hundred years?

Whatever else might be said about the wisdom, patriotism, and pertinacity of the
Scottish Commissioners in the 1705–6 Union negotiations, the Articles of Union they
agreed, together with the associated legislation, did secure the Scottish Church from
the dominion of Canterbury and York, did secure distinctive local government, and did
secure a precociously well-developed educational system along with those two; but
above all they secured the law. Time, chance and legislation have diluted the others. But
the courts and the law they administer have remained in being with substantial
integrity, still as stipulated in 1706 without subordination to any 'Court in
Westminster Hall'.

This would surely not have happened but for the conditions set by the Scots
Commissioners for Union as their sticking point once federation (the Scots'
preference) had been rejected by England as unacceptable. The stipulation of the
required fundamental provisions among the terms of the Union was an absolutely
necessary condition for the continuing legal integrity of Scotland. But of itself it would
not have been sufficient. For what would it have availed had the law been inadequate or
hopelessly obscure? A modernising community needs law that is both intelligible and
adaptable. The political and civil circumstances of life in Scotland in the later sixteenth
century and through the seventeenth had not given her Parliament or Parliamentarians
much chance to focus systematically on the law; the courts had been subjected to
considerable disruption also.

A clear expository statement of the law of Scotland was not lacking, though. The
work was primarily Stair's in the *Institutions*, which dealt exclusively with civil law. A
word must also be said, however, of his contemporary Sir George Mackenzie of
Rosehaugh, 'bluidy Mackenzie' of the repression of conventicles. As King's Advocate,
Mackenzie had maintained a harsh enforcement of the criminal law; but he also
produced in his *Law and Customs of Scotland in Matters Criminal* (1678), the first text-

book of that criminal law. (On the civil law, Mackenzie brought out an adaptation for Scots law of the *Institutions* of Justinian, which was useful for students and as a model for later work, but in depth and detail not a patch on Stair's work.) Taking the work of Stair and Mackenzie together with the earlier seventeenth-century *Jus Feudale* (completed around 1600, but first published only in 1655) in which Sir Thomas Craig of Riccartoun gave an account of the feudal land law, we find that Scotland came into the Union not only with her law guaranteed constitutionally, but also with that same law available in clear and systematic presentations of all its main parts.

All three writers mentioned were jurists of considerable distinction, but Stair's work stands out. For beauty and elegance of presentation, and for the lucidly systematic approach he takes to his subject, his work stands comparison with the other great works of European law in the seventeenth century. Read aloud, for example to a class of students, it has something of the majesty and cadence of the King James Bible. Taken in context, it belongs among the institutional statements of national law which, as a genre, sprung up all over Europe in the later seventeenth century and on into the eighteenth. But, in distinguished company, Stair's work wins particular distinction from the philosophical originality and rigour of his approach to legal exposition. This is not altogether surprising, since in his earlier life the young James Dalrymple of Stair served in the University of Glasgow as a Regent Master in Philosophy from 1641 till 1647. Though he afterwards passed Advocate and went into practice, subsequently serving as a (civil) judge both during the Protectorate and after the Restoration, and becoming Lord President of the Court of Session in 1671 (with an interruption in political exile in the Netherlands 1681–89 terminated with the fall of James VII), he retained an active lifelong interest in philosophy till his death in 1695, and this shows through to good effect in his legal writing.

The *Institutions* express the idea of law as a rational order ordained by a benevolent and reasonable deity. Since it is a rational order, humans as rational creatures can by reflection and deliberation, especially deliberation by and with wise and experienced judges, develop an understanding of its principles. In this, though Scriptural revelation is of profound assistance, it is not essential for a grasp of the first foundations. These set basic obligations for humans, to which they are bound in obedience to God. The obligations are to refrain from harming others and to treat them honestly; and to fulfil family responsibilities. Beyond these 'obediential' obligations, humans are free creatures, at liberty to dispose of themselves as they see fit, and to acquire such natural goods as they need for their own survival and their families', each then owing every other the obligation of respect for their acquired assets. Further, their freedom is in their own power, in the sense that they are able to bind themselves by engagements (promises and contracts). These engagements may be freely entered for any licit purpose, but one is naturally under an obligation to fulfil engagements freely made.

From these building blocks, Stair constructs a picture of the law as grounded in three basic principles, the principles of 'obedience, freedom and engagement'. As frail and fallen creatures, humans cannot live unaidedly by direct reference to the basic principles of a rational law of nature, but need to establish ordered societies to develop more detailed regulation ('positive law') along the lines of these basic principles, and to provide impartial judges to settle complaints about breaches of obligations, and to furnish appropriate and enforceable remedies. So the positive law is aimed at human convenience and utility within the framework of fundamental obligations; its principles are 'society, property, and commerce' that is, humans should set up societies for their mutual defence and support, and protection of their rights; in human societies, property should be protected, and people encouraged to develop their assets to the common advantage; and should engage in trade and commerce with each other to distribute the fruits derived from each person's utilisation of natural talents or acquired assets.

Within this broad framework of general principle, Stair argues that the law can best be envisaged and expressed as a structure of rights and obligations. The underlying principles indicate a rational structure for the exposition of the rights and obligations in appropriate detail, and for a discussion of how they can be transferred among persons, and how they can be cognised and enforced by actions in the courts. The exposition of all these matters in the *Institutions* has the same clarity and elegance as the explanatory framework devised by the author.

Not merely did Stair succeed in his own terms, but he (as likewise Mackenzie and Craig) provided a model for successors in the eighteenth and nineteenth centuries. A series of very able commentators proceeded to give further and more up-to-date elucidations of Scots law. Outstanding among many significant writings are the work of three Edinburgh Professors of Scots Law, John Erskine (*Principles of the Law of Scotland*, first edition 1754; *An Institute of the Law of Scotland*, 1773), David Hume (*Commentaries on the Law of Scotland respecting Crimes*, 1797) and George Joseph Bell (*Commentaries on the Mercantile Jurisprudence of Scotland*, 1804). These works continued the institutional tradition set by Stair, and came to be recognised as works of particular authority on the law for succeeding generations. Both through scholarly study and through the activity of practising lawyers and judges, Scots law remained (and yet remains) a sturdy and independent member of the family of European legal systems. The courts and the members of the legal profession have played a leading and distinctive role in Scottish society, conscious of their trusteeship of a particular and in some respects admirable version of the omnipresent human attempt to order society according to a government of laws, not of the unbounded discretion of governments or officials.

Why can I call this a 'particular and in some respects admirable' member of the family of legal systems? To start with the question of particularity, it is important to stress that the originality and excellence of Stair's work, or that of the other institutional writers, was originality in representation and exposition of law, not in its invention. The law that Stair stated in his *Institutions* was the inheritance of many generations, an interweaving of many traditions, not a new-minted code. Without the work of the institutional writers, the inheritance might have withered and died. They modernised and made available the terms of the inheritance, but did not devise them. Stair himself in the original Preface to his work, addressed to King Charles II, laid stress upon the antiquity of the Scottish monarchy and its roots in the choice of the people rather than in conquest, and exhorts the king to take satisfaction in the antiquity and native vigour of the laws of the oldest of his kingdoms, the one to which his ancestors were wedded with a 'virgin Crown'.

Recent scholarship has indicated that Stair's point is grounded in sober fact, not mere prefatory flight of fancy or piety. Where earlier scholars of great authority saw Stair's work as a substantial reinvention of Scots law from the embers of the earlier materials, more recent work has identified strong threads of continuity in Scots law from the earliest times of the Scottish kingdom through to the seventeenth century – and, indeed, beyond that to the present day. Let us investigate these threads.

The earliest detectable element in Scots law is the Celtic, originating in the law brought by the Gaelic-speaking settlers of Dalriada from Ireland, and in due course mingling with traditions of the indigenous Pictish people with whom they became united in the ninth century AD. This in turn must have come to incorporate a good deal of the law and custom of the Nordic countries in the period of the Viking invasions and of Norse suzerainty over the Hebrides. (Unlike Orkney and Shetland, which remained Norse till much later and retained a form of udal law, the Hebrides came within a version of feudal law.) Certainly, the longest-enduring home of an originally Celtic body of law, in the Hebrides and adjacent mainland under the Lordship of the Isles, from the thirteenth to the sixteenth centuries, must have witnessed a substantial infusion of Norse custom into the Celtic heritage. The law governing family relationships and land-holding in north and west Scotland must have long had elements of this inheritance, and some of what is commonly if loosely understood of the 'clan system' in Scotland long reflected and even continues in a shadowy way to reflect this.

But in terms of formal legal doctrine, the law of land-holding in Scotland came to belong to the 'feudal system'. This originated in the customs of the Germanic tribes in their conquest of Western Europe right up to the bastions of Moorish Islamic rule in the Iberian peninsula, and was developed particularly by the 'Norman' descendants of Norse Vikings in northern France, spreading to England by conquest in 1066, and in the following century to Scotland by a process of imitative adaptation. The Norman influence in Scotland arrived by intermarriage and importation of warriors and servants of Scottish Kings engaged in modernisation of their kingdom. Feudalism originally involved the granting of land by a warrior leader as a purely personal 'fee' to a follower. But with the growth of settled authority and relatively fixed and defensible kingdoms, fees (or 'feus' as we call them in Scotland) came to be regarded as heritable by right in the family of their original holder, in return for continuing services. The landholder held land of the king, giving services for it; reciprocally, the king guaranteed protection and justice to his 'vassal'. He in turn could sub-grant land on a similarly reciprocal engagement to persons who counted as his vassals, and a chain of such tenures could exist. This process of extending the chain or of inserting new links in it was known as 'sub-infeudation'.

Where royal power existed through conquest and was centralised quite early, as in England, the practice of sub-infeudation could be and was banned by legislation from as early as the thirteenth century. In Scotland, it has lasted in various forms right up to the present day. It is easy to see its uses and relevance in a country occupied by a clan-conscious people whose traditional chiefs were also, in many cases, powerful territorial magnates and tenants-in-chief of the Crown, holding peerages of the realm and high offices of state often on a more or less hereditary basis. Scarcely less interesting is the way in which in the nineteenth and twentieth centuries it made possible the adaptation of the ancient forms of land-holding of a warrior society to the needs of a capitalist economy in one of the earliest industrialised parts of the world. (But with the advent of full registration of land-titles in Scotland, and redemption of feu-duties, the remaining survivals of feudal land-tenure have now become anachronistic and unhelpful, to say the least.)

Although the development of feudal law in Scotland diverged from quite early times from England's path of development, the energy, success and prestige of the English monarchs and their legal staffs made their law a significant model for reference by Scots lawyers throughout the Middle Ages and indeed later. This had a considerable influence both on the substantive legal doctrines that governed the holding of land and also, even more, on the judicial systems and processes for enforcing rights and settling disputes of right in relation to land. Dr Hector MacQueen's recent work has shown the extent of Scotland's debt to England in the early development of judicial forms and remedies, while also indicating the way in which independent practices and traditions took shape here.

In a feudal kingdom, land is not only property, it is the whole basis of civil government. People's relationship to the land determines their subsistence and survival; their relations to each other are mediated through their mutual rights and duties in relation to the occupancy and use of land and the services, whether military, monetary or menial, they must render in return for it. Legislation, adjudication and executive government all revolve around these relationships. The defence of the realm is absolutely dependent on the response of the chief men to the call for their proper share of knights and soldiers, or sailors, oarsmen and sea-warriors, to the feudal host; and their response depends on the response of their vassals, and so on. Law and justice are part of a complex set of reciprocal duties in this setting. Maintenance of internal peace against criminal inroads upon it is as vital a part of the public responsibility of the king as is the upholding of external security. Royal officers like the Justiciar or the Sheriffs in their localities have a vital part to play in this.

In relation to the constitutional aspect of the totality of legal relations, one must recall the powerful rhetoric of the Declaration of Arbroath of 1320, repeated in varying forms time after time since by spokespersons for Scottish constitutionalism. The request to the Pope to acknowledge the independence of the Scots after their long struggle under the leadership of King Robert to shake off English conquest is couched in terms that make clear the conditional position even of a militarily successful monarch. The clear assertion of Arbroath is that the Scots' allegiance to their monarchs is owed to them only as senior representatives of the chosen and native royal house and line. The reciprocity of the bond of allegiance obliges the people to respect and obey the monarch acting within law; accordingly, it obliges the monarch to respect and act within law and to defend the people's rights as his or her own. Failure by the subject is treason; failure by the monarch entails forfeiture of the right to rule in favour of another of the same line better able to carry out the duties of kingship. The doctrine is one that has, with variations, been repeated century by century and generation by generation well beyond the end of feudalism as a living form of government in favour of its survival as a technical form of property law. It is the peculiarly Scottish assertion of the Rule of Law as higher in authority than the highest human ruler, and of its guarantee of the independence of the whole people as a prerequisite of the independence of each person.

Land and relationships of land-holding were the special sphere of temporal authority. Even in that sphere, the need for literacy in dealing with the written materials of the law gave the clergy a special place in the development and administration of the law in earlier times. This was markedly so in Scotland. But it was not only in the royal Courts that clergymen had a prominent legal role to play. It cannot be too much stressed how much of the law affecting everyday lives in the Middle Ages and subsequently fell within the jurisdiction of the Church and its law, the canon law. Areas of this jurisdiction included most of the laws of family relationships and marriage, and also that of succession to moveable property. This was a matter distinct from the landed, or technically 'heritable', property that sits at the heart of the feudal relationship. Whereas feudal law and government demanded primogeniture and the succession whenever possible of a single male heir to do service for land and to maintain the integrity of government, no such necessity attached to moveable property such as money or mercantile assets. Here, the rule of the canon law permitted the making of wills, but also restricted their effect in favour of certain fixed shares which each legitimate family member might claim as of right from the estate of a parent.

The rule that family members have 'legal rights' in a deceased person's moveable estate persists to this day in Scotland, marking a restriction on the capability of anyone to disinherit their family by will. Whether this is a chance survival or a continuing marker of the rather strong sense of family (or even 'clannishness') that some detect in Scottish society is a matter for conjecture. There is certainly evidence of a widespread popularity of the view represented by the legal norm. The reform most strongly advocated is not one that would abolish legal rights, but one that would extend them to immovable ('heritable') property as well.

Since the Reformation, the rules of the canon law in relation to marriage, wills, moveable property and contract have largely ceased to be implemented through courts of the Church (though all of Session, Presbytery and General Assembly are courts with their own jurisdiction). The influence of canon law has been fully assimilated into the general secular law of Scotland, administered in the ordinary courts of the land. One little relic that remains as a reminder of times past is the practice of the universities (and not only the Scottish ones) in granting the degrees known as 'LL.D.' and 'LL.B.' – the double 'L' signifies 'Laws', or 'Both Laws', as the Latin version of the Doctor of Laws or Bachelor of Laws degree parchment makes clear.

To speak of 'both laws' is to bring the narrative to the point of introducing what may even be the greatest of all the originating influences that have gone into the making of Scots law. The 'two laws' of the medieval and Renaissance universities of Europe, the universities that trained the clerics who staffed the Scots courts both ecclesiastical and secular, and that formed the models for the universities of Scotland founded in fifteenth and sixteenth centuries, were the civil law and the canon law. By 'civil law' here is to be understood the Roman Civil Law. This originated in the ancient Roman Republic, and then developed through five centuries of Roman Empire before its collection in the sixth century AD by order of the Emperor Justinian into the three great works subsequently known as the *Corpus Juris Civilis*. These comprise the *Institutions*, which was a basic textbook of the law, the *Digest*, which was a vast compendium of readings about the whole range of legal subjects put together by a 'scissors and paste' method from the huge body of classical writings on the law, and the *Codex*, which was a collection of enactments by the emperors on various subjects over the years. As an addendum, there was also a book of *Novellae Constitutiones* by way of Justinianic law-reform.

The collapse of the Western Roman Empire with the invasion of barbarian tribes led to a death of formal legal learning during what is known, perhaps misleadingly, as the 'Dark Ages'. But in the twelfth century, in Bologna, the *Corpus Iuris Civilis* was rediscovered and the systematic study of law as a learned discipline resumed, with scholars dedicating themselves to mastery of the huge mass of material in the *Digest*. The influence of such civilian studies throughout Europe cannot be overestimated. The systematisation and development of law throughout Europe became deeply indebted to reflection on the Roman law. To varying extents in various parts, the Roman law was simply 'received' as the governing law except in so far as local law or custom were adequately established. In Scotland, while no formal reception ever took place, the training of the lawyers before and after the Reformation ensured that they were thoroughly instructed in the civil law (as well as, pre-Reformation, the canon law). Hence the rule of Roman law was always available for adoption or imitation in a difficult case where native legal materials were lacking. The prestige of Roman law as a rational body of law, coupled with the theoretical picture of law as (in Stair's phrase) reason versant about the rights of man, conferred legitimacy on the adoption of a Roman solution, or on the use of general Roman models for construction and reconstruction of domestic legal doctrines, in the development of Scots law.

By this process, Scots law came to partake very substantially of that European legal tradition which is called 'civilian' in contrast to the 'common law' tradition prevailing in England, most of the Commonwealth, and the USA. The very circumstances that drew Scotland into the orbit of the Romanising civilian tradition pulled England away from it. The Scottish War of Independence from England from 1286 to 1320 led to an alliance with France, and the outbreak of the Hundred Years' War between France and England guaranteed the continuance of this 'Auld Alliance'. Indeed, it carried on right up to the time of the Scottish Reformation in the 1560s. One consequence was a resort by Scots to the universities of France (particularly Paris) and other parts of the Continent, while England increasingly cut herself off from such contacts. Even after the Reformation and the Union, Scotland maintained active Continental links, especially with universities in the Netherlands. Several thousand Scots, most of them intending advocates, enrolled in the Universities of Utrecht and Leiden during the seventeenth and eighteenth centuries, bringing back with them the most advanced and up-to-date learning in the civil law and the 'Roman-Dutch' law that emerged in the Netherlands from the civilian tradition. These links were broken only when Napoleon's conquests first excluded Scots from Dutch contacts, and then so drastically changed the law of much of Continental Europe through codification as to break any subsequent basis for continued direct educational ties between Scots law and European learning. In the following century, the prestige of Oxford and Cambridge recovered greatly, and in due course outstripped that of the Scottish universities. In many cases, bright Scots with legal aspirations took to seeking at least a part of their higher education in the south. For the first time in six hundred years, Scotland's legal-intellectual links became closer with England than with the Continent.

The legal system that had developed over these centuries was a unique amalgam of native custom adapted to feudal tenures and feudal law, canon law and civil law, systematised in the writings of institutional authors, first among them Stair, and elaborated through the precedents and decisions of the courts. The common modern conception of law (of which, more later) no doubt stresses particularly the role of statute law, and the role of Parliaments as law-makers enjoying a legitimate title through endorsement by the popular electorate. But the lawmaker is by no means always as important to the development of a legal system as the law-applier. Stair himself, for example, argues that there is special strength and virtue in a process of development of law through debates in particular cases, where all the details can be carefully thought over, and where previous precedents that prove 'inconvenient' (he means something like 'at odds with the general run of legal principles') can be abandoned or overruled. So, over time, case law grows up through the deliberations of courts and lawyers, deliberations that look essentially to the principles underlying the particular rules or rulings handed down case by case. Law as a body of rational (or 'reasonable') principle is, in his view, better served by this process than by legislation, where a whole legal scheme has to be thought out from the beginning, and the experimental element of precedent is lacking.

Especially as of Stair's time of writing, when Parliaments met intermittently, and without the backing of legislative draftsmen, law commissions or bureaucratically staffed government departments, his view about the merits of case law has some persuasiveness. In fact, though, on certain fundamental points, basic to main branches of our law, the old Parliament of Scotland did some excellent work, for example in relation to the registration of deeds recording titles to land, or in support of every person's right to adequate legal representation before the law courts, especially when accused of crime. The development of the law was perhaps somewhat more of a partnership in experimentation between courts and legislators than Stair acknowledged. Yet the stress he laid on the case law element is of vital importance to the understanding of the character of Scots law. He is indeed right that Scots law was and has continued to be greatly indebted to the judges whose precedents have elaborated it, and that in its particular context Scots law's judge-made character has been part of its strength.

Nowadays, it is customary to contrast the 'civilian' or 'Romano-Germanic' legal systems of Continental Europe and other countries marked by their influence (Japan, Turkey, Latin America, Quebec, for example) with the 'common law' systems deriving from England (England and Wales, Ireland, most of the Commonwealth, the United States, and so on). One characteristic line of contrast is as to method: civilian systems are codified, and the judicial role is primarily that of interpreting and applying a code; precedent is not so much a source of law as a basis for uniformity in interpretation of codified law; the common law, on the other hand, though frequently dominated by statute law on particular points, is fundamentally precedent-based, case law more than statute law. The courts, staffed by judges drawn from the practising bar, work out the law after considering adversarial arguments advanced by counsel for opposing interests.

On this point of contrast, Scotland belongs methodologically more with common than with civil law. But the contrast is actually quite modern, being no older than Napoleon's early nineteenth-century codifications of French law; an older element of contrast, as to the content of legal doctrine, would look more to the origins and history of legal principles and legal doctrines than to the method of their development and application. By that test, Scots law has an infusion of the civilian far stronger than anything to be seen in English law, and Scots 'common law' is very different in origin and content than the 'common law' of Anglo-American tradition. Adversarial argumentation in the courts and judicial decisions thereon have worked out over the centuries a quite distinctive style and body of law here.

At this point, it becomes urgent to say a word or two about the courts that have borne the burden of administering justice and developing law in Scotland over the centuries. In present-day Scotland, we have two distinct courts, one for civil matters and the other for criminal, but they are staffed by the same judges. The Court of Session is our civil court, founded originally around 1532, but having continuity with earlier judicial officials of the King's Council; the High Court of Justiciary, developing out of the functions of the medieval Justiciar or Justiciars is the supreme criminal court. The Court of Session sits only in Edinburgh, and is divided into an Outer House in which single judges ('Lords of Session', 'Senators of the College of Justice') preside over debates on and trials or proofs of litigation upon questions of civil law, including the nowadays very important matter of judicial review of governmental and administrative decision-making, and an Inner House whose two divisions (presided over by the Lord President of the Court of Session and the Lord Justice-Clerk) hear appeals ('reclaiming motions') from the lower courts. The High Court of Justiciary retains from medieval times the practice of going on circuit throughout the country for trials of the most serious crimes. Individual Lords Commissioners of Justiciary preside over these trials, sitting with juries of fifteen laypersons who may reach their verdict by majority vote. The pannel (the accused person) is indicted in the name of the Lord Advocate, and the prosecution is conducted by an Advocate Depute or in particularly serious cases by the Solicitor-General or even very occasionally the Lord Advocate in person. Appeals from trials go to the High Court sitting as an Appeal Court of three or more judges in Edinburgh, usually presided over by the Lord Justice-Clerk or the Lord Justice-General. The latter office has in modern times always been held by the Lord President, who is Scotland's senior judge, our 'chief justice'.

Local jurisdiction is exercised both civilly and criminally by sheriffs sitting in Sheriff Courts in the various sheriffdoms into which Scotland is divided. Originally the local representative of the feudal monarch, the sheriff was a local dignitary of high rank, usually of the nobility and almost inevitably enjoying substantial independent power as well as that deriving from tenure of royal office. Sheriffdoms became hereditary in the great families of Scotland such as the Grahams of Montrose, the Scotts of Buccleuch and the like. But the functions were in post-feudal times carried out by appointed lawyers acting as 'sheriffs depute' who in turn appointed 'sheriffs substitute' who did most of the judicial work, subject to a process of supervision and appeal. Modernisations since the 1747 Abolition of Heritable Jurisdictions Act have led to rationalisation of structure and procedure and abandonment of archaic terminology. We now have a Sheriff Principal in each of the sheriffdoms, with first instance work being carried out by sheriffs simply so-called. They are qualified lawyers (advocates or solicitors) of substantial standing and experience who have jurisdiction over all local subjects of civil law, and summary criminal trials for most of the less grave criminal offences and trials on solemn procedure with juries for intermediate crimes (there being an upper limit of two years' imprisonment as the most serious penalty a sheriff can impose). Appeals lie to the Sheriff Principal locally, or (depending on subject matter) to the Court of Session or the High Court in Edinburgh.

Finally, there are District Courts with lay justices dealing with comparatively trivial offences, and, in relation to juvenile justice, a very important system of Children's Hearings in which lay members of Children's Panels deliberate under advice from the Reporter to the Children's Panel about how to deal with children up to sixteen years old who are in trouble either for their own misdeeds or through the neglect or misconduct of adults. The Hearings can act only with consent, and any disputed question must be dealt with in the Sheriff Court, as must the most serious crimes when committed by children or young persons. A considerable array of administrative tribunals also exists, and many public and local authorities have significant decision-making powers affecting individuals. In general, decision-making in such spheres of public law is subject to review by the appropriate procedure before the Court of Session.

From its foundation in the sixteenth century, the Court of Session has been at the centre of the 'College of Justice', of which its judges are 'Senators'. Other parts of this

College comprise the Faculty of Advocates, whose members have had historically the exclusive right (now extended, since June 1993, to solicitors with substantial experience of court practice) of audience before the Court of Session and the High Court. The Faculty is presided over by its own elected Dean, who almost invariably goes on to appointment as a judge, and it has other officers, including a librarian. For long, the Advocates' Library (founded by Mackenzie of Rosehaugh) functioned in effect as Scotland's National Library, and indeed in 1938 the non-legal books were gifted to the nation for the National Library that sits on George IV Bridge directly adjacent to the Advocates' Library in Parliament House by the High Kirk of St Giles in Edinburgh's Parliament Square.

The other element in the College of Justice is the Society of Writers to Her Majesty's Signet (the 'W.S. Society'), who exercised the function of 'writing', preparing writs and the like, rather than speaking before the courts. In parallel to the W.S. Society in Edinburgh were other local legal faculties such as the Royal Faculty of Procurators of Glasgow and the Society of Advocates in Aberdeen, which organised local bodies of law agents acting both as writers and as advocates in the Sheriff Courts. The various societies and organisations of law agents were brought together in 1947 into the Law Society of Scotland which under Act of Parliament and subject to the supervisory power of the Lord President governs, represents and exercises professional discipline over all solicitors in practice in Scotland.

Without going into details, it can be seen that there has been both professional and organisational continuity in the law of Scotland and in its professional practice and judicial administration over a great space of time. The guarantees of 1707 have in the main been honoured, and reforms and modernisations of courts or professional bodies have usually been in response to indigenous rather than extraneous pressures for change. The British Parliament has quite frequently engaged in legislation affecting the organisation of the Scottish legal system, but normally in a manner respectful of its constitutional distinctiveness.

There are, however, other sides to this picture. Not noted yet in our discussion of courts has been the fact of ultimate appeal to the House of Lords. This exists only in civil matters, and the legitimacy of the House of Lords' appellate role in respect of Scotland depends on the nicety that the House was never a court sitting in 'Westminster Hall', but rather a chamber of the Parliament that sat elsewhere in the Palace of Westminster. From the time of the Union till 1876 the House of Lords exercised an ultimate oversight over Scots civil law in almost entire ignorance of its content and origins, and did considerable damage to the integrity of the law. At the same time, in respect of England, though the House could and did take the advice of the English judges as never of the Scottish, its performance was not a matter of universal satisfaction, and abolition was seriously contemplated in the 1870s. In 1876, however, the House of Lords in its judicial function was reformed by the Appellate Jurisdictions Act, since when there has always been at least one – and more recently, by practically binding convention, at least two – Scottish Lords of Appeal in Ordinary. In recent times, the House of Lords has rarely incurred the criticism of intervening aberrantly in Scots law, and during this century a line of particularly distinguished Scottish Lords of Appeal such as Lord Dunedin, Lord Macmillan and Lord Reid have exercised a very considerable, and some would say 'Scotticising', influence upon English law, pushing it in the line of general and equitable principle that some have discerned as the peculiar character of Scots law at least since Stair's day.

In the criminal law, there has been no appeal to the Lords, and the special character of the law owes much to its early centralisation in a system of public prosecution (with Advocates Depute in the High Court and Procurators Fiscal in the Sheriff and District Courts) governed by the Lord Advocate, Scotland's senior law officer of the Crown. This enabled prosecution practice to blend with judicial precedent and juristic commentary (in addition to Mackenzie and Hume already mentioned, one should add reference to Macdonald's nineteenth-century treatise on criminal law, and the brilliant contemporary work of Sheriff, formerly Professor, G.H. Gordon) in developing a body of criminal law now quite distinctive in the western world as the only one whose law relating to most serious crimes remains chiefly enshrined in common law, with relatively small regulation by statute. The degree to which general principles rather than detailed rules can be invoked in our criminal law can indeed give rise to concern for the sake of civil liberty and the protection of the Rule of Law. But in general it seems reasonable to say that the great body of criminal law in Scotland, by virtue of its customary character, remains in close touch with popular attitudes to wrong-doing. That, rather than notorious survivals like the 'Not Proven' verdict (an alternative acquittal to 'Not Guilty') or robust rationalities like the majority verdict, is what gives Scots criminal law its special character.

Most problematic really for the health of Scots law now is the fact of its lacking a legislature of its own. As noted earlier, modern law everywhere is ever-increasingly enacted law, based on the will of the democratic legislature, and, in an ever more interdependent world, enacted in response to intergovernmental decisions whether at European Community level or through multilateral treaty. Thus it comes about that in spheres like financial or commercial law, or company law, Scots law is reformed through processes in which *de facto* Scotland and Scots law are largely unrepresented, even when, as now, a Scots Advocate and ex-Dean of Faculty sits as the first ever Lord Chancellor of Great Britain who is not an English barrister by training. Although we have a Scottish Law Commission, and although most reform of private law affecting individual and local life emerges from Scottish agencies rather than being imposed through mainly English ministries, it is a serious question whether the vitality and integrity of Scots law can persist in modern conditions without recovery of legislative institutions answerable to the Scottish electorate, and without ministers possessed of responsibilities exercisable in international forums.

Within the European Union, to be sure, Scots law has by the decision of UK prime ministers since Edward Heath had greater representation than might have been feared, through Lord Mackenzie-Stuart, the first UK judge in the European Court of Justice (and sometime President of the Court) and Judge (formerly Professor) David Edward, who sits in Luxembourg at present. This is welcome in itself, but leaves Scots law still with less representation than the law of Luxembourg or of Ireland. If it were counter-observed that English law is by the same token equally (or more) under-represented, one might nevertheless reply that it seems unlikely to be forgotten or neglected by British officials in their everyday work, a point which does not so well apply to Scots law.

These remarks perhaps go to the limits of appropriateness in a work such as the present. Suffice it here to repeat that in any account of Scottish culture, a prominent place belongs to the distinctive and long-matured law of this realm. Its past and present are not without their glories. A patchwork of influences has come together here in a body of coherent practical principles that seems in a way curiously well adapted to 'metaphysical Scotland', perhaps because itself one of the moments that shaped the national spirit captured in that phrase. The future is for political choices, not for works of history.

Books for Further Reading

M.C. Meston, W.D.H. Sellar and Lord Cooper, *The Scottish Legal Tradition*, ed. S.C. Styles (new enlarged edition, Edinburgh, 1991)

D.M. Walker, *The Scottish Legal System* (Edinburgh, 1992)

D.M. Walker, *The Scottish Jurists* (Edinburgh, 1985)

T.B. Smith and R. Black (eds.) *The Laws of Scotland: the Stair Memorial Encyclopaedia* Vol. 5, article on 'Constitutional Law'; and Vol. 22, articles on 'Sources of Law' (Edinburgh, 1987)

T.B. Smith, *A Short Commentary on the Law of Scotland* (Edinburgh, 1962), pp.3–38

The Stair Society, *Sources and Literature of Scottish Legal History* Vol. 1 (Edinburgh, 1936) and Vol. 20, *An Introduction to Scottish Legal History* (Edinburgh, 1958)

Hector L. MacQueen, *Common Law and Feudal Society in Medieval Scotland* (Edinburgh, 1993)

James Dalrymple, first Viscount Stair, *Institutions of the Law of Scotland*, ed. and intro. D.M. Walker (Edinburgh, 1981; reprint of second edition, Edinburgh, 1693)

Note: In the above suggestions for further reading appear the names of Lord Cooper, Sir Thomas Smith and Professor David Walker; Lord Cooper as scholar and judge (Lord President, 1947–54), and Professors Smith and Walker as scholars and authors together achieved in the present century an intellectual revival of Scots law perhaps even comparable to the revival in the seventeenth century on which the present essay has focused.

Scottish Education, 1700–2000

NIGEL GRANT AND WALTER HUMES

INTRODUCTION

W riting in 1983, the editors of *Scottish Culture and Scottish Education 1800–1980* criticised what they called the 'Acts and facts' tradition of Scottish educational history.[1] They suggested that narrative histories (such as H.M. Knox's *Scottish Education 1696–1946*),[2] which concentrated on the development of the statutory system and viewed it as a story of steady progress, failed to address important questions of a critical and interpretative nature. What was needed, they argued, was an attempt to locate Scottish education within a much broader cultural context, encompassing social, economic and political change, science and technology, religion and the arts. The challenge that these observations contained has been taken up by a number of writers – such as Anderson (1983),[3] McPherson and Raab (1988),[4] and Carter and Withrington (1992)[5] – and our present understanding of the history of Scottish education represents a marked improvement on that of a decade ago, though much work remains to be done. Our principal aim in this chapter is to discuss a number of key themes which recur, in various guises, throughout the period. These include virtue and learning, language and culture, reform and control, bureaucracy and power. It is impossible to be comprehensive in an essay of this length and no attempt will be made to give even coverage to the period as a whole. We hope, however, that readers will be encouraged to reflect critically on traditional assumptions about Scottish education and perhaps stimulated to undertake further research of their own.

HISTORY AND MYTH

History is always in danger of reinforcing myth, and the history of Scottish education is particularly liable to this. It is still often claimed that Scottish education sprang fully

64. *The Old College, Edinburgh University. The outside of the quadrangle is by Robert Adam*
(1789) and the inside by William H. Playfair (1819–27). The dome was built in 1879.
Edinburgh, which was founded in 1583, is the most recent of the four older Scottish universities
and the first founded after the Reformation. The others were all founded under the authority of
papal bulls: St Andrews in 1412; King's College, Aberdeen, in 1495 (followed by Marischall
*College in 1593); and Glasgow in 1451. (*RIAS*)*

armed from the head of John Knox; that it has always been democratic and egalitarian, based on a broad general schooling for all and providing for the 'lad o' pairts' opportunities to advance through sheer native wit and solid hard work, irrespective of social status or wealth. It is claimed that the Scottish schools have always been sufficient unto themselves, and have established stability and high achievement that would be threatened by any departure from well-established practice.

It would be as well to admit that those, like all myths, do contain an element of truth. It is true, for instance, that Scotland was early in trying to establish something like a national system of education. It is impossible to ignore John Knox's plan in the *First Book of Discipline* (1560),[6] albeit before our period; this was a scheme for a school in every parish, a secondary school in every burgh, development of existing universities, provisions for compulsory attendance and financial support for the poor. The scheme was to be for the good of society as a whole 'sa that the commonwealthe may have some comfort by them', an ideal far ahead of its time. It was at first (and this is less well known) too far ahead for the Scottish Parliament, which turned the plan down, although it passed several Acts in subsequent years in pursuit of the ideal. Something like it developed much later and more slowly; compulsory schooling was not achieved until 1872, free schooling not until 1918.

There is *some* substance in the notion of the 'lad o' pairts', the poor boy with a bag of meal on his shoulder and sound learning in his head, progressing through the parish schools up to university. Nor did this apply only to those destined for higher education or the professions, as witness the story of David Livingstone working his way up through night-school, or Robert Burns acquiring a sound basis for his own wide reading at Alloway Mill school. The significance of the case of Burns has been obscured by McKenzie's rather patronising description of him as the 'heaven-taught ploughman'. The hand of heaven must be conjectural, but that of John Murdoch, his teacher, is factual. According to Burns's early biographer, Currie, he was by no means unique; writing in 1880, Currie observed:

> A slight acquaintance with the peasantry of Scotland would serve to convince an unprejudiced observer that they possess a degree of intelligence not generally found among the same class of men in the other countries of Europe. In the very humblest condition of the Scottish peasants every one can read, and most persons are more or less skilled in writing and arithmetic; and under the disguise of their uncouth appearance, and of the peculiar manners and dialect, a stranger will discover that they possess a curiosity, and have obtained a degree of information corresponding to these requirements.[7]

Examples of this growing reputation abound during the eighteenth and nineteenth centuries. T.B. Macaulay, writing in 1859 about the 1696 Act for the Settling of Schools, stated:

> Before one generation had passed away, it began to be evident that the common people of Scotland were superior in intelligence to the common people of any country in Europe . . . This wonderful change is to be attributed, not indeed solely, but principally, to the national system of education.[8]

Sydney Smith, among many others, describes the Scots as 'perhaps . . . the most remarkable nation in the world', and makes particular reference to 'knowledge amongst the lower classes of society'.[9] Among the upper classes, we find the sister of Elizabeth Grant refusing the hand of an otherwise desirable suitor because his ignorance of history equipped him so poorly for rational conversation.[10]

But we must not get carried away. The lad o' pairts did exist, but he needed exceptional determination if he was the son of a craftsman or a crofter; the son of the teacher or the minister found things rather easier. For every one who made it to university, there were hundreds who left school with little more than basic literacy and a rote knowledge of the Bible and the Shorter Catechism. The case of Elizabeth Grant's sister is a useful reminder of the value attached to general culture, but it is also a reminder that for girls such matters were usually limited to the better off; there are not many cases of the 'lass o' pairts'.

It must also be remembered that schooling was not always a liberating or enabling experience. It is true that the parish schools did spread literacy more widely than in most countries, including England; but they were often under-equipped, badly under-funded and poorly staffed. Even when schooling was effective, it covered a limited range of knowledge and skills; the creative and physical aspects of the curriculum were relatively neglected. While the nurturing of the able child could be impressive, that of the average or below average was less so. It may well be that education in Scotland was more widespread than elsewhere, was less class-ridden and more open to the talents, and may even have embodied some notion of a broad-based education for personal development; but some caution should be exercised to avoid overstatement.

Scottish universities have often been held up as bastions of the 'democratic intellect', with a humane breadth of curriculum open to talent irrespective of class.[11] But again some caution is called for. The curriculum was broad in that there was little specialisation from the seventeenth century to the early nineteenth, embracing the classics, mathematics, natural philosophy, moral philosophy and logic; there was little time for anything else, and some of the studies were not taken to great depth. It may be the very curricular breadth that gave rise to doubts in England in the nineteenth century that the Scottish universities could rightfully claim that name. It is even possible that it was not until courses began to diversify during that century that Scottish universities came into their own as innovating institutions, free of the religious tests (and ecclesiastical politics) of their southern counterparts.

But it can also be emphasised that higher education, throughout most of this period, was much more widely available in Scotland's four universities (five for a time) than England's two. Entry certainly was not open, but it was more widely available and free of most of the class and religious constraints. It is true that standards were often low by modern criteria, but that was so of Oxford and Cambridge as well. The reservations about the Scottish universities' right to the title were mainly Oxbridge snobbery; the ethos of the Scottish universities was totally comprehensible in Europe. Even now, higher education is more widely available in Scotland than in England, though it lags behind most European countries, North America and Japan.

The Golden Age never really existed in quite the sense that mythology suggests. For all its early advances, education in Scotland was flawed, and in any case many things that characterised it in the eighteenth and nineteenth centuries are ones which few nowadays would wish to revive – such as the authoritarian pedagogy, the often brutal discipline maintained in the schools (what Christopher Smout called 'smashing facts into children',[12] by no means confined to Scotland), the way our concern for high standards often fell into pedantry, the obsession with formal examinations, and the joylessness which the Calvinist ethic so often visited upon the school – these, surely, are not what Scots would want to have as the signal features of their system. Its achievements, especially in the early centuries, are undoubted, but it is as well to remember that it had a dark side as well. When all these limitations are admitted, however, it is still true that the Scottish population was probably the best educated in the world for about three hundred years from the end of the sixteenth century.

VIRTUE AND LEARNING

It has sometimes been suggested that Scottish education in the past has been more interested in virtue than in learning. T.C. Smout, for example, has said that the aim of the parochial and burgh schools from the sixteenth century 'had been to give all people enough literacy to read the Bible and to inculcate a set of rules about acceptable social behaviour'.[13] The educational efforts of the Society in Scotland for Propagating Christian Knowledge (SSPCK), established in 1701, which by 1758 had founded 176 schools,[14] were directed towards the 'further promoting of Christian knowledge and the increase of piety and virtue, within Scotland, especially in the Highlands, Islands and remote corners thereof'.[15] As in England, where conflict between members of the Established Church and Nonconformists served to delay the introduction of a national system of schooling, so in Scotland religious conflict significantly affected educational provision, though it could be argued that not all of the consequences were negative.

The Disruption of the Church of Scotland in 1843, when 470 ministers, under the leadership of Dr Thomas Chalmers, left to form the Free Church of Scotland, led to an extension of educational facilities throughout the country. The Free Church of Scotland decided to set up its own system of schools and within five years had founded some five hundred, largely staffed by teachers who had left the Church of Scotland to join the new denomination. In the longer term the Free Church found this educational commitment a serious financial strain. Repeated attempts were made in the 1850s and 1860s by the Lord Advocate James Moncrieff to establish a system of non-sectarian, publicly funded schools which would tidy up the messy situation created by the co-existence of variously funded schools managed not only by the Free Church and the Church of Scotland but also by United Presbyterians, Episcopalians and Roman Catholics. Moncrieff's bills were defeated, despite majority support from Scottish MPs, because English MPs feared the consequences for the Church of England if the Established Church in Scotland were deprived of its privileged position.[16]

When reform finally did come, with the 1872 Act, the effects were dramatic. Within a few years some 80 per cent of the schools run by the Presbyterian churches had closed; the Act guaranteed the teaching of religion according to Presbyterian tenets and this satisfied most adherents of the Established and Free Churches. By contrast, Roman Catholic schools increased from 22 in 1872 to 224 in 1910.[17] This expansion took place mainly in the south-west of Scotland, to which Irish immigrants came in sizeable numbers in the years before the First World War. The provisions of section 18 of the 1918 Education Act allowed the Catholic schools to be brought into the public system with safeguards for the role of the Church in appointing teachers and the time spent on religious instruction and observance. This arrangement, which has been

65. The original buildings of Glasgow University, founded under a papal bull of 1450, and extensively rebuilt between 1654 and 1656. They were demolished in 1870 and replaced by a railway goods station. This is one of John Slezer's drawings from Theatrum Scotiae *of 1693.*
(National Library of Scotland)

jealously guarded by the Catholic hierarchy ever since, undoubtedly allowed considerable improvements in the standards of Catholic education to take place and helped to produce a Catholic middle class, in the face of considerable bigotry and discrimination. Sectarianism has steadily declined and there are now some indications at local level, involving co-operation between Catholic and non-Catholic parents, that the views of the hierarchy lag behind those of church members. The possibility of full-scale integration, however, remains remote.

The history of Scottish education cannot be properly understood without reference to the part played by religion. For centuries many children would not have received an education at all had it not been for the efforts of the churches. Those efforts, it is true, were often narrowly sectarian and as much concerned with control as enlightenment. The gradual decline of religious belief has meant that most Scottish children – Roman Catholics excepted – now receive an education that is non-denominational if not avowedly secular. There are some grounds for thinking that the pendulum has swung too far in the direction of learning and away from virtue. Perhaps significantly, the Scottish Consultative Council on the Curriculum in 1991 felt it necessary to publish a document entitled *Values in Education* which seeks to reassert the importance of the social, moral and spiritual dimensions of children's development.

LANGUAGE AND CULTURE

The ambivalent attitude of Scottish education, and Scottish society, can be seen in the policy of the educational system towards Scottish culture, and in particular towards

Scotland's indigenous languages, Gaelic and Scots.[18] Gaelic came into Scotland in about the sixth century (some say earlier) from Ireland, and was for centuries indistinguishable from Irish. Scots (as it is now called) developed from the northern form of Anglian brought into Lothian by Northumbrian incursions. What we now call Gaelic was simply one form of the Goidelic tongue spoken in Ireland, Scotland and the Isle of Man, just as what we now know as Scots was one of the many forms of 'Inglis' spoken in the southern parts of the British Isles.

The earliest assaults on the Gaelic language fell outside the period being discussed here, notably the Act of Privy Council of James VI (1616), which envisaged the establishment of the 'trew religioun' and the use of schools to ensure that 'the vulgar Inglishe toung shall be universallie plantit, and the Irishe language, which is one of the chief and principall causis of the continewance of barbaritie and incivilitie amongis the inhabitants of the Highlandis and Islandis, shall be abolisheit and removit'.[19] This policy was to continue until modern times.

The main reason appears to have been religious. Many of the Highland clans were Catholic, and politically disaffected. But the Church of Scotland, when trying to ensure a supply of Gaelic-speaking clergy for the Highlands, was quite happy to encourage a supply of 'Irish' bibles and catechisms. (Acts of Enabling of 1699, 1701, 1702, 1714 and 1717.) English, however, remained the language to be promoted in the schools, particularly by the SSPCK. Then came an apparent change of heart. In 1767 the SSPCK admitted Gaelic as the medium of instruction in the schools (though the parish schools continued to use English only). Apparently, the English-only policy proved hard to sustain when the children spoke nothing but Gaelic. It was necessary to teach them in Gaelic until they had learned enough English to switch after the 'pacification' of the Highlands post-1746 had made Gaelic seem less threatening.[20]

In any event, from the latter part of the seventeenth century to the passing of the Education (Scotland) Act of 1872 seemed a period of expansion of Gaelic schooling. It should be noted, however, that this was not accompanied by any developments of higher levels, and that the Highland Clearances were shifting the balance of society by removing much of the population from the land. The Gaelic schools were not intended to foster or develop the language, but to ease Gaelic monoglots into an English-speaking society. When the 1872 Act was passed, it gave no recognition to Gaelic at all, and the 1918 Act made a grudging and token concession. Children were taught only in English, and were punished for lapsing into Gaelic at school. This was still going on well into the 1940s. Meanwhile, the Gaelic-speaking population continued to bleed away to the Lowlands and beyond, thus devaluing the culture even for those who stayed at home.[21]

The haemorrhage continued unabated until the 1970s, when some stabilisation was achieved. It was partly economical, partly educational, as is quite common in peripheral societies. Scotland sends more young people than England into higher education; by the same token, the Highlands and Islands send more, proportionally, than does Scotland as a whole. But there is no higher education in the Gàidhealtachd, and getting on has therefore meant getting out. Since the Highland economy has not been able to employ all these graduates, it has also meant staying out. The very fact that success was equated with leaving meant that staying behind was associated with failure, thus devaluing the culture even at home.

The erosion of Gaelic did not pass unchallenged. The major language promotion movement, An Comunn Gàidhealach (The Highland Association) was founded in 1891. Celtic studies were established in the ancient universities a century ago, and are offered in Glasgow, Edinburgh and Aberdeen.[22] Gaelic is available as a school subject, though even now it is still often taught in English. By the middle of the present century, Gaelic development had been reduced to an academic and cultural token presence, and the decline continued.

Then, slowly at first, things began to change. In 1958, some Gaelic-medium instruction was officially introduced in bilingual areas, and in 1962 learners' papers were introduced in the Scottish Certificate of Education. Comunn nan Leabhraichean (the Gaelic Books Council) was founded in 1969, BBC Gaelic schools' broadcasting in 1970, the Gaelic College at Sabhal Mòr Ostaig in Skye in 1973, the publishing company Acair in 1977, Radio nan Eilean (Radio of the Isles) opened in 1979, and the highly successful beginners' programme *Can Seo* (*Say This*) appeared on BBC in the same year. These developments may have indicated a change of mood; more important, they began the building of a support structure that any language needs to survive.

The first major political breakthrough was the Local Government (Scotland) Act of 1975. This created Comhairle nan Eilean, the Western Isles Council, which established a bilingual policy in its administration in 1977, and launched a bilingual project (Proisect Dà-Chànanach). Bilingual education extended to secondary schooling in the Isles, and Gaelic-medium school units began to grow and multiply; eleven are open, and more are planned. Similar developments have been taking place in Highland Region since 1978. Developments have also been noticeable in the Lowlands, particularly since the 1980s. The 1991 Census, however, reported a drop in the number of Gaelic speakers in Scotland from 80,000 to 65,000, though this should be partially offset in the future by a rise in the number of speakers under the age of ten; in spite of a more supportive attitude by the media, this is a desperately small base for a language revival to be built on.

The position of Scots is rather worse. This is ironic, since Scots is easier for an English-speaker to learn; it is as close to English as Catalan is to Spanish, or Danish to Swedish.[23] It is spoken, in one form or another, by a larger proportion of Scots, though the absence of any census data makes it impossible to be more precise. It was the vehicle for a rich culture in the sixteenth century, was the language of Barbour, Dunbar, Henryson and Lyndsay, and was the standard language of Court and courts, school and Kirk, spoken by Scots of every class for every purpose. The Union of the Crowns in 1603 removed the Court to London, and with it the apparatus of royal patronage of literature, and the publication of the Authorised Version of the Bible alienated the 'standard' language. There was no Scots version – none was needed – since the English one was readily comprehensible; but it planted the idea that Scots was no longer a standard language. Scots hung on in popular use, but increasingly provincialised, a trend which continued apace during the eighteenth century. During this time, the legal profession continued to use Scots, but the upper classes (who spent more and more time in London) and the aspiring upwardly mobile middle classes sought to ape the 'correct' English of the south. The status of Scots as a language was forgotten; even Burns published his poems chiefly 'in the Scottish dialect', and adopted spelling conventions based upon English. Scots, in effect, broke down into a series of local dialects. The schools, of course, strove to instil 'correct' English to the exclusion of all else; Scots speakers, like Gaelic speakers, were also subjected to pressure and even punishment.[24]

This is largely still the case. True, some schools have accepted Scots literature, as have some universities, but this is kept in hermetically-sealed compartments; the language is otherwise stigmatised as 'bad English', 'uncouth', 'slovenly', 'coarse', 'debased' and so on – social but linguistically meaningless judgments. The provincialisation of Scots, in marked contrast to what happened to Catalan, Norwegian and Slovak, is perhaps one of the clearest examples of the dependency into which Scottish culture fell from the loss of effective statehood.

REFORM AND CONTROL

In terms of pedagogy, Scottish education in the nineteenth and early twentieth centuries is usually characterised as formal, didactic, with a strong emphasis on basic literacy and numeracy, and the rudiments of religion. Scotland's credentials as a progressive, reforming example are not generally thought to be strong. There are, however, important exceptions. The work of Robert Owen (1771–1858) and David Stow (1793–1864) is significant in this respect. Both were aware of the experimental, child-centred work of Froebel and Pestalozzi in Europe, as well as of the monitorial systems of Bell and Lancaster, which they found too rigid and insufficiently humane. Owen, a Welshman who had come to Scotland via Manchester, developed his own system at New Lanark where he first managed and then owned a cotton mill. The children of the mill workers were given an education in which play, singing and dancing were, in the early stages at least, given more importance than the acquisition of formal skills. Owen's idea was to create a community in which the happiness principle of the utilitarians was to find expression: he described New Lanark as an 'institution for the formation of character'[25] and claimed that, if the environment was properly controlled, society could be transformed. His ideas were elaborated in *A New View of Society* (1813). Owen has been variously described as a utopian, an early socialist and a philanthropist. In recent years, however, his credentials as a progressive educator and social reformer have been challenged on a number of counts. It has been suggested that he was a self-publicist and that too much reliance has been placed on his *Autobiography* (1857–58). Again, it has been argued that not enough credit has been given to David Dale,[26] Owen's father-in-law, for the enlightened work that undoubtedly went on at New Lanark. Most seriously it has been claimed that economic motives were more potent in determining Owen's actions than educational ones.[27] The system increased profits by regulating the supply of labour and thus represented a sound investment in social control. These revisionist interpretations can be taken too far. While there are certainly respects in which the educational work of New Lanark can be linked to the 'factory model' more obviously embodied in the monitorial system, Owen's important contribution was to challenge the social, intellectual and moral belief that the condition of the poor was directly attributable to some innate 'nature'. 'Nurture' had the power to transform. In his own words:

> Any character, from the best to the worst, from the most ignorant to the most enlightened, may be given to any community, even to the world at large, by applying certain means; which are to a great extent at the command and under the control, or easily made so, of those who possess the government of nations.[28]

Unlike Owen, David Stow's involvement in education was motivated by his deep religious beliefs. He was stimulated to act by witnessing, in the streets of Glasgow, daily examples of squalor and degradation. He first started a Sunday evening school (in

1816) but formed the view that this was inadequate to counteract the evils to which children were subject. He then decided to start a day school for children under six 'before their intellectual and moral habits were fully formed, and consequently when fewer obstacles were presented to the establishment of good ones'.[29] Habit formation was central to Stow's approach and he drew a distinction between *teaching*, which was merely the communication of facts, and *training*, which involved the promotion of socially desirable dispositions, thoughts and actions. An important element in this was peer group influence which he regarded as much more potent than corporal punishment. He felt, however, that the whole process needed to be under the control of a mature adult and, for this reason, was critical of the monitorial system which depended on the direction of younger children by older children. Stow was also a strong advocate of co-education, though for reasons that would displease feminists: he believed that girls *morally* elevate boys, while boys *intellectually* elevate girls.

Stow concluded that educational advance depended principally on the quality of teachers. Trainee teachers were attached to the schools founded by Stow in the Drygate and the Saltmarket, thus establishing the 'model' or 'demonstration' system that survived well into the twentieth century.[30] Teacher training in Scotland effectively dates from 1828 though it was not until 1837 that the Dundas Vale Training College of the Church of Scotland was opened. Following the Disruption of 1843, however, Stow had to sever his link with the institution he had been instrumental in establishing because of his Free Church beliefs. He subsequently established the Free Church Normal College.

Both Owen and Stow sought to lessen the dehumanising effects of industrialisation and argued – in Owen's case, as part of a radical vision of society – for the civilising power of education. By the end of the nineteenth century demands for universal schooling had been conceded but reforming voices have continued to be heard. The introduction of a mass institutionalised system of education, under state control and with its own burgeoning bureaucracy, has led to regular assertions of the importance of the principle of freedom in education. The views of A.S. Neill (1883–1973) and R.F. Mackenzie (1910–87) are well known. Less well known is Patrick Geddes (1854–1932), a polymath, who achieved distinction in a number of fields – botany, publishing, social reform, town planning and international development. He met and corresponded with several American educators who were involved in the promotion of progressive educational theory and practice, including John Dewey. Their advocacy of active learning methods and integrated curricula appealed to Geddes. He was highly critical of the prevailing practices of elementary and secondary schools which he described as 'prisons for body and mind'[31] whose main function was to serve the needs, not of children, but of 'textbook perpetrators' and 'examination-machine bureaucrats'.[32] For Geddes, real culture depended not on a heavy emphasis on formal teaching of the three Rs, policed by a schools inspectorate intent on applying 'standards', but on first-hand observation, exploration and discovery by the individual learner. Although in many respects a maverick figure, with a view of education that many would regard as romantic, his importance lay in his ability to detect the negative effects of institutionalised control of schooling. His scathing references to the 'decaying educational mandarinate'[33] were not calculated to disarm but they reflected misgivings, which have continued to surface from time to time, about the role of the Scottish Education Department and the rest of the administrative machinery that maintains the schooling system.

BUREAUCRACY AND POWER

Scotland has a separate administrative structure for its educational system and this is often seen as clear evidence of cultural distinctiveness from England. An examination of the history of the Scottish Education Department (now the Scottish Office Education Department) reveals a rather more ambiguous picture. The Scotch Education Department – as it was called until 1918 – was set up by the 1872 Act, but its headquarters remained at Dover House in London until 1939. In the early years there was considerable dissatisfaction within Scotland at the limited powers of the department: the Duke of Richmond referred to it disparagingly as 'simply a room in Whitehall with the word "Scotland" painted on the door'[34] and a recent historian of the Scottish Office has described it as 'virtually one with the English Board of Education'.[35]

After the appointment of Henry (later Sir Henry) Craik as the first Permanent Secretary the position began to change, though the critics – such as S.S. Laurie, the first Professor of Education at the University of Edinburgh, and Sir James Donaldson, Principal of St Andrews University – were to remain vocal. A product of the Whitehall bureaucracy and later a Unionist MP, Craik had a clear vision of the way he wanted the department to develop. Along with his successors Sir John Struthers and Sir George Macdonald, Craik exercised strong central direction of Scottish education and introduced numerous important reforms, including the restructuring of post-primary education, the introduction of leaving certificate examinations and the improvement of teacher training. In the period just before the First World War, the Scotch Education Department 'received nothing but praise' from the Royal Commission on the Civil Service under Lord MacDonnell's chairmanship.[36] Certainly in terms of administrative efficiency that praise would seem to have been justified. The policies of Craik, Struthers and Macdonald have, however, been subject to criticism. T.C. Smout has observed that the admirable aim of making public secondary education available to all those who could benefit from it was undermined by two accompanying assumptions: first that pupils could be accurately classified at the age of twelve as 'academic' or 'non-academic' and, second, that 'academic' pupils would be mainly – though not entirely – middle class.[37] Sir George Macdonald was disarmingly frank on this subject when he said that 'the school population falls into two parts – the majority of distinctly limited intelligence, and an extremely important minority . . .who are capable of responding to a much more severe call'.[38] These assumptions, which had administrative and economic attractions, were strengthened by the extravagant claims of the mental testing movement, well developed in Scotland, which purported to measure intelligence accurately and so provide justification for differentiated provision.

The system of secondary schooling which emerged under Craik, Struthers and Macdonald rests uneasily with the democratic and egalitarian beliefs that surround Scotland's educational history. Perhaps the class divisions were less marked than in England but they were there nonetheless. H.M. Paterson has observed 'if Scottish schools were ever democratic, they were democratic in a particular way which emphasised social division, competitive liberalism and individual achievement at the expense of others.'[39]

It might be argued, of course, that it is not the job of administrators to develop social policy: that is the task of politicians and it is they who should be held accountable for failures. This raises the important question of the relation between politicians and officials within the SED, a relation which has been subject to fluctuation in terms of

66. The Royal High School, Edinburgh, built to the design of Thomas Hamilton between 1825 and 1829. During its long history the school (now removed to the suburbs) has occupied many buildings, but this is the most magnificent. Between 1977 and 1980 the hall of the building was adapted to act as the House of the Scottish Assembly proposed under the Scottish Act. This was frustrated when the Conservative Government repealed the Act after the Referendum of 1979. The Government announced in September 1993 that they would offer the buildings for sale. The school itself has made a remarkable contribution to Scottish culture. As Lord Brougham said in 1825, it was 'the most important school in Scotland, and was intimately connected with the literature and progress of the kingdom'. (An early twentieth-century photograph from the RIAS collection)

their relative powers. Until 1939 all senior administrative staff came from the inspectorate but, since then, a clear division between career civil servants and Her Majesty's Inspectors (mostly with a background in teaching) has developed, with a fair amount of rivalry between the two. In the late 1950s and 1960s, under John Brunton,[40] the inspectorate was in the ascendancy: more recently, under the managerial ethos of the 1980s, the career civil servants have come into their own. At different times politicians have either sought to intervene to take charge of policy or left things largely to their officials, especially if issues other than education dominated the political agenda. Tom Johnston, Secretary of State between 1941 and 1945, in retrospect complained of his failure to import into the school system 'the first necessity of all education, a culture of good citizenship'.[41] His explanation was in terms of official obstruction:

> True, we got an advisory council on education and recommendations about the prime necessity of turning out good citizens; we produced a splendid pamphlet on the subject; but the polite, though obviously reluctant, acquiescence of the do-nothings and the Petronella dance-like side-steppings of the pundits filled me with foreboding that we were not going to break far into the existing codes.[42]

Well-established bureaucracies are, by their nature, resistant to change and it takes a strong interventionist style to disturb their procedures. One politician who did precisely that was Michael Forsyth who introduced a series of radical reforms in the 1980s, based on market, consumerist principles such as choice, standards and accountability. Interestingly, Forsyth was attacked by the Educational Institute of Scotland and others as an Angliciser seeking to foist an alien cultural importation on the Scots. To the extent that Forsyth's programme derived from New Right ideology this criticism had some force. But it could also be argued – and here again the ambivalence of the Scottish dimension of our education system becomes apparent – that from its origins the SED was run by personnel whose first loyalty was not to education, nor even to Scotland, but to the machinery of the British state. Not enough is known about how the SED has related to other government departments – most notably the Treasury and the Department of Education and Science (now the Department for Education) – but there are grounds for thinking that careful observance of civil service conventions has played as important a part in policy outcomes as any nationalist sentiments.[43]

PRESENT AND FUTURE

The current policy agenda in Scottish education, based on the market ideology described above, includes devolved financial management of schools, teacher appraisal, the incorporation of further education colleges (from 1 April 1993) and the progressive implementation of the 5–14 Development Programme. A major change on the horizon, which is likely to have profound implications for education, is the reform of local government. School boards have been in place for some time and opting out of local authority control is already a possibility. A radical option would be to remove schooling from a restructured local government system altogether. The implications of such a move for democratic government, especially given Scotland's delicate constitutional position, are a matter of some concern.

In the field of higher education, some attempt has been made to strengthen the Scottish dimension by revised funding arrangements and the creation of new universities. Prior to the 1960s Scotland had four universities (St Andrews, Glasgow, Aberdeen and Edinburgh). Following the Robbins Report (1963), which heralded expansion throughout the UK, four new universities were created. Two of these, Strathclyde and Heriot-Watt, were colleges of technology elevated to university status and widely diversified in function; one, Dundee, had been a branch institution that acquired independent status, and one, Stirling, was purpose-built on a new site. Stirling was determinedly innovative, which was reflected in the structure of its courses, as were the former colleges of technology, and all followed the English nomenclature for degrees. Note should also be taken of the creation of the Council for National Academic Awards (CNAA), set up to validate degrees in institutions without the right to award their own.[44] Not surprisingly, this largely followed English models and practices (with occasional attention to the 'peculiar features of the Scottish system'), and in the view of many has been a major force in the anglicisation of higher education in Scotland. The Council has now been abolished, but the thinking behind it, and the practices developed, are still influential.

The next leap was in 1992, when the decision was taken to abolish the 'binary divide' (and the CNAA), and put all institutions of higher education on an equal footing.[45] Non-university institutions were given a choice: in the absence of the CNAA, they could apply for university status in their own right, as did Napier

(Edinburgh), Robert Gordon's (Aberdeen), Paisley and Glasgow Polytechnic with the Queen's College, which eventually became Glasgow Caledonian University. They could merge with existing universities, as did Jordanhill with Strathclyde, Moray House with Heriot-Watt, and Craigie with Paisley. Or they could associate with universities which would validate their degrees. Northern College (with campuses in Aberdeen and Dundee) was linked with the Open University, and Glasgow has taken St Andrew's College of Education, the Glasgow School of Art, the Royal Scottish Academy of Music and Drama and the Scottish Agricultural College under its wing. Separate funding councils for higher education have been created for Scotland, England and Wales. Whether the Scottish Higher Education Funding Council (SHEFC), in the absence of any Scottish legislature, can really act as a Scottish body in Scottish interests, remains to be seen.

Before these changes were put in place, the SED kept tight control over the institutions it funded directly: it is questionable whether SHEFC will provide an adequate barrier to protect the academic freedom of the twelve universities which Scotland now has if the role of the Scottish Office remains unchanged. Once again, the centrality of constitutional and political questions to the functioning of Scotland's educational system is apparent.

CONCLUSION

James Scotland has remarked that 'much of Scotland's pride in her educational tradition is unreasoning and unreasonable'.[46] Nonetheless, he concludes his two-volume history with the sentence: 'At its best the Scottish tradition in education has served the people of Scotland well.'[47] A much less sanguine verdict is offered by T.C. Smout in a chapter significantly entitled 'The Aims and Failures of Education':

> It is in the history of the school more than in any other aspect of recent social history that the key lies to some of the more depressing aspects of modern Scotland. If there are in this country too many people who fear what is new, believe the difficult to be impossible, draw back from responsibility, and afford established authority and tradition an exaggerated respect, we can reasonably look for an explanation in the institutions that moulded them.[48]

This is reminiscent of Tom Johnston's complaint about the failure of Scotland's schools to promote a 'culture of good citizenship'. Those who run the system would, of course, deny the charge. They would point out that as we move towards the end of the century many reforms are being put in place – in primary, secondary, further and higher education – which are designed to improve knowledge and skills. What is missing, however, is adequate attention to the cultural dimension, the structure of values, attitudes and beliefs by which the Scots define themselves. Also missing, of course, is a mechanism by which Scots can control their own education. Until these issues are properly addressed – and it will be a painful process – the gap between aspiration and achievement, between myth and reality, will remain.

Notes

1. W.M. Humes and H.M. Paterson (eds.), *Scottish Culture and Scottish Education 1800–1980* (Edinburgh, 1983), Introduction.

2. H.M. Knox, *Scottish Education 1696–1946* (Edinburgh, 1953).

3. R.D. Anderson, *Education and Opportunity in Victorian Scotland* (Oxford, 1983).

4. A. McPherson and C.D. Raab, *Governing Education: a Sociology of Policy since 1945* (Edinburgh, 1988).

5. J. Carter and D.J. Withrington (eds.), *Scottish Universities: Distinctiveness and Diversity* (Edinburgh, 1992).

6. J. Knox *et al.*, *The First Book of Discipline* (1560), Cit. W.C. Dickinson, G. Donaldson and I.A. Milne, *A Source Book of Scottish History*, Vol. 2, T. Nelson (Edinburgh, 1958), pp.176–77.

7. J. Currie, *The Life of Robert Burns* (London, 1826), p.2.

8. T.B. Macaulay, *History of England*, Vol. 4 (London, 1858).

9. S. Smith, *The Letters of Sydney Smith*, ed. N.C. Smith, 2 Vols. (Oxford, 1953), Vol. 1, pp.21–22.

10. E. Grant, *Memoirs of a Highland Lady*, 2 Vols. (Edinburgh, 1988), Vol. 2, p.105.

11. G.E. Davie, *The Democratic Intellect* (Edinburgh, 1961, 1981).

12. T.C. Smout is referring to the once common practice of beating children with a leather strap (the 'tawse' or the 'belt') for laziness, indiscipline or even failure to learn. The last was rare, and the practice in any case was abolished in the 1970s.

13. T.C. Smout, *A Century of the Scottish People 1830–1950* (London, 1986), p.212.

14. J. Scotland, *The History of Scottish Education*, Vol. 1 (London, 1969), p.99.

15. Ibid, p.97.

16. See W.H. Bain, "Attacking the Citadel': James Moncrieff's Proposals to Reform Scottish Education 1851–69', in *Scottish Educational Review*, X, 2 (1978), pp.5–14.

17. Scotland, op. cit., Vol. 2, pp.43–44.

18. K. MacKinnon, *Gaelic: a Past and Future Prospect* (Edinburgh, 1991); B. Kay, *Scots – the Mither Tongue* (Edinburgh, 1986); N. Grant,'The education of lingusitic minorities in Scotland', in *Aspects of Education*, 36, pp.35–52.

19. K. MacKinnon, *The Lion's Tongue* (Inverness, 1976).

20. K. MacKinnon, *Gaelic: a Past and Future Prospect*.

21. K. MacKinnon, *Occupation, Migration and Language Maintenance in Gaelic Communities*, Hatfield Polytechnic, Occasional Papers, BSS 15.1.

22. W. Gillies (ed.), *Gaelic in Scotland/Alba agus a Ghàidhlig* (Edinburgh, 1989).

23. N. Grant and J. Docherty, 'Language policy in education: some Scottish-Catalan comaparisons', in *Comparative Education*, 28, 2, 1992, pp.145–66.

24. B. Kay, op. cit.; Grant and Docherty, op. cit.

25. R. Owen, *A New View of Society and Other Writings*, (London, 1927), p.93.

26. See D.J. McLaren, *David Dale of New Lanark*, (Milngavie, 1983).

27. See D. Hamilton, 'Robert Owen and Education: a Reassessment', in Humes and Paterson (eds.), op. cit., pp.9–24.

28. *A New View of Society and Other Writings*, p.3.

29. See G.A. White, *Silk and Saints: David Stow and Infant Education 1816–1836*, unpublished M.Ed. thesis (University of Glasgow, 1983).

30. See M. Cruickshank, *A History of the Training of Teachers in Scotland*, (Edinburgh, 1970), pp.32–39.

31. Quoted in P. Boardman, *Patrick Geddes: Maker of the Future* (North Carolina, 1944), p.269.
32. Ibid, p.266.
33. Ibid, p.278.
34. Quoted in Scotland op.cit., Vol. 2, p.5.
35. J.S. Gibson, *The Thistle and the Crown: a History of the Scottish Office*, (Edinburgh, 1985), p.19.
36. Ibid., p.46.
37. Smout, op.cit., p.226.
38. Quoted in H.M. Paterson, 'Incubus and Ideology: The Devlopment of Secondary Schooling in Scotland, 1900–1939', in Humes and Paterson (eds.) op.cit., p.208.
39. Ibid., p.205.
40. See A. McPherson and C.D. Raab, *Governing Education* (Edinburgh, 1988), pp.86–93.
41. Quoted in Gibson, op.cit., p.107.
42. Ibid., p.107.
43. See W.M. Humes, *The Leadership Class in Scottish Education* (Edinburgh, 1986).
44. The CNAA took English practice as its norm, but used to provide panel members on validation in Scotland with a document outlining the peculiar features of the Scottish system.
45. The binary divide represented the division between universities, with the right to award their own degrees, and the institutions without this right. It also indicated perceived differences in status and funding, and occasioned considerable friction before it was abolished.
46. Scotland, op.cit., Vol.2, p.257.
47. Ibid., p.275.
48. Smout op.cit., p.229.

Books for Further Reading

R.C. Anderson, *Education and Opportunity in Victorian Scotland* (Oxford, 1983)
R. Bell and N. Grant, *Patterns of Education in the British Isles* (London, 1977)
T.R. Bone, *School Inspection in Scotland 1840–1966* (Edinburgh, 1968)
J. Carter and D.J. Withrington (eds.), *Scottish Universities: Distinctiveness and Diversity* (Edinburgh, 1992)
M Cruickshank, *A History of the Training of Teachers in Scotland* (Edinburgh, 1970)
G.E. Davie, *The Crisis of the Democratic Intellect* (Edinburgh, 1986)
G.E. Davie, *The Democratic Intellect* (Edinburgh, 1964), 2nd edn
J.S. Gibson, *The Thistle and the Crown: a History of the Scottish Office* (Edinburgh, 1985)
R. Houston, *Scottish Literacy and the Scottish Identity* (Cambridge, 1985)
W.M. Humes, *The Leadership Class in Scottish Education* (Edinburgh, 1986)
W.M. Humes and H.M. Paterson (eds.), *Scottish Culture and Scottish Education 1800–1980* (Edinburgh, 1983)
A. McPherson and C. Raab, *Governing Education* (Edinburgh, 1988)
J. Scotland, *The History of Scottish Education*, 2 vols. (London, 1969)
T.C. Smout, *A Century of the Scottish People 1830–1950*, (London, 1986)

The Fading Vision: Scottish Politics in the Twentieth Century

ANDREW MARR

Politics, like more conventional productions of culture, is about dreams – as well as about the attempt to turn dreams into reality. Scotland's political culture has, particularly during our own century, been both rich and distinctive. It may not have done much for the native land, but it has often been exhilarating and even, in its own way, beautiful. It has had its dreary and ugly moments too, but as one of the great mass expressions of the Scottish imagination, it deserves its chance to dress up smartly and have a day out in a book about culture. Actually, it has never been possible to separate the cultural from the political in this country. Scotland's professional writers and artists have, during this century at least, been deeper-dyed in politics than their rivals in England. The first and most obvious example is the Scottish Renaissance writers of the 1920s, led by Hugh MacDiarmid. But today's left-wing realist writers like James Kelman and William McIlvanney are their heirs; as are the nationalist novelist Alasdair Gray and the conservative polemicist and novelist Allan Massie. Those writers who have been less overtly political, from Edwin Muir then to Douglas Dunn now, have also found themselves driven towards political writing. The values and arguments of twentieth-century Scottish politics, notably socialist egalitarianism versus Tory romanticism, and Nationalism versus Unionism, have saturated the written culture. And not only the written culture. Who would deny that the folk-song revival or much of contemporary Scottish rock is political culture? In painting, the modern reaction against sticky, lurid pastiches of the great French masters, and towards a grimmer northern realism has produced one of the new art movements that is both political and (as these things go) popular.

But, of course, the country's distinctive political culture goes far deeper than the occasional novelistic or painterly outcrop. Swarming around them is the more immediately recognisable political culture. A tough, rich surface, this; it is littered with a huge range of material things that remind each generation of what went before – the constitution of the Independent Labour Party; old copies of *Scots Independent*;

67. Part of the self-government demonstration in Edinburgh on 12 December 1992 during the European Summit. At the end of the march, leaders of all opposition parties signed a joint declaration which demanded the recall of the Scottish Parliament and appealed to European governments to recognise Scotland's right to national self-determination.

parliamentary speeches; trade union banners; pamphlets by the Tory Thistle Group; party political broadcasts; Church of Scotland videos. Below these obvious creations of political culture, and supporting them, lies the fecund, mysterious subsoil of politics – the dreams of millions of Scots, both those who made and broke political movements, and those who only supported, voted for, or feared them.

When a Militant supporter and an old-style Labour Tribunite argue most passionately, steaming up the windows of some inadequately heated Co-op hall, their words are as much a product of this country's political culture as the first edition of Hugh MacDiarmid's *Second Hymn to Lenin*. When Nationalists mull over the nature of Robert Burns's patriotism late one 25 January, their most private thoughts are the political culture. And when Edinburgh bankers and lawyers meet in the New Club to brood or tut-tut about the radical tykes over in the City Chambers, they are the living extension of a political culture that would have been recognised by Walter Scott or James Boswell.

To understand Scotland's political contribution this century, it is essential to recall where it came from – that alien-but-familiar place called Victorian Scotland. It was there that the radical idealism of socialist Scotland was born. Victorian Scotland had produced a Liberal-dominated politics that was high-minded, moralistic and factional. The key to most of what followed was Presbyterianism. If the Church of England was once (strange to recall) described as the Tory Party at prayer, then the Liberal Party in Victorian Scotland could be described, only a little unfairly, as the political wing of Presbyterianism. That gave it a huge dominance, at least as great as the dominance Labour has enjoyed in Scotland since the 1960s. A century ago, nearly 80 per cent of Scottish marriages were conducted by one or another of the rival Presbyterian Kirks. Catholics accounted for a mere 10 per cent and they were virtually cut out of political influence. The Scottish Episcopalians, supporters of the 'lairds' kirk', were a tiny group, with only 46,000 communicants in 1900. These religious differences were mirrored by the size and influence of the political parties.

What did Presbyterianism give to politics that might be called distinctively Scottish? The reformers' old insistence on Scripture, and the consequent need for widespread education, then schisms, furiously debated in villages and towns across Scotland, bred a more bookish, logical and argumentative political culture than most of England possessed. Religion and rationalism, or at least reasoning, then seemed more closely connected than a modern observer would readily admit. In a little-known essay published in *The Economist* in April 1869, and entitled *The Uses of Scotch Liberalism*, Walter Bagehot gave a characteristically clear contemporary summary of how the English saw the difference:

> The Scotch Liberal . . . is essentially a rationalist, a man who looks directly from cause to effect, who reasons out his principles in his own mind, and once satisfied, applies them unflinchingly. The *perfervida vis* of Scotchmen is really to a great extent what the French call having 'the courage of their opinions', and is the precise quality English Liberals are apt to want.

I think Bagehot underestimated the idealistic, even romantic, aspects of high Victorian Liberalism in Scotland, but his basic point is sound. Since the First World War, partly because of the rise of socialism and partly because of the decline of religion, the Scottish Liberals have been a minor chord in the country's political life: keen facilitators for constitutional change and the keepers of the radical flame alive in rural Scotland, but rarely truly important in the big arguments.

Second, the long battles for a more democratic Kirk, from the epic struggles of the Covenanters through to the rivalries of the various anti-establishment kirks of Victorian times, helped inculcate a democratic spirit among some groups of Scottish workers. We should not romanticise the connection between plain, free spirits in the rural presbyteries and the democratic instinct; for many Scots of all classes, the Kirk was more burden than staff, and for many poorer Scots, it was a complacent defender of the bourgeoisie. Some of the most radical Presbyterians were among the most fervent supporters of property. Even so, centuries of Presbyterian self-organisation and hostility to bishops had their political consequences.

Third, I think it is undeniable that the Manichaean vision and self-righteousness of Calvinism re-emerged in uncompromising revolutionary form in twentieth-century socialism. Just consider the imagery used by the Scottish republican and Marxist leader John Maclean at his trial in 1918:

> No human being on the face of the earth, no government, is going to take from me my right to speak, my right to protest against wrong . . . I am not here, then, as the accused: I am here as the accuser of capitalism dripping with blood from head to foot.

It is not only the appropriation of a Christian image that is striking; the confrontation between Maclean the agitator and the Crown's Court unmistakably echoes the famous confrontations between John Knox the agitator and Queen Mary. Consider Knox's defence of his right to criticise: 'Yea, Madam, to me it appertains no less to warn of such things as may hurt [Scotland] as it does to any of the nobility, for both my vocation and my conscience crave plainness of me.' Two causes; one voice.

The dominance of Presbyterianism and Liberalism was also entangled with the early eruptions of modern Nationalist sentiment. The constitutional position of the Kirk under the Act of Union had continued to be a live issue throughout most of the nineteenth century, and the trauma of the Disruption provided later generations with an image of noble rebellion, at once patriotic and godly. Ironically, when Gladstone precipitated the decisive political event of late-Victorian Scotland, the Liberal split over Irish Home Rule, this both gave birth to the first modern Scottish Home Rule movement; and, by sundering the Liberal Party, opened the way to the twentieth-century struggle between Presbyterian Unionism and Home Rule socialism. The anti-Catholic Tories marching through Glasgow in the 1930s, and the Red Clydesiders, can be seen as rival mutant strains of Liberal Presbyterianism. In one direction, the old Liberal Party lost the anti-Catholic, anti-Home Rule Liberal Unionists, who eventually fused with the Tory Unionists. In the other direction it lost the 'Lib-Labs', leading, via the Scottish Labour Party, to both modern socialism and modern left-wing Nationalism. They may have been at war through most of this century; but they are all children of the same Liberal mother.

SOCIALIST IDEALISM

The arrival of socialism in Scotland is an old tale, well told elsewhere. The early socialist trade union leaders and Lib-Lab agitators bore the hallmarks of radical liberalism. They were keen temperance men, often strong Christians, mostly self-educated and determined to shift the Liberals leftwards. New Liberalism in Scotland had been both radical and patriotic, supporting the Highland crofters in their battles with landowners and campaigning for more genuinely Scottish candidates. The Young Scots Society was hostile to the Boer War, and the bridge between the more radical Liberals and the new socialism was a broad and easily crossed one. The first Labourites were rooted in the more militant unions, such as the mineworkers. They mixed Morris with Marx much as their English comrades did. A distinctively Scottish tinge was apparent, however, in their Home-Rulery. By the war, a clearly Scottish note is evident in the speeches of Independent Labour Party men like Maxton and Buchanan, who used the Burns cult and a diffuse Scottish Nationalist sentiment to underscore their socialist analysis. Later, in 1924, Maxton inveighed against 'English-ridden, capitalist-ridden, landowner-ridden Scotland', as if the terms were interchangeable.

To what extent has Labourism in Scotland been a distinct movement since then? For much of its history, the Labour Party north of the border has been tightly integrated into the national British movement. It has had its own trades union congress, some independent unions and a continuing interest in Home Rule, although sometimes that has been the cause of a very small minority. Glasgow's municipal socialism was a distinctive achievement and in many smaller Scottish burghs, an imaginative and energetic assault on old social evils brought great local results. However, through the middle of the century, from the 1930s to the 1960s, one would be hard put to distinguish anything essentially Scottish, rather than British, about the party's thinking, though of course its members made a contribution to the British party.

Anyone looking for a peculiarly Scottish socialist tradition would probably have turned instead to the Nationalist republican fringe, or the highly educated, articulate and influential Communists of Fife. The Unionist heyday of the Labour Party produced two quite outstanding leaders, Tom Johnston and Willie Ross. Both were essentially practical politicians, deeply rooted in their native culture. Had the cards fallen differently it might have been Johnston, not Attlee, who led the British Labour Party to its victory in 1945; as it was, he more than anyone was responsible for the achievements of post-war corporatism in Scotland, including the Hydro Board and the Forestry Commission. Willie Ross, a devout and headmasterly Presbyterian, built up Labour into an unbeatable-looking Scottish political machine, which he ruled with a tawse of iron. But in the context of this cultural history, I think the two most interesting periods for Labour were the 1920s and the devolutionary era, running from the late 1960s to the present day.

Scottish Labour in the 1920s was dominated by the moral force and vigour of the Clydesiders, rather than by the national leadership of Ramsay MacDonald, the former Liberal and pacifist, who was moving slowly but decisively to the right. Labour's breakthrough had been achieved because of the First World War and the extension of the franchise in 1918, which tripled the size of the Scottish electorate. Then the achievement of Irish Home Rule released Catholics from the particular demands of that cause, and started to bring the first flood of Catholic workers into the Labour ranks. MacDonald, high-minded, talented and emotional, was worried by Glasgow's 'hair-raising reputation', and much of Labour's internal struggle during these years was a tug of war between MacDonald and the rest of the respectable leadership, keen to spread Labour's appeal, versus the Clydesiders and the Independent Labour Party (ILP), dominated by the Clydesiders. The ILP was a dominant force in Scottish socialist politics and its decline, after losing the battle for influence in Parliament, was followed by the decline of Scottish Labour politics as a distinctive force itself. 'ILP' and 'Scottish socialist radicalism' are not quite equivalent terms, but the overlap in the 1920s was clear.

The ILP Clydesiders proved, in argument after argument between the wars, that they were simply further left and less compromising than the Labour Party's national leadership. Whether the issue was slum clearance or macro-economics, national insurance or Spain, they were to be found urging solutions that frightened the middle classes and irritated the MacDonald leadership. MacDonald felt that they were scaring off millions of voters, particularly in England, and so holding back the cause of socialism by self-indulgent theatricals. They thought he was selling out the Vision Splendid to the imperatives of the London establishment. Both, of course, were right.

Yet years of caricature of the Clydesiders, both by hostile critics, from *Punch* to *The Times*, and by the equally blur-eyed romantics of the left, have obscured their views and importance. There is truth in the impression of fervent and impractical revolutionaries, who were eventually ground down by the unimaginative and corrupting influence of Westminster. But they saw themselves as practical and down-to-earth politicians too. John Wheatley, who organised the Catholic Labour voters, produced a Housing Act which stands as one of the party's few solid achievements before 1945. Home Rule, which the Clydesiders pushed unsuccessfully in Bills in 1924 and 1927 was seen as a practical affair: as George Buchanan, the portly, clerical sponsor of the earlier bill, explained to the Commons:

> [in Glasgow] you have the tragedy going on day after day, a death rate of four times the number of children than the death rate in a well-to-do division, and this is not because our people are poor, or Scottish, or Irish, or drunkards. It is not even because this Parliament is brutal towards our people. It is because this Parliament cannot devote the time to the work, and furthermore because it has no knowledge of the problems with which we are confronted.

Ultimately, though, the Clydesiders were caught in the trap that has maimed all radical movements in Britain: the cautious conservatism of middle England which, by virtue of sheer numbers, dominated the House of Commons and thus the British political system. The Labour leadership, in 1924 and 1929–31, felt the urgent need to the respectable. The primary motivation was not, despite MacDonald's legendary fondness for grand society hostesses, personal corruption; but the need to spread the party's electoral base far enough to fully replace the Liberals as the national anti-Tory force – something that was only finally achieved in 1945, under very different circumstances. This meant that the radicalism, the Home-Rulery, the parliamentary aggression and indeed the very language of the Scottish radical Labourites was irrelevant to the purpose of the party leadership – indeed, hostile to it. The socialist vision proclaimed relentlessly on Glasgow Green from the rent-strikes of the First World War through to the 1930s – proclaimed in heightened prose which mingled the argumentative steeliness of religion with the democratic sentiment of Burns – was as nothing to the arithmetic of the Commons benches. A whole Scottish radical tradition, which had risen from the country's Victorian experience, and poured from the early twentieth-century cities, was quietly and effectively dammed by the British Parliament.

Did it stagnate? The sheer dullness of Scottish Labourism from the 1940s to the early 1960s may suggest so. But these were the years of achievement of British Labourism, the years of the building of the welfare state, of slum-clearance and the creation of new homes which did not then seem fated to become the new slums. And many Scottish socialists played a significant part, not least by helping produce the Labour parliamentary majorities that made it possible. It would be intellectual élitism of the worst sort to equate their dourness and party discipline with conservativism: they may have been grey and unimaginative, but they were also doggedly determined to achieve concrete advances. Less blethers, mair action, heids doon. Johnston and Ross, as I have suggested, were big figures, who dreamed big dreams and changed the face of Scotland, for all their lack of enthusiasm for fiery, Clydesiderish rhetoric.

Even so, when discussing the Scottishness of Scottish socialism, we can leap ahead, so far as Labour is concerned, to the devolutionist era. Even here, devolution was a top-down project: it was a plot cooked up in London by Harold Wilson, Dick Crossman and others to stop the spread of Scottish Nationalism. The arid, administrative nature of the word itself should be enough of an indication that there was never a spontaneous uprising of feeling in Scotland for devolution. That said, the most aggressive and adventurous Labour Home Rulers of the 1960s and 1970s, men like Harry Ewing, Jim Sillars, John P. Mackintosh and Alex Kitson, were rediscovering a Home Rule tradition that had been confined to the fringes of the movement for a generation. Some, like Kitson, were carriers of the tradition through the Home Rule-supporting Scottish trade unions; others, like Sillars, were converts, who felt the scales were torn from their eyes.

They may have started by knee-jerking to the Nationalist threat, but they advanced beyond that, to create a variant of British socialism which stressed the northern radical, the danger of Whitehall centralism and the rightness of local solutions to local problems. The 'Watchdog group' was a centre of intellectual excitement, as was the short-lived breakaway Scottish Labour Party (SLP), which was launched in early 1976 and quickly torn apart by Trotskyist entryism and personal feuding. Going back now to look at the election literature and constitution of the SLP, one is struck by how much its creators – above all Sillars – were intent on trying to reach back to the origins of Labour in Scotland. They were trying to recover some of the fire and primal purity of the movement they felt had become compromised and wearied by years in power in London. (In tone, indeed, it was not so different from the later SNP '79 Group' of Nationalist-socialists.) For their Labour foes, such as Tam Dalyell and Neil Kinnock, those years of 'compromise' had brought Scotland, like the rest of Britain, almost every modern socialist gain – better housing, the National Health Service, transplanted industries. So they stressed the danger of pandering to nationalism and the importance of a strong, central socialist state. This was a real argument about the nature of left-wing politics – one that Gramsci would have enjoyed, and Willy Brandt would have understood – and its implications which went well beyond the immediate cause of stopping the SNP.

Finally, of course, the SLP died and so did devolution, destroyed by the 1979 referendum. This is not the place to rehearse again the complex arguments about why the referendum failed to reach the 40 per cent hurdle of 'yes' voters required by Parliament, other than to recall that it took place against the background of the 'winter of discontent' and profound anti-Callaghan feeling. The political inheritance of the long and bitter devolution battle inside the Labour Party was the reappearance of a strong Home Rule faction, one which survived and grew during the 1980s and has become dominant inside the Scottish party today – at local level, if not among the MPs.

Apart from wanting a Scottish parliament, what has it offered that is not shared by the average Labour supporter in, say, Tyneside or Essex? The answer can only be a conscious belief in the democratic and radical Scottish tradition, however vaguely apprehended – a belief that the Scottish people remain more keenly democratic, readier to pay taxes to transfer wealth and more hostile to the atomised social vision of libertarian Tories, than their English neighbours. Deep idealism? Naïve Nationalism, tinged with racism? Or a little of both? The Scots may have voted against Margaret Thatcher, but they bought their council houses, used her legislation on parental choice, and pocketed any income-tax cuts on offer. It is a rum thought that the very existence of an influential strain of distinctively Scottish social radicalism should now be a matter for serious debate. The Vision Splendid, ninety years on, has no more substance than a dream.

THE NATIONALISTS

Modern Scottish Nationalism had a mixed origin, and the mixture has affected it ever since. On the one hand there were the overtly Nationalist groups which had started early in the century, and were often cultural or reactionary – in the true sense of that abused word – Jacobite song-singers and fantasists. On the other hand was the Home Rule tradition inside the mainstream parties, above all the Liberal and Lib-Lab tradition which has already been discussed.

The political catalyst which led to a fusion of outright Nationalists and fervent Home Rulers was the failure of Scotland's Labour MPs to achieve self-government for their country during the 1920s. This persuaded a growing number of people that a new party was needed and led directly to the founding of the National Party of Scotland in April 1928.

Most of its influential founders were, or had been, socialists. The National Party leader between the wars, 'King' John MacCormick, had started as a Labour supporter at Glasgow University. The new party's sugar-daddy, a tannery owner and one-time anarchist called Roland Eugene Muirhead, had previously funded the Scottish Labour paper *Forward*, and backed the Lib-Lab Scottish Home Rule Association. Its most famous, or notorious, early propagandist, was R.B. Cunninghame Graham, former radical Liberal aristocrat and (with Keir Hardie) a founder of the Scottish Labour Party. Any observer of the early beginnings of the party would have thought it a safe prediction that it would have been staunchly socialist. Yet it never was: indeed, within a few years, it was denouncing class politics as alien to Scotland, campaigning vehemently against Irish immigration and negotiating a merger with the right-wing Scottish Party, partly to obtain the kudos of having the Duke of Montrose as one of its leaders. Since the war between the Nationalists and the Labour Party in Scotland has been one of great dividing-lines in modern Scottish politics, it is perhaps worth dwelling on this apparent paradox.

I think it goes to the heart of the ambiguous Nationalist appeal. For although the list of National Party founders included many self-described socialists, it did not include a single mainstream trade unionist or working-class Labour figure. These were, after all, years of depression at home and revolution abroad: even for Labour's natural Home Rule radicals such as the Red Clydesiders, there were other priorities. After Ramsay MacDonald split the Labour Party by forming his National Government, the

Scottish Labour left and the waning Independent Labour Party were struggling to keep socialism alive as a powerful native force. It didn't help that, just as the National Party of Scotland was looking around for support at home, the country's Labour and Communist supporters were becoming ever more involved in the crusade against the extreme nationalist-fascists of Italy, Spain and Germany. At the same time, general left-wing support for the Soviet Union and socialists across Europe was identified as specifically anti-nationalist. As Jimmie Maxton wrote afterwards:

> When the Scottish Nationalists came to us, who were the supporters of International Socialism, and told us that if we were to secure their support we would have to place nationalism in front of international socialism in our programme and in our activities, I declined to do it.

Nor was the National Party similar in tone or composition to Labour. The new party attracted the in-betweeners of politics, disaffected aristocrats, poets, small businessmen, lawyers and self-employed people. Its centres were Edinburgh, the east coast towns and the Highlands, not Glasgow or the industrial belt. Because of this make-up and perhaps because of its regional spread, it was forever struggling for respectability. It yearned for support from the (by now conservative) Kirk and from the leaders of Scottish society. Many Nationalists were beguiled by a general, benign Home-Rulery among Conservative and Liberal politicians. Figures like Churchill, Lord Beaverbrook, the already mentioned Duke of Montrose, Bob Boothby and the Scottish Liberal leader Lady Glen-Coats had all expressed enthusiasm for Home Rule. Could not a more respectable and moderate National Party help shape and lead a broad Scottish coalition for constitutional change? It was this hope that led MacCormick to fuse the National Party with the right-wing Scottish Party in 1934, thus forming the SNP.

Yet MacCormick's struggle for respectability was a futile one. The Liberals were a meagre force to rely on as allies. And though MacCormick drove his party rightwards, and expelled many of the more extreme or maverick supporters, the poets and the hardline Nationalists, he never had the slightest chance of winning over mainstream Conservative Unionist opinion. Perhaps he mistook nods and winks from a few mavericks for the real thing. At any rate, the party was trapped, shunned by organised Labour and despised by business leaders and the aristrocracy alike. Right from the beginning, and still today, the Scottish Nationalist appeal attracted many similar types to English Liberalism: the banner of choice for the awkward squad, the dreamers, the defiantly individualist. It has made for a lively and unpredictable party, but rarely for a mass movement.

At a deeper level, the strategic catch-22 for Scottish Nationalists has never been satisfactorily resolved, and perhaps cannot be. Should they be moderate, prepared to go for Home Rule as an interim measure, ready to work with all other groups to build a consensus? Or should they stand firmly on their Nationalist principles and fight at the ballot-box to win a mandate for the change they want?

If they go for the consensual path, they find themselves betrayed or ignored by the other parties. John MacCormick broke with the SNP in 1942 in search of the consensual path: on the surface, the argument was about resistance to wartime conscription, considered unacceptable by hardline nationalists, but really it was about strategy. He then founded his Scottish Convention which swept Scotland after the war with its 'covenant' demanding Home Rule. Millions signed. It seemed to be a great triumph for the consensual approach, particularly since the SNP was languishing in near-total obscurity at the time. But MacCormick found his grand movement simply ignored by Westminster: the Labour and Tory MPs there were playing by the parliamentary system, and MacCormick's attempt to create a national consensus was outside it.

Similarly, the SNP, on a roll because of Scotland's oil wealth and disillusion with Labour during the 1960s and 1970s, underwent great internal agonies in trying to respond to Labour's devolutionary riposte. The SNP backed devolution, even though its leaders understood full well that devolution was intended to disarm the nationalists. They gambled that the halfway house would become the slippery slope. But when Labour was only able to offer a weak form of devolution, and then was unable to deliver it because of the 40 per cent hurdle in the 1979 referendum, the SNP too was swept away in the ensuing election. The third attempt to create a national consensus for change, the Scottish Constitutional Convention of the late 1980s and early 1990s, was badly damaged by the SNP's refusal to take part. This was partly caused by personal pique and internal bickering, but those in the SNP leadership who declined to work with Labour had the memories of the 1940s and 1970s to use as justification for their stand.

So much for the consensual approach, thus far. Yet the electoral route has been no more successful. Until the 1970s, the SNP was only a marginal party so far as Westminster seats were concerned. There were the odd by-election excitements and interesting polls, but nothing to really alarm the mainstream parties. Then came what seemed like the breakthrough: the October 1974 election was the SNP's electoral high point, when it added four to the seven seats it had won in the February election, giving it eleven MPs and just over 30 per cent of the vote. It has come nowhere near that performance since, despite high hopes in the 1980s. No doubt the first-past-the-post electoral system is partly to blame, but the SNP must live with that for the time being. When pro-Nationalist moderates are harangued about the implausibility of doing deals with Labour or the Liberal Democrats, then they can simply point to the hardliners' electoral (un)success. The truth is, neither approach has worked.

The SNP's current leader, Alex Salmond, has moved the party gently leftwards, and believes that electoral success in the Labour heartland will be, sooner or later, essential if the SNP is to achieve independence in Europe. Yet he has been of the moderate tendency in the past when it comes to strategy. The SNP has a young and talented leader, stronger support than it did amongst working-class Scots, and a plausible-sounding programme. Its rhetoric and arguments have echoed across the Scottish political landscape for more than sixty years and at times dominated it. Yet Scotland is not noticeably nearer to independence now than it was when the National Party was founded at a Bannockburn rally in 1928.

TORIES, OR UNIONISTS, OR BOTH

Scotland's most successful modern political party has been one of Scotland's weakest parties: the Scottish Conservative and Unionist Party. It has achieved this paradoxical position because of the huge strength of the English Conservatives at Westminster, making it the northern wing of the most successful party in the UK, and one of the most successful parties in Europe. The Scottish Tories have had their political obituaries written many times. They have only eleven of the seventy-two Scottish seats. Their constitutional Unionism is unpopular in Scotland. Yet they are still there, still in control, and modern Scotland is increasingly shaped in their image. Despite the dominance of socialism and Nationalism in this century's Scottish politics, the country today owes more to the values of Conservatism – the dominance of the free market, the spread of home-ownership, the weakening of trade unionism and local government – than to any other creed.

The Conservatives' enemies have often tried to portray the party as alien to Scotland, somehow less Scottish than any other. And there is a certain surface plausibility about the argument. After all, the Liberal Democrats can trace their political ancestry back to the party which dominated Scotland throughout the nineteenth century. Labour has been dominant through much of this century and is still by far the most popular party. And what could be more Scottish than Scottish Nationalism? Beside their rivals, and despite their brief dominance of the electoral map in the 1950s, the Scottish Tories have found it hard to define their distinctively Scottish character. They are certainly a Nationalist party, but their flag is, and has always been, the Union Jack. For much of their modern history, they were defined first and foremost by their allegiance to Westminster, and the union with a larger neighbour: from 1912 to 1965 there was officially no 'Conservative Party' north of the Border, only the 'Scottish Unionist Association'.

Conservatives have responded, with some force, that many of their beliefs and political inheritance are distinctively Scottish. Free trade was a central tenet of the Scottish Enlightenment. Though Margaret Thatcher distorted Adam Smith by failing to highlight his rich social philosophy, in economics he was the high priest of market solutions. And across large swathes of rural and small-town Scotland, Conservative values, whether they be enthusiasm for the Royal Family or a hatred of taxation and government generally, have continued to dominate. The conservative instinct and the Conservative stress on the market are general and widespread human values and it is ultimately absurd to deny them the accolade of Scottishness. They may not be especially Scottish, but then neither are socialism or Nationalism. They may not be roaringly popular in Scotland, but then neither is modern Scottish poetry. Many people (including this writer) would say that, since the most 'Scottish' aspect of modern Toryism was, for many years, its militant Orange Order strand, then the less specifically Scottish the party becomes, the better for Scotland.

It is harder to establish achievements of the Scottish branch of the Conservative movement which have been both positive and distinctive to Scotland. Indeed, I think there is only one: the creation and extension of the Scottish Office itself. Administrative devolution was the Unionist response to nationalism, the bureaucratic alternative to the party's occasional flirtations with devolution (in the early 1900s, then under Edward Heath, and including the federalist enthusiasms of the Thistle Group of the 1960s). It may be the shadowy administrative government-in-waiting that has never had a parliament to fully legitimise it, but the Scottish Office has succeeded in giving a tartan tinge to the Westminster system and can perhaps explain some of the Unionist success. Ian Lang's recent additions to its powers are probably the furthest possible extent of such 'bureaucratic devolution'.

CONCLUSION

If there is one big theme in the story of Scottish politics this century that runs through most of this chapter, it is surely the decline of a quasi-religious vision. What made Scottish politics different was the impact of Presbyterian idealism on the country, a vague amalgam of strongly-held democratic beliefs and visionary language – the hope, if not of a godly society, then at least of a goodly society. That seems to me to have been defeated by the prosaic and the down-to-earth. A melancholy theme? Well, at least we no longer loathe one another because of our religious inclinations – if a lot of the fire has gone, then so too has a lot of the hatred. Life in the lost twentieth century, the country that might have ruled itself but didn't, must remain a matter for conjecture. Nor, of course, does the story end here. I have left until last the faint and weak possibility that the 'civil politics' of cross-party, and no-party, action for constitutional change in Scotland might be the harbinger of a new kind of Scottish politics for the century ahead. These are grim times for groups such as the Scottish Constitutional Convention (virtually dead), Scotland United (struggling for survival) and the smaller organisations such as Common Cause. Party politics has both failed to serve Scotland very well, and yet maintained a stranglehold as firm as ever on political activity. Still, it is just possible that the 'civil politicians' may be early prophets of different ways of doing business in the century to come. Now get you out and drink to that.

Books for Further Reading

Jack Brand, *The National Movement in Scotland* (London, 1978)

David Daiches, *Scotland and the Union* (Edinburgh, 1977)

I. Donnachie, C. Harvie and I.S. Wood (eds.), *Forward! Labour Politics in Scotland 1888–1988* (Edinburgh, 1988)

Owen Dudley Edwards, *A Claim of Right for Scotland* (Edinburgh, 1989)

Michael Fry, *Patronage and Principle* (Aberdeen, 1987)

Tom Gallagher (ed.), *Nationalism in the '90s* (Edinburgh, 1991)

H.J. Hanham, *Scottish Nationalism* (London, 1969)

Christopher Harvie, *Scotland and Nationalism* (London, 1977)

James G. Kellas, *The Scottish Political System* (Cambridge, 1973)

Neil MacCormick (ed.), *The Scottish Debate* (Oxford, 1970)

Andrew Marr, *The Battle for Scotland* (London, 1992)

James Mitchell, *Conservatives and the Union* (Edinburgh, 1990)

Tom Nairn, *The Break-Up of Britain* (2nd edn; London, 1981)

Paul H. Scott, *Scotland in Europe: a Dialogue with a Sceptical Friend* (Edinburgh, 1992)

Paul H. Scott, *Towards Independence: Essays on Scotland* (Edinburgh, 1991)

Will Storrar, *Scottish Identity: a Christian Vision* (??, 1990)

Publishing, Journalism and Broadcasting

IAN BELL

Few things symbolise the condition of the Scottish press better than the fact that the only mainstream newspaper recently to have endorsed the idea of an independent Scotland is one which otherwise acts as a berserk accomplice to the only party rejecting national self-determination. This is more than bizarre: it marks a significant moment in the history of media which have never, in Scotland, lacked for self-regard.

There is black comedy of a sort to be had, perhaps, in the fact that the *Sun*'s patriotic Scottish management were obliged to troop to London to win permission for their decision to support the SNP ahead of the 1992 general election. The image is almost too perfect, too typical, too suggestive of all those who went before. But Mr Rupert Murdoch, from whom the Nationalists' blessings flow, has a casual attitude to nationality: once an Australian, he is now – for reasons of multinational business – a citizen of the United States, albeit with 'Scottish roots'. It disturbed his equilibrium not at all to allow the *Sun*'s Scottish edition to 'fight for independence' a few years after the same newspaper, in reference to public spending on Scotland, had carried the headline 'Will ye stop your snivelling, Jock?'

There is nothing new, historically speaking, about the process. The first periodical to appear in Scotland was a simple reprint of the *London Diurnal Occurrances*, published in 1642. *Mercurius Scotius*, which appeared at Leith in 1651, was the first to claim, as the *Sun* does today, to be edited and printed in Scotland. Yet it, like most which followed in the eighteenth century, filled its pages with material lifted from London publications. The *Scots Magazine*, our oldest surviving journal, appeared in 1739 declaring an intention to promote the 'prosperity' of Scotland, but as Mary E. Craig[1] has recorded, the London periodicals had two advantages, which they retain. First, they were located in the political capital. Second, they used a language – English – 'which had of late taken on new value for Scotsmen'. Of seven known Scottish periodicals operating in 1750 – the *Edinburgh Evening Courant*, the *Caledonian Mercury*, the *Glasgow Journal*, the *Glasgow Courant*, the *Aberdeen Journal*, the *Scots*

Magazine, and the wonderfully titled *An Exortation to the Inhabitants of the South Parish of Glasgow and the Hearers in the College Kirk* – only the last and the *Scots Magazine* did not filch most of their material from London. Of the two, only the *Scots Magazine* showed any sign of what might be called cultural ambition.

The dependence on London, especially helpful to Edinburgh publishers situated at the terminus of the mail route, set a pattern. A contributor to the 1987 *Scottish Government Yearbook*[2] asserted: 'It is hard to see how the *Sun*, even if it produced a Scottish edition, could get over the mismatch between its very obvious political ideology and the very different ideology which prevails in Scotland.' But Murdoch's sheet did, with no difficulty at all, just as the *Daily Express* had endorsed Mrs Winnie Ewing at the 1967 Hamilton by-election and supported devolution for Scotland until a change of ownership at the title produced a Pauline conversion in 1977. National identity is, for the media, a marketing device. The indigenous media embrace it, one might argue, because they have no choice.

Craig wrote, of an eighteenth-century country of one million souls: 'There was scarcely a suggestion of the existence of an intellectual life in Scotland in any of the domestic newspapers.' In her period Edinburgh enjoyed a cultural renaissance that now seems like an attempt to heal the scars of the Union. Glasgow, meanwhile, got on with the business of becoming the Empire's tobacco market before finding cotton to be a better British bet.

Most of Scotland's major newspapers have long histories. The *Aberdeen Press and Journal* claims to have been born in 1748, though the modern title was in reality created from an amalgamation with the *Free Press* in 1922. The *Herald* began as the *Glasgow Herald* (formerly the *Glasgow Advertiser*) in 1783. D.C. Thomson's *Courier & Advertiser* was founded in 1801, the *Scotsman* in 1817. But while James G. Kellas has described Scottish newspapers as independent or as 'autonomous members of London publishing companies'[3] this is a charitable stretching of the meanings of the words 'independent' and 'autonomous'.

The media of communications are neither politically nor culturally 'stable'. It is easy to assert that they are crucial to the formation and preservation of national identity but a good deal harder to prove: the relationships are never clear and rarely simple. The pressures to which publishers, broadcasters and film-makers respond are primarily economic. Given that modern communications tend invariably to globalisation, the idea of 'national media' may even be self-contradictory. Where, and in whom, does the media's version of national identity then reside? Whatever the maps or the politicians say, we are all citizens of a trans-national electronic commonwealth. Add to that an increasing concentration of ownership (of which Mr Murdoch is the exemplar) and the republic becomes an oligarchy; the behaviour of the Scottish *Sun* unexceptional. When newspapers, television and radio have devolved edition structures and centralised policy-making, it is merely sensible to serve the local audience: local news, local politics, local 'culture'. The exploitation, if you like, of the indigenous.

Scotland and its newspapers are not, in that sense, unique. The pressures of anglicisation are well known and well charted; the pressures of globalisation (an ugly word for an ugly process) are if anything more powerful. Other small countries and other media share the experience, and broadcasting offers clearer examples than print. Yet the history of the Scottish media shows a pattern that was in place before communications satellites, video tape or computerised typesetting. Christopher Harvie[4] has noted that in 1920 twenty newspapers, each of them Scottish-owned, served Scotland's major centres of population. By 1940 there were nineteen titles, eight of which were English-owned. By 1980, however, there were only fifteen papers. Four were in Scottish hands; two were English-owned; and no fewer than nine were the property of multinationals.

Recently, the *Herald* has come back into Scottish hands after a spell with the Lonhro conglomerate, but both Edinburgh and Aberdeen are dominated by newspapers owned by a subsidiary of the International Thomson Organisation. The *Scotsman* regards itself as Scotland's national newspaper yet it is run by the precisely designated Thomson Regional Newspapers. The *Sun*, as we have seen, is Murdoch's; the *Daily Record* and *Sunday Mail* are part of the Mirror Group stable. Only D.C. Thomson (Thomson-Leng), publishers of the *Sunday Post*, can claim an unbroken history of Scottish ownership. Yet that newspaper, viciously reactionary and mindlessly couthy in equal measure, has been as destructive of the Scottish identity as any, not because it ignores Scottishness but because it neuters Scottishness, remaking the nation in the image of the theme park, where myths do service for truths. So successful has the *Post* been over the years that its tartanry ('the *Honest* Truth') is now accepted as the genuine article by many Scots.

Yet while the Thomson title may be the worst, it is not alone. Others are less brazen, more sincere, more scrupulous. But from a leader in the federalist *Scotsman* counselling caution, always caution, to an angry electorate, to the opportunism of the *Sun*, to the annual ersatz festivities of a television Hogmanay show, the media have followed grudgingly and led rarely. They have for decades, perhaps for centuries, acted as a distorting mirror. The exceptions have been rare and have not long survived. Part of the argument of this survey is that the Scottish media as a whole have been complicit in the denial of the Scottish identity and have, as an ironic consequence, laid the seeds of their own eventual destruction. After all, what is the point of indigenous media if they forever frustrate, wittingly or unwittingly, the nation which supports them? It is a self-contradictory proposition.

At first sight, the charges seem ludicrous. Over the last two decades the *Scotsman* and the *Herald* have tracked – and sometimes stimulated – the debate over Scotland's cultural and political identity. The Labour-supporting and devolutionist *Daily Record*, the country's best-selling daily newspaper, continues to serve the largest block of voters with unwavering journalistic selectivity. Whether they succeed or fail, our broadcasters take their duties to Scotland seriously, and are bound by law to do so. If any political grouping has reason to feel disenfranchised, you might think, it is the Conservative Party which, in sharp contrast to England, now has no newspaper it can truly call its own. Scottish Tories certainly think so.

The idea that Scotland's media are in rude independent health is supported, to take one inadvertent example, by a writer like John Osmond.[5] Drawing on Michael Steed's core-periphery model of British political geography, he divides the morning press into five 'zones', of which only the first three need concern us:

1. London-based 'national' dailies, doubling up as the only morning papers for the south-east inner core.
2. A changing situation in Manchester, with most major London dailies having distinctive northern editions.
3. An almost fully separate Scottish press, with only limited penetration from papers published in England.

As far as it goes, this is perfectly true. The combined circulation in Scotland of English quality papers comes nowhere near the circulation of the *Herald* alone. Historically, English titles have found the distribution challenges posed by Scotland's geography to be a game not worth the candle. But for the most part, foreign media groups have solved their Scottish problem either by buying Scottish titles – a process exemplified by Roy Thomson's purchase of the *Scotsman* from Sir Edmund Findlay in 1953 – or by establishing Scottish editions of English titles. Beaverbrook, it should be remembered, launched the *Scottish Daily Express* as far back as 1928 as a 'devolutionist' response to the Home Rule ferment of the period, providing Murdoch with his model for a *Sun* with, in newspaper jargon, 'a kilt on it'. Thomson used the *Scotsman* as a stepping-stone to the Scottish Television franchise, his 'licence to print money' (compelling the BBC, in the process, to offer separate Scottish news bulletins).

To that extent, the Scottishness of the Scottish press is merely superficial, if by Scottishness it is meant a willingness to reflect the views of the majority. The *editorial* positions adopted by the broadsheet press in Glasgow, Edinburgh, Dundee and Aberdeen during the last four general election campaigns have demonstrated as much. The *Herald* and *Scotsman* have, for example, covered the self-determination debate in minute detail; they have measured the growth of the demand for it in endless opinion polls; they have questioned the government's mandate on scores of occasions. Yet neither has been willing to endorse Labour or the SNP with conviction, though the former is Scotland's biggest party and the latter the focus of explicit dissent from 'Britishness'. The refusal is fundamental, for between them these two parties represent the vast majority of Scots. Scotland's 'opinion-formers' have declared themselves to be a minority in their own land. It seems not to make even commercial sense but it was, broadly speaking, ever thus.

Until the late 1950s all the main Scottish titles – with the exception of the *Daily Record* and the *Sunday Mail* – were Tory. After the Thomson purchase the *Scotsman* embraced Liberalism; in 1970 and 1974 it flirted with Nationalism before returning to the Lib-Dem fold. The *P&J* deserted the Tories for the SNP in the late 1960s but endorsed the Alliance in 1983. The 'Scottish' *Daily Mail* played the devolution card until its closure in 1968 but the *Herald* did not come out for an assembly until 1975. By 1983, all the main titles (save the *Record* and *Sunday Mail*) were offering their affections to the Conservatives or the Alliance.

Does this matter? It is easy to argue that Labour voters in England have rarely been well represented by the predominately Tory London papers, but this misses the point: the appeal of the Scottish titles turns on their Scottishness, however genuine. They are, or claim to be, part and parcel of the national unit. But if the nation dissents from the British settlement and defies British political trends how truly national is Scotland's national press?

In reality, the political relationship of, in particular, the *Herald* and the *Scotsman* with the London core mirrors the relationship between the Scottish media as a whole and the English capital while echoing an old pattern. Again, the reasons are at bottom economic. Neither newspaper will alienate its crucial readers within the business community – perceived to be almost wholly Unionist – any more than Scottish Television would seek to withdraw from the British independent television network. The banner of nationalism in the press is thus borne, laughably enough, by the *Sun*, while the *Record* trudges dutifully behind the Labour carthorse. It is all explicable, but it lays bare the myth of an independent Scottish press.

Equally, the Scottish media seem unwilling to recognise, and ill-prepared to meet, the challenge of global culture. Scottish Television alone, perhaps, has seen the threat, having been given a stark warning by the Thatcher-inspired television franchise auctions. Scottish is a prosperous company, but tiny in global terms. These are, economically, the only terms which count. The broadcaster, having fought its way into the inner councils of the network, and having demonstrated a commitment to Scottish culture while making and selling the thrillers and game shows the market demands, is ripe for a take-over attempt by a foreign competitor, whether English or Continental. And as we have seen with the press, it is perfectly possible to run a Scottish outpost whether your headquarters are in London, Manchester or Milan.

The problem of the Scottish media is easily put: how do you represent, report or foster a national identity − even if you are sure what it is − when everywhere communications are falling into the hands of multinationals who, by definition, have no country? How can you even begin when you seem uncomfortable with your own role within the nation? How can you do it when your nation's existence goes unrecognised? Assimilation has long been a problem for the Scottish media confronted with the demands of a larger neighbour. At the end of the twentieth century, the challenge is vastly more complex.

In other words, the simple possession of 'our' newspapers, 'our' broadcasters, 'our' publishers and 'our' film-makers would not resolve many questions: it never has. Today, across the globe, a shadow war is being fought between defenders of cultural identity and the multinationals. At a conference on cultural policies in Mexico City in 1982 (Mondicault '82), Jack Lang, then the French minister of culture, asserted:

> Culture and artistic creation . . . is today victim of a system of multinational financial domination against which we must organise ourselves . . . Is it our destiny to become the vassals of an immense empire of profit?

To which a French critic replied:

> While waiting for further episodes of *Dallas*, Moroccan television is showing another series, *The Conquest of the West*. In French! This is a double insult to the Arab viewer who cares nothing about America and does not understand French. Thus American imperialism is transmitted to the Third World via Paris.[6]

A Scot might, with equal conviction, subsitute London for the French capital. Ownership of the means of transmission, like ownership of the means of production, is not itself a panacea. Culture is imported and exported: the media are conduits.

There is a belief, still prevalent and still partly true, that the Scots have a peculiarly close relationship with their media and that, in consequence, the media are more tenacious in their Scottishness. T.C. Smout and Sydney Wood[7] have caught the image in one recollection of a nineteenth-century working man, 'a dour, stern, Calvinistic Scotsman, a man of few words . . .':

> On his way home from work he would buy the *Evening Citizen*, the only evening paper then published in Glasgow which upheld Liberalism. After supper, the paper was unfolded and the old man began the reading of the four pages; woe betide if any noise or talking was indulged in by the family until the task was completed.

Harvie asserts[8] that at the time of the 1872 Education Act 14 per cent more Scots children than English children were at school. Similarly, by 1960, Edinburgh held the British record for books borrowed per head per annum from public libraries. 'The Scots,' he writes, 'read newspapers avidly' and 'probably' bought more, in the central belt at least, than people elsewhere in Britain. Writing of recent trends, Kellas[9] supports the claim: in the 1980s morning dailies were read by 84 per cent of Scots when the UK figure was 75 per cent; the figures for Sunday titles were 88 per cent and 78 per cent respectively.

The phenomenon had historical roots: the *Glasgow Herald*, be it remembered, was born in the eighteenth century. The *Edinburgh Review*, the inspiration of Henry Brougham, Francis Horner, Francis Jeffrey and Sydney Smith, appeared in 1802 and was selling 14,000 copies by 1818.[10] After 1817 there was, too, *Blackwood's*, raised to its eminence by John Gibson Lockhart and John Wilson ('Christopher North'), while in 1827 Adam Black bought the copyright to the *Encyclopaedia Britannica*. Chambers, Thomas Nelson and Oliver and Boyd all conspired to give Edinburgh its reputation as a publishing centre.

Yet in the first half of the nineteenth century, when the story properly begins, these media pioneers had for the most part been involved, like most of the Scottish middle class, in sealing the Union − or at least healing the wound it had left − rather than preserving the Scottish identity. Robert Louis Stevenson, a subtle Unionist, could concede that the enforced relationships between Scotland, Ireland and Britain 'were equally obnoxious to the majority of the lesser nations most directly concerned',[11] but the mainstream press granted no such doubts. The *Edinburgh Courant*, first among the Tory papers and perhaps the first 'national' title, died in 1886 when the *Scotsman*, formerly Whig, became Unionist. Scottishness, indeed, was expressed best in matters of religion, in the *Free Church Witness* (1840–60), notably under the editorship of Hugh Miller, and the *Scottish Guardian*. Chartist papers aside, a typical example of the Scottish relationship with London was the *British Weekly*, founded in 1886 by a Free Church minister. Though it was published in London it nevertheless enjoyed a wide following north of the Border. Professor W.B. Blaikie, another Free Church man, had led the way with the explicitly-titled *North British Review*, launched in 1844.

Neither the *Scotsman* nor the *Herald* have been found guilty of disloyalty at any time in their long histories yet both have long promoted a disputable version of Scottishness. They have lived the contradiction: Scotland's *national* newspapers refuse seriously to question the political settlement fundamental to the United Kingdom. In the nineteenth century book publishers depended for their prosperity, in a parallel process, on cheap reprints, tracts (religious nationalism, once again) and English sales. Those who did not actually move to London, as Adam Black and others did, entered a long decline. This has only been arrested, to some extent, in the last two decades by the efforts of a few hardy individuals amid something of a literary renaissance. Nevertheless, most major Scottish authors retain London publishers.

The tension between nationhood and the media was always present in the nineteenth century. Even the unstamped press of the 1830s, with titles such as the *Scottish Patriot*, was regarded as more closely involved with Chartism and nascent trade unionism than with Scottishness as such. And though the vernacular had not disappeared, it was ignored increasingly by the 'opinion-formers' of North Britain.

In his remarkable book, *The Language of the People*,[12] William Donaldson has demonstrated, however, that discursive Scots prose not only survived in the local newspapers of Scotland in the second half of the nineteenth century but actually flourished. Changes in technology and the repeal of the Stamp Act in 1855 produced a communications revolution which, in marked contrast to the modern experience, caused newspapers to proliferate. More importantly, these newspapers could survive on Scottish sales alone. They were, Donaldson writes, 'intensely anti-imperialistic, routinely anti-clerical, thoroughly secular in spirit, fundamentally egalitarian in [their] hatred of hypocrisy, sham and artificially maintained class privilege' and free of the 'yokelry' of Barrie and his ilk.

Dr Donaldson proves his claim by extensive quotation but leaves a question: what happened? If the prose tradition lasted longer than we have been led to believe why did it falter in this century, at least in the press? Why did anglicisation and the modern Kailyard of D.C. Thomson triumph? Why was the Scottish voice suppressed as surely as the Clyde Workers Committee's paper *The Worker* was stilled by the government in 1915?[13] Why, for that matter, did the Scottish press become what it is today — thoroughly anglicised, often foreign-owned, yet oddly parochial? Of the newspapers he has studied, Dr Donaldson writes: 'By their agency Scotland achieved print autonomy, perhaps for the first time.' And, perhaps, for the last.

He suggests that proof of the Victorian revival fills a gap in our received cultural history, proving, at least, that there was something between Scott and MacDiarmid which belonged to the people themselves. Yet the tradition of which he writes is again quiescent, not least in the press. Why? Christopher Harvie has suggested[14] that the rush to imitate Northcliffe's 'new journalism' had a lot to do with it. If so, it seems only to prove that the Scottish media were utterly vulnerable to outside forces. There is no reason why that should have changed.

Technological progress does not halt the concentration of press ownership into fewer and fewer hands. Equally, the subordinate economic position of the Scottish media means that its workers are notably migratory, drawn to London where the money, political power and real action are. It is not a new phenomenon. Macaulay, Carlyle, Buchanan, Barrie and Buchan beat a path that is still well-trodden. John Gross[15] has described both the eagerness of the likes of the young Jeffrey 'bent' (in Cockburn's words) 'on purifying himself of the national inconvenience' (his accent) and the impact of Scots on the London press:

> They helped to create not only the great quarterlies and monthlies, as is well known, but the weeklies as well; the first editors of the *Spectator*, the *Economist* and the *Saturday Review*, for example, were all Scotsmen. And right through the nineteenth century critics and essayists made their way south across the border.

Before long, however, the newspapers excavated by Donaldson — the *Aberdeen Weekly Free Press*, the *Glasgow Commonweal*, the *Johnstone Gleaner* and the rest — were suffering death by Scotland's anglicisation, even if the end came later for Scots prose than many had previously thought. The Kailyard, a publishing phenomenon aimed at the middle classes and created to serve a London-dominated industry, won in the end. Meanwhile, the continual migration of some of the best and brightest talents impoverished, as it continues to impoverish, Scottish publications.

Scotland's political situation enfeebled Scotland's media, and continues to do so, whatever linguistic revivals there have been. At the end of the nineteenth century and the beginning of the twentieth a devotion to Liberalism created some illusion of distinctiveness, but it did not answer the enduring question: how can you have national media without a nation? 'Regions' are more often than not a bureaucratic convenience for media owners as much as they are for politicians; they can be changed by a line on the map and are assigned an importance, if any, according to metropolitan perceptions of them. The idea that Scotland's media have somehow matched its legal, religious and educational establishments in maintaining their distinctiveness is a myth. In the late twentieth century the country's inability to maintain one independent political journal has, for example, come to seem emblematic of many things (although a new quarterly, *Scottish Affairs*, was launched in 1992).

The problem of regionalism is best seen in the history of the BBC in Scotland. John Osmond, for example, quotes a remark made a few years ago by Lord Annan:

> BBC staff have to be more aware than other journalists that their first commitment is to serve the national community and the national interest. To do this, while remaining loyal to the facts, requires political sophistication.

Those two sentences carry more baggage than Annan perhaps intended. But look at the Corporation's map of Britain. There is an East and South-East Region, a South-West Region, Wales, the Midlands, Northern Ireland, the North-East, the North-West, and Scotland. Yet in BBC jargon Scotland is something called a National Region. Is it the 'nation' to which Annan referred? Hardly. Is it, then, a component of that nation? If so, why has it earned its curious title and what, in reality, does the title mean?

In reality, it means next to nothing, and has not since March 1923, when radio began under the aegis of the then-private British Broadcasting Company and the leadership of the quixotic Scotsman John Reith. Christopher Harvie has recalled that from the early 1930s until the late 1950s 'the BBC in Scotland became a by-word for puritanical parochialism', but that was the least of its problems. Harvie adds:

> The Scottish BBC was in fact a paradigm of the fate of regional organisations within otherwise highly centralised UK bodies. The nominated Broadcasting Council was selected to represent the Scottish establishment, and it tended to concur with an equally conservative local executive. If talented radicals could be got rid of by promoting them to positions at the centre, who would complain, least of all at Broadcasting House?

Little has changed. Elsewhere, Harvie has written of the *Scotsman* and the BBC in the late 1950s as 'bastions' of Unionism; as social glue, in other words, and Made in Britain. Consider the tortured logic which granted BBC Scotland its curious status, as described in a recent history:

> The BBC Regions were too large to represent communities with a common sense of social and cultural identity. Scotland was a nation of regions and so could not easily be treated as a single region as the BBC sought to do. In Scotland, the BBC was given the status of 'National Region'. It was regarded as a Region because Scotland represented only one part of the unitary BBC covering the whole of the United Kingdom; it was regarded as a National Region because it served a nation, thus distinguishing it from one of the BBC's English regions.[16]

In 1938, the Controller (Public Relations) at the BBC responded to a complaint about this absurdity by claiming there was 'no deprecatory connotation' involved before proceeding to perfect mandarin honesty: 'the term "Region" is one of administrative convenience'. Today, funding and overall strategy are decided in London, increasingly so according to some critics. Access to the 'network' – by which broadcasting success is judged – is also in London's gift. Fundamentally, however, the BBC's role as the 'social glue' of the British nation-state would be rendered impossible if real autonomy were to be granted to BBC Scotland. What was true under Reith remains true, and no amount of homegrown comedy shows, outside broadcasts from Ibrox Park, or reports on the General Assembly of the Church of Scotland will change it. Formal control of the policy and content of programmes lies with the Broadcasting Council for Scotland – but its members are appointed by the BBC. If anything, the elevation of Mr John Birt to the director-generalship of the BBC shows every sign of reversing such decentralisation as has been allowed hitherto.

It has been argued[17] that even by recognising the 'national unit' in, for example, political and industrial reporting Scotland's television broadcasters have, since 1957, exposed Scots to the 'Scottish dimension' in their affairs:

> We need only see television as accepting, transmitting and reinforcing a framework of assumptions, already established and taken for granted, that politics was all about the economic management of a national unit. The only framing assumption that specifically Scottish television news and current affairs coverage did not share with national (British) television news and current affairs coverage was the identity of the national unit in question.

This sounds oddly comforting, until its implications are grasped. It presupposes that all involved recognise that the 'unit' in question is national; it presupposes real autonomy for the reporters (usually employed to service what London calls 'opt-outs'); and it presupposes that control of resources are vested in Scottish broadcasters to do the job they wish to do. None of those suppositions stand much scrutiny. The short and mostly disastrous history of BBC Radio Scotland, founded in 1978 in response to commercial radio, shows as much. On television, the very order of precedence imposed from London – 'national' news followed by 'local' news – defines the role of the Scottish broadcast media.

The history of commercial television in Scotland has followed a pattern parallel to that of the BBC. While Roy Thomson interfered only rarely in the editorial content of his newspapers, he took his licence to print money seriously. From the late 1950s until the 1980s STV, as it was, was a paradigm for cheap, profitable, 'regional' televison. Kept out of the UK network by an effective English cartel of larger companies and content, like the BBC, merely to fill a quota of programmes paying lip service to Scottishness (by which, for the most part, was meant sport, religion and anything upon which tartan might be decked), the station's impact on Scottish culture was neglible when it was not pernicious.

The station's creative lethargy was matched only by its profitability. Both were a consequence of its role as, in effect, a branch office of an industry run from London and Manchester. As in newspapers, such talent as there was fled south while Scottish viewers were left to forage among imported English and American programmes and risible misreadings of Scottish realities.

In the late 1980s that began to change. Sensing the nature of the coming broadcasting revolution, Scottish first set about winning its franchise (which it did, for next to nothing) and then began to pursue the idea that, in television terms, Scotland could become an exporter. The risks in the strategy are as great as the potential rewards, but it is an option unavailable to the press. The station is now divided into two parts – a broadcasting division making local programmes; and Scottish Television Enterprises, serving the export market. Alastair Moffat, who runs STE, has been explicit: 'STE needs to expand steadily, and to do that we should break out over Hadrian's Wall to become more British, to climb up the major league.'[18]

It is not a statement calculated to please media patriots, yet it is no more than a recognition of reality in the modern broadcasting environment. Moffat's remark could also stand for the dilemma which has faced all of Scotland's media over the last two centuries. How to resist 'becoming British'? How to survive outside 'the major league'? How to be a Scottish information carrier when Scotland does not, politically speaking, exist, when multinational culture encroaches, and when assimilation by England has the force of economic necessity, whether for the newspapers bought over by multi-nationals, the generations of journalists who have trekked south, or the television stations all too aware of satellites in the sky and America's cultural power.

Scottish Television may, with luck, survive, and has already bought into 'British' breakfast television. Its hard-won role as a network 'player' is, one might say, devolution in action. The fate of Grampian Television, tiny in industry terms, or of the hybrid Border TV, tiny in every sense, is probably sealed. The sheer weight of technology in the service of multinational companies, the political paradox of Scotland's constitutional position, and the centripetal pull of London suggest that a decline which began with the Union can only accelerate.

In sum: if Scotland has not lost its identity since 1707, its media have seemed determined to shed theirs. Even the moments of glory – the heyday of the *Edinburgh Review*, say – look like a dazzling distraction. The journal functioned, whether it realised it or not, to facilitate assimilation and succeeded only in ensuring its own destruction as a *Scottish* publication. Today, nationhood and the media are increasingly antipathetic, but the case of Scotland – a self-proclaimed national media without a nation – has resembled a slow suicide. The paradox is uninhabitable.

History shows that ownership of the media has slipped steadily from Scottish hands. But it also demonstrates that ownership, in itself, was never enough to protect those forms of communication which regarded – and still regard – themselves as fundamental elements of the Scottish identity. Mr Murdoch's *Sun* is a symbol, and it promises no illumination.

Notes

1. *The Scottish Periodical Press 1750–1789* (Edinburgh and London, 1931).
2. D. Hutchison: 'Political Writing in the Scottish Press', in D. McCrone (ed.), *The Scottish Government Yearbook 1987* (Edinburgh).
3. James G. Kellas, *The Scottish Political System* (Cambridge, 1989, 4th edn).
4. *No Gods and Precious Few Heroes – Scotland 1914–1980* (London, 1981), p.123.
5. *The Divided Kingdom* (London, 1988).

6. A. Mattelart, X. Delcourt and M. Mattelart, *International Image Markets – In Search of an Alternative Perspective* (London, 1984), pp.14–17.

7. *Scottish Voices, 1745–1960* (London, 1990), pp.185–86.

8. Ibid., p.122.

9. Ibid., p.200.

10. Trevor Royle, 'The Literary Background to Stevenson's Edinburgh', in J. Calder (ed.), *Stevenson and Victorian Scotland* (Edinburgh, 1981).

11. Charles J. Guthrie, *Robert Louis Stevenson – Some Personal Recollections by the Late Lord Guthrie* (Edinburgh, 1920).

12. *The Language of the People – Scots Prose from the Victorian Revival* (Aberdeen, 1989).

13. See Stanley Harrison, *Poor Men's Guardians – a Survey of the Struggles for a Democratic Newspaper Press, 1763–1973* (London, 1974).

14. 'Nationalism, Journalism and Cultural Politics', in T. Gallagher (ed.), *Nationalism in the Nineties* (Edinburgh, 1991).

15. *The Rise and Fall of the Man of Letters* (London, 1969), pp.19–20.

16. W.H. McDowell, *The History of BBC Broadcasting in Scotland, 1923–1983* (Edinburgh, 1992), p.32.

17. S. Kendrick, 'Scotland, Social Change and Politics', in McCrone, Kendrick and Straw, *The Making of Scotland: Nation, Culture and Social Change* (Edinburgh, 1989), p.82.

18. *Scotland on Sunday*, 29 August 1993.

Books for Further Reading

There is, perhaps unsurprisingly, a dearth of useful material on the Scottish media. Official histories of newspaper houses reflect their origins and 'media studies' have yet to give birth to a comprehensive history. Several titles identified in the Notes contain worthwhile passages, however, and Donaldson's *The Language of the People* is a classic. Otherwise, see in general the *Scottish Government Yearbook* series, McDowell's *The History of BBC Broadcasting in Scotland, 1923-1983* (Edinburgh, 1992) and Maurice Smith's press study, *Paper Lions* (Edinburgh, 1994).

Notes on the Contributors

IAN BELL

Born and educated in Edinburgh. He is a former literary editor of the *Scotsman*, the Scottish editor of the *Observer*, and a contributor to several other publications including the *Herald*. *Dreams of Exile*, his award-winning biography of Robert Louis Stevenson, was published in 1992 and his novel, *Whistling in the Dark*, in 1994.

ALEXANDER BROADIE

Educated at the Royal High School, the University of Edinburgh and Balliol College, Oxford. Professor in philosophy at the University of Glasgow, Fellow of the Royal Society of Edinburgh, and first recipient of the triennial Henry Duncan Prize for Scottish Studies awarded by the Royal Society of Edinburgh. Chief areas of research are logic and philosophy in medieval Scotland, and philosophy of the Scottish Enlightenment. Author of *The Tradition of Scottish Philosophy* (1990).

ALASDAIR CAMERON

Senior Lecturer in the Department of Theatre Film and Television Studies at the University of Glasgow. He was published widely in the field of Scottish theatre, sits on the board of several theatre companies and is also a freelance arts journalist.

STEWART CRUICKSHANK

Senior Producer, Entertainment, BBC Radio Scotland. His many productions include *Beatstalking: the History of Scottish Rock Music, Simple Minds: the Street-Fighting*

Years and *242 is Calling You: the Story of Pirate Radio in Scotland*. He has for ten years produced *Beat Patrol*, Scotland's premier independent rock music programme. His other activities include membership of the Advisory Panels for Sound City and New Music World and his secret past includes Edinburgh's Mowgli and The Donuts.

NIGEL GRANT

Born in Glasgow and went to school in Inverness before returning to Glasgow where he studied English literature and language. He has been Professor of Education at Glasgow University since 1978. His writings include *Soviet Education* (1964, 1966, 1972, 1974); *Society, Schools and Progress in Eastern Europe* (1969); with R.E. Bell, *Patterns of Education in the British Isles* (1973); *A Mythology of British Education* (1971); with Lowe and Williams, *Education and Nation-Building in the Third World* (1971); and *The Crisis of Scottish Education* (1982). He is also the author of many articles on education, and was secretary of the AdCAS Working Party that wrote the pamphlet, *Scottish Education: a Declaration of Principles* (1988).

FORSYTH HARDY

First film critic of the *Scotsman* (1932). Co-founder of the Edinburgh Film Guild (1930) and the Edinburgh International Film Festival (1947). Founder member of the Scottish Film Council (1933). Chairman of BBC Scotland's Arts Review (1945–75). Author of *John Grierson: a Documentary Biography* and editor of three volumes of John Grierson's writings. Director of Films of Scotland Committee (1955–75), producer of 150 films including the Oscar-winning *Seawards the Great Ships* (1961). Hon. President of Edinburgh Filmhouse. Hon. Vice-President of Edinburgh International Film Festival. Hon. Adviser of Grierson Archive, University of Stirling. Member of British Council's Scottish Advisory Committee.

HAMISH HENDERSON

Born Blairgowrie, 1918. Educated at Blairgowrie High School, Dulwich College and Cambridge University. Served as an Intelligence Officer with 51st Highland and other infantry divisions in Egypt, Libya, Tunisia and Italy, 1940–45. Completed *Elegies for the Dead in Cyrenaica* in 1947 and translated Gramsci's *Letters from Prison* in 1950. Collected Scottish folk music with Alan Lomax and was a founder member of the School of Scottish Studies at Edinburgh University in 1952. He discovered Jeannie Robertson, the great ballad singer, and worked among the Scottish travelling people. From 1970 to 1990 he collaborated with Timothy Neat in the production of documentary films. His numerous essays on Scottish folklore were collected in *Alias MacAlias* (1992).

JOHN R. HUME

Born in Glasgow in 1939, and educated at Hutchesons' Boys' Grammar School, Glasgow University and the Royal College of Science and Technology. From 1964 to 1984 he was a lecturer (latterly senior lecturer) in the Department of History, University of Strathclyde. There he specialised in economic and industrial history with particular reference to Scotland. Since 1984 he has been an inspector, first of ancient monuments, more recently of historic buildings, in what is now Historic Scotland. He was appointed Chief Inspector of Historic Buildings in October 1993. He has written widely on industrial history and archaeology and has published, as sole author or jointly, more than twenty books and booklets including (with Michael S. Moss) studies of heavy industry in Scotland and Northern Ireland and of whisky distilling in Scotland.

WALTER HUMES

A lecturer in education at Glasgow University since 1976. He became editor of *Scottish Educational Review* in 1991. His main publications have been *Scottish Culture and Scottish Education 1800–1980* (edited with H.M. Paterson, 1983) and *The Leadership Class in Scottish Education* (1986), which offered a highly critical view of educational management. His current research interests are in the field of policy studies.

JOHN LENIHAN

A graduate of the Universities of Durham and Glasgow. He has spent most of his career in the management of technology related to health care. He was a visiting professor of chemistry in the University of California in 1976 and professor of clinical physics in the University of Glasgow from 1973 to 1983.

MICHAEL LYNCH

Born in Aberdeen, educated at Aberdeen Grammar School and the Universities of Aberdeen and London. He taught at University College, Bangor, before coming to Edinburgh University, where he is now Professor of Scottish History. Formerly editor of *The Innes Review*, he is presently joint literary secretary of the Scottish History Society. His books include *Edinburgh and the Reformation* (1981) and *Scotland: a New History* (2nd edn, 1993), and he is currently engaged as general editor of the forthcoming *Oxford Companion to Scottish History*.

RODERICK J. LYALL

Professor in Scottish Literature at the University of Glasgow. Born and educated in Perth, Australia, he taught English at Massey University, New Zealand, before moving to a lectureship in Glasgow in 1975, being appointed to a titular chair in 1987. He has published widely on medieval and Renaissance Scottish literature, including an edition of Lyndsay's *Thrie Estaitis*, and is at present working on a critical study of Alexander Montgomerie.

ANDREW MARR

Chief political commentator for the *Independent* in London. Before that, he was political editor of the *Economist* and the *Scotsman*. He was born in Glasgow in 1959, brought up in the Carse of Gowrie, and educated in Dundee, Edinburgh and Cambridge. He is a regular broadcaster and his first book, *The Battle for Scotland*, was published by Penguin in 1992.

MALCOLM NICOLSON

Senior Research Fellow in the Wellcome Unit for the History of Medicine, University of Glasgow, having previously been Wellcome Lecturer in the History of Medicine at the University of Edinburgh.

KEVIN McCARRA

Football correspondent of *Scotland on Sunday*. He is author or co-author of *Scottish Football: a Pictorial History*, *100 Cups: The Story of the Scottish Cup* (with Hugh Keevins), and *One Afternoon in Lisbon* (with Pat Woods). He has also edited *Glasgow's Glasgow* and co-edited (with Hamish Whyte) *A Glasgow Collection: Essay in Honour of Joe Fisher*. In 1983 he organised the Scottish Football exhibition which toured Scotland. He lives in Glasgow and is currently working on a history of Clyde FC.

NEIL MacCORMICK

Neil MacCormick has been since 1972 Regius Professor of Public Law and the Law of Nature and Nations at Edinburgh University. He was previously a lecturer in St Andrews University (Queen's College, Dundee, 1965–67) and Fellow and Tutor in Jurisprudence of Balliol College Oxford (1967–72).

He is author of four books on philosophy of law, and has edited or co-edited ten others. His best-known work is on legal reasoning, as exemplified by *Legal Reasoning and Legal Theory* (1978) and *Interpreting Statutes: a Comparative Study* (edited, with R.S. Summers, 1991) and the institutional theory of law (see MacCormick/ Weinberger, *An Institutional Theory of Law*, 1986). His current work is on legal theory with reference to problems of the European community.

He has been a visiting professor in Sweden, Texas, Canada, Germany and Australia, and has lectured in Europe, Japan and New Zealand. Vice-President of the Royal Society of Edinburgh. He is a long-term Member of the National Council of the Scottish National Party, and has contested four parliamentary elections as an SNP candidate.

CHARLES McKEAN

Secretary and treasurer of the Royal Incorporation of Architects in Scotland since 1979. He is also an architectural historian and writer, author of *The Scottish Thirties*, *Edinburgh – Portrait of a City*, and many papers. He is founder and general editor of the RIAS/Landmark Trust Illustrated Architectural Guides to Scotland, of which he has been the author of five. He is an Honorary Fellow of the RIBA, and an Honorary Member of the Saltire Society.

DUNCAN MacMILLAN

Curator of the Talbot Rice Gallery, and reader in Fine Art at the University of Edinburgh. He is an acknowledged expert on Scottish art, both historical and contemporary. He is author of *Scottish Art 1460–1990* which was awarded the Saltire Society/*Scotsman* Prize for Scottish Book of the Year, 1990–91. He has published a number of other books, articles and exhibition catalogues on Scottish art, historical and contemporary.

JOHN PURSER

Born in Glasgow and educated at Fettes College, Edinburgh, the University of Glasgow and the Royal Scottish Academy of Music and Drama. He is a composer, broadcaster and writer. His works range from opera to solo guitar, poetry to the thirty-programme series for BBC Radio Scotland on the history of Scottish music. His plays include *Carver*, a full-length radio play about Scotland's greatest composer. His *Scotland's Music* (1992) won the McVitie Prize for the Scottish Writer of the Year.

PAUL H. SCOTT

Born in Edinburgh and educated at the Royal High School and Edinburgh University. Spent many years abroad as a diplomat. He returned to Edinburgh in 1980 and since then has been active in many Scottish causes and has written on historical, literary and political subjects. He is Convener of the Advisory Council for the Arts in Scotland (AdCAS), President of Scottish PEN and of the Andrew Fletcher Society, Convener of the Scottish Centre for Economic and Social Research, Vice-Chairman of the Saltire Society and Convener of the Awards Panel for the Scottish Book of the Year, a member of the Council of the Association for Scottish Literary Studies and of the Campaign for a National Theatre in Scotland. He was a member of the group which drew up *A Claim of Right for Scotland* and has been on the Councils of the Edinburgh International Festival, the National Trust for Scotland and the Cockburn Association. A frequent contributor to several newspapers and periodicals. Rector of Dundee University from 1989 to 1992. He is a Vice-President of the SNP and spokesman on Education, the Arts and Broadcasting. His most recent books are *Towards Independence: Essays on Scotland* (1991); *Andrew Fletcher and the Treaty of Union* (1992); and *Scotland in Europe: A Dialogue with a Sceptical Friend* (1992).

ROBBIE SHEPHERD

An authority on Scottish dance music who has presented BBC Radio Scotland's weekly session of Scottish bands on 'Take The Floor' for the past twelve years. Born in Dunecht, a village near Aberdeen, his love of the music goes back to his childhood, listening to 78 rpm records of such as Jimmy Shand, Jim Cameron and Adam Rennie. His role of compere and commentator at Highland Games first brought him to the attention of the BBC. He has built up a great store of information on the dance, the music and the tunes over the years and is a fervent Scot, particularly pertaining to his own north-east corner.

DONALD SMITH

After completing post-graduate studies in Scottish literature, history and theology at New College and the School of Scottish Studies, Donald Smith became the Director of the Church of Scotland's Netherbow Arts Centre in 1983, and is actively engaged in the development and promotion of Scottish literature, theatre and visual arts, as well as in many aspects of contemporary Church life. Since 1989 Donald Smith has also been Curator of the John Knox House Museum and is currently Secretary to the Church of Scotland's Advisory Committee on Artistic Matters and a member of the Scottish Catholic Heritage Commission.

SARA STEVENSON

Curator of Photography at the Scottish National Portrait Gallery and in charge of the Scottish Photography Archive. She has arranged many exhibitions and has written extensively on photography. At various times she has been Vice-Chairman or Chairman of the Scottish Society for the History of Photography; a member of the International Advisory Board of the *History of Photography* and of the Scottish Arts Council's *Photography Review*.

DERICK THOMSON

Born Lewis, 1921. Taught at Edinburgh, Aberdeen and Glasgow Universities. Professor of Celtic at Glasgow, 1963–91. Founder/editor of *Gairm* quarterly (1952–). Author of many books and articles, among them *An Introduction to Gaelic Poetry* (1974, 1990), *The Companion to Gaelic Scotland* (1983) and *The MacDiarmid MS Anthology* (1992). He has published several collections of poetry from 1951 to 1992, including his Collected Poems, *Creachadh na Clàrsaich*.

RODERICK WATSON

Reader in Literature at the University of Stirling, and series editor of Canongate Classics. He has written and lectured widely on Scottish literature and cultural identity, also producing critical studies of Hugh MacDiarmid, Norman MacCaig and Edwin Morgan and a literary history, *The Literature of Scotland*.

List of Plates

List of Abbreviations

EIF   Edinburgh International Festival
NGS   National Galleries of Scotland
NLS   National Library of Scotland
NMS   National Museums of Scotland
NTS   National Trust for Scotland
RCAHMS   Royal Commission on the Ancient and Historical Monuments of Scotland
RIAS   Royal Incorporation of Architects in Scotland
SNGMA   Scottish National Gallery of Modern Art
SNPG   Scottish National Portrait Gallery

Index

(*page-numbers in italic refer to illustrations*)